Writing from Start to Finish

The 'Story Workshop' Basic Forms Rhetoric-Reader

Writing from Start to Finish

The 'Story Workshop' Basic Forms Rhetoric-Reader

JOHN SCHULTZ

Columbia College (Chicago)

BOYNTON/COOK PUBLISHERS, INC.

Acknowledgments

CAMBRIDGE UNIVERSITY PRESS. Excerpt from *The Stars in Their Courses,* by Sir James Jeans. Reprinted by permission of the publisher.

CHANDLER & SHARP PUBLISHERS, INC. Excerpt from *Eskimos and Explorers,* by Wendell H. Oswalt. Copyright © 1979 by Chandler & Sharp Publishers, Inc. Reprinted by permission of the publisher.

DELACORTE PRESS—SEYMOUR LAWRENCE. Excerpt from *How Children Fail,* revised edition, by John Holt. Copyright © 1964, 1982 by John Holt. Reprinted by permission of Delacorte Press—Seymour Lawrence. A Merloyd Lawrence book.

DODD, MEAD & COMPANY. "The Mating of the Mantis" from *The Insect World of J. Henri Fabre,* edited by Edwin Way Teale. Reprinted by permission of the publisher.

DOUBLEDAY & COMPANY, INC. Excerpt from *The Art of Survival* by Cord Christian Troebst. Copyright © 1965 by Doubleday & Company, Inc. "Pencil Sharpeners" from *How Does It Work,* copyright © 1961 by Richard M. Koff. Both reprinted by permission of the publisher.

FARRAR, STRAUS & GIROUX, INC. Excerpt from "The Marvelous Mouth" from *The Kandy-Kolored Tangerine-Flake Streamline Baby* by Tom Wolfe. Copyright © 1963, 1965 by Thomas K. Wolfe, Jr. Excerpt from *Close Quarters* by Larry Heinemann. Copyright © 1974, 1975, 1976, 1977 by Larry Heinemann. Both reprinted by permission of the publisher.

GENERAL ELECTRIC CO. Excerpt from *Power Maker for America, General Electric.* Courtesy General Electric Co.

HARCOURT BRACE JOVANOVICH, INC. Excerpts from *The Robber Barons* by Matthew Josephson, copyright 1934, 1962 by Matthew Josephson. Excerpt from "Old Mortality" in *Pale Horse, Pale Rider* by Kath-

Library of Congress Cataloging in Publication Data

Main entry under title:

Writing from start to finish.

   1. College readers.   2. English language—Rhetoric.
I. Schultz, John, 1932–
PE1417.W72 1982   808'.042   82–14595
ISBN 0-86709-039-1

For information address Boynton/Cook Publishers, Inc.
P.O. Box 860, Upper Montclair, NJ 07043

ISBN: 0-86709-043-X

Printed in the United States of America

84 85 10 9 8 7 6 5 4 3

Acknowledgments

erine Anne Porter, copyright 1937, 1965 by Katherine Anne Porter. Excerpt from *All the King's Men* by Robert Penn Warren, copyright 1946, 1974 by Robert Penn Warren. Excerpts from *The Road to Wigan Pier* by George Orwell from *The Orwell Reader*. Copyright 1949, 1965 by Harcourt, Brace and Company, Inc. All reprinted by permission of the publisher.

HARPER & ROW, PUBLISHERS, INC. From pp. 49–54 in *Mules and Men* by Zora Neale Hurston (J.B. Lippincott Company). Copyright 1935 by Zora Neale Hurston; renewed © 1963 by John C. Hurston and Joel Hurston. From pp. viii–xiii from the Introduction in *Native Son* by Richard Wright. Copyright 1940 by Richard Wright; renewed © 1968 by Ellen Wright. Excerpt from *Paper Lion* by George Plimpton. Copyright © 1964, 1965, 1966 by George Plimpton. From pp. 111–2 and 114–6 in *The Nature of the Universe* by Fred Hoyle. Copyright 1950, © 1960 by Fred Hoyle. Excerpt from pp. 118–9 in *Einstein: The Life and Times* by Ronald W. Clark (Thomas Y. Crowell). Copyright © 1971 by Ronald W. Clark. "The Laser: Humanitarian Hope or Doomsday Device?" by Harry J. Partin in *Technical English: Writing, Reading, and Speaking*, Third Edition, by Nell Ann Pickett and Ann A. Laster. Copyright © 1980 by Nell Ann Pickett and Ann A. Laster. All selections reprinted by permission of the publisher.

HARVARD UNIVERSITY PRESS. Excerpt from *The Letters of Gustave Flaubert*, selected, edited, and translated by Francis Steegmuller. Copyright © 1979, 1980 by Francis Steegmuller. Reprinted by permission of the publisher.

THE HARVEST PUBLISHING CO. "When Will You Be a No-Till Farmer?" by Dick Lehnert. Reprinted by permission from *Michigan Farmer*, March 1, 1980.

HOLT, RINEHART AND WINSTON, PUBLISHERS. Excerpts from *The Man Who Loved Children* by Christina Stead. Copyright 1940, © 1968 by Christina Stead. Excerpt by Jane Goodall from *Primate Patterns*, edited by Phyllis Dolhinow. Both reprinted by permission of the publisher.

INTERNATIONAL PUBLISHERS. Excerpts from *Pages from a Worker's Life* by William Z. Foster and "Open Letter to President Wilson" from *ABC of Color* by W.E.B. DuBois. Both reprinted by permission of the publisher.

LIVERIGHT PUBLISHING CORPORATION. "At Melville's Tomb" and "A Letter to Harriet Monroe" are reprinted from *The Complete Poems and Selected Letters and Prose of Hart Crane*, edited by Brom Weber, by permission of the publisher. Copyright 1933, © 1958, 1966 by Liveright Publishing Corporation. "Parapraxes" from Lecture II is reprinted from *Introductory Lectures on Psychoanalysis* by Sigmund Freud, translated by James Strachey, by permission of the publisher. Copyright © 1966 by W.W. Norton & Company, Inc. Copyright © 1965, 1964, 1963 by James Strachey. Copyright 1920, 1935 by Edward L. Bernays.

MACMILLAN, LTD. "The Allegory of the Cave" from Plato's *The Republic*, translated by John Davies and David Vaughan. Reprinted by permission of Macmillan, London and Basingstoke.

MACMILLIAN PUBLISHING CO., INC. Excerpt from *The Informed Heart* by Bruno Bettelheim. Copyright © 1980 by The Free Press. Excerpt from *The Golden Bough*, Abridged Edition, by Sir James G. Frazer. Copyright 1922 by Macmillan Publishing Co., Inc., renewed 1950 by Barclays Bank Ltd. Both reprinted with permission of the publisher.

HAROLD MATSON COMPANY, INC. Excerpt from *Book of the Eskimos* by Peter Freuchen. Copyright © 1961 by Peter Freuchen Estate. Reprinted by permission of the Harold Matson Company, Inc.

MODERN LANGUAGE ASSOCIATION OF AMERICA. "Problems of Collecting Oral Literature" by Mac-Edward Leach, *PMLA* 77 (1962), 335–40. Reprinted by permission of the publisher.

THE MOUNTAINEERS. Graphic illustration of ice-axe arrest from p. 265 of *Mountaineering: The Freedom of the Hills*, Third Edition. Reprinted with permission of the publisher.

W.W. NORTON & COMPANY, INC. Selection, pp. 53–58, from *The Art of Scientific Investigation* by W.I.B. Beveridge, 1950. All rights reserved. Revised edition, 1957. Excerpt from *The Mute Stones Speak, The Story of Archeology in Italy* by Paul MacKendrick. Copyright © 1960 by Paul MacKendrick. Both reprinted by permission of the publisher.

OXFORD UNIVERSITY PRESS. Excerpt from *The Sea Around Us* by Rachel L. Carson. Copyright © 1950, 1951, 1961 by Rachel L. Carson; renewed 1969 by Roger Christie. Reprinted by permission of the publisher.

PACIFIC NEWS SERVICE. "Why Nothing Seems to Work" by Rasa Gustaitis. Reprinted by permission of the publisher.

PETERSEN PUBLISHING COMPANY. "Hard Starting—Causes and Cures" from *How to Tune Your Car*. Reprinted by permission of the publisher.

RANDOM HOUSE, INC. Excerpt from *The Death and Life of Great American Cities* by Jane Jacobs. Copyright © 1961 by Jane Jacobs. "Prologue" from *Basic Research Methods in Social Science* by Julian L. Simon. Copyright © 1969 by Random House, Inc. "The Master Thief" and "The Cat and Mouse in Partnership"

Acknowledgments

by the Brothers Grimm from *Tales of Grimm and Andersen*, introduced by W.H. Auden. Copyright 1952 by W.H. Auden. Excerpt from *Blue Collars and Hard Hats: The Working Class and the Future of American Politics* by Patricia Sexton. Copyright 1971 by Random House, Inc., 1972 by Vintage Books. All reprinted by permission of the publisher.

SCHOCKEN BOOKS, INC. Excerpts from *The Diaries of Franz Kafka: 1910–1913* by Franz Kafka. Copyright © 1948, 1975 by Schocken Books, Inc. Excerpt from "In the Penal Colony" from *The Complete Stories* by Franz Kafka. Copyright © 1946, 1947, 1949, 1954, 1958, 1971 by Schocken Books, Inc. Reprinted by permission of the publisher.

BETTY SHIFLETT. "Cairo, U.S.A. 1971" was first published in *Evergreen Review;* "How to Melt, Blacken, and Break" was first published in *f 1.* Both are reprinted by permission of the author.

THE STEPHEN GREENE PRESS. Excerpt from *Cross-Country Skiing Today* by John Caldwell. Copyright © 1977 by John Caldwell. Reprinted by permission of the publisher.

TRUST OF IRVING SHEPARD. "Letter from Jack London to Messrs. N. Clark & Sons, December 29, 1913." Reprinted by permission of the Trust.

UNIVERSITY OF CALIFORNIA PRESS. Excerpts from "How Desert Animals Handle Water Loss" from *An Island Called California* by Elna Bakker. Copyright © 1971 by the Regents of the University of California. Reprinted by permission of the publisher.

UNIVERSITY OF CHICAGO PRESS. Excerpt from *The Year of the Gorilla* by George Schaller. Copyright © 1964 by the University of Chicago. Excerpts from *Lay My Burden Down* by B.A. Botkin. Copyright 1945 by the University of Chicago. All rights reserved. Both reprinted by permission of the publisher.

VIKING PENGUIN INC. Excerpt from Introduction by Malcolm Cowley to *The Portable Faulkner.* Copyright 1946 by The Viking Press, Inc. Copyright renewed 1974 by The Viking Press, Inc. Used by permission of the publisher.

ROBERT WERNICK. "Let's Spoil the Wilderness." Reprinted by permission of the author.

ZIFF-DAVIS PUBLISHING COMPANY. "Turbochargers" from "Car and Driver" Magazine. Copyright © 1980 by Ziff-Davis Publishing Company. Reprinted by permission of the publisher.

Preface

Writing from Start to Finish sets forth an approach to the teaching of writing originated by the author—the Story Workshop® Basic Forms approach—that will be new to many teachers of composition, but is familiar to many others who have used it successfully in their writing classes for a number of years at Columbia College (Chicago) and more recently in the Dallas County Community Colleges and in other colleges and high schools. The approach has been very effective with "open admissions" classes as well as more advanced classes. Teachers who have used it in a comprehensive way have found their students making unaccustomed progress in writing.

Astute teachers of writing have observed and frequently puzzled over the eliciting and organizing effect of how-to's, letters, and journals, the impact of content and perception upon expression, the relationship of speech to writing. These forms and principles are presented here, not in the all too common ad hoc fashion, but with a profoundly different emphasis, and given a theoretical and practical prominence within a broad ordering of "basic forms" that will be new to most teachers of composition. Yet all successful writers use "basic forms" approaches intuitively, by osmosis, by hook or by crook, just as we use the grammar of our language without thinking about it.

Basic forms contain a built-in sense of audience and naturally relate oral forms to written forms, establishing a bridge for the indispensable two-way traffic of speech and writing. The Teacher's Manual to *Writing from Start to Finish* sets forth classroom techniques, informed by Story Workshop Basic Forms principles, that will, over the course of a semester, help the teacher create in the classroom a dynamic learning involvement, enabling students to make significant progress in their writing. The audience focuses explored in this text (and in the Teacher's Manual) develop the most crucial audience of all for writing, that is, the writer himself or herself, who in the process of writing must incorporate teller and listener, writer and reader, conceiver and appreciator, and carry out the task of writing from start to finish. The development of this internal listening capacity has been overlooked, or overleaped (leaving the student behind), in most composition classes.

The introductory section is titled "To the Teacher." However, many teachers may wish to ask their students to read it, in order to stimulate their curiosity and let them begin to understand the theoretical background for the whole Basic Forms approach and the closely associated in-class activities and programs. One of my hopes is to get teachers, many of whom feel a quiet desperation about teaching writing, to believe in the abilities of their students (there is little research to suggest that our students are less capable than students of other generations) by providing forms, approaches, and challenges that will help them make contact with and develop their innate writing abilities and respect their writing achievements. Every section in this text contains one or more examples of compelling undergraduate writings, some of them written by students who would not have been predicted to be good writers. These writings stand beside the professional writings in the book, and you would not be able, in most cases, to tell the difference if you were not informed in advance or by the content of the work.

The bibliography for the introductory essay "To the Teacher" and for "The Process of Writing" is located in the Teacher's Manual to *Writing from Start to Finish*.

I want to thank Wallace W. Douglas, Richard Ohmann, Jon Wagner, Beverlye Brown, and James Hall for their helpful readings of portions of this manuscript (and the last two for their permission to use pieces they wrote in response to assignments in the text); Robert Boynton, my editor, who gave the book careful, insightful attention; James E. Miller, Jr. and Michael F. Shugrue for their encouragement of this project; Richard Larson for the questions that led me to write the introductory essay, "To the Teacher"; the English Department at the University of California at Berkeley for Guest of the Department research privileges; the many teachers who have used Story Workshop Basic Forms approaches and kept up a productive dialogue about their use; Charles Freilich, who saw the manuscript through many stages; and Mirron Alexandroff, President of Columbia College, for his close long-term interest in the Story Workshop program. I must especially thank Betty Shiflett, who read and commented most helpfully on several drafts of the book.

For agreeing to let me use selections they wrote as students in Story Workshop classes, I want to thank the following people: Randall Albers, Andrew Allegretti, Daniel Andries, George Bailey, Ronald Booze, Chris Burks, Reginald Carlvin, Sandra Crockett, Phyllis Crowley, Cloteria Easterling, James Elder, Joan Engel, Michael Finger, Gary Gaines, Jeanette Haynes-Morris, Ann Hemenway, Scott Hoeppner, Andrew Hyzy, Allan Johnson, Kevin Kotowski, Marina MacMichael, John Madler, Dino Malcolm, Marilyn Mannisto, Tom Nawrocki, Mike Schwarz, Shawn Shiflett, Chris Sweet, Paula Trent, and Sharon Weber.

Contents

Preface

To the Teacher   1

**I THE HOW-TO FORM—TECHNICAL, EXPOSITORY,
AND ARGUMENTATIVE ESSAY**   25

    Introduction *25*

        From *Cross-Country Skiing Today* John Caldwell *28*
        "How to Make Lasagna" Phyllis Crowley *34*

    Writing Your How-To: The Subject *38*

        From *Moby Dick* Herman Melville *39*
        "How to Make Chitterlings" Chris Burks *42*

    Writing Your How-To: The Audience *45*

        "How to Hit" Tom Nawrocki *45*

    Writing Your How-To: Your Authority *49*
    A List of the Major Elements and Characteristics of the How-To Form *50*
    How to Do Something You're Not Supposed to Do *51*
    How-To Subjects *52*
    Writing Your How-To: All-at-Once *53*

II THE PROCESS OF WRITING   57

    Working Methods: Getting Started, Build-up, Continuing, and Rewriting *57*
    Process Techniques for Essay   *62*
    Seeing-in-the-Mind *64*
    Spoken Language and Written Language *73*
        What About the Difficulties of English Spelling? *79*
        Moving from Speech to Writing *80*
        "Cosmetic" Grammar and Grammar of Sense and Meaning *81*
        What We Need Is a Mixed Diction *82*
        Punctuation *83*
        Voice *85*

Journals and Notebooks *86*

From *Diaries: 1910–1913*   Franz Kafka *87*
"Journal Entry"   Ann Hemenway *91*
A Journal Activity *93*
Writing in Your Journal *94*

The Letter Form—Essay and Fiction   96

From *The Letters of Gustave Flaubert 99*
"Open Letter to President Wilson"   W.E.B. DuBois *102*
"Dear Emily"   Beverlye Brown *104*
"Gus Is Dead"   James O. Elder *107*

Exaggeration *109*
Comparisons *111*
   Metaphor and Audience *112*
   Gesture and Metaphor *113*
   Other Gestural Correspondences *114*
Active Verbs *115*

**III HOW-IT-HAPPENS—TECHNICAL, EXPOSITORY,
ARGUMENTATIVE, AND FICTIVE**   **118**

How Things Happen: Subjects and Principles; Perception and
      Expression of Instances and Patterns *118*

From *How Children Fail*   John Holt *118*
"Baltimore School Days"   Joan Engel *122*
"Rats"   Mike Schwarz *123*
From *Pages from a Worker's Life*   William Z. Foster *128*
From *The Year of the Gorilla*   George Schaller *133*
From "The Behavior of the Mountain Gorilla"   George Schaller *137*
From *The Voyage of the Beagle*   Charles Darwin *138*
Journal Instances for "Parents, Children, and No"   John Schultz *140*
"Parents, Children, and No"   John Schultz *142*

Writing Your How-It-Happens Instances *146*

Monsters *148*

From "The Garlic Monster"   Andrew Allegretti *149*
"The Bread Monster"   Shawn Shiflett *150*

Telling and Writing Your Monster *151*

Parodies and Satires *152*

"Magical Mechanical Machine"   Scott Hoeppner *153*
"How Far Would You Go?"   Gary Gaines *153*
"Station Break"   Cloteria Easterling *155*

Writing Your Parody *155*

Comparison and Contrast of Short Instances to Develop Patterns *156*

From *Paper Lion*   George Plimpton *159*
From *Origin of Species*   Charles Darwin *160*

From *The Golden Bough*   James G. Frazer *161*
From *The Man Who Loved Children*   Christina Stead *162*
"Elaine's and Sheila's Dreams"   Ann Hemenway *163*

Writing Your Comparison and Contrast of Short Instances *163*
How-It's-Done, How-It-Works, How-It-Occurs *164*

"The Stud Ace"   John Madler *165*
From *The Jungle*   Upton Sinclair *168*
From *The Sea Around Us*   Rachel Carson *169*

Description of a Mechanism *171*
Pencil Sharpeners *171*
Turbochargers *171*
"Scissors"   Marina MacMichael *173*
From *"In the Penal Colony"*   Franz Kafka *173*

Writing Your How-It's-Done, How-It-Works Telling *176*
Writing Your Description of a Mechanism *176*

Model-Telling *177*

From *Lay My Burden Down*   B.A. Botkin *178*
From *Moby Dick*   Herman Melville *180*
From *All the King's Men*   Robert Penn Warren *183*
From *Close Quarters*   Larry Heinemann *184*
"The Mating of the Mantis"   J. Henri Fabre *186*

Writing Your Model-Telling *188*

Model-Summary *188*

From *The Robber Barons*   Matthew Josephson *188*
"Chimpanzees' Touching Behavior"   Jane Goodall *189*
From "Old Mortality"   Katherine Anne Porter *190*

Model Extended Comparisons (Analogies, Similes, Metaphors,
          and Figures) *191*

From *The Death and Life of Great American Cities*   Jane Jacobs *196*
"The Search Party"   James O. Elder *199*

Writing Your Model Comparison (Analogy, Simile, Metaphor, Figure) *201*

Model-Character-Telling *202*

From *The Man Who Loved Children*   Christina Stead *202*
"Cool Willie"   Ronald Booze *205*
"Route Manager"   James Hall *207*

Writing Your Model-Character-Telling *209*

Model-Type-Telling *210*

From *The Robber Barons*   Matthew Josephson *210*
From *Blue Collars and Hard Hats*   Patricia Sexton *211*

Writing Your Model-Type-Telling *211*

Model-Place (and Model-Instrument)-Telling *212*

From *Book of the Eskimos*   Peter Freuchen *212*
From *Eskimos and Explorers*   Wendell H. Oswalt *215*
From "The Encantadas or Enchanted Isles"   Herman Melville *216*
From *The Voyage of the Beagle*   Charles Darwin *218*
From "Blackhawk"   George Bailey *219*

Writing Your Model-Place-Telling *221*

IV POINT-OF-VIEW—ESSAY AND FICTION   **222**

Point-of-View *222*

From "Problems of Collecting Oral Literature"   MacEdward Leach *223*
From *The Kandy-Kolored Tangerine-Flake Streamline Baby*
    Tom Wolfe *224*
From *The Man Who Loved Children*   Christina Stead *224*
From *Einstein: The Life and Times*   Ronald W. Clark *228*
"Wordsworth Visioning and Re-Visioning"   Randall Albers *229*

Using Point-of-View Structure in Your Writing *231*

Opposites *232*

"Morgan"   John Schultz *232*
From *The Informed Heart*   Bruno Bettelheim *233*
From the Introduction to *Native Son*   Richard Wright *235*
"Marge"   Sharon Weber *239*

Writing Your Opposites *241*

Story-Within-a-Story *242*

From *Moby Dick*   Herman Melville *243*
From "Jonah" *247*
"Adam and Eva Mae"   Reginald Carlvin *248*

Writing Your Story-Within-a-Story *254*

Dialogue Form *255*

The Allegory of the Cave Plato *255*
"Which Is Better—Anticipating Something or Getting It?"
    Ann Hemenway *260*

Writing Your Dialogue *262*

Letter on Behalf of Yourself *262*

"Jack London to Messrs. N. Clark & Sons" *263*
"At Melville's Tomb"   Hart Crane *264*
"A Letter to Harriet Monroe"   Hart Crane *264*
"To: Ward Heeler, 51st Ward"   Andrew Hyzy *267*
"Resume"   Jeanette Haynes *269*

Writing Your Letters on Behalf of Yourself *271*

"Let's Spoil" Approaches to Argument and Persuasion *272*

"Let's Spoil the Wilderness"   Robert Wernick *272*
"Let's Give Babies Drugs"   Paula G. Trent *277*

Writing Your "Let's Spoil" Argument *279*

V GROUP ADDRESS—ARGUMENTATIVE ESSAY AND FOLKTALE   281

Course of Reasoning in Support of a Public Issue *281*
  Assignment 1—Solar Energy vs. Nuclear Energy *281*
  Assignment 2—Handgun Control vs. Unrestricted Gun Ownership *282*
  "Euthanasia" Marilyn Mannisto *283*

Writing Your Side of a Debate *287*
Eulogy of a Normally Uncelebrated Object *288*

  "The Book of Matches" Chris Sweet *288*

Writing Your Eulogy of a Normally Uncelebrated Object *291*

Folktale *292*

  "The Master Thief" The Brothers Grimm *293*
  From *Mules and Men* Zora Neale Hurston *297*
  "How to Melt, Blacken, and Break" Betty Shiflett *300*
  "The Cat and Mouse in Partnership" The Brothers Grimm *302*
  "A Cat and a Chick Hooked Up" Sandra L. Crockett *304*
  "Prologue" to *Basic Research Methods in Social Science* Julian Simon *306*

Writing Your Folktale *308*

VI HOW-IT-HAPPENS—INSTANCE COLLECTIONS AND GENERAL
   ESSAYS   309

How-It-Happens Instance-Collections *309*

  "How People Relate to Cancer" Marilyn Mannisto *309*
  From "D to the Knee! Stone to the Bone!" Dino Malcolm *316*

Writing Your How-It-Happens Collection of Instances *320*

General Essays—Combining Personal Observation, Research Through
        Reading, and Other Research Methods *321*
Speeches *321*

  "Oration by Chief Seattle" *321*
  "On the Murder of His Family" James Logan (Tah-gah-jute) *322*
  From *Introductory Lectures on Psychoanalysis* Sigmund Freud *323*
  "When Will You Be a No-Till Farmer?" Dick Lehnert *325*
  From "The Gospel of St. Mark" *327*

Definitions *328*
Cause and Effect *331*

  "Hard Starting—Causes and Cures" *331*

Comparison and Contrast—Division and Classification *333*

  From *Motion Will Be Denied* John Schultz *333*
  From *The Jungle* Upton Sinclair *337*
  "Cairo, U.S.A. 1971" Betty Shiflett *338*
  "Einstein and Frankenstein" Michael Finger *345*

Writing Your Essays—Content, Clustering of Instances, and Organization *348*

General Essays—How-It-Happens—Research Through Reading *350*

From *The Art of Survival*   Cord Christian Troebst *351*
"Why Nothing Seems to Work"   Rasa Gustaitis *354*
From *The Art of Scientific Investigation*   W.I.B. Beveridge *356*
From the Introduction to *The Portable Faulkner*   Malcolm Cowley *359*
"Workerology"   Reginald Carlvin *361*

Writing Your General Essay—How-It-Happens—Research Through
    Reading *368*

VII HOW-TO-DO-IT-BETTER—ARGUMENTATIVE ESSAY   372

How-to-Do-It-Better—Technical Form *372*

From *Moby Dick*   Herman Melville *372*
"How to Play Pinball Better"   Kevin Kotowski *375*
How to Eat a Hostess Ho Ho Better   Sue Ferraro *377*

Writing Your How-to-Do-It-Better Technical Form *378*

How-to-Do-It-Better—Parodic and Satirical Social Proposals *379*

"A Modest Proposal"   Jonathan Swift *379*
"Dear Henry"   Daniel Andries *384*

Writing Your Parodic and Satirical How-to-Do-It-Better Proposal *389*

Writing from Start to Finish

The 'Story Workshop' Basic Forms Rhetoric-Reader

To the Teacher

The "Story Workshop"® Basic Forms Approach*

Before there was writing, there was oral telling.

The forms of discourse in oral language are elaborated into the forms of discourse in written language, bridging the seeming dichotomy of speech and writing, with continuous two-way traffic. As anthropologists and linguists have taught us, preliterate languages, wholly oral and gestural, are as intrinsically complex as any language that uses writing. The Incas had no form of writing, yet their language had a complex verb structure and their engineers could "run" a perfect irrigation contour for twenty miles and perform other engineering feats.[1] How were preliterate peoples able to codify and transmit among themselves their knowledge, history, wisdom? How were they able to maintain the grammar of their languages without codified and written rules? The speakers of any language develop an intuitive understanding of the grammar and general syntax of their language. Far from letting their speech go "in one ear and out the other,"[2] (and their gestures go in one eye and out the other?), as asserted by those who seek to abolish phonetic writing's direct connection to speech, preliterate peoples intuitively used (as we still use today) "basic" forms of oral discourse. They used them (as we still use them today) to abstract and organize mental seeing, express concrete perceptions, and make messages memorable in the minds of hearers. Abstraction in writing, in all fields, comes originally from mental seeing in interplay with language. The broad family of basic forms includes imagery (with vivid gesture), how-it's-done and how-to tellings, model-tellings, folktales (using structures that vary from one language and culture to another but always with an organizing movement of voice), other structures of repetitions keyed to imagery such as formulary sayings[3], and the basic audience sense and flexible structures of speeches using the personal pronouns of "I," "you," and "we." Though in writing the basic oral forms of discourse become expanded and changed according to the special potentials and limitations of writing, these same oral forms pro-

---

*Story Workshop is a servicemark of John Schultz who originated and developed the Story Workshop method of teaching writing in 1965, U.S. Patent and Trademark Office Reg. No. 1080612.

1. Hiram Bingham, *Lost City of the Incas: The Story of Machu Picchu and Its Builders*, Duell, Sloan, and Pearce, 1948. Atheneum, 1963, p. 10. And: *The Ancient Civilization of Peru*, J. Alden Mason, Harmondsworth, England, 1957, 1968, pp. 230–236. Though the Incas used the quipu (knotted strings) for statistical record-keeping, and an abacus for calculating, their literature and science, their wisdom, depended upon mnemonic devices of oral language, i.e. upon basic forms, sometimes associated with the quipu.

2. Dominic W. Massaro, "A Stage Model of Reading and Listening," in *Visible Language*, Vol. XII, No. 1, Winter 1978, p. 4.

3. Walter J. Ong's studies of the use of formulary sayings in oral cultures and of the relationship of orality to literacy may be found in various publications, including *Rhetoric, Romance and Technology* (Cornell, 1971) and an article by Ong in *Profession 79* (MLA, 1979).

vide in writing both the flexible structure of expression and the connection to the wellsprings of concrete and abstractive perception. Since anyone who learns to write effectively uses these natural forms of discourse intuitively, consciously or unconsciously, by osmosis, by hook or by crook, we make written expression more effective and greatly clarify and facilitate the process by which students learn how to write when we develop a clear and active understanding of these natural forms of discourse and their connection to writing.

The basic forms of discourse elicit and organize the expression of our thinking and directly and immediately involve sense for the audience, whether present or imagined. In origin their purpose was—and is—to organize and set forth abstractive seeing with speech and gesture in order to meet immediate and long-term teller and audience needs: to convey usable information, persuade cooperation, store the knowledge of the oral culture, and artfully involve people in a common history and experience. We use these basic forms daily, as our forefathers used them thousands of years ago, as we learn to speak language itself, without thinking about them. The tremendous transformational potential of the more complex oral forms made the great development of writing possible. Let's examine the development of these basic discourse forms to show how we use them naturally in writing and can use them consciously and powerfully.

Before there was oral telling, there was seeing in the mind.

The image that we tell in speech and gesture or in writing "can overleap the intervening space and be reformed in the head of somebody else" (Bronowski, *The Visionary Eye*), so that the receiver can act accurately upon the information carried by the image. Seeing-in-the-mind includes visualization, conceptualization, symbolization, perception from the other senses, empathy, sense for points of view, the capacity for making concepts and the connections between concepts, and for pictorial seeing in the mind as clearly and with as much impact as one sees in a vivid dream. With seeing-in-the-mind, we conceive and anticipate the spatial and time and other relationships that we need and desire so urgently to communicate to other human beings. Yet we should seldom expect to "see" our mental seeing like film or television unrolling in our minds. Such strictly pictorial seeing would thoroughly inhibit our full seeing processes for concretion and abstraction. Writing abstracts from seeing-in-the-mind and *with* seeing-in-the-mind to find what we have to say.

In common speech, we say "I see" in order to say "I understand." When we exclaim at a funny story, "Oh, I can just see it!" we're registering the seeing in our minds. Our mental seeing occurs in our dreams, daydreams, etc., everyday problem-solving, and abstract reverie. Without seeing-in-the-mind human beings cannot remember or anticipate how to get from one place to another, how to find something left in the attic, how to solve any problem, and have no materials or tools for abstracting patterns and insights. In his *Autobiography,* Albert Einstein spoke of the importance of using (and used himself) the abstracting reverie of seeing-in-the-mind: "When . . . a certain picture turns up in many such series [of memory-pictures], then—precisely through such return—it becomes an ordering element for such series, in that it connects series which in themselves are unconnected. Such an element becomes an instrument, a concept. . . . It is by no means necessary that a concept must be connected with a sensorily cognizable and reproducible sign (word); but when this is the case, thinking becomes by means of that fact communicable." With seeing-in-the-mind, we can generate from our hypotheses a range of consequences that we "see" require further experiment and solution. Einstein used seeing-in-the-mind as a tool, to pose problems and solve them. We see to solve and solve to see. We tend to work out problems in a narrative problem-solving movement, like a story we see and tell ourselves about how the problems might be solved. In practice, when we begin to experiment with our ideas, we find—that is, we see—more solutions. We expect from our seeing-in-the-mind a result that will be understood by others. We expect them to be able to say, "Oh, I see!" If they can't say, "Oh, I see!" we know we haven't succeeded yet, which can be a fault of our expression or of our audience's reception.

Our seeing-in-the-mind exerts a pull upon language in order to produce the verbal-visual image that will communicate information to others. This verbal image is the primary discourse form, capable of handling complex technological and argumentative as well as other human needs. Seeing-in-the-mind and language is the combination (in coordination with hands, opposed thumb, bipedalism, sexuality, laughter, and other specific human attributes) that made human technology and art, human *life*, possible. Other primates, such as Japanese macaque monkeys who learn how to wash potatoes, separate wheat from sand, swim, dive for kelp, show the capacity for anticipatory seeing in procuring food and pass this seeing from one generation to another by observation and apparent remembrance of observation. But they do not have language. In human evolution, seeing-in-the-mind developed prior to language and, among human infants today, still develops prior to language. When the child, at about twelve months of age, *sees* in his mind that the thing which we hold behind our back, or things left in the next room or at a friend's house, are still *somewhere* and can *return,* seeing-in-the-mind is at work. The child is already showing "the ability to make images of absent things" (Bronowski). Children see objects and actions in their minds, and work out a kind of "substrate of grammar" with these mentally-seen objects and actions (Paivio), then build language in further interplay with seeing-in-the-mind. The power of utterance precedes seeing-in-the-mind, but is not in itself language. The child's seeing-in-the-mind draws upon the separate capacity of the power of utterance and builds it into language. This becomes the source for the deeply evocative power of named objects and sensory words which is particularly stimulating in learning how to write. The separateness of the capacities of language and seeing-in-the-mind is demonstrated when we observe that the object signified by the word "ball" in English is accomplished by "pelota" in Spanish, and by other sounds in other languages. Language gains its original meaning from seeing-in-the-mind, but the word "ball", in a person's language development, becomes free of any original sight of a ball and may be used not only for the whole class of objects but metaphorically as well.

Our mental seeing pulls magnetically upon language and gesture, with an urgency of sense of address and a pressure for precision, to express perceptions of how things work. At the same time, we use language and gesture to explore, discover, and elaborate meaning from our mental seeing. When we see how to do something and tell someone what we see so the other person can do it, or when we try to tell the imagery of a dream so someone else can see it, our hands move involuntarily to describe actions and visual concepts and we find our gestures and language discovering meaning. Again and again students do their first effective writing when they see an event, process, imagined concept, or dream clearly in their minds and tell it (orally and in writing) so someone else can see it. Their grammar also becomes clearer, their sentences better formed, which suggests the original closeness of seeing-in-the-mind and language. The relationship of seeing-in-the-mind and language is powerful and complex. Though language is built in interplay with seeing-in-the-mind, they are two separate capacities which, brought together, make human accomplishments and human life possible. Nevertheless, though brought together at crucial points in human evolution and human development, they can drift or be forced unnaturally apart, with generally adverse effects upon oral and written communication. When we find, in brain-damage research, that disturbances in oral language are reflected in similar and even greater disturbances in writing, we see the integral connection of oral language, seeing-in-the-mind, and writing coming out in strong relief.

We've heard much in popular scientific literature about the differing capacities of the right and left hemispheres of the brain: of the left hemisphere's concerns with language, logic, analysis and linear thinking, and of the right hemisphere's concerns with pattern, rhythmic, intuitive, and visual configuration thinking. The two hemispheres are coordinated by the "professor" of the connecting corpus callosum. This is actually a simplistic view of the division of the brain's work, particularly when this view attempts to describe the relationship of perception and language. For instance, visual, spatial configuration, pattern and gestalt perceptions are largely a function of the right hemisphere, while representational detail and other pictorial thinking can often be located in the left hemisphere (the left temporal lobe generates vivid fantasy and memory seeing, when electrically stimulated during brain surgery); and though overall syntax is located in the Broca's area in the front of the left parietal lobe in the left hemisphere (just back of your left temple), sense for language rhythm and gesture can be located in the right hemisphere, while the meaning of language, along with many other essential analytic capacities of intelligence, has yet another location in Wernicke's area in the angular gyrus area at the rear of the left parietal lobe (approximately above your left ear), near the area that can generate pictorial seeing. We should note that significant fiction writing ability, unlike other skills that can survive damage to un-involved areas of the brain, does not survive damage to the right hemisphere (or to the left, for that matter), though the right is not ordinarily considered a "verbal" hemisphere. Right hemisphere gestalt perception and left hemisphere detail perception collaborate with language capacities of right and left hemispheres to produce the verbal image. Writing calls into play *all* areas of the brain, a rapid shuttling back and forth between the two hemispheres according to the needs of the moment during the process of writing. No wonder that writing ability of any kind is affected by damage to *any* area of the brain: writing, the "supremely complex" skill, draws upon all areas of the brain simultaneously.

An additional complexity is that women show a greater dispersal of verbal and related capacities throughout both hemispheres, while men's right and left hemispheres tend to be more rigorously defined in their functions. Since many teachers have observed that girls tend to do better than boys in English classes, these rough mappings of capacities in the brain may help us begin to understand why both boys and girls do better in writing when teachers change to more inclusive composition approaches that emphasize visual, gestural, and form perception. Such approaches enable boys to take leadership along with girls in the composition classroom.

If persons are damaged in Wernicke's area but retain Broca's area intact, they lose all sense of the meaning of language and speak in a parody of an empty grammatical style, in a continuous rush, using such sentences as "The dog was bitten by the man," grammatically sound but without meaning; these persons do not recognize the absurdity in their empty but grammatical style. If persons are damaged in Broca's area, with Wernicke's left intact, they can still speak meaningfully though haltingly.* Language and the forms of discourse are meaningless without the content given by the perceptual complexity of verbalized seeing-in-the-mind, a complexity compounded at the very least of left hemisphere detail and right hemisphere gestalt capacities, and of Wernicke's area capacities for analysis, meaning, and language, and Broca's area capacities for syntax.

---

*Most of the material on brain-damage research is summarized from *The Shattered Mind,* by Howard Gardner, Knopf, New York, 1975.

So the coordination of language and perceptual capacities *is* complex. If we concentrate our efforts on only one area, such as Broca's grammatical capacity (as many approaches to the teaching of writing do), we will find other more important areas such as Wernicke's atrophying, as surely as other human organs and capacities atrophy without use. Such an analysis should make us focus our compositional approaches on the "all-at-once-ness" of writing—on content, seeing-in-the-mind, audience, intention, the relationship of speech to writing, and form.

If we're seeking the most fundamental of human utterances, we go back to the baby's cries, gurgles, smiles, and other signs that bring the parent to the baby and bind the parent-baby relationship. Daily the infant accomplishes rhetorical acts and becomes skilled at persuasion, using the power of utterance and expression, before he or she can properly speak "words." Still, though we find here the basic rhetorical components of speaker, speech, audience, and occasion, we do not find in the baby's utterances the other essential characteristics of the discourse forms that have enabled human beings to handle complex needs for transferring usable information persuasively. That comes with the ability to express with speech and gesture the imagery generated in our minds. Given the complexity of the relationship of language capacities and perception, it should not surprise us that, as anthropologists and linguists have seen, there is no such thing as a primitive human language. So when we begin our study of the basic forms of discourse, we find ourselves dealing first with the verbal image, a form capable of handling very complex perceptions in almost infinitely flexible ways.

Imagery, told with speech and gesture, is the first communicating form to transfer how-it's-done information to a listener so that the listener can "see" the information and thereby believe it and act upon it. Image, the primary basic form, at once the abstracting method and product by which our perceptions internally "speak" to us, pushes its concrete-abstractive relationship into our attention, first to deliver usable information to ourselves, then through language and gesture to others. In fact, we begin with the seeing and the seeing immediately begins abstracting what we need to know. Seeing involves us in the process of solving, while at the same time it "speaks" to us, that is, catches our attention with perceived relationships that have already begun the solving. I put quotes around "speaks" to suggest how the abstracting sense pulls or summons our attention to these relationships. For instance, if I see in my mind that a bottle of cider rolling around in the back of my station wagon may strike something and break, I can act to rearrange things to prevent the accident. The audience is myself. This "speaking" of our seeing-in-the-mind pulls on our attention without necessarily using language. However, mental seeing also exerts a magnetic urging upon gesture and language to transfer concepts vividly from one mind to another mind. When a mechanic gives a hard upward flip of his fingers off his thumb and uses the phrase "a little rock" to show how a rock was spun up by the tires to puncture the oil filter, the gesture and phrase transfer a visualized concept precisely to the receiving mind. The "intention" of our seeing is to transfer the image and its message to ourselves or to others.

Seeing-in-the-mind is at once *concrete* and *abstractive*. Mental imagery should be distinguished from seeing-in-the-mind. Seeing-in-the-mind is the full capacity and process, while imagery is one of its most important methods and products. Those who hear an image and see the gestures that accompany it have a persuasive understanding of the information that has been transferred to their minds, a communication distinct from and more objectively complex than such information as "I am hungry" or "I am in pain" or "I am frustrated" given by the baby's cries. The latter are useful to both baby and parent and perform the rhetorical purpose of securing attention and bringing the parent to the baby, involve the parent in reading the signals to determine the need, but do not transfer a specific relationship, seen in the teller's mind, that can be seen also in the hearer's mind and applied in other contexts. Imagery persuades us by the inherent logic of its clarity, making it the immediately available natural form to convey complex information that can be reformed with a high degree of accuracy in the seeing-in-the-mind of the hearer.

Image relates *something to something else,* such as relating "ball" to the direction of "up" and "down" with a gesture for the action of the ball. "Ball fa' down" employs the something to something else relationship as clearly as "When you are old and grey and full of sleep/And nodding by the fire . . . ."

Potentially, seeing-in-the-mind can be expressed in a medium other than speech, yet it "speaks" nonverbally, pushing across to our internal awareness the abstractive image relationships that take our attention. For a moment, in its inception, simultaneously concrete and abstractive, an image hovers, purely itself, part of the separate capacity of seeing-in-the-mind, and could reactively enter any medium capable of conveying it in a more or less successful outcome, though it is fundamentally coded to be expressed in words, gestures, and enactment. Among humans, seeing-in-the-mind, this most private of experiences, is made public through the universally available human medium of oral-gestural language, with its visual, poetic, and musical resources, sometimes accompanied by sketches (originally in dirt, sand, etc). Possible image relationships are, for all practical purposes, infinite. The basic image is virtually the basic sentence.

Let's follow the development of an image. A speaker, such as a small boy, may use a word to name an object or an action but the word is not an image.

Ball

This is pointing and naming. Such a single word, when voiced or read, may cause us to see an object or a class of objects and may trigger a process in the mind that produces an image, but it does not transfer a specific image with essentially the same relationship to each hearer that the hearers can then apply in other contexts.

If the boy says:

Girl and ball

this is still pointing and naming and comes closer to image, but does not give an essential relationship that can be transferred to other situations. It associates a person with an object, may have vivid associational impact in the hearer's mind, but it does not transfer to each hearer essentially the same relationship that can be applied precisely in other contexts.

If the boy adds to the pointing and naming a gesture of the hand moving from up to down to give both the verb and the spatial relationship of the perception, "Ball go poomp, daddy," we have the essential relationship of an image, with gesture supplying precision as the connecting and qualifying verb. If we go one step further and find the verb elicited by the gestural sense, we have a verbal image:

Ball fa' down, daddy.

Here we see *something and something else* related by a gestural verb sense, a perception of physics, one of the simplest forms of *how-it's-done* (or how-it-works) imagery and one of the simplest sentences: The verb relates "down" to an implied "up" and gives the relationship of what happens between "up" and "down." The boy has imaginatively seen that when the ball is held up and dropped, the ball will, without intervening obstacles, "fa' down." Because of the persuasive push and "speaking" of his seeing-in-the-mind, because of its intention to be communicated, he needs to involve the audience, to demonstrate it to his father, which adds the audience relationship. Such basic experimental inductive thinking and expression will be used throughout the boy's life, to one degree or another. If we are culturally familiar with the image's elements, it communicates essentially the same relationship to us, which can be applied by the teller and hearer to other contexts, or experienced in other contexts, whether it's "Ball fa' down" or "When you are old and grey and full of sleep/And nodding by the fire. . . ." Yeats expected us to see a woman in a chair nodding by the fire.

You probably have had the experience of remembering vividly the gesture that someone, perhaps a mechanic or repairman, used in telling you how something occurred or how something was done. You may remember—*see* the gesture in your mind—long after the words are forgotten. When we tell someone orally how to do something, such as how to fix a machine or how to get from one place to another, we communicate the precision of the image, and its abstract concepts, by gesture and by bodily and facial expression in association with language. You would have to fold your hands in your arm-pits or otherwise restrain or suppress them to prevent yourself from gesturing. Linguists speak of gesture as "embedded" in language, or as "paralinguistic." Gesture functions for us, as it functioned for early peoples, to give precise imaginative seeing, metaphorical concepts, spatial concepts, verb connections and qualifications, reactions, points of view, and so forth. In other words, no matter how hard one may try, gesture will not be divorced from the language of ordinary discourse, except by dedicated suppression. In fact, we can more properly speak of language in origin as oral-gestural language. Through oral-gestural language preliterate peoples communicated abstractive perception to each other, as, in all fields and areas of activity, we still communicate abstractive perception today. Too often teachers and students do not realize the importance of finding the correspondences (verbs, metaphors, and other words and devices) that move gestural perception and concepts into writing.

Imaginative seeing of what would and *could* happen, what *could* be done and *how* to do it, communicated by oral-gestural language, was originally anticipatory, making cooperative hunting, gathering, and tool-making possible. With the abstraction and precision of image accompanied by gesture, we are able to pull essential relationships from the plethora of detail that rich imaginative seeing gives us. Without this leaving out, this intuitive concrete-abstractive process that produces imagery and movement of imagery, we would be glutted hopelessly by our undifferentiated mental seeing and would not be able to communicate with other people at all, let alone swiftly.

Formulary sayings constitute one group of basic forms in oral cultures. Formulary sayings in each oral culture employ the particular resources of that culture's language to draw upon imagery of seeing-in-the-mind to create memory aids that make the message easily recalled. *A stitch in time saves nine* is a formulary saying—once you've heard the rhyme, you can hardly forget it. Among preliterate English-speaking peoples rhymes, alliteration, and other poetic mnemonic devices delighted the hearer at the same time that they made laws, recipes, and other "wisdom" memorable. Anglo-Saxon laws were rhymed so persons could remember them. The witches' incantatory recipe in *Macbeth* is another example. Nowadays we often hear such imaginative formulary poetry in jump-rope rhymes, "signifying" rhymes, and songs in work and play activities. In the Gulf Coast states, formulary sayings are at work in the rhyme that distinguishes the poisonous coral snake from the harmless one by the placement of the colored rings: "Red on black is a friendly Jack/Red on yellow will kill a fellow." Formulary rhymes help "store" such information as: "Thirty days has September, April, June, and November . . .etc." Each fall and spring we make sure which way to move our clocks with the time change: "Fall back, spring forward." Stereotyped metaphors get across certain meanings succinctly, surely, and often humorously: "sleep like a log," "climb like a monkey," "work like a dog," "busy as a bee," etc. Obviously, formulary sayings are alive and prevalent in speech today, just as the broader family of basic forms is intuitively, unavoidably alive in our ordinary use of oral and written language. The formulary saying is one form in the larger family of basic forms. Meant to be succinct and rigidly formed in oral telling, the formulary saying's transformational power is limited in writing, but not entirely unuseful. Certainly, in English, rhyme forms are capable of considerable extension and transformation in poetry, but none of the formulary forms have the transformational capacity of verbal imagery and other forms in the broad family of oral basic forms.

Preliterate peoples rely upon clear imagery and demonstration keyed with the full family of basic forms for communicating usable information persuasively. We find the first level of the basic forms in how-it's-done, how-it-works (non-instructional process) imagery. Actually, we could argue that even this first level is "instructional" in that its seeing-in-the-mind "speaks" to the perceiver nonverbally. Next comes the more complex *how-to imagery*, which puts together all the techniques of mental seeing, utterance, language, audience sense, gesture, in particular adding the argumentative dimension and the other rhetorical modes of thinking and expression. All other forms and modes are derived and elaborated from how-to imagery.

When we add the instructional and argumentative dimension to how-it's-done perception, involving the "you" as learner and doer in the more complex how-to form, we become capable of transferring clear, usable perception and persuading cooperative effort. E.g.:

> When you throw it [a frisbee], do you just close your eyes, aim in the direction of your player, and pray? No good, Charlie! Keep your eyes open, aim at your partner, make sure your arm is straight toward him or her, and fling it with an even stroke. Now is that so hard?

The most important dimension of basic forms potential, after image, is the physical movement of voice in time connecting and organizing all the elements of the expression, abstracting with the process of imagery to find what it needs in order to get the message across to the audience and to leave out what it does not need. Strong imaginative seeing generates movement in language, and such movement makes possible longer and more complex presentations of informative imagery, with more demand for rhetorical artfulness.

The how-to image (and the movement over time of the voice giving the how-to imagery) emerged not only to convey complex technical information but also to persuade the hearer to cooperate in the proper doing of the skill. The arts of necessity gave rise to the necessity of art, and came early to bear upon how-to imagery. The pictorial arts of Stone-Age religion developed in close association with the how-tos of hunting, gathering, and tool-making.

In addition to the use of imagery for its inherent persuasive clarity, we attempt in the how-to to persuade by reasoning, charming, proving, wheedling, illustrating, demanding, demonstrating, teasing, coaxing, cajoling, soothing, threatening, intimidating—using whatever expression, impulse or technique will work to secure people's effort toward a common goal. Rhetoric, properly understood, is the most necessary and most practical of human skills. The writing class should permit students to exercise the full range of persuasive impulses and techniques in their writings. The very form of the how-to, with deep roots in our common evolutionary heritage, calls upon a natural urge to artfully engage the audience, employing any appropriate techniques of language, e.g. imagery, tongue-in-cheek teasing, and so forth, as can be seen in a writing class that knowledgeably develops the form. All the principal characteristics of discourse forms can be found in, and are elaborated from, the movement of how-to imagery.

Here is a written example that helps demonstrate both the function of oral basic forms and their connection to the written versions. It's from *Cross-Country Skiing Today,* by John Caldwell:

> You've seen pictures of a good skier in full flight: right arm reaching out ahead to set the pole, matched by the forward-driving left leg; left arm and right leg extending backward, almost parallel. If you draw lines from arm to arm and leg to leg you'd see why we call this x-c signature "the diagonal."
>
> Although the stride is a natural elongation of walking, if you're like me and try too consciously to correlate these movements, you may get all mixed up. But if you master the steps—meaning the stages—described below, you'll be well on your way. Thereafter it's only a matter of lots of practice. And your work will be repaid, for a good diagonal combines power (provided by the thrust of legs and poling action) with moments of relaxation as the limbs swing forward once more.

The fact is that we may or may not have seen pictures of "a good skier in full flight," but after reading these two paragraphs we can *see* in our minds and gesturally sketch to ourselves the movements and imagine ourselves as skiers in "flight." The author addresses "you," the natural inbuilt audience of the how-to, and refers directly to "me," himself, the speaker. From his seeing the demonstration in his mind, he not only abstracts the essential diagrammatic image and definition of "the diagonal," but also compares the abstract image to a "natural elongation of walking," a familiar image in our minds. Overall we feel a persuasive intention at work, the speaker involving the "you" as learner and doer. By making us see and identify with his and our human tendency to get "mixed up" when we try too consciously to correlate these movements, he further familiarizes us with the comparison and the problem. Through the "sustained speech" of alphabetic writing, he moves the seeing-of-his-mind into our minds. Thousands of readers (or hearers) can carry out the same instructions from the specific imagery transferred to their minds. Such image, language, and rhetorical principles may be observed at work in the speech and gestures of everyday how-to telling. Throughout the process of this perceiving and telling, as in other basic discourse forms, we are comparing and contrasting instances, perceiving effect and cause, analyzing, defining, dividing and classifying, and generally using intuitively the modes of thinking and expression that we call the rhetorical modes.

Form is not a matter of arbitrary decision or imposition. Forms grow out of the interplay of imagery, language, and the need and purpose of communication. Yet form also acts with an independent power (as Baudelaire observed) not only to organize and relate content to the audience, but also to *evoke* content and help us to *see* the meaning in our seeing. Form draws meaning to it, and meaning seeks form.

Because of our need to understand what has happened in the past and to anticipate and predict needs for present and future, we have need for basic discourse forms to organize our thinking and to express perceived patterns of behavior. The *model-telling* form grows from the sequence and process of the how-it's-done and the learning and doing situation of the how-to. "See, daddy, ball always fa' down" is a model-telling of how it usually happens when the ball is dropped. If you say (and we daily make such statements), "Every time you step out the door, the cold hits you in the face . . ." or "When I came home, we would always . . ." and then, with imagery and narrative, however brief or long, give a model of what would usually happen, you are intuitively using the model-telling form. Sometimes we summarize instances that give patterns and frequently we mix imagery of what "always" happens with summaries of instances. When vivid imagery gives a model of a pattern of behavior, it will be recalled by the hearer, a kind of storage in the memory, and its information will be predictively usable by him or her.

Model-tellings can be observed readily in everyday oral and written discourse, in technical, scientific, narrative, expository, and poetic oral telling and writing. Though derived from characteristic aspects of the how-it's-done and how-to forms, the model-telling may be used in those forms too, which illustrates the combining of forms in ordinary discourse. Fundamentally, the model-telling uses the present tense and/or the conditional mood (would) and the implied or directly addressed "you." The model-telling's use of the present tense is sometimes called "the historical present," which implies a model of a pattern of actions. However, the model-telling is by no means limited to "the historical present"; it makes characteristic use also of the conditional mood and other tenses—indeed, it shows its great flexibility in using all pronouns and tenses according to the needs of the material and context. The purpose of the oral model-telling in origin was to greatly increase our ability to predict behaviors of people, animals, plants, natural forces, and so forth, by presenting imagery that would stay clearly in the mind. The following examples of model-tellings are taken from written works and show the connection of the oral basic forms to their written counterparts.

Here is a model-telling of how it usually happens at noon on board the whaling ship *Pequod,* told to the "you," using the present tense and the conditional mood. Though it occurs in a fictional work, it could just as well be used in social science writing to give a model of status behavior in an institution:

It is noon; and Dough-Boy, the steward, thrusting his pale loaf-of-bread face from the cabin-scuttle, announces dinner to his lord and master; who, sitting in the lee quarter-boat, has just been taking an observation of the sun; and is now mutely reckoning the latitude on the smooth, medallion-shaped tablet, reserved for that daily purpose on the upper part of his ivory leg. From his complete inattention to the tidings, you would think that moody Ahab had not heard his menial. But presently, catching hold of the mizen shrouds, he swings himself to the deck, and in an even, unexhilarated voice, saying, "Dinner, Mr. Starbuck," disappears into the cabin.

When the last echo of his sultan's step has died away, and Starbuck, the first Emir, has every reason to suppose that he is seated, then Starbuck rouses from his quietude, takes a few turns along the planks, and, after a grave peep into the binnacle, says with some touch of pleasantness, "Dinner, Mr. Stubb," and descends the scuttle. The second Emir lounges about the rigging awhile, and then slightly shaking the main brace, to see whether it be all right with that important rope, he likewise takes up the old burden, and with a rapid "Dinner, Mr. Flask," follows after his predecessors. (From *Moby Dick,* Herman Melville)

Here is a model-telling in the past tense, of the way it "always" happened for the writer on ambush in Viet Nam:

Every time we went out we sat watching the cart trails or a footpath or a rice paddy, until first light or the first rush of blood in our ears when all of a sudden there he was, skylarking down the trail right at us. And then we blew him away with a claymore, and watched him fly and bounce and roll. Some quiver, some wiggle, some are stiff right away. Every night for weeks, months. Years maybe. (From *Close Quarters,* Larry Heinemann)

You can practically hear the oral telling of it and see the teller's gestures for the verbs. The one line "Some quiver, some wiggle, some are stiff right away" summarizes instances of patterns.

Now look at the model-telling in a piece of reportage:

I could not be seen arriving for interviews with white people in cabs driven by black people. There would be no interview. A regular white cab took me to Bob's Restaurant on Washington, where a huge young man at a back table kept a revolver stuck under his belt, half-hidden by a fat belly. From Bob's I walked around the corner to the black United Front. Often at night two cabs were necessary with a neutral switch point in between. The black cab would be crowded with many people and silent because of my unexplained presence. With one notable exception, the white drivers called me "Baby" in an intimate, gritty way. The necessity behind the cloak-and-dagger performance rapidly took on the weight of a stone. (From "Cairo, U.S.A., 1971," Betty Shiflett)

In "The Mating of the Mantis," Henri Fabre employs personification in a natural scientist's model-telling of how the praying mantes act at mating time:

It is near the end of August. The male, that slender swain, thinks the moment propitious. He makes eyes at his strapping companion; he turns his head in her direction; he bends his neck and throws out his chest. His little pointed face wears an almost impassioned expression. Motionless, in this posture, for a long time he contemplates the object of his desire. She does not stir, is as though indifferent. The lover, however, has caught a sign of acquiescence, a sign of which I do not know the secret. He goes nearer; suddenly he spreads his wings, which quiver with a convulsive tremor.

Model-comparisons, model-character-tellings, model-place-tellings, model-instrument-tellings, and other variations are flexibly and widely used in all modes and kinds of oral and written discourse.

Movement of voice in time not only organizes the imagery of the how-to and model-telling forms that help us control our environment through transfer of useful information, but also makes possible speeches and storytelling with a wide range of technical, entertaining, and argumentative purposes. Among both preliterate and literate peoples, speeches influence and stimulate an audience toward an issue at hand, and storytelling (including story enactment) entertains and stimulates our sense of belonging to a people, affirms cultural beliefs, mores, history, and gratifies our complex needs for story. Speeches may also entertain audiences, and storytelling may argue a point or transfer technological information. Music and enactment may accompany storytelling. Among preliterate or folk storytellers, the standards of artfulness are high. The group that hears the imagery, model-tellings, repeated structures, poetic and formulary devices of a folktale (characteristic techniques that help the tale "stick" in the minds of the listeners) can reconstruct it more or less true to the original telling days, weeks, or months later. Recall of any part of the structure of the folktale begins to stimulate recall of the full story.

In speeches among preliterate peoples vivid imagery conveys the message to the audience.

Every part of this soil is sacred in the estimation of my people. Every hillside, every valley, every plain and grove, has been hallowed by some sad or happy event in days long vanished. The very dust upon which you now stand responds more lovingly to their footsteps than to yours, because it is rich with blood of our ancestors and our bare feet are conscious of the sympathetic touch. Even the little children who live here and rejoice here for a brief season love these somber solitudes and at eventide they greet shadowy returning spirits. And when the last redmen shall have perished and the memory of my tribe shall have become a myth among the white man, these shores will swarm with the invisible dead of my tribe and when your children's children think themselves alone in the field, the store, the shop, upon the highway or in the silence of the pathless woods, they will not be alone. (Oration by Chief Seattle)

Among classical orators this natural use of seeing-in-the-mind to act as memory aid, organizer and conveyor of meaning, was developed consciously as a kind of "inner writing." Cicero tells us that Simonides, who originated the classical art of memory, prescribed that orators "must select places and form mental images of the things they wish to remember and store those images in the places, so that the order of the places will preserve the order of the things, and the images of the things will denote the things themselves, and we shall employ the places and images respectively as a wax writing-tablet and the letters written on it." (From *The Art of Memory,* Frances Yates)

When drawing upon the imagery of our seeing-in-the-mind as we make our arguments, speaking to a small audience or to an intimate familiar audience (however large), it would be unnatural for us not to use the personal pronouns "I," "you," and "we." In writing as well as in speech, the use of the personal pronouns and the intimate sense of audience comes first and should, because of its sustained connection to speech, always be preferred over the neutral approach to audience in which all personal pronouns are avoided. The natural, appropriate use of the personal pronouns should be the first permission rather than the last permission that we give ourselves in the "sustained speech" of writing.

Personal pronouns often imply eye-contact with the audience. In other kinds of oral narration or how-it's-done telling, we use the third person and keep our eye (and our audience's eye) on the imaginative seeing without direct eye contact of teller with the audience. When I use "I" for myself as the speaker in expository and argumentative discourse and "you" or "we" for the reader, these personal pronouns connect to an internal sense of speaking to an audience during the process of writing, and help me to organize and express the content. Sometimes while writing in the third person, I can feel the "I" and "you" and "we" in the wings or out in the audience, so to speak, without naming them explicitly, and get the same benefit. The appropriate use of all pronouns makes up the basic forms audience sense.

Because writing is done for future audiences, the teaching of composition has generally overlooked, or overleaped, the necessity for using an *immediate* audience to help develop the *imagined* audience sense; for the imagined audience is also an immediate audience, a stand-in for the future reader. A psychiatrist in a case history writing class had so little sense for his audience when he was writing alone that he worked out an ingenious solution for his need: he hired his son to sit near him so he could look up at the boy while he was writing. A law professor discovered that his students consistently did their most effective writing when he asked them to imagine themselves as lawyers writing a memo to the head of a law firm, with the purpose of making the head of the firm understand the facts of a case. Writing for immediate audiences, such as writing for others in one's class, in forms with a built-in imagined audience that directly connects to the internal sense of composition, stimulates and helps develop our internal sense of audience. Rather than use such approaches in an occasional ad hoc way, we can develop them in a comprehensive program with correspondingly larger benefits.

Oral basic forms techniques are able to handle complex materials. They reached their artistic culmination in preliterate times with the long stories that were told, sung, and acted in many cultures by accomplished storytellers. Once there was scholarly debate about whether the Homeric epic story-poems, the *Odyssey* and the *Iliad,* were originally written or orally told. The weight of the debate tended toward the side that asserted they had to have been written. Then Millman Parry, through a study of the tale-singers of Yugoslavia, discovered the modern-day use of the techniques that demonstrated how the epic story-poems could be orally transmitted by accomplished tale-singers using a variety of poetic memory-aid devices, including formulary techniques keyed with vivid imagery, names, and (I may add) forms such as speeches, stories-within-a-story, model-tellings, and other basic forms. In *Preface to Plato,* Eric A. Havelock argues for the instructional nature of the formulaic techniques of Homeric verse and suggests that Homer's oral epics developed in close association with literacy. At a time when the Greeks were emigrating to islands near Asia Minor, Homer's tales, sung and told in public performance, were used to keep the Greeks Greek. Instructional and informative purpose inherently characterizes the broad family of the basic forms.

With the invention of phonetic writing, especially in its most advanced form of the alphabet, speech and writing become directly connected, that is, the written language becomes a secondary form of the spoken, a kind of "sustained speech" (Britton, Diringer), making it possible for the powers of speech and abstractive seeing to be explored in the potentials of the fixed medium of writing.* Because of the nature of "sustained speech" in alphabetic writing, almost infinite re-writing becomes possible. Oral basic forms provided a certain dimension of "sustained speech" for oral discourse, a kind of "inner writing," helping the oral teller to stabilize in memory what he or she had already told and to add to and heighten it by modification. Using the genius of the oral form antecedents, written basic forms expand the tremendous economy and concentration of basic forms techniques. In the "sustained speech" of the permanent medium of writing on the page, the basic forms were elaborated through direct phonetic correspondences for speech elements and indirect correspondences for gestures (e.g., verbs, metaphors, comparisons, juxtapositions, etc.).

In written tellings we take for granted techniques that find the right correspondences for oral methods and expand them to exploit the potentials of writing, as exemplified in the three following excerpts from materials that were originally orally told.

> One day an old man and his wife were sitting in front of a miserable house resting awhile from their work. Suddenly a splendid carriage with four black horses came driving up, and a richly dressed man descended from it. (From "The Master Thief," a Grimms' tale)

> You see in de very first days, God made a man and woman and put 'em in a house together to live. 'Way back in them days de woman was just as strong as de man and both of 'em did de same things. They useter get to fussin' 'bout who gointer do this and that and sometime they'd fight, but they was even balanced and neither one could whip de other one. (From "Why Women Always Take Advantage of Men," by Zora Neale Hurston)

> You say you can't throw a frisbee straight. You want to throw it toward someone and it veers off into another direction. You say you throw it up—it flies up; it stops in mid-air; it flies back directly towards you, over your head, and hits someone on the head. Is that what's troubling you, son? (From "How to Throw a Frisbee," by Allan Johnson)

---

*Though the meaning elements of early writing systems were principally visual, any writing system to be writing must function with a close correspondence to spoken language (Yuen Ren Chao).

When phonetic writing became directly and precisely connected to elements of the oral language, it became capable of reaching into our internal world that "speaks" to us with concrete-abstractive mental seeing and other "non-verbal perceptions." "A barefoot boy in a blue shirt running down the street . . ." is the image that the language psychologist Vygotsky uses as an example of *thought*, when he says "I can conceive of all this in one thought but I put it into separate words." Thus, in this case, he identifies *imagery* as *thought*. The world of "inner speech" uses what Vygotsky calls "predication," with understood subjects, felt verbs, a sense of words as much as the words themselves, "a fluttering between word and thought," a darting interplay of perception and words, a sense of thoughts that escape or miscarry words; it also uses, we may add, the non-verbal "speaking" of relationships that take our attention, and the outright sounding and dramatizing of speech in our minds. These are the most reactive levels of language and perception. Language, in that it combines perception, feeling, form, aim, purpose, and sense of audience, is not the mirror of thought/imagery, though it may seem at times nearly to mirror thought; nor is it only the medium—the language of discourse is the *outcome* of the reactive interplay of perception and language and all other factors.

The "sustained speech" of alphabetic writing connects to this inner world of perception and speech, as well as to our external speech and gesture, and makes possible the more elaborate development of perceptions and patterns. Through extended note-taking, in such forms as journals, diaries, logs, etc., we are able to put elusive instances, thoughts, and observations onto paper where we can see, study, and dwell upon them in order to discover patterns and connect series of patterns to produce the concepts on which the development of science and technology is based. Writing is capable of giving particular attention to recording and interpreting instances and patterns of instances that are produced by the highly selective and abstractive process of the seeing-in-our-minds. Because we can see our speech on the page before us, rather than have its sounds depend upon memory as we speak them aloud, the "sustained speech" of phonetic writing also makes possible the more elaborate development of sentences and paragraphs, which often aids the organization of complex thought. Such syntactical development should never be the primary or principal emphasis in writing and should seldom be treated separately from the full writing task, for the full writing task has eliciting and organizing power beyond the separate treatment of any of its single aspects. Robert Frost observed that no amount of deliberately and ingeniously varied sentence structures can make sentences dramatic. "All that can save sentences is the speaking tone of voice somehow entangled in the words and fastened to the page for the ear of the imagination. That is all that can save poetry from sing-song, all that can save prose from itself." And only the basic oral forms can save written discourse from itself. The great dimension of the permanent medium of writing opens up when we can use the power of speech to develop sentences on the visible page.

Those elements of a "basic form" most clearly identifiable—such as pronouns of address, audience sense, characteristic verb tenses, and the intrinsic intuitive structure and purpose of the form—are the elements that make it most useful in eliciting and organizing oral and written expression. Basic forms elements can be readily recognized in such forms as how-it's-done (process) writing, instructional how-tos, letters, journals, model-tellings, speeches, expository and argumentative essays (lecture address), stories-within-a-story, advertising forms, business and technical reports, street and game poetry, songs, and so forth. The combination of basic forms elements changes according to purpose, content, and context.

By now we can see that the process of oral and written composition occurs within a sort of *compositional theater of the mind* that includes seeing-in-the-mind, the verbs and phrases (the "predication") of inner speech, internal listening, basic forms, tenses, sense of address, oral language and gesture, the full cast of the pronouns of address, all playing their parts in the production. A basic form emerges from the process of this theater incorporating many of the elements of the theater's workings. For instance, we witness the small-group address of some how-tos, folktales, and speeches elaborated into the imagined lecture (or letter) address of writing to an audience of interested professionals or laymen.

If you read a few pages of *The Golden Bough* by James G. Frazer or *Introductory Lectures on Psychoanalysis* by Sigmund Freud, or the insect essays of Henri Fabre, as examples of early modern scientific writing, you find that these authors used imagery and other basic forms pervasively, developing them from clear oral antecedents. Juxtaposed with passages from many contemporary *impersonal* scientific and expository writings, you find by comparison that Frazer, Freud, and other early modern scientific writers used the full personae of pronouns of address—you, we, I, he, she, they, one, someone, and many variations of the third person, a veritable novelistic or theatrical cast of characters. They also used varied verb tenses—present, past, future, and the conditional mood—integrally and intuitively related to sense and context of address and form of the passage, rather than paving the writing over with one uniform tense. They wanted to be understood by those who picked up their books and read them, so they intuitively incorporated into their writing the explicit basic forms elements of the compositional theater of the mind. The writer who invites the reader to participate as both conceiver and appreciator, writer and reader, gains greater reader involvement, stimulation of the reader's curiosity, clarity of transfer of thought, a better chance of getting across what he or she has to say. To enable the reader or hearer to see what you see, understand what you understand, was Plato's definition of communication.

Many contemporary scientific, technical, and other expository writings attempt to expunge every mark of "personal" or "subjective" awareness, every sign of the compositional theater of the mind. Such writing avoids pronouns of address wherever the sentences can be formed to avoid them, uses only neutral pronouns if pronouns cannot be avoided—"it," "one," and occasionally "he" and "she"—and enforces uniformity of tense. The aim of such writing is impersonal objectivity no matter what the cost, no matter what abstractive perception, audience sense, and clarity of communication are paved over. Yet, try as they will to be purely impersonal, these writings cannot expunge the *present tense* from expository address to *future* audiences—the ultimate "subjective" tense of inner language and perception, the tense of the compositional theater of the mind's direct framework address to its immediate internal audience of the imagined future reader, and the fundamental tense of the basic forms. We see the present tense in the direct framework address of such works as *Tom Jones, Vanity Fair,* and many other classic and contemporary works. Within its framework, the compositional theater uses appropriate tenses in relating the material to the reader in the past-present-future context of oral and written discourse.

The unexpungeable present tense in expository writing that strives for *impersonal* objectivity forces us to consider that there may be no such thing as "impersonal" knowledge, and even the striving for it is a wrong effort in a wrong direction. Further, the present tense in these writings suggests that every other sign of the mind's compositional theater has been cut from the visible work or allowed only minimal participation in it. Our attempts to be "neutral" and "objective" by expelling from the process of writing the signs of the mind's utterly necessary compositional processes, divorces us from the most important wellsprings of concrete-abstractive seeing-in-the-mind, sense of address, and language expression. To the extent that we do not use these composing processes fully and effectively, we diminish the clarity and power of writing.

In the following excerpt from George Schaller's "The Behavior of the Mountain Gorilla," we have clear examples of how seeing-in-the-mind functions from the first gathering of data (the journal entry), through the abstracting processes of finding the patterns in the data, to the final abstract presentation, in which imagery performs the necessary function of rendering the message accurate and stable in its communication to various readers. An examination of the tenses of this passage, in relation to the context of the materials, also reveals Schaller's overall basic forms sense: past tense model-tellings (the past tense occurs because of the contextual relationship of the writing to observations in the past), present tense address to reader, and present tense journal entries.

Definite dominance interactions were observed 110 times (Table 3-3). Dominance was most frequently asserted along narrow trails, when one animal claimed the right of way, or in the choice of sitting place, when the dominant animal supplanted the subordinate one. Gorillas showed their dominance with a minimum of actions. Usually an animal low in the rank order simply moved out of the way at the mere approach or brief stare of a high-ranking one. The most frequently noted gesture involving bodily contact was a light tap with the back of the hand of a dominant individual against the body of a subordinate one.

Table 3-3 Dominance interactions between age and sex classes

Dominant Animal	Silver-backed Male	Black-backed Male	Female	Juvenile	Infant	Total
Silver-backed male	13	1	26	9	2	51
Black-backed male	—	—	2	3	—	5
Female	—	4	12	13	11*	40
Juvenile	—	—	—	4	8	12
Infant (One year or older)	—	—	—	—	2	2
Total	13	5	40	29	23	110

*Tabulated only if infant was not in direct contact with its mother at the time.

One example from my field notes illustrates a typical dominance interaction:

A juvenile sits under the dry canopy of a leaning tree trunk during a heavy rain storm. A female walks toward the juvenile who rapidly vacates its seat, while she appropriates the dry spot. Shortly thereafter the silverbacked male arrives and pushes the female with the back of his hand on the lower part of her back until she is out in the rain and he is under cover.

Dominance was largely correlated with body size. Silver-backed males were dominant over all black-backed males, females, and young. (From "The Behavior of the Mountain Gorilla," by George Schaller, in *Primate Patterns*, ed. Phyllis Dohlinow.)

If Schaller had made only abstract statements about gorilla dominance behavior, the volatile connotations of such words as "dominance" and "asserted," plus the usual mythical distortions about gorillas in people's minds, would cause many distortions. Indeed, virtually all abstract statements become victims to such distortion. If writing lacks abstractive imagery, the message becomes unstable in its communication to another mind. Even an abstract statement such as "a minimum of actions" needed for a dominant gorilla to assert himself could easily be misunderstood. The image of the final sentence, the most frequently noted gesture being "a light tap with the back of the hand of a dominant individual against the body of a subordinate," gives the precise, clearly seen and understood qualification that accurately characterizes gorilla dominance. All of the patterns of gorilla behavior are abstracted from the imagery of journal entries. Seeing-in-the-mind is crucially present from beginning to end of the abstracting process, the first and the last, to provide the basis, substance, method, and accurate qualification of the discussion. All effective writing, in all fields, originates in the abstracting processes of pattern-perception in seeing-in-the-mind. Even people who claim to work solely with abstraction in language are actually working with abstractions that originated in the seeing-in-the-mind of other people. The *separateness* of our language capacity, though originally built and coordinated by seeing-in-the-mind, enables language to express a high degree of abstraction of meaning, i.e., of carrying to a high degree of abstraction meaning found by image, pattern, cluster, principle, and configuration perception in seeing-in-the-mind.

How is language able to move so far into abstraction without necessarily breaking its lifeline connection to seeing-in-the-mind? Language "distances" itself from the building of meaning by seeing-in-the-mind, but continues dynamically to receive and change meaning at the behest of the intentions and perceptions of our seeing-in-the-mind, though language is by no means simply an obedient servant but expresses the "outcome" (Vygotsky) of its encounter with seeing-in-the-mind's powerful intentions and perceptions. This "distancing" allows word meanings to change in context with other words, in context of forms, and in context of audience, and for abstract, oblique, irrelevant, deceitful, half-truthful, non-sensical (playful as well as no-sense), very flexible manipulation to occur. How do we investigate the relationship of meaning to language which, though imperfectly understood, is broad and powerful? If someone argues that there is a precise impression behind every word, we may ask—how far behind? Is there such a thing as a single investiture behind each word? What do we gain with language's "distancing" from seeing-in-the-mind? What do we gain from language's clear association with seeing-in-the-mind? Does the transformational capacity of language's "distancing" from seeing-in-the-mind depend for its meaningfulness upon the lifeline connection to seeing-in-the-mind? For instance, many of the verbs that English absorbed from Latin and French have become usefully general and abstract, i.e., "distanced" in their use, but have a clear seeing-in-the-mind impression of meaning in their etymological origins. The word "capable" originally meant "to hold," to "seize and be able to hold." In Indo-European, the word "holy" was connected intimately with impressions of "whole, healthy."

Here are examples of how seeing-in-the-mind impressions not only give words meaning but also dynamically provide the impulse or influence to bend or change the meaning of language. In my late teens, I was instructed by an English teacher that the word "livid" meant "bluish" rather than "reddish with anger" or "extremely angry, spluttering with anger," which was what I wanted it to mean. In one blow, the seeing-in-the-mind impression of "bluish" dislodged my original impression of "reddish" or "furious." "Bluish" provided a strong enough dose of seeing-in-the-mind to accomplish the overthrow of my previous meaning. Along with that English teacher, *The New American Webster's Handy College Dictionary* (Copyright 1951, 1955, 1956, 1957, 1961, 1972) allows only: "dull bluish in color, as in a bruise." Nevertheless, more English-speaking people share the seeing-in-the-mind impression and impulse that "livid" means "reddish" or "extremely angry" than share the notion that it means "bluish or ashen." So that *The American Heritage Dictionary* (Copyright 1969, 1970) will allow livid to have as a third meaning: "Extremely angry; furious," but not "reddish." *Webster's New College Dictionary* (Copyright 1976) allows "reddish" along with "bluish" and "extremely angry." Obviously the meanings that come to prevail in the usage of common speech are often forced upon dictionaries. If the word "livid" can mean "bluish" or "reddish" or "extremely angry," then our seeing-in-the-mind can, potentially, make a word mean whatever it wants or needs it to mean, so long as our listeners share this understanding.

There are also cases in which a seeing-in-the-mind impression of meaning is difficult to dislodge. The seeing-in-the-mind meaning of "extremely angry," commonly associated with "livid," is evidently one of them. Seeing-in-the-mind bears upon our private use and interpretations of language as well as upon widely shared meanings. When I was in my teens I thought the word "inchoate" meant "chaotic" rather than rudimentary, only because I found the word in the context of the phrase "inchoate chaos"—I loved it, even though my meaning was redundant—and did not bother to look it up in a dictionary. I'll probably never be able to use the word "inchoate"—should there ever come an occasion, other than an ironical one, for using it—without the echo or association of "chaotic" occurring for me; so that, though the accepted meaning of "rudimentary" intruded heavily upon my original impression behind the word, it did not completely dislodge the ghost of it, possibly because "rudimentary" is more abstract than "bluish" or "reddish" or "furious." Nevertheless, our English abstraction of "rudimentary" derives from concrete Latin meanings of "rough, raw, beginning," and "inchoate" from origins of "to begin, to harness," both words having been more precise and different in their original meanings, which came more directly from the speakers' seeing-in-the-mind.

In a broader cultural development, the word "silly," from its Old English seeing-in-the-mind meaning of "blessed, happy," changed its impression of meaning through changing societal attitudes toward persons deemed to be "blessed," to "pitiable," to "unreasoning, stupid, frivolous"; i.e., we English-speaking peoples no longer think of such aberrant behavior as "blessed" but as "silly" in our modern meaning for it. However, the German word from the same root retains a meaning similar to the original. "Dolor" in Spanish carries meanings of "sadness" and "melancholy" that are not carried by the English words "pain," "ache," or "hurt." Our word "pain" is derived from Latin and Greek meanings of "penalty," while "dolor" has its source in Latin meanings "to feel pain, to grieve." "Ache," in Proto-Indo-European, means "fault, guilt" or "to cause mental pain." Rather than use the word "pain" to give a direct impression of the experience of pain, we may use it to sheathe us from, or make oblique, the sensation of "pain" or our association with it (Wittgenstein, Holub). Children seem to realize that "hurt" more directly relates to the experience or sensation of pain, so that they say "I hurt, Mommy," rather than "I feel pain," or "It is painful," for "pain" involves more "distancing" and "obliquity" from the sensation. My son used the word "knee" to mean "hurt," because, being a vigorous fellow, his most frequent association with "hurting" was in his knees. Later, when jolted or bumped, he would sometimes look up at his parents to see from their expression if he was "hurt" and other times look at himself to see if he was "hurt," whereas with other kinds of "hurt" he reacted—howled—without waiting for interpretation from his or anyone else's point of view. Human beings work out the meaning of their words in action with perception, with audience, and with other words. So seeing-in-the-mind, early and late, continually gives meaning to, in interplay with, language.

Seeing-in-the-mind meanings not only give precision and range to words but also provide the capacity that makes possible continual, dynamic change in meanings and use. Even our prepositions such as "of," "in," "with," "by," "after," etc. are relational, involving an abstract seeing-in-the-mind spatial sense to give them their meaning, as in ". . . and nodding by the fire." Indeed, a seeing-in-the-mind impression makes it possible for us to agree on the impression of meaning to be carried by the word. The closer the "distancing" or the more precise the relationship of the word to seeing-in-the-mind, the more precise the use of the word and the more force it has for conveying meaning. If language were not powerfully and fundamentally involved in receiving meaning from, and creating "outcomes" of thought with seeing-in-the-mind, its "distanced" (useful and un-useful), abstract, irrelevant, non-sensical, non-sequitur, non-meaning occurrences would have no significance for us and could not be named as such. Language, in its "distanced" freedom in relation to seeing-in-the-mind, nevertheless occurs in powerful interplay with seeing-in-the-mind, so that the "outcome," what we express, does not belong purely to one or the other capacity.

However, when we break the lifeline of our language's connection to the concretizing, abstracting and analytical processes of seeing-in-the-mind, our language becomes extremely imprecise—not to mention dull—in its communication to readers. Allan T. Paivio's research in *Imagery and Verbal Processes* finds that wholly abstract verbal expression, i.e., writing and speech without clear basis in concrete imagery, is uncertain and unstable in its communication to reader and listener. A psychiatrist found that the "pure" abstractions of a case history were misunderstood by his readers, but the abstractive imagery of his original journal entries was clearly understood. Seeing-in-the-mind and language are capacities that, despite their original close association, and despite the original building of language from seeing-in-the-mind, can, as we mentioned earlier, drift or be forced apart. If language is divorced from seeing-in-the-mind, or if seeing-in-the-mind is used only for performing such menial duties as supplying vivid "detail," language loses its power of exploration and abstraction. As with other human organs and capacities, as suggested earlier in our discussion of what brain research reveals about the connection of the area of brain concerned with language meaning to other language involved areas, lack of use causes atrophy of the capacity or the coordination of capacities.

Francis Bacon warned us, as have other scientists/thinkers, against the danger of desiring greater order and equality of priorities than actually exist in the complex universe we perceive. Heeding this warning complicates our lives, because our need for order and simplification is also one of our most positive and productive traits. For instance, few subjects can be more complex than the relationship of language and perceptual capacities. People turn away from examining (or utilizing) the complexity of this relationship as if from the dazzle of the sun, and, as in Plato's *The Allegory of the Cave,* try to make shadows and fragments function as reality, in an order much removed from, and not at all parallel to, the powerful reality which is not so orderly as we would often desire. Students are unknowingly but frustratedly chained as they confront the shadows of the conventions of writing, projected before them by texts, teachers, and approaches. This fragmenting and scrambling of priorities—for example, emphasizing isolated sentence structures and formal grammar, rather than the actual process and context of a whole essay or other writing task—confuses people who are learning to write and prevents their best powers from reaching the real task of writing. Because word meanings change in the overall context, and because the relationship of meaning to language, though imperfectly understood, is broad, powerful, and positive (Rummelhart), writers can work better with sentences and paragraphs within a whole discourse form. If a student is having trouble with sentences and paragraphs, it is symptomatic of deeper troubles in the whole process and task of writing. We can do more to rectify the deeper problems evidenced by faulty sentences and paragraphing by working with regular assignments of whole discourse forms, directing our students first and foremost to emphasize effectiveness in getting across what they have to say in writing to an audience, using whatever language techniques will do the job.

We should keep ourselves warned against this anxious need for more fixed order and simplification than actually exist in our universe of perception and expression. When we see the aspects of one form, such as the sequence and process of the how-it's-done and the learning situation of the how-to, changing and transforming into another form, such as the very flexible model-telling, which in turn gives the transforming power of forming to other derivations, we are witnessing the dynamic order of a dynamic universe. ("There are some enterprises in which a careful disorderliness is the true method," says Melville, tongue-in-cheek.) Rather than turn away from the dazzle of the dynamic universe and declare that "nothing makes any difference," we should let our eyes clear and push ourselves to recognize that the dynamic order is not only the way things really happen, but also the *best* way for things to happen. We should coach ourselves to take advantage of the immensely flexible order and transforming power of forms and forming.

Many teachers have asserted that students today receive a language conditioning drastically different from and less productive than that of students prior to the 1960s. On the other hand, some historians of composition (Ohmann, Douglas) would dispute the notion that students today are any less "literate" than students of previous generations, and would say that "literacy crises" have been chronic in our history. However that may be, at age 18, the average student comes into our composition classroom having received 12,000 hours of schooling (what quality and depth of reading and writing experience?) and watched and heard 15,000 hours of television (about 3½ hours a day). In addition, the student has listened to a great deal of radio and electronically delivered song, watched many movies, and been exposed to written advertising that simulates certain kinds of fragmented oral language and direct personal address. The depriving effects upon perceptual, verbal, and motivational capacities are undoubtedly immense. The usurpation of time that could be devoted to other activities, particularly to imaginative play (social or individual), which is acknowledged to be the most important learning process for children, affects their willingness and capacity to engage in imaginative problem-posing and problem-solving. Television watching not only reduces the time spent in play, reading and other activities, but reduces the generative seeing-in-the-mind produced by imaginative play and its major extensions, the reading of strongly evocative literature, the enactment of story, and the use of story in visual arts.

The average preschool child watches 54 hours of television per week, or 7½ hours per day. Observers note that television watching tends to anesthetize the child's impulse to play (probably because it diminishes the imaginative seeing that produces the impulse), and tends to render the child irritable, uncooperative, and impatient of even simple demands. The rigidly passive, addicting effects of television watching—the immobility of the viewer's body, the fixed eyes, the reduction of time and impulse for imaginative play and reading, the increase of muscle and nerve tension without release through play or other activity, the narrowness of the sense experience, the medium's inherent lack of technical variety, the emphasis upon quick-changing image techniques, the usurpation of direct experience—all these and more skills-diminishing effects of television watching are not readily overcome by the approaches commonly used in our classrooms. In fact, classroom approaches often appear to be chosen to avoid or mask the problem, rather than engage it.

Further, the language of the television experience is flat and shallow when compared to almost any natural oral telling (both factual telling and storytelling) among preliterate or literate peoples. It's a peculiar kind of oral language at that, scripted or otherwise script-influenced (Ong), often fragmented in ways that no natural oral language is ever fragmented. This language of scripted or script-influenced fragments not only employs fewer verbs than would occur in oral language, but also leaves out the rich variety of verbs, adjectives, and adverbs suggested by gestures. The "cool" attitude of the medium of television tends to suppress gesture, and gesture is obviously excluded from the medium of radio and electronically delivered song. Perhaps our modern experience with oral-gestural language and imaginative perception has not been as rich and various as the experience in decades past of people who developed their oral-gestural expression in close association with reading, and not as rich as the oral-gestural expression of preliterate peoples.

Yet, despite the depriving effects of this saturation media exposure, there is something left for us to work with. In conducting writing-across-the-curriculum and composition teacher-training seminars, I hear teachers again and again comment that students show liveliness, intelligence, and capability in speech, when compared to the same students' awkward, stiff, frozen incapacity in writing. In addition, storytelling and discussion among student peers can be lively, imaginative, and astute. I hear many teachers ask, "How can you get students who are verbal geniuses with speech and gesture in the hallway to use that power in writing?" Here is what I tell these teachers:

Not all the fault of students' lack of success with writing should be laid at the screen of television, but much of it at the door of the classroom. If writing and reading were taught differently, the negative effects of television would be lessened. Seeing-in-the-mind is essential to develop the power of pleasure in reading, which is the most important single enabling factor in learning how to read with facility; and inward hearing is essential to an awareness of meaning of language (built from seeing-in-the-mind). Observations from different fields indicate the close relationships among external hearing, inward hearing, and the apprehension of meaning in language. Fast typists can transcribe a page without remembering immediately afterward a single word; the meaning has gone in one eye and out the other, so to speak. Children blind from birth learn to speak and read relatively easily, but children deaf from birth have great difficulties in learning to read. Throat surgeons forbid patients who've had throat surgery to read, because the throat muscles work silently as the reader scans the page. This throat muscle movement is not detectable by pressure of fingers, so inward hearing is deeper, subtler, and more pervasive than simple sub-locution, i.e., sounding words as you read them. Inward hearing is built by external hearing. Yet nowadays, in our educational institutions, reading and writing are only sporadically *heard*. Teachers who avoid approaches that connect speech, audience, writing, reading, and imaginative seeing-in-the-mind have forced not only external but *internal* silence and blindness upon writing and reading and made these most complex and exciting of human skills dull and uninvolving.

Teachers of rhetoric and writing usually agree upon certain creed-like statements but seldom give them practical attention. Rhetorics, for instance, remark on the "interchangeability and interpenetration" (Brooks and Warren) of the modes of discourse in ordinary speaking and writing, while also stating wisely that style is the expression of a personality apprehending the elements of the full writing task. "Style and content are inseparable, and the very cleavage between them is a symptom of something gone wrong." (Brooks and Warren) "Writing is an art, with choices abounding." (Young, Becker, and Pike) Well, something's gone wrong all right, and the cleavage between style and content runs right through the writing classroom. Texts, administrators, and teachers assume, advocate, prescribe that students need to study and practice isolated aspects of writing. They assume that students should practice sentences (bits and pieces of isolated grammatical formations), then paragraphs (and other bits and pieces), then five paragraph essays, before they try to write whole discourse or any full writing task that calls into play all aspects of writing at once. They compare this practice of the separate "bits and pieces" approach, rather inappropriately in each case, to a musician practicing scales before he or she plays music, to a swimmer learning the various strokes before he or she swims. Texts and teachers tell students "you must learn the strokes before you can learn to swim," and therefore you must master isolated tasks of formal grammar, sentences, and paragraphs before you can write to communicate effectively to an audience. Yet we can see that something's wrong with the analogies, for the swimmer is actually swimming as he or she learns the strokes, and the musician's scales are carried out in almost immediate relationship with playing music. As a matter of fact, a music teacher would not begin with scales. In most sports and arts, the coaches and players practice virtually immediately the "whole" activity at the same time that they practice the parts. For instance, the novice archer must perform the complete act of drawing the bow, however clumsily, to practice shooting arrows.

The basic and dynamic usefulness of wholistic approaches to learning is backed up by anthropological observation. The activity of *play* is the primate's—and even more so the human primate's—most important form of learning; and one of the main characteristics of play is that it wholistically combines so many elements all at once. (Dohlinow) Primates excluded from play—from wholistic learning activity—do not develop necessary skills. Texts, teachers, and administrators claim that they simplify the process of writing into divisible, supposedly easily mastered parts, only to find (if they are open enough to observe any pattern that differs from their assumptions) that they have mired their students in hundreds of unrelated "bits and pieces" of skills, so that they hear the more intelligent students say, in effect, "I think I see where you want me to go, but I don't see how to get there from here." For eight years, the Chicago Public School system has employed, by administrative imposition, a "bottom-up" approach to the teaching of reading, requiring students to master 283 separate reading skills (it was originally 500, reduced to 283 by union negotiations), which now produces 11th grade students who, having mastered the 80% of the skills regarded as sufficient by the program's goals but having never read a whole book, are actually semiliterate. After eight years of schoolwide implementation, the majority of Chicago public school 11th grade students read no higher than the 25th percentile on a national scale (the 10th percentile is virtually the "chance effect" range). Do school systems (texts, teachers, administrators, etc.) "simplify" reading and writing into so many "bits and pieces" of skills for the students' sake?

Actually, many teachers of writing observe that those students who read actively for their own interest and pleasure (difficult to accomplish if you're continually distracted by trying to concentrate on 283 separate skills) are the ones who tend to grasp writing as a whole, all-at-once activity, rather than as a helter-skelter assemblage of "sentences and paragraphs and grammars and admonitions and modes and forms." But even these students tend to sicken with the unholy (unwhole, unhealthy) diet of "bits and pieces" of skills. In other words, from the very beginning, even in the course of learning how to roughly form words on paper, students need to work with and be carried by the "whole" activity of writing and have control and responsibility for their discourse (Graves), trying to get something across in writing to someone else as effectively as they can, relying upon and building from the resources of their own language.

Rather than accept defeat or abridgment of our goals before this unfortunate compounding of negative conditioning, we can seize the advantage of our observations that students do well in oral discussion and work well in groups, that is, in immediate audiences. We can and should prize and cultivate a dynamic standard English over a rigidly codified one—a powerful mixed diction that will welcome the unique voices of all writers and better achieve our language goals. We can benefit from the foothold of the students' power of speech by relating natural oral discourse forms to their written counterparts. We can move in the directions suggested by modern research in composition, that is, stimulating and sustaining the process of writing by directly relating perception, reading, speaking, listening, and writing. We can coach our students to put emphasis first and foremost on effectiveness in getting what they have to say in writing across to an immediate audience, using activities that help them draw upon and combine the language they use with peers, world, parents, teachers, and other audiences, thereby helping their sentences become better-formed and their use of discourse forms to be more naturally effective—better than occurs when we divide their concentration by emphasizing formal grammar and other isolated "bits and pieces" of the conventions of writing. We can and should invest the writing course from the very beginning with the principle that style, within a community of writing models, is the expression of an individual voice and personality apprehending the elements of the full writing task. We *can* help our students learn to write better than even the best student writers of their parents' generation, as I believe the undergraduate writings in this text will begin to demonstrate.

At this point many teachers of writing may look with wistful longing toward the prospect of this dynamic world in the teaching of writing and still be restrained by one base fear: If I let students write "the way they speak," will they write grammatically? First, it is inaccurate to talk abut writing "the way one speaks." Rather, we should say: Yes, they will write better-formed sentences if they're allowed to draw upon and build continuously and instinctively from the sentences they use in casual speech and when talking with peers, that is, if they're allowed to develop the powers of their speech and perception in the potentials of writing in close association with oral reading and silent reading. The following summation of research comes as a bemusing shock to teachers in the writing-across-the-curriculum and composition teacher-training seminars that I've conducted.

"Everyday speech," "casual speech," and "working-class speakers," according to William Labov's research, reveal proportionately more well-formed sentences than middle class or educated speech and speakers.[4] Time and time again I have seen doubtful teachers try in-class writing and reading aloud of the writing, in which the students address their writings directly to other students,* and be startled that it produces, when regularly used over the period of a semester, better-formed expression than these teachers are accustomed to seeing from their students. A major emphasis upon formal grammar actually hinders students in learning to write effectively. In its place, at the right time and priority, in the context of full composing processes, exploration of the grammar of sense and meaning will have a good effect in developing a powerful mixed diction. Indeed, this exploration is most effective if oral reading and hearing of the writing heighten recognition of the grammar of sense and meaning. Most of the problems of expression will be handled best by working with full writing processes and forms, in a context that relates reading, speaking, writing, and listening.

When writers rely on their intuitive grammatical sense and put their effort and concentration on getting across what they have to say to their immediate classroom

---

4. *Language in the Inner City: Studies in the Black English Vernacular,* by William Labov, University of Pennsylvania Press, Philadelphia, 1972, p. 222.
*See *Teacher's Manual* for a description and discussion of these techniques and approaches.

audiences, their expression becomes better-formed. Whenever students have an immediate sense of address urging them to clarity, such as in a how-to or a letter or a journal or other basic form, when their seeing-in-the-mind is actively exerting a pull upon their language, their writing stands a chance of becoming compelling. The same person writes dull stuff when he or she tries to write an essay that doesn't yet have the advantages of active seeing-in-the-mind, sense of address, and other clearly defined flexible characteristics of a basic form. When we're exploring a basic form, our emphasis on the obvious characteristics of the assigned form make a big difference in helping students learn how to write. The way we involve the students in our assignments makes a big difference. The in-class audience approaches we've discussed in the Teacher's Manual must be carried out regularly, without any equivocation on our part; we must put our emphasis first and foremost upon the sheer communicating effectiveness of the writing over any other priority.

Because the basic forms relate oral language forms to written language, they provide a natural bridge from speech to writing and enable us to draw upon the familiar language that we speak rather than forcing us to learn an "alien" language called writing. Across this bridge the students' best powers of perception, speech, gesture, and listening can move and come readily to bear upon the problems posed in their writing.

I

The How-To Form

Introduction

How often has someone, in giving you directions, left out essentials of the task or blurred them because they didn't see it the way you would see it? The how-to form is implicit or explicit in the oral or written telling of anything we do. From cooking a meal to persuading a jury, from playing a game to fixing a car, from obeying rules to modifying them, from job to sport to play, it focuses on the physical and psychological skills, competencies, techniques, make-sure points, and attitudes for doing whatever it is effectively. The how-to is a fundamental form of on-the-job writing. The naturalness and variety of the how-to make it pleasurable to write. It is also one of the most common forms of published writing. All forms of engineering and industry and communications, all of the sciences and social sciences, most professions, most trades, require clear technical perception and effective writing.

The telling and demonstrating of how-to instructions that can be clearly recalled and followed has been the responsibility of how-to tellers and the how-to form throughout human evolution. Our dependence upon the cooperative use of technology (from rocks, bones, sticks, and fire to cybernetics) makes the how-to basic and crucial. The how-to puts a strong emphasis upon vivid imagery, course of reasoning, and persuasion.

Here is part of a how-to that was told orally and then retold by the author in writing: (It's from "Getting the Most Out of Frisbeeing," by Allan Johnson.)

> You say you can't throw a frisbee straight? You want to throw it toward someone and it veers off into another direction? You say you throw it up—it flies up; it stops in mid-air; it flies back directly towards you, over your head, and hits someone on the head? Is that what's troubling you son? Well, the problem is in handling the thing: you're holding it wrong. Let me explain:
>
> The way you're doing it is placing four fingers under its groove and your thumb on its edge. Wrong! You place *three* fingers under the groove, one finger (index) on the rounded edge, and thumb on top.* When you throw it, do you just close your eyes, aim in the direction of your player, and pray? No good, Charlie! Keep your eyes open, aim at your partner, make sure your arm is straight toward him or her, and fling it with an even stroke. Now is that so hard?

Defines problem as the "you" sees it—uses "veers" as gestural verb.

Defines problem as the teller sees it—transfers gestures into writing

Demonstrates and compares how-not-to-do-it and how-to-do-it gestures

Why does he use the foil of "Charlie"? How does he take the needs of the reader completely and immediately into account? How does he use his authority? What does his teasing accomplish? Where do you feel eye-contact?

---

*There are accomplished frisbee throwers who differ about the placement of the fingers.

What verbs act as correspondences for gestures? The writer addresses "you," using the foil of a "Charlie" (whom the reader can see at a certain distance distinct from himself or herself), and imagines the how-to as a speech-demonstration, merging his own way of speaking with Standard English and conventions of writing. In his imagined speech-demonstration, he finds verbs and other devices to act as correspondences for gestures.

You mean we can write the way we talk? Yes, begin with the way you speak, tell it to the page, so you can develop your own voice in the potentials of writing. Almost immediately you become involved, as did the author of "Getting the Most Out of Frisbeeing," in having to find indirect written correspondences—verbs, metaphors, etc.—for certain oral-gestural effects.

How-to writing is a particularly important kind of technical and expository writing. Liking to describe their field as "writing for the world's work,"[1] technical writers assert that technical writing takes the reader completely into account. The major technical writers "abhor the grey language, or the so-called 'objectivity,' of the petty technical mind." Technical writing accomplishes little by perpetual "parts-listing."[2] Major technical writers use the full range of rhetorical, poetic, narrative, and technical methods to relate the needs of the subject to the needs of the reader. When writing takes the reader and the reader's needs into account, it becomes emphatically and intrinsically imaginative *because you must see the material in your mind's eye and imagine and sense the audience during the writing.*

The primary basic form is the image, the how-to image. The oral how-to draws upon seeing-in-the-mind for its imagery, told with language and gesture, related directly to the "you" audience of a single person or small group.

> To fully appreciate the Italian flair for creating works of intricately interdependent layers, levels, strata, and tiers, examine a pile of several kinds of fruit in any Italian grocery, or St. Peter's Cathedral, or the Mafia, or The Church, or Dante's *Inferno.* Lasagna is built somewhat along the same principle.

When you see this imagery in your mind and tell it orally to someone, you probably stack one hand on top of another and use other gestures to indicate "layers, levels, strata, and tiers." You invent ways to get gestural perception into writing.

> In this poling motion you should begin to think about pushing each arm far enough to the rear so that your hand passes by your thigh.

Here we see the image principle *of the relationship of something to something else:* "so that your hand passes by your thigh." Now examine the image principle with further, *exaggerated* instructional emphasis:

> I ask my skiers to continue pushing back with the arms, whether they are using them one or two at a time, so that I can see *some daylight between their arms and legs* (italics mine).

". . .*some daylight between their arms and legs*" makes the image relationship spring out clearly.

Seeing-in-the-mind of likenesses and contrasts *of the relationship of something to something else* produces metaphors and other comparisons:

---

1. "Teaching Writing for the World's Work," by Fred H. Macintosh, in *The Teaching of Technical Writing,* ed. by Donald H. Cunningham and Herman A. Estrin, NCTE, Urbana, IL, 1975, p. 23.
2. "What Can the Technical Writer of the Past Teach the Technical Writer of Today?" by Walter James Miller. Ibid. pp. 198–216.

Here comes a really good builder of coordination and strength. In it you propel yourself along the track using just one arm at a time, alternately, while you keep your skis steady, like a sled's runner.

The author gesturally-demonstratively sees the steady skis, with which the reader-pupil may not be so familiar, side by side with the sled's runners, with which the reader is almost certainly familiar. What comparison could be used for an audience unfamiliar with sleds?

In the following passage, exaggerated imagery and comparisons of gestural origin take into account the seeing needs of the untutored audience, showing how and why the whalemen make sure the line is coiled unkinked in the tub.

As the least tangle or kink in the coiling would, in running out, infallibly take somebody's arm, leg or entire body off, the utmost precaution is used in stowing the line in its tub. Some harpooners will consume almost an entire morning in this business, carrying the line high aloft and then reeving it downwards through a block towards the tub, so as in the act of coiling to free it from all possible wrinkles and twists.

When you're writing, see in your mind's eye what you have to tell at the moment of writing (or rewriting) and tell it so someone else can see it. That is basic. Joseph Conrad said that the task of his writing was "by the power of the written word, to make you hear, to make you feel—it is, before all, to make you see." Most writers emphasize the essential principle of seeing and making you see. Hearing, touch, smell, or taste also provide what we need to know and sometimes enable us to see something visually in a fresh, effective way.

Through striking verbal and gestural imagery, the how-to teller impresses information on the minds of hearers so they can recall and use it effectively. The basic elements of oral-gestural how-to tellings show clearly in good written how-tos, with verbs (and sometimes nouns, adjectives, adverbs), metaphors, comparisons, and other language devices providing the correspondences for gestures.

Here's a classical example from the Latin technical writer Vitruvius, of the 1st century B.C., in which we sense clearly the author's imagined lecture-demonstration as he discusses with us how to design a town better:

> The town being fortified, the next step is . . . the laying out of streets and alleys with regard to climatic conditions. They will be properly laid out if foresight is employed to exclude the winds. . . . Cold winds are disagreeable, hot winds enervating, moist winds unhealthful. We must, therefore, avoid mistakes and beware of the experience of many communities. For example, Mytilene in the island of Lesbos is a town built with magnificence and good taste, but its position shows a lack of foresight. In that town when the wind is south, the people fall ill; when it is northwest, it sets them coughing; with a north wind they do indeed recover but they cannot stand in the streets owing to the severe cold.

> *States problem thesis*
> *Elaborates imagery of problem—Make-sure point "We must . . ."*
>
> *Example*
>
> *Imagery—how-not-to-do-it, make-sure emphasis—cause and effect*

Who was the writer's audience then? Who is the audience now? You. And *we*.

* * *

Here follows a set of how-to selections, one by a well-known writer, one by a professional who is well-known in his field but not otherwise known as a writer, and three by undergraduates in writing classes. For three of the selections, you'll find keys for important, characteristic elements of how-to writing in the margin. Thus, as you read, you may easily pick up the key with the sweep of your eye to the left or right and relate it to the particular passage.

In a few cases I have analyzed the structure of paragraphs in the margin. You will find "classic" paragraphs in the selections, and yet other paragraphs with structure and rationale that vary widely from one selection to another. You should compare the paragraphs of each reading selection with other selections, to give yourself clues, not necessarily prescriptions, for how to paragraph your own writings.

When the marginal key coaches you to "See it" or "Do the gestures," make a particular effort to see in your mind the imagery and do the gestural demonstration to find out what it has to tell you. From beginning to end in the reading selections, you should try *to see everything*—imagery, objects, actions, people, metaphors, comparisons, sequences, and whatever else takes your attention—whether or not the coaching of "See it" is in the margin.

You may wish to read all the way to the bottom of the page, or even to the end of a selection, to maintain the flow of your reading, before looking to see the relationship of the marginal keys to principles at work in the passages.

From

Cross-Country Skiing Today
John Caldwell

Direct I-you address

A New Approach—and Why

Entices you with a new and better way to learn— implied problem and answer to it

In this edition I'm going to put forward a new method, or you could call it a new chronology, for learning to ski x-c (cross country). . . .

Dialogue form— develops definition of the underlying problem (use of arms and legs) that affects the learning process

This new system starts out by emphasizing certain arm movements.

Hey, wait a minute! you say—the *legs* are the most important parts of the body in skiing!

I agree. So I'll say it too. The legs are the most important limbs in skiing x-c, and provide by far the most strength, power and stability. I merely emphasize the use of the arms in this method because I think it's a good way to learn. For the following reasons:

Compares and contrasts North Americans and Europeans to emphasize and clarify underlying problem—See North American catching ball with hands, European with feet

1. *In beginning to learn a skill sport, most North Americans are far more adept with their arms than they are with their legs.*

You recall the old trick of testing arm *vs.* leg coordination by throwing a ball to someone: If he catches it with his hands, he's from North America; if he traps it with his feet he's from Europe. This difference occurs because of the North Americans' in-grained preference for such games as baseball, basketball and our brand of football, as compared with the European's being brought up on soccer, where touching the ball with your hands is a No-No unless you're the goalie.

Identifies audience—begins answer to the underlying problem, begins building confidence in pupil

Thus I find that North Americans generally have good control of their hand and arm movements—which makes it quite easy to teach them basic x-c skiing movements by starting with emphasis on the arms.

Further entices you with the new and better approach

On the Flat

What You'll Arrive At: The Diagonal Stride

A well-executed diagonal stride is the hallmark of a practiced x-c'er. You've seen pictures of a good skier in full flight: right arm reaching out ahead to set the pole,

> Defines the goal of learning, the "problem"—see the "skier in full flight"—do the gestural demonstration—see the precise exaggeration

matched by the forward-driving left leg; left arm and right leg extending backward, almost parallel. If you draw lines from arm to arm and from leg to leg you'd see why we call this x-c signature "the diagonal."

> Addresses "you," the pupil—demonstrate and draw gestural lines of the diagonal—see it

Although the stride is a natural elongation of walking, if you're like me and try too consciously to correlate these movements, you may get all mixed up. But if you master the steps—meaning the stages—described below, you'll be well on your way. Thereafter it's only a matter of lots of practice. And your work will be repaid, for a good diagonal combines power (provided by the thrust of legs and poling action) with moments of relaxation as the limbs swing forward once more.*

> Makes comparison to further understand problem—see "natural elongation of walking" in your mind's eye
> Gives you anticipation—motivation boost
> See "thrust of legs" and "moments of relaxation"—motivation boost for learning

Technically speaking, nearly all phases of hill-climbing—as well as flat skiing—use the diagonal: that is, alternate legs and arms move in a co-ordinated fashion.

> *Note:* This technique is referred to as the "single stride." I use the term myself but I can't explain its derivation: what would a double stride, or even a triple stride, be like? Probably rather difficult maneuvers. . . .

There are four steps in the following sequence leading up to the diagonal, or single-stride, technique. The diagonal will remain the classic method of traveling on x-c skis for a long time to come, despite a slight trend away from it in the racing camp. This is the stride that you will use in judging your own proficiency—or another skier's. This is the one you will most enjoy practicing, or skiing with, too.

Step One: The Double-Pole

Are you ready to go? I will assume that your equipment is ready and your skis work—that is, they are waxed correctly or are waxless skis that work in given conditions. I will also assume that you are skiing in tracks, packed out especially for x-c skiing.

> Gives assumptions that define the Model Learning Situation

The first exercise takes place on the flat or on a very gradual downhill. It's called double-poling, and you simply reach forward slightly and place both poles in the snow at enough of an angle so that, when you push down on them, the force will propel you forward along the tracks. Keep your elbows close to your body.

> See it—image—definition of double-poling—from "reach forward and place both poles" to "elbows close to your body"—do the gestures

---

*I can testify that I learned how to cross-country ski from reading Caldwell's book, putting into practice the instructional imagery, and then adding some refinements from watching other skiers. It helped to read some of the sections, then ski, then read some more, practice, review, and so on.

You may find you don't have enough strength to do this. If so, you'll have to train your arms gradually and build them up. Meanwhile, you can try this exercise on a slightly steeper downgrade where you can coast without pushing on the poles. Begin coasting, then give a push with the poles to get the feel of it. After a few times you'll have the ability to go back to the flatter—i.e., less steep—downhill.

Try It Uphill

After your arms get stronger you can try double-poling on the flats—and then, believe it or not, *up* some gradual hills.

If you are a teaching purist you're going to get after me right now and ask how in the world this poor skier can get back up the hill if I haven't taught him how to walk or climb.

That's a good question and I'll answer it this way: This sequence is aimed primarily at teaching the single-stride, or diagonal. I would hope that the teacher or the reader (pupil in this case) would get the whole sequence in mind before going out, and so perhaps would be able to apply the next steps to get back up the gradual hill.

I'll admit this will not work with some beginners. With them, there are two choices left. You let the beginner improvise. You might be surprised at what he will be able to do to get back up that little old hill.

Or you tell him to take off his skis and walk back to the beginning point.

Step Two: Single-Poling

Here comes a really good builder of co-ordination and strength. In it you propel yourself along the track using just one arm at a time, alternately, while you keep your skis steady, like a sled's runners.

Place each pole at an angle so the force will propel you forward as you push down and back on it. In this poling motion you should begin to think about pushing each arm far enough to the rear so that your hand passes by your thigh.

Again it will be easier to start on a gentle downgrade. If you progress so you can do this on the flats, then on gradual uphills, you will have developed excellent strength and coordination, both of which will come in handy doing the diagonal stride. However, it's not necessary to be able to do this exercise uphill before proceeding to the next step.

Step Three: One Step Double-Pole

In this exercise you reach forward with both arms simultaneously, as in the double-pole, and at the same time, slide one ski forward. Then push with the arms.

Practice so that you can slide either leg forward, and pole, using both arms forcefully. A good drill is to alternate your legs. Start with the left ski sliding ahead, pole, then coast a bit; slide the right leg ahead, double-pole, and coast. Continue.

See it—imagery, sequence—do the gestural demonstration—give gestures for the verbs—slide, pole, alternate, coast, double-pole

At this point you may begin using your legs for some power. As you double-pole, give a little push, or bounce (here called a *kick*), off the leg you did not slide forward. If your skis aren't holding, or if you push too hard off this more stationary leg, your ski will slip back. If this happens, don't push back so hard with the rear leg. Instead, try pushing (kicking) *downward* more.

See and give gestures for the verbs—double-pole, push, bounce, kick—give gestural demonstration for precision and feeling of the right action

Review of 1 Through 3

Make sure points

A review is a good idea at this time. Make sure you can do the three preceding exercises fairly well. Pay attention to your arm-swing, so it is relaxed as it goes forward and there is enough extension beyond your hip as the arms push to the rear. I ask my skiers to continue pushing back with the arms, whether they are using them one or two at a time, so that I can see some daylight between their arms and hips.

Pause and gathering for climax

Gestural imagery

Increase of coaching demand—teasing—see "daylight between arms and hips"

Step Four: The Diagonal Itself

To do the diagonal simply reach forward with your right arm and at the same time slide your left leg ahead; pole with your right arm and give a little push off your right leg. Then reach forward with your left arm, slide the right ski ahead and push with your left leg.

Gesture demonstration of definition of the diagonal—imperative sentences

It's like walking. You alternate: right arm and left leg ahead, left arm and right leg behind.

Comparison—"like walking"—restates main problem, goal, and definition

Climax

If you've followed the sequence leading up to the diagonal, you haven't concentrated much on using your legs. But you ought to begin now. As you pole, give a slight push down and back with the more stationary leg—which has completed its glide and is ready to extend behind you—just as I suggested you do in the one-step double-pole.

Begins fresh emphasis on main problem—see "give a slight push down and back"

When everything goes well you will glide a bit on the forward ski, then reach forward with the other arm and slide its opposite leg ahead simultaneously, pole, and push off the stationary leg, and soon you've got it. After a while you will gain some rhythm and will be able to glide along in near effortless fashion.

Do gestural demonstration for precision of sequence and verbs—push, extend, glide, reach, slide, gain

Motivation—satisfaction

How to Correct Common Diagonal Faults

The more accomplished you get with the diagonal, the more likely you are to acquire a few individual flourishes that will keep you from feeling too mechanical. Don't worry about them; they'll distinguish you from an automaton. For instance, I seem to cross one arm in front of my body, but not the other. And we had one boy on the U.S. Team who ran with his head cocked to one side.

Conclusion

Teasing reassurance—distinguishing individuality from real problems

Make sure point

Motivational
mixture of
increased
coaching demand
and easing up

Problem—cause
and effect

Answer

Problem—cause
and effect

Image—how-to-
do-it—from
"driving the front
arm" to "better
extension"

See the image of
problem

See—image—
better skiers—
comparison and
contrast

See—image of
why not to do
it—"wear
themselves out"

Image of the
answer

Problem—how to
find it—cause and
effect

Precision of
imagery—
analysis—see it
from "someone
sight on you from
ahead or behind"
to "tip over into
the snow"

Answer

Gives imagery of
problem so you
can see it in your
own mind and
correct it

The basic rule to follow in using the diagonal stride is this: *Try to make all your movements directly ahead.* Use economy of motion by making only those movements which contribute to carrying you straight along the track.

The following are a few common faults that should be guarded against in the diagonal because they can keep you from getting the most out of your effort. They don't spoil your enjoyment when you're out cruising around, but they can add up to disappointment in competition.

Not enough drive forward. To improve, you may have to develop more strength and balance. Skiing is the best way to do this. You can try skiing occasionally without poles. This helps the balance.

Not enough extension. To correct this, concentrate on driving the front arm out straight—e.g., reaching forward with your pole without bending your arm. Although most skiers don't use a straight arm out front, the straight arm sometimes is helpful in getting better extension.

Upper-body bob. If someone watches you ski from the side he can tell how much motion of the upper body you have. As the better skiers glide along the flats, their heads stay at just about the same height from the track all the time. Others bounce up and down in their strides and eventually wear themselves out—or get sore backs.

To eliminate this bob, try relaxing your back, even to consciously rounding your shoulders slightly at the end of your glide.

Side-bending. This could be a balance problem, and it's easy to spot by having someone sight on you from directly ahead or behind. Sometimes if the tracks are too far apart, or if you are skiing too much on your edges instead of on the flat of your ski, you will bend from side to side with each stride.

Sometimes it happens because you swing your arms too wide, instead of straight ahead.

Skiing without poles will often remedy this situation, especially if you use tracks that are very close together, so close that your bindings hit each other occasionally. Then, if you side-bend too much, you will tip over into the snow. Soon you'll learn to stop bending.

Hanging the rear leg "out to dry." If you ski with a fast tempo, there is hardly time to leave that leg out there, to the rear, so if you're one of those fellows who lift their rear leg too high, try skiing with a faster tempo.

Conclusion cont.

It also will help if you concentrate on keeping the rear foot as close to the snow as possible. This in turn can be helped by pointing the rear hand downward toward the snow as you finish your poling motion. (Racers are so conscious of this that they seem at full extension to be holding that rear pole with only thumb and forefinger.)

Gestural image for answer

Gestural image— touch

Commentary

Writing has many advantages over film, television, and other electronic media for relating information and instruction. For three thousand years, writing has had the advantage of being available in a more or less convenient, fixed, relatively compact, inexpensive, portable medium, from clay tablets to the printed book—particularly in the five hundred years since Gutenberg's invention of moveable type. But further, because writing, the "supremely complex" skill, involves all parts of the mind,* it draws deeply and widely and subtly upon the teller's capacities, enabling you to handle simultaneously a complexity of seeing-in-the-mind, voice, form, points of view, and sense of address with simplicity, efficiency, and effectiveness. Film-makers, for all the immediacy of the medium, find it laborious, virtually impossible, because of the limitations of film, to develop the internal points of view that are unique to writing. For instance, take the *Upper-Body Bob* two paragraphs in HOW TO CORRECT COMMON DIAGONAL FAULTS. You could do most of the imagery in film, but you would at the same time have to speak most of the writing to get across the problem and the answer, the feeling and sense of "relaxing your back" and "rounding your shoulders."

Caldwell's cross-country skiing how-to begins immediately in the imagined situation of a coach giving a speech-demonstration to the "you." This situation is *imagined* because the author sees it in his mind while instructing the "you" at the moment of writing. Notice the imperative verbs: "Start with the left ski sliding ahead, pole, then coast a bit; slide the right ski ahead, double-pole, and coast. Continue." Actually use your hands and body to do the gestures for the sequences of verbs and actions. You may notice while doing the gestures that they (or your gestural sense) are the source for many verbs in writing.

By initially enticing the reader with a new approach to learning to cross-country ski, Caldwell raises suspense and expectation, and then states the full "problem" and the goal of learning, the developed diagonal stride. He establishes the model learning situation and his assumptions about your equipment. His imagined speech-demonstration helps him organize the written how-to. Sometimes his visual presentation on the page, italicized sentences and phrases, headings, capitalization, suggest a strong pause and sweeping eye contact with the audience to gather concentration for a new aspect of learning the skill. Eye-contact is also associated with getting the attention of the "you" for either a sequence of actions or for emphasis of a point.

Throughout, his demand increases at times and eases at times, a pulse of heightening and easing of teacher demand. He uses the personal pronoun "I" in relation to the "you" to emphasize the imagined speech demonstration and the authority of the teller. At one point he changes the persona of the "you" in order to teasingly admonish an imagined fellow-teacher for lack of confidence in the pupil. Directly after the climax of the process of explaining the full diagonal itself, he reviews the learning stages to achieve an assured answer to the full problem of how to cross-country ski.

---

*We know this because if *any* part of the brain is damaged, writing is in some way affected, unlike other skills that are unaffected by certain kinds of brain damage. See *The Shattered Mind* by Howard Gardner (Knopf, 1975).

Just as Caldwell recommends review for the skier, now is a good time to review the marginal coachings, to look over and put together the basic aspects of how-to telling and writing (and of telling and writing in general). Actually do gestural demonstrations to yourself for the metaphors, similes, and other comparisons indicated by the marginal keys. You may notice while doing them that gestures (or gestural sense) were the source for many of the comparisons, as well as verbs and other devices.

Each of our reading selections shares the essential characteristics of the how-to form. Using these principles, the authors respond inventively from beginning to end, trusting and cultivating their voices, and connecting physical voice, sense of address, imagery, and gesture to writing.

*   *   *

Read the next selection from beginning to end and watch how the essential demands of the how-to form are inventively met.

How to Make Lasagna
Phyllis Crowley

To fully appreciate the Italian flair for creating works of intricately interdependent layers, levels, strata and tiers, examine a pile of several kinds of fruit in any Italian grocery, or St. Paul's Cathedral, or the Mafia, or The Church, or Dante's *Inferno*. Lasagna is built somewhat along the same principles.

If your kitchen is makeshift, substandard, defective or outmoded, never mind. A dash of outrageousness in its immediate environment mysteriously brings out more of the essence of lasagna than do completely circumspect accoutrements. Let's say you're guilty of owning one of these kitchens, that 25 guests are expected at seven, and you haven't straightened up the house. Well, don't. Relegate that task or forget it. Lasagna will tolerate nothing else but your total conscious state for the four hours it takes to make.

You may use the recipe that follows as a shopping list. But remember, you can't pin down lasagna in a recipe, just as you can't assure that gin, vermouth and olives however flawless their combination will always result in a classic martini. There has to be something in the martini besides gin, vermouth and an olive. There has to be gestalt. Lasagna requires a lot of gestalt, but since nobody knows what it is, gestalt doesn't appear below. Do not proceed without it, however:

The meatballs
  Ground chuck, 3 pounds*
  Parsley
  Eggs, 3
  Bread crumbs, about two cups (use really good bread.)

The seasonings:
  Salt
  Pepper
  Garlic
  Bay leaves, 2

---

*The protein does not have to be confined to ground beef. You can use poultry, seafood, or just about anything in the vegetable kingdom. [Author's note]

> Oregano
> Basil
> Dill
> Thyme
> Vinegar, about half a cup
> Table sugar, a tablespoon and some
> Chili sauce, half a bottle of the good stuff
> Chianti, half a bottle
> Parmesan cheese

Other things you use:
> Butter, about ½ pound
> Purple onions, about 6
> Canned tomatoes, 3 large cans
> Water, as you go
> Green peppers, about 4
> Mushrooms, 2 large packages
> Table celery, finely cut—5–6 stalks
> 2 pounds of ricotta

So here you have the general makings of one of those freewheeling, imprecise, impertinent dishes that tell you what they need as they cook along. Just imagine you're Pavarotti, stepping on stage to do King Gustaf. You know he respects Verdi but is not going to be confined by him.

All Italian dishes begin with garlic, even spumoni. So get two fat, gleaming garlic cloves with outer skins just the tiniest bit brittle. Flick at each with a fingernail and check the noise for tone. A sound thunk tells you a clove is sound inside. Whichever knife isn't as dull on one side as on the other will have to do, as will the hand-sized carving board you probably own, with the large, unsanitary, black crack. As you chip away at the garlic, toss a stick of butter into the frying pan. Don't let the butter get past tepid. Before adding the roughly chopped garlic, swish the butter around once. Throw in another butter stick and turn off the gas. That stick will get absorbed at the other ingredient's leisure. Chop six purple onions you have, it is to be hoped, chosen only after comparison with several dozen other purple onions. No one can really afford six purple onions but you must have them today for they are to their pale cousins what crabmeat is to tuna fish.

You might imagine, because lasagna does not require dainty handling, that your course for the afternoon will be easy. But the dish makes subtler demands. What they are, no one can define precisely. Be alert for them.

Right now, melt yet more butter in a saucepan and add the onions. Then just hack around, swirling the entire purple mixture over low heat. Toss it, after a couple of minutes, into the garlic. Set the combination aside, on the sink, maybe. If the butter congeals that's perfectly okay. Just don't let it get hot because then it will render.

Order the cat from the room. Her interest in your adventure is not innocent.

Produce three one-pound four-ounce cans of tomatoes and toss contents into the huge dented pot suspected of having Macbeth's coat of arms on it somewhere. Again, low heat. Half a cup of vinegar follows the tomatoes into the pot summarily as does the tomato paste from three eight-ounce cans.

Next, a scant tablespoon of sugar. Oh, keep stirring. Use a wooden ladle. Never, never stir lasagna with a metal implement. Use your wooden ladle even if it couldn't pass any known Board of Health test; use it if, withal, it has authority, character, tone, air, countenance, the complexion of a mercenary in the Sahara, and if it is strong enough to keep your brew from sticking. If this occurs, señora, you had best lose yourself in the night or, worse, profane this peerless dish by attempting to substitute for its sauce some unspeakable red plastic substitute from a jar. At this juncture, you need salt and two crisp, fragrant, shiny, unfragmented bay leaves. Toss in oregano as the bay leaves sink into your sibilant, warm, red mess, and some basil. And throw in half a bottle of chili sauce if you keep a decent brand about the place.

With an eye on all, chop, seeding first, four green peppers and pile them over the onions and garlic that are cooling their heels on the sink. Stir in the peppers but not violently, or you will have spillage since your heap is six inches high by now, or should be.

To the sauce—you kept stirring, didn't you, while chopping and adding the peppers?—add a half cup of water. Ride constant herd on this sauce now.

Since you must hang around in the kitchen for the next two hours anyway, you can make little clean-up dashes in between stirs, but this is tricky. You can also amuse yourself by getting together your mushrooms and celery. Use a lot of mushrooms, a cascade of them. After all, how often do you make lasagna? You don't want to be counted among those lasagna makers who, because of some weird, subservient attitude toward money, skimp.

By the way, have you got everything for the last stages? It isn't a bad idea to turn off everything while you check because you probably haven't. If you do have to return to the store, shut the kitchen door, not that we don't trust the cat.

Now that you're back with the Parmesan and the ricotta, get busy. Jesus, you haven't much time. Get the sauce going.

You're not letting it bubble? A tad more water, quick, and ply that wooden ladle. Get at the bottom of the cauldron. Stir downward toward upward, not the other way, not just round and round. Don't let anything stick down there. A scorched bottom is fatal.

A potentially serious crisis point approaches, the moment you choose to dump the garlic mushroom celery etc. mix into the sauce. If you break down, if panic seizes you, the fact that you won't be the first, confronted by this challenge to do so, might make your disgrace easier to bear.

Having chosen, you stir and fold the mix into the sauce. Taste. You'll find you need more salt, much more pepper, more oregano. Take out the bay leaves. Add half a bottle of Chianti. Add a little thyme, perhaps. A little dill—fresh is nice. Fool around for a while.

Assuming you have been clever and have done a few preparations this morning, get the things from the icebox. You used four or five pounds of ground chuck, lots of parsley, snipped with a scissors, three eggs, pepper, paprika, bread crumbs (shredded), salt, and all of this resulted in meatballs. They are tiny and round and hard. You used a teaspoon of meat mix for each. You have thousands. Brown them in the pan, batch after batch, and toss each batch into the sauce from the pan. You had better have a *very* high pot.

The noodles you know about. You'll need two packages. A dab of Bertolli olive oil when the noodles begin to boil insures non-stick, ethnically synchronized noodles. When they're cooked, get over to the sink with them as best you can—they have required a large pot and boiling water and are fairly dangerous. Flush the noodles with cold water. Drain very efficiently or you will have runny lasagna.

Get the ricotta. You have the sauce, you have the noodles, you have the cheese. The moment has come when you begin to build, to integrate. Steady. Here again, what proportion of what ingredient is correct in relation to the position, texture, and tone of another ingredient, or several, cannot be conveyed. However that may be, you have to know.

Layer two brownie pans with noodles. Trim the noodles to size with scissors. Let us hope they were cooked and drained carefully and therefore did not pull apart, or fuse, or act up otherwise. Carefully pour some of the sauce over the noodles. During the building process it might be a good idea to give the sauce a stir now and then—just because you turned it off doesn't mean it's stopped cooking. Its internal temperature is so hot it's probably cooking itself, to an extent. If all of the meatballs, during this stirring and building don't keep their shape, don't worry. They sort of tend to merge anyway but cooking the meat meatball style is infinitely preferable to free form, and you will reap rewards in flavor and texture, for your effort. You begin to suspect this since the aromas in your kitchen are sheer magic and cause an occasional passerby to pause and stare at the window.

To the noodles and the sauce, add ricotta, in dollops here and there. Apply another layer of scissored noodles, then the sauce, then the cheese. Remember layers, levels, strata, tiers. Repeat the process until the ingredients are incorporated. You have now built your dish. Shake the can of Parmesan over the two pans for quite a while.

Forty minutes in the oven will do to interlock all components and charge the air even more fragrantly.

Very soon after the pans are brought forth, the diners will arrive.

When the hushed crowd eddies around your magnificent gently steaming golden-brown, autumn orange, beige, ochre and sienna complex, remember the old Italian proverb, "Art is the concealing of art," and to all entreaties reply you will be glad to give them the recipe but they must understand that you have in this dish a secret thing you are not prepared to reveal at the present time.

Commentary

Teasing, exaggeration, self-parody, and fun of the writing invest this how-to from beginning to end. For instance, the author suggests with the series of teasing comparisons in the first sentence the main problem of lasagna-making, building "layers, levels, strata, and tiers"; this also begins the answer to the problem.

The organization is two-leveled: First, the author establishes the suspense of seeing how the dish works out step by step; then she introduces a sort of sub-plot, telling of "your" making the fabulous dish in an ever-recurring situation of urgency in which "25 guests are expected at seven" and the cat must be ordered from the kitchen. You may also have to rush back to the store to get other ingredients and make clean-up dashes from the kitchen into the house "but," because of the peculiar demands of lasagna, "that's tricky."

Taking into account the reader's need for understanding, she frequently exaggerates important points, e.g., the admonition to use a wooden ladle, the fun and urgency of the situation, the "huge dented pot suspected of having Macbeth's coat-of-arms on it somewhere," watching the "bay leaves sink into your sibilant, warm, red mess . . . ," etc.; and the timing of certain phrases of address "—you kept stirring, didn't you?—" teasingly exaggerates a make-sure point, a motivational nudge of the elbow to the reader.

Metaphors, similes, and other comparisons, spring from the imaginative seeing of things side by side in our minds. Frequently, exaggeration draws forth and projects comparisons. *Do* an exaggerated gestural demonstration for a "cascade" of mushrooms. Not all comparisons originate from the gestural sense, but whether from gestural or other origin, they tend to relate the less familiar to the familiar, such as "Six purple onions that are to their pale cousins what crabmeat is to tuna fish." But how is a wooden ladle with "the complexion of a mercenary in the Sahara" a relation of the less familiar to the more familiar? It reverses the principle and relates the over-familiar of the ladle browned with age to the exotically familiar of the complexion of a mercenary in the Sahara; it also implies that the ladle is a soldier in your service.

The strictly necessary sequence of cooking lasagna enforces a certain basic order for the writing, as with any how-to. What happens with the out-of-sequence telling of the preparation of the meatballs? Tongue-in-cheek, it implies that the self-parodic "you" has resources that are just beginning to be revealed, and it emphasizes prior planning and preparation in a dramatic, ironical way.

Look at the sentences and their lively verbs. You no doubt recognize immediately what happens when noodles "fuse." Throughout lasagna-making you are asked to examine, toss, throw, melt, hack, bring, stir, check, drain, flush, add, apply, build, etc.; "A potentially serious crisis point *approaches*"; "*Relegate* that task or *forget* it"; "If the butter *congeals*"; "Half a cup of vinegar *follows* the tomatoes"; "*amuse* yourself"; "*skimp*"; "*stir* and *fold* the mix"; "*to interlock* all components and *charge* the air even more fragrantly";" When the hushed crowd *eddies*"; and so on. Every paragraph, nearly every sentence, sports the energy, precision, and gestural sense of active verbs.

Read aloud pages of "Lasagna" and *Cross-Country Skiing Today* alternately to yourself, to a friend, to the class. In "Lasagna," the "I" of the teller merges with the "you" in a self-parodic characterization that sweeps along with the urgency of the situation. How is that different from the "you" and the teller of *Cross-Country Skiing Today?* How does the precision of haste and urgency contribute to the sense that the author of "Lasagna" knows what she's talking about? Read the passages slowly and concentrate on seeing the imagery and anything else you may notice, any similarities and differences, anything that takes your attention, comparing the methods and approaches of the two writers.

Writing Your How-To: The Subject

Think of a skill you know how to do well, and of telling it to someone so that person can do it too, a job or sport or game or whatever, *something you do with your hands* or in which your hands and body play a significant part, i.e., a skill that requires physical-mental coordination, something you have done again and again, something you do well, something you enjoy doing. Think of telling it to someone, of gestures you would use. Start writing your how-to.

Some of you will say you have "writer's block." Some of you will say that the blank page becomes a wall between you and what you have to say. Well, in fifteen years of teaching writing, I've had a number of students who have promptly claimed "writer's block," and most of them completed the semester's work. Some of you will say, "I can show you how to do it, but I can't write it." I say, "Fine, if you can tell and show us, you're well on the way to knowing how to tell it in writing. As a matter of fact, you can start telling us right now—in writing. Pick out a student in the class and tell it to that person now—in writing." Put pen or pencil to the paper, or fingers to the typewriter. Make the pencil move,* the fingers type.

---

*"Make the pencil move" is a copywriter's prescription for when you feel blank.

Make sure your how-to is a skill activity that you know how to do reasonably well. See the *characteristic* objects, *characteristic* situations, *characteristic* things that happen. See the special twists that you know about. See the points that the "you" must make sure of. Lay out a sequence of make-sure points, though many of these will occur to you in the process of writing. You don't have to wait to figure out everything. You can write notes and discover the rest of it as you write.

Imagine yourself demonstrating your how-to to your audience. See yourself, (the authority) and "you" (the audience) as actors in it. See the usual situation of doing whatever it is. Let your hand be an extension of your voice. Concentrate on telling your how-to to someone. See it, and tell it so the someone can *see* it and *do* it.

* * *

In the next reading selection, "The Line," look and listen for exaggeration. Again, read the piece all the way through, and then look back at each of the marginal coachings. Watch how the author, from beginning to end, defines the whale-line. Actually, "The Line" is more of a how-it's-done, how-it's-used, and how-it-works form with pronounced how-to characteristics, particularly in its simulation of a tour-guide speech addressed to a small group "you." Reading "The Line" aloud will make its language more familiar to you.

"The Line"
From Moby Dick
Herman Melville

With reference to the whaling scene shortly to be described, as well as for the better understanding of all similar scenes elsewhere presented, I have here to speak of the magical, sometimes horrible whale-line.

Suggestion of problem, the magical dangerous whale-line—teasing of suspense

The line originally used in the fishery was of the best hemp, slightly vapored with tar, not impregnated with it, as in the case of ordinary ropes; for while tar, as ordinarily used, makes the hemp more pliable to the rope-maker, and also renders the rope itself more convenient to the sailor for common ship use; yet, not only would the ordinary quantity too much stiffen the whale-line for the close coiling to which it must be subjected; but as most seamen are beginning to learn, tar in general by no means adds to the rope's durability or strength, however much it may give it compactness and gloss.

Suggestion of tour-guide speech to the audience, the reader

Make-sure point—"too much stiffen"

Of late years the Manilla rope has in the American fishery almost entirely superseded hemp as a material for whale-lines; for, though not so durable as hemp, it is stronger, and far more soft and elastic; and I will add (since there is an aesthetic in all things), is much more handsome and becoming to the boat, than hemp. Hemp is a dusky, dark fellow, a sort of Indian; but Manilla is as a golden-haired Circassian to behold.

Comparison

Exaggeration

The whale-line is only two thirds of an inch in thickness. At first sight, you would not think it so strong as it really is. By experiment its one and fifty yarns will each suspend a weight of one hundred and twenty pounds; so that the whole rope will bear a strain nearly equal to three tons. In length, the common sperm whale-line measures something over two hundred fathoms. Towards the stern of the boat it is spirally coiled away in the tub, not like the worm-pipe of a still though, but so as to form one round cheese-shaped mass of densely bedded "sheaves," or layers of concentric spiralizations, without any hollow but the "heart," or minute vertical tube formed at the axis of the cheese. As the least tangle or kink in the coiling would, in running out, infallibly take

"You" address—

Tour-guide demonstration

Gestural imagery, metaphors and comparisons—do the gestural demonstration

Paragraph build-up

somebody's arm, leg, or entire body off, the utmost precaution is used in stowing the line in its tub. Some harpooners will consume an entire morning in this business, carry-

ing the line high aloft and then reeving it downwards through a block towards the tub, so as in the act of coiling to free it from all possible wrinkles and twists.

In the English boat two tubs are used instead of one; the same line being continuously coiled in both tubs. There is some advantage in this; because these twin-tubs being so small they fit more readily into the boat, and do not strain it so much; whereas, the American tub, nearly three feet in diameter and of proportionate depth, makes a rather bulky freight for a craft whose planks are but one half-inch in thickness; for the bottom of the whale-boat is like critical ice, which will bear up a considerable distributed weight, but not very much of a concentrated one. When the painted canvas cover is clapped on the American line-tub, the boat looks as if it were pulling off with a prodigious great wedding-cake to present to the whales.

Both ends of the line are exposed; the lower end terminating in an eye-splice or loop coming up from the bottom against the side of the tub, and hanging over its edge completely disengaged from everything. This arrangement of the lower end is necessary on two accounts. First: In order to facilitate the fastening to it of an additional line from a neighboring boat, in case the stricken whale should sound so deep as to threaten to carry off the entire line originally attached to the harpoon. In these instances, the whale of course is shifted like a mug of ale, as it were, from the one boat to the other; though the first boat always hovers at hand to assist its consort. Second: the arrangement is indispensable for common safety's sake; for were the lower end of the line in any way attached to the boat, and were the whale then to run the line out to the end almost in a single smoking minute as he sometimes does, he would not stop there, for the doomed boat would infallibly be dragged down after him into the profundity of the sea; and in that case no town-crier would ever find her again.

Before lowering the boat for the chase, the upper end of the line is taken aft from the tub, and passing round the loggerhead there, is again carried forward the entire length of the boat, resting crosswise upon the loom or handle of every man's oar, so that it jogs against his wrist in rowing; and also passing between the men, as they alternately sit at the opposite gunwales, to the leaded chocks or grooves in the extreme pointed prow of the boat, where a wooden pin or skewer the size of a common quill, prevents it from slipping out. From the chocks it hangs in a slight festoon over the bows, and is then passed inside the boat again; and some ten or twenty fathoms (called box-line) being coiled upon the box in the bows, it continues its way to the gunwale still a little further aft, and is then attached to the short-warp—the rope which is immediately connected with the harpoon; but previous to that connexion, the short-warp goes through sundry mystifications too tedious to detail.

Thus the whale-line folds the whole boat in its complicated coils, twisting and writhing around it in almost every direction. All the oarsmen are involved in its perilous contortions, so that to the timid eye of the landsman, they seem as Indian jugglers, with the deadliest snakes sportively festooning their limbs. Nor can any son of mortal woman, for the first time, seat himself amid these hempen intricacies, and while straining his utmost at the oar, bethink him that any unknown instant the harpoon may be darted, and all these horrible contortions be put in play like ringed lightnings: he cannot be thus circumstanced without a shudder that makes the very marrow in his bones to quiver in him like a shaken jelly. Yet habit—strange thing! what cannot habit accomplish?—gayer sallies, more merry mirth, better jokes, and brighter repartees, you never heard over your mahogany, than you will hear over the half-inch white cedar of the whale-boat, when thus hung in hangman's nooses; and, like the six burghers of Calais before King Edward, the six men composing the crew pull into the jaws of death, with a halter around every neck, as you may say.

Perhaps a very little thought will now enable you to account for those repeated whaling disasters—some few of which are casually chronicled—of this man or that man being taken out of the boat by the line, and lost. For when the line is darting out, to be seated then in the boat, is like being seated in the midst of the manifold whizzings of a steam-engine in full play, when every flying beam, and shaft, and wheel, is grazing you. It is worse; for you cannot sit motionless in the heart of these perils, because the boat is rocking like a cradle, and you are pitched one way and the other, without the slightest warning; and only by a certain self-adjusting buoyancy and simultaneousness of volition and action, can you escape being made a Mazeppa of, and run away with where the all-seeing sun himself could never pierce you out.

Again: as the profound calm which only apparently precedes and prophesies of the storm, is perhaps more awful than the storm itself; for, indeed, the calm is but the wrapper and envelope of the storm; and contains it in itself, as the seemingly harmless rifle holds the fatal powder, and the ball, and the explosion: so the graceful repose of the line, as it silently serpentines about the oarsmen before being brought into actual play—this is a thing which carries more of true terror than any other aspect of this dangerous affair. But why say more? All men live enveloped in whale-lines. All are born with halters around their necks; but it is only when caught in the swift, sudden turn of death, that mortals realize the silent, subtle, ever-present perils of life. And if you be a philosopher, though seated in the whale-boat, you would not at heart feel one whit more of terror, than though seated before your evening fire with a poker, and not a harpoon, by your side.

Margin annotations, left: Climactic build-up cont. / Conclusion

Margin annotations, right: Exaggerated metaphor—comparison— / Alliterative onomatopoeisis: z's, s's, g's, and w's / Metaphorical imagery of gestural origin / Metaphor—comparison / Metaphor—comparison

Commentary

In the early paragraphs, our speaker acts as a sort of tour-guide, telling us how-the-line-works and how-you-make-the-line-work. In the course of the telling, the speaker's character and relationship to us change. By the end of it, the character of the "you" has changed too. Told largely in the present tense, the tense of "ideal" time in the model situation of a how-to, "The Line" tells us *the way it happens and the way it can happen with the line.* In the next chapter, "Stubb Kills a Whale," the author shifts to the past tense again to tell a specific narrative incident. This demonstrates the integral relationships of verb tense to form, sense of address, and pronouns of address, relationships which are natural in our use of language.

Our tour-guide speaker suggests the main problem and danger of the line in the first sentence, particularly in the phrase "the magical, sometimes horrible whale-line." If you follow the building of each paragraph, you come to a climax and conclusion, except for two paragraphs. How does paragraph three function in relation to paragraph two? How does the eighth function in relation to the seventh?

Do gestural demonstrations to yourself for the metaphorical imagery in paragraph four, and anywhere else in "The Line" that reveals gestural sense. You'll find that gestural precision of seeing often produces vivid imagery and strong metaphors that move the reader toward more precise understanding. Other metaphors come from the side-by-side perception of likenesses, e.g., the analogy of the half-inch bottom of the whale-boat to "critical ice." The rich and playful voice of "The Line" discovers metaphorical nuance in such words and phrases as "eye-splice," "slight festoon," "hovers at hand to assist its consort," and "caught in the swift, sudden turn of death," the latter echoing and extending previous technical imagery. Watch and listen for other language techniques, such as alliteration and onomatopoeia, in association with imagery and metaphor.

Trace the development of the danger of the line, from the more or less technical tour-guide telling in the beginning, to the teasing philosophical meditation at the end. Melville often exaggerates and teases to heighten suspense, and to heighten make-sure and warning points.

When you read "The Line" aloud in class, concentrate on seeing its objects and actions and metaphors so everyone else in the class can see them. If reading aloud to the entire class scrambles your concentration or intimidates you, pick a classmate and address it to him or her as a letter, looking up occasionally at that person. Read one word after the other without trying to impose a pause, and without stumbling ahead for the end of the sentence, and you will find that the sentences take care of themselves. You may also—alone in your room—read it aloud to yourself, listening to the voice of it *in your voice,* as you concentrate on seeing the objects, actions, people, imagery, comparisons, etc. Do the gestures wherever suggested in the marginal keys and wherever you sense them.

You may find that you want to parody Melville's style in your writing. If you're attracted to the style of any of the how-to selections, you can copy it, imitate it, or parody it (that is, make fun of it), incorporating the structure and characteristics of the style, as a way of stretching and making more flexible your English voice, and developing your own sense of style.

*   *   *

We move to a very different kind of English voice in the next selection, in which we hear suggested dialect alongside Standard English. When the phrasing seems different from the way you would say it, sound it either aloud or to yourself and see how much more familiar your own voice makes it.

*How to Make Chitterlings**
Chris Burks

Imagery—see it—"the neighbors gather"—appeal to tradition for motivation and argument

Teasing—motivation

Down home, when the hogs are shiny with fat, the neighbors gather in my grandma's backyard to watch the slaughtering of her hogs. Each year four or five hogs are changed into porkchops, pork roast, pickled pig feet and ears, neckbones to be boiled and smothered with white potatoes, cracklin for bread, ham and lean bacon sugarcured, sausage seasoned with plenty of sage and kidneys for stew. The women bargain with grandma for the surplus fat while the men wait, impatiently wait, for grandma to announce the chitterling dinner date.

---

*The author spells it "chitterlings" but she, as do most Black vernacular speakers, pronounces it "chit-'lins."

The main attraction are two ancient black kettles that steam with fresh cooked chitterlings. For two days the stank of the chitterlings assaulted the air with rudeness. Yet no one minded as they knew each morsel would be tender and succulent; full of flavor.

The problems with having a chitterlings dinner in the city are the lack of fresh chitterlings. You can buy chitterlings in 5, 10, and 20 pound pails. However, since they have been chemically treated and frozen some of the original taste is lost. Please note— the best time to purchase chitterlings (frozen or, if you are lucky, fresh) is the winter months. It is during this time pigs are slaughtered but also the heat of summer adds to the risk of trichinosis and spoilage.

In order to cook chitterlings you must possess two things: a huge pot and a strong nose. If you are squirmy when it comes to a foul smell I suggest you have porkchops for dinner as chitterlings give off an offensive odor; like an outhouse in the summer.

It's also wise to plan the dinner for a Sunday so you will have ample time to cook and clean them. A pail of chitterlings is packed tightly and frozen. They require more time than other meat to defrost. Generally 12 to 16 hours. It's advisable to leave them out overnight.

I feel it's most comfortable to clean them in a spotless kitchen after a nice hot bath. This insures that the meat is clean and also prevents your stomach from turning at the filth.

Pour the defrosted chitterlings into a clean sink. Each chitterling is one long intestine of the hog. It is wiggly and split down the middle like a busted balloon. The frozen chitterlings are freed of the waste matter except for a few specks here and there. Fresh chitterlings are caked with a huge amount of waste matter and require more time and a steel stomach to clean. Therefore, if this is your first time cleaning chitterlings I advise you use frozen ones.

Run cold water into the sink . . . COLD, not Hot, as hot makes them slimy and activates the odor before it's necessary.

Annie Banks used hot water the first and only time she attempted to cook chitterlings. The smell was so strong that she became dizzy and vomited on top of the chitterlings. She threw the 20 pounds of chitterlings and waste out, and has not eaten another bite since.

Therefore I urge you to USE ICE COLD WATER.

You may want to sprinkle a little salt over them. I don't know why! There are several wives' tales for this:

1. According to grandma, salt kills any filth
2. Aunt May says salt helps remove the fat.
3. Mama says it's just the thing to do when cooking chitterlings.

But, as I've said, it probably don't make a difference. I've never not done it, so I can't tell you.

Add two cups of vinegar to the water as this helps loosen the fat; also if you let this set for two to three hours it will cut down the odor later. Be sure to keep changing the water and adding the vinegar as it is important that the water stay ice cold.

After they have soaked, hold one chitterling at the tip. Stretch it open with both hands. Once it's open, you will see globs of white fat dotted with black, brown and green

---

The model learning situation

Imagery—see it—"two ancient black kettles that steam"

Teasing—repulsion of the problem and attraction of feast

Cautionary point—"the best time to purchase"

Clear statement of the problem—direct address

Emphasizes problem

Cautionary point—"plan the dinner for a Sunday"

Simile—comparison—"like a busted balloon"

Describes the problem

Cautionary point

Make-sure point

Example

Emphasis—make-sure point

Teasing—more development of tradition and sense of community of the audience

First-person clarification

Further development of answer to the problem

Imperative gestural form of verbs—"hold," "stretch"

Simile—
comparison—
gestural origin
"like a claw"

Image—
metaphor—re-
lating unfamiliar
to the familiar
"tiny web design"

waste matter. Using the fingers of one hand like a claw, firmly grip this and pull it off. You will have to repeat this several times in each spot. The spot is cleaned when the skin is faintly translucent. You will see tiny web design inside the skin. Do this continuous along each intestine. You may wish to cut the chitterlings in half as one intestine is sometimes two feet long. Also, the intestine is full of dips and curves, you should be particularly attentive to these areas as a small particle may be curled there.

Climax

Once the chitterlings are freed of fat and waste matter, rinse them carefully under running water with quick spot checks. Place them in a large pot, approximately 10 to 12 quarts. Cover with water, add two cups of vinegar per 20 pounds and place over a high heat and cover with a lid.

Conclusion

While waiting for the chitterlings to boil, skin and cut four onions in half; place these on top of the boiling chitterlings. According to your own personal taste you may want to add crushed red pepper.

The onions and vinegar will tone down the smell of the chitterlings but for an added measure you may do the following: Unscrew the top on the lip (the handle), place a pared apple on top and drop a grain of salt on the inside of the apple.

Allow 10 to 12 hours cooking time. I prefer a low heat overnight. If the chitterlings is covered with plenty of water they will simmer into a mellow flavor. Add salt to taste.

Commentary

Burks merges her personal voice and the voice of her background with Standard English elements to tell how to make chitterlings. Do you sense that she is writing for a double audience, one familiar with chitterlings and one not? One that will pronounce the word "chitterlings," and one that will pronounce it "chit'lins"?

When you sound this how-to to yourself, or out loud, you may notice that the less familiar elements of the author's langauge become more familiar, particularly if your own speech is not Black English vernacular. We can hear or generally understand the dialects of English in our own English voices, whether or not we speak the dialect as a part of our background, though we may not be able to reproduce or speak the dialect ourselves and may not understand unfamiliar dialectal elements. Standard English is also a kind of dialect—a coordinating dialect for all English speakers—though scholars of the English language have no precise agreement on all of its features. We can hear the dialects of English *as* English, because we hear the underlying principles that govern them. We can also use alphabetic symbols to represent our dialects rather precisely in writing, even though we may need a glossary for some terms and constructions. In other words, *you can—and should—for all practical purposes connect your voice to your writing*. The greatest writers in our language have always cultivated the connection of their spoken and inner language to their writing. Fortunately, it's a two-way street, which means that writing and reading can, when you *hear* them in your voice, influence and help you change your language and develop your speaking, thinking, and writing, drawing always upon the resources of your voice.

While addressing one audience familiar with chit'lins, the author keeps an eye to another audience unfamiliar with them. In fact, she was writing for the mixed audience of a class, where she expected her writing to be read aloud. In dealing with her sense for the double audience, she mixes spoken and Standard written English. She teases and gets involvement of both audiences with the main problem and the end delectable result—teasing them out of their squeamishness and into an appreciation of the preparation of chitterlings. In her imagined gestural-demonstrations, she uses the command form of the verbs (the imperative form), which allows her to deal directly with the reader and the "problem." The writers of our how-to selections take the reader into account and adapt what they have to say to make the reader understand it.

Writing Your How-To: The Audience

Most writing is addressed to "mixed audiences." Put together two or three or four persons with different backgrounds, and you have a "mixed audience." Most literature is written for mixed audiences—or for anyone-who-can-see-and-hear-it, which is both a fundamental kind of telling what you see in your mind so someone else can see it and a most advanced form of "ideal" literary audience. Of course, all of these audience elements exist in certain degrees for any kind of writing at any time.

The "mixed audience" is the most common audience and the one you should ordinarily anticipate and imagine during your writing. Your class is probably a good example of a "mixed audience." Technical reports are frequently organized in two parts, the first being addressed to a "mixed audience," and the second to persons trained in the particular expertise.

When you write a how-to, you merge the "mix" of the anticipated audience with the "you" in your mind. Assume that your full expertise must be made available in the language that gets it across to the "mixed" audience. For instance, if you are an electrical engineer and your supervisor is a mechanical engineer, you need to know how to write a report for such a supervisor who is only partly familiar with your subject and background. Imagine one or two experts in the audience who are there to see that you instruct the newcomers properly, as does Caldwell in *Cross-Country Skiing Today*. You address the "you" in the course of your writing, keeping an eye to the mix of needs of the audience that may or may not share your skills, attitudes, values. In the course of your writing, you may find your pronouns of address transforming naturally, according to the needs you feel in a particular passage, to the we, I , he, she, they, one, it, someone, anyone (and other versions of third person). Verb tenses, too, will change occasionally with changing relationships of form, content, and sense of address.

* * *

Read the next how-to all the way to the end; then look back and study each of the marginal coachings. Watch the course of reasoning as you read.

How to Hit
Tom Nawrocki

The most difficult feat to consistently accomplish in American sports is hitting a baseball during a major league game. There is no other sport which allows you to be successful only thirty percent of the time. Yet the ball-player who hits .300 these days is not only kept around, he is also paid several hundred thousand dollars a year. Only thirteen men since 1900 have successfully hit a baseball forty percent of the time, the last being Ted Williams who in 1941 hit .406. Out of the hundreds of thousands of names that are immortalized in the Baseball Encyclopedia, only one man has gotten a base hit

States problem

Authoritative knowledge of the author

Teasing motivation boost

Authority—the
author knows
what he's talking
about

Question reader
automatically
asks—used as
lead sentence for
paragraph

Imagery—precise
description and
definition of the
problem—see it
from "trying to
hit a round ball
with a round bat"
to "no guarantee
it won't be
snagged . . ."

Metaphorical
jargon with
precise technical
imagery—ground
out, line drive,
"sweet spot",
easy dribbler

Conclusion of
paragraph

Topic sentence of
paragraph—states
particular problem

Defines and
describes the
problem and
begins answer of
how to meet it

Make sure
points—"must
begin your stride"
and "your
concentration
must be so
intense"

See it—gestural
slow-motion
exaggerated
precision of
process—"You
must determine if
the red string
. . . ."

See it—image—
exaggerated
emphasis on
make-sure
point—"You will
have the
consolation of
seeing"

everytime he came to the plate during his major league career. Clarence William Pickup played one game for the Philadelphia Phillies in 1918, came to the plate once, got a base hit, and promptly retired to become the only major league player to carry a 1.000 lifetime batting average.

Why is it so difficult to hit a baseball? Consider the fact that you are trying to hit a round ball with a round bat. The circumference of the ball is seven inches while the bat may be slightly larger. This makes the point of impact on the bat approximately one square inch. If that point of impact occurs too high on the rounded surface of the bat, a foul ball or popup results. If it occurs on the lower portion of the bat, the ball careens into the dirt for an easy ground out. If the point of impact occurs on the thin line exactly level with the pitched ball, a line drive should occur. However, if the point of impact is more than five inches away from the fat end of the bat, the "sweet spot," the line drive will actually be an easy dribbler. Also when a line drive does occur, there is no guarantee it won't be snagged by one of the nine defensive players in front of the hitter.*

The factors that make up the art of hitting are legion, but none is as important or critical as reading the pitch. Consider the fact that the baseball will leave the pitcher's hand and travel the sixty-feet, six-inch distance to home plate at a speed that normally exceeds ninety miles per hour. As a batter your reaction time must be split second. As the ball leaves the pitcher's hand you must begin your stride into the ball. At this point your concentration must be so intense upon that baseball that you *must* be able to perceive the rotation on the ball. You must determine if the red string that laces the baseball's seams is spinning sideways, indicating a curveball, or spinning end over end in the fashion of a fastball. If you read the pitch as a curve, you must now adjust your stride forward so that your moving foot steps closer to the plate in order to reach the ball that will be curving away from you. If, however, you have mis-read that pitch and you are striding into a fastball, you will have the consolation of seeing each of the red threads grow larger in their zipper-like pattern as the ball rises directly into your forehead. Nobody mentions the fact that standing in the batter's box can be dangerous, but all hitters have a secret fear of being hit in the head by a pitched ball. Ray Chapman, shortstop for the 1920 Cleveland Indians, was having his best season as a hitter batting .303 when he was struck in the head by a Yankee pitcher's fastball and killed. He was the last hitter killed, but there have been players either injured or intimidated enough to retire from the game forever.

Development of paragraph

Paragraph build-up

Climax of
paragraph

Conclusion of
paragraph

---

*Although the catcher assumes his defensive position behind the batter, the catcher is still responsible for the fifteen foot area of fair territory directly in front of the batter. Hitting coaches instruct batters to think of *nine* defensive players in front of them [Author's note.]

As you begin to realize what a baseball pitched at high velocity can do to you, you begin to see the need for total concentration. In order to successfully hit a pitched ball, your concentration must be focused not only on the pitcher on the raised mound sixty feet in front of you, but more precisely, on the area above his right or left shoulder where he will release the ball. This area is referred to as the window.

Watch a pitcher take his warm up tosses before you hit against him. Even these easy, loosening-up throws will all come from the same general area, no more than a foot above or to the side of his throwing shoulder. As you take your position in the batter's box, forget about looking into the pitcher's eyes, or watching him paw the dirt in front of the mound with his spiked shoe. These are unnecessary distractions. Your eyes should be focussed on the window, defining its size on the distant background above the centerfield wall. Most ballparks keep this section closed to fans so the hitter can see the ball better. In fact, most parks have painted this background green in order to make the white baseball stand out. An intelligent hitter will select some landmark in this background such as a section of brick, a public address loudspeaker, etc., as the center of his window in order to focus on the same spot everytime. In this way, as soon as the pitcher releases the ball, the hitter picks up the rotation of the ball immediately and begins to decipher not only the type of pitch it is, but also its direction and velocity. Thus, a hitter will not be surprised by a pitch, and also he will be able to adjust soon enough to react immediately to a fastball, or delay the fraction of a second necessary for hitting an off-speed curveball.

How important is visualizing the window of a pitcher? Consider the case of Luis Tiant, a right-handed pitcher currently with the Boston Red Sox. At the age of 35, which Tiant miraculously maintained for three years, he was washed up as a major league pitcher. This happens to all of them sooner or later. The fastball loses its rising action and becomes a straight ball, while the curve begins to flatten out and not break, thus becoming a swerve-ball rather than the sweeping downward arc it should be.

When a pitcher loses his stuff, he either sees the reality of aging and retires, or goes down to the minor leagues, chasing the elusive ghost of "one last chance." Tiant chose the latter. Most veteran pitchers going down to the minors try to work on some new pitch like the knuckleball, forkball or spitball that requires manual dexterity rather than sheer arm power. Tiant *did* develop several new pitches in the minor leagues, but primarily, he worked on a new delivery.

Left margin:

Paragraph build-up

Climax

Conclusion

Right margin annotations:

See it—

Make-sure point

Special point—metaphorical concept (figure) of "the window"

Topic sentence of paragraph—focuses concentration

See it—develops special point—"throws will all come from the same general area"

See it—

Imagery—from "forget about looking into the pitcher's eyes" to "Your eyes should be focussed on the window" to "An intelligent hitter will select . . ."

Imagery to develop the use of "the window" concept

Develops answer to main problem

Begins secondary how-to for pitcher—to emphasize special point of "window" for hitter

States secondary problem of sub-form or substory of Luis Tiant

Gestural verbs, imagery and metaphor to describe problem—from "loses its rising action" to "sweeping downward arc"

Anticipation

Compares and contrasts Tiant with other pitchers

Ordinary answer to the problem

Anticipation of better answer

Emphasizes
importance for
the hitter of
understanding
"the window"—
imagery of Tiant's
"gyrations"

In his wind-up before releasing the ball, Tiant contorts his body in several different directions with his back actually to the hitter at one point, before he delivers the ball. It is common for hitters to watch a pitcher's head or eyes during this wind-up because it seems natural for a pitcher to stare at his target the moment before releasing the ball. Tiant, before throwing, looks everywhere but in the direction of home plate—the sky, the ground, third base, everywhere. Because of this, when he finally throws the ball, the hitter has been mesmerized by Tiant's gyrations and is surprised by the pitch. Thus, hitters say that Tiant has "an explosive fastball" when actually they have been lulled to a state of distraction by Tiant's gestures.

Tiant's better
answer to the
problem

Image of Tiant's
success and
hitter's problem
with "the
window"

However, Tiant wouldn't be a twenty-game winner for the past three seasons because of this aforementioned feat alone. Tiant must also be given credit for realizing the importance of the window, and then expanding it. Luis Tiant rarely delivers the ball from the same spot within his window. On one pitch he will come over the top of the shoulder, while the next one will come directly from the side, parallel to his elbow. Because of this, a hitter cannot focus on one exact spot within the window; he must visually back-up and study the entire arc from Tiant's head to his right thigh. This is the reason that Luis Tiant, the oldest 39-year-old in baseball, can still get the smart hitters along with the rookies.

However, Tiant is an unusual case; the exception to the rule. If you, as a hitter, concentrate on first of all learning how to read a pitch, and then finding windows, your hitting is bound to improve.

There are no natural hitters, but if you watch, perceive and concentrate, that's what people will call you.

Commentary

Nawrocki states the problem and challenge in the first sentence, suggests the peculiar demand of the challenge in the second, and the reward in the third. Immediately he shows that he's done his homework on the historical background of the problem and ends the paragraph with a summarized anecdote that clinches an easy, authoritative relationship with his audience. In the next paragraph, he takes the time to elaborate the problem, further demonstrating that he knows what he's talking about. In the long third paragraph, he sets up the model learning situation, changes pace and uses another technique altogether: a slow-motion exaggeration of the process of the hitter's "reading" of pitched balls and what he must do with each different reading to carry out the answer to the problem. In the fourth paragraph, he restates and develops problem-and-answer to emphasize danger and the need of concentration. He closes with an announcement of the figure of the "window."

In the fifth paragraph, he exaggerates to explore the concept of the "window" as a major contribution to the answer to the problem. The figure of the "window" evidently resulted from a hitting coach's gestural tracing in the air over the shoulder of a pitcher, and his seeing-in-the-mind of his gestural tracing to come up with the comparison that makes the figure. What happens if you say "area" and do not liken it to "window"? What happens if you say "rectangle" instead of "window"? How does the figure of the "window" *help you to see what you need to see?*

In paragraph six, the author re-emphasizes the batter's problem in the contest with the pitcher, as he begins to tell the substory of pitcher Luis Tiant's inventive manipulation of the "window" to solve his pitching problem. He virtually entrances us with the Tiant story while making us see the crucial importance of the window concept, a basic principle of sleight-of-hand in which you seem to be doing one thing while you're also doing something else. The substory ends with a boost of motivation for pitcher and hitter.

Rather than try to deal with all aspects of hitting, the author narrows the subject to the sequence and process of "reading" the pitch and using the "window." Using slow-motion exaggeration to stimulate and explore his seeing-in-the-mind, he perceives precise correspondences in writing for what would ordinarily be told by a hitting coach with slow-motion gestures. Illustrative drawings would be too cumbersome. An excellent film could probably be made from Nawrocki's treatment, but many factors would become elusively complicated and the Tiant story would require a verbal retelling. With writing's economy and access to points of view, he conveys simultaneity and vivid precision of process.

Reread the passages and *do* gestural demonstrations to yourself for the different pitched balls and the batter's relationship to each, and of the "window" concept and the batter's and pitcher's relationship to it. See what the gestural demonstration tells you.

Writing Your How-To: Your Authority

The telling of the how-to to the "you" tends to draw forth your authority: You know what you're talking about. Thus, a person who is not James Beard may write an effective, entertaining "How to Make Lasagna"; one who is not a well-known sports writer, coach, or player may write an instructive "How to Hit"; one who is not Zora Neale Hurston may write a fine, partly dialectal "How to Make Chitterlings." We could tear the relevant pages out of Caldwell's book and present them to a novice skier without giving any suggestion of who the author is and find that the novice learns to ski from the convincing seeing and telling of necessary how-to elements. You know what you're talking about, step by step, and you have the confidence to tell it—using images, phrasing, exaggeration, verbs, comparisons, metaphors, make-sure points, and so on—so your audience can see it and do it.

The imagined learning situation (the usual where and when) is incorporated into the writing, e.g., the batter at the plate being coached by the teller of "How to Hit," the cleaner of chitterlings in preparation for Sunday dinner being coached by the teller of "How to Make Chitterlings," the self-parodic "you" of "How to Make Lasagna" being coached in urgent preparation for the party of guests expected at seven, and so on. Probably you often see yourself as both the doer and the teller.

You merge the how-to's inbuilt sense of address with your perception of your audience's needs, which helps control the range and amount of material you see, seek, and write about. Your imagination may abound with things and possibilities for the how-to, so you make many decisions about what's to be left out and what's to be included, according to the needs of the how-to and your audience. No matter what kind of writing it is, this process is necessarily imaginative and inventive, *because you conceive and feel an anticipated future audience during your writing* and *see* in your mind the content you want to communicate to the audience.

You need to move your audience to perceive, believe, and do what they might not otherwise perceive, believe, and do—or would not perceive so clearly, believe so willingly, do so effectively. In some cases, it means changing the audience's mind or persuading the audience to try out a different understanding of a subject. This requires a convincing course of reasoning and persuasion. In rhetoric, "argument" is the term for a course of reasoning. *The facts and sequence of how to do whatever it is are essential to the argument of a how-to.* The way facts are presented can be as crucial as the necessary sequence. The need for reasoning and persuasion functions integrally with both oral and written how-tos, from the simplest, most urgently told image to the most strictly technical how-to writing.

Just about anything done in the telling/writing of a how-to contributes to persuasion and motivation: teasing, demanding, charming, exaggerating, urging, rewarding, prodding, berating, reasoning. Clear telling is fundamentally convincing in itself, with boosts of motivation supplied by enhancements of satisfactions, make-sure points, and why-to-do-it emphases. The effective how-to writer uses whatever will work to enhance the argument.

When you read your writing aloud, you may, just by looking around at your immediate audience, perceive persuasive challenges—or find out what you need to do to solve problems of persuasion.

A List of the Major Elements and Characteristics of the How-To Form:

1. *Beginnings.* Begin in a way that seizes or charms or teases your reader's interest. Probably begin with the problem and/or the motivation.
2. *In the most fundamental form of the how-to, the "you" sense of address and the present tense of the verbs emerge naturally:* You may use other pronouns of address as they come to you, as they seem right: I, we, one, he, she, they, it, anyone, someone. The pronoun "one," e.g., "One begins to understand . . . ," gives more distance and is sometimes more arch than the "you," and should be used only when the distance feels effective. Frequently the how-to uses the imperative or command form of the verbs, e.g., "Hold this . . ." or "Take that . . .", in which the "you" is understood.
3. *Authority.* You know what you're talking about. Your authority comes not from your being famous in a field, but from your ability to see the how-to in your mind and tell it so someone can see it, and understand it, and do it.
4. *Imagery and Image-Principled Relationships.* You see it in your mind and tell it so someone else can see it. See it, hear it, touch it, taste it, smell it. We see to solve, and solve to see.
5. *Course of Reasoning (Argument).* The how-to uses the classic structure of argument: statement of problem (thesis), development and elaboration of problem and answer, climax, and conclusion.
6. *Persuasion.* Throughout its structure, the how-to pays attention to *the audience's motivation:* to the why-to-do-it, the feelings, rewards, and satisfactions of doing it. The how-to usually begins and ends with a boost of motivation.
7. *Model Learning or Doing Situation.* Characteristic occurrences, mistakes, actions, attitudes, objects, and perceptions.
8. *Sequence and Process—step by step.* The sequence of doing something usually affects and often determines effectiveness.
9. *Exaggeration.* We will see how exaggeration, too often misunderstood and excluded from the canon of the teaching of writing, can be supremely important for getting things across to the reader precisely and surely.
10. *Gesture.* Nothing is more natural or wonderfully precise than gesture with language. You discover written correspondences of verbs, imagery, concepts, metaphors, and other comparisons and language tricks that you invent for gestures.
11. *Active verbs.* Verbs result from the clear seeing of the material, relating it to the audience. Verbs often come from gestural sense.
12. *Metaphors, similes, analogies, figures, and other comparisons.* Metaphor usu-

ally results from seeing things side by side in our minds, that is, we see likenesses and contrasts of the unfamiliar and familiar. Metaphors often take the
place of gestures in writing.

13. *Make-sure points.* The how-to tells the things that you must make sure of or
    the how-to will fail or not work so well.

14. *Eye contact.* In the written how-to, you inventively transfer eye-contact
    through timing, parentheses, paragraphing, and other devices that you invent
    in the process of writing.

15. *How-to-do-it-better points.* Emphasize them.

16. *The how-to ends often with an extra boost of motivation,* to close the argument.

If you refer to the above summary while you're writing your first draft, you may
divide your concentration with too many "bits and pieces." After you've written a first
or rough draft, you should use the summary as a way of helping you make notes for
things that need attention in your how-to. In the next draft, as you retell the whole how-
to, you try to meet the challenges of those notes.

How to Do Something You're Not Supposed to Do

Simply to get along in life, we all develop ways of doing things that we're not supposed to do. The how-to-do-something-you're-not-supposed-to-do draws upon people's
creativity for solving otherwise impossible problems generated by impossible demands.
Often in "worst" jobs or other trapped situations people are required to do things
they're not supposed to do, and to do them well enough to survive and continue working—or living.

Avoidance of something you're not supposed to do has even caused the fall of civilizations. The Incas could have completely stopped Pizzarro's conquistadores and pre-
served their way of life deep in the Andes if they could have brought themselves to cut
their magnificent rope bridges that dipped across the sheer chasms of the Andes, a
criminal and sacrilegious act that normally incurred the death penalty. New creative
frontiers open when someone does well something he or she was not supposed to do. In
the 17th and 18th centuries dramatists and other storytellers challenged the academical-
ly sacred notion that stories must occur within the time period of one day and night and
within one place of no more than five miles radius. One generation's "cheating" may
become the next generation's way of working. Some of the simpler principles of the
"New Math," really mental shortcuts, such as adding or multiplying by tens and then
tacking on the remainder, were considered cheating in my time in grade school.

Occasionally the how-to-do-something-you're-not-supposed-to-do assignment
elicits material that is considered outright criminal by some conventional definitions.
Many teachers and students tend to avoid such material, even pretend that it has no
place in their activities. These "illegal" how-tos, that seem to clearly violate accepted
rules, laws, regulations, or procedures, may be the very subjects that lead to strong,
important writing. We don't learn much, don't help the development of our morality or
our awareness of the world, by excluding them. Once, in a writing class in which this
assignment was developed, every member of the class gave namby-pamby, inoffensive
oral tellings of how-to-do-something-you're-not-supposed-to-do subjects (such as how
to park in a no parking zone or get a free ride on the bus), then told really strong subjects privately to me in the hallway. The stronger subjects came to their minds in the
class, but they set those subjects aside and looked for something less guilty-seeming. A

Vietnam War veteran said that he'd set aside the subject of a "mechanical ambush," the use of which is clearly forbidden by the Geneva Convention's Rules of War but, as he put it, "done by just about everybody over there." He added that he'd then considered and set aside several other "disapproved" skills before he told something inoffensive. Yet he sensed that the avoided content could lead to strong writing of articles, essays, stories, and novels. And it did. You should return to those how-to-do-something-you're-not-supposed-to-do subjects that vividly take your attention but which you set aside because you're afraid of telling about them.

The how-to-do-something-you're-not-supposed-to-do essay uses the essential structures, elements, and characteristics of a "legal" technical how-to, but because of its emphasis upon doing something that is unusual, unapproved, out of the ordinary, and unwritten, it makes emphatic use of narrative example and illustration, comparison and contrast of ways of doing things, and figurative language, in order to familiarize the audience with things unfamiliar to them and to be clear about special points and needs.

How-To Subjects

Though just about anything to be made or done or accomplished, in any situation, can be the subject of a how-to telling or writing, telling about skills that emphasize use of the hands, feet, and body especially stimulates writing. The following list, compiled from successful how-tos written by students in various writing classes, gives a sense of the possibilities:

How to make an Italian scoungli salad; how to hit a good iron shot; how to form a band; how to give an old woman a bath; how to build a rabbit cage; how to raise rabbits without going broke; how to persuade a jury; how to tie-die; how to garden for fun and profit; how to drive a car (how not to drive a car); how to play pinball; how (and why) to buy used clothes; how to make a basic skirt; how to relate to cancer patients; how not to pick up a man; how to fit into the disco scene (or any other social scene); how to make your boss like and promote you (also things not to do); how to get sick; how to lose weight through illnesses; how to make divinity candy; how to wash a dog; how to grow mushrooms in your own home; how to be a teen (how to avoid being crushed by love in high school); how to rock-climb; how to pole a pirogue; how to procrastinate; how to salvage underwater; how to manage dogs and drive a dog team; how to ride a horse (make sure you give him his reward); how to find and catch poisonous snakes; how to signify; how to play stick ball; how to submit poems to a magazine (with parodic how-not-to-do-it elements); how to turn a child into a brat; how to kill a chicken; how to survive as a supermarket employee; how to embalm a body; how to climb a palm and use coconuts; how to obtain and use fake IDs (a how-to-do-something-you're-not-supposed-to-do); how to steal a cattle-crossing sign (and display it in your dorm room); how to pick up women; how to improve your backhand in tennis; how to wash your car by hand; how to skin a cat (in this case, barbering a cat); how to use a Chinese brush; how to get the most out of Frisbeeing; how to conceive and draw your own Super-Hero comic book story; how to walk two Doberman Pinschers for Profit and Conservation (recycling of furniture and other items picked up on the walks); how to raise an avocado tree; how to survive (in one of many situations, from wilderness to your own bedroom); how to do an appendectomy on a stuffed animal; how to get a job (a particular job); how to get yourself messed over; how to build a tree-house, and many more.

Writing Your How-To: All-at-Once

Everything in writing happens at once: seeing-in-the-mind; voice; sense of form and urgent address to the imagined audience; sense of movement and what to leave out and what to put in. Of these simultaneously realized capacities, in initial writing or in rewriting, the more clearly you *see* the material in your mind, the more the seeing tends to urge forth language and gesture that move your perceptions precisely into the mind of someone else. Almost everything we discuss in this book about writing will be associated with, or produced by, or abstracted from, or qualified by, or organized from, the seeing, telling, recalling, of seeing-in-the-mind perception and the patterns and concepts that result from it.

Rather than try to tell everything there is to tell about cooking or water-skiing or rock-climbing or street games or fishing, you should narrow your subject so you can concentrate sufficiently on what you have to tell to your audience. You may begin mentally rehearsing or "daydreaming" the speech-demonstration, and then see and tell those images and passages on paper. Some persons do not feel the preliminary rehearsal as strongly as others, but virtually all writers experience an interplay between mental rehearsal and writing once they get started. You may also find, as do many writers, that when you sit down to blank paper with a blank mind and make the pencil move or the fingers type, you find yourself getting into the writing. Inward hearing of the language as you make the pencil move or the fingers type stimulates your seeing and sense of movement.

A reasonably effective technology could not exist, from the bow and arrow to the blender in your kitchen, without the heightened precision of make-sure consciousness. It helps to make a list or outline of make-sure points for your how-to. When you've located the sequence of essential make-sure points in your how-to, you've probably laid out a structure for telling the how-to. Here are tellings of make-sure points:

From an oral telling: When you set about taking blood from the big vein underneath the femoral artery of a baby and by mistake you hit the artery, the arterial pressure bounces back on the plunger against your thumb. Without taking any blood, you must carefully withdraw the needle, and then find the vein, from which the blood seeps more slowly.

From "How to Drive a Tractor": When filling the tractor with gasoline, be careful you don't bang those cans against each other. One spark and I'll be scraping you off the side of the barn over there, and you won't be in one piece either. A full gas barrel would just burn like a torch, but one that's the least bit empty will explode in a minute.[1]

From "How to Create a Super-Hero Comic Book Story": . . . you should leave plenty of room for the word balloons (character dialogue) and captions (descriptions and time indications). Use your T-square and draw them out with your pencil. Each letter syould not be over a quarter of an inch square.[2]

From an oral telling: When you're shooting marbles, you must make sure to keep your wrist straight and rigid and your eye on the marble you want to hit and imagine a line from the shooting taw in your thumb and finger to the marble you want to hit.

---

1. By Cliff Wilkerson, in *Best of Hair Trigger*, Columbia College, Chicago, 1981.
2. By Jim Labatt, in *Best of Hair Trigger*, ibid.

From an oral telling: When transplanting a gardenia plant, you make sure you knock the dirt down firmly in the new pot with your fist, or else the plant will die. You put it in the shade of a closet door so it can rest and get over its "shock" and not suffer too much leaf drop. Don't fertilize it for two weeks, so it can rest.

From an oral telling: You make sure you get a tennis racket where your grip will place your thumb no further than the first knuckle. If your grip reaches your second knuckle, the racket will twist and you will hit the ball wildly. You keep your head down so you can always watch the ball. You never stand still on your feet, you're always moving, swaying. You look for the seams of the ball when it's flying toward you, never take your eyes off the ball, never let your eyes shift to the racket instead of the ball. You always stand sideways to the ball. You swing the racket as if you're going to smack someone on the ass.

From outlines of make-sure points, articles can be written about shooting marbles, transplanting gardenia plants, and playing tennis. The more you take the reader into account in the seeing and telling of a how-to, the more the make-sure sense emerges and sharpens every perception, every sentence. Many how-to writers discover the make-sure points *as they write*.

Try to write or sketch out a complete movement, beginning to end, no matter how fragmentary, and then retell it (perhaps more than once) to complete it. Things that you orally tell to others, or in inner speech to yourself, may be starting points for passages. Get them into your writing. Try writing your how-to as a letter or memo addressed to a specific person. At the top of the page, put the name of the real or imagined person, someone with whom you feel "you can get away with murder," say whatever you need to say, someone whose presence and character you can feel in your imagination (perhaps someone from the class), and tell the how-to directly to that person. Actually write the salutation, "Dear. . . ." Try to keep that person, that "you," in mind throughout the writing. Or imagine telling your how-to as a speech-demonstration to a person or group of persons interested in doing the skill, keeping an eye to the mix of the audience. Frequently the imagined audience (made-up persons) exerts the stronger pull upon your voice and imagination. If you lose the sense of the "you" or of any other audience in your writing, keep writing, because often the writing "carries" the sense of audience in spite of the dullness you feel. Try to see what you have to tell, listen to your voice, imagine yourself looking up at your audience and talking to them. Use contractions— "can't," "don't"—to get the sense of talking to someone. Read over your own writing to find what's coming through most effectively. Be writer and reader at once. Keep writing.

You may write a preliminary draft, or notes and fragments, before you find the problem that the "you" (the reader) will have with the how-to—or the problem in the mind of the "you." You can write notes and fragments and then organize and retell them.

State the problem as early as possible, in the first sentence if possible, in a way that seizes the reader's interest, in close association with why-to-do-it, and then answer the problem step by step. State the problem early unless you have an important reason for engaging the audience and delaying the statement. How a problem works out, step by step, normally intrigues us. Four of our how-to selections state or suggest the problem in the beginning sentence. Each does it in a way unique to the particular how-to; only "How to Make Chitterlings" wisely delays the statement of the problem, teasing your suspense for a few paragraphs. The elaboration of the problem (and of the main body of your how-to) is usually intertwined with the development of the answer, of what to do and how to do it, attention to sequence and process, persuasion, suspenseful telling and organization, and storysense. If you haven't found the problem to begin with, then write and discover it while you're writing.

How the problem is worked out and answered generates the storysense that puts everything together. When you see the how-to from the point of view of the reader and discover the reader's problem, you see *more*, see it more surely, sense the "you" of the audience and yourself as the speaker-demonstrator becoming actors in the how-to, and feel the rightness of choices of expression.

Beginnings often generate the suspenseful impulse. In their beginning sentences, each of our how-to authors teases suspense as well as stating or suggesting the problem: "The most difficult feat to consistently accomplish . . ."; "To fully appreciate the Italian flair for creating works of intricately interdependent layers . . ."; ". . . I have here to speak of the magical, sometimes horrible whale-line"; "In this edition I'm going to put forward a new method . . ." "How to Make Chitterlings" also teases suspense in the first sentence, though without stating the problem: "Down home, when the hogs are shiny with fat . . ."

The sequence of a how-to usually parallels, or borrows from, the necessary sequence for the effective doing of whatever it is. Thus, the how-to form virtually enforces an appropriate sense of order.

Sometimes a how-to-do-it-better sequence for doing something becomes a new organizing principle and requires new invention for the writing. Caldwell starts with declaring that he's shifting emphasis from the legs to the arms, because he's found it to be helpful in teaching the sport, so he develops early his reasoning for altering the ordinary sequence. Examine the sequence and process of each of the how-to readings.

For those perceptions that you would ordinarily tell with gestures, actually do your gestures and let them suggest verbs, metaphors, other comparisons, and anything else that will work. No less an authority than Aristotle advises the writer, when seeking the right words, to get up and do it, to use gestures in demonstration to yourself. Look for what your gestures tell you, what they make you see, what they pull out of you. Be ready to try anything that will be effective to get what you have to tell across to your audience.

Exaggerate the how-to, exaggerate teasing the "you," and see what you find out. With its frequent tongue-in-cheek exaggeration and teasing, the how-to form often contains its own parody or self-parody (as in "How to Make Lasagna" and "The Line"). Or you may parody a foil, a "Charlie," as in "How to Get The Most Out of Frisbeeing." This teasing may occur naturally in the telling of how-tos because the how-to form is so basic, and human beings have always welcomed and needed humor and playfulness. Laughter is a peculiarly human capacity, and peculiarly integral and necessary to human activity.

Your teacher may ask you to state orally in the class the how-to you're going to tell and write—tell something about it, then start the writing and read it aloud to the class. You and other students and your teacher may read aloud some of your handed-in how-tos. Listen for the writing that comes through especially clearly and effectively *for whatever reason,* no matter what kind of language is used to tell it. Does it get through to you? Can you see it? Can you do it? Can you remember it? Can you retell it? Do you feel it's so effective that you're reluctant to give the person credit for it? These are some of the ways of identifying what comes through effectively.

The parody of a particular form or genre may at times be enticing to any writer. When you do a parody of a how-to (or of any form), *you should use your inventive powers to meet the demands of the point-by-point structure and elements of the form. The parody of a form goes much further than off-hand sarcasm or poking fun. A parody fully and imaginatively incorporates the main structure and characteristics of the form or genre.* Sometimes the parody accomplishes a very serious argument, as we shall see in the PARODIES section.

In dreams you are confronted with bizarre or witty how-tos and how-it's-done and other technical sequences. Write them in your journal. They may trigger stories or other writings, or be complete in themselves. Kafka tells technical how-it's-done and how-it-works sequences for the strange machine in "In the Penal Colony."

Rewriting and rephrasing begins with the first rehearsal/daydream/voicing of images and passages in your mind and with the first oral telling to other persons; it begins with your in-class writing, or with your journal writing, or with your first notes and scribbles about the subject, and continues integrally with everything you do to complete the writing. To rewrite your how-to, use the list of major elements and characteristics of the how-to form. Most writing is revision and rewriting of one sort or another. Sometimes when you read a draft you find a stronger beginning in the movement and this becomes a key to reorganizing the piece. *You can reorganize your writing around strengths, high points, relating them to the necessities of the form and the needs of the audience;* you may cut, modify, reduce, or alter your writing in order to effectively communicate the subject of the form to the audience. *Sounding your writing aloud or "silently" to yourself,* or to your class or a friend, can help you with rewriting. In rewriting, you choose strengths and move in the direction of strengths, of what gets the subject across to the audience *however and for whatever reason.* The perfecting and clarifying of language can be *better* handled when you're working with choices of strong and vivid material. Often students point out weak material as the stronger when, for some reason, it seems "grammatically correct" to them. The most vivid material may sound like "someone talking"and actually be more naturally grammatical. We want *your* voice on the paper. Get it down in whatever way will tell them what you have to say.

There's nothing worse than asking the reader to "read between the lines" when anyone can see that there's nothing but blank paper between the lines. Somewhere you may have heard admonitions to "leave it to the reader's imagination," or "understate it," or "be subtle" or "suggest" or "let the reader read between the lines," to the point that it could seem to any student that everything important must be on the white paper between the lines. Be aware when you feel embarrassed or restrained about telling clearly things that need to be said. Your obscurity or subtlety or obliquity at moments that sorely need clarity is lost upon the reader. Be clear. Exaggerate. Even be blunt. The first person to appreciate it will be the audience that hears and reads what you have to say. In the process of telling effectively what you have to say, you will discover and develop flexibility and fineness of expression.

Because how-to skills are so integral and basic to our minds and to everything we do, how-tos draw upon, lead toward, and draw forth compelling areas of experience that often result in fiction, poetry, journalism, scientific and other forms of analytic writing.

There's always an avid demand for written how-tos that show fresh ways (or tell in a fresh way) how to do something. If you are inclined to seek publication for your how-tos, it's likely that there are meeting points between some of your interests and some kinds of magazine, newspaper, or even book publishing.

Here are simple tests for the effectiveness of a how-to. Can the audience see and understand the proper sequence with proper emphases? Have you made sure of the make-sure points that the "you" needs to understand? Have you persuaded the audience—boosted it with motivation in the beginning, motivation along the way, an extra boost at the end, so that the reader will have the impetus of wanting to know how to do it effectively? Have you moved the seeing and understanding of your mind into the reader's mind? Can the "you," the reader, go out and do, adequately, what you've told?

II

The Process of Writing

Working Methods: Getting Started, Build-up, Continuing, and Rewriting

Most writers develop their own ways for getting started and continuing writing. These usually turn out to be life-long experiments, changing with the writers' intentions, problems, resolutions, and writing tasks, yet developing within patterns that hold for effective writers of all kinds, including effective student writers. This section sets forth some of the techniques and kinds of writing used in one way or another by a variety of writers that will help you get started and continue writing. Experiment with them in your own writing.

A major pattern for most successful writers is the use of the notebook or journal, along with a strategy of writing a first draft from beginning to end as fast as possible, no matter how ragged or incomplete, so there's "something to work with." After that, most writing becomes *re*writing—retelling and rewriting. Many writers use letter, notebook, and journal writing to support *re*writing. The Russian novelist Dostoevsky developed a notebook of trial passages, ideas, reminders, in interplay with a rough first draft, and then rewrote as much as time and money would allow. D. H. Lawrence, a writer who wanted to tell it all in "the heat" of a single draft, though obviously not at one sitting if he was working on a novel or long essay, rewrote but in a different way: Lawrence's rewriting strategy was to set aside a draft and then write the movement again from memory, with a different point of view or other significant changes, but without looking at the previous draft. Flaubert wrote rough drafts quickly, then rewrote intensely, so that each manuscript page became a "tangle" of additions, crossings-out, cuttings, and retellings, as he pushed toward greater precision and heightening. He also sounded words and passages carefully in his rewriting (as do many other writers), using direct connection of writing to speech to arrive at "rightness" of expression. Yet he also wrote wonderful, vivid letters and journal passages, mostly in complete sentences but with many incomplete, run-on, or fragmented sentences, too; these may be true first drafts without any prior notes. Few readers would argue that Lawrence's writing is as fully realized as Flaubert's or that Dostoevsky's passages that received the least rewriting are as good as those that received more attention. These three writers developed rewriting approaches that suited their personalities, abilities, aims, and situations.

Only an occasional important writer claims to need to get every paragraph right before he or she continues. Writing is so wonderful, complex, and individually demanding that there would have to be a few. How they do it and keep a sense of movement is known only to the gods of their agony. However, even these writers do not necessarily follow "rigid rules" and "inflexible plans."

Most of the successful student writers I've known use modifications of Dostoevsky's, Lawrence's, and Flaubert's approaches, though not many rewrite at length in Flaubert's way. The self-discovery process of intensive rewriting simply cannot be effectively guided or taught in one or two years. But learning how to do basic, adequate rewriting is within your reach.

You've heard that good writing should be "succinct," "terse," "to the point." That's one of those partial, sometime "truths" that, applied more than one-tenth of the time, can really entangle your writing efforts. The actual goal of writing is to get across effectively what you have to say. Students usually say too little rather than too much. *The most important basic steps in rewriting are to resee and retell your writing and give more, say more, of what you know about the subject. If you find a stronger beginning further on in your first draft, move it to the front.*

Most students have to meet deadlines as Dostoevsky did, which means finally that you rewrite according to the time and space available. If Dostoevsky was not pressured by a deadline, he would retell and rewrite a section of a novel twenty times, but usually time permitted him only three or four rewrites. I'm frequently amazed at the way some students can develop journal passages and notes, a pencilled first draft, a typed second draft, get feedback, make changes that range from choosing different words and phrases to moving around whole passages, and then do a final draft. Indeed, the foregoing would be an elaborate process for many good student writers. Sometimes they move from the pencilled first draft to a typed second draft, more in the Lawrence way. Only an occasional page will be rewritten in Flaubert's way, to make it come right. But they are always retelling and rewriting, from the first mental sights, oral tellings, notes and journal entries, to the handed-in draft.

An article, "Rigid Rules, Inflexible Plans, and the Stifling of Language: A Cognitivist Analysis of Writer's Block," by Mike Rose, published in *College Composition and Communication,* December, 1980, gives the results of a study of ten student writers, five of them successful and five unsuccessful. It clearly supports the use of the strategies suggested by modifications of Dostoevsky's, Lawrence's, and Flaubert's approaches. Students who have the most trouble in writing successfully are those who stick to rigid rules and inflexible plans. Such persons labor over the first paragraph of an essay for hours, entangled in trying to find a first sentence that will "catch the attention of the audience," or a thesis statement, or three points to develop the thesis, not even letting themselves get the first draft started, as Flaubert did, to have something to work with. Worse, I may add, they also try to make sure that each sentence is phrased in formally correct grammar. They write stiffly, awkwardly, generally unsuccessfully, nearly paralyzed and stammering with attempts to make rigid rules work, and seldom get the writing finished, as if they were tying themselves hand and foot and trying to play tennis or football. They also seldom use an active audience of friends and classmates to help them find out what they need to know about their writing. Writing is not just work for these students, it is agony.

Hemingway, who did intensive rewriting, once said of Ezra Pound's critiques of his manuscripts that when Pound was right he was so right there was no denying it, and when he was wrong he was so wrong there was no denying it. "Get it right the first time" was one of the wrongest things Pound ever said to prose writers, a rule that he apparently didn't obey in writing his poetry.

Make plans and rough outlines, yes, but be ready to change and develop them in different ways according to the wisdom of what you discover as you write. The professional writer and the successful student writer take advantage of surprise discoveries in the process of writing, even to the point of redoing the whole piece, if necessary, when they find that the writing itself "has a different idea." Rigid rules and inflexible plans stifle the flow of language and perception and don't allow you to accept the ever-changing complexity of writing. In fact, writing is a complex problem-posing and -solving process, and rigid rules and inflexible plans are simply not complex enough to deal with the writing process.

Successful, nonblocking student writers have their rules too, such as "If the rule doesn't fit or work for me, I'll change it or modify it." Successful student writers "*try* to keep the audience in mind," but if their feeling for the audience becomes indistinct or uncertain, they continue writing anyway. They always seek people to give them feedback on their writing. "When stuck, write" is the one rule that the nonblocking, successful student writer uses religiously. Write to find your thesis, write to find what you have to say. Get feedback. Act upon the feedback according to your own best perceptions about it. "Often, but not always" and "Sometimes, but not all the time" give you two important qualifications for any of the "good" rules about writing—and just about anything else. When stuck, write. When stuck, start telling your material to yourself and to the page. When stuck, make the pencil move, the fingers type. When stuck, sleep on it, but always come back to the writing, for it is in the writing that you will discover the subconscious solutions that are coming to you.

The experience of successful professional and student writers suggests strongly that the problems posed by any writing task are solved most effectively in the writing process itself, in a rich interplay of many writing activities.

If we recognize writing as "sustained speech," sustained by the page as we work it out, we have the opportunity to develop and heighten it in rewriting almost infinitely. "Sustained speech" makes it possible for you to keep a rich interplay going between your mental rehearsal and your writing and rewriting. "Sustained speech" makes it possible for you to plunge ahead and keep your writing moving, with pauses to reread what you've written and cross out lines and phrases and write in others. "Sustained speech"* makes it possible to keep a dialogue going with your own writing, with yourself as reader, with yourself listening to other readers in your mind. Many writers have said that their writing was not so much finished as finally "abandoned." We rewrite to an acceptable closure and "abandon" the piece of writing.

There is a trite admonition about rewriting that I must warn you about. That is the idea that you rewrite with a "cold critical eye." There is nothing "cold" about a productive process of rewriting. It may be positively heated and excited with the involvement of all your perceptions and faculties; it may be the most pleasureable part of writing. Certainly it should be "warm" and alive, even if calm. The "cold critical eye" can destroy good writing. Many times I've seen it happen that new and experienced writers alike make the writing worse when they try to rewrite, because they try with "a cold critical eye" to manipulate the writing in ways that don't work with the writing's own logic and magic. They muck up or cut up the best writing, stupidly expand the worst, and reformulate it in a way that doesn't work as well as the original, all in the name of "cold critical rewriting." Rewriting demands sensitivity to the wisdom of the essay, report, poem, or story. The story is wiser than we are. The essay is wiser than we are. You need to listen for and feel the wisdom and the strengths of the writing in order to rewrite effectively. Reading your writing aloud to a friendly audience helps you hear the wisdom, strengths, weak or flat places, and directions to develop. Fiddling with the writing without gaining any sense of the warmth and wisdom of the essay, story, or poem can cripple good writing or make it awkward. Of course, "fiddling" can sometimes be a way to

---

*I had developed the basic concept of "sustained speech" before I heard James Britton use the term in conversation. I owe the term itself and some suggestions of the concept to him.

get into a feeling for the writing which will help you tell the difference between strengths and weaknesses, to know places to expand, places to cut, places to heighten. Just about every recommendation concerning writing and rewriting needs to be qualified by "Often, but not always," or "Sometimes, but not all the time," or "Occasionally, but only occasionally," and so forth. This means that you have to be alert not only to your own individual differences but also to the individual differences of various writing tasks as you explore universal principles.

It's probably foolish, even if convenient, to divide writing into "prewriting, writing, and rewriting." Writing is an all-at-once activity. From mental rehearsal onward, most writing, at whatever speed, is rewriting, a constant, reflective, revisioning push of sustained speech toward greater clarity and effectiveness that occurs rapid-fire (or in "the calm grass-growing mood," as Herman Melville put it), with frequent swift crossing-out and rewording on the page. This retelling occurs in mental rehearsal, before words are even put to paper; it flashes backward and forward in the more or less perceived movement. Thus, we see that most *pre*writing is also *re*writing, that is, reseeing and retelling. Because of the nature of sustained speech in writing, the stages of mental rehearsal, prewriting, writing, and rewriting interpenetrate. With your sense of movement and your internal listening, you make many choices in the sustained speech of writing to find what you can most effectively say to your audience.

When I took notes on what I saw and heard in the Chicago Conspiracy trial, in the act of notetaking itself I was already writing my book about the trial. Everything I wrote on the book after those notes was, in a sense, rewriting. When I started writing passages in my notebooks, and then the first draft of the first article at my typewriter, you could say that I was not so much writing the first draft as *re*writing my notes, using the "sustained speech" of writing to rearrange and cluster impressions into patterns, tell them more fully, and give the story as, at the moment of writing, I remembered and perceived it. One incident would be expanded as a narrative illustration, while another became part of a cluster or pattern. Reporter's notes phased into notebook passages, which phased into draft writing at the typewriter, which phased into cuttings and rearrangements for the magazine articles on the trial, which were later retold and reworked to become parts of the book.

Rewriting is always somewhat different for each writer and each piece of writing. When you realize that most of the great potential of writing is made possible by rewriting, you have found the most important clue to the world waiting to be explored beyond your first drafts. Nevertheless, there are those times when a first draft may be the right one and require only some editing and polishing, and there are those amazing young student writers who are able to take a few notes or write a first pencil draft and then go to the typewriter and write a good draft that they hand in. But even then, they have gone through a rewriting and retelling process.

Because rewriting carries throughout the writing process, I have dealt with it before even mentioning *pre*writing. You may have heard the term "prewriting" used to include notetaking, free-writing, field notes, and journal writing. Actually prewriting means—or should mean—the activities that we stimulate, encourage, and develop *before* we put pen to paper, fingers to typewriter, voice to dictaphone, or whatever tool or machine we use. Prewriting should mean among other things our indulgence of our idiosyncrasies, such as the smell of the rotten apple that Goethe (some say Schiller) used to get started and keep writing, or the pencils that Hemingway had to sharpen. Above all, prewriting should mean the essential activities of mental rehearsal, stimulation of memory, fantasy, daydream, seeing-in-the-mind (visualization, conceptualization, and seeing right now with the vividness of a dream), our inner telling about the subject, our oral telling of it to someone, our initial sense of audience and organization. Yet, we cannot say that these activities are *limited* to prewriting because *they are urgently essential to all phases of writing*. We cannot cut the writing process into pieces, for to cut it into pieces means that we separate capacities and activities that should be working together in all phases of writing.

Any kind of writing, as any other kind of problem-solving, needs access to the imaginative state of mind, its sense of organizing movement, concentration, leaps of seeing and thinking, ready flow of perceptions, words, and syntactical responses, and the sense to make distinctions among them. In technical and expository writing as well as fictional and poetic writing, you need the concentration and movement of perceptions that allow for the sense of telling what you have to say to yourself as audience, so that the "you" in you merges with your sense for whatever audience is your focus. You need a heightened kind of internal listening. Any person of normal capacities has experienced the imaginative state of mind many times, but probably in problem-solving work or play other than writing.

Mental rehearsal, notetaking, free-writing, oral telling of imagery that we see in our minds, oral telling about our subject to someone else, field journals, personal journals, and letter writing help us not only get into but sustain the imaginative state of mind necessary for a writing task and for any other problem-solving activity. They are used in rewriting as well as in "prewriting." They may actually be—and sometimes should be— as complete as any other form of writing or expression, while they may also function as a build-up and accompaniment of a writing task, to bring to bear your associational processes, whatever catches your attention, your basic sense of audience, preliminary development of passages, and any observations or imagery about what you have to say.

In the free-writing activity in the Journals section, you can see the revisioning push of making "rewriting" choices in spontaneous mental rehearsal. The interplay of seeing-in-the-mind and language makes up the wellspring of writing that both gives and needs constant stimulation. In free-writing, journal writing and letter writing, you begin to see and hear firmly and dependably the strength of connecting your perceptions, your voice, your spoken language, to your writing.

In your journal writing, in which you use all the modes and forms of thinking and writing, in which the first draft is usually the only draft, you may find yourself rewriting as you go along. Passages of journal writing may be as complete in themselves as any other kind of writing, up to a natural ending or to the point where the passages break off. Yet the journal is also an important form of writing done for its own sake and for *your* sake, for basic development of perceptual and writing skills, as well as for exploration and build-up for specific writing tasks.

Letter-writing (or using imagined letter-writing as a form for writing that you need to do) stimulates the internal sense for telling your material to an imagined present audience, prodding you into effective expression and organization. All of these activities and principles work together to help you get started, build up, and sustain writing of all kinds.

What is an essay? Many students have a notion that the academic research essay is the only kind of essay, writing that is dry, rigid, and alien to them. Actually an essay means any kind of writing that sets forth a subject. Virtually every piece of writing in this book, from the how-to to the general essay, is a kind of essay. Most of the writing that you read in magazines is a kind of essay. Here is the definition of the word "essay" taken from *The American Heritage Dictionary*:

> **es·say** (e-sā') *tr. v.* **-sayed, -saying, -says. 1.** To make an attempt at; try: *"The Lieutenant essayed a few initial pleasantries"* (S.J. Perelman). **2.** To subject to a test; try out. —*n.* (ĕs'ā, ĕ-sā' *for senses 1, 2; only ĕs'ā for sense 3*). **1.** An attempt; endeavor. **2.** A testing or trial of the value or nature of a thing: *an essay of his capabilities.* **3.** A short literary composition on a single subject, usually presenting the personal views of the author. [Old French *essaier, assaier,* from *essai, assai,* a trial, from Vulgar Latin *exagiāre* (unattested), to weigh out, from Late Latin *exagium,* a weighing, balance, from Latin *exigere,* to weigh out, examine. See **exact.**] —**es·say'er** *n.*

Liberate the word essay in your mind so it can mean an attempt to set forth a subject (to move any subject to the reader) in writing.

Let's also liberate the word "argument" from meaning only quarrel or contention between people. In rhetoric, it means course of reasoning as you attempt to move your audience to understand or believe something about a particular subject.

> **ar'gu·ment** (är'gyU-mUnt) *n.* **1. a.** A discussion in which disagreement is expressed about some point; debate. **b.** A quarrel; contention. **c.** *Archaic.* A reason or matter for dispute or contention: *"Sheathed their swords for lack of argument."* (Shakespeare). **2. a.** A course of reasoning aimed at demonstrating the truth or falsehood of something. **b.** A fact or statement offered as proof or evidence. **3. a.** A summary or short statement of the plot or subject of a literary work. **b.** A topic; subject; theme: *"You and love are still my argument."* (Shakespeare). **4.** *Logic.* The minor premise in a syllogism. **5.** *Mathematics.* **a.** The independent variable of a function. **b.** The **amplitude** (*see*) of a complex number. [Middle English, from Old French, from Latin *agūmentum,* from *arguere,* ARGUE.]

> **ar·gu'men·ta·tion**(är'gyU-mñUn-tā'shUn) *n.* **1.** The presentation and elaboration of an argument. **2.** Deductive reasoning in debate. **3.** A debate.

Try the following process for doing an essay:

1. Write down notes, passages, thoughts, images, that come to you about your chosen subject. Be alert for any passages that feel like beginnings, that have organizing power. Or at least make a list of suggestions and reminders to yourself.

2. Address a first draft as a letter to someone (perhaps someone in your class or another friend "with whom you feel you can get away with murder"), trying to organize as best you can what you have to say from a supposed beginning to a supposed end. If possible, start it in class with the person you're addressing it to right there in front of you.

   Keep on writing and listening to your voice, even if it doesn't seem to be working as it should, even when you think you've lost the sense of your audience.

3. Finish the draft and set the writing aside for a day or so. Do a different piece of writing or other work before you come back to it.

4. Reread the writing and then read it aloud to someone. At least read the beginning part aloud. In class, you will probably read only the beginning part aloud for purposes of rewriting. Listen to other students' writings for clues and suggestions that may affect your writing, for what comes across strongly and clearly and what passages in their writings tell you about your own writing. In private, you may be able to read your whole essay or other writing aloud to a friend. Mark passages and take notes about what these readings suggest to you.

5. Be particularly alert for stronger beginnings that you may hear in reading your writing aloud. You may find the stronger beginning somewhere on the second or third page. The stronger beginning may give the impulse that helps you reorganize the whole piece. Be alert for any organizational and thematic strengths, for wherever the writing seems to be getting across what you have to say to your audience. *In reading aloud, you can often hear statements that need support and example.* Be alert for them. Say more about them. You may hear also what's not getting across clearly, and where the audience needs to have something said in a different way.

   (Use an occasional in-class writing period for rewriting, to begin to organize what you have to say to the immediate audience of someone in the class and the class itself. Try to keep your feeling for the audience while you're writing alone. Usually you'll find that your audience sense gets better week by week and that you'll have breakthroughs.)

6. Assemble all your notes and impressions, reread the piece, make notes for all passages to be shifted and changed, find your strong beginning, sleep on the matter for one night, then retell the essay as soon as possible. In the draft that you're going to hand in, make an effort to type it clearly and make it as readable as possible.

In this process, from Step 1 to Step 6, many surprises happen. You may hear writing getting across clearly that you doubted could be understood. You may hear that other writing is muddled when exposed to the audience. Many surprise perceptions are generated by the audience and by your own reading and thinking about your writing. Good perceptions may come suddenly or after you've given your mind a night's sleep to dwell on them, or very frequently in the process of writing itself.

Studies show that many students spend much less time doing their writing assignments than they spend in other kinds of study. I encourage you to spend *more* time on the various stages of your writing, particularly to retell your drafts, to *say more* and make your writing more effective. You'll gain many learning benefits for school and career. If you're particularly pressed for time, pay attention to steps 1 and 2, and if possible step 6. If you do have to do a writing assignment the night before you must hand it in, then try to reread what you've written in the process of writing your first draft and tell what you have to say as fully as you can. In the final copy (at two o'clock in the morning), you can also make additions and changes as you go along.

If fear for your grammar keeps making you stop the flow of your writing and tie yourself in knots, then you must make yourself concentrate on what you have to say, on the person you're addressing it to, on saying it in your own voice, on letting your hand be an extension of your voice, *on keeping the writing moving in your own voice.* Trying to make sure that each sentence is "grammatically correct" is another rigid rule that will put clamps and blinders on your writing, whereas trying to say what you have to say in your own voice as effectively as you can to your audience will be the best help for making your sentences better-formed, your grammar clearer.

In any of these writing activities, you should "Listen to your voice, see it (what you see in your mind), and tell it so someone else can see it." If you're trying to get your first draft down on paper as fast as you can, you should "See it (or get the sense of what you have to say about your subject) and tell it to the page, listening to it and making sure that someone else can see it too. Tell it as fully as you can, as fast as you can. Tell it so someone else can understand it. Keep moving." In your speeded-up, heated-up process of writing (or the calm "grass-growing" process), you experience a continuously reflective, spontaneous, responsive effort of seeing and reseeing, telling and retelling that moves toward making what you have to say effective. The finding of the right pace appears to integrate the necessary faculties of writing into what you feel as a flow, or forward thrusting movement, or expanding state of mind. In oral reading, "slow down" appears to be the most effective principle for finding the pace that brings together all necessary relationships. In writing, the practice of telling it "as clearly as you can as fast as you can" to your imagined audience so the audience can understand it appears to find the pace that integrates the necessary elements of the process for many writers. Tell it as fast as you can, but take the time to tell it fully. Writing has an alternating flow-and-pause rhythm. Use the pauses to reread what you've just written, picking up the movement and making changes. The speed of the work varies according to the need of the particular draft, the movement and moment of writing, as well as the particular kind of writing.

Finally, let's say something about the tools of the trade. Get yourself a notebook, such as a spiral notebook, that will keep your journal and first draft writings together. Find the paper, pens, pencils, notebooks, typewriter, and working situation that suit you. Make sure you have them. Learn to type.

Your own curiosity about your subject, about your writing, about your research, about how to get across effectively what you discover as you write is one of your best helps.

Begin the life-long experiment of working out the methods that work best for you.

Seeing-in-the-Mind

Every example of writing in this book draws upon seeing-in-the-mind and tries to tell what it has to say so that you, the reader, can see and understand it, too. Writing abstracts from seeing-in-the-mind, and *with* seeing-in-the-mind, to find what we have to say. In common speech, we say "I see" in order to say "I understand." When you exclaim at a joke, "Oh, I can just see it!" you're registering the seeing-in-your-mind. We see in our daydreams, in our dreams, in our memories, in our everyday problem-solving. We can't find a remembered something in the attic, or give or follow directions, without seeing-in-the-mind. *Seeing*, rather than *perceiving*, is the right word and concept, because seeing connotes and involves a process of understanding, includes everything meant by perceiving, and gives the sense of mental distance that occurs with seeing-in-the-mind. Einstein spoke of the importance of using the reverie of seeing-in-the-mind to find the series of connections that lead to visual conceptualization (pictorial analogies). These in turn lead to hypotheses with a range of practical consequences that also require seeing-in-the-mind. (See the Einstein selection on page 228.)

> Indeed what is certainly true is that all important human work in the arts and in science consists exactly in fashioning in one's head a hypothetical situation which can overleap the intervening space and be reformed in the head of somebody else. . . . (*The Visionary Eye,* by Jacob Bronowski, The MIT Press.)

We see to solve and solve to see.

When you try to solve a mechanical or applied mathematical problem, a problem around the house, with a machine, or in some kind of play, you notice yourself, even when you're away from the scene of the problem itself, seeing how to solve it (or how to begin to solve it) in your mind's eye. You tend to work out these problems in a narrative problem-solving movement, like a story you see and tell yourself of how it might be done. When you begin to experiment with your ideas and see more solutions in practice as you do so, that's a kind of solving to see. For instance, in an applied mathematical problem-solving example, when you know the length of a pipe, the thickness of the metal, and the radii of the inner and outer diameters, you see the circular opening of the pipe in your mind's eye and lay the concepts of inside and outside radii upon it in order to figure out the volume of metal in the pipe. You work it out in a narrative problem-solving movement.

We expect from our seeing-in-the-mind a result that will be understood by others. We expect them to say, "Oh, I see!" If they can't say "Oh, I see!" we know we haven't succeeded yet. We expect to have an answer to the question of the volume of metal in the pipe that will be the same as the answer arrived at by the others who do the problem. We expect people to be able to share literature they have read. We expect to be able to see from other points of view. Einstein expected that we all could see (in the imagined experiment of the box falling in space) what happens with the shaft of light that enters a hole on one side of the box and crosses to the other side, as viewed simultaneously by the man in the box and by the viewer from the outside.

Seeing-in-the-mind is the fundamental capacity that made human technological developments possible. As a teacher of writing, I've been struck with the effect of vivid seeing-in-the-mind upon people's writing. Even persons with poor writing skills tend to write clearly when they see clearly in their minds what they're telling. They write clear, well-formed sentences when they see a dream or personal experience or imaginative experience clearly and tell it so someone else can see it too. They write clearly not because their knowledge of formal grammar has increased, but because their seeing and intuitive grammatical sense make them form adequate sentences. This suggests that communicating seeing-in-the-mind is an original function of language, a meeting of two capacities that made us uniquely human.

> There comes a stage in a child's life before he is twelve months old, when he visibly takes the great step . . . one day there comes a moment when the child is aware that the toy behind your back is still a toy—it is still somewhere, it exists, and it will return. . . . The ability to make images for absent things, and to use them to experiment with imaginary situations, gives man a freedom which an animal does not possess. . . . A child's play is concerned with this pleasure; and so is much of art, and much of science too. At bottom, pure science itself is a form of play. (*The Visionary Eye*, by Jacob Bronowski, The MIT Press)

> Imagination is of great importance not only in leading us to new facts, but also in stimulating us to new efforts, for it enables us to see visions of their possible consequences . . . visualizing the thoughts, forming mental images, stimulates the imagination. . . . Pictorial analogy can play an important part in scientific thinking. (*The Art of Scientific Investigation*, by W.I.B. Beveridge, W. W. Norton.)

For example, the German chemist Kekule conceived the "benzene ring" (the structure of the benzene molecule) when he sank into a half sleep after trying to write about it. Long rows of the atoms wriggled and turned like snakes in his mind. "One of the snakes seized its own tail and the image whirled scornfully before my eyes. As though from a flash of lightning I awoke; I occupied the rest of the night in working out the consequences of the hypothesis. . . . Let us learn to dream, gentlemen." Jonas

Salk, the inventor of the vaccine against polio, has credited his scientific discoveries to his ability to see, in images, complex chemical reactions.

A great many writers from Joseph Conrad to Virginia Woolf, William Faulkner and others, have testified to how important seeing-in-the-mind was to their writing. Faulkner speaks of imagining characters, following them, and writing down what they do. In a letter, Virginia Woolf, attempting to answer a friend's question about how she writes, says that first she sees something and from this seeing comes the "wave" of feeling and perception that urges itself into words. We may infer from the work of other writers that seeing-in-the-mind plays an equally crucial role with them. In every kind of human endeavor, seeing-in-the-mind is basic to thinking—in art, engineering, architecture, psychology, history, city planning, physics, chemistry, etc.

Seeing-in-the-mind is more than simply seeing detail or finding imagery to support a statement. *Seeing* is visualization and conceptualization, but it is also, and begins with, seeing-in-the-mind right now as clearly and with as much impact as one sees in a dream, daydream, or reverie. Seeing involves us in the process of abstracting and solving.

The principle of image enables us to leave out much undifferentiated and unessential seeing. Without the image-principle, without the leaving out of inessentials, we would be unable to communicate. For instance, in George Schaller's studies of the mountain gorilla, we have demonstrations of the function of seeing-in-the-mind in scientific observation and writing, from the very beginning to the completion of the work. Seeing-in-the-mind provided the basic field journal observations, then the image-principle for making the abstractions from the observations, and finally the precision for the patterns. The image of dominant gorillas using mainly "a light tap with the back of the hand" against the body of a subordinate gives an accurate understanding of the workings of dominance among gorillas.

How do we take from our concrete-abstractive seeing what we need to know? How do we accomplish it sometimes so swiftly? How are we able to know what are the important relationships? How are we able to pick what to tell? Actually we appear to notice something that catches our attention, possibly related to the needs of an audience to understand it, and we the see-er and listener are also part of the audience in our minds. The principle *of whatever takes your attention* is crucially important in abstractive seeing. It may not always be right, it may sometimes be off-center, it may be imperfect, it occasions much trial and error, but it can also be amazingly swift and accurate; it is our best and surest capacity for perceiving and telling what is really essential, what we need to tell.

In fact, we begin with the seeing and the seeing immediately begins abstracting what we need to know. Seeing involves us in the process of solving, while at the same time it "speaks" to us, catches our attention with relationships, that have already begun the solving. I put quotes around "speaks" to suggest how the abstracting sense pulls or summons our attention to these relationships. For instance, below I describe a common kind of seeing-how-things-work and seeing-how-to-solve-it perception that came to me virtually without words, with a sense of verbs and felt verbs, and yet it "spoke" to me with the image relationships that took my attention. The audience of this mental seeing was myself. I had no anticipation of telling it to others, though I did later tell it in journal writing.

I had a gallon bottle of cider in a grocery sack in the cargo area in back of the upright backseat of my station wagon; plus another sack of groceries. With my eyes on the street and the traffic, I heard the bottle turn over and roll back and forth in its sack. It rolled violently with the stop and go and turn of the car and I saw in my mind's eye that it could break against something. I then visualized that if

I stood the bottle of cider in the corner where the backseat met the side of the car and then propped the sack of groceries against it, it would not roll around. I stopped the car—I rearranged the sacks in the corner in the way that I had visualized; it worked exactly as I had seen it would work.

I abstracted an important principle of physics here without naming it as such. A round bottle would tend to roll back and forth in the cargo area, gathering forces of inertia from the stop and go and turn of the car and might soon strike something with enough force to break.

Seeing-in-the-mind is inherently inventive.

This "speaking" of our seeing-in-the-mind pulls on our attention without necessarily using language. Theoretically, the seeing could move into any medium capable of expressing it. Among humans, this most private of experiences is made public through the universally available human medium of oral-gestural language, perhaps with accompanying sketches (originally in dirt or sand). Mental seeing exerts a magnetic urging upon gesture and language.

Here's a written account of the communication of a seeing-how-things-work perception originally given in oral-gestural language:

When I was driving north through the mountains (in Mexico) toward Saltillo, the red oil light flashed on the dashboard and I went really tense and scared that I would not reach Saltillo and a garage in time. At a Pemex station in Saltillo, after the oil filter was changed, I asked the *maestro* (master mechanic) what caused the accident. With the absolute confidence of a Mexican master mechanic, he spoke rapidly and vigorously to me and used the word "piedrito" (little stone) simultaneously with a hard upward fountain-like flip of his fingertips off his thumb to show how the little stone flipped, flew, spun, was flung up by one of the tires like a bullet to hit the oil filter hard enough to puncture it. He was looking directly at me and speaking vividly of the probable cause that he saw in his mind, and gave the visualized concept with the vigorous, extraordinarily precise gesture associated with his oral language. Thus, he accomplished the clear transfer of the image-principle from his mind to my mind, as Plato defined the goal of communication. I understood him perfectly.

The more vivid our seeing, the more involuntary and precise are the gestures that accompany our oral telling of it. To tell the Mexican maestro's concept in writing, I use verbs, metaphors and other comparisons to provide more or less precise correspondences for the gestural-conceptual imagery. When people deliberately try to suppress their impulses to gesture, they often must do so by folding their arms and clamping their hands in their armpits always to the diminishment of the precision and vividness of their telling. Persons committed to academic, bureaucratic, or "finishing school" language removed from common speech habitually condition themselves to avoid gesture by hooking their arms over the backs of their chairs and slumping backward instead of forward, or by forcing their hands to hold onto the edges of their chairs or other objects. Thus, they keep the sense of always being removed, in control, and never "caught" in a dynamic relationship with their audience. They diminish the discovery power of seeing-in-the-mind, its conceptual power, its pleasure. They diminish its dynamic relation to the audience. They work only with what is entirely known to them. In order to avoid gesture, imagery, and the abstractive power of imagery, they may retreat to language that tends to be empty of meaning, empty of visualization, empty of pull upon gesture, a kind of meaningless utterance socially approved in many bureaucratic and educational situations, so their hands can rest in their laps or on their desks. Even so, their fingers often raise or twitch or move with the suppressed gestural impulse coming from the seeing-in-their minds.

Here's a conclusion from some interesting research:

For example, the fact that concrete noun-abstract noun pairs are easier to learn than abstract-concrete pairs has implications in regard to an old question in communication and pedagogy, namely, is it more effective in communicating ideas to move from the relatively abstract and general to the more concrete and specific? The research I have described suggests that it may be more effective to begin with concrete, picturable examples and then move to the abstract or general ideas suggested by them, than to proceed the other way around. (*Imagery and Verbal Processes,* by Allan T. Paivio, Holt, Rinehart and Winston, Inc.)

In fact, we both see to solve and solve to see. When what we tell is "picturable," it is simultaneously formed and forming, already abstracted and potentially moving toward further concretion and abstraction.

Often we begin impulsively to gesture when we're hunting for an appropriate expression for our perceptions, and as we gesture and see what we're trying to say in our minds, we find the words we want. Gesture both expresses the seeing of our mind's eye and stimulates it. Gesture pulls language after it. Gesture is a key to pulling together and coordinating the capacities of abstractive seeing-in-the-mind and language.

Originally utterance of sound, as distinct from language, was not built from seeing-in-the-mind. Rather, it appears that at a crucial point in our evolutionary development the two capacities began to be pulled together, to meet, to work together. Language utilizes but is different from the capacity to utter sounds to give warnings, commands, and to attract attention. Because mental seeing is essential to technological perception and because it exercises such a precise urging upon utterance, it was the primary power in the bringing together of these separate capacities. Upon seeing-in-the-mind children build the language that stands for imaginatively seen and understood things. We may conjecture that early, people-like creatures, able to see fairly clearly in their own minds how something worked and how it could be done, uttered sounds to get attention, pointed at objects and gestured so that pointing gave the noun and gesture the verb. These creatures came up against situations somewhat removed from the actual situation, and because the necessary objects were not present, needed to be able to communicate an imagined perception, e.g., "we need a stick." In the urgency of the situation they uttered sounds for the noun-objects and used gestures for the verbs, until certain utterances came to mean noun-objects. Here we see how the urgency of seeing-in-the-mind reached out inventively to find whatever human capacity could be developed to communicate its perceptions.

The urgency of seeing-in-the-mind exerts a compelling influence in selecting the language that most effectively expresses the perception. Such mental seeing is a primary source for bringing self-generated content into the assigned writing task. Even though the full syntactical sense is not retained in the meaning-area at the rear of the left parietal lobe, this area does possess the basic subject-predicate sense. In this area of the brain, the capacities of hearing, speaking, and seeing are closely conjoined.

Seeing-in-the-mind is the primary, essential capacity and activity for virtually any kind of problem-solving and storytelling.

The empirical conclusion from the research on meaning and associative learning can be restated firmly: Imagery-concreteness is the most potent of any meaning attribute yet identified among relatively familiar and meaningful items. . . . (*Imagery and Verbal Processes*)

Even in the very first level of image abstraction, we see and tell some relationships and not others. If we told all of our undifferentiated seeing with no distinctions, we would glut ourselves and our audience and provide no understanding. Certain relationships in our seeing take our attention *for whatever reason*. Pushed at us by the abstracting sense of our seeing, they "speak" to us without immediate use of words, and they pull upon our attention and our oral-gestural language. We learn to trust this concrete-abstracting capacity that helps us form the image of our seeing so that we can "tell" it to ourselves and to others. We find that, even with our most unique seeing-in-the-mind, such as the bizarre and complicated imagery of our dreams, our internal seeing and listening help us to form what we have to say so that someone else can see and understand it. The more we develop our seeing-in-the-mind, the more we can heighten the use of our capacities at all levels.

> We are led to believe in a lie,
> When we see *with* not *through* the eye.
> —William Blake

Through our eyes, we see with the abstracting power of the mind's eye.

* * *

The other senses, plus the capacity for empathy, also contribute to the concrete-abstractive perception of seeing-in-the-mind. Sometimes hearing, touch, smell, or taste provide the perception that enables us to see something *visually* in a fresh, effective way; sometimes another sense provides essential perception from its own source.

Hearing

In the evolutionary world of tens and hundreds of thousands of years ago, hearing provided us with many precise, essential perceptions, as it does today. The following passage from the early German technical writer, Georgious Agricola, writing about how miners did their work in 1556, illustrates the importance of imagery of sound in the process of doing something:

> . . . where the vein is seen to be seamed with small cracks, they drive into one of the little cracks one of the iron tools I have mentioned; in each fracture they place four thin iron blocks, and in order to hold them more firmly, if necessary, they place as many thin iron plates between two iron blocks, and strike and drive them by turns with hammers; whereby the vein rings with a shrill sound; and the moment when it begins to be detached from the . . . wall of rock, a tearing sound is heard. As soon as this grows distinct the miners hastily flee away; then a great crash is heard as the vein is broken and torn and falls down.

This is the expository telling of a man who has been described as one "of the first technical writers to stuff his pride and university degrees into his pocket and to interview the working technician for what he could contribute."[1] The third person "they" establishes it as the how-it's-done form rather than the fundamental how-to that usually uses the "you" person of address. In "How to Drive a Tractor,"* we are told that while filling the tank with gasoline:

---

1. "What Can the Technical Writer of the Past Teach the Technical Writer of Today?" by Walter James Miller in *The Teaching of Technical Writing*, ed. by Donald H. Cunningham and Herman A. Estrin, NCTE, Urbana, 1975.
*By Cliff Wilkerson, in *Hair Trigger II*, Columbia College, Chicago, 1978.

You'll get to where you can tell, by the sound of the gas splashing in the tank, how near the top you are. It starts out sounding like when you pour water in an empty bucket, then after a while like water running in the creek and when it's nearly to the top it fades to a whisper. When you don't hear it whispering to you any more you know it's time to stop turning the crank.

In an excerpt from a how-to that I wrote about stalking:

You stay still for fifteen minutes or so against a tree or other backdrop, then you become aware of something faraway in the stillness of the woods on all sides. You feel a startle of excitement; you seem to know what's happening before you can say what it is coming toward you from the distances through the trees, slowly at first, then like the ripple of a pond contracting inward upon you. The sounds of the forest are rippling toward you! It means you are "disappearing"! You will never lose your excitement for it, this excitement that occurs in spite of you, as the contracting ripple of forest sounds comes closer and closer until, like a magician's cloth swept away, that ripple closes over your head, and you find you are as invisible as you will ever be. Don't move. Not even your eyes. A colony of wild canaries will play around you, nearly light in your hair. It is the most extraordinary, liquidly peaceful, expansively exciting feeling, state of mind. When a noise takes your attention, turn your head very slowly toward it.

Other special techniques of language appeal to the sense of hearing: technically, alliteration means the repetition of the sound at the beginning of a word; however, prose-writers and poets use sounds within as well as at the beginning of words, to develop onomatopoetic effects.

For when the line is darting out, to be seated then in the boat, is like being seated in the midst of the manifold whizzings of the steam-engine in full play, when every flying beam, and shaft, and wheel, is grazing you.

Melville heightens the comparison of the movement of the line to the movements of the steam engine with the sibilant s's, z's, and "juh" sound of the g, and the whirring of the w's set off by the labial b's and m's, and by the f's and p's. Writers exploit and heighten these natural techniques of our language. Melville faced an interesting choice in the above sentence: It would often be effective to rewrite a sentence using active verbs in place of more passive verbs, but in this case he would have lost three z-sounds of "is's." If you substituted near synonyms for z-sound words, the sentence would lose still more effect.

For modern prose-writers and poets to leave out the natural resources of alliteration, assonance, rhyme, cadence, chime, contrast of broad and narrow vowels, contrast of consonants, and so on, makes for a major loss of language effects and a flattening of their writing.

Touch

In our perceptions of how to do things we make certain distinctions with touch. Melville invites you to tell by touch that "the ordinary quantity" of tar would "too much stiffen the whale-line for the close coiling to which it must be subjected."

The suggestion of touch makes for precision in the following coordination of motions in how to cross-country ski:

It also will help if you concentrate on keeping the rear foot as close to the snow as possible. This in turn can be helped by pointing the rear hand downward toward the snow as you finish your poling motion. (Racers are so conscious of this that they seem at full extension to be holding that rear pole with only thumb and forefinger.)

In the servicing of a tractor you should

be sure to keep that grease gun in the shade because if you try to pick it up in the middle of the afternoon when the sun's beating down, that piece of metal can get hot enough to blister your hand.

In cooking, you need to feel the texture of food with the palate. You pull on the leg of a roasting chicken to see when it waggles loosely enough to indicate that the bird is done. The sense of touch gives us important signals in almost every activity.

Smell

The smell of smoke, gas, and other kinds of fumes, warns us of danger. The sense of smell has always given us warnings and pleasure. When the gasman checks for gas leaks, he sniffs at the joints of the pipes. Horticulturists sniff soils, fertilizers, plants. A painter can tell the difference between different kinds of paint by smell. Smell is helpful in cooking. How is the sense of smell used in different kinds of mechanical work? In other activities?

The sense of smell powerfully evokes memories, almost more powerfully than any other sense, jolting us with the momentary reliving of the memory.

Taste

In cooking, taste tells us what spices or other treatment the food needs; how far along it is; when it's just right. How would you describe a taste to someone who has not cooked the dish before?

Taste has also been used as a way of determining the presence of dangerous or unwanted substances. Sometimes we dab something from the tip of a finger to our tongue as a cautious way of deciphering a substance.

Point of View

Seeing-in-the-mind also gives us access to point of view, and through the experience of point of view to empathic seeing. A young girl cringes at the blinding of the bearcub by the claws of the cat in *The Incredible Journey,* by Sheila Burnford, when the story is read aloud, but does not cringe at such imagery on television, because the dimension of the internal point of view in reading stories is not present. The storytelling of oral-gestural language makes us see the "picture" in our minds, react to it in our own seeing-in-the-mind, whereas television puts the picture outside of us and seems also to put it outside of our minds. In recall of imagery from Orwell's essay "A Hanging," a person using gestures in recall-telling takes the hanged man's heels (as does the doctor in the story) and gives them a downward jerk to ensure the breaking of the man's neck; someone on the other side of the class winces with the powerful empathic identification given by the gestural-verbal image—winces and then laughs with recognition: he has been forced by the conveyed image, that overleaped the intervening space between him and the teller and reformed itself clearly in his mind, to participate both as the doctor and the hanged man. Seeing-in-the-mind coordinates words and gestures, point of view and imagery.

Remember the imaginative play you did as a child, the imaginative play you see children do, the inventing of problems and solving them? Remember your daydreams, your adult imaginative play, your daydream problem-solving? In such imagining, you frequently see (or feel) yourself as a physically separate actor, i.e., with a spatial distance between you the storytelling perceiver of the daydream and you the separate participant. You often use the first person and present tense, but sometimes you tell the daydream to yourself (or act out the imaginative play) with you the participant as a third person he or she. You see other third person hes or shes. You may tend to use the present tense, but you may also construct the daydream so that you use the past tense most satisfyingly in reports or in other stories-within-a-story concerning yourself. Sometimes you feel that the teller merges with the participant.

Writing becomes more complicated than most simple daydreams, but daydream problem-solving, storytelling, reverie, and imaginative play, that sort of seeing-in-the-mind, and similar states of mind (which you develop in the process of writing), can help you with any writing task, whether fictional, poetic, technical, or expository. In adult imaginative play, we perceive and pose problems, obstacles, and possibilities, and solve them in our writing and other forms of expression.

When we get into further developments of expository and technical writing, we will find that statements and perceptions of patterns have been abstracted from seeing-in-the-mind. We will find that image and sense of image have also provided the precise qualifications that make the abstracted passages accurate. We will also encounter a large amount of writing virtually divorced from its concrete-abstractive basis, devoid of qualification through imagery, and we will ask if that writing is as effective as it could be. We will find that seeing-in-the-mind and language can drift or be forced apart, and that communication and comprehension are adversely affected.

Further Advice for Developing Your Seeing-in-the-Mind

Let's correct an unhelpful misunderstanding about imaginative seeing. *You don't need to close your eyes to stimulate your imaginative seeing.* If you stop to think about it, you'll see that in oral tellings and in writing you have to keep your eyes open in order to focus on the audience or on the tools of pencil, typewriter, and paper. In our most vivid seeing, our eyes will shift from our audience to the seeing-in-our-minds, much as our eyes move in REM in sleep. So the seeing happens naturally in association with oral and written telling. As a matter of fact, if you close your eyes and have to concentrate on keeping your eyes closed, you divide your concentration by keeping your eyes unnaturally rigid, which inhibits your imaginative seeing. When you're daydreaming or in a reverie, you naturally stare into space with your eyes open—or perhaps they move as in the telling of vivid imagery. You don't need to close your eyes or imitate some burlesque version of hypnosis in order to stimulate imaginative seeing. However, if closing your eyes now and then makes you slow down and see what you have to tell, then do it—now and then.

For those perceptions that you would ordinarily tell with gestures, actually do the gestures and let them suggest verbs, metaphors, comparisons, and anything else that will work. Follow Aristotle's advice. When seeking the right words, look for what your gestures tell you, what they make you see, what they pull out of you. Be ready to try anything that will be effective to get what you have to tell across to your audience. The seeing of perceptions in your mind stimulates your telling of them to your audience, makes you see the needs and challenges of your audience more clearly, and helps you feel and trust the things and actions that most strongly take your attention.

A few persons may have trouble "seeing" what they have to tell. You should not expect to see it as film or television unrolling in your mind. Such seeing would thoroughly inhibit your concrete-abstractive processes. The sense of mental seeing and abstraction, the most private of experiences, varies from one person to another, one kind of perception to another. Sometimes your seeing may happen as vividly as a dream, sometimes you may sense the structure of the image without direct seeing of it, with many combinations and variations being possible and useful. Trust your sense for the way it happens for you. Your seeing will contain many possibilities and choices.

You often generate seeing in your mind with language, while concentrating on the imagery of objects and actions and sounding and hearing what you have to tell. Looking at what you have to tell from the "you's" point of view generates seeing. Just as the unbroken wall of the blank page happens for everyone, so does blankness of seeing. The more you hear your voice, the more you'll find your seeing; the more clearly you see your perceptions, the more clearly you'll hear your voice. The movement of your voice in writing generates seeing; gesture stimulates seeing; exaggeration brings forth seeing; seeing stimulates language; your sense of the audience's needs stimulates seeing. If you feel your seeing go blank or that you're not seeing clearly, listen to your voice, exaggerate, do gestures *and anything else you figure out on your own,* to get your seeing started. Keep on writing, because your writing may "carry" the seeing in spite of the blankness you feel. Many times a writer does good writing when dead tired, because defenses are down and the writing happens unimpeded by contradictory impulses.

But don't wait around for clear vivid magical urgent seeing and clear definite sense of audience, as if you're waiting for a bus that never comes. Start writing. Make the pencil move, the fingers type. Try to see what you have to say. Listen to your voice. Be ready to experiment and play around and try anything as you write until you begin to find what you need. Keep writing. Often, when you read the writing later, you find that you wrote well.

Spoken Language and Written Language

"A dramatic necessity goes deep into the nature of the sentence. Sentences are not different enough to hold the attention unless they are dramatic. No ingenuity of varying structure will do. All that can save them is the speaking tone of voice somehow entangled in the words and fastened to the page for the ear of the imagination. That is all that can save poetry from sing-song, all that can save prose from itself."

Robert Frost, Introduction, *A Way Out*

"Writing was in its origin the voice of an absent person."

—Sigmund Freud

"Alfred has shiny six motorcycles."

No matter what dialect of English you speak, you know that sentence is not an English sentence. You don't have to know the formal grammar rule to know why it's not an English sentence. I've read that and similar sentences to many groups of teachers and students and I have yet to encounter a single person who could state the formal rule: adjectives of number precede adjectives of quality. Teachers and students alike simply know it's "not right."

You don't need to be taught formal grammar in order to be able to write. You don't need to be taught formal grammar in order to be able to recognize good English grammar.

As in baseball the hitter keeps his eye on the ball not on the bat, in tennis on the ball not on the racket, in archery on the center of the bull's eye not on the point of the arrow, in horseback riding on the wall or point beyond the fence to be jumped not on the fence, so in writing we get the best results when we keep our eye on what we have to tell not on the grammar of our sentences. Just as our peripheral vision and subconscious awareness keep track of the bat, the racket, the point of the arrow, the fence to be jumped, so our intuitive sense for the grammar of our language keeps track of the grammar of sense and meaning. In the sports mentioned above, the necessity of keeping your eye on the point that makes the accomplished act possible is essential *from the very beginning of training*. In writing, it is similarly essential to keep your concentration on the "ball," on what you have to say, *from the very beginning of writing*. If we divide our attention by glancing continually at the myriad rules of formal grammar instead of concentrating on what we're trying to say, we disrupt and scramble the necessary process for writing effectively.

Students who have poor writing skills frequently come to my office to discuss *the problem*. I ask a student, "What's the problem?" already knowing what "the problem" will be. The student says, "I can't write sentences. I don't know sentences." I listen to the student talk for a few minutes, and I hear one complete sentence after another coming out of his mouth. Nearly 75% of what he says is spoken in complete sentences. I'm not sure that my own rate of sentence completion in speech would be that high. I tell him, "I've been listening to you for the past few minutes and I hear one complete sentence after another. What do you mean you don't know sentences?" We discuss it. Like the man in Moliere's play who was amazed to learn that he'd been speaking prose all his life, the student goes away bemused and amazed to hear that he's been speaking sentences all his life. Now the question is: Will he be able to hear the sentences in his writing?

Given half a chance and the right kind of work, contexts, and points of concentration, most students can learn to hear the sentences they speak and the sentences they use in the sustained speech of writing. Often the context, particularly the audience context of the writing itself, determines whether or not you are able to "hear" your sentences in writing. For example, a teacher who was trained in my department for a couple of years got a job as supervisor of a writing lab in a community college; in a letter he told me about a young woman who had come to him for help about her writing:

Teacher: What seems to be the trouble?
Student: I can't write sentences. (the old refrain)
Teacher: Well, I'd like to see some of your writing.
Student: But I can't write!
Teacher: Write anything. Write a letter
Student: (*Hesitating*) Is it all right if I write a letter to my mother?
Teacher: Sure.
          (*Student writes for several minutes, then hands the paper to the teacher.*)
Teacher: (*Reads it.*) Well, the sentences are fine here!
Student: But I was writing to my mother!

In writing to her mother, she was able to *"hear"* her sentences. In her "school" writing, she was *not* able to "hear" her sentences. Then why not imagine that she's writing a school essay to her mother? Rudolf Flesch, author of "Write the Way You Talk," condensed for *Reader's Digest* from his book *Say What You Mean*, says, "What you need is instruction in the basic principles of professional writing. . . . The pros— magazine writers, newspapermen, novelists, people who write for a living—learned long ago that they must use 'spoken' English and avoid 'written' English like the plague." Flesch recommends that you "*talk* to your reader. Pretend the person who'll read your letter or report is sitting across from you, or that you are on the phone with him. . . . One helpful trick is to imagine yourself talking to your reader across a table at lunch. . . . Go over what you've written. Does it look and sound like talk? If not, change it until it does." Notice that Flesch advocates using the sustained speech of writing in order to *re*write until the writing sounds "like talk," like the address of one person to another person. Strangely enough, that means using a dimension of writing that is *different* from speech in order to make writing sound *more* "like talk."

Developmentally, hearing and speech come before writing and are essential pre- requisites to its acquisition. "Genetically we know that speech comes first because chil- dren who are deaf have great difficulty in learning to read—shutting off the channels of sight has little effect on acquiring language, but shutting off those of sound is almost fatal to it."[1] We also know that "Disturbances in oral language are accompanied in practically all cases by equivalent or greater difficulties in written language. This is because writing appears to be 'parasitic' upon the capacity for oral communication, and also because writing is about as complex a skill as most normal individuals possess."[2] It should not surprise us then that for students to try to learn to read and write through sight alone without oral sounding of the language, is nearly impossible. Yet that is virtually what is asked of students in our educational institutions, in which reading and writing nowadays are only sporadically *heard*.

If you have trouble with your sentences when you write assigned papers, you can imagine yourself writing them to a friend or relative or to an imagined someone with whom you can "get away with murder." Not only will your writing become more effec- tive but your sentences will become better-formed.

You've probably heard many people advise you that writing is very different from speech and you must carefully learn its different rules and procedures, particularly learn formal grammar. They seem to be asking you to master a foreign language in order to be able to write. Their reasoning goes like this.

Writing is different from speech.

Therefore:

You must learn formal grammar in order to be able to write.

Not all good reasoning is syllogistic, but elementary logic teaches you to recognize the fault in the above sequence. It should be stated:

Writing is different from speech.

It is different because. . . .

Therefore, you need to learn formal grammar in order to be able to write.

The people who say that you need to learn formal grammar in order to be able to write have never developed for you or themselves why and how writing is different from speech and why those differences make it imperative for you to learn rules that amount to learning a foreign language. If they do begin to examine the *real* differences between writing and speech, they will not find much to support the conclusion of their strange logic. Only after we have seen all the connections between writing and speech can we determine what needs of writing make certain conventions and formalization helpful for

1. *Aspects of Language*, by Dwight Bolinger, Harcourt Brace Jovanovich, New York, 1975.
2. *The Shattered Mind*, by Howard Gardner, Knopf, New York, 1975.

developing the different dimensions of writing, which are actually *made possible by the connection and correspondences of the sound medium of speech to the visible medium of writing*. However, since these people have put the cart before the horse and are asking both the horse and the vehicle to perform in unnatural ways, we will sort out the confusion and get the power of oral-gestural language back up front where it will be able to pull the vehicle (the medium of writing) much more easily and efficiently.

There are those who advocate that writing is—or should be—separate from speech, as unconnected as possible. Others advocate that writing should be almost a transcription of speech. My own position is different from either of these. I think it's a position that will be particularly helpful to you, and I think it deals realistically with the close connections between speech and writing as well as the differences. I believe that writing is, can, and should be very closely connected to our language as we speak it, in whatever English voice or dialect, so it can draw continuously upon the power of speech. However, writing has tremendous potentials beyond the capacity of speech, or else there would be no reason for it.

Before I examine the connections and differences, I should deal with some of the questions and issues that make life and learning miserable for many students in writing classes: Is most speech ungrammatical? Is *my* speech ungrammatical? What if my particular dialect differs from the kind of speech that I hear my teachers speak? What if I'm a black dialect speaker or an Appalachian or other dialect speaker?

A massive study of the use of formal grammar approaches in the teaching of writing in Auckland, New Zealand high schools (reported in *Research in the Teaching of English*, Spring 1976, Vol. 10) concluded after three years' work with 248 students that the grammar approaches did not significantly affect the students' acquisition of composition skills. In fact, the grammar-trained students ended the study with a more negative attitude toward writing. The case against the teaching of formal grammar as a way of teaching writing is stated succinctly for many writers, teachers, and researchers by Michael F. Shugrue in *English and Reading in a Changing World* (NCTE): ". . . The teaching of formal grammar has a negligible or, because it usually displaces some instruction and practice in actual composition, even a harmful effect on the improvement of writing." In *A Writer Teaches Writing*, Donald Murray observes that many good, even great writers, have had only a skimpy knowledge of formal grammar. Shakespeare and other great English writers, who wrote prior to the codification of English according to Latin (not English) rules in the eighteenth century, had no training in formal English grammar. Chinese scholars and writers developed a literature for thousands of years without benefit of a formal published grammar. They, as the pre-eighteenth century English writers, were trained in writing (or rhetoric) and calligraphy, not in formal grammar. However, all writers recognize that use of the grammar of sense and meaning is a skill that they need to develop along with their general skill of writing. Spelling and other mechanical skills should not be confused with grammar. Obviously, we need to be able to spell, to punctuate, and to use the mechanical conventions of writing with reasonable facility or we simply cannot be understood by our readers. Most of these skills are also best taught within the context of full writing processes, though spelling and certain aspects of handwriting may be taught separately or adjunctively to full writing processes. Part of the purpose of this chapter is to help you to learn how to develop skill with the grammar of sense and meaning and confidence in the use of the mechanical conventions of writing.

In *Errors and Expectations* (a book about the problems of the so-called "basic" writing student in college), Mina Shaughnessy said somewhat wryly in a footnote: "If we are to accept William Labov's research on the matter, in fact, they (students) have probably been producing more 'well-formed' sentences than their teachers."

> Our own studies . . . of the grammaticality of everyday speech show that the great majority of utterances in all contexts are complete sentences, and most of the rest can be reduced to grammatical form by a small set of editing rules. The proportions of grammatical sentences vary with class backgrounds and styles. The highest percentage of well-formed sentences are found in casual speech, and working-class speakers use more well-formed sentences than middle-class speakers. The widespread myth that most speech is ungrammatical is no doubt based upon tapes made at learned conferences where we obtain the maximum number of irreducibly ungrammatical sequences." (*Language in the Inner City: Studies in the Black English Vernacular,* by William Labov, University of Pennsylvania Press, Philadelphia, 1972.)

These conclusions are based upon tapes made of conversations from many social backgrounds and situations. Most educated persons wince and laugh with recognition at the final sentence in Labov's summation of this research. The fact is that learned persons speak ungrammatically, get tangled in clauses and lose their subjects and predicates, because they try to take into account all the consequences of their statements as they form them and to duplicate in speech the kinds of sentence structures that can only be sustained in writing, a kind of backhanded evidence of the connection between speech and writing. If teachers are really interested in going "back to the basics," they should direct students to the sentence structures that students use in everyday speech with peers and family, as the proper and most effective foundation for developing the potentials of writing.

Read this sentence to Standard English speaking friends (White or Black) in off-guard moments and ask them to reproduce it from memory:

I aks Alvin do he know how to play basketball.

Read this sentence aloud to friends who are black vernacular speakers:

I asked Alvin if he knows how to play basketball.

I have read these examples to many groups of teachers and students.* An occasional white teacher or student can reproduce the black dialect sentence precisely, but most of them add the "if" or "whether," transforming it into their own dialect, or they turn "aks" into "asked." Black vernacular speakers usually turn the second sentence into a version of the first sentence. This demonstration lets teachers know that they would have just as much difficulty in trying to reproduce a dialect different from their own as a native speaker of the dialect has in trying to reproduce and incorporate Standard English. *However, the experiment also demonstrates that we usually can hear the meaning of sentences in other dialects of our language, though we cannot reproduce the many features of them in our own speech.* English dialects draw upon the basic grammar of English. Further, the passages demonstrate that alphabetic writing can be used to give representation to dialect speech as well as to Standard speech. As Labov suggests in *Language in the Inner City,* language change must be accomplished in subtler and more powerful ways than can ever be done by red-pencilling student papers until they "bleed." As a matter of fact, "error-correction" on paper has a distinctly negative effect upon students' acquisition of writing skill. Language behavior change must be accomplished through the power of speech and peer relationships, and the interrelating of the skills of silent reading, oral reading, speaking, listening, and writing.

---

*These examples are taken from *Language in the Inner City,* by William Labov, ibid.

In a way it is strange that we should have any debate at all about the connection of alphabetic writing and speech, because the original purpose, the very genius, of the alphabet was, and is, that each element of its system corresponds to a specific sound element in the language to be represented. Alphabetic writing can represent, come to the service of, whatever dialect you speak.

Here we have the classic statement for the purpose, function, and genius of alphabetic writing:

> In the picture-writing and the pure ideographic scripts, there is no connection between the depicted symbol and the spoken name for it; the symbols can be 'read' in any language. Phonetic writing is a great step forward. Writing has become the graphic counterpart of speech. *Each element in this system of writing corresponds to a specific element, that is sound, in the language to be represented* [my italics]. The signs thus no longer represent objects or ideas, but sounds or groups of sounds; in short, the written forms become secondary forms of the spoken ones. A direct relationship has thus been established between the spoken language and the script, that is, writing has become a representation of speech. The symbols, being no longer self-interpreting pictures, must be explained through the language they represent. The single signs may be of any shape, and generally there is no connection between the external form of the symbol and the sound it represents. Phonetic writing may be syllabic or alphabetic, the former being the less advanced stage of the two. (*The Alphabet,* by David Diringer, Hutchinson, London, 1968.)

Linguists have pointed out that any writing system must closely correspond to a language as it is spoken. "Visual symbols do not begin to be writing until they have a close correspondence to language." (*Language and Symbolic Systems,* Yuen Ren Chao, Cambridge University Press, 1968.) Chinese ideographs and Egyptian hieroglyphics are "speakable." The Chinese ideograph for "man" 人 can be read in any dialect of Chinese, even pronounced as a different word still meaning "man" in different dialects of Chinese. In English alphabetic writing, the "m," "a," "n," and the combination "man," can be read in many different words with different meanings, such as "manners," "mangle," "mandolin;" the three letters "m," "a," "n," and the word or syllable "man," have meaning *only* as secondary forms of sounds in our spoken language. In Chinese, however, you combine *visual* elements that have *emblematic* meaning in themselves to make words. For instance, here we combine the symbol sun 日 with the symbol moon 月 to make another symbol 明 that means bright. This symbol can be spoken in any dialect of Chinese, and theoretically (according to Diringer) has the meaning "bright" in any language. (Obviously, certain special poetic effects can be achieved with Chinese characters.) In alphabetic writing, the symbols b–r–i–g–h–t or m–a–n do not have emblematic meaning in themselves; they receive meaning solely from spoken English, from their precise correspondences to elements of speech. The spelling c–h–a–t, meaning talk in English, means cat in French, gaining its meaning solely from spoken French. The English language that you speak every day is the language our alphabetic symbols represent.

You've probably heard the saying that "a picture is worth a thousand words." In fact, if pictures could do everything that words can do, our writing would have remained pictorial.

So, though the earlier forms of writing were speakable, they were cumbersome and lacked precision of language representation when compared to the alphabet, which was "invented" by Sumerian peoples just north of Canaan 3500 years ago, and perfected into a full alphabet with addition of the vowels by the Greeks beginning about the ninth century B.C. Imagine if you had to learn 185 basic syllable symbols instead of 26 a–b–c–'s. Imagine if you had to learn a separate symbol for each word in order to be able to write—if you had to learn the 9,000 or so symbols actually employed by Chinese scholars, or the 80,000 Chinese characters existent. No wonder the Chinese have sought so mightily to develop an alphabet. With English alphabetic writing, you coordinate 26 symbols with elements of your speech and begin to develop the "sustained speech" of writing.

The first purpose of alphabetic writing was to record business transactions, to provide a witness fixed in the clay, "the voice of an absent person," as Freud said. However, there would be only limited purpose for writing if its sole purpose had proved to be the transcription of speech as it is spoken. In fact, alphabetic writing, as human beings have been discovering for 3500 years, has the potential for "sustained speech." When we speak, our words disappear as soon as they are spoken, to be remembered by speaker and hearer according to how successfully memory techniques and organizing forms are used. In alphabetic writing, we develop "sustained speech" in the extraordinary dimension of past-present-future progression on the pages right before our eyes, speakable to our ears and minds, a dimension unequalled in any other medium. This unique playback and playforward nature of alphabetic writing enables us to look and listen backward and forward from any point in what we're writing or reading. The advantages of alphabetic writing compared to speech are paradoxically made possible by the precision of its connection to speech, not by its supposed independence from that connection. With the connection of speech to the visible medium of writing, the entire human brain becomes involved in writing.

Writing's dimension of "sustained speech" makes intensive rethinking and rewriting possible, from simple retelling to very complex reformulation.

What About the Difficulties of English Spelling?

The irritations surrounding the complications of the English spelling system stoke up a sort of smoke screen that makes the debate on the relationship of spoken to written language seem distractingly attractive. Printing, introduced into England by William Caxton in the midst of the Great Vowel Shift in the language, helped to complicate the relationship of our spelling to our pronunication, because it tended to preserve hundred-year-old Middle English spellings, which were probably regarded as "Standard" at the time. The result was a disorganization of our spelling system that has continued until today.[3] Yet, even though the language has certainly acquired its share of inconsistencies, the patterns of English spelling have in the main been demonstrated to correspond impressively with our pronunciation.[4]

The following poem by Richard Krogh addresses the famous, frustrating complications of English spelling:

Beware of heard, a dreadful word
That looks like beard and sounds like bird.
And dead; it's said like bed, not bead;
For goodness sake, don't call it deed!
Watch out for meat and great and threat
(They rhyme with suite and straight and debt).

---

3. Morton Bloomfield, "A Brief History of the English Language," *The American Heritage Dictionary*, New York, 1970, p. xvii.
4. *Research in the Teaching of English*, Vol. 13, No. 3, October, 1979.

A moth is not a moth in Mother,
Nor both in bother, broth in brother.

It's the sounding of precisely understood alphabetic correspondences that makes the wit of the poem possible.

Because of the complications of the English spelling system, many people have mistakenly conditioned themselves to feel that our written language must not be directly correspondent to the spoken. "What is meant is that the spelling does not directly *reflect* the way in which a word is pronounced. This, of course, is true; but the generally accepted corollary that English orthography bears little relation to English phonology is in fact quite false. . . . The pronunciations of words are quite generally *predictable* from their spellings. In trying to prove the contrary, it is not sufficient to cite a random set of orthographic vagaries, a handful of letters indicating the same sound, a handful of sounds being indicated by the same letter, and so on."[5]

Learn how to spell. Use a dictionary. Learn to sound the word and see it in your mind at the same time. Adequate spelling makes writing readable.

Moving from Speech to Writing

Most of us are aware of the challenge of trying to move a successful oral telling into writing. If you're doing writing that seeks to directly represent someone's speech, you might use the "you knows" and "likes" and other such slangy words and phrases that people use for emphasis and to keep contact with their audience. However, in most writing, such repeated words and phrases are redundant and actually obstruct the audience's appreciation of writing's sustained speech. In writing we do not try to duplicate speech with all its hesitations, disruptions, etc. Rather, we use sustained speech with an immediate audience that we imagine in our minds, to draw upon the power of our perception, speech, gesture, and intuitive sense of grammar.

In speech, we use "got," "gotten," "get," and "getting" a great deal, and make abundant use of linking verbs "is," "was," and other forms of the verb "to be." Usually gestures, facial expressions, bodily expression, and voice nuances accompany our speech, suggesting active verbs, understood clearly as such by our immediate listening audience. In writing, we express such perceptions with explicit active verbs (sometimes with nouns, adjectives, and adverbs, but particularly with verbs). If you speak certain dialect forms, such as "black dialect" in urban areas and white "hill" speech in the south and southern midwest, you won't use the "is" and other forms of "to be" in certain sentences. If you want to bring such dialect speech into writing, you have to be mindful of the dialect's features and how you represent them with written symbols. In much of the writing you do, you will begin to incorporate active verb forms in place of "is," was," etc.

Here's an example of the transfer of an oral telling to writing. We might tell someone:

> Well, he got there, you know, going like this (giving a back and forth slouching of our shoulders to indicate how he slogged tiredly into camp) about nine o'clock (big sigh), dead tired. (Rummaging motions with the hands) couldn't find any food anywhere. Well, he was, you know, pissed. . . . (we give expression of glaring around us).

---

5. Wayne O'Neil, "The Spelling and Pronunciation of English," *The American Heritage Dictionary*, New York, 1970, p. xxxv.

We might write it, to get across our perception:

> Well, he slogged tiredly into camp at about nine o'clock, slouching his shoulders back and forth, shifting his pack. Dead tired, he let the pack down with a big sigh. He rummaged around in the camp, but couldn't find any food anywhere. Really pissed, he glared around him, looking for someone to blame.

The great wealth of verbs, nouns, adjectives, and adverbs in our language makes possible a transfer of our perceptions from speech and gesture to writing. In the HOW-TO section, we discussed how to use metaphors, exaggeration, audience sense, imagery, and other methods to get into writing the concepts and perceptions of speech and gesture.

In oral-gestural language, we often keep the referent points of our meaning understood by physical means that are not directly present in writing. We must take our reading audience into account and be aware that the surface features of the language, and transitions and connections of one thought to another, need more attention in writing than in speech, in order to make our meaning clear. A grammar of sense and meaning helps us to keep our referent points straight. At the same time, the connection of speech to writing, sounding your writing aloud to a present audience, and hearing your writing in your voice, are your best helps in finding transitions, connections, and referent points in writing.

"Cosmetic" Grammar and Grammar of Sense and Meaning

There are rhetorics and usage handbooks which produce lists of "common errors" in speech that are deemed not desirable in writing. Some of those "lists" contain three or four hundred items, rather ponderous to memorize. Actually, since there is no general agreement among scholars about these "errors," the list could include many more than three or four hundred items, which would convey a message to most students that they should be very cautious with the language that they use in writing. So the "lists" end up placing an emphasis that suppresses the spontaneity of language and chokes the lifeline connecting the power of speech to writing.

In principle, I can alert you to two kinds of "common errors," one "cosmetic," and one having to do with sense and meaning. The difference between "aint" and "isn't" or "aren't" is "cosmetic." There's no difference of grammatical meaning between "He aint coming," and "He isn't coming," though there may be a difference of emphasis, since many of us use "aint" ironically. There's no difference of meaning between "My uncle cannot read very good" and "My uncle cannot read very well," though again some of us may use "very good" with an ironical emphasis. Subject-verb disagreement, which often occurs in the speech of educated persons as well as in the speech of other folks, is more a matter of "cosmetic" appearance than of sense. "The man and his people is coming" makes the same grammatical sense as "The man and his people are coming."

At the same time, you don't need a grammar handbook to tell you that the following sentence is not grammatical: "Alfred has shiny six motorcylces." Without knowing the formal grammatical rule, any English speaker will say that the sentence should be formed, "Alfred has six shiny motorcycles. Lucky man." Most of the grammar you use in writing falls in this recognition category. You know the grammar without being able to name it.

Reading aloud your writing to an audience, sounding it in your voice, is one of the best ways to hear the grammar of sense and meaning.

For instance:

They (the English people) kept on throwing their garbage out of their windows well into the next century.

When the English teacher who wrote the above sentence read it aloud in the context of a very interesting piece of in-session writing about garbage disposal in Elizabethan England, he laughed out loud with recognition of the "squinting modifier." The misplaced modifier made it sound as if the people were throwing their garbage into the next century, rather than into the streets. The grammar of sense and meaning could be fulfilled as follows:

Well into the next century, they (the English people) continued throwing their garbage out of their windows into the street.

When you read your writing aloud to an audience, you can hear the grammar of sense and meaning.

Here's something we might say when looking up a mountainside:

Because the road don't meet the trees, they can't get there.

Does the "they" refer to the "trees" or to other plural objects or persons? Actually, our speaker meant to say:

Because the road don't meet the trees, our people can't get there.

That handles the grammar of sense. The matter of "cosmetic" grammar in the same sentence, in which the speaker should use "doesn't" instead of "don't," is another matter.

"Cosmetic" grammar can be very important, depending on the social situations in which you want to give a certain appearance to your language. *You can learn much of what you need to know from reading, oral reading, and listening.* Theoretically, virtually every question you have about the conventions of written language can be answered by what you see and hear in your reading.

What We Need Is a Mixed Diction

"What we need is a mixed diction," said Aristotle, meaning the mixture of common words of speech with less well known words, colloquial words with formal language, to gain clarity and distinction in our writing. Twenty-three centuries and several languages later Sheridan Baker quoted Aristotle in his argument for an English diction mixing Anglo-Saxon and Latinate words.[6] Baker argued for what already existed, against those who feel that we should use only or mainly the short, tough, concrete Anglo-Saxon words, and against those who would use only Latinate "soup." He argues, as did John Crowe Ransom, that some of Shakespeare's power comes from his mixing of Anglo-Saxon and Latinate words:

This my hand will rather
The multitudinous seas incarnadine,
Making the green one red.

Baker believes that the contrast of the two extremes of Latinate and Anglo-Saxon words generates "incomparable zip" in our use of English. For another example, he offers Faulkner's description of Dilsey in *The Sound and the Fury:*

---

6. *The Practical Stylist,* by Sheridan Baker, Harper & Row, New York, 1981, pp. 88–90.

. . . a paunch almost dropsical, as though muscle and tissue had been courage or fortitude which the days or the years had consumed until only the indomitable skeleton was left rising like a ruin or a landmark above the somnolent and impervious guts. . . .

The "grand Latin preparation" makes the impact of the short Anglo-Saxon "guts" almost "unbearably moving," Baker says.

Yes, today, "what we need is a mixed diction." As in Aristotle's time, as in Shakespeare's time, as in Faulkner's time, as in Baker's time, what we need in the writing of English-speaking America today is a diction that mixes the Anglo-Saxon, the Latinate, and the powerful personal speech and dialect usage that students bring to the classroom. After Sweet Daddy Seeky has finished his story of how original sin originally came about (see "Adam and Eva Mae," by Reginald Carlvin p. 247), he leaves the barber shop:

. . . And with that, he recovered his sky and cane and joined the baddest looking hammer I'd seen in a long time who was waiting for him outside on the sidewalk, wearing an outfit that left very little to the imagination but a whole lot to the temptation.

Notice the mixed diction of Anglo-Saxon, Latinate, and vernacular elements. We need the power of that mixture in our writing today as much as Shakespeare needed it in his day and for the same reason.

Acceptance of a "mixed diction" means that a dynamic standard English replaces a rigidly codified set of rules and procedures called Standard English. A dynamic standard English is a greater and more effective resource, always our best language resource. Dynamic standard English not only allows you to begin with your own voice and familiar language, but recognizes that those are valid instruments of communication, and encourages their development in your writing. Dynamic standard English allows you to advance from the base of your own natural voice to incorporate other voices and constructions from your reading and listening as you progress through your studies. In past generations, many speakers of English dialects as different from Standard English as any dialects that we encounter in the composition classroom today, as different as any English dialect that you might speak, have used the familiar language of their voices to develop a very effective dynamic standard English. We could use Samuel Clemens (Mark Twain) of Missouri, Richard Wright, and Zora Neale Hurston as examples, and hundreds more who were less renowned but nevertheless successful in their writing. Many writers and teachers and other professional persons today have gone through a similar long-term process of language acquisition. Writers. Teachers. Doctors. Engineers. Physicists. Businessmen. Economists. Journalists. Editors.

Develop the language you speak in the "sustained speech" of writing.

Punctuation

In speech, we have the immediate audience before us and we use pauses, emphases, and inflections to make clear what we have to say. Some of the pauses are voluntary, some are involuntary. The pauses that we use to organize our spoken sentences are largely involuntary and correspond roughly to the punctuation of writing. "It is virtually impossible to commit a 'comma blunder' when speaking. If we examine a spoken sentence, we see [and hear] that 'pauses' do keep separate thoughts from running into one another."[7] In writing, certain formal conventions help the reader understand the

---

7. Betty Shiflett, "Story Workshop as a Method of Teaching Writing," *College English*, November, 1973.

syntax and meaning of our sentences, such as paragraphs, capitals at the beginning of a sentence, other punctuation, and a grammar of sense and meaning. Rather than mark arbitrary pauses for elocutionary emphasis, modern syntactical punctuation organizes the *meaning* of what we have to say in writing, just as natural pauses organize the meaning of what we speak.

Punctuation goes a long way toward helping the reader apprehend swiftly and surely what you, the writer, have to say. Punctuation symbols correspond to speech signals that may be interpreted by different people as "pauses," "breaks," "clicks," things that happen that you can hear—sometimes the break is so brief that the word "pause" gives a connotation of disproportionate length. These speech signals help organize the way we put our words together. When a teacher asks, "Can't you *hear* the pause in your voice?" meaning the pause of punctuation, that teacher almost always fails to distinguish between a syntactical pause and a pause for elocutionary emphasis. The syntactical pause is one in which the pause or stop or slight break or click, or whatever it's to be called, occurs involuntarily in order for the sentence to make sense. On the other hand, the pause for elocutionary emphasis is one of choice and can vary widely from one reader to another. Writers vary in their ways of using syntactical punctuation but they usually "stay within the rules," that is, they stay within the variable limits for what kind of a syntactical pause—comma, semicolon, colon, period, dash, parentheses—will be used. Actually, the syntactical "pause" may be very brief, because you can read material aloud deliberately fast and still hear the distinctions between the various syntactical signals of punctuation. Using the word "pause" for punctuation can mislead many students. The notion that a sentence stops at the end of a breath is completely false, since you may be able to read several sentences in one breath.

Writing was historically well developed before punctuation as we know it came fully into play. Before 300 B.C. the Greeks did not even have the benefit of separation of words. theirwritingwouldhavelookedlikethis. Aristotle used only separation of words and a marking for the paragraph. Elizabethan letter writers used hardly any punctuation. Aristotle's writing and the Elizabethans' letter writing would have resembled, in appearance anyway, the punctuationless writing of many "basic" writing students. Actually, punctuationless writing is easier to understand than writing bespattered and broken up by inappropriate punctuation sprinkled helter-skelter for emphasis.

Throughout the medieval period and into the seventeeth century, there were writers who used "elocutionary" punctuation, a kind of notation to indicate breath pauses for emphasis. Because elocutionary punctuation for emphasis, without attention to natural syntactical divisions, can vary hugely from one individual and situation to another, some of these elocutionary-punctuated writings can be more difficult to understand than punctuationless writing, in which you can "hear" the punctuation of meaning as you read it. In Shakespeare's time syntactical punctuation, or punctuation for sense and meaning according to the natural syntactical divisions of the language, was just coming into use. Shakespeare himself used a combination of syntactical and elocutionary punctuation. Ben Jonson was a strong advocate of syntactical punctuation, which finally won dominance because it is the most universally understood and the most useful. Writers nowadays use syntactical punctuation, with occasional punctuation for an appropriate individual emphasis.

Here's a sample of late seventeenth century prose punctuation of a recipe. Sentences are generally separated by commas, as are clauses, one semicolon is used, and the period is used to end the paragraphs.

To boil lobsters to eat cold the common way.

Take them alive or dead, lay them in cold water to make the claws ruff and keep them from breaking off, then have a kettle over the fire with fair water, put in it as much bay salt as will make it a good strong brine, when it boils scum it, and put in the lobsters, let them boil leisurely the space of half an hour or more, according to the bigness of them, being well boild take them up, wash them, and then wipe them with beer and butter, and keep them for your use.

To keep lobsters a quarter of a year very good.

Take them being boild as aforesaid wrap them in course rags having been steeped in brine and bury them in a cellar in some sea-sand pretty deep.[8]

Read the recipe aloud and repunctuate it according to modern syntactical punctuation.

If you type up a passage from a book without including any punctuation and then hand the passage to someone to real aloud, the person who reads it can begin to hear the sense of the syntactical meaning and begin to punctuate the passage. (Misreadings occur too, often humorous and instructive, sometimes wildly different.) Reading it aloud in a deliberate monotone without allowing any voluntary pause, making yourself keep moving, begins to expose the involuntary syntactical punctuation. Usually it helps your "hearing" of the punctuation if you read three sentences at a time, or several lines of writing that you want to punctuate, rather than try to worry one sentence or line to death. Meaning and syntax are embedded in the movement of the overall expression, rather than in the single separable sentence or line. Use of these approaches over a period of time can help clear up your punctuation. In fact, concentrating your effort on what you have to say and on getting it across to your audience helps make your punctuation clearer, partly because punctuation is so closely associated with meaning that if you concentrate on getting your meaning across to the audience it becomes more obvious, to your ear, where punctuation is needed. If you use punctuation just because you think you should sprinkle your writing with punctuation marks, you will make more of an inarticulate mess than if you simply concentrated, as Elizabethan letter writers did, on getting across what you have to say to your letter receiver and not bothering with the punctuation at all.

How to use the paragraph, period, comma, semicolon, colon, parentheses, dashes, exclamation marks, question marks, quotation marks can be figured out by watching and listening to what happens in literature that you read, referring to a good style and usage handbook for "rules" and the range within the rules, and listening to your writing in your voice.

Voice

Speech is a way to voice, speech is a part of voice, but voice is more than speech. Voice is gesture got into writing, voice is culture (including the personal background of the writer), voice contains the powers of the unconscious and the conscious and the possibility of style. Voice is also the movement of a telling/writing through time, everything that connects words and perceptions, the economy of which is to use what it needs and to leave out what it does not need. Voice is the articulation of all perceptions in verbal expression, written and oral, including the so-called nonverbal which we want to get into writing too.

---

8. *Maine Coastal Cooking,* Down East Books, Camden, Maine, 1980.

Voice is the expression of the whole person, an extension of speech, an extension of the body. "Style is the full and pointed development, the full flowering, of your own voice," of your sustained speech in writing. "It is not something that you acquire solely by exterior means, as some systems of teaching rhetoric imply. We ask you to 'Listen to your voice, listen *for* your voice,' discover your voice and its potential for expressing perception, *believe your voice.* . . ."[9] It's altogether possible that you have never heard your own voice, and particularly have never heard it in writing. Voice gives perception and compels belief. Seeing-in-the-mind spurs voice into life, and voice delivers seeing with the living authority that makes it seen, understood, and felt by a reader or hearer.

"Discovering one's own voice, and getting to know it, are as healthgiving as getting acquainted with one's own body. The vitality released in the recognition of voice flows powerfully back into your writing."[10]

When you begin to get the speaking tone into your writing, you may begin to hear your voice in passages, have a feeling of it here and there, and then, in a breakthrough, write something in which you feel the strong movement, authority, presence, of your voice. The discovery of voice will happen somewhat differently for different writers at different times and with different pieces of writing. Voice comes from the "waves" of feeling from your seeing-in-the-mind, from your sense of audience, form, theme, and from the interplay of all these factors. Write your way into it. Experiment with how the process occurs for you.

Journals and Notebooks

A writer's journal knows its own laws, and it knows all laws. Nothing is alien to it, nothing is excluded from it. In your journal, *you write whatever takes your attention for whatever reason.* Yet the journal differs from the popular conception of a diary, since in the journal you use language not only to record but to *find out* what you think, to find out what's happening in your imaginings, perceptions, feelings, thoughts, and observations. Journals, reporter's notes, and field notes are essential tools for recording instances of the way things happen with any subject, of what takes your attention about the subject, in order to discover patterns, progressions, comparisons, concepts. A personal journal can be a pleasureable and exciting way to discover what you see, think, and feel about yourself, other people, your dreams, your troubles, your speculations, your joys, your struggles. A journal can be an effective way to develop your thinking and writing abilities. Even people who do little writing in their careers find a journal to be important in their lives (and their careers).

Anything goes in the journal.

Drawing directly upon the way you talk, think, and listen to yourself, the journal lays the foundations for and allows crucial explorations of all kinds of writing. It can use all forms and modes, and its entries may break off, end naturally, be complete in themselves. Because language is its chief medium of expression (many people draw in their journals, too), the journal generates a continuous interplay between your language, perception, and thought. It helps you cultivate your internal listening, your internal "you." There are students who can hardly write effectively in any form of writing, but who can, in their journals, make *any* form of writing work. Indeed, they can virtually tear out

9. Betty Shiflett, ibid.
10. Betty Shiflett, ibid.

passages of their journals, type them up, and satisfy the needs of other forms. It perplexes and frustrates them that they cannot write well outside their journals. Journal writing becomes the way for them to develop their other kinds of writing. Sometimes they say they have the feeling of "someone actually listening" when they write in the journal. The listening is their internal listening. A student who wrote well in his journal and in other kinds of writing but was having trouble with his novel found that he rushed more in writing the novel than in writing the journal entries. Actually, he also wrote swiftly in his journal but with a difference—in the journal, he made the effort to tell everything as clearly and fully as he could, as fast as he could. He slowed down and began writing the novel more the way he wrote in his journal. "Write as fast as you can, but slow down and tell it as fully as you can" sounds paradoxical but is actually a useful way to coach yourself in writing.

The journal may include reporter's notes and field notes, but differs from them, being more broad and complete in both range and execution. Reporter's notes are usually rapid notations made of things said and observed—they act as reminders and give authority of fact for the reporter's story; they must be used quickly or the reporter loses the mental context of the notes. Field notes, such as those used by an observing scientist or naturalist (see the Schaller and Darwin entries), may be more or less complete but also act mainly as reminders; back at the home base, they are rewritten and developed in journal style to make sure all immediate observations and thoughts are on the page. Personal or professional, long-term or short-term in its explorations, the journal is exploratory writing with imaginative, factual, scientific, rhetorical, fictional, and poetic directions, always with the potential of being complete in itself, even when you are using the journal to gather material for a book, article, or story.

When you write in your journal regularly, you become more aware of your internal listening. Your internal listening stands in as the present responder for your future reader and shapes what you write. The future reader may be yourself or any other audience you anticipate.

Watch how the authors of our journal selections freely use exploratory principles. Be alert for what you sense of their internal listening as they write.

* * *

Our first set of entries is taken from the journal of Franz Kafka. (He called his journal a diary, though he treats it as an exploratory journal rather than as a daily record.) He wrote these entries (along with a hundred others) in the few months prior to and including the writing of his first major story, "The Judgment."

From

Diaries: 1910–1913

Franz Kafka

This morning my nephew's circumcision. A short, bow-legged man, Austerlitz, who already has 2,800 circumcisions behind him, carried the thing out very skillfully. It is an operation made more difficult by the fact that the boy, instead of lying on a table, lies on his grandfather's lap, and by the fact that the person performing the operation, instead of paying close attention, must whisper prayers. First the boy is prevented from moving by wrappings which leave only his member free, then the surface to be operated on is defined precisely by putting on a perforated metal disc, then the operation is performed with what is almost an ordinary knife, a sort of fish knife. One sees blood and raw flesh, the *moule* bustles about briefly with his long-nailed, trembling fingers and pulls skin from some place or other over the wound like the finger of a glove. At once everything is all right, the child has scarcely cried. Now there remains only a short prayer during which the *moule* drinks some wine and with his fingers, not yet entirely unbloody, carries some wine to the child's lips. Those present pray: "As he has now entered into the covenant, so may he enter into knowledge of the Torah, a happy marriage and the performance of good deeds."

*   *   *

Yesterday in the factory. The girls, in their unbearably dirty and untidy clothes, their hair disheveled as though they had just got up, the expressions on their faces fixed by the incessant noise of the transmission belts and by the individual machines, automatic ones, of course, but unpredictably breaking down, they aren't people, you don't greet them, you don't apologize when you bump into them, if you call them over to do something, they do it but return to their machine at once, with a nod of the head you show them what to do, they stand there in petticoats, they are at the mercy of the pettiest power and haven't enough calm understanding to recognize this power and placate it by a glance, a bow. But when six o'clock comes and they call it out to one another, when they untie the kerchiefs from around their throats and their hair, dust themselves with a brush that passes around and is constantly called for by the impatient, when they pull their skirts on over their heads and clean their hands as well as they can then at last they are women again, despite pallor and bad teeth they can smile, shake their stiff bodies, you can no longer bump into them, stare at them or overlook them, you move back against the greasy crates to make room for them, hold your hat in your hand when they say good evening, and do not know how to behave when one of them holds your winter coat for you to put on.

*   *   *

Dreamed recently:
I was riding with my father through Berlin in a trolley. The big-city quality was represented by countless striped toll bars standing upright, finished off bluntly at the ends. Aside from that everything was almost empty, but there was a great forest of these toll bars. We came to a gate, got out without any sense of getting out, stepped through the gate. On the other side of the gate a sheer wall rose up, which my father ascended almost in a dance, his legs flew out as he climbed, so easy was it for him. There was certainly also some inconsiderateness in the fact that he did not help me one bit, for I got to the top only with the utmost effort, on all fours, often sliding back again, as though the wall had become steeper under me. At the same time it was also distressing that (the wall) was covered with human excrement so that flakes of it clung to me, chiefly to my breast. I looked down at the flakes with bowed head and ran my hand over them.

When at last I reached the top, my father, who by this time was already coming out of a building, immediately fell on my neck and kissed and embraced me. He was wearing an old-fashioned, short Prince Albert, padded on the inside like a sofa, which I remembered well. "This Dr. von Leyden! He is an excellent man," he exclaimed over and over again. But he had by no means visited him in his capacity as a doctor, but rather only as a man worth knowing. I was a little afraid that I should have to go in to see him too, but this wasn't required of me. Behind me to the left I saw, sitting in a room literally surrounded by glass walls, a man who turned his back on me. It turned out that this man was the professor's secretary, that my father had in fact spoken only with him and not with the professor himself, but that somehow or other, through the secretary, he had recognized the excellences of the professor in the flesh, so that in every respect he was as much entitled to an opinion on the professor as if he had spoken to him in person.

* * *

I have just read in Flaubert's letters: "My novel is the cliff on which I am hanging, and I know nothing of what is going on in the world."—Like what I noted down about myself on May 9th.

Without weight, without bones, without body, walked through the streets for two hours considering what I overcame this afternoon while writing.

* * *

The invention of the devil. If we are possessed by the devil, it cannot be by one, for then we should live, at least here on earth, quietly, as with God, in unity, without contradiction, without reflection, always sure of the man behind us. His face would not frighten us, for as diabolical beings we would, if somewhat sensitive to the sight, be clever enough to prefer to sacrifice a hand in order to keep his face covered with it. If we were possessed by only a single devil, one who had a calm, untroubled view of our whole nature, and freedom to dispose of us at any moment, then that devil would also have enough power to hold us for the length of a human life high above the spirit of God in us, and even to swing us to and fro, so that we should never get to see a glimmer of it and therefore should not be troubled from that quarter. Only a crowd of devils could account for our earthly misfortunes. Why don't they exterminate one another until only a single one is left, or why don't they subordinate themselves to one great devil? Either way would be in accord with the diabolical principle of deceiving us as completely as possible. With unity lacking, of what use is the scrupulous attention all the devils pay us? It simply goes without saying that the falling of a human hair must matter more to the devil than to God, since the devil really loses that hair and God does not. But we still do not arrive at any state of well-being so long as the many devils are within us.

* * *

August 10. Wrote nothing. Was in the factory and breathed gas in the engine room for two hours. The energy of the foreman and the stoker before the engine, which for some undiscoverable reason will not start. Miserable factory.

* * *

A dream: I found myself on a jetty of square-cut stones built far out into the sea. Someone, or even several people, were with me, but my awareness of myself was so strong that I hardly knew more about them than that I was speaking to them. I can remember only the raised knees of someone sitting near me. At first I did not really know where I was, only when once I accidentally stood up did I see on my left and behind me on my right the distant, clearly outlined sea with many battleships lined up in rows and at anchor. On the right New York could be seen, we were in New York Harbor. The sky was gray, but of a constant brightness. I moved back and forth in my seat, freely exposed to the air on all sides, in order to be able to see everything. In the direction of New York my glance slanted downward a little, in the direction of the sea it slanted upward. I now noticed the water rise up near us in high waves on which was borne a great cosmopolitan traffic. I can remember only that instead of the rafts we have, there were long timbers lashed together into gigantic bundles the cut ends of which kept popping out of the water during the voyage, higher or lower, according to the height of the waves, and at the same time kept turning end over end in the water. I sat down, drew up my feet, quivered with pleasure, virtually dug myself into the ground in delight, and said: Really, this is even more interesting than the traffic on a Paris boulevard.

* * *

September 23. This story, *The Judgment,* I wrote at one sitting during the night of the 22nd-23rd, from ten o'clock at night to six o'clock in the morning. I was hardly able to pull my legs out from under the desk, they had got so stiff from sitting. The fearful strain and joy, how the story developed before me, as if I were advancing over water. Several times during the night I heaved my own weight on my back. How everything can be said, how for everything, for the strangest fancies, there waits a great fire in which they perish and rise up again. How it turned blue outside the window. A wagon rolled by. Two men walked across the bridge. At two I looked at the clock for the last time. As the maid walked through the anteroom for the first time I wrote the last sentence. Turning out the light and the light of day. The slight pains around my heart. The weariness that disappeared in the middle of the night. The trembling entrance into my sisters' room. Reading aloud. Before that, stretching in the presence of the maid and saying, "I've been writing until now." The appearance of the undisturbed bed, as though it had just been brought in. The conviction verified that with my novel-writing I am in the shameful lowlands of writing. Only *in this way* can writing be done, only with such coherence, with such a complete opening out of the body and the soul. Morning in bed. The always clear eyes. Many emotions carried along in the writing, joy, for example, that I shall have something beautiful for Max's *Arkadia,* thoughts about Freud, of course; in one passage, of *Arnold Beer;* in another, of Wassermann; in one, of Werfel's giantess; of course, also of my "The Urban World."

I, only I, am the spectator in the orchestra.

* * *

My stupid laughter today when I told my mother that I am going to Berlin at Whitsuntide. "Why are you laughing?" said my mother (among several other remarks, one of which was, "Look before you leap," all of which, however, I warded off with remarks like, "It's nothing," etc.). "Because of embarrassment," I said, and was happy for once to have said something true in this matter.

* * *

May 4. Always the image of a pork butcher's broad knife that quickly and with mechanical regularity chops into me from the side and cuts off very thin slices which fly off almost like shavings because of the speed of the action.

Kafka wrote in his journal most of his adult life, started many stories and fragments of stories in it, and generally used it as a way of finding out not only what he was thinking, seeing, and imagining, but also the *style* of his thinking and imagining, and the patterns of his life. He writes about dreams, recent events, observations, self-observations. In some entries, not present here, he includes playwriting scripts, passages researched through reading, lists, and other forms. His journal, which provided him with an arena in which he tried out any impulse to any kind of writing, also tells directly of the anxieties, joys, hopes, despairs, and struggles of his life.

* * *

The next set of entries is selected from the journal of a young woman who was an undergraduate at the time she wrote these passages. She explores patterns concerning characters in a novel she's writing, memories of a childhood friend, states of mind, present events and past events, with some observations about reading and literature.

Notice that the authors appear to write swiftly in their journals yet slow enough to tell their perceptions as fully as they can, which is exactly the way they did write in their journals.

Journal Entry
Ann Hemenway

I started a journal entry a while ago—about dreams, somewhere. I was in one of my more meditative moods. I *like* dreams. I've slept enough in the last two days, you'd think I'd remember something about my dreams. I think I've been bitten by a tse-tse fly . . . this afternoon I fell asleep while reading *Nausea,* but I know why I did that. The translator had no sense of rhythm, or else Sartre doesn't, which I doubt, and I couldn't get pulled into the work. Maybe it was the continual use of the present tense, although it shifted tense all over the place, so that's not necessarily true, but somehow that present tense had the effect of making it seem sterile—no, I think it was the lack of rhythm that made it seem sterile. Anyway, I fell asleep and woke up with post nasal drip, a yellow prickling hand that I had to pound against the arm of the couch to wake up and a head that I should have done the same thing with. That narcotic sleep drugged and no dreams to console me, just a dead feeling at the back of my head. So . . . I lit a cigarette that tasted absolutely *foul* and I put it out immediately because I could feel the cylindrical shape between my lips and it felt terrible, like something hideously foreign, and I read some more.

And became impatient with Antoine, which is why I skipped and read the end after skipping to the part where he meets his mistress again for the first time in five years. I get impatient ("Afternoon of the Faun" is playing on the radio and it's lovely) with people who cry, "I exist, I exist, or do I exist?" and "What is existence?" because I climbed on that merry-go-round in jr. high and now, since I've happily jumped off the damn thing, I'm bored with watching the miserable people bobbing up and down on those dumb question marks. At the height of my existential crisis, it was Easter of my senior year in high school and I was taking one of the many confused night walks I took in those days. (I miss those, you can't take them in the city. I used to walk to the outskirts of town to the farms in the summer, walking along the cooling tar past rows of cornfields and leaning over fences to call to a pony in the muddy or drydust farmyard in front of a greasy dilapidated house and the sound of the crickets would rise with the scent of the long grass and I would be exquisitely depressed and lonesome). . . .

. . . But I was talking about dreams. Sheila dreams in red, or an off-red purple (they say psychotics connect word with color, I guess I'm psychotic, because so do I) and her dreams are out of focus, blurred, as though everyone was encased in angora sweaters. Her dreams are dark and full of shadow—a woman puts her hand on a table, a woman Sheila doesn't know and Sheila, outside her dream keeps asking if that's herself, Sheila, when she's fifty, but the woman's hair is blonde streaked with brown and there's a stairway behind her that leads to a room with a bay window overlooking a lake. The woman lifts her hand from the table and the imprint is a powdery, yellow smear on the dark varnish. Flea powder, Sheila knows (the next day those words are in the middle of a piece of onion skin paper), and the woman turns and climbs the stairs, slowly with painful steps, her back hunched, gripping the railing and leaning with all her weight. She is older than fifty, she is seventy, or a hundred. She climbs the steps and hobbles across the bare floor to the bay window, which is now a pair of French doors and she opens them, pushing them heavily and goes to the grass outside, each foot smashing the grass and leaving green footprints. The woman stops, her black sweater glistens in the sun; she stops and looks at the lake, but the lake has no beach, no rocks, no swamp around it. It stops dead at the grass; a huge lake, one of the great lakes, with no waves, no movement. Thirty feet from the french doors it ends, desolate, no horizon in the distance, no curve, just a straight line with grass on either side and grey-blue water ahead as far as Sheila can see. And the woman turns and looks at Sheila, who stands behind her, and says, the yellow powder cracking in the wrinkles of her face, her widow's hump poking through her sweater, the woman says, "This is all it is."

Elaine's dreams are sharp and glittering like broken glass. They are noisy, full of movement, full of people. J. T., her artist friend is wearing a tri-cornered hat made from newspaper as they sit in his basement art studio. His studio has high, wide ceilings and only stick figures drawn on the yellowed walls. J. T.'s skull-like head grimaces under the big paper hat as he sips green liqueur from a crystal glass. Elaine is wearing a pink party dress with puffy sleeves and a satin sash—just like the one she had in first grade—and stiletto heels. J. T. puts his glass down on the bench where he sits and begins to blow a light blue balloon and the veins at his temples expand with every puff.

Elaine thinks she must do something too, so she takes a pencil and begins to draw on the wall across from J. T. J. T. nods at her. Good, good, he says as she draws lines and circles and odd geometric shapes. Suddenly, she is finished; her hand stops moving, and when she steps back to look at it, she sees she has drawn *Guernica*. J. T. claps her on the back and says genius and babbles and exclaims, stomping up and down and snorting as his big hat falls over his feverish eyes until his cadaver-like jaw is the only part of his face that shows. Elaine keeps insisting that she has no talent at all, that it makes no sense, that she didn't actually draw it, or didn't think about what she was drawing and would he please just shut up and not tell anybody about it and not to talk to her about it because it doesn't matter to her; but J. T. takes the pencil and writes, By Elaine, in the corner of the drawing and Elaine is furious and begins to leave. As she reaches the door, George comes in with a thin, skim-milk pale girl on his arm. They are dressed in grown-up clothes: George is wearing a tie, the girl is wearing a black spaghetti strapped dress and has eyeliner on her eyes, but no eyelashes. Elaine's party dress is suddenly even more starched and stiff, and the sleeves are beachballs on her arms, and she feels like a munchkin, or that she's about to do a tapdance, and she feels huge and gawky and young.

George and the girl stand stiff in the doorway and stare at Elaine's drawing. They are formal and aloof, the girl holds George's black-suited elbow and George's chin is high and they look as though they're about to be presented to the Queen of England. "Very good," says George, cold and pompous. Elaine ducks her head and wants to say that she doesn't normally dress this way, that it's a joke, but George and the girl know it's not a joke and they keep standing in the doorway, and Elaine can't leave and can't change her clothes.

*   *   *

The first real letter I ever got had a dream in it. It was from Berit, written on kitchen pad paper in crayon from Door County, Wisconsin. I was eight or nine years old. Berit wrote about her dream in which the mother of a friend of ours gave the friend a diary (which I think was spelled dairy) and the friend "goofed" on one of the pages, "So

Val's mother got her another one, see? And I said, Val why din't you just rip the other one ount? You could have kept the dairy. I was really mad, see?"

Berit was and is one of the world's worst spellers. For years she spelled 'else' e–l–a–s. In that same letter she drew a perfectly horrible picture of a "gookily sore" she had. "Its real ugly, see?" It was sketched in purple and black and red crayon and had the various parts delineated such as, "Gookily part," "bruse," and "Scab"—with arrows.

One summer she was into glow paint and she wrote a letter with instructions on how to see the glow paint she had put on the letter during the day.

"Hold the envelope in the light for about 30 sec. Then, pull your grubshirt over your head so that the neck part is on top of your head. Hold the envelope under the grub shirt and look down and read the secret message. Or elas you can go in the closet." Spoil-sport that I am, I probably went in the closet.

How does George write letters? Goddamn you, George, you fucking elusive creature. I can see your handwriting—slanted and smeary. Are you left handed? Yes, you are, but I can't read your words. Writing is such an effort for you, the way you have to rigidly curl your hand over the word and pull backwards . . . the way your elbow curls around your paper until your arm is a circle around the pencil. Poor George. But what do you write? What do you say? I see a drawing on the paper, but I still don't know. Fuck you, George.

What particularly took your attention about the way Hemenway uses her journal to explore and tell herself about personal events, states of mind, speculative insights, memories, imaginative character explorations? Notice, throughout the journal entries, how she lets what she sees in her mind press for language to express it and lets language and movement stimulate and pull out the insights that are tugging at her attention, as did Kafka in his journal. Notice (and see step by step) the dramatic narrative telling of each of the dreams and how she reveals the characteristic gestures, actions, and attitudes of herself, Sheila, Elaine, J. T., George, and Berit.

A Journal Activity

Free-writing activities stimulate the interplay of perceptions and language, building upon the "waves" of feeling from mental sights that Virginia Woolf talked about. Somewhere in the midst of free-writing, you usually feel a sense of movement and expanding awareness taking hold. Not every writer needs free-writing to get started, but virtually every writer can benefit from free-writing and have fun to boot. In free-writing you become aware of *yourself* as the natural immediate audience for your writing, of the "you" in you.

The free-writing activity that follows, an adaptation of an exercise developed by Peter Elbow in *Writing Without Teachers* (Oxford University Press, New York, 1973) can be done with pencil, pen, or typewriter. You're not bound by any rules of punctuation, syntax, sense, or organization; you should deliberately unbind yourself from any such rules. You roll paper into the typewriter and begin typing, or put pencil to paper and begin writing.

Here's a free-writing example taken from my notebook, done on a typewriter:

splutter blue sparks leaping shmeepping a line of sheep flowing along a deep narrow path over a ridge, like a white waterfall spray rainbows tremor spastic colon deep in the earth the sides of the fault ground and urged apart, like a tremendously shouldered weightlifter groaning with pulling vacuum cups apart tee hee tease backseat battery smell of acid biting smell of acid oscillates in the top of your head, rocking you rock rock rock sprained thumb robert Andrews stands outside Braun's Drugs something flutters in the wire wastebasket by the telephone pole something flies a bird a sparrow flies from the wires in the sky flourish crapgame steamtable flush They raised the gates of the dam and when the water lunged, as if it were the biggest bull in the universe, into the narrow canyon, they danced on top the walls clapping at the sight of houses torn loose and bounding light as chips on top the torrent, houses suddenly collapsing like something made of popsicle sticks against the walls of the canyon red amethyst chill climb sting scoop pinch collate tackle smooth your way smooth as the fine dust on top cement when it's first finished silky dust on top cement when it's hard and still dark milky green and smelling cleanly of the inside of Mount Vesuvius That was a crashing good poem, if only it hadn't burnt to a simple crisp in the eruption, only to be found two thousand years later and the light black cinders of the paper placed between glass and treated with lemon juice and the words come out to tell us once again: Your boats sail into my harbor/We live on the hill and watch them all day from our garden /From the stern of your boat a diver arcs,/like the curve of a fine white fish, tiny below us/in the immense clean circle of blue water and sun and sky/The red poppies sway beside us/We smile and touch hands on the arm of the chair straighten expand lengthen tuck chuckle blurt fluff wheeze train tidy

"Splutter," the first word I sounded to myself without knowing what would happen next, produced "blue sparks," which produced "leaping". At that point, already tired of the obvious direct associations of words, I made the silly mocking rhyme with "shmeeping," which by rhyme association with "sheep," triggered the flow of sights that began with "a line of sheep." With the sight and feeling of "in the earth the sides of the fault ground and urged apart," I sensed the need of a metaphor to get the perception across to myself and to any other audience and came up with "like a tremendously shouldered weightlifter etc." When a sight quit or exhausted itself, I gave a series of words such as "flourish crapgame steamtable flush." "Flush" suddenly caused the sight of the letting loose of all the water behind a dam. When in my mind I saw and smelled cement dust drying on top of new cement, I tried for metaphorical perception, "silky dust on top cement," and "smelling cleanly of the inside of Mount Vesuvius," which, in a surprise movement, triggered the imaginative event of the poem burnt in the eruption and resurrected two thousand years later, a story within the story. I ended with a riffle of verbs, avoiding direct associations from one verb to the next, that is, I rejected verbs that were directly associated with previous verbs until each surprise "unassociated" verb (from a deeper level of association) sprang out, producing more imaginative impact and more sense of movement and pleasure. Direct associations might have produced only straighten, jerk, topple, fall, smash, etc.

Writing in Your Journal

In your journal you write anything you wish. You write even if you think you don't want to write, because you find that the interplay between perception and language draws you into the movement of writing. *Talk to your journal. Listen to your voice in your journal.* You can—and should—try any of the forms and modes set forth in this book. Write about your job, your love life or lack of it, research through reading that interests you, imagined societies, imagined technology, imagined machines, fantasy appliances.

When a movement takes hold in your journal writing, as in any writing, follow it. You write dreams, images, memories, lists of thoughts; you write about objects, actions, and whatever event or subject takes your attention. You may write starts at (or complete) stories, poems, speculations, and essays in your journal that can then be moved readily to the typed page, separate from the journal. You tell personally observed and experienced events, events that happened during the week, imagined events, and mixtures of personally experienced and imagined events, *as happening right now in your mind's eye,* that is, *you see an event happen again in your mind's eye and tell it as you see it happening at the moment of your writing.* You tell these events in first or third person. Your seeing pulls on your language, your language tugs at your seeing. That's where the special strength of your writing comes from, from the perception and language that take your attention *while* you're writing. Even though you will probably be handing in journal passages and reading aloud from your journal in the class, your journal should be private and you will give permission to have any entries read aloud in the class.

Be aware that the journal is—or should be—private while you're writing, that you can tell anything you please in any way you please, that *you* decide what other people may read. You may discover that not all the censors are in the external world, as you come up against the censor in yourself and must find ways to lessen the censor's hold on your perceptions or get around it. You need to be able to take any risk in your journal and to find out how willing you are to be complete and frank with yourself. Everyone has balking points. Usually those balking points hide strong and good perception.

If you'll set one rule for yourself in your journal, *that you want your writing to get across effectively to your audience in whatever way* (you are the first audience), you can then make your own rules or set yourself important challenges and tasks as you go along. One of the best challenges is: "Write in complete sentences. Tell the entry as fully and clearly as possible. Jack up your effort enough to write in complete sentences." If you use fragmented sentences and entries punctuated only by dashes, you may find that you are not able to fully understand your own writing at a later time: You yourself are a part of the future audience (maybe the only audience) for your journal. Writing in complete sentences in your journal, in the complete sentences of your voice, stimulates the development of your writing abilities now as well as helps make your writing intelligible years later. You can set yourself other "rules" or tasks, such as: "Write in complete sentences and make a point of using active verbs." or: "Write in complete sentences and make a point of varying sentence structures and lengths according to possibilities I feel in my voice." You can set yourself any tasks you wish.

"But what do I write about in my journal?" In one round of journal readings in a writing class, we heard passages about an old people's home with the smell of urine in the air; a committee of young lawyers meeting to decide the complicated matter of whether or not the "dumb" son of one of the founders of the firm can become a junior partner; an insomniac night in which the man who can't sleep walks out to Lake Michigan to watch the sun rise; a trip by a father and son to pick up a German shepherd puppy and their meeting with the kennel owner who had had her throat cut once in a robbery and wears a turtleneck sweater to conceal the scar; a tornado that makes trees snap off and leap across the street; a how-to about playing tennis; a beginning of a research-through-reading essay about meteorology; an unemployment office where the only white faces are among the employees behind the counters; a cat that fell four stories and only chipped a tooth; a man's dialogue with his image in the mirror, done in script form; a couple of dreams: one about a new device for eavesdropping and one in which a woman sees her wraith in a kittenish tam coming toward her in the reflection of a glass door; and a telling of living alone for the first time in a long time.

Much journal writing is done naturally in the first person, but sometimes when you write about yourself in the third person in the journal (as "he" or "she"), it permits you to see and tell the event or dream or imagined event without the constraint of fearing that you're exposing your sensitive thoughts and feelings. Actually, the technical reason for this release is just as important as the relaxation of the psychological inhibition, in that the third person helps you to see yourself as a separate character with some distance and actual space between you and the "he" or "she." It provides effective distance from which to perceive persons and relationships, the space around the persons and the space for the relationships. Writing about yourself in the third person can be a way of "telling it to the stove," as the King instructed the Goose Girl in the folktale of the same name, when she said she could not relate her awful tale directly to anyone. You may even write about some events using a name different from yours or use whatever device will conceal your identity, such as having some events told in the story-within-a-story form. The journal can use all pronouns as personae for the sense of address—I, you, we, he, she, they, one, someone, anyone, whatever pronouns are appropriate and natural for what you're writing.

Writing in a journal is a way of experimenting, exploring, probing and developing, always potentially complete and sufficient unto itself. Rewriting may occur in the journal, and the journal may also be used as a way to rewrite other forms of writing.

Though journal writing may not usually come to a formal or balanced end, its entries may still come to a natural breaking off point and be complete in ways that cannot be duplicated in any other form.

In the How-It-Happens section, journal writing will be used to explore particular subjects.

Write three or four entries a week in your journal.

Anything goes in the journal.

The Letter Form

Everyone has written letters—or notes, memos, messages—to people they know well, and undoubtedly felt that such writing was easier than writing essays or research reports for unknown audiences or for people they didn't know well. Most of you certainly found it easier in high school to write notes and stories and letters that you passed among your friends than the compositions required by your English teacher. The private writing that you did for your high school peers, from what I've seen and what I remember from my high school days, generally contained better writing than much of the writing done for English classes—and the sentences were better-formed, too. Even writing an angry letter to an "unfriendly" audience allows you to retain the organizing confidence of your anger.

We see it happen again and again. The letter's clear sense of audience helps you organize what you have to say. When you're writing letters to friends, you draw upon the language you use in your ordinary talk with them. It's when you're writing or talking to an audience with whom you feel you can't trust your own language that your sentence sense becomes entangled.

Many people find it difficult to write to a broad, unknown audience, but much easier to write to one person. The fact that everyone else can read it, too, as if the letter were written to them, or as if they were listening in, is the grand bonus, the trick, of the game. Many people will write well for the first time when they write to a single person they pick out in class. Musicians and public speakers often pick out one face in the audience and play or speak to that person. The rest of the audience hears the performance too and probably is not aware that the performer is playing to one person. Other players and speakers are able to handle the sense of address to the large array of faces and persons in the audience, picking out the liveliest, most attentive faces and playing to them. Many people find it difficult to read aloud to a broad audience of faces, as in a class, but can read effectively to one person in the audience, just as the musician or public speaker plays to one person. Many students who do not read well out loud to the whole class will read clearly when they address the writing to one person in the class. John Steinbeck said that he would always try to get the feeling of telling his stories to a friend, because then the writing would begin to flow. Other writers seek the feeling of telling their writing to a listening presence in themselves, Barbara Tuchman, the historian, speaks of "the complicated fugue" that occurs between herself and her imagined reader during her writing. A successful student writer referred to this process as "living with the reader."

If we test the letter sense of audience in the oral reading of literature in the classroom, we see and hear some interesting changes take place. For instance, when you're reading a passage of Orwell or Melville or Woolf aloud in class, you'll be startled to feel how well it works when you pick out one person in the class and address that person, "Dear . . . ," and read the passage as a letter to him or her, almost as if the passage had been written originally as a letter. Perhaps most writing is addressed to a very basic "you," a listener and reader, in yourself, as the letter reading exercise suggests. The letter reading activity works not only with expository writing, but with fictional narrative and poetry as well. Try reading aloud any reading selection in this book to a person you pick, with the salutation "Dear. . . ." and see how the sense of audience works.

Letters can be used as a way to cultivate your sense of address to your audience, as a way to start and continue essays and other writings, as a way to build your basic writing skills, and as a form in itself. The letter sense of address exerts a pull on your voice for effective language, stimulates and puts together the capacities you need for any kind of writing and helps you organize your perceptions and ideas; it uncovers your authority to tease the audience and tell the odd, different, and fantastical notions that come to you. A student writer said, "The letter form enables you to tell about the most outrageous things" with perfect authority of image, voice, sense of address, etc. Other student writers have commented that the letter form helps them skip through time, organize material that happens in different times and places, and take leaps to organize factual and expository content.

Your teacher may start letter writing by asking you to pick out a person in the class, orally tell the person you've picked something of what you're going to write about, then write your letter to that person. Sense of address and sense of the listener in yourself are among the main keys to clear, effective, lively writing. You try to move what you see into the mind of your letter-receiver. You may read aloud in the class some of the letters you start there. Try to keep the clear physical sense of writing to the person you've picked. When you're writing in the class, look up at the person now and then to get the sense that you're getting across to him or her. When you're writing alone at home or in your room or wherever, look up at the person in your imagination.

Pick a person (or imagine one) with whom you feel you "can get away with murder, say anything," as one writer put it. Try different persons now and then, though you may find that one person works particularly well for you. Put that person's name at the top of the page, "Dear so-and-so," and write your letter so he or she will understand what you're trying to say. Invent a person. You may find it particularly powerful to write to an imagined person. Write passages in your journal as letters. Write a letter to yourself. See if you can say anything, "get away with murder," with yourself.

Your teacher may ask you to read aloud the "letters" you start in class, to the person to whom you addressed them, looking up at him or her when you feel your eyes naturally "pulled up" by what you feel in the writing. You can ask the person if he or she understands it. Your listening to someone else's letter being read to you, hearing when their writing is coming through effectively, will stimulate your internal listening to your own writing. When you're writing your "letters" in the class, begin to be aware of the rest of the class listening in.

You can write accounts of events, fictional narrative (fantasy or realism), essays, political arguments, any form or mode of writing you can think of, as letters. In the finished draft you can remove the name of the person from the salutation and from wherever else you've used it in the writing. In some cases, the letter itself may be the final suitable form of the writing. If you use the letter form to write an essay, *I advise you to cut out of the final typed draft the salutation and any tag-ends that reveal that it was written as a letter*. The unknowing teacher of whatever subject may well comment on your easy style and natural organization, but be offended if you reveal that the essay was written as a letter.

When you get the sense of telling the seeing-in-your-mind to an audience, such as in a letter, you often put together naturally the necessary skills for writing effectively. The letter sense of address helps you see more clearly in your mind's eye what you have to tell and need to tell. Many teachers have observed, "Of course, students may write well, even overcome basic skills obstacles, if they have something to say." Don't hesitate. See something in your mind and "have something to say." Your awareness of your content and your "sense of address," your sense of telling that content to someone, is what is usually meant by having "something to say."

If you feel you lose the sense of writing to your picked person when you are away from that person or when the movement of the writing gets longer, or the sense of the "you," singular or plural, fades, keep writing, because the *writing* may "carry" the sense of the "you," the organizing sense of address, in spite of the lack you feel. You may be dead tired, feel that you have lost all seeing, voice, and sense of audience, but if you continue writing, you find the next day that the writing was better than you thought. When you're physically tired, your defenses may be lowered and your writing can draw upon more capacities of your mind. Keep listening to your voice and *for* your voice as you write. Use contractions—can't, isn't, don't—to get the feel of your voice. Imagine yourself looking up at the "you" or talking to him or her. Writing is such a complex activity, drawing upon all areas of the mind, that it may employ our minds, our capacities, even when we're not aware of it.

You can use the letter form to rewrite essays, stories, reports, and other kinds of writing, to organize the material in the right voice for the particular audience. You can try rewriting an essay or report by addressing it as a letter to someone you pick. You may want to try such rewriting after you've been successful in writing to fellow and sister students. If you have a piece of writing that you feel should have worked, because you saw it vividly and felt strongly about it, but somehow something went wrong in your writing about it, you may find it helpful to rewrite it as a letter addressed to a classmate, or an imagined person, or anyone else you choose.

Among our letter reading selections, we have an account of travel, a public political letter, and two imagined letters. Gustave Flaubert writes his letter to Louis Bouilhet, who was the sort of friend to whom Flaubert could say anything. Bouilhet was also Flaubert's most helpful, even most demanding critic and reader. W. E. B. DuBois took on the difficult task of writing to a President of the United States whom DuBois felt was not living up to a campaign promise. Beverlye Brown writes an imagined letter by a mother whose daughter wants to marry a man who cannot provide what the mother feels is enough money to support a marriage. James Elder's imagined letter is to a friend in prison from a friend outside, a letter that meant vastly different things to sender and receiver.

Compare the kinds of audiences and what the authors tell and how they tell it in each of the letters. How does the language change with each audience?

From

The Letters of Gustave Flaubert
(translated by Francis Steegmuller)

To LOUIS BOUILHET

> March 13, 1850. On board our *cange*,
> 12 leagues beyond Assuan.

In six or seven hours we are going to pass the Tropic of that well known personage Cancer. It is 30 degrees in the shade at this moment, we are barefoot and wearing nothing but shirts, and I am writing to you on my divan, to the sound of the *darabukehs* of our sailors, who are singing and clapping their hands. The sun is beating down mercilessly on the awning over our deck. The Nile is flat as a river of steel. On its banks there are clusters of tall palms. The sky is blue as blue. O pauvre vieux! pauvre vieux de mon coeur!

What are you up to, there in Rouen? It's a long time since I had any of your letters, or rather I have so far had only one, dated the end of December, which I answered immediately. Perhaps another has arrived in Cairo and is being sent on to me. My mother writes that she sees you very seldom. Why is that? Even if it bores you too much, go once in a while anyway, for my sake, and try to tell me everything you can about what is going on in my house in every conceivable respect. Have you been in Paris again and seen Gautier and Pradier? What has happened to the trip to England for your Chinese story? *Melaenis* must be finished? Send me the end, you bloody bastard. I often growl out some of your lines, if you want to know. I must without further delay withdraw as vociferously as possible the objection I made to your word *vagabond* as applied to the Nile:

"Que le Nil vagabond roule sur ses rivages."
There is no designation more just, more precise and at the same time more all-embracing. It is a crazy, magnificent river, more like an ocean than anything else. Sandy beaches extend as far as the eye can see on both its banks, furrowed by the wind like sea shores; it is so enormous that one doesn't know where the current is, and sometimes you feel enclosed in a great lake. Ah! But if you expect a proper letter you are mistaken. I warn you seriously that my intelligence has greatly diminished. This worries me: *I am not joking*—I feel very empty, very flat, very sterile. What am I to do once back in the old lodgings? Publish or not publish? The *Saint Antoine* business dealt me a heavy blow, I don't mind telling you. I've tried in vain to do something with my oriental tale, and for a day or two I played with the story of Mykerinos in Herodotus (the king who slept with his daughter). But it all came to nothing. By way of work, every day I read the *Odyssey* in Greek. Since we've been on the Nile I have done four books; we are coming home by way of Greece, so it may be of service to me. The first day on board I began to write a little; but I was not long, thank God, in realizing the ineptitude of such behavior; just

now it's best for me to be all eyes. We live, therefore, in the grossest idleness, stretched out all day on our divans watching everything that goes by: camels, herds of oxen from Sennar, boats floating down to Cairo laden with negresses and with elephants' tusks. We are now, my dear sir, in a land where women go naked—one might say with the poet "naked as the hand," for by way of costume they wear only rings. I have lain with Nubian girls whose necklaces of gold piastres hung down to their thighs and whose black stomachs were encircled by colored beads—they feel cold when you rub your own stomach against them. And their dancing! Sacré nom de Dieu!!! But let us proceed in proper order.

From Cairo to Benisuef, nothing very interesting.

. . . At a place called Begel el-Teir we had an amusing sight. On the top of a hill overlooking the Nile there is a Coptic monastery, whose monks have the custom, as soon as they see a boatload of tourists, of running down, throwing themselves in the water, and swimming out to ask for alms. Everyone who passes is assailed by them. You see these fellows, totally naked, rushing down their perpendicular cliffs and swimming toward you as fast as they can, shouting: "Baksheesh, baksheesh, cawadja christiani!" And since there are many caves in the cliff at this particular spot, echo repeats "Cawadja, cawadja!" loud as a cannon. Vultures and eagles were flying overhead, the boat was flashing through the water, its two great sails very full. At that moment one of our sailors, the clown of the crew, began to dance a naked, lascivious dance that consisted of an attempt to bugger himself. To drive off the Christians he showed them his prick and his arse pretending to piss and shit on their heads (they were clinging to the sides of the *cange*). The other sailors shouted insults at them, repeating the names of Allah and Mohammed. Some hit them with sticks, others with ropes; Joseph rapped their knuckles with his kitchen tongs. It was a *tutti* of cudgelings, pricks, bare arses, yells and laughter. As soon as they were given money they put it in their mouths and returned home the way they had come. If they weren't greeted with a good beating, the boats would be assailed by such hordes of them that there would be danger of capsizing.

In another place it's not men who call on you, but birds. At Sheik Sa'id there is a tomb-chapel built in honor of a Moslem saint where birds go of their own accord and drop food that is given to them—this food is then offered to poor travelers—You and I, "who have read Voltaire," don't believe this. But everyone is so backward here! You so seldom hear anyone singing Béranger's songs! ("What, sir, the benefits of civilization are not being introduced into this country? Where are your railway networks? What is the state of elementary education? Etc.")—so that as you sail past this chapel all the birds flock around the boat and land on the rigging—you throw them bits of bread, they wheel about, pick it up from the water, and fly off.

At Kena I did something suitable, which I trust will win your approval: we had landed to buy supplies and were walking peacefully and dreamily in the bazaars, inhaling the odor of sandalwood that floated about us, when suddenly, at a turn in the street, we found ourselves in the whores' quarter. Picture to yourself, my friend, five or six curving streets lined with hovels about four feet high, built of dried gray mud. In the doorways, women standing or sitting on straw mats. The negresses had dresses of sky blue; others were in yellow, in white, in red—loose garments fluttering in the hot wind. Odors of spices. On their bare breasts long necklaces of gold piastres, so that when they move they rattle like carts. They call after you in drawling voices: "Cawadja, cawadja," their white teeth gleaming between their red or black lips, their metallic eyes rolling like wheels. I walked through those streets and walked through them again, giving *baksheesh* to all the women, letting them call me and catch hold of me; they took me around the waist and tried to pull me into their houses—think of all that, with the sun blazing down on it. Well, I abstained. (Young DuCamp did not follow my example.) I abstained deliberately, in order to preserve the sweet sadness of the scene and engrave it deeply in my memory. In this way I went away dazzled, and have remained so. There is nothing more beautiful than these women calling you. If I had gone with any of them, a second picture would have been superimposed on the first and dimmed its splendor.

I haven't always made such sacrifices on the altar of art. At Esna in one day I fired five times and sucked three. I say it straight out and without circumlocution, and let me add that I enjoyed it. Kuchuk Hanem is a famous courtesan. When we reached her house she was waiting for us; her confidante had come to the *cange* that morning escorted by a sheep all spotted with yellow henna and with a black velvet muzzle on its nose, following her like a dog—it was quite a sight. Kuchuk had just left her bath. She was wearing a large tarboosh topped with a gold plaque containing a green stone, and with a loose tassel falling to her shoulders; her front hair was platted in thin braids that were drawn back and tied together; the lower part of her body was hidden in immense pink trousers; her torso was entirely naked under purple gauze. She was standing at the top of her staircase, with the sun behind her, sharply silhouetted against the blue background of the sky surrounding her. She is a regal-looking creature, large-breasted, fleshy, with slit nostrils, enormous eyes, and magnificent knees; when she danced there were formidable folds of flesh on her stomach. She began by perfuming our hands with rosewater. Her bosom gave off a smell of sweetened turpentine, and on it she wore a three-strand golden necklace. Musicians were sent for and she danced. Her dancing isn't at all up to that of the famous Hasan I mentioned earlier. Still, it was very agreeable and of quite a bold style. In general, beautiful women dance badly. (I except a Nubian we saw at Assuan—but that was no longer Arab dancing; more ferocious, more frenetic, tigerish, negroid.)

That night we visited her again. There were four women dancers and singers, *almehs*. (The word *almeh* means "learned woman," "bluestocking," but has come to signify "whore"—which goes to show, Monsieur, that in all countries literary ladies . . . !!!) The party lasted from six to half-past ten, with intermissions for fucking. Two rebec players sitting on the floor made continual shrill music. When Kuchuk undressed to dance, a fold of their turbans was lowered over their eyes, to prevent their seeing anything. This modesty gave a shocking effect. I spare you any description of the dance, I'd write it too poorly. To be understood it has to be illustrated with gestures—and even that would be inadequate.

When it came time to leave, I didn't. Kuchuk wasn't too eager to have us spend the night with her, out of fear of thieves who might well have come, knowing there were foreigners in the house. Maxime stayed alone on the divan and I went downstairs with Kuchuk to her room. We lay down on her bed, made of palm branches. A wick was burning in an antique-style lamp hanging on the wall. In an adjoining room guards were talking in low voices with the serving woman, an Abyssinian Negress whose arms were scarred by plague-sores. Kuchuk's little dog slept on my silk jacket.

I sucked her furiously, her body was covered with sweat, she was tired after dancing, she was cold. I covered her with my fur pelisse, and she fell asleep, her fingers in mine. As for me, I scarcely shut my eyes. My night was one long, infinitely intense reverie. That was why I stayed. Watching that beautiful creature asleep (she snored, her head against my arm; I had slipped my forefinger under her necklace), I thought of my nights in Paris brothels—a whole series of old memories came back—and I thought of her, of her dance, of her voice as she sang songs that were for me without meaning and even without distinguishable words. That continued all night. At three o'clock I got up to piss in the street—the stars were shining. The sky was clear and immensely distant. She awoke, went to get a pot of charcoal and for an hour crouched beside it warming herself, then she came back to bed and fell asleep again. As for the *coups,* they were good—the third especially was ferocious, and the last tender—we told each other many sweet things—toward the end there was something sad and loving in the way we embraced.

At 7 in the morning we left. I went shooting with one of the sailors in a cotton field, under palm trees and *gazis.* The countryside was lovely. Arabs, donkeys and buffalo were making their way to the fields. The wind was blowing through the fine branches of the *gazis,* whistling as it does through rushes. The mountains were pink, the sun was rising. My sailor walked ahead of me, bending to pass under bushes, and with a silent gesture pointing out to me the turtledoves he saw on the branches. I killed one, the only one I sighted. I walked pushing my feet ahead of me, and thinking of similar mornings—of one among others, at the Marquis de Pomereu's at Le Héron, after a ball. I hadn't gone to bed, and in the morning went out in a boat on the pond, all alone, in my lycée uniform. The swans watched me pass, and leaves from the bushes were falling on the water. It was just before the beginning of term. I was fifteen.

In my absorption of all those things, *mon pauvre vieux,* you never ceased to be present. The thought of you was like a constant vesicant, inflaming my mind and making its juices flow by adding to the stimulation. I was sorry (the word is weak) that you were not there—I enjoyed it all for myself and for you—I was excited for both of us, and you came in for a good share, you may be sure.

. . . Just now we have stopped for lack of wind; the flies are stinging my face. Young DuCamp has gone off to take a picture. He is doing quite well—I think we'll have a nice album. As regards vice, he is calming down; it seems to us that I am inheriting his qualities, for I am growing lewd. Such is my profound conviction. When the brain sinks the prick rises. That isn't to say that I haven't collected a few metaphors. I have had a few stirrings. But how to make use of them, and where? . . .

Open Letter to President Wilson
W. E. B. DuBois

Sir: On the occasion of your inauguration as President of the United States, *The Crisis* took the liberty of addressing to you an open letter. *The Crisis* spoke for no inconsiderable part of ten millions of human beings, American born, American citizens. . . .

Sir, you have now been President of the United States for six months and what is the result? It is no exaggeration to say that every enemy of the Negro race is greatly encouraged; that every man who dreams of making the Negro race a group of menials and pariahs is alert and hopeful. They are evidently assuming that their theory of the place and destiny of the Negro race is the theory of your administration. They and others are assuming this because not a single act and not a single word of yours since election has given anyone reason to infer that you have the slightest interest in the colored people or desire to alleviate their intolerable position. A dozen worthy Negro officials have been removed from office, and you have nominated but one black man for office, and he, such a contemptible cur, that his very nomination was an insult to every Negro in the land.

To this negative appearance of indifference has been added positive action on the part of your advisers, with or without your knowledge, which constitutes the gravest attack on the liberties of our people since emancipation. Public segregation of civil servants in government employ, necessarily involving personal insult and humiliation, has for the first time in history been made the policy of the United States government.

In the Treasury and Post Office Departments colored clerks have been herded to themselves as though they were not human beings. We are told that one colored clerk who could not actually be segregated on account of the nature of his work has consequently had a cage built around him to separate him from his white companions of many years. Mr. Wilson, do you know these things? Are you responsible for them? Did you advise them? Do you not know that no other group of American citizens has ever been treated in this way and that no President of the United States ever dared to propose such treatment? Here is a plain, flat, disgraceful spitting in the face of people whose darkened countenances are already dark with the slime of insult. Do you consent to this, President Wilson? Do you believe in it? Have you been able to persuade yourself that national insult is best for a people struggling into self-respect?

President Wilson, we do not, we cannot believe this. *The Crisis* still clings to the conviction that a vote for Woodrow Wilson was NOT a vote for segregation. But whether it was or not segregation is going to be resented as it ought to be resented by the colored people. We would not be men if we did not resent it. The policy adopted, whether with your consent or knowledge or not, is an indefensible attack on a people who have in the past been shamefully humiliated. There are foolish people who think that such policy has no limit and that lynching, Jim Crowism, segregation and insult are to be permanent institutions in America.

We have appealed in the past, Mr. Wilson, to you as a man and statesman; to your sense of fairness and broad cosmopolitan outlook on the world. We renew this appeal and to it we venture to add some plain considerations of political expediency.

We black men still vote. In spite of the fact that the triumph of your party last fall was possible only because Southern white men have, through our disfranchisement, from twice to seven times the political power of Northern white men—notwithstanding this, we black men of the North have a growing nest egg of 500,000 ballots, and ballots that are counted, which no sane party can ignore. Does your Mr. Burleson expect the Democratic Party to carry New York, New Jersey, Pennsylvania, Ohio, Indiana, Illinois, by 200,000 votes? If he does will it not be well for him to remember that there are 237,942 black voters in these States. We have been trying to tell these voters that the Democratic Party wants their votes. Have we been wrong, Mr. Wilson? Have we assumed too great and quick a growth of intelligence in the party that once made slavery its cornerstone?

In view of all this, we beg to ask the President of the United States and the leader of the Democratic Party a few plain questions:

1. Do you want Negro votes? 2. Do you think that a Jim Crow civil service will get these votes? 3. Is your Negro policy to be dictated by Tillman and Vardaman? 4. Are you going to appoint black men to office on the same terms that you choose white men?

This is information, Mr. Wilson, which we are very anxious to have.

The Crisis advocated sincerely and strongly your election to the Presidency. *The Crisis* has no desire to be compelled to apologize to its constituency for this course. But at the present rate it looks as though some apology or explanation was going to be in order very soon.

We are still hoping that present indications are deceptive. We are still trying to believe that the President of the United States is the President of 10,000,000, as well as

of 90,000,000, and that though the 10,000,000 are black and poor, he is too honest and cultured a gentleman to yield to the clamors of ignorance and prejudice and hatred. We are still hoping all this, Mr. Wilson, but hope deferred maketh the heart sick.
1913

Dear Emily
Beverlye Brown

Dear Emily,

I apologize for my late reply to your recent letter. Aunt Phyllis just left on Friday. Her presence as you can remember from our childhood visits to Trenton can be wearing in that she seems always on the verge of some small but startling surprise. But she is a delight, sprightly and wizened now, a face full of smiling, crinkly wrinkles. She had just come from Helen's, who has recently started working as a secretary for Glen; they wanted to "keep everything in the family," as Helen put it. But even in the interests of a family business, of which as you know Phyllis highly approves, still she had a great deal to say on the subject of wives working, of which she of course disapproves. (And I must admit I'm inclined to agree.) She was especially funny about wives and husbands working together, "like strapping a goat and an ass in the same harness." When I looked a little surprised, she laughed and passed it off as one of her "left-field" analogies and said she wouldn't say who was the goat and who the ass, that the incongruity should suffice. You would have enjoyed her I know. But delightful or not, it was time-consuming to have her here.

Still I can hardly lay my late reply to the door of her visit. Jenny is home from school and has been in a round of parties for the Anderson-Pollock wedding. You remember Blair Anderson I know; she is that inordinately pretty girl who moved to Demopolis from Birmingham two years ago. You met her at our Christmas Eve open house last year and remarked on her white, white skin and the fineness of her very black eyebrows. I do believe she is one of the loveliest girls of her age I've seen. Her figure is model perfect and showed to every advantage in her wedding dress. But never you mind what a pretty thing she is. The wedding was a dreadful event! Jenny thinks I didn't notice, but she hardly came home a day without smelling of some kind of liquor. I expected them to drink a little sherry in the afternoons, and I knew, though I thoroughly disapprove, that she would most certainly introduce herself to cocktails at some of the dinner parties. But every day! I didn't say a word to her. We have been round the mulberry patch about practically everything else. She has unearthed this thoroughly unsuitable boy from Southwestern, an aspiring seminary student with definitely "modern" opinions, as her latest beau. I am afraid however that "beau," that lovely, old-fashioned term, does not cover what she is feeling for this young man. She is livid over my objections. I have forbidden him to visit her this summer, hoping to cool things a little between them before fall and school resume. I know your first reply will be that my objections will drive her even more quickly to him. But there is a method in my madness in that Frank too is home from school, and I'm hoping that they will strike up again as they were. Really, it would be hard to convey how furious she is with me! And I am genuinely alarmed.

After watching this wedding as a bystander (I went to none of the wedding parties due to a long-standing un-pleasantness between myself and Liz Pollock) I am more and more convinced that it is madness for girls to marry so young, cutting short their education and whatever else might emerge in the late teens or early twenties. You know Blair was only nineteen in April! Oh dear, I know I sound like one of Charles dreadful sociology books or one of those awful articles on parenting in the *Journal*. But truly Emily, I am honestly frightened. I could see after one look at this Marsh (he insisted on coming to help Charles pack Jenny's things in the car at the end of spring term; he was so forward, one of those cheerful talky sorts who is accustomed to charming people) that Jenny is positively inflamed by him. And he is obviously infatuated with her. I know he will, if he hasn't already, press her to marry him when he graduates and leaves Southwestern for seminary next spring. And then what? What on earth she plans to do married to a new-fangled Elmer Gantry (I know that is at best a rude observation but he impressed me as just that sort) I simply cannot imagine. She has no notion of what her life would be like; the deprivations, the constraints, even more than are usually placed on a woman, of a minister's wife. At least this would be so unless he were completely beyond the pale of any conventional ministry, which I half suspect he will be. And whichever side of the fence he takes, I do not know which would be worse.

I've been reading one of Charles' books, *The Mute Stones Speak, A Short History of Archaeology in Italy*. (You see I do read, although Charles and Jenny both act for the most part as if I were lobotomized before I ever went to school.) There's a passage that struck me, a description of an early Etruscan tomb:

> In the central recess in the farthest wall is a bed for a noble couple. It is flanked by pilasters bearing medallions of husband (on the left) and wife (on the right). On the husband's side appears the end of a locked strongbox, covered with raised studs or bosses, with a garment lying folded on top. On the wife's side is a sturdy knotted walking-staff, a garland, necklaces, and a feather fan. The couch has lathe-turned legs; it is decorated with a relief of Charon and the three-headed dog Cerberus, with a serpent's tail. The couch rests on a step on which a pair of wooden clogs awaits their master's need. Above the couch, and continuing all the way around the room, is a frieze of military millinery: helmets with visors, helmets with cheek-pieces, the felt cap worn under the helmet to keep the metal from chafing, swords, shields, greaves or shin guards, and a pile of round objects variously interpreted as missiles, decorations for valor, or balls of horse-dung. The central pilasters, with typical Etruscan economy are decorated only on the sides visible from the door. What is represented is the whole contents of an Etruscan kitchen. Identifiable objects include a sieve, a set of spits for roasting, a knife-rack, an ink-pot, a dinner gong, a game board (not unlike those provided in English pubs for shove-ha' penny) with a bag for the counters, and folding handles, a ladle, missing spoons, an egg beater, pincers, a duck, a tortoise, a cat with a ribbon around its neck, playing with a lizard, a belt, a pitcher, a long thin rolling pin for making macaroni, a pickaxe, a machete, a coil of rope, a pet weasel teasing a black mouse, a *lituus* (the augur's curved staff), a wine-flask of the familiar Chianti shape, a knapsack, and a canteen. Over and flanking the door are *bucrania* (ox-skulls), wide shallow sacrificial basins, and a curved war-trumpet or hunting-horn. Surely never a household embarked better equipped for the next world. This tomb is as good as a documentary film; nothing ever found by archaeology brings Etruscan daily life more vividly before our eyes.

Pardon the long-windedness of the quotation, but I thought that passage painted a lovely picture of a husband and wife, their life, even their journey to the next life, surrounded by all the useful and beautiful objects needed to make their mutual journey together. Now granted the Etruscans were pagans and the passage does not exactly prove the point I'm getting at, still it seemed cogent. But when I talk, or rather "try" to talk to Jenny about the necessity of material comforts in a marriage she is so scornful. I know she thinks I'm grasping and crudely old-fashioned and out-of-date. What she calls me to my face is "materialistic." If only I could make her see how bare her life would be without a good deal of what she now calls "superflous and immoral opulence." (Where she gets these phrases I can only imagine, most likely from PhD's still wet behind the ears.) And as if this family were opulent! Really, it's ludicrous. One could hardly call the life of a college professor and his non-working wife "opulent." How she plans to live with this alarming ministerial student (I think he's even considered becoming a missionary) I can only in my most horrified daydreams imagine.

I know she thought my own religious bent would dispose me to like him, but the fact that I have been a devout parishioner "for lo these many years" as Charles puts it, has nothing whatever to do with my approving Jenny marrying a Methodist minister, or preacher, as he calls himself. (She insists that he prefers the colloquial title. Another modern attempt, I suppose, at informality which supposedly leads to equality of some sort. To my mind it simply leads to that mindless lowering of standards which seems to be everywhere around us now.) A nice Episcopalian parish priest would be one thing, but a Methodist preacher! *I think not.*

Well, as I said, she has been alternately furious and morose at our not allowing him to visit. For once Charles agrees with me on something concerning Jenny and supports my objections to the boy. So now we both must suffer either her sulks or the loud banging of doors at any hour. I have tried to be patient and because I feel we are strained to the breaking point, I have not mentioned all the drinking at Blair's wedding parties. I think it is, on Jenny's part, a passing rebellion. She looks so dreadful every morning, one almost feels sorry for her. She has not a drinker's constitution, and for that if for no other reason, I refuse to worry myself that the drinking would become a habit. But even in the midst of reassuring myself of that, I have awful starts about the most unlikely persons becoming alcoholics. You may deduce from all this Emily dear that I am, to use one of Jenny's recent phrases, "coming unglued."

And as if all this were not enough, Blair's wedding itself was an awful mixture of tradition and modern insanities. All the proper accoutrements coupled with completely unbridled behavior. Too many parties. Too much drinking. At the wedding reception the best man pushed his way into the suite at the Club where Blair was changing for the honeymoon and attempted to handcuff himself to her. He was totally inebriated and caused a perfectly horrendous scene. Blair, poor child, was hysterical and had to be sedated before she could leave. The only good thing I can say about the entire affair is that Buster (the bridegroom) is certainly in a position to take good care of the bride and any family they might have. But I have my doubts as to their prospects for any real happiness. Blair is, though I am fond of her, coldly calculating, especially for a girl her age, and I strongly suspect she married the poor boy for his money. And despite what Jenny thinks I would never advocate her marrying someone she did not love. Why she cannot see that both love and the reasonable prospect of material comfort are pre-requisite for a marriage I simply do not know.

As you can see, my summer thus far has been anything but restful. Please write soon. I feel so in need of a friendly voice. But by all means, be frank. I do want your genuine opinion of my alarms about all this wedding activity, actual or planned. If I'm a hopeless old dinosaur, you are the only one, Emily dear, who could tell me so with any success.

Much love,
Kathrine

Gus Is Dead
James O. Elder

Maxwell held the envelope up to the light to see where it was safe to tear, he quickly ripped the end off, and dumped the contents into his lap. His palms grew moist with perspiration as he unfolded the letter and began reading:

"DEAR MAX

GUS IS DEAD. He got killed on 16th street trying to stick up a store-front preacher with a toy gun. I know it sounds crazy but its true. He got shot four times in the chest and once in the head and they say he still lived long enough to crawl in a hallway and die. Me and Gus never did get along, but I figured you'd prefer to hear about him from me rather than some stranger, who didn't know him at all, or luck out and get blowed away by stumbling across it in the Jerline Gazzete or whatever the fuck y'all read down there, because regardless of how I might have felt about him I always knew that you loved him like a brother. . . ."

Max's hands trembled so uncontrollably that he had to put the letter down; the opposing corner edges where he'd gripped it were damp, warm, and crumpled. He shut his eyes and took a long, deep breath. Then he looked at the letter lying there on the bed beside him and slowly began shaking his head from side to side—at that very moment he hated Sleepy's guts for bringing him that letter. As hard as he'd fought the violence and the nightmares of being institutionalized by fantasizing about the serenity of the outside world, Sleepy had conspired with the prison to let the outside world reach into his cell and violently slap him into a nightmarish stupor. He'd always thought that Gus would fade out with a needle in his arm in the back room of some musky lit 'SHOOT-ING GALLERY'—and that he could accept—but not like some mangy, suicidal dog with his tail stuck between his legs, moping across the Dan Ryan Expressway during rush hour. He had a sudden flash of Gus kneeling in a piss-stained hallway with buckets of blood oozing from his mouth and nostrils: only his vision wasn't of the Gus who was killed—it was the dope addict who was drooling into his breakfast the last time he'd seen him at Nick's, and in so doing had made him feel so embarrassed that he left the restaurant without finishing his food or saying hello—no, not in the least, his vision was one of youthful innocence, of the Gus who'd died so long ago that he'd forgotten he was dead— the black, lanky kid with the nappy hair and the crooked smile, the make-believe brother that always came thru when needed; to punch somebody out or to enlighten him to the majestic beauty of a pigeon in flight. Maxwell had his choice of visions; and he chose. But either way Gus was dead and the thought of it nauseated him. He blamed the heat for the queasy feeling in his gut, wiped his sweaty palms off the bed sheet, lit a ciga-rette, and reluctantly picked the letter up and started reading again—and in THIS he had no choice.

"Gus's habit had him by the balls Max and wouldn't let go. He joined the 'program' a couple of times but the best he could manage was to swap habits: a methadone habit for a heroin habit. I rapped with him a few times since the last time we seen him nodding in Nick's, and I swear Max, You wouldn't have recognized him; He had these crusty looking scab-sores all over his face and hands, and his skin was so burnt out he'd turned ash-gray. Little Mickey told me that he'd gotten so down and out that he'd started shooting T's and Blues and that part of his ass had fell off—can you imagine that—that's why he'd quit taking baths, because whenever he'd wash with a rag part of his flesh would peel off. I don't know what you and the good ol' boys down there be getting off on, but if it's them T's and Blues Max I really wish you'd ice it; that shit is worse than rat poison.

Gus had gotten to the point where he looked like a winehead, dressed like a winehead, and smelt like a winehead, and even though he wasn't, you sure'n the hell couldn't tell the difference by looking at him, and Max you know a booster can't steal shit looking like a winehead. All of the shopping mall security guards in and around Chicago knew him by sight, smell, and name; and they would snatch him time they spotted him; and the 1st district policemen didn't even allow him downtown, day or night. Since his shabby appearance had blown his main hustle—and his habit was too wicked to handle a package—he started burglarizing apartments.

"He made out O.K. at first. I mean, he was stealing shit as fast as Sears could deliver it. But once while he was burglarizing a third floor apartment over on Douglas this niggah came home early from work and busted him; Gus had the man's clothes, T-V, radio, and meat from the freezer all stockpiled by the front door, and was in the process of disconnecting the stereo system in the front room when he heard the jingle of door keys. Time the niggah saw his shit sitting by the door he up'd with his piece and started shootin'. Knowing that death stood between him and the front door, Gus jumped from the third floor window as a bullet grazed his back. Gus broke his collar bone, two fingers, and his right leg in two places; but he still managed to get away before that niggah could get down stairs and kill him. He walked with a real bad limp after that, and lost his nerve for burglarizing completely. But he still had that habit to feed. And right around then is when he started stickin' up with that toy pistol; a black plastic, snub nose 38 they said in the papers.

"Anyway, late last Sunday night he spotted this mark sitting in a mint green Cadillac countin' a lump of cash. He eased up on him from the passenger side of the car and threw the toy pistol up in his face, and told him to give it up. Now the preacher said that he didn't know the gun was a toy, but people on the street say otherwise. Anyway, the preacher went on to say that when he'd given Gus the money that he had in his hand that Gus demanded him to give him the money that he had in his pocket and that if he didn't he was going to 'blow his fuckin face off', and that's when he reached into his suit coat pocket, pulled his gun, and shot him. Jive niggah shot him five times before he hit the sidewalk. Some people say the preacher is an ex-pimp hustling behind some bullshit religion that he invented, and that he knew that Gus's gun was a toy, and that's why he went for his piece even though Gus had the drop on him; they also say that Gus never got a chance to even smell that money let alone touch it.

"Me and Joyce went to the funeral and I swear it was the wildest thing I ever seen in my life, Max, people were screamin' and hollerin' and kicking over benches, and ol' deacon Crawford got drunk and threw up on the podium right in the middle of his 'LITTLE BOY LOST' speech; but that's another story and I'm running out of paper. I hope those six years pass like six days. I'll be down to see you as soon as I can, and remember that 'good time' is the quickest way out.

LOVE,

P.S. CONNIE'S HOME."

Possible Assignments:

- Write accounts of travel or any other event in letter form (addressed to someone in the class or to an imagined person or to anyone else).
- Write an open letter to a public figure arguing for or against something.
- Write a story in letter form, fantasy or dream, and incorporate the character of the letter recipient into the story.
- Write a letter exchange, a bundle of letters, telling a story and revealing the

characters of the letter writers (see the short story, "A Bundle of Letters" by Henry James).

- Write a letter to a group of people.
- Write a letter in which you imagine the letter writer and the letter receiver.
- Write a letter to a friend (or imagine a friend) to whom you can say anything.

Exaggeration

If you watch an effective teller of an everyday how-to giving directions, you find that exaggerated gestures and exaggerated imagery move toward precision, toward greater clarity, toward meeting the need of the audience. Exaggeration also enables beginning and professional writers to overcome restraints that result in inadequate or imprecise written and oral expression. In other words, what you as the teller feel to be exaggerated actually achieves the clarity and thrust necessary to get the image, or message, or instruction across to the reader. Exaggeration brings forth and brings together all of the essentials. Yet, you will find manuals, how-to books, fiction, and essays that rigidly avoid exaggeration and suffer serious losses in substance and precision, because they do not see the task as the reader sees it, do not take the reader's point of view into account, and do not exaggerate the presentation in ways sufficient to move everything into the reader's mind. I can testify to the effectiveness of exaggerated graphic illustrations for conveying technique in snow and ice mountain-climbing. Let me use it as an example for what should be got into the writing itself. If you slip on certain steep slopes without being roped to other members of your party, you alone must somehow arrest your wild flight, usually with your ice-axe, or you will, as one climber put it, simply "sail away." In glissading down Popocateptl in Mexico, down three thousand feet of snow with safe runouts into volcanic sand, my son and I were able, because of what we remembered from what we'd seen the day before in a mountaineering book, to accomplish the ice-axe arrest several times, and to conveniently descend several thousand feet in a few minutes, where we sat for a while with astounding headaches due to oxygen loss from exertion. Then, on review, I saw that it had been *not* the text but the vivid, caricatural, *exaggerated* graphic illustrations that had moved precision of seeing and under-standing into our minds. Unlike the written text, which scrupulously avoided the "you" address (and avoided taking the point of view of the learner and seeing it as the learner sees it), the caricatural graphic illustrations used the command form of the verbs, the understood "you," and left the gasping climber finally arrested with his feet dangling over a precipice, having clearly abstracted the crucial elements for a successful ice-axe arrest.

You may wonder why I don't use "heightening" or "emphasis" in place of exaggeration. Instead, I say that we exaggerate to *achieve* "heightening" and "emphasis," and to do much more. To heighten or to emphasize means to heighten or emphasize what is already there. To exaggerate means to bring forth *what is not yet there.* Exaggeration calls upon sources that have not yet been called upon. Our language does not have a word for such positive, "truthful" exaggeration. However, even to qualify exaggeration with adjectives such as "positive" and "truthful" cramps the free, *accurate* style of it. In the common spoken language "to exaggerate" can mean to bring forth strongly, clearly, freely, effectively, what is not yet there. In theater training, exaggeration is used in this sense.[1] We exaggerate in order to discover, draw forth, and project with precision what is not yet there in the telling and the presentation.

Writers often know that something more is needed at certain points in their writing, but do not allow themselves to exaggerate to get it. Somehow many writing teachers—though not usually writers themselves—believe that exaggeration is proper in illustrations, but improper in writing. You should not hesitate to "tease out" what *is not yet there;* to exaggerate the expression of the perception in order to draw upon resources that are *not yet touched, not yet there.* Editors resort to graphic illustrations because they know you must make the reader *see* in order for the reader to understand. Good writers *make the reader see.* In our how-to selections, we find exaggeration used to accomplish precision, often with make-sure points, metaphors, figures, comparisons, verbs, adjectives, adverbs, how-not-to-do-it points, satisfactions, and teasing for certain effects.

Examine the following passages, in which exaggeration strongly influences the authors' choices of tone and timing; of verbs, adjectives, adverbs; of metaphors and other comparisons; and of other words and expressions and techniques that serve the cause of getting the point across to the reader.

> Oh, keep stirring. Use a wooden ladle. Never, never stir lasagna with a metal implement. Use your wooden ladle even if it couldn't pass any known Board of Health test; use it if, withal, it has authority, character, tone, air, countenance, the complexion of a mercenary in the Sahara, and if it is strong enough to keep your brew from sticking. If this occurs, Senora, you had best lose yourself in the night or, worse, profane this peerless dish by attempting to substitute for its sauce some unspeakable red plastic substitute from a jar.

> Thus the whale-line folds the whole boat in its complicated coils, twisting and writhing around it in almost every direction. All the oarsmen are involved in its perilous contortions; so that to the timid eye of the landsman, they seem as Indian jugglers, with the deadliest snakes sportively festooning their limbs.

---

1. Viola Spolin uses exaggeration in exercises in *Improvisation for the Theater,* Northwestern University Press. It was in workshops conducted by Spolin that I came across the use of the term in a professional context. Copywriters are familiar with the use of exaggeration. So are fiction writers, poets, essayists, and scientists. Personification is a form of exaggeration used by scientists. (see "Imagination in Scientific Discovery," p. 356, and "The Mating of the Mantis," p. 186.)

For two days the stank of the chitterlings assaulted the air with rudeness. Yet, no one minded as they knew each morsel would be tender and succulent; full of flavor.

As the better skiers glide along the flats, their heads stay at just about the same height from the track all the time. Others bounce up and down in their strides and eventually wear themselves out—or get sore backs.

In Flaubert's letter, he exaggerates to make clear and bring out the humor of the scenes.

On the top of a hill overlooking the Nile there is a Coptic monastery, whose monks have the custom, as soon as they see a boatload of tourists, of running down, throwing themselves in the water, and swimming out to ask for alms. Everyone who passes is assailed by them. You see these fellows, totally naked, rushing down their perpendicular cliffs and swimming toward you as fast as they can, shouting: "Baksheesh, baksheesh, cawadja christiani!" And since there are many caves in the cliff at this particular spot, echo repeats "Cawadja, cawadja!" loud as a cannon. Vultures and eagles were flying overhead, the boat was flashing through the water, its two great sails very full.

In a very real sense, Flaubert (through the translator) is telling exactly what occurred. Yet if we rephrase the passage using tamer verbs, adjectives, adverbs, passive constructions, and a weaker simile for "loud as a cannon," we see how exaggeration brought forth what was not yet there, to give the reader the experience of the scene. Because of the "all-at-once" nature of writing, and the interpenetration of forms and techniques, I could just as well have used this passage to demonstrate the use of active verbs, imagery, the model-telling (see Model-Telling chapter), and other facets of writing.

Exaggeration triggers invention of telling devices. In exaggerated slow-motion, the author of "How to Hit" gives fine precision, with verbs and participles, to the sequential telling of the batter's perception of pitched balls: ". . . you must be able to perceive the rotation on the ball. You must determine if the red string that laces the baseball's seams is spinning sideways, indicating a curveball, or spinning end over end in the fashion of a fastball."

There are times when exaggeration would be inappropriate for a particular passage or a particular how-to. If you see the subject as the reader sees it and take the reader into account, you will be sensitive to appropriateness. In the following section on comparisons, we will see how exaggeration helps us to abstract concepts as well as express them. Without exaggeration we would lose much discovery, much invention, much precision.

Comparisons

The many kinds of comparisons—such as metaphor, simile, figure, analogy—all result from the basic thinking process of comparing, juxtaposing, apposing perceptions, that is, seeing things side by side in our minds and relating the unfamiliar thing to a familiar thing in order to make an understanding more clear or more effective for the reader or listener, and for ourselves as writers and thinkers about our subject. Metaphor, simile, figure, analogy, and comparison are distinct terms that overlap, like circles lying partly upon and partly free of each other. A metaphor transfers a term from the object it ordinarily designates to an object that it can designate only by an implicit comparison, e.g., "the high noon of his career," "a glittering river of coal." A simile compares two unlike things, making its comparison explicit by use of *like* or *as,* e.g., "she feels like a munchkin." A figure takes one object and uses it by comparison to build a comprehension of another concept, e.g., "the window" for the area over the pitcher's shoulder where the pitched balls come from. An analogy takes one thing and another thing dissimilar in function and position and compares their likenesses without necessarily creating a pure metaphor, simile, or figure, e.g., comparing the expanding universe to a swelling balloon with dots on it. Metaphor and comparison are often used as catch-all terms for the various kinds of comparisons. We use metaphors, similes, figures, analogies, and other comparisons instinctively in our everyday language.

Metaphor and Audience

Metaphor takes vigorously into account the audience's need for immediate understanding, by relating the unfamiliar to the more familiar thing or action, or by turning the principle around to relate the usual to the unusual, or the overly familiar or hard-to-describe familiar to the exotically familiar and suggestive. Many descriptions, comparisons, figures, verbs, and other devices are of gestural origin, that is, we see our gestures (or the sense of them) reflectively in our minds and come up with imaginative correspondences. Metaphors of gestural origin carry into writing gesture's vivid, immediate sense of address. For instance, if you gesturally demonstrate "the intricately interdependent layers, levels, strata, and tiers" of the introductory statement of "How to Make Lasagna," you see what it begins to tell you about how to layer noodles and sauce. When a tennis player tells you to "swing the racket as if you're going to smack someone on the ass," his seeing of his own gesture causes him to come up with the comparison. If you tell someone to "put in lots and lots of mushrooms" for lasagna, you gesture instinctively with your words. In writing, you see the gestures in your mind and come up with the comparison of "cascades" of mushrooms.

The following comparison, relating the unfamiliar to the familiar, would be recognized by all human beings everywhere:

If you drew lines from arm to arm and from leg to leg you'd see why we call this x-c signature "the diagonal."

Although the stride is a natural elongation of walking, if you're like me and try too consciously to correlate these movements, you may get all mixed up.

The comparison of the diagonal stride to "a natural elongation of walking" permits us not only to see and identify with it, but also with the tendency to become confused when trying "too consciously to correlate these movements." (It further allows the author to ingeniously identify with the reader without condescension: "if you're like me.")

An example of relating the hard-to-describe familiar to the exotically familiar and suggestive is the comparison of the color of an old wooden ladle to "the complexion of a mercenary in the Sahara."

In the following comparison, "pale cousins," as a replacement for white onions, establishes an even greater, more humorous contrast and distance between purple and white onions:

No one can really afford six purple onions but you must have them today for they are to their pale cousins what crabmeat is to tuna fish.

The following simile sharpens the reader's perception of a particularly crucial moment in a process, using comparison to an object common in our society:

Each chitterling is one long intestine of the hog. It is wiggly and split down the middle like a busted balloon.

In a primitive society, or even in a less urban society, it could easily be more familiar to say that "a busted balloon is like a split and wiggly intestine."

In the following passage a metaphor and simile get across to us not only the visible image but the way the girl feels:

Elaine's party dress is suddenly even more starched and stiff, and the sleeves are beachballs on her arms, and she feels like a munchkin, or that she's about to do a tapdance, and she feels huge and gawky and young.

You've probably heard that you shouldn't "mix your metaphors." That's useful guidance when properly understood within a specific context, but many persons trying to learn how to write unnecessarily inhibit their use of metaphor because of this injunction, only to find that later teachers complain that they don't show much capacity for comparisons. Is Melville "mixing his metaphors" in the following passage? What is the difference between a series and a "mixing" or "confusing" of metaphors? If we gesturally examine the series of metaphors in this passage, we find each one used to make an essential comparative distinction for how the line is, and is not, coiled into the tub:

Toward the stern of the boat it is spirally coiled away in the tub, not like the worm-pipe of a still though, but so as to form one round, cheese-shaped mass of densely bedded 'sheaves', or layers of concentric spiralizations, without any hollow but the 'heart', or minute vertical tube formed at the axis of the cheese.

Modern-day readers still understand comparisons such as "worm-pipe of a still" and "one round, cheese-shaped mass," which were more immediately familiar to readers in Melville's time; these comparisons relate unfamiliar elements of the whale-line to familiar elements of the readers' experience. These comparisons also tell us something about the life of Melville's time, and suggest Melville's clear sense of audience.

Gesture and Metaphor

In the passage below, gestural demonstration produces not only the comparisons but also the command verbs:

After they have soaked, hold one chitterling at the tip. Stretch it open with both hands. Once it's open, you will see globs of white fat dotted with black, brown, and green waste matter. Using the fingers of one hand like a claw, firmly grip this and pull it off. You will have to repeat this several times in each spot. The spot is cleaned when the skin is faintly translucent. You will see tiny web designs inside the skin.

"Like a claw" and "tiny web designs" provide correspondences for gestures that give you crucial information.

At first sight the following image and its accompanying comparison in the form of a simile may not seem to be precisely gestural in origin:

. . . the American tub, nearly three feet in diameter and of proportionate depth, makes a rather bulky freight for a craft whose planks are but one half-inch in thickness; for the bottom of the whale-boat is like critical ice, which will bear up a considerable distributed weight, but not very much of a concentrated one.

However, if we duplicate the process of telling and discovery, we'll likely find ourselves gesturing for elements such as "bulky freight," "planks . . . but half-inch in thickness," "bottom of the whaleboat," "critical ice," "distributed weight," and "concentrated weight." Once again the simile "like critical ice" tells us something about the audience that Melville imagined at the moment of writing: a Northern Temperate zone audience. What metaphor would successfully relate the same principle to a person familiar only with the tropics or subtropics?

Gesture and metaphor often occasion conceptual discovery. For instance, scientists may use the abstractive power of gesture to "draw forth" and describe the structures of molecules, the behavior of atomic particles, and so forth. In other parts of this book, we'll examine the function of gesture in conceptual discovery and expression.

Frequently the insight of the gesture comes out in an impulse, the gesture emerging naturally with the perception; but sometimes abstractive perceptions will pull on your attention and you'll think about them for a while (hours, days, sleep on them) before your seeing-in-the-mind forms clearly, or your gestural impulses develop, and then words come for telling your seeing. You can also gesturally explore such tugging perceptions to find out more clearly what you are perceiving.

Melville referred to metaphor as being like a turning beacon that sweeps its light in every direction, thereby using a simile to explain what a metaphor does.

Other Gestural Correspondences

You won't find correspondences in metaphors or verbs (see ACTIVE VERBS) for all of your gestural perceptions. There can be as many language inventions as there are perceptions that require them. For instance, in "How to Get the Most Out of Frisbee-ing," a gestural correspondence was found as follows:

> You place *three* fingers under the groove, one finger (index) on the rounded edge, and thumb on top.

In the oral telling, the teller could gesturally show the index finger without naming it. The parenthesis suggests the teller's realization of the imagined speech-demonstration in his writing and gives a moment of suggested eye-contact with the reader.

Gestural and bodily telling also play a significant part in the two-way seeing of point of view, and in the telling of perceptions of spatial relationships, and of rhythm and space-time concepts.

When a speaker restrains hands and body, tellings of conceptual imagery flatten and lose substance, depth, precision, vividness, point of view. So does writing lose substance, depth, precision, vividness, and point of view when authors suppress their gestural sense. Obviously you need to let yourself gesture freely and clearly if you're going to find metaphors, similes, comparisons, figures, and other devices for your telling and writing. You should use gesture as if your life depended on it, in oral tellings and in writing, for long ago in our evolutionary history our lives did depend upon it, and we're essentially the same persons now as our counterparts were then.

Active Verbs

If the author of *Cross-Country Skiing Today* were coaching pupils directly, he would use demonstration and gesture keyed with his words. In writing, he invents from various perceptual-language resources to accomplish correspondences for gestural precision and sense of address; for one, he draws upon the rich treasury of verbs in the English language: "You *reach* forward, "*slide* one ski," "*push* with the arms," "*practice*," "*alternate*," "*start*," "*coast*," "*double-pole*," "*continue*," "*give* a little push or bounce," and so on. Then come the participles, which also tell with the precision of verbs, such as "*using* both arms," "*sliding* ahead," "if your skis aren't *holding*," "try *pushing (kicking)*," "*relaxing* your back," "*rounding* your shoulders." Gerunds, derived from verbs, used as nouns, with -ing endings, also contribute precision: "elongation of *walking*," "the *following*," the problem of "*side-bending*," and so on.*

In oral tellings and conversation, we often use precise gestures to qualify a few basic verbs such as "is," "go," "come," and so on. For instance, an oral telling of "How to Get the Most Out of Frisbeeing" could have occurred as follows:

> You say you can't throw a frisbee straight? You want it to go toward someone and it goes off into another direction? (gesture of frisbee going off to one side)

In the writing, a verb provides the gestural correspondence:

> You want it to go toward someone and it *veers* off into another direction?

The verb *veers* could also occur in the oral telling, instantly accompanying the gesture of hands, eyes, head.

English is a language particularly rich in verbs. Verbs help achieve precision of written expression. Verbs of Old English, Norse, and Germanic origin tend to retain their immediate gestural sense and meaning, e.g., reach, slide, slip, throw, melt, hack, bring, stir, drain, hit, start, hunt, hurdle, cart, clip, while many of the verbs that English absorbed from Latin and French become more general, e.g., examine, continue, practice, relegate, assist, approach, decipher, amuse. But in their etymological origins, these verbs from French and Latin had clear gestural sense and meaning, too: "to examine" meant to weigh accurately, a weighing, a consideration; "to relegate," to send away, send back; "to assist," to stand beside, help. Some verbs of Latin and French origin retain their explicit gestural character, e.g., pounce, coast, push, veer.

With many verbs, you find immediately direct gestural correspondences. For the verb "hovers," for instance, you can give a specific image by holding your hand flat in the air and making it wobble, oscillate—a nearly perfect gestural correspondence. "Assist" must usually be explained with other words as you act it out with your gestures. Such acting out with gestures and language is important for oral and written expression. Look over the readings and find the verbs that can be expressed by direct gestural correspondence and those that must be explained and acted out at the same time.

In "The Line," when Melville seeks to demonstrate to you how strong the whale-line is, he makes precise distinctions of meaning with two verbs, "suspend" and "bear":

---

*Sometimes people are confused when asked to identify parts of speech. However, since we use the parts of speech all the time and use them accurately, according to our intuitive sense for the principles of the English language, we, in a real sense, know them without knowing them, i.e., we use the parts of speech without being able to name them as such. Many fine writers have possessed only the most rudimentary knowledge of the terms of abstract grammar. However, our being able to identify a few basic parts of speech, such as nouns, verbs, participles, adjectives, adverbs, and pronouns, facilitates our discussion of certain aspects of writing.

By experiment its one and fifty yarns will each *suspend* a weight of one hundred and twenty pounds so that the whole rope will *bear* a strain nearly equal to three tons.

If you used one of these verbs in place of the other, the sentence would still make approximate sense; but the precision of one of the yarns *suspending* a weight without apparent strain, and the whole rope *bearing* a strain of nearly three tons, would be lost.

Here is John Caldwell telling you how to do the telemark turn, in which the precision of verbs is crucial for making the actions clear:

To *do* it, *slide* one ski ahead of the other as you *go* downhill. *Slide* it so that the binding of the forward ski is about alongside the tip of the *following* ski. Then *stem* the forward ski—to the left if it's your right ski that is ahead—*weight* it or *edge* it slightly, *use* your arms for balance, and you should *go* around. *Bring* your skis together to *complete* the turn.

I also italicized *"following,"* which in this case is a participle used as an adjective, giving the verb's precision.

In the next passage from "The Line" I have italicized verbs and participles. I have not italicized the linking "to be" verbs—is, was, were, and other forms of "to be"— because, though indispensably useful, they are not active verbs.

When the *painted* canvas cover is *clapped* on the American line-tub, the boat *looks* as if it were *pulling* off with a prodigious great wedding-cake *to present* to the whales.

Both ends of the line are *exposed;* the lower end *terminating* in an eye-splice or loop *coming* up from the bottom against the side of the tub, and *hanging* over its edge completely *disengaged* from everything.

This arrangement of the lower end is necessary on two accounts. First: In order to *facilitate* the *fastening* to it of an additional line from a *neighboring* boat, in case the *stricken* whale should *sound* so deep as to *threaten* to *carry* off the entire line originally *attached* to the harpoon. In these instances, the whale of course is *shifted* like a mug of ale, as it were, from the one boat to the other; though the first boat always *hovers* at hand *to assist* its consort.

We've already examined the play and precision of verbs in "How to Make Lasagna" and the imperative gestural verbs of "How to Make Chitterlings." We've examined verbs in "How to Hit" and "The Line" in association with the techniques of exaggeration and metaphor.

Notice the frequent metaphorical character of some verbs and participles in the tongue-in-cheek, exaggerated ironies of Burks' "the stank of the chitterlings assaulted the air" and of Melville's oarsmen surrounded by the convolutions of the line as if they were "Indian jugglers, with the deadliest snakes sportively *festooning* their limbs." By exaggerating in slow-motion the hitter's perceptions of the pitch, with gesturally precise verbs and participles, Nawrocki enables himself to examine a complicated, nearly instantaneous process.

Even without the command form of address, verbs—particularly active verbs— carry a direct sense of address and give precision of perception, perhaps because of their gestural sense.

A good exercise is to juxtapose pages of the reading selections, that is, a page of *Cross-Country Skiing Today,* of "The Line," and of "How to Make Lasagna," or of any of the other selections. Read aloud a page of one and then a page of another, exaggerating and listening to the verbs. You can do this activity in the class, or by yourself. See the action of the verbs, exaggerate the verbs, listen to them.

You need to see and feel the imagery and scene and characters in whatever you have to tell in order to respond with the most effective verbs and expression. Often you find them by trying again, repeating the seeing. The language psychologist Lev Vygotsky has pointed out that the language of inner speech, which is close to seeing-in-the-mind, tends toward "predication," which is the use of verbs and the sense of verbs.

III

How-It-Happens

How Things Happen: Subjects and Principles; Perception and Expression of Instances and Patterns

One of the most important and most common modes of thinking is finding patterns through comparison and contrast of observed instances of behavior. Everyday we watch and compare instances of the behavior of fellow employees on a job, peers in social situations, teachers, animals, plants, birds, insects, machinery, traffic, etc. When we extend this way of thinking into comparison of patterns of behavior, it lays the bases for perceiving connections that lead to new concepts in science, technology, art, the study of culture, and so forth. The "it" in how-it-happens is the principle of the pattern perceived.

Instances may simply be lists, but usually they are developed more fully by the scientist, artist, or other writer, in a kind of continuous journal exploration, an interplay between observations, thought, and feeling. This interplay is what finally leads to the series of connections, the abstraction of patterns, new concepts. Yet, long after the concepts have been realized by the author, the process of this interplay of observation and thought in a journal or essay is still useful, instructive, pleasurable, and compelling to us as readers. We share again, while reading the completed work, in each individual exploration.

* * *

In journal form, John Holt explores a pattern that compelled his attention about the behavior of children in school-learning situations. He found himself asking: "Why do children sometimes not only resist understanding but often turn things around in their minds, even when the teacher feels he or she has been very clear? Can a child have a vested interest in failure?"

From
How Children Fail
John Holt

February 13, 1958 I can't get Nell out of my mind. When she talked with me about fractions today, it was as if her mind rejected understanding. Isn't this unusual? Kids often resist understanding, make no effort to understand; but they don't often grasp an idea and then throw it away. Do they? But this seemed to be what Nell was doing. Several times she would make a real effort to follow my words, and did follow them, through a number of steps. Then, just as it seemed she was on the point of getting the idea, she would shake her head and say, "I don't get it." Can a child have a vested interest in failure? What on earth could it be? Martha, playing the number game, often acts the same way. She does not understand, does not want to understand, does not listen when you are explaining, and then says, "I'm all mixed up."

There may be a connection here with *producer-thinker* strategies [We used the word *producer* to describe the student who was only interested in getting right answers, and who made more or less uncritical use of rules and formulae to get them; we called *thinker* the student who tried to think about the meaning, the reality, of whatever it was he was working on.] A student who jumps at the right answer and misses often falls back into defeatism and despair because he doesn't know what else to do. The thinker is more willing to plug on.

It is surprising to hear so many of these kids say, "I'm dumb." I thought this kind of thing came later, with the bogey, adolescence. Apparently not.

My room group did fairly well today at the number game. [At certain periods, two-thirds of the class was away at art or shop classes, and the rest stayed with me for "room period," a special class, invented by Bill Hull. We met in a small room just off the classroom. There we played various kinds of intellectual games, did puzzles, and held discussions in a way as little like ordinary classroom work as possible. On this occasion we played a game like Twenty Questions, in which the teacher thinks of a number, and the students try to find it by asking questions to which the teacher may answer "Yes" or "No."] Laura was consistently the poorest asker of questions. It happened that on several occasions her turn came when the choice of numbers had been narrowed down to three or four, and she guessed the number. This made her feel that she was the official number guesser for the day. In one game she made her first guess at an individual number when there were still twelve numbers left to choose from—obviously a poor move. Once she guessed, others started doing the same, and wasted four turns on it. Later on Mary got the idea that she was a mind reader, and started trying to guess the numbers from the beginning. The rest of her team became infected with this strategy for a while, before they went back to the plan of closing in on the number.

On the whole they were poised and collected and worked well as a team, though they didn't eliminate enough numbers at a turn. Thus, knowing that the number was between 250 and 300, they would say, "Is it between 250 and 260?" instead of taking a larger bite.

Nancy played well; but after a point the tension of the game got to be too much for her, and her mind just stopped working. She didn't get frantic, like Nell or Martha, or make fantastic guesses; she just couldn't think of anything to say, and so said nothing. A safe policy.

February 18, 1958 Intelligence is a mystery. We hear it said that most people never develop more than a very small part of their latent intellectual capacity. Probably not; but *why* not? Most of us have our engines running at about ten percent of their power. Why no more? And how do some people manage to keep revved up to twenty percent or thirty percent of their full power—or even more?

What turns the power off, or keeps it from ever being turned on?

During these past four years at the Colorado Rocky Mountain School my nose has been rubbed in the problem. When I started, I thought that some people were just born smarter than others and that not much could be done about it. This seems to be the official line of most of the psychologists. It isn't hard to believe, if all your contacts with students are in the classroom or the psychological testing room. But if you live at a small school, seeing students in class, in the dorms, in their private lives, at their recreations, sports, and manual work, you can't escape the conclusion that some people are much smarter part of the time than they are at other times. Why? Why should a boy or girl, who under some circumstances is witty, observant, imaginative, analytical, in a word, *intelligent,* come into the classroom and, as if by magic, turn into a complete dolt?

The worst student we had, the worst I have ever encountered, was in his life outside the classroom, as mature, intelligent, and interesting a student as anyone at the school. What went wrong? Experts muttered to his parents about brain damage—a handy way to end a mystery that you can't explain otherwise. Somewhere along the line, his intelligence became disconnected from his schooling. Where? Why?

This past year I had some terrible students. I failed more kids, mostly in French and Algebra, than did all the rest of the teachers in the school together. I did my best to get them through, goodness knows. Before every test we had a big cram session of practice work, politely known as "review." When they failed the exam, we had post-mortems, then more review, then a make-up test (always easier than the first), which they almost always failed again.

I thought I knew how to deal with the problem: make the work interesting and the classroom a lively and enthusiastic place. It was, too, some of the time at least: many of these failing students actually liked my classes. Overcome children's fear of saying what they don't understand, and keep explaining until they do understand. Keep a steady and resolute pressure on them. These things I did. Result? The good students stayed good, and some may have got better; but the bad students stayed bad, and some of them seemed to get worse. If they were failing in November they were still failing in June. There must be a better answer. Maybe we can prevent kids from becoming chronic failers in the first place.

OBSERVING IN BILL HULL'S CLASS:

February 24, 1958 In today's work period three or four people came up to you for help. All were stuck on that second math problem. None of them had made any effort to listen when you were explaining it at the board. I had been watching George, who had busied himself during the explanation by trying, with a pencil, to ream and countersink a hole in the side of his desk, all the while you were talking. He indignantly denied this. I showed him the hole, which silenced him. Gerald was in dreamland; so for the most part was Nancy, though she made a good recovery when asked a question. Unusual for her. Don listened about half the time, Laura about the same. Martha amused herself by turning her hand into an animal and having it crawl around her desk.

Watching older kids study, or try to study, I saw after a while that they were not sufficiently self-aware to know when their minds had wandered off the subject. When, by speaking his name, I called a daydreamer back to earth, he was always startled, not because he had thought I wouldn't notice that he had stopped studying, but because *he* hadn't noticed.

Except by inflicting real pain on myself, I am never able to stay awake when a certain kind of sleepiness comes over me. The mind plays funny tricks at such times. I remember my own school experiences of falling asleep in class while listening to the teacher's voice. I used to find that the "watchman" part of my mind that was saying, "Keep awake, you fool!" would wake me when the teacher's voice began to fade. But the part of my mind that wanted or needed sleep was not so easily beaten. It used to (and still does) counterfeit a voice, so that as I fell asleep an imaginary voice continued to sound in my head, long enough to fool me until the watchman no longer had the power to awaken me. The watchman learned, in turn, that this counterfeit voice was liable to be talking about something different, or pure nonsense, and thus learned to recognize it as counterfeit. Many times, I have dozed off with a voice sounding inside my head, only to have the watchman say, "Hey! Wake up! That voice is a phoney!"

Most of us have very imperfect control over our attention. Our minds slip away from duty before we realize that they are gone. Part of being a good student is learning to be aware of the state of one's own mind and the degree of one's own understanding. The good student may be one who often says that he does not understand, simply because he keeps a constant check on his understanding. The poor student, who does not, so to speak, watch himself trying to understand, does not know most of the time whether he understands or not. Thus the problem is not to get students to ask us what they don't know; the problem is to make them aware of the difference between what they know and what they don't.

All this makes me think of Herb. I saw the other day why his words so often run off the paper. When he is copying a word, he copies about two letters at a time. I doubt whether he looks beyond them, or that he could tell you, in the middle of a word, what the whole word was. He has no idea, when he begins to copy a word, how long the word is going to be, or how much room it may take up.

April 21, 1958 I watched Ruth during the period of the Math test. At least four-fifths of the time she was looking out the window; or else she played with her pencil, or chewed her fingernails, or looked at Nell to see what information she might pick up. She did not look in the least worried or confused. It looked as if she had decided that Math tests were to be done, not during the regular test period, when everyone else does them, but during conference period on Friday, with teacher close at hand, so that if she got into a jam she could get instant help.

She seems to find the situation of not knowing what to do so painful that she prefers to do nothing at all, waiting instead for a time when she can call for help the moment she gets stuck. Even in conference period today she did next to nothing. She was trying to sneak something out of her desk. She moves rather jerkily, so every time she raised the desk lid, I saw it out of the corner of my eye and looked at her. This was rather frustrating for her; however, she kept right on trying for most of the period, not a bit abashed by being caught at it all the time.

Remember when Emily, asked to spell "microscopic," wrote MINCOPERT? That must have been several weeks ago. Today I wrote MINCOPERT on the board. To my great surprise, she recognized it. Some of the kids, watching me write it, said in amazement, "What's that for." I said, "What do you think?" Emily answered, "It's supposed to be 'microscopic.'" But she gave not the least sign of knowing that she was the person who had written MINCOPERT.

On the diagnostic spelling test, she spelled "tariff" as TEARERFIT. Today I thought I would try her again on it. This time she wrote TEARFIT. What does she do in such cases? Her reading aloud gives a clue. She closes her eyes and makes a dash for it, like someone running past a graveyard on a dark night. No looking back afterward, either.

Reminds me of a fragment of the Ancient Mariner—perhaps the world's best short ghost story:

Like one, that on a lonesome road
Doth walk in fear and dread,
And having once turned round walks on,
And turns no more his head;

Because he knows, a frightful fiend
Doth close behind him tread.

Is this the way some of these children make their way through life?

Holt begins the journal as a dialogue with himself: "I can't get Nell out of my mind. When she talked with me about fractions today, it was as if her mind rejected understanding." The pattern pulls on Holt's attention, though he cannot yet verbalize what it is. He writes to find out what the pattern is. To begin a trial exploration, he explains what he means by "producer-thinker" strategies, then gives another example of how several children performed in a classroom game, then continues the dialogue with himself about intelligence and learning, then tells of the seeming anomaly of a boy who was the "worst" student in the school but very intelligent in his life outside the school. The third entry, about a class Holt has observed, is addressed to the teacher of the class. In the fourth, he discusses, in his dialogue with himself, Ruth's behavior during a math test and Emily's attempts to spell "microscopic." Throughout the journal that became the book *How Children Fail,* Holt lets observations pull on his attention and writes to find out what the patterns are. The different ways he explores each journal entry may suggest ways for you to approach your how-it-happens instances. Do you differ with him in interpreting what the children are doing at certain points?

We call the passages "instances," though we could also call them incidents, events, episodes, tellings, accounts. If we understand the word "instances" properly, it's the most accurate word for our purpose. Within each passage is a core or central instance that could be stated in one or two lines—or be developed meaningfully in a more extended telling as you see in these instance collections. You may use one-line or one-sentence instances as support for or contrast with other marked patterns.

* * *

Here's a list of one-line instances that one author set down before she started telling each instance more fully in her how-it-happens exploration of school experiences in Baltimore in the early 1940s during World War II. She briefly noted each of the incidents that came to her mind, sometimes with a suggestion of an image that caught her attention, and sensed overall patterns emerging in the instance collection. She chose to see and write about herself in the third person.

Baltimore School Days
Joan Engel

Helen walked out of Stoneleigh School, wheeling her bike along, and saw her mother and dad coming up the walk to get her.

The children on the playground traded cards, and on the bus two cards, valuable ones, accidentally landed in Helen's lap and she kept them.

Mrs. Miller had a red face and yelled and Helen knew she didn't want her for a teacher but she got her.

Her first strong sexual feelings were for a "bad boy" in third grade who was in their class but was older and at recess she admired his ring.

Her teacher called her over in class and told her to stay away from that boy.

Mrs. Spencer's son was killed in the war and her window wore a gold star.

Mrs. O'Brien's son was killed when he ran across the street.

The Air Raid Wardens knocked at the door, wearing white helmets.

On the way home from school a boy pinched her nipples.

At Peggy's Halloween party they put their hands in spaghetti.

She played Queen of the Fairies with Mary Rose using sticks from the recently cut hedge for wands.

She got a cat, but it spit on her father and she had to give it back.

She watched herself in her neighbor's crystal ball.

Her mother cried when her period started.

She played strip poker with Susanne and Susanne's older brother and some other boys.

She fell deeply in love in Junior High and spoke the boy's name all the time.

He asked her to a dance and she got a high fever before the dance but went anyway.

Helen lent her cast-off evening gown to a girl who didn't have one.

They practiced chorus kicks to "Put Another Nickle in the Nickolodcan."

At Meadowbrook swimming pool they played "Mona Lisa."

She swam at Beaver Pond at night.

She didn't go to Saylor's Lake with Janet but stayed home with her parents.

She picked violets on the mansion grounds.

The new girl came to school and cried all the time and Helen made friends with her.

* * *

The following instances are excerpted from a collection called "Rats," written by Mike Schwarz while he was an undergraduate. He compares and contrasts, juxtaposes, people's encounters with rats and attitudes toward rats.

Rats
Mike Schwarz

There is a high, gray rippled metal fence, supported by a four foot foundation of concrete that surrounds the limestone quarry on 29th and Poplar. The huge hole is a whopping four city blocks square, and at least three hundred feet deep. The air down there is often ten degrees warmer than street level, and in the winter months young kids have been known to sneak down via the long twisting road that slithers like an earthworm down along one side of the crevasse. There are narrow holes in the fence where the bolts have rusted, and you can look down at the road, and the machinery on the bottom, and it all looks like a Tonka Toy set for a small child.

On one side, there is a now useless dumping area. Useless because there was a popular idea several years ago to fill the thing up with garbage and make a park out of it. The program had to be scrapped when the rat population became such a problem that

Summary-telling about the quarry

Illustrative incident of a woman's reaction to rats and of other people's reactions to her

people who lived in the area became fearful for their lives. One neighborhood woman recalled an encounter with one of the larger rodents. Eyes glaring, she said, it had somehow broken into her home and was seated on her sub-pump. Butcher knife in hand, she went after it not out of bravery, but out of a mother's protective instinct for the saiety of her child. The rat, upon first seeing her, just crouched slightly. She moved closer slowly. Slowly the knife raised above her head, and the rat, not more than three feet away now, just twitched his nose. Closing her eyes in anticipation of the gruesome sight of a skewered, gnawing rat, her arm stabbed downward. The rat, acting quickly, but not quickly enough, jumped out of serious harm's way. The knife, however, did manage to slice through the base of his thick tail. The woman happened to open her eyes just in time to see the rat scurry up the stairs, and out the door she had left open to quickly jettison the lifeless corpse (had she killed it).

After the initial shock of the incident, she confided in her neighbors. Most of them took her rather lightly. Joking, they asked her, "Cut off his tail with a butcher knife? Did you ever see such a sight in your life?" Even her husband had asked if she would use it to make a rat tail comb. This levity did not amuse her, and not only did she refuse to speak to the neighbors for several weeks, but it was rumored that her husband slept downstairs on the pool table for more than a month after.

Summary telling
of how people act
when they have
the rats trapped

The garbage, of course, had to be burned. Crews of men with protective leather boots stood out in the street waiting, large cans of poison sprays in their hands, for the rats to run from the flames in packs. Some died on the way up from exhaustion and smoke inhalation. Many were burned along with the trash. It is an eerie thought that lying among the rusted tin cans with singed labels, and hard weathered chunks of cindered garbage that carpet the quarry's floor, are the ghosts of many rats.

*   *   *

Model-place-
telling of the
theater and
where people sit
and why

There was a movie theatre located on Thirty First and Lowe Ave. called, appropriately enough, The Lowe Theatre. It serviced mostly the younger members of the community, showing such epic films as "The Ghost and Mr. Chicken." It had no marquee or balcony (I think it had one, but I also remember hearing that it collapsed soon after the building was completed) and a filthy little lobby that smelled of dust. The candy counter was covered with streaks of tape covering the cracks in the glass, and someone was always unscrewing the salt so that the next user would dump the entire contents on his popcorn. There were only three aisles, dividing the four sections. Mostly, everyone sat in the back row center. During a Saturday matinee it was the only safe place to sit. Throughout the film, like a background sound track, one could hear the steady pink pink pink pink of the Boston Baked Beans. They were the biggest selling candy. Not because of the taste, to be sure (every one hated them), but they hurt well enough if you hit someone in the head with one.

Narrative
example. See it
from "A lot of
things flew about"
to "and the black
splotch
remained. . . ."

A lot of things flew about during a show, popcorn boxes mostly, but one industrious kid snuck in a small balloon filled with black paint. As Don Knotts approached the blood covered keys of the organ which played by itself, a large black splash swept across his nose. Like a hand grenade it had been tossed on target. The house lights went on and the manager stormed into the center aisle. "Whose the god-damn painter?" he growled. Looking around, meeting everyone's eyes one at a time, he pointed back to the screen. The projector hadn't stopped and the image was hardly visible, but the black splat was as plain as day. "So you know how much that's gonna cost me? Everybody, let me see your hands." As if he were in a hold up, the manager demonstrated. Walking up and down the aisles he checked for tell-tale paint marks. There were none. "Now I'm gonna tell you. You want this place to look like a pig sty, that's how it's gonna stay. And

let me tell you, if I ever find out who did this I'll kick his ass from here to Chinatown."
Storming out, his face contorted by anger and frustration, the picture continued, and the
black splotch remained until the day the Board of Health closed the Lowe down, and
condemned it.

There was a popular joke at the time that went like this, "Going to the Lowe?
Don't drop your popcorn or you'll have to sit with your feet up for the rest of the show."
The reason? Rats.

Everybody knew they were there, but while no one was hurt, it was almost laugh-
able. They'd jump along the wall from radiator to radiator, flickering shadows in the
darkness. It was a game to spot one, until one hot July when someone had his leg dangling at the wrong place at the wrong time and the inevitable finally occurred. The rat bit
him on the ankle, and caused a considerable amount of swelling.

Model-telling of patrons' reactions to rats. Incident that changed "the game."

Scuttlebutt had it that he had been given the series of painful shots as a precaution
against rabies. The family decided to sue, but the theatre (a shaky financial establishment anyway) declared bankruptcy. The building was sold to a man interested in opening an electronics store. He had the rows of ripped leather chairs with back rests that
mothers warned their children not to touch, torn out, and entirely gutted the structure.

* * *

Rats come and rats go, but mostly they come. Where they come from is the river
front. You can see them, if you go to the fishery that sits quietly on the south bank. A
large bridge suspends across the river, and the rats use this to come to and fro. If you
want to sneak up on a rat and surprise him, here's what you do. You go down behind the
fishery, turn the headlights in your car off (don't go without a car). Pull up slowly to the
edge of the water, don't get too close. Many a rat scarer has ended up in the drink for
being careless. Wait awhile, until you can hear the scuttering of little feet under your
car. Watch out the front window, look toward the water. When all is quiet, and the ro-
dent population has finally turned out, suddenly TURN ON YOUR LIGHTS, AND KICK
ON YOUR BRIGHTS. Man, those rats will jump out of their skins. They'll race for the
waterfront and hide in the muddy weeds. Sound like fun? Try it sometime. Try it with a
girl friend. Threaten to make her walk home alone if she doesn't act right to you. You
never know, it might work.

Parodic how-to. Locate how-to elements and characteristics.

* * *

There is a triangle of small businesses located in an otherwise unpopulated area
just south of Chicago's famous Loop. The first, and largest in size of the three, is an auto
grave yard. Surrounded by a warped, weather beaten fence (made of ill fitting chunks of
plywood carrying the faded message "Monocko's Auto Parts) are the gutted hulls of
smashed, useless cars. Grizzly reminders of fatal accidents. Up through the floors of
these empty, rusted junks grow weeds, tall and straight. To the imaginative mind, they
almost appear to be oversized planters.

Model-place-telling

It is no secret to the owner of this waste field that residing in great numbers on his
property are large, dangerous rats. There is little he can do but acknowledge it. Rats
tend to live in areas where they can move about freely, and any attempt to get rid of
them will ultimately end in vain. Instead, he has learned to live with them. That is why
he carries a large baseball bat, fully covered with black tape, with him whenever disman-
tling a part from a car. He uses it to beat hard on the frame of the car before doing work
of any kind. This scares the rats away, and so far he has never been bitten, although
there have been many close calls.

Suspenseful change in place telling—"it is no secret. . . ."

Model-telling of owner's reactions to rats

Once, after pounding on the dented hood of a car he needed the left front door
from, he sat on the ripped interior, and began working from the inside. It was cold out,

Narrative
example. See it
from "Once, after
pounding . . ." to
"mouth gaping,
on the hard
ground . . ."

and his hands were covered with warm, bulky gloves that made it difficult to hold the screw driver. It slipped down through a hole rusted away near the brake pedal. Reaching through it, he started groping for the tool, when something began tugging at one finger on his hand. Scared and panicked, he pulled, struggling to release his hand, but the rusted tin cut through the skin along his arm, and several stitches were needed.

Later that day he returned to the car, with his bat, and a hammer. The bat, of course, was used to bang away on the hood. The hammer was to pound out the hole in the floor. It took him somewhat longer with his left hand, as the stitches were in the right.

He pounded hard, orange chips flying everywhere, until his curiosity was satisfied. He had noticed small, toothy indentations on the middle finger of his glove, and thought that a rat might have been what scared him. He had almost dismissed that thought, however, because a rat's teeth would have chewed right through the leather. Unless it was a small rat, or a weak one. Or a rat on the verge of death. Like the one he found, mouth gaping, on the hard ground underneath the car.

Model-place-
telling

The second business of the three is a small, make-shift fruit stand, that pops up suddenly in the spring, and disappears by mid-autumn. Judging from the quality of their produce, it is hard to believe they throw anything away, but it's true. Day after day the burst melons pile on top of the dark, rotted leaves of lettuce that line the bottom of the garbage cans. When these cans are full, they continue to dump on top of them, and at night the piles of edible garbage attract the rats from the auto yard across the street. As

Narrative of
incident that
changed the
situation

long as the rats confined their meals to the early morning hours, the owner was content to leave them alone. But one evening he accidentally left his rear door open, and rats in multitudes rushed in to gorge themselves on fresh fruit and vegetables.

Opening the stand as usual the next day, he noticed shreds of green tissue (used to wrap the pears) scattered around the floor. He checked a crate near-by, and found a rat, tail curled about its furry body, sleeping soundly. Enraged, he screamed and kicked the box over, stomping his foot through the wooden slats. The crate caught above the ankle, and he was hopping and kicking when an elderly woman walked in with the intention of buying corn. The rat scurried out through her frail, black stockinged legs, and she leaned against the frame of the doorway, mouth open in a silent scream. The owner, who as yet did not notice her, was swinging a broom under a table yelling, "C'mon outta there you sonofabitching rats!." The old woman gasped for air, and stumbled out the door. The owner turned, and face flushed with embarrassment, he followed her out, and pretended to be sweeping. "Can I help you with anything?" he asked. "Pears are special today." She waved him away, and leaned weakly against the bus stop.

Model-place-
telling

Narrative of
puzzling
occurrences
concerning a rat
trap. Note
familiarity: "(it
would jam on
dimes)"

The third and most prosperous business of the three is a full service gas station. Because of its location, right across the alley from the fruit stand, the owner of this six pump, two rack garage has had several problems with the rats. Not to mention the sour smell of rotted fruit that persisted even stronger than the fumes of gas and oil. On one of these occasions, the owner was almost convinced he had the smartest rat in the world, because for three days, it appeared he had stolen the bait without tripping the trap.

One afternoon, after making a pot of coffee, this owner reached for his box of sugar only to find it had fallen down behind a cabinet. One side of the box had been chewed through, and checking the heavy sliding door in the back by the auto racks, he saw that it had been left about an inch from the ground. Fearing the rat might still be lurking around, he went over to the metal strong box that held his most expensive tools, and produced a brown stained rat trap. Putting three nickels into his candy machine (it would jam on dimes) he bought a bag of peanuts and put one under the trigger for bait. After setting the trap, he decided to place it along the base boards of the wall near the cabinet where he'd found the box of sugar.

When closing time came, he checked the trap, and discovered the bait was gone, but the trap was still set. He touched the trigger lightly with a rag. The metal bar sprung back with a muffled snap. The trap was fine, but the rat must have managed somehow to work the peanut out. He set the trap again with another peanut and closed up for the day. Again, in the morning, the trap was set, and the bait gone. He set it once more, and it happened still again. Setting it a fourth time, he kept a watchful eye. Toward midday, he noticed the trap was engulfed by a quivering black mass of ants. Working together, they carried the peanut away, until he killed them with a huge pan of boiling water.

Another time, though, he did catch a rat in the trap. But it was so large the bar wasn't enough to kill it. He had to pick it up with a pair of long-nosed pliers, and carry it outside to a garbage can full of water. The wood on the trap made it float, and the rat had to be held under the surface for fifteen minutes before he finally died. But for every rat killed, many more are born, and it will be some time long in the future before all of the rats are gone from this triangle of small businesses located just before the outskirts of Chicago's famous Loop.

*   *   *

Rats weren't the only problem to plague Finnigan Park. In truth, the building was old and outdated. A new park was designed to replace the old one. A new field house, more baseball diamonds, tennis courts, even an indoor swimming pool. The new building was built in one summer, because it was really just "assembled," like an erector set. Piece by piece the prefabricated parts were put together. Occasionally vandals would delay the progress by pouring bags of cement in the empty pool, just after a heavy rain, or by kicking down wooden frames within the hollow structure. But the workers always managed to continue.

Soon after its completion the old building was demolished. The fence around the outdoor swimming pool was uprooted and dismantled. Kids hurled junk by the armloads into the slanted floor of the huge cement hole. The rats from the building wandered aimlessly through the junk at night, always avoiding the pool to bypass it on their way to the alley. Occasionally, though, one did manage to fall in, and there was no way of getting out. The shallow end of the pool was two feet high.

The next day, the workmen would come and begin tearing the insides out after knocking over walls with a ball and chain. Old men sitting on benches watched the destruction. Sometimes they turned around and spat. The rat ran from side to side, over and over again looking for a way out. At four o'clock it finally came.

The workmen knock off around three, and most of the grammar schools in the area ring the final bell somewhere about three-fifteen. This means by three forty-five, the park is swarming with kids. By four, one of these will have noticed the rat trapped on the bottom of the pool.

Bricks certainly aren't scarce on a demolition site, and this kid would only have to walk maybe two or three feet away to gather quite an armful. By throwing them down hard on the concrete, they break into nice, easy to handle chunks. The rat is running along the sides of the pool endlessly, so the hunter would have to walk the circumference of the pool in order to get a clear shot. Arm cocked behind his head, he fires! The dull thud that echoes up says that he's missed. He tries again, and again. Soon more kids wander over to see what he's doing, and fascinated they join in the fun. Behind them, the wind blows through the trees, scattering the autumn-colored leaves across the field.

The rat darts one way, then the next. It seems to have no feet, just wheels that instinctively know when to turn. The crowd grows, and the bricks come down in a steady rain. One strikes the rat in its hind quarters, throwing it to one side. Apparently stunned, it just sits there, leaning against the side wall. One youth dashes to the side

Narration of
another incident

and struggles with a heavy chunk of sidewalk. Another helps him, and carrying it one on each end they swing counting . . . one . . . two . . . three . . . The huge chunk lands on the rat's head, smashing it paper thin. Most of the kids continue throwing stones. Twenty minutes later, everyone is gone.

"Rats" is a sort of fictional realism, that is, the author took many anecdotes, observations, and other "research" about rats and fictionalized it. He imagined the incidents, saw them happening in his mind during his writing, and retold them as fictional realism.

The storyteller in "Rats" speaks directly and authoritatively to us in his own voice. Locate words, phrases, sentences, that give you the feeling of the storyteller talking directly to you, almost as a citizen of the area, or as a researcher familiar with it. He stands at a little distance and tells us about his research, inviting us into the process of discovery. Locate moments that indicate the author's familiarity with the scenes. Describe the different attitudes toward rats by people in the several instances.

How does the author draw you suspensefully into the tellings of the instances? How do the voice and imagery together make you see and feel the events? In the first paragraph, notice how the author tells the scene from a distance, from his own researcher's point of view. In the second paragraph, notice how he tells it both from the storyteller's point of view and the point of view of the woman trying to kill the rat on her sub-pump with a butcher knife, almost as if we are looking over her shoulder and have access to some of her feelings at the same time. Examine the point of view of the other instances.

* * *

In the following set of "instances," each entry is about a particular aspect of hoboing.

"Hoboing"
From *Pages from a Worker's Life*
William Z. Foster

DANGERS ON THE ROAD

Railroading in those years was very dangerous for train and engine crews, but incomparably more so for hoboes. Besides hunger and cold, the hobo was confronted with a maze of perils. Death laid in wait for him at every turn. The hobo might dash his brains out or be cut to pieces while jumping on or off a rapidly moving train; he might fall from the top of a swaying box-car or be swept off by a low bridge of whose presence he was unaware; he might have his head torn off by a car or railroad structure that was not "in the clear"; he might be crushed between telescoping cars or mangled in wrecks. Broken bodies of hoboes were constantly picked up along the railroad right-of-way, and hurried off to nameless graves in local Potter's Fields.

Experienced hoboes, wise to the ways of the road, like veteran soldiers in war, were able to shield themselves somewhat from the thickly-strewn hazards. But green hoboes, "gay cats," walked into these dangers blindly and were mowed down in hundreds. The latter exposed themselves to disaster especially in their frantic efforts to hide from trainmen and bulls.

One of the deadliest and prolific sources of death to hoboes was the shifting of loads in cars. Often, by rough switching in yards or by a heavy application of the airbrakes on the road, the cars were so violently jerked as to literally catapult their loads against the car ends, smashing them out. Worst of all cargoes in this respect was lumber, especially planed lumber. Expert boes were always very careful about riding in cars with loads liable to shift, and especially to keep away from the chief danger spot, the forward-end of the car. But greenhorn hoboes were frequently killed or badly injured.

Once in Avery, Idaho, while beating my way over the Milwaukee, I was walking through the local yards when I noticed a knot of railroad men gathered around a freight car in a train that had just arrived from the West. I went over and found a horrible sight. It was a box-car loaded with planed lumber, and on the heavy grades in the Bitterroot Mountains the slippery, treacherous load had shifted so hard as to break out the whole forward-end of the car. A hobo had been killed in the shift. His bones were crushed like pipe-stems and his flesh was smeared against the shattered car-end. I shuddered and passed by as they gathered up what they could of the shapeless mass and put it into a wheelbarrow.

Low bridges also killed many hoboes. Trainmen knew where these fatal obstacles were located, but even they often got caught. To a hobo who did not even know of their existence such bridges were a deadly menace, especially in the dark. One night, while I was beating my way east through Maryland over the Baltimore & Ohio railroad, a hobo was riding several cars ahead of me. He wanted to cross over a couple of cars to an open gondola where the riding would be easier. But hardly had he climbed to the top of the box-car when he crashed into a low wagon-road bridge and was instantly killed.

A special horror that all expert hoboes constantly bore in mind was the danger of being locked in a car and left at some isolated point to starve. Railroad annals record many cases where this occurred. It could easily happen. A trainman or yard-bull going along a train finds a box-car door unlocked and locks it. The green hobo inside, afraid of being arrested or ditched, keeps still. Then on the road the train crew sets out this particular car on a siding because of a "hot-box," a pulled "lung" (wrecked coupling) or for some other reason. The hobo locked inside, not knowing what all the switching is about, is careful to make no noise that might attract the train crew. Finally, however, when he hears the train whistle he becomes alarmed and tries to get out. If the car is at some frequented spot he is not so bad off; the worst that will happen to him is to be slugged or thrown in jail. But if the car happens to be at some desert siding, maybe miles from the nearest house, then this unfortunate hobo faces the prospect of dying from hunger and thirst. Many's the time trainmen and car inspectors have opened foul-smelling box-cars and discovered dead hoboes, starved to death.

RIDING THE TRUCKS

Much skill was needed in hoboing, especially in the mountain and desert regions of the West. As a rule the best hoboes were native-born Americans. They possessed a knowledge of the railroads and the country which gave them a self-confidence such as the foreign-born hobo seldom acquired.

There were many methods of beating one's way over the railroads. First, there were those slick elements who—through faked passes, stolen hat checks and other devices—"rode the cushions." But the bulk of the hoboes did not know how to work these dodges, and rode the freight and passenger trains.

On a freight train there were many places to ride—inside box-cars and gondolas, in ice-boxes of refrigerator cars, on body rods under the cars, on the locomotive tenders, etc. Only greenhorns rode the "bumpers" between the cars, because here they were most exposed to shacks, police and accidents. From one hundred to three hundred miles of road was a day's run for a 'bo by freight.

But "fast" hoboes scorned freights and rode passenger trains whenever possible. On passenger trains, or "rattlers," they rode the "blinds," the "rods," the side-boxes on Pullman diners, vestibules, the steps, the men's washrooms and the car tops. They also rode the locomotive pilots, or "cow-catchers," and even the engine brakebeams.

But when it came to really getting over the road in a hurry, the expert hobo made for the trucks, or wheel structure under the passenger coaches. There, hidden in a maze of axles, wheels and springs, it was difficult for police or trainmen to find him. He could ride day and night and make long "jumps." I remember once how Frank Little, one of the fastest hoboes in the I.W.W., and a brave fighter who was lynched in Butte during the war while leading a miners' strike, held down the trucks of the Overland Limited from Chicago without a break all the way to Ogden, Utah. There, hungry and exhausted, he got off, ate and slept, caught the Limited twenty-four hours later and rode her right into Oakland, California.

Riding the trucks was something that only experienced hoboes ventured. It was packed full of danger. One had to know precisely what he was about, or face disaster. Even with all his skill he might easily be cut to pieces. When a 'bo crawled into the trucks he usually had only a minute or two to do so, and if, once inside, he found he had made a mistake and there was no place for him to ride in that particular kind of truck, he was a good candidate for Potter's Field, as he would hardly have time to get out before the train started.

My first ride on the trucks was on the Northern Pacific, between Missoula and Butte, Montana, on my way to New York. I'll never forget the experience. I had made two coast-to-coast trips already and considered myself an expert hobo, before I finally ventured upon trying the trucks, my favorite riding place on rattlers being the tops.

Missoula was a tough town at the time, with hostile shacks and bulls, and there was no chance to ride a freight or the tops of a rattler. So I decided to hit the trucks. It was about a three-hour run to Butte. But just how to get into the trucks was not altogether clear. I had no time to lose, as the passenger train was about to pull out. Selecting a rear car, I crawled over the brakebeam and across the axle. I was now in the very heart of the truck. I had to figure out instantly how to place myself in order to ride, for the train began to move. To get out alive from the truck would now have been impossible.

The way I rode was as follows: There was a brakerod, or bottom rod, connecting the two brakebeams of the truck. It was so low it cleared the rails by only a few inches. Upon this slender rod I had to sit. There I balanced myself by bracing my shoulders against the truck frame on one side and my feet against the truck frame on the opposite side. This left me riding sidewise to the direction of the train, with my feet raised as high as my head. The thin rod cut into my seat, the whirling axle was within three or four inches of my elbow, and the roaring wheels were even closer to my shoulders and feet. It was a cramped, uncomfortable and dangerous position, but a good one for knocking off the miles, and this was all that counted.

As the train rapidly gained headway, the one-inch brakerod I was sitting on sagged heavily under my weight. The car rumbled over a switch, and the rod cleared the rails by hardly more than an inch or two. My heart "popped into my mouth." I shivered at such a narrow margin and tried not to think of what would happen to me if the brakerod should come loose, bend down more or break outright, or if we should run across one of those pieces of wire that are frequently to be found snagged in the ballast between the tracks. In any of these cases I should be instantaneously cut to pieces, as hundreds of hoboes had been before me.

In my narrow quarters, I had nothing between me and sudden death but the slender brakerod. I had difficulty in balancing myself on my precarious perch, with the jerking and bouncing of the truck. The roar of the train was so deafening that I could not even "hear myself think." I was pelted with stones and half smothered with dust, picked up by the rushing train. Many a hobo has been knocked off the trucks by such stones or actually suffocated while crossing long sections of dusty roadbed. And an even greater danger, I was peppered with hot coals dropped by the locomotive. Fortunately I knew enough not to ride too close to the head-end of the train, because there hoboes are sometimes badly burned by the spray of blazing coals, and even forced to let go their hold and fall beneath the wheels.

The first stop out of Missoula was Garrison, a one-and-a-half-hours' run. I did not think I could stick it out that far. My situation was alarming. But as time went on I began to get a little used to the terrific roar, the cramped quarters, the unnatural and painful position of my body, the precariousness of my brakerod seat and the acute sense of danger; so that when we reached Garrison I decided to ride it out to Butte, and I did. Arrived there, I felt that now I was indeed a real hobo.

After that I made dozens of divisions on the trucks of rattlers. The trucks became my favorite place to ride, and so accustomed to all their inconveniences did I become that I eventually had to watch out for a special danger of the experienced hobo, that of falling asleep on the trucks and tumbling beneath the wheels. I later made many a long and hard trip on the trucks, but I never had such a thrilling ride as that first one from Missoula to Butte.

DEATH AT MY FEET

On the railroads sudden death grasps at the hobo from most unexpected quarters. I had scores of narrow escapes. A day's riding that did not contain some deadly peril was exceptional. And usually the danger situation developed so swiftly that one hardly had time to think before it was all over.

How unexpectedly a hobo may get into mortal difficulty was illustrated to me one night in The Dalles, Oregon. I was just finishing a transcontinental trip from Galveston, Texas, and The Dalles was my destination. It was a very hostile town, and they were sentencing hoboes to four months in jail. I had heard this, so I rode on the top (roof) of a passenger coach several cars back from the engine, in order not to be "glommed" by the bulls in the depot.

The train pulled into the station, and I could see the police giving her the once-over at both ends and along the sides. What was I to do? I simply had to get off at The Dalles, as the next stop was many miles away. Evidently I couldn't go to either the head or hind-end of the train, so I decided to leap to a string of box-cars on the next track. It was a difficult jump, as there was a gap of several feet and I had a very bad take-off from the rounded passenger car-roof, which was covered with ice.

I waited until the train started to pull out and then rose to jump. Just then a 'bo beside me shouted, "For Christ's sake, don't jump, you'll be killed," and he clutched at my coat-tail. He got enough of a grip to check my jump. But I managed to light on the very edge of the box-car. There I teetered precariously for a moment or two on the verge of falling between the moving cars, which would have been certain death. Fortunately, I caught my balance and righted myself. Quickly I clambered down from the box-car and disappeared in the yards, evading the police. In spite of the cold night I was covered with sweat. It was just an everyday incident in the life of a hobo.

Many times, while hoboing, I found myself in similarly dangerous situations, but my most agonizing experience occurred while I was beating my way over the Great Northern. I was eastbound and had just hopped a freight train leaving Havre, Montana. The yards were full of bulls, so I couldn't look her over and find an inside place to ride, but had caught her on the fly. I grabbed the first thing that came along, a gondola loaded with coal. It was a bitterly cold night, far below zero, and I had to locate a better place, so, although it was extremely hazardous for a 'bo to wander over a train top at night, I decided to do it in the hope of finding an open end-door or top-door of a box-car.

I started forward on the swaying, surging train, and I had crossed a few box-cars when I struck another gondola. It was here that I nearly came to grief, trying to climb from this gondola to the roof of the adjoining box-car. Ordinarily it was not difficult to stand on a gondola-end, throw myself over to the box-car end and elbow up onto the running board on the box-car roof. I had often done it before. But this time, as I was trying to get my elbows upon the roof running-board, the box car gave a big lurch that broke my grip, and in a fraction of a second I found myself hanging at arm's length from the roof running-board.

This put me in a strange position. Hanging from the box-car roof, I had no footing beneath me. A couple of feet below were the narrow, swaying couplers. To let go and drop down upon the jiggling couplers would mean almost certainly to fall beneath the wheels. For there was hardly a chance that I could maintain my balance on the couplers, leaping and dancing as they were, long enough to spring back upon the gondola-end. If I were to let go death would be the result.

Evidently to get out of my predicament I had to climb up onto the box-car roof. But how? The box-car end was quite flat and smooth, with no toe-hold anywhere. There was no brakestaff or end-door upon which to get a purchase for my foot. I tried several times to "chin" myself up to the roof running-board and then clamber up onto the roof. But with my exhaustion from hard riding, the wild swaying of the box-car, with my hands in gloves, and my poor grip on the roof running-board, I simply could not make it. After many fruitless attempts, I dropped back to my old position of hanging at arm's length from the roof flat against the smooth car-end.

Things began to look black. I did not dare to drop down upon the couplers and I could not climb onto the roof; I had no idea when the train would stop, and there was no way to notify the train crew of my difficulty. Besides, it was desperately cold. I did not know what to do. I felt I was facing death. But I was more angry than frightened; angry that I, an expert hobo, had allowed myself to get into such a jam.

I realized that sooner or later I would be forced to let go. The strain was so great I felt my arms were being pulled from their sockets. My fingers seemed to be paralyzed, or frozen. I became truly alarmed. The hungry-looking wheels appeared to be reaching up for me. I finally resolved upon a plan. I would hang on as long as I could, but if I reached the end of my endurance before the train halted, I would let go, drop onto the swaying couplers and then, practically with the same motion; try to leap clear of the speeding train.

It was a desperate expedient, with only a faint hope for success. I tried not to think of where my flying leap from the rapidly moving train might land me, even if I escaped falling beneath the wheels. But my plan offered a better chance for me than to drop onto the swaying couplers and try to balance myself there even long enough to grab the top of the gondola. I was certain that if I tried the latter I would be thrown beneath the wheels and ground to pieces.

With my desperate plan in mind, I hung on to the roof running-board. How long I don't know. I felt it was an hour or more. My arms were numb, my strength was rapidly failing and my mind was in torture. The agony seemed endless. Suddenly I heard the engine "whistle in" to a station. A quick flash of relief passed over me. The pain seemed to leave my arms and I grew stronger. Now I really did hang on for dear life. The train slowed down and stopped. I dropped on the coupler and got off the train. I was almost in a state of collapse, but our stopping place was only a desert siding and I had to keep going. I managed to find a satisfactory place on the train and rode out the division. For two weeks afterward my sore arms and three frozen fingers were constant reminders of how I almost left my bones along Jim Hill's railroad, and to my dying day I shall not forget this odd adventure.

Notice how Foster begins not only entries but paragraphs with a definite statement, gives details and instances to support the statement, and concludes paragraphs and entries with strong wrap-up statements. Examine "Dangers on the Road," which tells of the special ways hoboes can get killed, for its definite beginning statement of what the entry will be about, its examples and illustrations, and its strong concluding statement and image. Examine the beginnings, the development, and the endings of other entries. Despite the similarities of a strong structure for each entry, how does Foster also treat each entry differently? Locate passages in which he tells us how things were done. Locate entries that make a general statement of pattern and then give a narrative example to support the statement. Describe the pattern of each paragraph in "Dangers on the Road."

Find phrases and words in any entry, such as the use of the participle "jiggling" in "the jiggling couplers" in "Death at My Feet," which demonstrate the use of common adjectives, verbs, and adverbs to make an unusual situation come through clearly. Locate the hobo slang that gives us the feeling of "being there" and also tells precisely what's happening.

* * *

The following selections, one from *The Year of the Gorilla* by George Schaller and the other from *The Voyage of the Beagle* by Charles Darwin, were developed from extensive field notes and journal entries kept over long periods of time, 500 hours of direct observation for Schaller, four years nine months and two days on the *Beagle's* voyage for Darwin. Schaller and Darwin were observers who deliberately went to see what patterns would emerge from instances of, as in Schaller's case, the behavior of mountain gorillas and, in Darwin's, the observations of animals, birds, and plants found on the *Beagle's* voyage.

"A Gorilla Day"
From **The Year of the Gorilla**
George Schaller

Characteristically, the gorilla sits and reaches for food in all directions, only to move a few steps and sit again. The only sounds are the snapping of branches, the smacking of lips, and an occasional belch. Infants stay with their mothers and probably learn what to eat and what not to eat by watching them. In this way, food habits are handed down from generation to generation, a primitive form of culture. Once I saw a youngster take a partially eaten *Vernonia* branch from the hands of its mother and gnaw out the remains of the pith. And on another occasion an infant pulled down the lip of its mother and extracted a bit of bed straw which it then ate. Sometimes infants bite into plants which the adults do not use. One tiny fellow stuffed some lichen into his mouth but hurriedly spat them out. When another infant began to gnaw on the petiole of a *Hagenia* leaf, which adults do not consume, its mother reached over and took the leaf away from it. Yet in all my hours of observation I never saw a mother actually hand food to her infant, like Kortlandt, the animal behaviorist, who watched female chimpanzees in the wild give pieces of paw-paw fruit to their young.

Infants also have to learn how to eat certain foods. The leaf of the bed straw, for example, has three rows of small hooks, which readily adhere to fur and are abrasive to the skin. Adults handle the vine carefully, as one entry from my field notes illustrates:

> A sitting female reaches forward and with her right hand bends some *Senecio tri-chopterygius* toward her, and with her left hand pulls off strands of *Galium*. After examining the vine closely, she removes several dry leaves with her lips. Then she picks out several dry *Galium* stems between thumb and index finger, using first one hand and then the other. Finally she pushes the *Galium* several times against her partly-opened lips while twisting the vegetation around in her hand, thus forming a tight green wad in which all leaves adhere to each other. She stuffs the mass into her mouth and chews.

Small infants have not yet learned to make this tight wad, and they laboriously stuff the long strands into the mouth.

Feeding slows down considerably as the morning progresses, and the apes become leisurely gourmets as they wander about, choosing a leaf here, a bit of bark there. The following observation from my report illustrates this leisurely feeding behavior in Junior, the blackbacked male of Group IV, during a half-hour period.

> Junior sits and peers intently at the vegetation, reaches over, and bends the stalk of a *Senecio trichopterygius* to one side. He stretches far out and with a quick twist decapitates a *Helichrysum*. After stuffing the leafy top into his mouth, he looks around and spots two more plants of the same species, which he also eats in similar fashion. He then yanks some wild celery, including the root, from the ground, and with rapid sideways and backward jerks of the head bites apart the stalk before gnawing out the pith. The sun appears briefly, and Junior rolls onto his back. But soon the sun hides behind a cloud, and Junior changes to his side, holding the sole of the right foot with the right hand. After about ten motionless minutes, he suddenly sits up, reaches far out, slides his hand up the stalk of a *Carduus afromontanus*, thus collecting the leaves in a bouquet which he pushes with petioles first into his mouth. This is followed by a leafy thistle top, prickles and all, and a *Helichrysum*. He then leaves his seat, ambles ten feet, and returns to his former place, carrying a thistle in one hand and a *Helichrysum* in the other. After eating the plants he sits hunched over for fifteen minutes. The rest of the group feeds slightly uphill, and Junior suddenly rises and moves toward the other members, plucking and eating a *Helichrysum* on the way. A giant senecio has been torn down by another gorilla, and Junior stops and rips off a leafy top. From the stem he bites large splinters until only a two-inch section of pith remains in his hand, which he eats. A strand of bed straw follows, and just before he moves out of sight, a final *Helichrysum*.

Gorillas require about two hours of feeding to become satiated in the morning, and each animal is so intent on filling its belly that it has little time for anything else. Scattered over fifty yards of terrain, the gorillas are frequently out of each other's sight in the dense undergrowth. But movement is usually so slow that there is little danger of their becoming separated from the group. Between nine and ten o'clock, the foraging generally comes slowly to a stop. The great amount of forage which the gorillas have by then consumed provides not only the needed nourishment but also the water. I have never seen gorillas drink in the wild. There is little permanent water at Kabara, for the runoff rapidly disappears in the porous soil and rock. But the vegetation is succulent, rain is frequent, and dew lies heavily on the foliage, all providing moisture for the gorilla's diet.

From midmorning to midafternoon is siesta time. The members of the group are pictures of utter contentment as they lie crowded around the silverbacked male, especially when the sun shines warmly on their bodies. Many loll on the ground, lying on their back, belly, or side, arms and legs askew; others lean in a sitting position against the trunks of trees. If gorillas had a religion, they would surely be sun worshippers. Once in awhile a gorilla constructs a nest in which to rest. These nests are in no way distinguishable from those built for sleeping at night except that the packed-down vegetation of the night nests indicates that they have been occupied for a long time. On December 14, one of the juveniles in group VII built himself such a nest in a *Hypericum* tree some twenty feet above ground. The youngster stood in a crotch and pulled in small pliable branches with one hand and stuffed them down under its feet. After breaking in about ten branches in this manner, the basic platform of the nest was constructed. The juvenile then pushed down on the mass with its hands and feet. Next it pulled in all protruding twigs, broke them, and packed them down along the nest rim. As a final touch, it snapped off several small branches that still reared up from the nest. The construction time was five minutes.

In effect, the leading silverbacked males of groups are dictators who by virtue of their size and position always get their way. But these males also are tolerant and gentle, and this is especially evident during the periods of rest. The females and youngsters in the group genuinely seem to like their leader, not because he is dominant, but because they enjoy his company. Sometimes a female rested her head in his silver saddle or leaned heavily against his side. As many as five youngsters occasionally congregated by the male, sitting by his legs or in his lap, climbing up on his rump, and generally making a nuisance of themselves. The male ignored them completely, unless their behavior became too uninhibited. Then a mere glance was sufficient to discipline them.

Sleeping, dozing, and sitting are not the only activities of the gorilla during the noon siesta. Some animals may be engaged with their morning toilet, scratching and grooming themselves. Much of the scratching starts in an exploratory manner with the fingers being merely moved against the grain of the hair, much as a man searches through the hair on his head. When something is noted, it is scratched off and occasionally eaten. A gorilla may groom itself very intently by slowly bending aside the hairs on the upper arm, or on another part of the body, to expose a piece of skin, which is then examined closely for possible imperfections, flaky bits of skin, or parasites. Females groom themselves twice as frequently as males, and juveniles do so more often than females. I could not find out why this difference exists, but somehow I cannot quite imagine that the average youngster merely shows a greater concern over his cleanliness than a female. Infants groom themselves rarely, probably because their mothers usually do it for them. When the youngster is small, the mother usually lays it in her lap or drapes it over one arm, then carefully grooms its pelage by parting the hairs. At such times her lips are pursed and her eyes watch her active fingers from a distance of six inches or less as if she were terribly shortsighted. She pays special attention to the cleanliness of the rectal region, which in youngsters is marked by a tuft of white hair like a fluff of cotton. The infants do not at all enjoy being turned upside down to have their anus inspected. They wiggle and squirm and kick, but the mother firmly persists with utter calmness. Never was a young gorilla chastised by being slapped. As the infants grow older, they tend to be groomed in a more cursory manner. For example, one two-year-old was sitting beside its mother when she reached over, gathered it into her arms, and affectionately nuzzled its shoulder before grooming its arm. The infant suddenly reached up and put both arms around her neck in an embrace.

It has frequently been asserted that, in general, grooming strengthens and maintains the social bond between members of a monkey or ape group. Gorillas, however, have the disconcerting habit of refusing to comply with the premature generalizations that have been made about primates. If indeed mutual grooming strengthens the social bond in gorillas, one would expect the activity to be frequent between adults, as is the case in baboons. Yet I never saw a female groom a silverbacked male, and between females I saw it happen only five times. Once, for instance, two females sat near each other. One reached over, tapped the other on the upper arm with the back of the hand, rose, and pointedly turned her rump toward the face of the sitting female. The latter then groomed the indicated area. Thus, grooming between adult gorillas seems to be mainly utilitarian, confined primarily to the rump and back and other parts of the body which the animal itself cannot reach with ease.

Juveniles seemingly use grooming as a means of initiating social contact with a female. Juveniles are at an awkward social age, being too young to function as full members of the group, yet too old to receive the preferential treatment that is accorded infants: they are like teenagers in our society. Occasionally a juvenile ambles by a female, presumably its mother, and suddenly begins to groom her or her small infant, thereby achieving the desired social contact. When, on rare occasions, a female does not want the juvenile by her side, she merely snaps at or swats it. Juveniles sometimes take small infants gently out of the arms of their mothers and carry them a short distance. But when the infant squirms or in any way shows distress, the mother immediately rescues it.

Schaller compares and contrasts instances to find patterns of likenesses. He gives statements of patterns that result from observation of many similar incidents, examples of how these similar incidents occur, examples of single events that either support or stand in contrast to the patterns, and two full journal entries of the kind that supplied the basic observations for the whole essay. The journal entries are fully developed in themselves and give us particularly illustrative, detailed tellings of what the author saw.

Anomalous instances not only make contrasts that point up distinctive patterns but also suggest other patterns, such as the suggestion that gorillas learn from experimentation. When Schaller compares and contrasts his instances of gorilla feeding behavior, he finds many instances that are so much alike that he tells a single scene unrolling before our eyes that gives a general pattern, "Characteristically, the gorilla sits and reaches for food in all directions . . .," then two individual incidents to illustrate points about feeding as learned behavior, another statement of pattern "Sometimes infants bite into plants . . .," then two incidents about infants and feeding as learned behavior, ending with another statement of patterns comparing gorilla and chimpanzee mothers' behavior in feeding and not feeding their infants. The excerpt ends with a discussion of dominance among gorillas, giving imagery that enables us to see clearly how their dominance relationships actually work.

He finds sufficient repetition of like instances about the midafternoon siesta that he can give another single scene for a pattern, "The members of the group are pictures of utter contentment as they lie crowded around the silverbacked male. . . ." Other model-telling images result from his comparing instances and finding enough repetition that one image can be made to demonstrate the pattern. He also makes statements about patterns, such as "The females and youngsters in the group genuinely seem to like their leader . . ." and contrasts patterns such as: "Females groom themselves twice as frequently as males, and juveniles do so more often than females." He makes you *see* each instance of gorilla behavior, each pattern.

Who does Schaller feel to be the audience for the journal and who the audience for the book?

* * *

Here's one brief excerpt from a research article, "The Behavior of the Mountain Gorilla," that Schaller wrote for an audience of professionals and students of primate studies. He uses the same basic observations for this article as for the book, *The Year of the Gorilla,* but treats the material in a different way. In the Study Methods excerpt, note how he makes pattern-statements for his two major methods of observation, compares and contrasts them, and then gives specific journal entries to illustrate the success of his best method. When we *see* what happened, we *understand* what happened. Schaller makes sure we see what happened.

From
"The Behavior of the Mountain Gorilla"
George Schaller

STUDY METHODS

Gorillas are usually not difficult to locate, for if a fresh trail is found the trampled vegetation, food remnants, dung, and other spoor aid in leading the tracker to the animals. In most areas, however, gorillas inhabit such dense vegetation that prolonged daily observations are difficult, if not impossible. The habitat with the best visibility was the Hagenia woodland in the Virunga Volcanoes, primarily because a shrub stratum was almost absent.

Two methods were used in observing gorillas. They were viewed from the cover of a tree trunk, with the observer remaining undetected by the animals; or they were approached by the observer slowly, alone, and in full view, to within about 150 feet, with the hope that after repeated contacts they would become habituated to his presence. The former method had only limited value, for the gorillas, with senses comparable to those of man, frequently detected me. The value of the latter method was shown by the fact that after from 10 to 15 prolonged contact periods some groups became so well habituated that their daily routine was little affected. Animals occasionally approached to within 15 feet of me, and once climbed into the same tree in which I was sitting. An excerpt from my field notes illustrates the casual manner in which group VII responded to my close proximity after 78 observation periods.

08:30 I advance inadvertently to within 30 feet of a foraging group. After I have settled myself on a low branch 5 feet above ground, a female with an infant on her back spots me, looks intently, and then continues to feed. A juvenile backs into the vegetation upon seeing me, and when the silver-backed male glances over from a distance of 45 feet he emits an annoyed grunt. However, the animals continue to sit and feed leisurely in the sun within 25 to 60 feet of my observation post.

09:30 Foraging slows down and ceases entirely as the animals rest in the sun within 40 to 60 feet of me.

10:30 Two animals begin to snack, and 10 minutes later the silver-backed male rises, looks at me seemingly startled and roars three times. He begins to feed and the whole group joins him. During the following 25 minutes the group moves some 500 feet and then settles into another rest area.

Compare the style of "The Behavior of the Mountain Gorilla" to the style of the excerpt from *The Year of the Gorilla*. Notice the pronouns that Schaller uses to refer to himself in the two different kinds of writing.

* * *

Compare Schaller's writing about gorillas to the following excerpt from Darwin's writing about tortoises in the Galapagos Islands.

"The Galapagos Tortoise"
From **The Voyage of the Beagle**
Charles Darwin

I will first describe the habits of the tortoise (Testudo nigra, formerly called Indica), which has been so frequently alluded to. These animals are found, I believe, on all the islands of the Archipelago: certainly on the greater number. They frequent in preference the high damp parts, but they likewise live in the lower and arid districts. I have already shown, from the numbers which have been caught in a single day, how very numerous they must be. Some grow to an immense size: Mr. Lawson, an Englishman, and vice-governor of the colony, told us that he had seen several so large, that it required six or eight men to lift them from the ground: and that some had afforded as much as two hundred pounds of meat. The old males are the largest, the females rarely growing to so great a size: the male can readily be distinguished from the female by the greater length of its tail. The tortoises which live on those islands where there is no water, or in the lower and arid parts of the others, feed chiefly on the succulent cactus. Those which frequent the higher and damp regions, eat the leaves of various trees, a kind of berry (called guayavita) which is acid and austere, and likewise a pale green filamentous lichen (Usnera plicata), that hangs in tresses from the boughs of the trees.

The tortoise is very fond of water, drinking large quantities, and wallowing in the mud. The larger islands alone possess springs, and these are always situated towards the central parts, and at a considerable height. The tortoises, therefore, which frequent the lower districts, when thirsty, are obliged to travel from a long distance. Hence broad and well-beaten paths branch off in every direction from the wells down to the sea-coast; and the Spaniards by following them up, first discovered the watering-places. When I landed at Chatham Island, I could not imagine what animal travelled so methodically along well-chosen tracks. Near the springs it was a curious spectacle to behold many of these huge creatures, one set eagerly travelling onwards with outstretched necks, and another set returning, after having drunk their fill. When the tortoise arrives at the spring, quite regardless of any spectator, he buries his head in the water above his eyes, and greedily swallows great mouthfuls, at the rate of about ten in a minute. The inhabitants say each animal stays three or four days in the neighbourhood of the water, and then returns to the lower country; but they differed respecting the frequency of these visits. The animal probably regulates them according to the nature of the food on which it has lived. It is, however, certain, that tortoises can subsist even on those islands, where there is no other water than what falls during a few rainy days in the year.

I believe it is well ascertained, that the bladder of the frog acts as a reservoir for the moisture necessary to its existence: such seems to be the case with the tortoise.

For some time after a visit to the springs, their urinary bladders are distended with fluid, which is said gradually to decrease in volume, and to become less pure. The inhabitants, when walking in the lower district, and overcome with thirst, often take advantage of this circumstance, and drink the contents of the bladder if full: in one I saw killed, the fluid was quite limpid, and had only a very slightly bitter taste. The inhabitants, however, always first drink the water in the pericardium, which is described as being best.

The tortoises, when purposely moving towards any point, travel by night and day, and arrive at their journey's end much sooner than would be expected. The inhabitants, from observing marked individuals, consider that they travel a distance of about eight miles in two or three days. One large tortoise, which I watched, walked at the rate of sixty yards in ten minutes, that is 360 yards in the hour, or four miles a day,—allowing a little time for it to eat on the road. During the breeding season, when the male and female are together, the male utters a hoarse roar or bellowing, which, it is said, can be heard at the distance of more than a hundred yards. The female never uses her voice, and the male only at these times; so that when the people hear this noise, they know that the two are together. They were at this time (October) laying their eggs. The female, where the soil is sandy, deposits them together, and covers them up with sand; but where the ground is rocky she drops them indiscriminately in any hole: Mr. Bynoe found seven placed in a fissure. The egg is white and spherical; one which I measured was seven inches and three-eighths in circumference, and therefore larger than a hen's egg. The young tortoises, as soon as they are hatched, fall a prey in great numbers to the carrion-feeding buzzard. The old ones seem generally to die from accidents, as from falling down precipices: at least, several of the inhabitants told me, that they had never found one dead without some evident cause.

The inhabitants believe that these animals are absolutely deaf; certainly they do not overhear a person walking close behind them. I was always amused when overtaking one of these great monsters, as it was quietly pacing along, to see how suddenly, the instant I passed, it would draw in its head and legs, and uttering a deep hiss fall to the ground with a heavy sound, as if struck dead. I frequently got on their backs, and then giving a few raps on the hinder part of their shells, they would rise up and walk away;— but I found it very difficult to keep my balance. The flesh of this animal is largely employed, both fresh and salted; and a beautifully clear oil is prepared from the fat. When a tortoise is caught, the man makes a slit in the skin near its tail, so as to see inside its body, whether the fat under the dorsal plate is thick. If it is not, the animal is liberated; and it is said to recover soon from this strange operation. In order to secure the tortoises, it is not sufficient to turn them like turtle, for they are often able to get on their legs again.

There can be little doubt that this tortoise is an aboriginal inhabitant of the Galapagos; for it is found on all, or nearly all, the islands, even on some of the smaller ones where there is no water; had it been an imported species, this would hardly have been the case in a group which has been so little frequented. Moreover, the old Bucaniers found this tortoise in greater numbers even than at present: Wood and Rogers also, in 1708, say that it is the opinion of the Spaniards, that it is found nowhere else in this quarter of the world. It is now widely distributed; but it may be questioned whether it is in any other place an aboriginal. The bones of a tortoise at Mauritius, associated with those of the extinct Dodo, have generally been considered as belonging to this tortoise: if this had been so, undoubtedly it must have been there indigenous; but M. Bibron informs me that he believes that it was distinct, as the species now living there certainly is.

When you read Darwin's writing aloud to yourself or in class, you'll find that the slightly unfamiliar sentence structure makes sense to you. Try exaggerating it as you read it aloud, for the fun of it and for clarity.

Darwin's work preceded Schaller's by more than a hundred years and is part of the foundation of modern biology. Can you point out methods of observation and writing that Schaller may have got directly or indirectly from Darwin's work?

We have a clear sense of Darwin's presence, often participation, in the events that he observes. What did he accomplish by trying to ride on the backs of the tortoises? How does he make you *see* the tortoises and their behavior? Compare Darwin's presence and participation with Schaller's in the events that they observe.

How does the authors' clear presence in certain passages help their telling of their story and help your understanding of it? Would the authors' first-person presence in other passages get in the way of the telling?

* * *

The next how-it-happens selections are excerpted from my journal entries about child-raising and from an essay about the subject that evolved from the journal work. The journal entries show the kind of observation that went into the collection of instances for the essay. The essay compares and contrasts patterns of the behavior of parents and children in the use of "no."

Journal Instances for "Parents, Children, and No"
John Schultz

The way Timmy sits on the floor. Back very straight. Head up. Head sometimes tilted back, big eyes, blue eyes, looking up at us.

* * *

Taking things to his mouth. He never really knows a thing until he tries to put it in his mouth. Whether small as a pebble or a nut, or big as a beachball, whatever the size of the object, he must put it in his mouth to know it. When it's a beachball, he takes it between his hands and takes a sort of deep breath with a little shake of his whole body and then puts the beachball to his mouth as if he is going to swallow it whole.

* * *

The joy he takes in moving things bigger than him. First, pushing a chair around the room so he could move and have support too while beginning to walk, besides testing his strength and his surroundings.

* * *

Sitting by a door and, with intense concentration, moving the door back and forth.

* * *

The meaning of "no." The lamp by my chair. The car keys that hang near Annie's lap and that he reaches for when he's sitting on her lap as we drive along. I say "no," for sometimes he actually turned off the motor while we were driving. The puzzlement, cautious reaching out to test in what way has "no" changed the object. Partly he realizes the object is still the same, partly he thinks the object must be different, transformed somehow by "no." He lays his hand with caution on a "no" object and looks at it for a long moment and then withdraws his hand.

"No" must be consistent or the object is instantly transformed back again, and he attacks it with his usual gusto.

So far I have made the "no's" stick. By using only my voice. No tapping his hands. Just voice.

* * *

There is a feeling of great power, of absorbing power, for both Timmy and anyone watching him, in his concentration on his play, such as when he moves his sprinkler-bucket and its handle back and forth, here and there, for time on end. He is so immersed in his concentration, he would never need to invent art, god, or work.

* * *

When he falls or bumps himself, he looks up to see our reaction in order to see if he has hurt himself. If we don't show that we feel he's been hurt, he'll take a lot of bumps and jolts. He cries when he has really hurt himself.

* * *

The more Timmy understands "no," the more freedom he has. He can crawl anywhere he wants in the entire house now without being watched, which means a world of tremendous variety down there on the floor on the level of legs of tables and chairs and people for him to explore.

* * *

Susie is starting to stand up by herself. She is testing it consciously. She lets go of my knee, while I'm sitting in the chair, and then she stands there all by herself, supported all around by air. She opens her mouth wide, laughing with the pleasure of the sensation of standing, no hands, supported by air all around her. Then *plunk* she sits down *bump* on the floor. There is a silence after the jolt, a look on her face of "How should I feel and what should I do because that was not altogether pleasant bumping down like that?" Then she tips herself over onto her hands and knees and crawls and grabs hold of my pants leg, laughing because she's pleased and pleased with us, still laughing, but not as loudly as when she's standing supported by air. She pulls herself upright by my pants leg, holds onto my knee with both hands, her little butt wobbling in and out as she tries to get her balance. She starts to let go a few times, hesitates, waits until she feels the support of balance and air; then she lets go of my knee, spreads her arms out in the air, and starts laughing, her mouth wide open again, and then plunk she sits down bump again. And she does it over again and again.

* * *

Sue is dainty and pleasing in size and weight and easy to handle. She is not heavy on the thigh when I carry her. Timmy was quite fat until he began to crawl really vigorously.

Sue crawls gracefully, lightly. Timmy crawled much faster, more energetically, pounding to wherever he was going back and forth in the household.

* * *

Timmy was dressing up the doll and putting rubber pants on it. It was an accurate sort of playing that he was doing. Susie was helping him, dragging around a diaper in one hand, laughing the way she laughs. Timmy did all sorts of things with the doll, put her in the high chair, etc. After breakfast, when I was sitting on the toilet, Timmy pounded on the door. "I've got to get in the bathroom," he said. I let him in. Immediately, he closed the door and sat down on the floor and put the doll over his legs and pulled up the dress and started really spanking the doll's bottom, spanking on the rubber pants and all. He became violent with all the punishment he was giving the doll, really spanking her, whacking her on the bottom, shaking her, pulling her hair, etc. Our spanking is seldom more than one or two whacks on the bottom. The doll, I thought at the time, may have been a substitute for Susie, but I'm not so sure now because I've seen the way children love to play "adult punishing child." After a while, Timmy dragged the doll to the bathtub, diligently, and began to wash its hair. Then he ran for a comb and combed its hair.

Parents, Children, and "No"
John Schultz

Parents, influenced by the attitudes of our general, bourgeois, nuclear-family society and by conflicting trends within it and by their situations and hopes and anxieties for their children and by what they "politically" believe about the "nature" of people, make decisions about feeding, weaning, bedtime, pacifiers, toilet training, crawling, space, trust, curiosity, joy, learning, game-playing, and sense of responsibility. Parents make decisions about "no."

Just as there is one well-represented, if not well-published view in our culture that children must generally be beaten and suppressed in order to be and become obedient and "good," there is its opposite sibling in the view that "no" implemented in any way at all will destroy children's spirit and curiosity forever. I think both views are idealistically defiant toward "human nature," reflect each other negatively, and are designed to govern everything under the sun with guilt, with negative moralistic avoidances.

There are two closely associated reasons for the parent to assume active responsibility for making "no" effective. One is that there are many objects and places in houses, streets and cities that are physically dangerous to a child, but are not known as such to him. The other is that if a child understands the "no" objects and "no" places clearly, then both child and parents have a much desired freedom of movement and less supervised personal occupation.

We knew directly of a lively, curious two-year-old who swallowed sleeping pills, pretty blue-green chloral hydrate pills. If it's guilt you want, you need only see yourself finding your small child huddled behind the toilet, cold and stiff and dead. We knew of children hit by cars and trucks in the street, children hurt by other machinery, maimed, suffering brain damage that would oppress them the rest of their lives.

"No" in its proper function encourages freedom and ability to choose, and proceeds from the adult's authority of perception. The child feels the authority in the parent's voice and body, varying from gentle to firm to deliberate or impulsive anger, and shares or agrees or learns with the belief of it. The child trusts in the adult's insistence that, for instance, deadly electricity moves in the innocuous-seeming wire.

When the object was immediately dangerous to Timmy, I said "no" with an urgent warning emphasis, brooking no hesitation, from concern for his safety. Otherwise, I tried to say "no" in an even, firm voice which gave him a chance to share and agree voluntarily in the discovery. Up to his first birthday, I had made the "no's" stick by using only my voice, not tapping his hands, not spanking, just my voice and the awareness of the relationship between him and me, between his desire to know and my letting him voluntarily become aware of what I knew.

He was puzzled when we said "no" about an object. He felt the impact of the "no," from something in the tone and manner of our speaking, however mild, and shook a little with it. Then he would reach out gravely with both hands toward the object, moving jerkily toward and away from it, until he put both hands flat upon it. He seemed to think that "no" in some way transformed the object, and he wanted to test and know it. Unless the object were nakedly dangerous to the touch at that moment, we allowed him to put both hands on it, look at it for a long moment and then, with an "unnh" noise and a "swallowing" shake of agreement throughout his body, withdraw his hands. Then he would look up at me, though still mildly puzzled in tone, and I too would make noises or say something in agreement. It would have been easy to misinterpret his reaching out toward the "no" object, to see it as disobedient rather than as an act to recognize the "no" and take it into his awareness of the world.

If "no" was not consistent, the object lost its transformation and Timmy approached it with his usual gusto. But quickly, with repetition, it became a "no" and the "no" held. Later, I would sometimes let my hand rest on his hand while I said "no" and sometimes I would repeat "no."

In Cuernavaca, Mexico, at about fourteen months of age, "no" changed for Timmy. Now if we said "no," even to outright dangerous things, it upset him. He either started to cry or was intolerably pushed and pulled inside by "no."

Then came another turn-around, epiphany moment for me when he started to crawl out an open door and down stone steps into the driveway. I understood something without verbally understanding it in my mind. I said, without moving from my chair on the other side of the room, "Timmy, do something else," and I knew it was right the instant I said it. He turned away and started "doing something else." It became another formula for "no" that did not upset him. "Do something else" gave him a chance to "do something else."

A few months later, "no" was reinstated.

Late one summer night, Timmy was deep among the "no's" about my chair, pounding back and forth around my legs as I read and wrote in my notebooks. I say "pounding" because in crawling he hit the floor hard and rapidly with his hands and knees most of the time.

There were several "no's" around the big chair. My ashtray on the arm of my chair was "no" because it spilled so easily. (He quit the pacifier before I quit smoking.) The cup of coffee on the arm of the chair was a "no," and the lamp and its cord beside the chair were "no's." He liked to crawl around my feet and play with things near me, usually so involved in his play that he was seldom disruptive of my work; I often found it pleasantly relaxing to have him nearby. He liked to haul himself up by the arm of the chair and hold on with one hand and with the other hand try intently to close upon the smoke rising from a cigarette in the ashtray.

At this time, Timmy obeyed "no" if it were repeated.

I became aware that he had been sitting for several minutes below the left arm of my chair in that particular silence that often meant that the object of his absorption was forbidden. I looked over the arm of the chair and saw that he was playing with the old dead cord that came out of the base of the lamp. At first, I said nothing. Then I thought, how does he know when it's hot? He should not play with any electric cord.

"No, Timmy," I said, looking over the arm of my chair.

He did not even look up at me. He continued playing with the cord. It was late at night, and father and son were in the house alone. I leaned my face over the arm of the chair near the ashtray and said, "No," and again, "No." My voice likely did not vibrate with that special conviction of warning. He ducked his head down, clutched the cord to his chest, and would not look up at me. Probably he had been playing with the cord for a few minutes, and now refused to permit "no" to transform the object. "No," I said, and "No" again, very firmly because I was beginning to feel that a different sort of authority was at issue: Electric cords and sockets should not be played with until the person knew enough about them.

It had been important to me that he respond to my warnings and directions and obey voluntarily, though I had not yet felt it to be an issue. I was becoming frightened now of Timmy's not responding to my voice and of what that implied in terms of a distintegrated relationship in which I would have to terrorize him with angry, disruptive, authoritarian "no's."

I said "No" yet again. Still, I did not take the cord out of his hands or tap or slap his hands. It was urgently important to me that he understand by voice alone. "No," I said, a degree more firmly yet, a hard knot in my chest. He ducked his chin down harder and clutched the cord to his chest and would not look up at me. "No, Timmy," I said, committed now to my firmness.

Then slowly he looked up at me, relaxing his hands that held the cord just a little. His lips were pressed down in a smirk, a smirking of deliberate obstinancy, as he tried with down-turned lips not to burst out with laughter. So "grownup" or "adolescent" was the look on his face, so rebellious and teasing, so aware of what he was doing, so challenging in manner, that I was terrified. I was shocked with the realization of his terrific separateness. I had never seen such a look on a child's face. I was ready to believe in changeling children and any diabolical form of transformation that would explain why my son was now transformed toward me as much as my "no" had ever transformed an object for him.

I was full of a continuous pulsing flash of terror. What should I do? Give a more authoritarian "no?" Spank? Shout? Then, seeing his lifted face so pent-up with laughing dare and rebellion, my terrified feeling turned suddenly around. I laughed out loud. I really whooped with laughter. Timmy laughed with gusto, too. He threw down the dead cord and crawled rapidly away from the lamp.

For months after this incident, he left electric cords pretty much alone without need of "no's." "No" generally became much easier and more trusted by him. What was avoided and what was enabled here? Where, in that moment of terror, did the wisdom of my laughter spring from?

The more Timmy understood "no," the more freedom he had, because we did not need to fear for his safety. It opened up a life of tremendous variety for him to explore and affirm down there on the floor, on the level of the legs of tables and chairs, and on the porch outside. . . .

Timmy's energy, persistence and curiosity were nearly relentless. There passed nearly a year before he again handled an electric cord. Late one morning when I was making breakfast in the kitchen, and I knew he was in the nearby storeroom-study, I became aware of that peculiar, deliberate silence that generally meant he was trying to do something forbidden. I looked in the door of the storeroom and there he was standing in the middle of a pile of papers, holding an electric plug properly and extending it properly, like a fencer, ready to insert it into the wall socket, but one slip and his fingers would have gone onto the contact points. I leaped, yelled, tore it out of his hands, slapped his hands, the only time ever, and yelled, "No, no, no!" He howled and rushed to his mother, and I was afraid of what his upset would do to his feeling for me. But in a few minutes he was his self again.

When the moment came that we trusted him with electric cords and with lighting the stove to cook his own breakfast, it was almost a ceremonial, certainly a decisional moment for him, a sort of rite of passage that made him feel good and proud and expansive and capable.

It is a practical fact that children are similar in their different ways, different in their similar ways, and different and similar in unique ways. So it was with Susie and "No."

Standing on her high chair and leaning on the table with one hand, she started to pull at a gallon of grapefruit juice. "No!" we said, nearly in chorus. Usually we found ourselves remonstrating with her again and again because she didn't obey as quickly or in quite the same pattern as Timmy. But I'd just recently had an experience of catching her eye and watching her as "no" became silently plain to her. I'd told her mother about it, and suggested that we should wait longer after we said "no" to her. So now we waited, watching, as Susie leaned on the table with that funny, experimental, partly hurt look of hers, keeping her hand testing the jar without taking it or giving in to the "no." I sensed something about her hesitation and I said to her mother, "I think we should go about our business."

With our attention gone, Susie suddenly withdrew her hand from the jar, clambered down to the floor, ran happily in a circle, and then ran, very pleased, to her mother and climbed in her lap and hugged her. "Oh, you wonderful little girl!" her mother said.

Yes, Susie wants to accomplish compliance "all by herself," without our attention upon her. If I listen to the children, I find that they often declare the principles by which they work and will work with us. Susie frequently insists, probably because of her relationship to her older brother who is always, *always,* two and a half years older, "*I* do it, *I* do it!" "I do it all by myself!" is her working principle. Yet it is one that we have to rediscover again and again, because it is hard to turn your back and let the "no" happen.

"Yes, it's yours, but put it back when we're ready to go," I said to her, as she frantically pulled her 'jamas out of the laundry bag. "O.k.," she said in that quavery tone of surrender, and clutched the 'jamas to her bosom until the last second and then willingly put them into the laundry bag herself.

In my studio she picks up some papers of mine, and I tell her to put them back on the desk. She says, "I don't want to." I repeat it and then wait until she does it "on her own." Later, when she handles a packet of X-Acto knives, I tell her with a firm sense of danger to put the packet of knives back. "I bleed?" she says, and promptly puts the X-Acto knives back on the table by the stove. She messes with some notebooks on a chair. "Straighten them, Susie," I say. When I repeat it, she says, "I *am*!", asserting to herself and to me that she does not need me to tell her again. When she steps on a stack of notebooks on the floor, "No," I tell her, "step somewhere else. Not on my notebooks." Then, wonderfully, she *twice* steps back and forth astraddle over the notebooks, beaming, to show me she recognizes and can do it.

She sometimes howls at "no," but soon her tone of crying becomes one of release. "I want I want I want" or "I don't want I don't want" conflicts often overwhelm her. With great conviction she asserts "I want" or "I don't want," as if these statements have persuasive moral power for her.

"Why are you doing that, Susie?"

"Because I *want* to."

Once, in our cabin on a vacation, I suddenly declared, "All right, all kids out of the house!" because they were making adult exchange impossible. First, I got Timmy to leave the house.

Susie said, as usual, "*Why?*"

"Because I *want* you to leave the house!" I said.

"Oh," she said, as if "I *want*" were morally correct and compelling, and she left the house and went out onto the lawn to play on the swings. . . .

After I'd made many journal entries, I realized by comparing them that the brief fragmented journal entries did not provide as much information about the subject as the more expanded entries which contained more seeing. Years later, I could still see and understand the more expanded entries clearly. The brief journal entries are more like reporter's notes, which are reminders meant for immediate use. In the essay itself, I felt it was imperative to make the reader understand by *seeing* what was happening with children and parents.

The essay excerpt argues why parents need to use "no" and make it effective, for the safety of the child and the freedom of both child and parent. It compares different cultural approaches to "no." Then, by comparing and contrasting instances of "no," the essay takes the reader into a process of discovery of the use of "no" and how it can be implemented in a better way. I follow, delineate, and abstract patterns for a boy-child and then compare them to the patterns for a girl-child, arguing for parental recognition of the individual differences of individual children. When you compare my journal entries with the excerpt from the essay itself, what differences do you notice between them?

Juxtapose, read one after the other, pages from Holt's *How Children Fail,* Foster's "Hoboing," Schaller's "A Gorilla Day" and "The Behavior of the Mountain Gorilla," Darwin's "Galapagos Tortoises," Mike Schwarz's "Rats," and my journal entries and essay excerpt, "Parents, Children and No." Compare and contrast the authors' voices, attitudes, imagery, statements of patterns, arguments, use of storyteller, first person or third person points of view, paragraphs, narrative developments, sense of the author speaking to you, and anything else that takes your attention. Recall and comment in class about what you notice in comparing and contrasting the different writings. Let yourself pick up on any suggestions that may help your writing. Some of these suggestions may simmer in your subconscious for a while and then surface in your writing.

Writing Your How-It-Happens Instances

Think of the "worst" or strangest or most oppressive job you've ever had, or any experience of prolonged duration, preferably from the years after your childhood. School. Family. Neighborhood. Army. Sports. Gangs. Love-life. Dangerous experiences. Or repeated human activities such as sleeping, dreaming, eating, sex, dying, child raising, leisure activities, teaching, learning. Think of a comparison of jobs, or of institutional or group experiences. Or observation of groups of people or of any other kind of behavior. Or a time of life such as teenage, undergraduate, or parenthood. It can be anything from the observation of two frogs in an aquarium to the experience of a street gang. It's important that you choose an area of experience with fairly well-defined patterns of behavior, such as jobs, schools, other institutions, neighborhoods, sports, or observations of animals, plants, machinery, or physical processes, etc., and that it be an area of experience of more or less prolonged duration from the years after your childhood.

Often students make the mistake of selecting their own childhood, which tends to be unproductive for them and their writing in the long haul, though some childhood memories may stimulate good writing for you. Institutional or group situations help pull you out of the subjective thrashing and confusion that tends to characterize new writers' efforts. They give you a clear context and enforce several kinds of relationships. Also, such situations have probably introduced you to the broader world of living and work, in which you have encountered a variety of incidents and people.

You have spent as much time in school, in your neighborhood, in playing a sport, on a prolonged job or jobs, in some other institutional or extended experience, as

Schaller spent in observing the mountain gorilla or even Darwin in field observation on the voyage of the *Beagle*. So you have had ample time and ample experience to give you plenty to work with when you set out to develop your how-it-happens assignment. Also we generally know more than we think we know about our subject. As we write, we remember more and discover more about it.

Possibly, your strongest memories of a prolonged job or group situation are not altogether pleasant. Frequently, students (and other writers) avoid the really strong material because of the unpleasantness associated with it. For instance, a student who was writing and telling instances about one job, revealed at one point his experience in years past with organized street gangs. At the teacher's encouragement, he began telling and writing a powerful set of how-it-happens instances about the gang experience, always surprised to find that his audience welcomed and was enthralled with the vivid writing. A young woman who began writing about a phone soliciting job, when asked to "go to those experiences that most strongly take your attention," shifted to a job experience in the "mailroom" of a supermarket chain. She was surprised at how much meaning she found in "that old job . . . that generally miserable experience." Another young woman began writing about her experience as a receptionist (because she thought she should be writing about a job), but later wrote much more strongly about her experience in an expensive private college. The ceremony of weddings, personally observed and researched through reading, provided another woman with rich factual and fictional material. A lawyer pursued his continuing interest in the relationship of courtroom performance to jury voting. You choose the subject, but in a sense the strongest subjects choose you, that is, the strongest subjects keep pulling at your attention or come at you with surprising power when you stop turning away from them. With your how-it-happens instances, you bring new knowledge to yourself and into the world; you rescue what would otherwise be lost if you did not explore and write about the subject.

You will be living with your how-it-happens subject, exploring it, finding out and telling more about it, throughout the rest of this writing program. If you find that instances from a different subject compel your attention, give the new one a few trial instances in your journal and find out how rich it is. Read one or two of them aloud in your class, if possible. If the new subject is stronger than the earlier one, switch to it.

Start out on your subject by writing a list of those events and images that you see and remember most clearly, or those that you *imagine* most clearly, the ones that take your attention. Write down any questions that come to your mind about the instances or the subject as a whole. List objects, sensory experiences, characteristic actions, characteristic gestures, characteristic behaviors, along with events or incidents. If you read the lists aloud in class, see what you notice in other students' lists that gives clues and suggestions for your how-it-happens subject. Such lists provide a preliminary view of the scope of your subject, suggest patterns, and serve as a reminder of instances that you can expand. Of course, you may also see many instances, a kind of list in your mind, without actually listing them on paper.

Begin writing instances as journal-like entries. Even before you make your overall list, you can go to the event or image that most clearly takes your attention, try to see it in your mind as you write, *and write it as fully as possible*. Tell the instances as you see them happen in your mind at the moment of writing. Conduct feedback with yourself and your imagined readers about whatever takes your attention in the instances. You may keep adding to the list as you write expanded instances.

Your instances can be *real* or *imagined*, or a mixture of the real that you remember and fictional imagining, depending upon the purpose and possibilities you feel in your material and upon the emphasis of your class.

Try different forms for different entries. Forms emerge naturally from the material as you're writing it. In some instances, you will combine several forms, without necessarily doing it consciously. Let it happen. You may write some entries as letters, memos, reports, public addresses, etc. Rely on your intuitive sense for the form, on what form you're attracted to. Your intuitive sense for forms is not infallible, but it is a good resource. See and tell your images and events so someone else can see them. Write those things that catch your attention in each instance. In most of the collections of instances that are presented in this book, a variety of forms are used to tell the instances, sometimes subtly, sometimes obviously. Frequently, the forms emerged subconsciously in the writing as the writer worked: the writer perceived the emergence of the form and explored and heightened it. Other times the authors deliberately sought material for particular forms and points of view. Instances suggest patterns. Let the patterns develop. Write to discover the patterns, and the imagery and the forms that reveal the patterns.

Take a place where an event occurs again and again (in a job, in a game situation, etc.), or see a kind of event that repeats itself in the same place (such as the days of a court trial, the events of dorm life, the work of a hospital, daily football practice). See different instances at different times of similar, or similar but different, behavior in this place. See at least three such instances. Write the third one first, working backwards to the second, then to the first so that you won't slight the last instances you see. Do this with different places in your subject area, or with only one place if there is only one.

Research through reading may be used in this exploration, too.

As we move from one form to another, look over your how-it-happens subject for material within it that could be used for that form. Play the particular form back and forth over your how-it-happens subject to find where it begins, almost magnetically, to take hold of material, organize and stimulate it.

With your how-it-happens subject, you are sustained by a whole body of interrelationships that, as you set them forth for your audience, keep leading you to further discoveries. *You can likely find in your how-it-happens subject the basic material and context for every writing assignment in this book. At the same time, you can reach outside your how-it-happens subject to other areas of your experience and imagination for any of the "forms" assignments.* You choose or let your material choose you according to its "pull" on your attention.

Monsters

You may wonder, since we've just spent so much effort on factual and fictionally realistic how-it-happens subjects, why I introduce Monsters in this section and Parodies and Satires in the next. Good monster-tellings require you to use seeing-in-the-mind not only to perceive patterns of occurrence but to form concepts from the patterns, to visualize and conceptualize the monster, even to take the monster's point of view. Good monster-tellings stimulate your reflective and conceptualizing faculties, your sense of movement, your sense for seeing and the words that tell your seeing. Conceiving of the sort of monster that you're going to tell about makes you compare instances of mishaps and disasters, little and large, similar and different, in which a pattern can emerge and you may glimpse the monster, the concept of the monster, the thematic pattern of the monster, the personification of the pattern.

In fact, a monster may be waiting right now in patterns of mishaps and disasters in your how-it-happens subject; no, not the obvious monsters, not a high school principal or teacher or boss (these will usually be more effective when realistically told), not those comic book or television or dinosaur or cartoon monsters (unless you have a particularly compelling and unique vision of them), but your own monster, the monster that only you see, that you will be the first to tell the world about—a monster that, in causing patterns of mishaps and disasters, has definite goals or a program in mind. Now you're beginning to feel the suggestion of a possible monster tugging on your attention? Not quite visualized perhaps, but emerging.

Think of a monster that's already at work in the mishaps and disasters of your life or of the lives of those around you, of the lives of people in your how-it-happens subject area or of everyone's lives.

What does the monster do? How does it cause mishaps and disasters? What is its purpose? What is its destiny, its goal? What keeps the monster alive?

*   *   *

The first reading selection is from an account of class recall of an oral telling.

From

The Garlic Monster
Andrew Allegretti

"It was a monster disguised as a meatball and it soaked up the garlic in the sauce . . ."—the student gives a gesture of the monster disguised as a meatball, inside the pot of sauce on the stove, with spaghetti drooping over its head, taking hold of the lip of the pot to peer over it and ducking down to hide when Mama Minelli comes into the kitchen (and now in the immediacy of seeing, the teller of the recall shifts to the present tense)—" . . . so that when Mama Minelli tastes the sauce . . ."—gestures of Mama Minelli reaching up to a shelf for a wooden ladle and dipping and tasting the sauce— ". . . and there is never enough garlic, so Mama Minelli reaches up . . ."—again a gesture of reaching—"for a clove of garlic and twists it over the pot. . . ." Other students join the recall. A gesture of Mama Minelli twisting a clove of garlic, ". . . and stirs, but again the garlic monster, disguised as a meatball, soaks up the garlic so that when Papa Minelli comes into the kitchen and tastes the sauce there is not enough garlic, and he twists a clove of garlic into the pot . . too, and so on with each member of the family, until the big dinner when the Italian sons in black suits and black ties sit on one side of the long table with their Anglo girlfriends, thin and fragile in white dresses, with clouds of blond hair, and the fat Italian daughters, all divorced (for some reason) sit on the other side, and Papa Minelli sits at the head of the table in a room draped with gold-tasselled red curtains and candles lit on the table, and then the garlic monster releases all of the stored garlic into the sauce and the room fumes and reeks. . . ." Gestures of waves of fumes rising from the plates of the Anglo girlfriends. The workshop is laughing again as strongly as they laughed when the oral telling was first told the week before. The oral telling/recall continues with vivid realistic images of the family.

Review and re-see the gestural images in "The Garlic Monster." Do the gestures yourself.

* * *

In "The Bread Monster" we have a unique twist upon the ageless conception of the evil child genius. Or is he evil? Is he even a child? Which is the monster, the child genius or. . . .?

The Bread Monster
Shawn Shiflett

First I go to the store. I grab two shopping carts—one for my right hand and one for my left. I glide the carts down the aisle to where the flour is and load both of them up; then on top of all that flour I balance the gallons of milk, bags of sugar, cans of shortening, salt, and last but not least the yeast. I use a five pound box of yeast—not just any box. No, the proper way to pick out a box of yeast is to put box after box up to your ear until you find one that has a heart beat. That's right, a heart beat—bum-bump-bum-bump-bum-bump. I put the yeast in one of the carts and head up front to the checkout counter. Inevitably the checkout girl will say something snotty like, "Planning on baking a little bread, huh?" but I just stare back at her and say, "You wouldn't understand."

I carry my ingredients home: it takes about five trips but believe me, it's worth the trouble. From my bedroom closet I take out my oil barrel, completely cleansed of oil of course: some kids hide *Playboy* magazines in their closets; I hide my oil barrel. As I take it out it gives off the sweet smell of past bread doughs I've made: Barbecue Bread, Boston Brown Bread, Cinnamon Crescent French Bread, French Bread Fix-Ups, Herb Bread, Herb-Buttered Bread, Onion Supper Bread, Parsleyed Bread Slices, Perfect Corn Bread, Perfect Wheat Bread, Perfect Rye Bread, Raisin Loaves, Sugarplum Loaves, Toast and Cheese Loaf. So you can see I'm good at what I do. Let's say that today I'm going to make Perfect White Bread. I listen to make sure no one else is home because the last thing I want to do is get caught with my barrel in public. I take my barrel out of the closet, roll it over to the stairs and then bounce it down the stairs one by one. Once downstairs I roll it into the middle of the kitchen, then take the ingredients out of the grocery bags and begin to pour, and pour, and pour them into the oil barrel. I don't have to measure anything because after making bread since I was six months old, I have developed an innate sense for measurement. The more yeast I add the more distinct the bum-bump-bum-bump-bum-bump becomes, so that when you think about it, I'm not really making bread, I'M GIVING BIRTH!

I run upstairs to my closet again and pull out my trusty two-by-four that I use for a stirrer. I run back down stairs, stick my two-by-four into my barrel and begin to stir, and stir, and stir. Then when everything is good and mixed I lean over the barrel and begin to knead the dough gently—a mother stroking her newborn son's hair couldn't be more gentle than the way I first touch my dough—but slowly I begin to grip and squeeze the dough until I'm practically falling into the barrel. My arms are completely submerged. I feel the dough; the dough feels me back, clings to me, caresses me, yes, even loves me. My hand movements become more and more violent, but the more I beat my dough the more attached to me it seems to get.

The moment has come. I pull my arms out of the barrel and lay wax paper all over the kitchen floor, then turn the barrel over on its side and let the dough crawl out— that's right, by this time it can actually crawl on its own power. Slowly, tentatively, like a baby exploring its new world for the first time, the dough ball leaves the comfort of the barrel. It sits there on the floor like a white oversized ball of silly putty. It pulsates—

bum-bump-bum-bump-bum-bump, and when I move, it moves as if following me with invisible eyes.

Now comes the scary part. I have to let the dough rise. It rises, and rises, and rises, until it touches the ceiling. I watch it from the kitchen doorway just in case I have to make a run for it. It rolls around on the wax paper, its trememdous weight sending vibrations through the foundation of the house. Suddenly it lunges at me—not out of viciousness, but out of love of its Daddy. IT SWALLOWS ME UP! I'M INSIDE THE DOUGH BALL TRYING TO FIGHT MY WAY OUT BUT IT WON'T LET ME GO! I HEAR THAT EAR SHATTER-ING BUM-BUMP-BUM-BUMP-BUM-BUMP! At this point it's hard to tell if I am making the bread or if the bread is making me! In the distance I hear the front door open and slam shut. OH, MY GOD! MOMMY'S HOME! I have to think fast. Not only will Mommy beat me if she sees me doing something as dirty as making bread, but besides that it's hard to breathe in all this dough. I hold my arms up over my head and spread my legs so that my body forms two large V's. I shift my weight from side to side so that I eventually gain momentum and roll the dough ball towards the stove. The dough ball is confused: What is Daddy doing? It's heart beat increases—bum-bump-bum-bump-bum-bump. I manage to punch one of my hands through the dough long enough to open the oven door, and then I leap inside the oven, dough covering and all. At first I contemplate staying in the oven with the dough—after all, what better way to die than to be baked as one with the life I have created. But no, I must escape so that I can create more life, more love, more bread. I eat my way out of the dough, then stuff the rest of the dough ball into the oven. It's a tight fit but I manage to pack it all in. I . . . I . . . DON'T WANT TO TURN THE HEAT ON, BUT I KNOW I MUST DO IT . . . MUST KILL MY BREAD, MY BABY. I turn the oven dial to three-fifty. Slowly the bum-bump-bum-bump-bum-bump fades. A faint, "Why are you doing this to me, Daddy?" echoes from inside the stove, then silence. I haven't time to even grieve: MOMMY WILL BE IN THE KITCHEN ANY MOMENT! I MUST HIDE MY BARREL AND MY TWO-BY-FOUR! I carry them back up stairs on my back—that's right, ON MY BACK—it's amazing the kind of physical strength you can muster in an emergency. No sooner do I have them hidden in my closet than I hear the sharp tapping of Mommy's high heels down in the kitchen. And then, WITHOUT POSSIBLY KNOWING HOW CRUEL SHE'S BEING, MOMMY YELLS UP THE STAIRS, "ERIC, WHAT SMELLS SO GOOD?"

Odd little fellow, isn't he? Is the story a sort of parody of Dr. Frankenstein and the monster he created? Which is the monster, the maker or the bread? Retell the story in class, giving gestures for the imagery of how the bread is made, how things are done.

Telling and Writing Your Monster

Dwell upon the patterns of the monster's actions until you see the occurrences from the monster's point of view.

See the monster, or see the monster's doings. Sometimes you see the actions of the monster, but not the monster itself. See at least three different instances of it doing its work. Write all three of them. As you see and tell about the monster in class, give the gestures that make us see how it functions. Give gestures from the monster's point of view. You may have the perception and feeling of the monster more as a force than a visible being; but can still give gestures of how it functions, that is, sometimes you can take the monster's point of view, particularly with gestures telling its actions, without directly describing it. Exaggerate what you see, tell, and gesture.

Give oral tellings about monsters in class, listen to other people's monster tellings and *see* them and see what they suggest to you for your telling and writing. Write about your monster in class. Read the writing aloud, and continue writing about the monster when you're writing alone. You can try letters about monsters, or stories-within-a-story, that is, stories that someone in a story framework tells to someone else. Some monsters are funny in the telling, some are deadly serious.

Parodies and Satires

Each author of our parodies imaginatively exaggerates the familiar characteristics of the form being parodied, its content, attitudes, tone, and language. If you examine closely the parodies presented in this section, you'll see how each author fulfills the requirements of each form closely, as do all good parodies, such as the requirements of the forms of radio, television, direct mail advertising, a newspaper column, etc. Ripe for parody are standardized tests, corporate reports, traditional or popular songs. Parodies usually satirize social attitudes, pretensions, trends, fashions, desires, greeds, motivations, behavior.

Parodies give you full authority of their execution. No one but you can perceive how you're going to make fun of whatever form you've chosen. You're the one who comes up with the concept. You're the one who uses the form to do a "job" on the original form and its content, in the slangy sense of doing a "job." Not all parodies are mean, but parody gives you full permission to be *mean*, to make mean fun of the form and content. You come up with the conception, take in the full structure of the form, make fun of it and its content, or use it to make fun of something else and give yourself permission to use whatever language and expression get the "job" done. You exaggerate with a vengeance.

The challenge of parodying particular forms and styles effectively helps many writers learn more about form, manner, and style, while it liberates voice and sense of movement. Notice the parodies of style in The Eulogy of a Normally Uncelebrated Object section. Notice the parody of a folktale, "Cat and a Chick Hooked Up," in the Folktale section, and Jonathan Swift's "A Modest Proposal" in the How-to-Do-It-Better section. You'll find parody and parodic characteristics in examples of other forms in this book. The how-to seems to invite tongue-in-cheek humor, virtually containing parody as a common characteristic of its form. In a true parody, you pay attention to and fulfill the form, its style, its voice, its persona, with an extravagant and precise attention to the form's elements and characteristics. Such an extravagant approach permits each author to assume unabashedly the voice and authority of the parody.

Examine "Magical Mechanical Machine" for characteristics of advertising forms, techniques, language, attitudes, and how it functions as a parody of a radio commercial or, if you put "Dear Reader" or "Dear Friend" at the top of it, as direct mail advertising. Examine "Station Break" for essential characteristics of the radio commercial form, language and attitudes. "How Far Would You Go?" parodies form, content, techniques, and appeals of television commercials, through a dramatic context in which the "autobiographical" viewer sees the commercial while he's sick and insomniac with the flu. How different would it be if we had only the detergent commercial and not the dramatic context? Each of the parodies executes a flight or dance of free-swinging, precise exaggeration from beginning to end.

Magical Mechanical Machine
Scott Hoeppner

Are you tired of all those kitchen gadgets that fall apart as soon as the warranty expires? Were you just saying to your neighbor this morning how you wish someone would come up with one item that does the work of all the rest? We at Upchuck Productions have come up with this gadget that does the work of all the other implements and more, better. Yes, it's the *Magical Mechanical Machine*, destined to become the housewife's best friend. This one machine blends, beats, brews, bakes, butters, boils, cuts, cubes, chops, chills, crushes, crumbs, cooks, cracks, creams, embalms, freezes, ferments, flakes, fertilizes, drains, dices, destroys, grinds, gels, grates, hacks, harasses, jostles, kneads, knifes, liquefies, mixes, marinates, mends, molds, mangles, mutilates, minces, manipulates, adds, substracts, multiplies, divides, purees, pastes, purifies, pulverizes, rotates, rips, stews, scrambles, tears, tosses, vegetates, whips and dials the police in case of emergencies all in the privacy of your own home. With a flick of your finger you can pulverize an entire carrot, with a flick of your carrot you can pulverize an entire finger. No food is too difficult for the *Magical Mechanical Machine*. Highly recommended for cannibals. You say you like bacon with your eggs in the morning? Not only does our machine fry the bacon, it goes out and kills the pig. Now, how's that for modern convenience. Still not satisfied? You still want more? Then listen up. The many uses of our *Magical Mechanical Machine* do not stop in the kitchen. Just change the blades and it becomes a hedge trimmer. Change the blades once again and it becomes a helicopter. Our machine can teach your children ten different languages, take the dog out after dinner, tell telephone solicitors what they can do with their siding and satisfy your husband when you have a headache. This is definitely the household device that you have been waiting for all your life. Listen to the latest sports scores and the weather while you mutilate a turnip. That's right, our handy machine gives you all the scores of the important games and even places your illegal bets and stands ready to erase all records of the bets if you are raided by the police. Yes, the *Magical Mechanical Machine* polishes your silver, places rhinestones on your asparagus, wallpapers your bedroom, projects your favorite porno movies, converts into a whirpoool bath and wards off evil spirits. This is a limited time offer so don't delay, act now. To order your *Magical Mechanical Machine* send your bank account, the mortgage on your house, and your first born male child to *Magical Mechanical Machine*, Upchuck Productions, Box 1000, Boston, Massachusetts. That is *Magical Mechanical Machine*, Upchuck Productions, Box 1000, Boston, Massachusetts. After three P. M. send to Fred, 291 Ocean Drive, La Junta, Colorado. Order today so you can mangle an eggplant tomorrow.

How Far Would You Go?
Gary Gaines

I know you won't believe this, but I swear on my Bruce Springsteen albums that every word is true. One night I was up kind of late. I had the flu and was feeling too miserable to sleep so I was watching one of those late night/early morning flicks on one of the UHF stations. I don't remember much about the movie except that it was one of those war films with a bunch of people with English accents in it.

Well, I was fumbling around with this jigsaw puzzle and I look up and see this commercial come on. It was one of those detergent commercials. It opened up with this guy and this young housewife sitting at a table with a box of this detergent between them. On the housewife's lap is a little boy, maybe four or five years old, in a t-shirt and jeans. He had blond hair and blue eyes and was really cute and all (you know, the All-American, kid-down-the-street type). So anyway, this lady's telling the guy how much she loves the detergent and all and how it keeps little Jimmy's clothes so clean and then Jimmy pipes up and says how good his clothes smell.

Well, I just figured this was more of the usual bullshit you get from commercials and was about to go back to the puzzle when these two guys in these railroad costumes, you know, the blue and white striped coveralls and cap, come in and the guy at the table says, "Now you go with these nice men, Jimmy, and we'll see you later." So they take the little kid away.

Then the guy starts offering the housewife money for the box of detergent and she keeps turning him down. "Now come on, Mrs. ——, I'll give you fifty dollars for that box of detergent." "No!" she says as he grabs the box off the table and holds it to her. Then the guy says, "Well . . . Mrs.——, let's see how much you really like your detergent. Why don't you just look at the monitor over there on the side?" Then they switch the picture to this railroad track and they got her little Jimmy tied to it. They go in for a closeup and there are tears running down the poor kid's face and he's struggling uselessly to get himself free. He keeps yelling, "Mommy, Mommy, Mommy . . ." The housewife's voice comes on and she starts consoling the kid, saying, "Don't worry, Jimmy, Mommy's here, everything's all right."

Then the picture shifts again and there's this diesel engine racing down the tracks with the detergent's logo painted across the side and the guy comes on saying, "When we see the engine go past the red marker flag, Mrs. ——, you'll have fifteen seconds to decide whether to keep your detergent or save little Jimmy's life by having us switch the engine onto another track. There goes the marker flag now! What'll it be, Mrs. ——?" Then it's back to a close-up of Jimmy still bawling his eyes out, repeating "Mommy, Mommy, Mommy," really quickly now in this high-pitched, sort of delirious-sounding voice as the roar of the engine gets closer. There's a little clock now in the upper right hand corner of the screen sweeping past the seconds.

They switch quickly back to the studio where you see the mother chewing on one of her fingernails with this confused look on her face, turning from monitor to detergent box and back again like she hasn't made up her mind yet. "I don't want to put any pressure on you, Mrs. ——," says the guy, "but there are less than ten seconds left." The housewife gives a little nod and continues trying to decide between the boy and the box.

Now they go to this shot of the oncoming train and little Jimmy by the bottom of the screen. He seems to have quieted down or maybe the roar of the train is just drowning him out. Anyway, when the clock is down to like three seconds the guy says, "Well, Mrs. ——?" "I'll keep the box!" says the housewife excitedly. It's just another second or two before the train goes screaming over the little kid, but they hold the camera on it just long enough to show little Jimmy's head tumble and roll down the side of the track bed.

Then it's back to the studio where they show the used-to-be mother holding the box of detergent with a big smile on her face, obviously feeling she's made the right decision. "Any regrets, Mrs. ——?" asks the guy. "Nope!" "There you have it, friends."

The last shot is a close-up of little Jimmy's head (nose up, eyes wide open, blood trickling out of his neck) lying in the weeds next to a box of detergent, the tracks off in the distance. And the guy's voice says, "How far would you go for your detergent?"

Station Break
Cloteria Easterling

. . . We will return to our program, "Frontier Tree Surgeon," in a moment, after these commercial messages.

Friends, ELVIS is gone but not forgotten. And to give you that little piece of ELVIS we all need, *Better Condos and Window Boxes* is offering you a "LITTLE PIECE OF ELVIS."

That's right friends, a little piece of Elvis. This isn't a record offer, or an offer of a life-size Elvis made from four hundred thousand toothpicks, like those other companies try to sell you. I mean we will actually send you pieces of Elvis Presley.

If you send $800,000.00 plus $40.00 shipping, handling, and postage, the employees of *Better Condos and Window Boxes* will, at midnight, sneak into Elvis' actual grave and remove pieces of bones, decayed flesh, or whatever else we find, and send it to you for our *LOW, LOW, PRICE!!!*

Be the first on your block to own Elvis. You can display him on a coffee table, in a den, or to brighten up a dark space.

Just remember for the LOW, LOW, LOW!!!! PRICE of $800,000.00 plus shipping, handling, and postage, you too can own a "LITTLE PIECE OF ELVIS."
SEND TO:
"LITTLE PIECE OF ELVIS"
P.O. Box 149
Back Room Deal, Nevada 00000
Or call our toll-free number: 1-800-5555555
Our operators are on the lines waiting for your calls NOW!!!!!!

Remember, send for this offer, because a little piece of Elvis will bring a little piece of happiness into your life.

Beyond the parody of the form itself, how does each of the examples satirize aspects of our society? What is the "point" made by each parody? What is the point of a woman being unable to choose between the life of her son and her box of detergent? Of a machine that can fulfill the actions of a hundred verbs, maybe more?

Parodies show you that you can approach the "holiest" of things on equal terms.

Writing Your Parody

You can parody any contemporary form of advertising or any form that would be used in any kind of communication. You can parody television forms, formats, shows, and commercials, and other selling forms such as direct mail, radio spots, newspaper advertising. You can parody television anchor men and women, newscast formats and reports, quiz shows, soap operas, sitcoms, and talk shows. You can imagine yourself the writer for your favorite anchor man or woman. You can parody documentary/instructional films, of which you have seen many. You can parody memos, reports, speeches, sales demonstrations, computer formats, and dialogues with computers. You can parody any of the forms put forth as basic forms in this book. Indeed, several of our reading selections have parodic attitudes and characteristics. You can parody oral telling forms, such as folktales, or oral poetic forms, such as street rhymes, game rhymes, counting rhymes, the "dozens," signifying rhymes, jump-rope rhymes, "it"-choosing rhymes, and so forth. You can parody genre, such as gothic romances and hunting and fishing stories. You can parody style.

Here is a passage from the Bible and a parody of it in modern bureaucratic prose. Read them aloud.

> I returned and saw under the sun, that the race is not to the swift, nor the battle to the strong, neither yet bread to the wise, nor yet riches to men of understanding, nor yet favor to men of skill; but time and chance happeneth to them all.
>
> —Ecclesiastes

> Objective consideration of contemporary phenomena compels the conclusion that success or failure in competitive activities exhibits no tendency to be commensurate with innate capacity, but that a considerable element of the unpredictable must invariably be taken into account.
>
> —George Orwell

In your how-it-happens subject area, you will find opportunities for parodies of commonly used forms, such as speeches, memoranda of in-house correspondence, instructional films, sales demonstrations, pep-talks, computer print-outs and "dialogues," and so on.

You should parody whatever form most strongly takes your attention, whatever impulse from your seeing of the parody makes you react strongly, whether or not it's part of your how-it-happens subject. If something outside your how-it-happens subject takes your attention for parody, go after it. Once you have a strong sense of the parody, you should try to do a draft of it in one sitting. Follow the impulse while it's strong.

Comparison and Contrast of Short Instances to Develop Patterns

Subject-by-subject or point-by-point are the two basic methods we use in comparing instances similar in similar ways, or different in similar ways, or similar in different ways, or very different. Usually we mix the two methods, responding to what we perceive, and might be hard put to say how we mixed them. In the first approach, we compare one subject to another subject, for instance, one quarterback to another quarterback. In the second approach, we juxtapose point by point the things we want to compare about the subjects. For instance, if we are comparing two football quarterbacks, we could, in the subject-by-subject approach, devote one paragraph or set of paragraphs to one quarterback and a second paragraph or set of paragraphs to the other quarterback. In this case, the occupation establishes a significant basis for the comparison. We could establish at the outset a possible thesis: The two quarterbacks have certain similarities but are not identical, and then compare their characteristics and abilities to support our thesis and see how it works out. Actually we may be more interested in contrasting whatever most clearly takes our attention about each of the quarterbacks. In the alternating point-by-point approach, we could compare the passing performance of each quarterback, their running or "scrambling" abilities, their inspirational abilities, their abilities to distract the other team, their outside interests in religion or partying, their training and team backgrounds, their personalities, interests, special abilities, and so on, point by point.

Comparison and contrast is a basic mode of thinking by which we begin to abstract patterns and perceive useful organizations of perceptions, thematic patterns, and concepts realized from patterns. Most people usually mix the subject-by-subject and point-by-point methods, responding to the things that take their attention about the subjects.

If you set out to garden, you compare patterns of your past experiences with various vegetables or flowers and come to your conclusions about what you will grow and not grow and how you will do it. If it's your first time in gardening, you may compare and contrast more than one person's experience and advice. If you start doing something on your own, you compare your experiences as they occur. You compare ways of doing things, the behavior of people, the molecules of different substances when subjected to heat or cold, and so on. Comparison and contrast is a basic mode of thinking, of exploring and making situations work, of extending and refining knowledge.

* * *

Examine the following examples of the use of comparison and contrast excerpted from the chapter "How Desert Animals Handle Water Loss" in *An Island Called California,* by Elna Bakker. In the first example, the stated subject is the desert animal's use of evaporation to cool its body; then several examples are compared and contrasted to support the thesis of the subject.

One device is to use the natural cooling resulting from evaporation. One of the first lessons taught in high school science classes is that when water changes its state from liquid to vapor there is an accompanying loss of heat. Man has made use of this handy little physical principle ever since the first tribesman thought to hang an oozing skin bag of water in a tree to catch the breeze. He could very well have been inspired by his own body. Countless sweat glands are scattered in much of the human skin. When perspiring animals are warm, water is shunted out into the sweat glands from the blood. The glands open, water is flushed out over the skin, it evaporates, and the body is cooled; a breeze is enjoyed on a hot day because it speeds evaporation. However, the human species is unusual, for most other terrestrial vertebrates have fewer sweat glands. Evaporative cooling can only occur where there is moist skin, or tissue such as the mucus secreting membranes of nose, mouth, throat, and the lung itself. Many desert animals open their mouths and some even pant while under heat duress, exposing as much moist surface as possible to the open air. The long, dripping tongues of overheated canine friends point up the usefulness of saliva as a moisture source for evaporative cooling. Some ground squirrels, the cactus mouse, and Merriam's kangaroo rat have been seen to actually spread saliva around on their heads and chests as a last-ditch method of keeping body temperatures below lethal levels.

In the second example, we see a clear statement of process of how certain desert species retain as much water as possible by using as little as possible to discharge waste. Bakker compares many instances of species' handling of water to perceive the pattern that makes the clear statement of thesis of process possible, then uses a few of the compared instances to support the thesis in the written presentation.

The wastes of vertebrate animals are usually discharged while suspended in fluid or in a moist state. Many desert species absorb most of the liquid passing through the lower intestines, and the discharged feces are relatively dry. In birds and reptiles, the urine is concentrated to the point where its solid particles precipitate out as crystals of uric acid. They are voided with the feces with little loss of water. In some of the desert rodents, urinary wastes are almost pasty in consistency, in contrast with the liquid discharge of more water-spending species. The desert tortoise has a water-storing bladder, an internal resource upon which it can draw when drought has killed or prevented the growth of the moist vegetation on which it feeds.

In the third example, we are told point-by-point about individual desert species that need a watery environment.

A number of desert animals are restricted to a damp or aquatic environment, if they are to survive. They rarely, if ever, expose themselves to desiccating air and heat. Toads and frogs are among those unable to live far from moisture. Both the red-spotted and spadefoot toads retreat to damp burrows and crannies when their pools contract after the swelling of winter. There is some evidence that they estivate, or enter summer dormancy, akin to hibernation or winter sleep. Neither food nor water is needed in what amounts to a state of suspended animation. The California treefrog also spends part of the time holed up in moist, underground pockets. For all three species, rainy spells are times of busy activity which are usually coincidental with an increased insect supply. They feast on juicy grubs and the emerged adults alike. Breeding usually takes place during the same period of optimum conditions; the tadpoles hatch in rain pools and renewed streams.

Though some aquatic forms such as the little desert pupfish are confined to permanent water, brine shrimp can exist for years as viable eggs encased in the dried mud of a playa bed. When rains and runoff create temporary lakes or puddles in these basins, almost miraculously they hatch into lively little crustaceans, swarming in the salty water. Fairy shrimp, near relatives, behave in the same way, but they cannot survive highly saline solutions.

* * *

The following reading selections compare several short instances to find patterns. Sometimes the short instances and their patterns support an argument for a particular point that was originally discovered from the comparison of the instances. Thus, the process of our thinking not only supplies us with our discoveries, but also provides the argumentative support for those discoveries.

The first selection, from *Paper Lion* by George Plimpton, simply compares the physical types and running styles of football players, each unique style emerging from (and suited to) the personality of the player. In the selection from *Origin of Species,* by Charles Darwin, we find short instances of the breeding of domestic animals compared and used as examples to illustrate how man-made selection so strongly influences the development of domestic animals and plants. Darwin selects instances that make a significant comparison possible. The patterns of these short instances support his argument that selection, whether man-made or natural, can choose best-suited adaptations and develop animal or plant varieties in the direction of those adaptations. Some of his instances come from personal observation and some from reading and other reports. He argues his thesis for selection carefully, comparing instances as examples to illustrate points.

James G. Frazer, in the excerpt from *The Golden Bough,* develops the patterns of world-wide superstitious behavior toward footprints. All of Frazer's instances, so far as we know, come from research through reading. Yet he makes you *see* the image of each instance juxtaposed with the images of other instances to find the pattern.

In "The Children and Sam's World and Henny's World," from *The Man Who Loved Children,* by Christina Stead, we find the comparison and contrast method used in fiction. Fiction writers frequently use comparison and contrast in subtle and powerful ways, contrasting and comparing characters, actions, consequences, etc. Strong narrative movement may develop from such comparison and contrast.

In the final selection, by Ann Hemenway, we have a distillation of an earlier journal entry, another fictional exploration. From the comparison of the two young women's dreams, Elaine's and Sheila's, what differences in their characters do you sense?

See what the use of comparison and contrast in these reading selections suggests for your writing.

From

Paper Lion

George Plimpton

Down on the field after a day or so, the players, who had been so many ciphers, one indistinguishable from another, began to take on identifying characteristics. Some were obvious. One was struck by the odd disparity of the football players' physiques— more than in any other team sport—from the lean, near emaciated stringiness of the defensive backs and flankers to the bulwarked heft of the linemen, many with pronounced bellies, who were set close to the ground, like cabbages. The range would be from such a player as Del Shofner, the Giants' flanker, lanky, sallow, with ulcers, who has been described as looking like a saxophone player after a hard one-night stand— from Shofner to Brown, the three-hundred-pounder of the Lions, the bulge of his thighs so enormous that to get one leg past the other produced a waddle of such distinction that the players seeing him in the locker room or emerging from the shower jawed at him about it, and imitated his walk.

Down on the practice field I would see Brown and the other big men endlessly circling the field after practice—distant figures against the trees, trying to remove a pound or two, so that their bulk could be moved with more agility.

The running styles were as different as the physical characteristics. Dick Compton, a small Texan scatback, ran with sharp exhalations when he had the ball, *ah-ah-ah,* like piston strokes—a habit he had picked up in high school which he felt gave power to his run. He could be heard across the width of a field. The "Gasper" some of the players called him, and he was also nicknamed "Roadrunner"—after the quick-running desert bird of his home state. Jake Greer also had a distinctive run—moving his spindly body in leaps like a high jumper moving for the crossbar, high, bouncy steps, and then he stretched out fast, and when he got to the defending back he feinted with his small high-boned head, sometimes with a tiny bit of toothpick working in it. Then he'd fly on past or off at an angle, his hands splayed out wide, looking back for the ball honing in to intercept his line of flight, and then he'd *miss* it—good moves but bad hands in those early training sessions, they said—and the shouts would go up, "Squeeze that thing, baby." "Hands, man, hands." Greer would circle back, stricken, staring into his big hands as if they had betrayed him as he bent down to pick up the ball. His face would remain long and melancholy, and when his signal came up again, Scooter McLean would shout: "Look like you want it, Al, come *on,* baby."

"Selection in Domestic Breeding"
From **Origin of Species**
Charles Darwin

Directs reader's curiosity toward changes in domestic animals, but withholds his main thesis statement

Let us now briefly consider the steps by which domestic races have been produced, either from one or from several allied species. Some effect may be attributed to the direct and definite action of the external conditions of life, and some to habit; but he would be a bold man who would account by such agencies for the differences between a dray- and race-horse, a greyhound and bloodhound, a carrier and tumbler pigeon. One of the most remarkable features in our domesticated races is that we see in them adaptation, not indeed to the animal's or plant's own good, but to man's use or fancy. Some

Comparison and contrast of instances to build support for thesis—from "a dray and racehorse" to "flower garden races of plants"

variations useful to him have probably arisen suddenly, or by one step; many botanists, for instance, believe that the fuller's teasel, with its hooks, which cannot be rivalled by any mechanical contrivance, is only a variety of the wild Dipsacus; and this amount of change may have suddenly arisen in a seedling. So it has probably been with the turnspit dog; and this is known to have been the case with the ancon sheep. But when we compare the dray-horse and racehorse, the dromedary and camel, the various breeds of sheep fitted either for cultivated land or mountain pasture, with the wool of one breed good for one purpose, and that of another breed for another purpose; when we compare the many breeds of dogs, each good for man in different ways; when we compare the game-cock, so pertinacious in battle, with other breeds so little quarrelsome, with "everlasting layers" which never desire to sit, and with the bantam so small and elegant; when we compare the host of agricultural, culinary, orchard, and flower-garden races of

Main thesis— "power of accumulative selection"

plants, most useful to man at different seasons and for different purposes, or so beautiful in his eyes, we must, I think, look further than to mere variability. We cannot suppose that all the breeds were suddenly produced as perfect and as useful as we now see them; indeed, in many cases, we know that this has not been their history. The key is man's power of accumulative selection: nature gives successive variations; man adds them up in certain directions useful to him. In this sense he may be said to have made for himself useful breeds.

Examples that expand the thesis—breeding is deliberate and conscious

The great power of this principle of selection is not hypothetical. It is certain that several of our eminent breeders have, even within a single lifetime, modified to a large extent their breeds of cattle and sheep. In order fully to realise what they have done, it is almost necessary to read several of the many treatises devoted to this subject, and to

Metaphor to emphasize human power—"the magician's wand"

inspect the animals. Breeders habitually speak of an animal's organisation as something plastic, which they can model almost as they please. If I had space I could quote numerous passages to this effect from highly competent authorities. Youatt, who was probably better acquainted with the works of agriculturists than almost any other individual, and who was himself a very good judge of animals, speaks of the principle of selection as "that which enables the agriculturist, not only to modify the character of his flock, but to change it altogether. It is the magician's wand, by means of which he may summon into life whatever form and mould he pleases." Lord Somerville, speaking of what breeders have done for sheep, says:—"It would seem as if they had chalked out upon a wall a form perfect in itself, and then had given it existence." In Saxony the importance of the principle of selection in regard to merino sheep is so fully recognised, that men follow it as a trade: the sheep are placed on a table and are studied, like a picture by a connoisseur; this is done three times at intervals of months, and the sheep are each time marked and classed, so that the very best may ultimately be selected for breeding.

What English breeders have actually effected is proved by the enormous prices given for animals with a good pedigree; and these have been exported to almost every quarter of the world. The improvement is by no means generally due to crossing different breeds; all the best breeders are strongly opposed to this practice, except sometimes amongst closely allied sub-breeds. And when a cross has been made, the closest selection is far more indispensable even than in ordinary cases. If selection consisted merely in separating some very distinct variety, and breeding from it, the principle would be so obvious as hardly to be worth notice; but its importance consists in the great effect produced by the accumulation in one direction, during successive generations, of differences absolutely inappreciable by an uneducated eye—differences which I for one have vainly attempted to appreciate. Not one man in a thousand has accuracy of eye and judgment sufficient to become an eminent breeder. If gifted with these qualities, and he studies his subject for years, and devotes his lifetime to it with indomitable perseverance, he will succeed, and may make great improvements; if he wants any of these qualities, he will assuredly fail. Few would readily believe in the natural capacity and years of practice requisite to become even a skilful pigeon-fancier.

The same principles are followed by horticulturists; but the variations are here often more abrupt. No one supposes that our choicest productions have been produced by a single variation from the aboriginal stock. We have proofs that this has not been so in several cases in which exact records have been kept; thus, to give a very trifling instance, the steadily-increasing size of the common gooseberry may be quoted. We see an astonishing improvement in many florists' flowers, when the flowers of the present day are compared with drawings made only twenty or thirty years ago. When a race of plants is once pretty well established, the seedraisers do not pick out the best plants, but merely go over their seed-beds, and pull up the "rogues," as they call the plants that deviate from the proper standard. With animals this kind of selection is, in fact, likewise followed; for hardly any one is so careless as to breed from his worst animals.

"Footprints and Magic"
From *The Golden Bough*
James G. Frazer

Again magic may be wrought on a man sympathetically, not only through his clothes and severed parts of himself, but also through the impress left by his body in sand or earth. In particular, it is a worldwide superstition that by injuring footprints you injure the feet that made them. Thus the natives of Southeastern Australia think that they can lame a man by placing sharp pieces of quartz, glass bone, or charcoal in his footprints. Rheumatic pains are often attributed by them to this cause. Seeing a Tatungolung man very lame, Dr. Howitt asked him what was the matter. He said, "some fellow has put *bottle* in my foot." He was suffering from a rheumatism, but believed that an enemy had found his foot-track and had buried in it a piece of broken bottle, the magical influence of which had entered his foot.

Similar practices prevail in various parts of Europe. Thus in Mecklenburg it is thought that if you drive a nail into a man's footprint he will fall lame; sometimes it is required that the nail should be taken from a coffin. A like mode of injuring an enemy is resorted to in some parts of France. It is said that there was an old woman who used to frequent Stow in Suffolk, and she was a witch. If, while she walked, any one went after her and stuck a nail or a knife into her footprint in the dust, the dame could not stir a step till it was withdrawn. Among the South Slavs a girl will dig up the earth from the footprints of the man she loves and put it in a flower-pot. Then she plants in the pot a marigold, a flower that is thought to be fadeless. And as its golden blossom grows and blooms and never fades, so shall her sweetheart's love grow and bloom, and never, never fade. Thus the love-spell acts on the man through the earth he trod on. An old Danish mode of concluding a treaty was based on the same idea of the sympathetic connexion between a man and his footprints: the covenanting parties sprinkled each other's footprints with their own blood, thus giving a pledge of fidelity. In ancient Greece superstitions of the same sort seem to have been current, for it was thought that if a horse stepped on the track of a wolf he was seized with numbness; and a maxim ascribed to Pythagoras forbade people to pierce a man's footprints with a nail or a knife.

"The Children and Sam's World and Henny's World"
From **The Man Who Loved Children**
Christina Stead

Sam tried to impart everything he knew to the children and grumbled that the *mother* taught nothing at all: yet their influence on the boys and girls was equal. The children grabbed tricks and ideas according to the need of the day, without thinking at all of where they got them, without gratitude; and Henny saw this and so did not bother her head about her children. She herself belonged to a grabbing breed. Henny would also tell fortunes, by the cards, over her tea, though never for the children. While she was dealing to tell the fortune of Aunt Bonnie (Sam's twenty-five-year-old sister and their unpaid maid of all work), or Miss Spearing (Henny's old-maid friend from schooldays), she would always begin a wonderful yarn about how she went to town, "more dead than alive and with only ten cents in my purse and I wanted to crack a safe," and how, in the streetcar, was "a dirty shrimp of a man with a fishy expression who purposely leaned over me and pressed my bust, and a common vulgar woman beside him, an ogress, big as a hippopotamus, with her bottom sticking out, who grinned like a shark and tried to give him the eye," and how this wonderful adventure went on for hours, always with new characters or new horror. In it would invariably be a woman with a cowlike expression, a girl looking frightened as a rabbit, a yellow-haired frump with hair like a haystack in a fit, some woman who bored Henny with her silly gassing, and impudent flighty young girls behind counters, and waitresses smelling like a tannery (or a fish market), who gave her lip, which caused her to "go to market and give them more than they bargained for." There were men and women, old acquaintances of hers, or friends of Sam who presumed to know her, to whom she would give the go-by, or the cold shoulder, or a distant bow, or a polite good day, or a black look, or a look black as thunder, and there were silly old roosters, creatures like a dying duck in a thunderstorm, filthy old pawers, and YMCA sick chickens, and women thin as a rail and men fat as a pork barrel, and women with blouses so puffed out that she wanted to stick pins in, and men like coalheavers, and women like boiled owls and women who had fallen into a flour barrel; and all these wonderful creatures, who swarmed in the streets, stores, and restaurants of Washington, ogling, leering, pulling, pushing, stinking, overscented, screaming and boasting, turning pale at a black look from Henny, ducking and diving, dodging and returning, were the only creatures that Henny ever saw.

What a dreary stodgy world of adults the children saw when they went out! And what a moral, high-minded world their father saw! But for Henny there was a wonderful particular world, and when they went with her they saw it: they saw the fish eyes, the crocodile grins, the hair like a birch broom, the mean men crawling with maggots, and the children restless as an eel, that she saw. She did not often take them with her. She preferred to go out by herself and mooch to the bargain basements, and ask the young man in the library what was good to read, and take tea in some obscure restaurant, and wander desolately about, criticizing shopwindows and wondering if, in this street or that, she would yet, "old as I am and looking like a black hag," meet her fate. Then she would come home, next to some girl "from a factory who looked like a lily and smelled like a skunk cabbage," flirting with all the men and the men grinning back, next to some coarse, dirty workman who pushed against her in the car and smelled of sweat, or some leering brute who tried to pay her fare.

Louie would sit there, on the end of the bench, lost in visions, wondering how she would survive if some leering brute shamefully tried to pay her fare in a public car, admiring Henny for her strength of mind in the midst of such scandals: and convinced of the dreary, insulting horror of the low-down world. For it was not Henny alone who went through this inferno, but every woman, especially, for example, Mrs. Wilson, the woman who came to wash every Monday. Mrs. Wilson, too, "big as she was, big as an ox," was insulted by great big brutes of workmen, with sweaty armpits, who gave her a leer, and Mrs. Wilson, too, had to tell grocers where they got off, and she too had to put little half-starved cats of girls, thin as toothpicks, in their places. Mrs. Wilson it was who saw the ravishing Charlotte Bolton (daughter of the lawyer, who lived in a lovely bungalow across the street), she saw "my lady, standing with her hands on her hips, waggling her bottom and laughing at a man like a common streetgirl," and he "black as the inside of a hat, with dark blood for sure." Louie and Evie, and the obliging little boys, tugging at the piles of greasy clothes on Mondays, puffing under piles of new-ironed linen on Tuesdays, would be silent for hours, observing this world of tragic faery in which all their adult friends lived. Sam, their father, had endless tales of friends, enemies, but most often they were good citizens, married to good wives, with good children (though untaught), but never did Sam meet anyone out of Henny's world, grotesque, foul, loud-voiced, rude, uneducated, and insinuating, full of scandal, slander, and filth, financially deplorable and physically revolting, dubiously born, and going awry to a desquamating end.

Elaine's and Sheila's Dreams
Ann Hemenway

Elaine's dreams are like windchimes made of broken glass, glittering in the sun, but Sheila's dreams are red, or off-red purple and her dreams are out of focus, blurred, as though everyone is encased in angora sweaters. As Elaine dreams, Sheila dreams her own dreams. But what did she do before she fell into this kind of sleep—Sheila's sleep—a sleep where she doesn't move, but lies on her side, open-mouthed, her head on the pillow and her hair falling across her cheek.

Writing Your Comparison and Contrast of Short Instances

Wherever possible choose a clear basis for comparison. Compare things that are significantly similar or different. If we explore Hamlet's pun ("I am but mad north-north-west. When the wind is southerly, I know a hawk from a handsaw."), we can compare and contrast a hawk (bird) and a hernshaw ("handsaw" was an Elizabethan word for "hernshaw," a kind of heron), or hawk (board with a handle on the bottom, used by a plasterer) and handsaw (the common tool); in either case we will have a significant basis (similarity and difference) for the comparison. However, if we compare hawk (bird) with handsaw (tool) we have a clear basis of difference but not significant similarity. Nevertheless, to try the latter comparison and contrast could be fun, instructive, and imaginatively stimulating in your journal writing, as a precise parody of a comparison and contrast assignment; it would force you to invent significant similarities and exploit the contrasts.

In most cases you will probably learn more by comparing and contrasting things that are similar in some essential way. Rather than contrast an automobile with a stone, unless we are comparing kinds of lethal weapons, we contrast it with other automobiles or forms of transportation, or with other things that occupy space or use energy, or whatever is the basis for the comparison. If we compare automobile and stone as lethal weapons, we have a significant basis. If we compare automobile and stone as forms of transportation, we don't learn much. You may prove me wrong by accepting it as a writing challenge. If Darwin compared breeding changes in domestic animals to geologic changes in certain mountain ranges, his course of reasoning would be immediately scattered. If Frazer reported all images of footprints from anywhere, rather than footprints that are used in sympathetic magic, his pattern would not be clearly revealed. However, though Plimpton makes the point that the running styles of each of the players are different, another study could compare many running styles and other factors influencing running ability to find patterns that could cause coaches to change football training. Many teams use computers to try to maximize such perception of patterns.

If, in doing a set of high school instances, I compare the gangbanger* with the preppy, I could write one or more paragraphs about the gangbanger and then one or more about the preppy. Then I could also list point by point the ways in which the gangbanger's and the preppy's backgrounds differ or are similar. I could extend the subject-by-subject or point-by-point comparison to jock, scholar, or whatever other types are available. Similar comparisons of types of people, or of individuals and their occupations, could be done in a set of job instances.

First, list the instances that particularly take your attention and see what they begin to tell you as you compare them. Patterns may be found in a leap of comprehension, or in a more deliberate sorting through of the instances. Find your pattern, state it, then use your instances to argue a point that you conceive from the pattern. If you don't feel you have a clear pattern, start writing and compare as you go. You can write two or three pages wholly inductively just to see what instance patterns you begin to perceive. If you perceive a pattern, state it, and support it with the instances.

Keep comparing and contrasting through all of your writing assignments. Keep using this important method of thinking.

How-It's-Done, How-It-Works, How-It-Occurs

The how-it's-done or how-it-works form tells how an activity, process, system, or concept is sequentially, chronologically carried out, or how it works or occurs, such as how the cardiovascular system of the body works, how a bureaucracy works, how a mechanism works or how a young man gets tattooed. Though process also plays a sig-

---

*In the memory of many of your teachers, "gangbanging" meant a kind of group sexual practice. In modern Black English vernacular gangbanger means a "gang member" or a particularly aggressive gang member.

nificant part in a successful how-to, as we've already seen, this form differs from the how-to in important ways.

How-it's-done perception precedes, as a way of perceiving and thinking, and actually helps lay the basis for, the more complicated how-to form. In the how-to, the second person "you" is usually the natural pronoun, addressed directly to the reader to involve him or her as a learning participant in what's being told. The how-it's-done form may use the "you," the third person singular or plural (he, she, they, someone, anyone, everyone), or the first person singular or plural (I, we). How-it's-done may display a variety of persuasive aims, but in it we do not necessarily try, as we do in the how-to, to persuade the reader of the reason and worth of doing whatever it is, though we do try to persuade the reader to believe in what we're telling, as we do in any form of writing. For instance, in our first reading selection, "The Stud Ace," the seeing and telling of the single incident of one young man's tattoing convinces us of the validity of what we're seeing, but doesn't attempt to persuade us to get a tattoo, whereas the true how-to of tattooing would probably attempt to persuade "you" of the value of tattooing or at least give "you" a set of clear instructions and implicitly suggest that "you" follow them.

The how-it's-done form deals with mechanisms of process, whether the processes are mechanical, social, physical, or psychological. Though it uses the basic techniques of single event narrative telling, it shades into the model-telling form, which gives us image or narrative of how something usually happens. Indeed, "The Sausage Room" and "The Moon and the Tides" are model-tellings of the processes of social and natural mechanisms, of how these processes happened again and again over a period of time. "The Stud Ace" is a process telling of a single event.

The description of a mechanism is another form of process telling. It uses imagery to tell us how a mechanical mechanism works. "Pencil Sharpener," "Turbocharger," and "Scissors" exemplify this kind of telling in factual technical writing. The selection from "In the Penal Colony" by Franz Kafka is a description of an imagined mechanism.

All three of our process writings, and our four descriptions of mechanisms, explain by making you *see* the processes.

* * *

In "The Stud Ace" we sense that our observer-teller is right there in the room with us, a "friend" of Stoney's.

The Stud Ace
John Madler

Stoney's had its entrance at the end of a short arcade off of Howard Street. It was one large, very white room with big fluorescent lights on the ceiling. The walls were covered with detachable panels with hundreds of different tattoo designs on them. Across the center of the room was a high counter, and behind the counter were two chairs and a small table holding a sterilizer for the needles, four vibrators laid out in a row on a clean towel. And on the second shelf were all the dyes in many small bottles, reds, blues, greens in any shade, and one big bottle of black.

Stoney was always in one of the chairs. The chairs were old barber shop chairs, and he would have one tilted way back with the footrest almost out straight in front. The back would be reclined and Stoney would be chain-smoking cigarettes and listening to the radio with his eyes closed. Stoney was very small, not more than four foot tall, and the chair almost swallowed him. He was about sixty, bald, and was covered with tattoos. He even had a watch tattooed around his right wrist and rings on his fingers. . . .

Things are kind of slow on a Saturday morning, and Stoney is in his chair listening to the radio. A kid comes in with two of his buddies. All three are dressed the same, sports shirts and faded blue jeans. All of them are kind of on the thin side. Stoney opens one eye and gives the trio the once over. Not one of 'em over eighteen, he thinks to himself.

The kid nervously looks around the walls at all the tattoos. Looking at each one and rejecting it as his buddies would point to this tattoo or that one, going, "Wow," and "Hey, look at this one." "That one," he says, "that one. I want to see that one," pointing to the panel in the back on the bottom row. Stoney takes the panel off the wall and hands it to the kid. The kid all but grabs it out of Stoney's hands and stares at a tattoo called The Stud Ace. His eyes get big, very big.

The Stud Ace was a background of a large black spade with a hand of four aces over it and the word "lucky" in a scroll under it. "This one, I want this one!" One of his buddies goes, "Wow." The kid looks at his buddies for approval, and it comes from the one who said "Wow." "Man, that's the toughest tattoo I ever saw. How much?" he asks. "Ten dollars," says Stoney. "Sold," says the kid, looking triumphantly at his two buddies as he throws his chest out even more. Stoney takes the ten, puts it in a small green cash box that's kept under the counter. "O.K., young fella, step right this way," Stoney says in a carnie barker's voice as he points to the chair. All three laugh at Stoney's little joke. The kid goes to the chair and sits down. "Right bicep?" Stoney asks. The kid nods. Stoney takes a cotton swab dipped in alcohol in his right hand, and in the other flips the sleeve of the kid's shirt so that the whole arm is bare as he carefully starts to swab the bicep to be tattooed. The kid gives a little jerk from the cool of the alcohol and resettles stiffly back in the chair. Stoney checks out the vibrator with short buzzes, fills and attaches a small bottle with black dye in it and tries the vibrator again. He jacks the chair up until the bare arm is in front of him, and tells the kid to keep his arm just so. Stoney gives the vibrator another short burst and says, "O.K." to the kid, as if asking for permission to start. The kid gives a nod, not taking his eyes off the needle of the vibrator. He never takes his eyes off of it as Stoney puts the needle on his arm and moves his head so that his eyes are only ten inches from the arm. At the last moment, the kid turns his head and looks straight ahead.

Stoney starts the tattoo, and the kid gives a small jerk and his knuckles turn first red and then white as he grips the chair arms. The kid is sitting rigidly in the chair as his eyes burn a hole in the wall. Stoney happily chatters away. "It's coming along nicely," he says. "That 'a boy, just keep your arm right where it is." The kid isn't hearing a word. His forehead breaks out in a sweat, big beads of sweat that run down his face and hang on under his chin before dropping off.

Stoney finishes the black outline of the spade and the four aces and the scroll with "lucky" in it. He says, "Just a second, got to refill the bottle." The kid just sits there. Stoney rapidly refills the bottle and is back at the kid's side. Down goes the needle, and Stoney starts to fill in the spade. A trickle of blood runs down the kid's arm, and as it does the kid's mouth opens a little and slowly, very slowly, as if it was all the blood he had, he turns white as a sheet and his eyes get glassy. Stoney looks up just in time to see the kid pass out and slump down into the chair.

Stoney goes to the counter for some smelling salts and waves it under the kid's nose. The kid stirs and slowly opens his eyes. Even before he can get his chin off his chest, the kid mutters, "I'm O.K., I'm O.K.," in a weak voice. "You're O.K.?" asks Stoney. "Yeah, O.K.," says the kid. Stoney starts again, but the kid never gets his chin off his chest. He sits there staring at the floor and wheezes over and over, "I'm O.K.,

I'm O.K.," and with each deep breath he sways slowly in his chair.

Stoney works as fast as he can, changing the vibrators for each new color. It's all the same to the kid. He can hear the vibrator and feel the needle going up and down all the time. Stoney finishes the tattoo with a small red star in one corner, explaining that it's his trademark. He steps back to admire his artwork and says, "O.K., son, it's all done!" But the kid just sits in the chair still hearing the vibrator and feeling the needle. "All done," Stoney says again, and gives the kid a slap on the back.

The kid slowly lifts his head and turns toward the voice. The corners of his mouth turn upward a little, in a silly smile. Unsteadily he gets out of his chair, takes two shaky steps and makes it to the counter. His buddies start to talk at the same time. "Hey, that's great, that's really great, tough, really tough. How do you feel, how was it, did it hurt?"

The kid lets go of the counter and hitching up his blue jeans says, "Nothing to it, didn't hurt much." Stoney comes over and gets a large square gauze pad from the counter, and while putting it over the tattoo says, "Leave it there for a couple of days to prevent infection." The kid proudly holds out his arm as Stoney puts two strips of adhesive tape at both the top and the bottom of the gauze pad.

The kid slowly turns around and heads for the door. His eyes never leave his arm that's slightly raised as if he could see through the pad to The Stud Ace. He'll be back, he says to Stoney, as they go through the door. "Ya, we'll be back," echo his two buddies.

Stoney goes over and turns up the radio and then goes back to his chair. He lowers the chair, extends the footrest, tilts the back and gets on it, proceeds to light up a cigarette, lean back, and close his eyes.

At one point, the observer-teller even seems to know what Stoney is thinking— "Not one of 'em over eighteen, he thinks to himself"—and at other points the observer-teller seems to know more or less what the "kid" is thinking, e.g., "It's all the same to the kid. He can hear the vibrator, etc . . . ," and "But the kid just sits in the chair still hearing the vibrator and feeling the needle." We recognize from our own oral tellings that these are ways in which we simulate point-of-view for humorous effects. Otherwise, the process of how one young man gets a tattoo in the company of two buddies is told by what can be seen or known or inferred from observation, from the outside, by a friend of Stoney's present in the tattoo parlor, a slight abstraction of the participant-observer. Can you find suggestions that our observer-teller may be relating a story that Stoney told him?

What do you learn about the process of tattooing from the sequential telling of "The Stud Ace?" What sort of person is Stoney? What sort of person is the "kid" who gets the tattoo? What can you infer about the social background of Stoney, the "kid," and the kid's buddies?

* * *

In "The Sausage Room" Upton Sinclair gives the pattern of what usually happens day after day in the sausage room, in a single chronological scene unrolling before our eyes, as observed by touring visitors, whose leisure contrasts with the desperately narrow life of the sausage room workers.

"The Sausage Room"
From **The Jungle**
Upton Sinclair

Elzbieta was used to working, but she found this change [to the sausage room] a hard one, for the reason that she had to stand motionless upon her feet from seven o'clock in the morning till half-past twelve, and again from one till half-past five. For the first few days it seemed to her that she could not stand it—she suffered almost as much as Jurgis had from the fertilizer [Jurgis had worked in the sickeningly dusty fertilizer plant] and would come out at sundown with her head fairly reeling. Besides this, she was working in one of the dark holes, by electric light, and the dampness, too, was deadly—there were always puddles of water on the floor, and a sickening odor of moist flesh in the room. The people who worked here followed the ancient custom of nature, whereby the ptarmigan is the color of dead leaves in the fall and of snow in the winter, and the chameleon, who is black when he lies upon a stump and turns green when he moves to a leaf. The men and women who worked in this department were precisely the color of the "fresh country sausage" they made.

The sausage room was an interesting place to visit, for two or three minutes, and provided that you did not look at the people; the machines were perhaps the most wonderful things in the entire plant. Presumably sausages were once chopped and stuffed by hand, and if so it would be interesting to know how many workers had been displaced by these inventions. On one side of the room were the hoppers, into which men shovelled loads of meat and wheelbarrows full of spices; in these great bowls were whirling knives that made two thousand revolutions a minute, and when the meat was ground fine and adulterated with potato flour, and well mixed with water, it was forced to the stuffing machines on the other side of the room. The latter were tended by women; there was a sort of spout, like the nozzle of a hose, and one of the women would take a long string of "casing" and put the end over the nozzle and then work the whole thing on, as one works on the finger of a tight glove. This string would be twenty or thirty feet long, but the woman would have it all on in a jiffy; and when she had several on, she would press a lever, and a stream of sausage meat would be shot out, taking the casing with it as it came. Thus one might stand and see appear, miraculously born from the machine, a wriggling snake of sausage of incredible length. In front was a big pan which caught these creatures, and two more women who seized them as fast as they appeared and twisted them into links. This was for the uninitiated the most perplexing work of all, for all that the woman had to give was a single turn of the wrist; and in some way she contrived to give it so that instead of an endless chain of sausages, one after another, there grew under her hands a bunch of strings, all dangling from a single centre. It was quite like the feat of a prestidigitator—for the woman worked so fast that the eye could literally not follow her, and there was only a mist of motion, and tangle after tangle of sausages appearing. In the midst of the mist, however, the visitor would suddenly notice the tense set face, with the two wrinkles graven in the forehead, and the ghastly pallor of the cheeks; and then he would suddenly recollect that it was time he was going on. The woman did not go on; she stayed right there—hour after hour, day after day, year after year, twisting sausage links and racing with death. It was piece work, and she was apt to have a family to keep alive; and stern and ruthless economic laws had arranged it that she could only do this by working just as she did, with all her soul upon her work, and with never an instant for a glance at the well-dressed ladies and gentlemen who came to stare at her, as at some wild beast in a menagerie.

The telling suggests that the touring visitors happen by frequently enough to be part of the model scene, too. The tourists observe the woman worker, but the worker herself doesn't notice the tourists. The telling does not try to persuade a "you" to do it. On the contrary, the telling persuades us that the sausage room is stunningly repetitious work and tries to get us to see its effect upon the human beings who work there.

What do we learn about the process of making sausages? What is the author's purpose in this telling? How does he show inside knowledge of the workers and the operation of the sausage room and at the same time see the room from the vantage point of the touring visitors? What sights do you recall after reading it?

"The Sausage Room" is rich with comparisons and metaphors. Sinclair compares the complexion of the sausage room workers to the adaptable colors of ptarmigan and chameleon and makes many more comparisons such as "sort of spout, like the nozzle of a hose," "work the whole thing on, as one works on the finger of a tight glove," "miraculously born from the machine, a wriggling snake of sausage of incredible length," "a big pan which caught these creatures," "quite like the feat of a prestidigitator," "only a mist of motion," "In the midst of the mist," and so on. The metaphors come from the author's seeing of gestures and other sights side by side in his mind with possible comparisons. Which comparisons seem to come from gesture? Which from direct sights? Which from a mixture of gesture and direct sights?

*   *   *

In this excerpt from *The Sea Around Us* Rachel Carson tells of the mechanism of the tides and the moon over millions of years, in short, deals with billions of instances in a chronological telling of how the furious tides rendered the early earth uninhabitable and how the tides changed steadily over time in relation to the moon.

"The Moon and the Tides"
From *The Sea Around Us*
Rachel Carson

If the history of the earth's tides should one day be written by some observer of the universe, it would no doubt be said that they reached their greatest grandeur and power in the younger days of Earth, and that they slowly grew feebler and less imposing until one day they ceased to be. For the tides were not always as they are today, and as with all that is earthly, their days are numbered.

In the days when the earth was young, the coming in of the tide must have been a stupendous event. If the moon was, as we have supposed in an earlier chapter, formed by the tearing away of a part of the outer crust of the earth, it must have remained for a time very close to its parent. Its present position is the consequence of being pushed farther and farther away from the earth for some 2 billion years. When it was half its present distance from the earth, its power over the ocean tides was eight times as great as now, and the tidal range may even then have been several hundred feet on certain shores. But when the earth was only a few million years old, assuming that the deep ocean basins were then formed, the sweep of the tides must have been beyond all comprehension. Twice each day, the fury of the incoming waters would inundate all the margins of the continents. The range of the surf must have been enormously extended by the reach of the tides, so that the waves would batter the crests of high cliffs and sweep inland to erode the continents. The fury of such tides would contribute not a little to the general bleakness and grimness and uninhabitability of the young earth.

Under such conditions, no living thing could exist on the shores or pass beyond them, and, had conditions not changed, it is reasonable to suppose that life would have evolved no further than the fishes. But over the millions of years the moon has receded, driven away by the friction of the tides it creates. The very movement of the water over the bed of the ocean, over the shallow edges of the continents, and over the inland seas carries within itself the power that is slowly destroying the tides, for tidal friction is gradually slowing down the rotation of the earth. In those early days we have spoken of, it took the earth a much shorter time—perhaps only about 4 hours—to make a complete rotation on its axis. Since then, the spinning of the globe has been so greatly slowed that a rotation now requires, as everyone knows, about 24 hours. This retarding will continue, according to mathematicians, until the day is about 50 times as long as it is now.

And all the while the tidal friction will be exerting a second effect, pushing the moon farther away, just as it has already pushed it out more than 200,000 miles. (According to the laws of mechanics, as the rotation of the earth is retarded, that of the moon must be accelerated, and centrifugal force will carry it farther away.) As the moon recedes, it will, of course, have less power over the tides and they will grow weaker. It will also take the moon longer to complete its orbit around the earth. When finally the length of the day and of the month coincide, the moon will no longer rotate relatively to the earth, and there will be no lunar tides.

All this, of course, will require time on a scale the mind finds it difficult to conceive, and before it happens it is quite probable that the human race will have vanished from the earth. This may seem, then, like a Wellsian fantasy of a world so remote that we may dismiss it from our thoughts. But already, even in our allotted fraction of earthly time, we can see some of the effects of these cosmic processes. Our day is believed to be several seconds longer than that of Babylonian times. Britain's Astronomer Royal recently called the attention of the American Philosophical Society to the fact that the world will soon have to choose between two kinds of time. The tide-induced lengthening of the day has already complicated the problems of human systems of keeping time. Conventional clocks, geared to the earth's rotation, do not show the effect of the lengthening days. New atomic clocks now being constructed will show actual time and will differ from other clocks.

Vivid imagery of the process persuades us of the validity of the hypothesis concerning the tides, of the dynamic mechanism of the moon and the tides, but Carson is not telling us how to do something or persuading us to do something.

Notice how the character of the scene is given by such phrases as "fury of the incoming waters," by such verbs as "inundate," "batter," "sweep," "erode," and by nouns made from adjectives such as "bleakness," "grimness" and "uninhabitability." What other such phrases, verbs, adjectives, nouns, other words, do you find that give particular tone, atmosphere, character to the scene and the process?

No longer is the observer present as a participant in the telling itself, in the sense of the friend in Stoney's tattoo parlor or of the touring visitors to the sausage room. The observer-teller is abstracted into the mind of the writer and the reader, still supremely important to the telling, still relating the author's seeing-in-the-mind to the reader's mind.

Notice how many processes are told, one coming out of the other. Each paragraph tells yet another process or develops an earlier one. Such a telling as "The Moon and the Tides" requires research of the kind that can only be found by reading the work of many researchers and by pulling together in your mind what you've found in the reading.

How does Carson make sure we see how the mechanism of the moon, the tides, and the earth's rotation works? Does she exaggerate to make sure we see it clearly and appropriately? "Twice each day, the fury of the incoming waters would inundate all the margins of the continents." What happens if we rephrase it still more or less accurately? "Twice each day, the incoming waters would cover all the margins of the continents." Find other sentences in which *positive exaggeration* sets forth clearly what the author has to tell.

Description of a Mechanism

These two descriptions of mechanisms are very different.

Pencil Sharpeners

They're so familiar, yet the operation of a pencil sharpener is far from a simple thing. You're probably aware that the sharpener has two striped rollers that move around the pencil point. What makes them move that way and why does the movement result in a sharpened pencil?

Let's work from the outside in. The crank turns a sort of yoke that carries end pivots for the two rollers. The rollers slant away from each other in a sharp Vee. One end of each roller carries a gear and the gears mesh with another larger gear built into the housing of the sharpener. This is an *internal gear*—one in which the teeth point toward the center rather than away from the center, as ordinary gears do.

Now we have enough to see how the peculiar spinning motion of the rollers is created. As you turn the crank you turn the yoke carrying the two rollers. The rollers are carried around the pencil point but at the same time the gears at their ends are also turned as they roll in mesh with the internal gear.

Pretend for a moment that you are very small and that you stand in the center of the sharpener, much as your pencil does. If the crank were rotated slowly you would see the rollers move around you as the moon turns around the earth. At the same time the rollers turn on their own axes and so the stripes seem to climb along the roller just like the stripes on a spinning barber pole.

The stripes are actually raised and sharpened welts spiraling around the rollers. The sharpened edge of the stripe cuts forward as the roller turns and makes a spiral cut around and back on the pencil point. Each edge takes off a thin sliver of wood and lead. Since there are four or five edges in contact with the tapered point of the pencil, four or five such slivers are removed in neat, tapered spirals, leaving a rounded needle sharp point on your pencil.

Turbochargers

Turbochargers are as simple as they are effective. Basically, a turbo is two pieces of rotating machinery joined by a common shaft. The hot side is a gas turbine driven by the exhaust from an internal-combustion engine. The flow path is tangential to the turbine wheel on entry, and axial as it leaves. Inside the turbine housing, energy from the hot, high-velocity exhaust stream is converted to shaft rotation by the turbine wheel. At peak speed, the turbine spins at roughly 100,000 rpm, and this rotation is transferred along a short driveshaft to the turbo's cold, or compressor, side. All airflow entering the engine (frequently with fuel) is ducted to the mouth of the compressor, a circular port that's concentric with the turbocharger's shaft. The spinning compressor wheel pumps the intake charge out a tangential passage and then into the engine's intake manifold under pressure.

Turbine housings are typically cast from ductile iron, while compressor housings are cast aluminum. Turbine wheels are precision-cast, nickel-based super alloys for durability in the harsh exhaust stream, while plain old aluminum alloy (but still cast and machined with great precision) works fine for compressor wheels. A central bearing housing holds everything together. Oil under pressure from the engine must be fed to the bearing housing to lubricate sleeve-type bronze or aluminum bearings.

How does the telling of the working of a pencil sharpener make "you" participate in the process? Could the description of the turbocharger be told with "you" and "we" as direct observer-participants in learning how the turbocharger works? Why or why not?

Compare also their use of verbs. Nearly all the sentences in the turbocharger description use linking verbs, like "is" or "are." Only three active verbs make sentences complete: "spins," "pumps," and "holds." Compare with the active verbs used in the pencil sharpener telling. In the turbocharger description, only the phrase "plain old aluminum alloy" has the sense of direct address. What elements of speech, of direct address to the reader, do you find in the pencil sharpener telling? The pencil sharpener and the turbocharger tellings are examples of two different kinds of telling, personal and impersonal. What are the advantages of each kind? Is one superior to the other? All of the time? Most of the time? Part of the time? Explain.

Are there points in either telling that you did not understand on a first reading but were able to work out and understand on re-reading? What would you add to make them clear on first reading. Rewrite "Pencil Sharpeners" and "Turbochargers" to make them clearer.

* * *

Here's another description of a mechanism. How does the author tell us the way a good pair of scissors should work by telling us how her scissors do not work? When we read the piece aloud, we find the humor in the author's deadpan attitude. What is she making fun of? Compare her description of her scissors to the description of the pencil sharpener and the turbocharger.

Scissors
Marina MacMichael

My scissors are constructed of two identically formed pieces of steel, inverted and fastened above the center with a rivet; but that is where their similarities to other scissors end.

The scissors are six inches long, with the handles consuming three inches of the length. Those handles are bright red and of equal size, each shaped like a cross section of an apple quarter. The shiny, red paint is chipping off in thin strips around all sides of the handles, exposing the chrome plating underneath.

The blades are in a state of deterioration. The chrome is cracking off, especially on the cutting edge, exposing dull, gray steel. The blades are no sharper to the touch on the cutting edge than on the outer edge, although they are not as thick, and they more or less rip the paper instead of slice it.

The two parts of the scissors are held together with a small rivet and two washers. The rivet is not crimped as tightly as it ought to be; thus the blades have approximately one-eighth inch between them. This separation adds to the ripping action of the scissors when in use.

When the scissors are moved back and forth, they make a sound similar to flatware being clanged against itself. When the scissors are in a closed position, the handles make contact, whereas the blades do not. The blades are closest together just above the rivet; the distance increases until there is a separation of about one-eighth inch or more at the points.

Read the descriptions of the pencil sharpener, turbocharger, and scissors aloud in class. As you read, make sure you try to see each step and make the audience see each step of how the mechanism works. Which aspects, if any, of the descriptions come through more clearly in the reading aloud?

* * *

Here's a description of an entirely different kind of mechanism.

Imagine a salesman or an engineer giving a lecture on the process of refrigeration to an intelligent but non-technical listener. That's the situation of the officer and the explorer and the machine of execution.

From
In the Penal Colony
Franz Kafka

"Won't you take a seat?" he asked finally, drawing a cane chair out from among a heap of them and offering it to the explorer, who could not refuse it. He was now sitting at the edge of a pit, into which he glanced for a fleeting moment. It was not very deep. On one side of the pit the excavated soil had been piled up in a rampart, on the other side of it stood the apparatus. "I don't know," said the officer, "if the Commandant has already explained this apparatus to you." The explorer waved one hand vaguely; the officer asked for nothing better, since now he could explain the apparatus himself. "This apparatus," he said, taking hold of a crank handle and leaning against it, "was invented by our former Commandant. I assisted at the very earliest experiments and had a share in all the work until its completion. But the credit of inventing it belongs to him alone. Have you ever heard of our former Commandant? No? Well, it isn't saying too much if I tell you that the organization of the whole penal colony is his work. We who were his friends knew even before he died that the organization of the colony was so perfect that his successor, even with a thousand new schemes in his head, would find it impossible to alter anything, at least for many years to come. And our prophecy has come true; the new Commandant has had to acknowledge its truth. A pity you never met the old Commandant!—But," the officer interrupted himself, "I am rambling on, and here stands his apparatus before us. It consists, as you see, of three parts. In the course of time each of these parts has acquired a kind of popular nickname. The lower one is called the 'Bed,' the upper one the 'Designer,' and this one here in the middle that moves up and down is called the 'Harrow.' " "The Harrow?" asked the explorer. He had not been listening very attentively, the glare of the sun in the shadeless valley was altogether too strong, it was difficult to collect one's thoughts. All the more did he admire the officer, who in spite of his tightfitting full-dress uniform coat, amply befrogged and weighed down by epaulettes, was pursuing his subject with such enthusiasm and, besides talking, was still tightening a screw here and there with a spanner. As for the soldier, he seemed to be in much the same condition as the explorer. He had wound the prisoner's chain around both his wrists, propped himself on his rifle, let his head hang, and was paying no attention to anything. That did not surprise the explorer, for the officer was speaking French, and certainly neither the soldier nor the prisoner understood a word of French. It was all the more remarkable, therefore, that the prisoner was nonetheless making an effort to follow the officer's explanations. With a kind of drowsy persistence he directed his gaze wherever the officer pointed a finger, and at the interruption of the explorer's question he, too, as well as the officer, looked around.

"Yes, the Harrow," said the officer, "a good name for it. The needles are set in like the teeth of a harrow and the whole thing works something like a harrow, although its action is limited to one place and contrived with much more artistic skill. Anyhow, you'll soon understand it. On the Bed here the condemned man is laid—I'm going to describe the apparatus first before I set it in motion. Then you'll be able to follow the proceedings better. Besides, one of the cogwheels in the Designer is badly worn; it creaks a lot when it's working; you can hardly hear yourself speak; spare parts, unfortunately, are difficult to get here.—Well, here is the Bed, as I told you. It is completely covered with a layer of cotton wool; you'll find out why later. On this cotton wool the condemned man is laid, face down, quite naked, of course; here are straps for the hands, here for the feet, and here for the neck, to bind him fast. Here at the head of the Bed, where the man, as I said, first lays down his face, is this little gag of felt, which can be easily regulated to go straight into his mouth. It is meant to keep him from screaming and biting his tongue. Of course the man is forced to take the felt into his mouth, for otherwise his neck would be broken by the strap." "Is that cotton wool?" asked the explorer, bending forward. "Yes, certainly," said the officer, with a smile, "feel it for yourself." He took the explorer's hand and guided it over the Bed. "It's specially prepared cotton wool, that's why it looks so different; I'll tell you presently what it's for." The explorer already felt a dawning interest in the apparatus; he sheltered his eyes from the sun with one hand and gazed up at the structure. It was a huge affair. The Bed and the Designer were of the same size and looked like two dark wooden chests. The Designer hung about two meters above the Bed; each of them was bound at the corners with four rods of brass that almost flashed out rays in the sunlight. Between the chests shuttled the Harrow on a ribbon of steel.

The officer had scarcely noticed the explorer's previous indifference, but he was now well aware of his dawning interest; so he stopped explaining in order to leave a space of time for quiet observation. The condemned man imitated the explorer; since he could not use a hand to shelter his eyes he gazed upwards without shade.

"Well, the man lies down," said the explorer, leaning back in his chair and crossing his legs.

"Yes," said the officer, pushing his cap back a little and passing one hand over his heated face, "now listen! Both the Bed and the Designer have an electric battery each; the Bed needs one for itself, the Designer for the Harrow. As soon as the man is strapped down, the Bed is set in motion. It quivers in minute, very rapid vibrations, both from side to side and up and down. You will have seen similar apparatus in hospitals; but in our Bed the movements are all precisely calculated; you see, they have to correspond very exactly to the movements of the Harrow. And the Harrow is the instrument for the actual execution of the sentence."

"And how does the sentence run?" asked the explorer.

"You don't know that either?" said the officer in amazement, and bit his lips. "Forgive me if my explanations seem rather incoherent. I do beg your pardon. You see, the Commandant always used to do the explaining; but the new Commandant shirks this duty; yet that such an important visitor"—the explorer tried to deprecate the honor with both hands, the officer, however, insisted—"that such an important visitor should not even be told about the kind of sentence we pass is a new development, which—" He was just on the point of using strong language but checked himself and said only: "I was not informed, it is not my fault. In any case, I am certainly the best person to explain our procedure, since I have here"—he patted his breast pocket—"the relevant drawings made by our former Commandant."

"The Commandant's own drawings?" asked the explorer. "Did he combine everything in himself, then? Was he soldier, judge, mechanic, chemist, and draughtsman?"

"Indeed he was," said the officer, nodding assent, with a remote, glassy look. Then he inspected his hands critically; they did not seem clean enough to him for touching the drawings; so he went over to the bucket and washed them again. Then he drew out a small leather wallet and said: "Our sentence does not sound severe. Whatever commandment the prisoner has disobeyed is written upon his body by the Harrow. This prisoner, for instance"—the officer indicated the man—"will have written on his body: HONOR THY SUPERIORS!"

The explorer glanced at the man; he stood, as the officer pointed him out, with bent head, apparently listening with all his ears in an effort to catch what was being said.

———

Kafka uses the compelling story-within-a-story principle here, of someone in the story framework giving a demonstration of something to another person in the story framework. This is an objectification of the situation that occurs in our minds as we write, which allows us to identify with the essential figures of teller and listener. How are the techniques of describing the execution mechanism similar to and different from the techniques used in the descriptions of the pencil sharpener, turbocharger, and scissors? Which of those three descriptions is it more like?

Most of us occasionally create unique machines in our dreams. We also fantasize machines and appliances and see how they work in our minds, and tell other people about them. Drawings and written descriptions of imagined mechanisms show up frequently in the annals of technical literature. Imagined mechanisms lead to inventions, to how-to-do-something-better mechanisms.

Read the full story of "In the Penal Colony." See what happens with the machine.

Writing Your How-It's-Done, How-It-Works Telling

Factual and fictional process tellings frequently use the present tense of verbs, because they tell the way the process usually occurs in ideal time, often called "the historical present." According to the needs of the context, some expository narrative and fictional narrative process tellings may use past tense, present tense, or the conditional mood. "The Stud Ace" uses the present tense, "The Sausage Room" the conditional mood (would), "The Moon and the Tides" past, present, and future tenses.

Look over your how-it-happens subject for events, places, activities, mechanisms that will more or less fit the assignment. Virtually any activity can provide the basis for a process telling. Write a single event of how something works or occurs. You may give some narrative and descriptive attention to the characters of the participants, such as happens in the feeling of tattooing in "The Stud Ace." Or write a model scene of how things happen the same way again and again in a workplace, as in "The Sausage Room." As you write, let what you see and feel and know about the work activity and its effects help you discover your attitude and tone.

Research a process, such as how the moon and tides work, or how the cardiovascular system works, or the processes of crowds, glaciers, hurricanes, weather systems, traffic, businesses, government agencies, family conflicts, political systems, and so on, and give a description of how the system or concept usually functions. Rely on personal experience and observation as well as material researched through reading. Use comparisons that will make the process clear to a mixed audience of readers.

Look at your chosen process or mechanism from beginning to end and write down notes of those things that most clearly catch your attention about it, that the reader needs to understand. You could imagine a person to whom you write a letter about this process. You might make letter, letter-writer and letter-recipient in some way part of the "story" too. See the imagery of the process and tell it so your reader can see it. Trust your impulses to use whatever pronouns come to you naturally. Trust your impulses to use the verb tenses that seem right. Imagine a "mixed" audience for your how-it's-done writing, perhaps the audience of your class with other persons you may add to it in your imagination as you write. Most of our process reading selections are directed toward "mixed" audiences of people who are probably not expert in the particular subject.

Writing Your Description of a Mechanism

Describe a mechanism that you find in your how-it-happens subject.

Describe a fantasy mechanism.

Use the story-within-a-story principle to tell how either the real mechanism or the fantasy mechanism works. Write it as a lecture, a demonstration. Use the speech of the demonstrator. Make sure your readers can see your place, situation, characters, and the workings of the mechanism being demonstrated.

Imagine and describe a fantasy mechanism or appliance for cleaning a house, cultivating farmland, cutting grass, living underneath the sea, moving traffic in a city, or performing any other function that comes to your mind.

Use any of the techniques of the pencil sharpener, turbocharger, scissors, and execution machine tellings if they seem appropriate.

Model-Telling

The model-telling is an image or narrative of the pattern of how something usually or characteristically happens, happened, will happen, or can happen. You recognize the everyday use of this form in such tellings as "When you're in the middle of a traffic jam and everybody's freaking out all around you . . ." or "When you step out of your door and the cold takes your breath away . . ." or "You wear the pouch on your belt, so when you're working you can reach your chaw handily. . . ." Oral model-tellings often use the "you" and the present tense. The "you" and the present tense also show up in written model-tellings, such as in the selections from *The Road to Wigan Pier.* The model-telling present tense is also called the "historical present." Model-tellings vary in length from one-liners to whole chapters, whatever length is needed. The chapter, "A Gorilla Day," in *The Year of the Gorilla,* is an extended model-telling, mixed with summary of characteristic gorilla behavior.

The model-telling establishes the pattern of a repeated experience, the "universality" or commonality of it; it gives visible knowledge of the pattern in a "scene unrolling before our eyes," a model of the repeated occurrence, e.g., "He would always raise his hand and wave and then duck his head a little as he approached us." The model-telling functions to bring order to our experience and to express that order to others. So accustomed are we to using this form that it tends to persuade us of "universality" of whatever pattern of experience is being set before us by the imagery. It may use any pronouns—he, she, they, it, I, we, you, someone, anyone—and any tense, present, past, future, or the conditional mood (would). In writing, it often uses the conditional mood. You should use the pronouns and tenses that feel right to you.

The model-telling is flexibly used in all written and oral expression—in everyday oral telling, in technical and scientific writing, in fiction, exposition, and journalism—and by every human being who speaks and tries to convey patterns of experience.

Flexibility is the key to this form's concept and use. The model-telling is an extension of the usual learning situation of the how-to and the model chronology of the how-it-works process form. One form grows out of another. The how-it-works mode of thinking extends into the learning situation and process of the how-to, which then transforms into the model-telling, which, as we will demonstrate, possesses enormous flexibility to meet many needs and uses. While you are reading these selections, think of—and see in your mind—instances in your how-it-happens subject area of how things usually occur in a place, activity, or time. Any job or school or other institutional situation offers many opportunities for model-tellings.

* * *

In the 1930s a massive oral history project was carried out by members of the Federal Writers' Project, who gathered thousands of oral accounts from still-living ex-slaves about their remembered experience in slavery. From these records, B. A. Botkin culled hundreds of transcriptions of the ex-slaves' oral tellings and published them in *Lay My Burden Down.* The tellers often use model-telling imagery and example and illustration to express patterns of experience.

Count the Stars Through the Cracks

I stayed round with Master's boys a lot, and them white boys was as good to me as if I had been their brother. And I stayed up to the big house lots of nights so as to be handy for running for Old Master and Mistress. The big house was fine, but the log cabin where my mammy lived had so many cracks in it that when I would sleep down there I could lie in bed and count the stars through the cracks. Mammy's beds was ticks stuffed with dried grass and put on bunks built on the wall, but they did sleep so good. I can 'most smell that clean dry grass now.

A Pretty Crop of Children

Yes, ma'am, my white folks was proud of they niggers. Um, yessum, when they used to have company to the big house, Miss Ross would bring them to the door to show them us children. And, my blessed, the yard would be black with us children, all string up there next the doorstep looking up in they eyes. Old Missus would say, "Ain't I got a pretty crop of little niggers coming on?" The lady, she look so please like. Then Miss Ross say, "Do my little niggers want some bread to gnaw on?" And us children say, "Yessum, yessum, we do." Then she would go in the pantry and see could she find some cook bread to hand us.

Whupping

Single incident illustration

I know so many things 'bout slavery time till I never will be able to tell 'em all. . . . In them days preachers was just as bad and mean as anybody else. There was a man who folks called a good preacher, but he was one of the meanest mens I ever seed. When I was in slavery under him, he done so many bad things till God soon kilt him. His wife or children could git mad with you, and if they told him anything he always beat you. Most times he beat his slaves when they hadn't done nothing a-tall. One Sunday morning his wife told him their cook wouldn't never fix nothing she told her to fix. Time she said it he jumped up from the table, went in the kitchen, and made the cook go under the porch where he always whupped his slaves. She begged and prayed, but he didn't pay no 'tention to that. He put her up in what us called the swing, and beat her till she couldn't holler. The poor thing already had heart trouble; that's why he put her in the kitchen, but he left her swinging there and went to church, preached, and called hisself serving God. When he got back home she was dead. Whenever your master had you swinging up, nobody wouldn't take you down. Sometimes a man would help his wife, but most times he was beat afterwards.

Another master I had kept a hogshead to whup you on. This hogshead had two or three hoops round it. He buckled you face down on the hogshead and whupped you till you bled. Everybody always stripped you in them days to whup you, 'cause they didn't care who seed you naked. Some folks' children took sticks and jabbed you while you was being beat. Sometimes these children would beat you all 'cross your head, and they mas and pas didn't know what stop was.

Model-tellings

Another way Master had to whup us was in a stock that he had in the stables. This was where he whupped you when he was real mad. He had logs fixed together with holes for your feet, hands, and head. He had a way to open these logs and fasten you in.

Then he had his coachman give you so many lashes, and he would let you stay in the stock for so many days and nights. That's why he had it in the stable so it wouldn't rain on you. Every day you got the same number of lashes. You never come out able to sit down.

I had a cousin with two children. The oldest one had to nurse one of Master's grandchildren. The front steps was real high, and one day this poor child fell down these steps with the baby. His wife and daughter hollered and went on terrible, and when our master come home they was still hollering just like the baby was dead or dying. When they told him 'bout it, he picked up a board and hit this poor little child 'cross the head and kilt her right there. Then he told his slaves to take her and throw her in the river. Her ma begged and prayed, but he didn't pay her no 'tention; he made 'em throw the child in.

One of the slaves married a young gal, and they put her in the big house to work. One day Mistress jumped on her 'bout something, and the gal hit her back. Mistress said she was going to have Master put her in the stock and beat her when he come home. When the gal went to the field and told her husband 'bout it, he told her where to go and stay till he got there. That night he took his supper to her. He carried her to a cave and hauled pine straw and put in there for her to sleep on. He fixed that cave up just a like a house for her, put a stove in there and run the pipe out through the ground into a swamp. Everybody always wondered how he fixed that pipe. Course they didn't cook on it till night when nobody could see the smoke. He ceiled the house with pine logs, made beds and tables out of pine poles, and they lived in this cave seven years. During this time, they had three children. Nobody was with her when these children was born but her husband. He waited on her with each child. The children didn't wear no clothes 'cept a piece tied round their waists. They was just as hairy as wild people, and they was wild. When they come out of that cave, they would run every time they seed a person.

The seven years she lived in the cave, different folks helped keep 'em in food.

Single incident illustration

Summary

Each of these experiences undoubtedly happened with variations each time, but the pattern of the experience was sufficiently significant that the tellers could give a central image that conveyed the overall pattern. How do the illustrative incidents in the first, fourth, and fifth paragraphs of "Whupping" differ from the model-tellings in the second and third paragraphs?

When the ex-slaves give patterns of past experiences, they tend to use the past tense, the first person "I" and "we," and the third person forms. Sometimes they use the conditional mood (would). The tellings start with a tense form that indicates the past such as "thought" or "was" and then use the dialectal form of the present tense as both a past tense and a model-telling present tense. Do you feel the interviewer or editor may have changed some of the tenses for the sake of the general reader's understanding? Why or why not? Refer to your own hearing of various dialects.

Though the first paragraph of "Whupping" is mainly devoted to an illustrative incident, there are model-telling elements in it. Find them. In paragraphs two and three examine when and where the "you" is used. In the illustrative incident in the fourth paragraph, what pronouns are used? How does the use of these pronouns differ from the "you" in paragraphs two and three?

What reasons can you find for the use of the past tense and the few dialectal uses of present tense forms, such as "give" and "pay," functioning as the past tense, in all four paragraphs? Why do these four paragraphs tend to stick to the past tense? Examine your own speech and oral tellings for similar occurrences.

*   *   *

The following examples of written model-tellings come from the factual narrative *The Road to Wigan Pier,* by George Orwell.

. . . you crawl through the last line of pit props and see opposite you a shiny black wall three or four feet high. This is the coal face. Overhead is the smooth ceiling made by the rock from which the coal has been cut; underneath is the rock again, so that the gallery you are in is only as high as the ledge of coal itself, probably not much more than a yard. The first impression of all, overmastering everything else for a while, is the frightful, deafening din from the conveyor belt which carries the coal away. You cannot see very far, because the fog of coal dust throws back the beam of your lamp, but you can see on either side of you the line of half-naked kneeling men, one to every four or five yards, driving their shovels under the fallen coal and flinging it swiftly over their left shoulders. They are feeding it on to the conveyor belt, a moving rubber belt a couple of feet wide which runs a yard or two behind them. Down this belt a glittering river of coal races constantly. . . . You can never forget that spectacle once you have seen it—the line of bowed, kneeling figures, sooty black all over, driving their huge shovels under the coal with stupendous force and speed. They are on the job for seven and a half hours, theoretically without a break, for there is no time "off." Actually they snatch a quarter of an hour or so at some time during the shift to eat the food they have brought with them, usually a hunk of bread and dripping and a bottle of cold tea. . . . Ducking the beams becomes more and more of an effort, and sometimes you forget to duck. You try walking head down as the miners do, and then you bang your backbone. Even the miners bang their backbones fairly often. This is the reason why in very hot mines, where it is necessary to go about half naked, most of the miners have what they call "buttons down the back"—that is, a permanent scab on each vertebra.

In these written examples, we see the same distinctive combinations of pronouns, tense, and patterns of happening as we found in the everyday oral model-tellings. Orwell tells the passages consistently in the present tense. Follow the "you" as he tells it and how you see things from the "you's" point of view. Watch how the author concentrates on vivid model imagery for the patterns of how the experience happens again and again.

*   *   *

"The Cabin Table" is excerpted from an extended model-telling.

"The Cabin Table"
From *Moby Dick*
Herman Melville

It is noon; and Dough-Boy, the steward, thrusting his pale loaf-of-bread face from the cabin-scuttle, announces dinner to his lord and master; who, sitting in the lee quarter-boat, has just been taking an observation of the sun; and is now mutely reckoning the latitude on the smooth, medallion-shaped tablet, reserved for that daily purpose on the upper part of his ivory leg. From his complete inattention to the tidings, you would think that moody Ahab had not heard his menial. But presently, catching hold of the mizen shrouds, he swings himself to the deck, and in an even, unexhilarated voice, saying, "Dinner, Mr. Starbuck," disappears into the cabin.

When the last echo of his sultan's step has died away, and Starbuck, the first Emir, has every reason to suppose that he is seated, then Starbuck rouses from his quietude, takes a few turns along the planks, and, after a grave peep into the binnacle, says, with some touch of pleasantness, "Dinner, Mr. Stubb," and descends the scuttle. The second Emir lounges about the rigging awhile, and then slightly shaking the main brace, to see whether it be all right with that important rope, he likewise takes up the old burden, and with a rapid "Dinner, Mr. Flask," follows after his predecessors.

But the third Emir, now seeing himself all alone on the quarter-deck, seems to feel relieved from some curious restraint; for, tipping all sorts of knowing winks in all sorts of directions, and kicking off his shoes, he strikes into a sharp but noiseless squall of a hornpipe right over the Grand Turk's head; and then, by a dexterous sleight, pitching his cap up into the mizen-top for a shelf, he goes down rollicking, so far at least as he remains visible from the deck, reversing all other processions, by bringing up the rear with music. But ere stepping into the cabin doorway below, he pauses, ships a new face altogether, and, then, independent, hilarious little Flask enters King Ahab's presence, in the character of Abjectus, or the Slave.

It is not the least among the strange things bred by the intense artificialness of sea-usages, that while in the open air of the deck some officers will, upon provocation, bear themselves boldly and defyingly enough towards their commander; yet, ten to one, let those very officers the next moment go down to their customary dinner in that same commander's cabin, and straightway their inoffensive, not to say deprecatory and humble air towards him, as he sits at the head of the table; this is marvellous, sometimes most comical. Wherefore this difference? A problem? Perhaps not. To have been Belshazzar, King of Babylon; and to have been Belshazzar, not haughtily but courteously, therein certainly must have been some touch of mundane grandeur. But he who in the rightly regal and intelligent spirit presides over his own private dinner-table of invited guests, that man's unchallenged power and dominion of individual influence for the time; that man's royalty of state transcends Belshazzar's, for Belshazzar was not the greatest. Who has but once dined his friends, has tasted what it is to be Caesar. It is a witchery of social czarship which there is no withstanding. Now, if to this consideration you superadd the official supremacy of a ship-master, then, by inference, you will derive the cause of that peculiarity of sea-life just mentioned.

Over his ivory-inlaid table, Ahab presided like a mute, maned sea-lion on the white coral beach, surrounded by his warlike but still deferential cubs. In his own proper turn, each officer waited to be served. They were as little children before Ahab; and yet, in Ahab, there seemed not to lurk the smallest social arrogance. With one mind, their intent eyes all fastened upon the old man's knife, as he carved the chief dish before him. I do not suppose that for the world they would have profaned that moment with the slightest observation, even upon so neutral a topic as the weather. No! And when reaching out his knife and fork, between which the slice of beef was locked, Ahab thereby motioned Starbuck's plate towards him, the mate received his meat as though receiving alms; and cut it tenderly; and a little started if, perchance, the knife grazed against the plate; and chewed it noiselessly; and swallowed it, not without circumspection. For, like the Coronation banquet at Frankfort, where the German Emperor profoundly dines with the seven Imperial Electors, so these cabin meals were somehow solemn meals, eaten in awful silence; and yet at table old Ahab forbade no conversation; only he himself was dumb. What a relief it was to choking Stubb, when a rat made a sudden racket in the hold below. And poor little Flask, he was the youngest son, and little boy of this weary family party. His were the shinbones of the saline beef; his would have been the drumsticks. For Flask to have presumed to help himself, this must have seemed to him tantamount to larceny in the first degree. Had he helped himself at that table, doubtless, never more would he have been able to hold his head up in this honest world; nevertheless, strange to say, Ahab never forbade him. And had Flask helped himself, the chances were Ahab had never so much as noticed it. Least of all, did Flask presume to help himself to butter. Whether he thought the owners of the ship denied it to him, on account of its clotting his clear, sunny complexion; or whether he deemed that, on so long a voyage in such marketless waters, butter was at a premium, and therefore was not for him, a subaltern; however it was, Flask, alas! was a butterless man!

Another thing. Flask was the last person down at the dinner, and Flask is the first man up. Consider! For hereby Flask's dinner was badly jammed in point of time. Starbuck and Stubb both had the start of him; and yet they also have the privilege of lounging in the rear. If Stubb even, who is but a peg higher than Flask, happens to have but a small appetite, and soon shows symptoms of concluding his repast, then Flask must bestir himself, he will not get more than three mouthfuls that day; for it is against holy usage for Stubb to precede Flask to the deck. Therefore it was that Flask once admitted in private, that ever since he had arisen to the dignity of an officer, from that moment he had never known what it was to be otherwise than hungry, more or less. For what he ate did not so much relieve his hunger, as keep it immortal in him. Peace and satisfaction, thought Flask, have for ever departed from my stomach. I am an officer; but, how I wish I could fist a bit of old-fashioned beef in the forecastle, as I used to when I was before the mast.

"The Cabin Table" first compares and contrasts the behavior at the dining table of each of the officers of the ship, then of officers and men in the forecastle (through Flask's memory), and finally of officers and harpooners (in the rest of the chapter not printed here), so that the different kinds of behavior are classified into categories.

The author tells the first four paragraphs in the present tense; the "you" shows up in the first and fourth paragraphs. With the fifth paragraph, the story changes to the past tense as it shifts to the narrative of the silent Ahab. In the sixth paragraph, the tenses shift back and forth from present to past. What do you notice about why they shift? What do you notice about other shifts of tense, to present tense and conditional mood?

"The Cabin Table" is rich with metaphorical comparisons and historical allusions. It sets forth a model of the status and power relationships on the *Pequod* and how these affect behavior. Specific incidents of all participants' behavior are compared and contrasted to moody Ahab's. All of this enhances our sense of Ahab's peculiar, solemn, foreboding destiny.

In your own how-it-happens subject area, look for examples of status behavior. For instance, how do doctors, nurses, administrators, technicians, orderlies, and others dress and act toward each other in a hospital? How about teachers, students, tutors, administrators, and assistants in a school? How about the boss, the foremen, and the workers on a job?

* * *

What follows is a model incident or instance, a composite scene extracted from the pattern.

"*Jack Burden Comes Home*"
From *All the King's Men*
Robert Penn Warren

It was always the same way when I came home and saw my mother. I would be surprised that it was the way it was but I knew at the same time that I had known it would be this way. I would come home with the firm conviction that she didn't really care a thing about me, that I was just another man whom she wanted to have around because she was the kind of woman who had to have men around and had to make them dance to her tune. But as soon as I saw her I would forget all that. Sometimes I forgot it even before I saw her. Anyway, when I forgot it, I would wonder why we couldn't get along. I would wonder even though I knew what would happen, even though I would always know that the scene into which I was about to step and in which I was about to say the words I would say, had happened before, or had never stopped happening, and that I would always just be entering the wide, white, high-ceilinged hall to see across the distance of the floor, which gleamed like dark ice, my mother, who stood in a doorway, beyond her the flicker of firelight in the shadowy room, and smiled at me with a sudden and innocent happiness, like a girl. Then she would come toward me, with a brittle, excited clatter of heels and a quick, throaty laugh, and stop before me and seize a little bunch of my coat between the thumb and forefinger of each hand, in a way that was childlike and both weak and demanding, and lift her face up to me, turning it somewhat to one side so that I could put the expected kiss upon her cheek. The texture of her cheek would be firm and smooth, quite cool, and I would breathe the scent which she always used, and as I kissed her I would see the plucked accuracy of the eyebrow, the delicate lines at the corner of the eye toward me, and note the crinkled, silky, shadowed texture of the eyelid, which would flicker sharply over the blue eye. The eye, very slightly protruding, would be fixed glitteringly on some point beyond me.

That was the way it had always been—when I had come home from school, when I had come back from camps, when I had come back from college, when I had come back from jobs—and that was the way it was that late rainy afternoon, on the borderline between winter and spring, back in 1933, when I came back home again, after not coming home for a long time. It had been six or eight months since my last visit. That time we had had a row about my working for Governor Stark. We always sooner or later got into a row about something, and in the two and a half years that I had been working for Willie it usually in the end came round to Willie. And if his name wasn't even mentioned, he stood there like a shadow behind us. Not that it mattered much what we rowed about. There was a shadow taller and darker than the shadow of Willie standing behind us. But I always came back, and I had come back this time. I would find myself drawn back. It was that way, and, as always, it seemed to be a fresh start, a wiping out of all the things which I knew could not be wiped out.

Notice the use of the conditional mood (would) in the first paragraph. How does the model-telling of the first paragraph differ from the summary of the second paragraph?

* * *

In "Ambush," the author tells first in present tense and then in past tense and conditional mood. What pronouns does he use in each passage? Why?

"Ambush"
From Close Quarters
Larry Heinemann

You've got to be nuts to do an ambush, to want to do it, to do it, to get your sorry ass talked into it. It sounds so simple—walk out, walk in, like falling out of bed. Every night, for months, a different route, a different spot, every night a brand-new can of worms. Listen, not even your own house back on the block looks the same at night. Everything was shades of gray and silver and black, even with an illumination round from a 105 floating down from two thousand feet. But after a while you catch on to the game. The deeper shadows among the bushes or the silhouettes glowing on the woodline or the lighter, almost white of the line of the horizon. And you learn to step light. The closer you get, the more quiet you've got to be. Toe-heel-toe. Stop. Listen. Watch. Does it smell funny? Move again. Listen. Stretch your neck and put your ear to it. What's the sound behind that sound? Gooks or rats or a swarm of mosquitoes? Keep moving, keep looking, keep listening. Hear that? Music from a radio in that ville over there. You get to the ambush site and set up slowly, one man at a time. Then you sit. Hour after hour, the woodline and the lonely bushes and the sorry clumps of kunai grass and the clouds that come and go. Everything becomes so familiar. Everybody sits within an arm's reach, behind camouflage, in a defilade if you can, all the claymores out, the grenades in your lap, and the pistol grip of the pig* in your hand. It is the oldest skill. You think about everything: God and the devil and pussy and *what*-the-*fuck*-am I-*doing*-here. You sing a song to yourself or crack a joke. You squirm because you've got to take a leak, but you hold it until your stomach aches, and wait for morning. And sometimes, if you're an FNG, a fucken new guy, you nod out, thinking the same things you were thinking before—God and the devil and pussy, damn I wish I had some pussy. Then something starts you awake. There is a flash of light, like somebody has cracked you across the face with the narrow side of a two-by-four. You startle. And there it is just the way you left it. The woodline and the bushes and the kunai grass. You sit there red in the face, not because you've nodded off, but because you have jerked awake and made the mistake of being heard. But it is a trick of the mind. It is only your eyes that have moved. You sit there dumb, like stones and logs, as still as lake water in the moonlight. The movement is underneath—the cool water rising, the warm slowly sinking. All you heard was your heart beating, slamming against your chest, screaming again and again.

Every time we went out we sat watching the cart trails or a footpath or a rice paddy, until first light or the first rush of blood in our ears when all of a sudden there he was, skylarking down the trail right at us. And then we blew him away with a claymore, and watched him fly and bounce and roll. Some quiver, some wiggle, some are stiff right away. Every night for weeks, months. Years maybe. Mac and his E-deuce, Atevo's shotgun, Steichen's seventy-nine. Rain or shine. From camp or some fire base or other, into the jungle or the rubber or the paddies north of Trang Bang. We would gather at the seven-four to sip some smoke, slap on some camouflage, and go. And after the first dozen or so I got used to the pig and preferred it. That and the two hundred rounds. I would come back in the morning, the second man back from point, my flak jacket smeared with mosquitoes, hating the rain. My eyes going bad and my mustache coming along. Out and back, just like falling out of bed, until I couldn't have told you the day or the date. My eyes went deeper and deeper into my head and my hair got a shade

*M-60 machine gun.

lighter, my hands got water-wrinkled and leathery, and I had a strength in my wrists I was sure could crush a wooden post. I would sit out there nights in the pouring-down rain or the insane moonlight and wonder why, why am I doing this? But after a while that faded, too, like clouds fade sometimes, slow and billowing, but billowing like a fire sucking the smoke into itself. I would sit there snug enough in my flak jacket, my belly and back sleek with sweat. My thighs and arms shivering, my stiff and wrinkled fingers around the pistol grip, and the grenades snuggled down comfortable, like breaking in a big ugly chair. Then early in the morning we would pass around the No Doz and the canteen. And when we could see each other plain and the dinks could see us plain, we got up in a gang, stood around working our legs and gathered in the claymores, and walked in. We got on line and moved off by the most direct route, calling the El-tee to say we were coming in. And as we moved off, the papa-sans came behind with their oxcarts, and the herd boys came behind them with the cattle and buffalo that dragged their nose-ring thongs between their legs. We walked with a long interval, stretched out fifty meters and more. We did the last hundred meters with our backs to the perimeter watching the woodline, stepping around and through and over the several concentric semicircles of armed claymores. When we passed between the tracks, Atevo and I made for the seven-three, Steichen for the seven-four, Mac the seven-two, and Stepik and Whiskey j. the six-niner. Like the fingers of a hand first pointing, then reaching flat to grasp. We would throw off the guns and hats and flak jackets and shirts and steel pots, and walk with a shuffle over to the artillery's mess tent for breakfast. The Romeo ambush was always the last to eat. We would straggle through the chow line voiceless, beyond complaining and wishing and sleep, into bizarre swirling dreams, coming down from that tight, circling ambush high. Our eyes wide and tight, staring down at cold, shriveled eggs, the dregs of instant potatoes, and no milk. Atevo and Steichen and I would sit on the cook's bunker outside the doorway, no shirts and all, stinking that morning mildew stink. The camouflage still on our faces, the streaks of grit thick and kind of artful, like the small subtle folds of sand that an inlet surf leaves when a slow tide gives way. We would sit there side by side just like we had done all night, wordless, eating soundlessly, but feeling the close heat of the other bodies. The dreams would come faster and faster, the forks moving slower and slower.

The wry humor of common colorful speech characterizes "Ambush," such as "You've got to be nuts . . . to get your sorry ass talked into it," "like falling out of bed," "brand-new can of worms," "like somebody has cracked you across the face with the narrow side of a two-by-four." Speech mixes with ironic, literary, almost romantically poetic metaphor, in such phrases as "like stones and logs, as still as lake water in the moonlight," "your heart beating, slamming against your chest, screaming again and again," "the first rush of blood in our ears," "skylarking down the trail," "sip some smoke, slap on some camouflage, and go," "the pouring down rain or the insane moonlight and wonder why, why am I doing this?" "like clouds fade sometimes, slow and billowing, but billowing like a fire sucking the smoke into itself." The "mixed diction" makes possible ironic exaggeration, metaphor, hyperbole, poetic imagery, to get across the truth of the experience. Heinemann juxtaposes and plays with language taken from talk, from inner speech and perception, from poetic and literary syntax and methods.

A mixed diction that draws upon your speech, your language background, your reading of poetry and prose literature, your listening to many voices, gives you a wide, powerful range of language effects.

* * *

In the following model-telling of the peculiar mating behavior of the praying mantis, which is told in the present tense, the author personifies the insects to make clear their behavior.

The Mating of the Mantis
J. Henri Fabre

Let us watch the pairing and, to avoid the disorder of a crowd, let us isolate the couples under different covers. Each pair shall have its own home, where none will come to disturb the wedding. And let us not forget the provisions, with which we will keep them well supplied, so that there may be no excuse of hunger.

It is near the end of August. The male, that slender swain, thinks the moment propitious. He makes eyes at his strapping companion; he turns his head in her direction; he bends his neck and throws out his chest. His little pointed face wears an almost impassioned expression. Motionless, in this posture, for a long time he contemplates the object of his desire. She does not stir, is as though indifferent. The lover, however, has caught a sign of acquiescence, a sign of which I do not know the secret. He goes nearer; suddenly he spreads his wings, which quiver with a convulsive tremor. That is his declaration. He rushes, small as he is, upon the back of his corpulent companion, clings on as best he can, steadies his hold. As a rule, the preliminaries last a long time. At last, coupling takes place and is also long drawn out, lasting sometimes for five or six hours.

Nothing worthy of attention happens between the two motionless partners. They end by separating, but only to unite again in a more intimate fashion. If the poor fellow is loved by his lady as the vivifier of her ovaries, he is also loved as a piece of highly-flavoured game. And, that same day, or at latest on the morrow, he is seized by his spouse, who first gnaws his neck, in accordance with precedent, and then eats him deliberately, by little mouthfuls, leaving only the wings. Here we have no longer a case of jealousy in the harem, but simply a depraved appetite.

I was curious to know what sort of reception a second male might expect from a recently fertilized female. The result of my enquiry was shocking. The Mantis, in many cases, is never sated with conjugal raptures and banquets. After a rest that varies in length, whether the eggs be laid or not, a second male is accepted and then devoured like the first. A third succeeds him, performs his function in life, is eaten and disappears. A fourth undergoes a like fate. In the course of two weeks I thus see one and the same Mantis use up seven males. She takes them all to her bosom and makes them all pay for the nuptial ecstasy with their lives.

From "Let us watch the pairing" through four paragraphs to "makes them all pay for the nuptial ecstasy with their lives," Fabre personifies the mantes with such words and phrases as "wedding", "slender swain", "impassioned expression", and many other terms, adjectives and expressions. "His little pointed face wears an almost impassioned expression. Motionless, in this posture, for a long time he contemplates the object of his desire. She does not stir, is as though indifferent." This is a kind of parody. What sort of storytelling, what sort of language, is Fabre making fun of? What does the personifying parody make you see? Personification exaggerates, draws forth, and helps heighten the image and the sense of the model-telling. Find other ways in which ironical personification works in "The Mating of the Mantis," affecting timing, choice of verbs, and other words. Biologists working in their laboratories personify the elements of diseases in their research. Other scientists personify the elements of their research subjects. Chemists say that the chlorine atom "wants" and "gets" an electron, and the sodium atom "donates" an electron, in order for the two to form sodium chloride. How do you think such personification helps scientists see and abstract? Examine Kekule's account of his discovery of the benzene ring in "Seeing-in-the-Mind" on page 65. Examine the observation of two frogs, "Einstein and Frankenstein," on page 345. The exaggerated personification that scientists use intuitively in their experimentation and informal discussion can be helpful in making concepts clear in writing.

* * *

Here's a model-telling put together from historical research, that is, research through reading, about the Globe theater in London in Shakespeare's time recounted by the nineteenth century French historian, H. A. Taine.

> On a dirty site, on the banks of the Thames, rose the principal theatre, the Globe, a sort of hexagonal tower, surrounded by a muddy ditch, surmounted by a red flag. The common people could enter as well as the rich: there were sixpenny, twopenny, even penny seats; but they could not see it without money. If it rained, and it often rains in London, the people in the pit, butchers, mercers, bakers, ⟩ past tense
>
> sailors, apprentices, received the streaming rain upon their heads. . . . While waiting for the piece, they amuse themselves after their fashion, drink beer, crack nuts, eat fruits, howl, and now and then resort to their fists; they have been known to fall upon the actors and turn the theatre upside down. At other times they have gone in disgust to the tavern to give the poet a hiding, or toss him in a blanket. . . . Above them, on the stage, were the spectators able to pay a shilling, ⟩ present tense
>
> the elegant people, the gentlefolk. These were sheltered from the rain, and if they chose to pay an extra shilling could have a stool. . . . It often happened that stools were lacking; then they stretched themselves on the ground: they were not dainty at such times. They play cards, smoke, insult the pit, who give it them back ⟩ past tense
>
> without stinting, and throw apples at them into the bargain. As for the gentlefolk, they gesticulate, swear in Italian, French, English; crack aloud jokes in dainty, composite, high-colored words: in short, they have the energetic, original, gay manners of artists, the same humor, the same absence of constraint, and, to complete the resemblance, the same desire to make themselves singular, the same imaginative cravings, the same absurd and picturesque devices, beards cut to a point, into the shape of a fan, a spade, the letter T, gaudy and expensive dresses, copied from five or six neighboring nations, embroidered, laced with gold, motley, ⟩ present tense
>
> continually heightened in effect, or changed for others: there was, as it were, a carnival in their brains as on their backs. ⟩ past tense

In this near-circus atmosphere, Shakespeare's plays, whether comic or tragic, were played.

Follow the pattern of the tenses here, from past tense to present tense, to past tense, to present tense, to past. How do these tense-shifts, and what is said in each passage of each tense-shift, work together? How does the author exaggerate to bring forth the model scene of the Globe?

The model-telling form possesses broad flexibility, used by virtually all authors in every kind of writing. Marcel Proust used this form powerfully and flexibly to tell the seven-novel story of *Remembrance of Things Past* and Gustave Flaubert developed it strongly in *Madame Bovary*.

Writing Your Model-Tellings

Look over your how-it-happens subject, and see which repeated activities or experiences are attracted to the model-telling form. How the students arrive in the school every morning, how everything is different on the morning of the big snow or the big rain, how the halls become active between classes and how they are during class periods. How the workers on the job act at the beginning of the workday, at lunch time, on breaks, at the end of the day. How a worker starts and conducts his job. The possibilities for model-tellings are immense and various.

Exaggeration helps to clarify and bring out the central images of the model-telling, the fact and truth of what happens again and again. You will find many instances of exaggeration in all of the oral and written model-tellings in this section, in good oral and written expression everywhere. You exaggerate to find what you're looking for, to bring forth what's not yet there.

Exaggeration draws out the concept of the model-telling, as it does of other forms, too. Exaggeration stimulates and propels metaphor, which clarifies understanding for the reader by comparing less familiar things to more familiar things. Exaggeration digs deep for the right verbs, the strong verbs and participles. Exaggeration brings forth the basic perception, strongly affects syntax which helps express the perception of the writing. Find examples for all of these uses of exaggeration in each of the model-telling reading selections.

Mixed diction draws upon colloquial, dialectal, informal, and formal language. It provides you with a range of means for effective exaggeration, for effective writing. See and exaggerate the perceptions and imagery that make clear the patterns that go into making the model incident, instance, chronology, telling. Try several model-tellings in your journal, from your how-it-happens subject or other subjects. One or two of them may feel stronger to you than the others. You can then continue to develop them and hand them in as part of your how-it-happens subject area assignments.

Model-Summary

The model-summary, rather than giving a single image or narrative scene to stand for a pattern of behavior, presents separate instances that weave a pattern. Wherever many similar, slightly different, or contrastingly different instances of behavior must be taken into account in order to give insight into, or information about, a pattern, we summarize rather than give a model-telling. Nevertheless, the model summary, following the transformational principles of one form growing out of another and combining with another, uses model-telling elements.

"The Panic of 1873"
From ***The Robber Barons***
Matthew Josephson

For ten days the mad rout continued. The stronger railroad chiefs, bankers and industrial captains fought each other mercilessly amid the wreckage of their broken hopes and enterprises. It was a *sauve qui peut* of rats. A Jay Gould flies about preying upon the rich debris; and in the vast confusion, hulking figures such as that of Cornelius Vanderbilt stand out, moving vigorously in their own defense. To the appeals of his fellows Vanderbilt is adamant. "He had no intention of being caught up in the whirlpool himself and engulfed with the rest of the ruined," writes his biographer. So a Morgan, a Rockefeller, a Carnegie rode out the storm with damage more or less, while in the jettison of great enterprises and invaluable assets younger adventurers, hitherto unknown, a Harriman, a Frick, plunged in to wrest many a prize from the financially dead and dying.

In the recoil of the forward movement all the services administered by the existing economic institutions, all circulation of things, is halted while the "flight of capital" continues and money passes out of circulation into hoarding. Where yesterday credit flowed liberally to finance stores of goods, to move commodities of all sorts, to aid the various projects of empire-builders, now no celebrated name, no merchandise commands any money value in the marketplace but gold itself, The wealth of mountains of ore, of iron foundries, of machines and factories, of rich farm lands, of ships and railroad tracks, is called nothing but illusion. From 1873 to 1879, according to important personages in the iron trade who were associated with Carnegie, "you could not give away a rolling mill"; nor could a 2,000-mile-long transcontinental railroad be sold even for a bagatelle. Now the constructive effort of those who yesterday were advancing the public good by seeking their own selfish ends is seen but as the dance of pursuers and possessors.

"Chimpanzees' Touching Behavior"
From *Primate Patterns*
Jane Goodall

A chimpanzee may seek to initiate physical contact with another chimpanzee (often, but not necessarily, a higher ranking one) in a number of behavioral contexts when it is afraid, agitated, or intensely stimulated by social activity or the sight of food. The gestures most frequently involved in the behavior are touching, holding the hand toward another, embracing, mounting, and grooming movements. In addition, one adolescent male frequently touched or held his own scrotum or penis under such circumstances. This type of behavior is illustrated by the following examples.

When chimpanzees were suddenly startled (for example, by a strange noise or sudden movement) they frequently reached out to touch another individual. When some violent social activity broke out in a group (such as fighting or branch-dragging displays) individuals not participating often reached out to touch or make grooming movements on each other; sometimes one mounted or embraced a companion. The same patterns often occurred when chimpanzees heard or saw others in the distance. . . . When chimpanzees were confronted with an especially large pile of bananas or saw us opening a big box of the fruit, the individuals concerned not only touched, patted, kissed, or embraced each other, but invariably uttered loud food "barks" at the same time.

One mature male embraced a three-year-old infant three times—twice after the adult had been attacked by another male and once when he had a sudden fright from seeing his own reflection in some glass. Even contact with the infant had a marked effect in calming him.

When a chimpanzee hurried to touch a high-ranking individual after being attacked or threatened by a less dominant one, it often looked around after the contact and made threatening sounds or gestures in the direction of its aggressor. Similarly, when an infant was suddenly frightened it often ran to its mother and suckled her, briefly held her nipple in its mouth, or simply reached out to touch her; he then looked around at the alarming stimulus (van Lawick-Goodall 1968*b*).

This type of contact-seeking behavior also occurs in other primates. On one occasion a gorilla was seen to reach its hand toward another when it suddenly saw a human observer; the second responded by taking the hand (Osborn 1963). An old baboon at the Gombe Stream Reserve was seen to reach out and touch another individual while threatening an observer (Miss Koning, personal communication). Hall (Hall and De-Vore, this volume) observed behavior in the chacma baboon that may be comparable; when a pair of animals was threatening another baboon, one sometimes briefly mounted the other, placing its hands lightly on its companion's back while standing slightly to the side and pointing its muzzle in the direction of the threatened individual. Man also shows a number of similar gestures in such situations. Frank (1958) notes that "a person who is strongly reacting emotionally, as in acute fear or pain, or grief, may be able to recover his physiological equilibrium through close tactile contacts with another sympathetic person." A small child may hold its mother's hand or skirt in the presence of strangers; similarly an adult may reach out and touch a companion or hold his hand when suddenly frightened or emotionally upset. In a different type of situation (probably comparable to a chimpanzee seeing a lot of food) two men may embrace or clap each other on the back when they suddenly hear good news.

"What Is a Beauty"
From *Old Mortality*
Katherine Anne Porter

"Tell me again how Aunt Amy went away when she was married." "She ran into the gray cold and stepped into the carriage and turned and smiled with her face as pale as death, and called out 'Good-by, good-by,' and refused her cloak, and said, 'Give me a glass of wine.' And none of us saw her alive again." "Why wouldn't she wear her cloak, Cousin Cora?" "Because she was not in love, my dear." Ruin hath taught me thus to ruminate, that time will come and take my love away. "Was she really beautiful, Uncle Bill?" "As an angel, my child." There were golden-haired angels with long blue pleated skirts dancing around the throne of the Blessed Virgin. None of them resembled Aunt Amy in the least, nor the type of beauty they had been brought up to admire. There were points of beauty by which one was judged severely. First, a beauty must be tall; whatever color the eyes, the hair must be dark, the darker the better; the skin must be pale and smooth. Lightness and swiftness of movement were important points. A beauty must be a good dancer, superb on horseback, with a serene manner, an amiable gaiety tempered with dignity at all hours. Beautiful teeth and hands, of course, and over and above all this, some mysterious crown of enchantment that attracted and held the heart. It was all very exciting and discouraging.

Miranda persisted through her childhood in believing, in spite of her smallness, thinness, her little snubby nose saddled with freckles, her speckled gray eyes and habitual tantrums, that by some miracle she would grow into a tall, cream-colored brunette, like cousin Isabel; she decided always to wear a trailing white satin gown. Maria, born sensible, had no such illusions. "We are going to take after Mamma's family," she said. "It's no use, we are. We'll never be beautiful, we'll always have freckles. And *you*," she told Miranda, "haven't even a good disposition."

Miranda admitted both truth and justice in this unkindness, but still secretly believed that she would one day suddenly receive beauty, as by inheritance, riches laid suddenly in her hands through no deserts of her own. She believed for quite a while that she would one day be like Aunt Amy, not as she appeared in the photograph, but as she was remembered by those who had seen her.

When Cousin Isabel came out in her tight black riding habit, surrounded by young men, and mounted gracefully, drawing her horse up and around so that he pranced learnedly on one spot while the other riders sprang to their saddles in the same sedate flurry, Miranda's heart would close with such a keen dart of admiration, envy, vicarious pride it was almost painful; but there would always be an elder present to lay a cooling hand upon her emotions. "She rides almost as well as Amy, doesn't she? But Amy had the pure Spanish style, she could bring out paces in a horse no one else knew he had." Young namesake Amy, on her way to a dance, would swish through the hall in ruffled white taffeta, glimmering like a moth in the lamplight, carrying her elbows pointed backward stiffly as wings, sliding along as if she were on rollers, in the fashionable walk of her day. She was considered the best dancer at any party, and Maria, sniffing the wave of perfume that followed Amy, would clasp her hands and say, "Oh, I can't *wait* to be grown up." But the elders would agree that the first Amy had been lighter, more smooth and delicate in her waltzing; young Amy would never equal her.

Like the model-telling, the summary tends to use the conditional mood (the "would") at times, or the present tense, but may use any tense appropriate to the content and context. "What Is a Beauty?" uses the past tense with occasional use of the conditional mood: ". . . Miranda's heart would close with such a keen dart of admiration, envy, vicarious pride it was almost painful; but there would always be an elder present to lay a cooling hand upon her emotions." In "The Panic of 1873," the past tense carries most instances, with the present tense occurring in some of the specific model-telling examples, e.g., "A Jay Gould flies about preying upon the rich debris; and in the vast confusion, hulking figures such as that of Cornelius Vanderbilt stand out, moving vigorously in their own defense." "Chimpanzees' Touching Behavior" begins with "A chimpanzee may seek . . . ," then uses the present tense in its model-telling elements and the past tense in reporting separate instances as they occurred at a time of observation in the past. The past tense instances are set side by side to show the overall pattern. (In "Chimpanzees' Touching Behavior" Goodall gives credit, in parentheses, for observations taken from studies done by other people.) Imagery, metaphor, active verbs, example, illustration, syntactical variation—all stimulated and brought forth by exaggeration—make the patterns of the model summaries clear. How does the use of short instances in these summaries differ from Darwin's in "Selection in Domestic Breeding," Frazer's in "Footprints and Magic," and Schaller's in "A Gorilla Day"?

Look over the readings for some of the techniques of exaggeration.

Model Extended Comparisons
(Analogies, Similes, Metaphors, and Figures)

In this section, we examine and write extended comparisons. When we use short comparisons, we generally do it without additional explanation because the short comparison makes a leap of comprehension from the unfamiliar to the more familiar. In the extended comparison, we often explain a good deal to the reader or listener as we develop it. We make complicated concepts, such as the expanding universe or the search for an escaped prisoner, clear to an audience that understands the terms of the comparison but not the unfamiliar concept or subject.

Seeing something side by side in our minds with something else gives us comparisons that communicate concepts more clearly to listeners or readers. Often the concepts that we communicate with gestures are done in writing with a comparison. Here are two different kinds of short comparisons from *The Road to Wigan Pier:*

"Down this belt a glittering river of coal races constantly."

"the unending rattle of the conveyor belt, which in that confined space is rather like the rattle of a machine gun."

When we transform the side by side comparison into a single image, such as in "Down this belt a glittering river of coal races constantly," we have a pure metaphor. If we rewrite the "glittering river" metaphor as a simile, such as "Down this belt coal races, like a glittering river," we find that it is not as effective. When we use "like" and sometimes "as," "as though," and "as if" to relate side by side comparisons, we have a simile, such as "the rattle of the conveyor belt" sounding "rather like the rattle of a machine gun." If we rewrite the simile as a pure metaphor, making it "the unending machine-gun rattle of the conveyor belt in that confined space," we find that the author's side by side comparison conveyed more strongly the din of the conveyor belt and "rather like" gave a wry tone missing from the pure metaphor. Everything in writing works together: tone, syntax, metaphor, imagery, and so forth. You will often feel instinctively whether or not to use the pure metaphor or the simile.

In extended comparisons, the above principles are carried further and additional discussion is added, in order to explain concepts that are unfamiliar to the audience. For instance, if laymen are told that a "resonant vibration" could cause a turbine to destroy itself, they might still not comprehend what could happen. However, most of us have heard the admonition that a group should not walk in step across a bridge, lest the bridge begin to sway and then collapse. If this kind of vibration is then identified as a "resonant vibration," and we're told by comparison that the same thing could happen to a turbine rotor and its buckets, we understand how a "resonant vibration" could destroy a turbine. The fact that my discussion of the comparison is lengthier than the comparison itself demonstrates the efficiency of comparison as a technique of communication.

In the humorous comparison of money-fund-selection to porcupine-hunting, we probably have no familiarity with actual porcupine hunting but are familiar with the porcupine's fabled prickles. Implicitly, the author compares our apprehension of choosing a money fund to our sense of avoiding the prickles of the porcupine. With the image of the tub, he shows us how we trap the porcupine without getting stuck by its quills and likens that to getting our "money under cover" first and then worrying about selecting the "best" money fund. In this case, the familiar image of the tub gets across the message of the comparison.

In the passage from *The Robber Barons,* concerning the causes of the financial panic of 1873, the author reduces the event to a visible and comprehensible size by comparing America's mad investment in railway building to a landowner's overextending his financial resources in building a drainage system. The comparison allows us to understand immediately the essential principle of the contribution of the "railway madness" to the general financial collapse.

When we compare waves striking the columns of a pier to the way sunlight struggles through the atmosphere, we make clear a complicated scientific concept of how the longer light waves march right through the atmosphere to the earth but the shorter light waves are "scattered" by the encounter with the atmosphere. Notice that the author uses another comparison within the overall comparison to give us a clear image of how the longer, larger waves travel relatively unaffected to the earth.

*   *   *

In the reading selections, we can see the imagery and gestures of the comparisons as if the authors were telling them orally to us, as they saw or sensed them at the time of writing. Wherever possible, do the gestures for each comparison, and see each comparison in your mind.

You've probably heard the warning that a group of people should never walk across a light bridge in step. They might set up a resonant vibration that would make the bridge sway and collapse. The same thing could happen to a turbine rotor and its buckets.

From "Better and Better Turbines Help Keep
Electricity Today's Greatest Bargain,"
Power Maker for America, General Electric.

If your curiosity about money-market mutual funds was rising along with interest rates, then there is no reason for that curiosity to have peaked even though rates may have.

Money funds are a good way for investors to enjoy peak returns for several weeks after interest rates start falling.

And if you are apprehensive because you don't know which is the best of the many funds available—well, relax, advises money-fund maven William Donoghue. Selecting a money fund is no more scary than hunting porcupines.

A porcupine hunter spots his prey, throws a washtub over it, and then figures out what to do next. Similarly, an investor should spot a reasonable-looking money fund and quickly invest.

"Get your money 'under cover,' and then worry about selecting the 'best' money fund," says Donoghue, publisher and editor of a money fund newsletter.

From the *Chicago Tribune,* Charles Storch

The settlers who had so swiftly opened the new lands could no longer sell the mountainous stores of grain which they brought forth. Nor could they buy the wares of merchants and manufacturers. The war in France, a crash in the bourse of far-off Vienna in 1872, timed with the frauds of the Union Pacific, had slackened the pace of railroad-building, and this in turn spread idleness to the factories, shops and mines who gave the materials for empire-building. Soon the till was bare. It was as if a landowner in possession of a rich estate had determined to spend twice the increment from his estate in drainage construction. The drainage was an excellent operation which would benefit the land when it was done; but in mid-career he must pause. His savings and his income were gone; a part of his land must now be sold to pay for the drainage system which, left incomplete, helped as yet in no way, and burdened him the more. So with America and its railway madness.

The whole country had strained its nerves to the utmost to build up, to double its transportation machinery within eight years, exceeding by far its needs for a long time to come.

From *The Robber Barons,* Matthew Josephson

Imagine that we stand on any ordinary seaside pier, and watch the waves roll-ing in and striking against the iron columns of the pier. Large waves pay very little attention to the columns—they divide right and left and re-unite after passing each column, much as a regiment of soldiers would if a tree stood in their road; it is almost as though the columns had not been there. But the short waves and ripples find the columns of the pier a much more formidable obstacle. When the short waves impinge on the columns, they are reflected back and spread as new ripples in all directions. To use the technical term, they are "scattered." The obstacle provided by the iron columns hardly affects the long waves at all, but scatters the short ripples.

We have been watching a sort of working model of the way in which sunlight struggles through the earth's atmosphere. . . .

From *The Stars in Their Courses*, Sir James Jeans

*   *   *

In the following selections, the comparison is developed with much more discus-sion of how the comparison explains the concept or subject.

Now we observe that the light from the galaxies is reddened, and the degree of reddening increases proportionately with the distance of a galaxy. The natural ex-planation of this is that the galaxies are rushing away from each other at enormous speeds, which for the most distant galaxies that we can see with the biggest tele-scope become comparable with the speed of light itself.

My nonmathematical friends often tell me that they find it difficult to picture this expansion. Short of using a lot of mathematics I cannot do better than use the analogy of a balloon with a large number of dots marked on its surface. If the bal-loon is blown up, the distances between the dots increase in the same way as the distances between the galaxies. Here I should give a warning that this analogy must not be taken too strictly. There are several important respects in which it is definitely misleading. For example, the dots on the surface of a balloon would themselves increase in size as the balloon was being blown up. This is not the case for the galaxies, for their internal gravitational fields are sufficiently strong to pre-vent any such expansion. A further weakness of our analogy is that the surface of an ordinary balloon is two dimensional—that is to say, the points of its surface can be described by two co-ordinates; for example, by latitude and longitude. In the case of the Universe we must think of the surface as possessing a third dimension. This is not as difficult as it may sound. We are all familiar with pictures in perspec-tive—pictures in which artists have represented three-dimensional scenes on two-dimensional canvases. So it is not really a difficult conception to imagine the three dimensions of space as being confined to the surface of a balloon. But then what does the radius of the balloon represent, and what does it mean to say that the balloon is being blown up? The answer to this is that the radius of the balloon is a measure of time, and the passage of time has the effect of blowing up the bal-loon. This will give you a very rough, but useful, idea of the sort of theory investi-gated by the mathematician.

The balloon analogy brings out a very important point. It shows we must not imagine that we are situated at the center of the Universe, just because we see all the galaxies to be moving away from us. For, whichever dot you care to choose on the surface of the balloon, you will find that the other dots all move away from it. In other words, whichever galaxy you happen to be in, the other galaxies will ap-pear to be receding from you.

From *The Expanding Universe*, Fred Hoyle

Hoyle uses the balloon comparison in this passage to make the concept of the expanding universe comprehensible to a general audience. He stimulates our seeing-in-the-mind so that we can perceive clearly the imagery of the comparison and the mechanism of the expanding universe. He invites, even needs to make sure of, our full intimate participation in his demonstration to make the comparison work. Note each time he uses you, we, I. What do the pronouns accomplish in association with various parts of the comparison? How does he strengthen the comparison by explaining the inaccuracies of the balloon analogy?

Seeing-in-the-mind finds comparisons (analogies, figures, similes, and metaphors) that strongly stimulate processes of discovery and actually help bring forth the new concept so that the inventor and the audience can understand it. Einstein used pictorial analogy to find and demonstrate the principles of both the Selective and the General Theories of Relativity (see the selection concerning Einstein's work in the Point of View section). Kekule half-dreamed the image or analogy of wriggling snakes of atoms swallowing their own tails, which demonstrated to him the structure of the benzene ring. The history of science, and of discovery in many fields, is replete with instances of invention through the imagery of analogy, gestural concepts, personification, for discovering patterns and concepts.

*   *   *

With such comparisons, the eighteenth century English engineer, John Smeaton, discovered the effective shape for the construction of the stone lighthouse.

On this occasion, the natural figure of the waist or bole of a large spreading oak presented itself to my imagination. Let us for a moment consider this tree: suppose at twelve or fifteen feet above its base, it branches out in every direction, and forms a large bushy top. . . . This top, when full of leaves, is subject to a very great impulse from the agitation of violent winds; yet partly by its elasticity, and partly by the natural strength arising from its figure, it resists them all, even for ages, till the gradual decay of the material diminishes the coherence of the parts, and they suffer piecemeal by the violence; but it is very rare that we hear of such a tree being torn up by the roots.

Let us now consider its particular figure. Connected with its roots, which lie below ground, it rises from the surface thereof with a large swelling base, which at the height of one diameter is generally reduced by an elegant curve, concave to the eye, to a diameter less by at least one-third, and sometimes to half of its original base. From thence its taper diminishing more slow, its sides by degrees come into a perpendicular, and for some height form a cylinder. After that a preparation of more circumference becomes necessary, for the strong insertion and establishment of the principal boughs, which produces a swelling of its diameter.

Now we can hardly doubt but every section of the tree is nearly of an equal strength in proportion to what it has to resist; and were we to lop off its principal boughs, and expose it in that state to a rapid current of water, we should find it as much capable of resisting the action of the heavier fluid, when divested of the greatest part of its clothing, as it was that of the lighter when all its spreading ornaments were exposed to the fury of the wind; and hence we may derive an idea of what the proper shape of a column of the greatest stability ought to be, to resist the action of external violence. . . .

From "What Can the Technical Writer of the Past Teach the Technical Writer of Today?" Walter James Miller

From the gestural impulse of his visual abstraction, Smeaton veritably traces in the air the figure of the trunk of the oak trees, exaggerating its natural figure and principles of resistance to currents of water and wind, thereby finding the basic design of the stone lighthouse. Then he begins to develop the visualized figure in the theater of composition of his mind. Keeping the context of the underlying principle in mind, he enlarges, magnifies, sharpens, abstracts the figure of the trunk of the oak tree. He exaggerates to bring forth both the concept and the writing of it. He brings "us" and "we" directly into the process of discovery, using precise active verbs and many gestural and metaphorical phrases.

*   *   *

Now read a passage from *The Death and Life of Great American Cities.*

"Hudson Street Ballet"
Jane Jacobs

Under the seeming disorder of the old city, wherever the old city is working successfully, is a marvelous order for maintaining the safety of the streets and the freedom of the city. It is a complex order. Its essence is intricacy of sidewalk use, bringing with it a constant succession of eyes. This order is all composed of movement and change, and although it is life, not art, we may fancifully call it the art form of the city and liken it to the dance—not to a simple-minded precision dance with everyone kicking up at the same time, twirling in unison and bowing off en masse, but to an intricate ballet in which the individual dancers and ensembles all have distinctive parts which miraculously reinforce each other and compose an orderly whole. The ballet of the good city sidewalk never repeats itself from place to place, and in any one place is always replete with new improvisations.

The stretch of Hudson Street where I live is each day the scene of an intricate sidewalk ballet. I make my own first entrance into it a little after eight when I put out the garbage can, surely a prosaic occupation, but I enjoy my part, my little clang, as the droves of junior high school students walk by the center of the stage dropping candy wrappers. (How do they eat so much candy so early in the morning?)

While I sweep up the wrappers I watch the other rituals of morning: Mr. Halpert unlocking the laundry's handcart from its mooring to a cellar door, Joe Cornacchia's son-in-law stacking out the empty crates from the delicatessen, the barber bringing out his sidewalk folding chair, Mr. Goldstein arranging the coils of wire which proclaim the hardware store is open, the wife of the tenement's superintendent depositing her chunky three-year-old with a toy mandolin on the stoop, the vantage point from which he is learning the English his mother cannot speak. Now the primary children, heading for St. Luke's, dribble through to the south, the children for St. Veronica's cross, heading to the west, and the children for P.S. 41, heading toward the east. Two new entrances are being made from the wings: well-dressed and even elegant women and men with brief cases emerge from doorways and side streets. Most of these are heading for the bus and subways, but some hover on the curbs, stopping taxis which have miraculously appeared at the right moment, for the taxis are part of a wider morning ritual: having dropped passengers from midtown in the downtown financial district they are now bringing downtowners up to midtown. Simultaneously, numbers of women in housedresses have emerged and as they crisscross with one another they pause for quick conversations that sound with either laughter or joint indignation, never, it seems, anything between. It is time for me to hurry to work too, and I exchange my ritual farewell with Mr. Lofaro, the short, thick-bodied, white-aproned fruit man who stands outside his doorway a little up the street, his arms folded, his feet planted, looking solid as earth itself. We nod; we each glance quickly up and down the street, then look back to each other and smile. We have done this many a morning for more than ten years, and we both know what it means: All is well.

The heart-of-the-day ballet I seldom see, because part of the nature of it is that working people who live there, like me, are mostly gone, filling the roles of strangers on other sidewalks. But from days off, I know enough of it to know that it becomes more and more intricate. Longshoremen who are not working that day gather at the White Horse or the Ideal or the International for beer and conversation. The executives and business lunchers from the industries just to the west throng the Dorgene restaurant and the Lion's Head coffee house, meat-market workers and communications scientists fill the bakery lunchroom. Character dancers come on, a strange old man with strings of old shoes over his shoulders, motor-scooter riders with big beards and girl friends who bounce on the back of the scooters and wear their hair long in front of their faces as well as behind, drunks who follow the advice of the Hat Council and are always turned out in hats, but not hats the Council would approve. Mr. Lacey, the locksmith, shuts up his shop for a while and goes to exchange the time of day with Mr. Slube at the cigar store. Mr. Koochagian, the tailor, waters the luxuriant jungle of plants in his window, gives them a critical look from the outside, accepts a compliment on them from two passers-by, fingers the leaves on the plane tree in front of our house with a thoughtful gardener's appraisal, and crosses the street for a bite at the Ideal where he can keep an eye on customers and wigwag across the message that he is coming. The baby carriages come out, and clusters of everyone from toddlers with dolls to teen-agers with homework gather at the stoops.

When I get home after work, the ballet is reaching its crescendo. This is the time of roller skates and stilts and tricycles, and games in the lee of the stoop with bottletops and plastic cowboys; this is the time of bundles and packages, zigzagging from the drug store to the fruit stand and back over to the butcher's; this is the time when teen-agers, all dressed up, are pausing to ask if their slips show or their collars look right; this is the time when beautiful girls get out of MG's; this is the time when the fire engines go through; this is the time when anybody you know around Hudson Street will go by.

As darkness thickens and Mr. Halpert moors the laundry cart to the cellar door again, the ballet goes on under lights, eddying back and forth but intensifying at the bright spotlight pools of Joe's sidewalk pizza dispensary, the bars, the delicatessen, the restaurant and the drug store. The night workers stop now at the delicatessen, to pick up salami and a container of milk. Things have settled down for the evening but the street and its ballet have not come to a stop.

I know the deep night ballet and its seasons best from waking long after midnight to tend a baby and, sitting in the dark, seeing the shadows and hearing the sounds of the sidewalk. Mostly it is a sound like infinitely pattering snatches of party conversation and, about three in the morning, singing, very good singing. Sometimes there is sharpness and anger or sad, sad weeping, or a flurry of search for a string of beads broken. One night a young man came roaring along, bellowing terrible language at two girls whom he had apparently picked up and who were disappointing him. Doors opened, a wary semicircle formed around him, not too close, until the police came. Out came the heads, too, along Hudson Street offering opinion, "Drunk . . . Crazy . . . A wild kid from the suburbs."*

Deep in the night, I am almost unaware how many people are on the street unless something calls them together, like the bagpipe. Who the piper was and why he favored

---

*He turned out to be a wild kid from the suburbs. Sometimes on Hudson Street we are tempted to believe the suburbs must be a difficult place to bring up children. [Author's note]

our street I have no idea. The bagpipe just skirled out in the February night, and as if it were a signal the random, dwindled movements of the sidewalk took on direction. Swiftly, quietly, almost magically a little crowd was there, a crowd that enveloped into a circle with a Highland fling inside it. The crowd could be seen on the shadowy sidewalk, the dancers could be seen, but the bagpiper himself was almost invisible because his bravura was all in his music. He was a very little man in a plain brown overcoat. When he finished and vanished, the dancers and watchers applauded, and applause came from the galleries too, half a dozen of the hundred windows on Hudson Street. Then the windows closed, and the little crowd dissolved into the random movements of the night street.

The strangers on Hudson Street, the allies whose eyes help us natives keep the peace of the street, are so many that they always seem to be different people from one day to the next. That does not matter. Whether they are so many always-different people as they seem to be, I do not know. Likely they are. When Jimmy Rogan fell through a plate-glass window (he was separating some scuffling friends) and almost lost his arm, a stranger in an old T shirt emerged from the Ideal bar, swiftly applied an expert tourniquet and, according to the hospital's emergency staff, saved Jimmy's life. Nobody remembered seeing the man before and no one has seen him since. The hospital was called in this way: a woman sitting on the steps next to the accident ran over to the bus stop, wordlessly snatched the dime from the hand of a stranger who was waiting with his fifteen-cent fare ready, and raced into the Ideal's phone booth. The stranger raced after her to offer the nickel too. Nobody remembered seeing him before, and no one has seen him since. When you see the same stranger three or four times on Hudson Street, you begin to nod. This is almost getting to be an acquaintance, a public acquaintance, of course.

I have made the daily ballet of Hudson Street sound more frenetic than it is, because writing it telescopes it. In real life, it is not that way. In real life, to be sure, something is always going on, the ballet is never at a halt, but the general effect is peaceful and the general tenor even leisurely. People who know well such animated city streets will know how it is. I am afraid people who do not will always have it a little wrong in their heads—like the old prints of rhinoceroses made from travelers' descriptions of rhinoceroses.

On Hudson Street, the same as in the North End of Boston or in any other animated neighborhoods of great cities, we are not innately more competent at keeping the sidewalks safe than are the people who try to live off the hostile truce of Turf in a blind-eyed city. We are the lucky possessors of a city order that makes it relatively simple to keep the peace because there are plenty of eyes on the street. But there is nothing simple about that order itself, or the bewildering number of components that go into it. Most of those components are specialized in one way or another. They unite in their joint effect upon the sidewalk, which is not specialized in the least. That is its strength.

The analogy of the life of the streets of the old city to a ballet helps organize, clarify, and demonstrate the message of the essay. The first paragraph develops the overall ballet analogy. The author returns to it periodically in the course of the essay, usually to make changes and modifications in the concept as she clarifies the alternations of the behavior patterns in the streets. In the second to the last paragraph, she returns to the ballet analogy again to make a final important qualification.

How does the ballet analogy help us understand the life of the "good" streets of the old city? How is "Hudson Street Ballet" also a full model-telling? Where does it use several instances to show patterns? What do you notice about the author's use of the first-person "I"? Examples demonstrate the strength of the ballet analogy. How does the use of people's names and anecdotal examples affect the telling?

* * *

Here's another extended analogy, this time based on a gameboard with a bull's eye in the middle.

The Search Party

James O. Elder

And the search party roared down on Nantuck County like it was the last piece of fish at a fish fry. They blocked off roads, searched cars, houses, and barns, knocked on doors, shook doorknobs, and arrested any Black man who had the cripple dog luck of being alone without a white man in the crowd to identify him. The FBI supervised the attack from the second floor of the Jerline Courthouse. The State Police manned communications and roadblocks on all major highways within a 30 mile radius of the prison. County police set roadblocks inside the State roadblocks. And the Lexington police department conducted the air search which was to begin immediately, or—as soon as it stopped raining. Local police from neighboring townships were put in charge of the foot soldiers who were comprised of off-duty prison guards and local volunteers who had seized this rare opportunity by the throat; for it wasn't often that these robust men of Nantuck County had occasion to brandish their shotguns and rifles in such a brazen and orderly fashion; to do so while wearing the scowls and grimaces of men in defense of their womenfolk was damn near more than this over-ripe troop of boy scouts could stand.

Now in order to get a clear picture of this awesome campaign against one man's freedom we must first play a game. Imagine you are hovering 3,000 feet in the air directly over the prison from where the prisoner escaped; it's 4:30 in the afternoon; it's raining like hell; and this siren is squawking like a chorus of wounded ducks. Draw a circle around the prison and paint the inside of it black—this circle should measure a half-mile across at any two fixed points. Now line the circle with 400 men wearing either red, yellow, blue, or green ribbons around their arms; the men wearing the red ribbons should be on the north side of the black circle, the yellow south, the blue east, and the green west. Now the purpose of the ribbons is to cut down on some of the confusion that arose seven years ago when two inmates escaped from the prison and a search group got lost and drifted into the wrong area and was attacked by another search group who thought that they were the enemy and by the time buckshot quit flying thru the air three members of the search party had been wounded. So it is important that the men and the ribbons are properly distributed around the circle. At no time should you have 300 men congregating on one side of the prison while there are only 100 left on the remaining three sides; nor should you have 198 men wearing red ribbons and only 2 wearing yellow. Yes, it is essential to the game that the men and the ribbons are properly distributed.

Now march off 20 miles from the black circle and draw another circle making sure to keep the black one in the middle. Mark all the highway intersections that cross this circle with an X—the X's will represent County roadblocks.

March off 10 more miles and draw yet another circle—still making sure to keep the first two in the middle—and this time mark all major highways that cross the circle with double XX's—the double XX's will represent State roadblocks.

Now if you have done this correctly we should have three circles surrounding the prison: the first one just outside the prison walls with the inside painted black; the second one 20 miles away from the prison with X's representing County roadblocks; and the third one 30 miles away from the prison with double XX's representing State roadblocks. Now this gameboard that we've just designed should resemble a bull's eye target with the black circle surrounding the prison being the bull's eye. Now you might be saying to yourself, "Damn, that's a big target." But really it's not. It is true, however, that if you walked from one State roadblock straight across the circle to one on the other side you would have walked 60 miles and it probably would have taken you from sun-up to sun-down and you'd still have 10 miles left over for breakfast the next morning—and that's only if you're a good walker walking on a good day. My point is that the size of the target doesn't matter—it's the purpose that counts—because targets, like all game boards, are designed for the games people play on them and not the other way around. How much fun do you think it would be to play darts on a target the size of a 3-story building? Not much I'm afraid. Why, the bull's eye would have to be at least 12 feet round in circumference and a blind man can hit that with his back turned. And therefore it would just be a matter of time before the other players got bored and quit, because nobody likes to play a game where it's impossible to prove that they're better than the people they're playing against. It doesn't take any talent to shoot an arrow into a tree if that tree just happens to be a Redwood, nor does it take any shrewd cunning to shoot a basketball into Grand Canyon. Why, it's simply no fun at all to play a game if the gameboard is not designed to meet the needs of the game you choose to play. There's no challenge to doing that because you'd have to make up your own rules as you went along—and some people refer to that as CHEATING. But then on the other hand a target can be as big as the moon and possess all the glitter and excitement of a Salem Witch Hunt if the game is designed for a target of that size; and on occasion it has been. Why, Russia and the United States have shot men at the moon and all they wanted them to do was to land in the light, stick a flag in the ground, and bring back some rocks. But, since the moon is 238,857 miles from the Earth, that was a challenge. So when you look down at this 60 mile wide bull's eye target don't think of it as being big, just think of it as being just the right size to play this game.

Now the objective of this game is to keep the Black man in the bull's eye. But, as we both well know, he has already escaped. So the objective now is to keep him confined to the second circle until he is caught. Now if he escapes from the second circle this same process must be repeated all over again in the third circle. But at all cost he must be captured before he breaks that third ring, because the farther he gets away from the bull's eye the less likelihood there is of him being caught, and the longer he remains at large without being caught, the greater the odds are that he'll break that third ring. So, as you can see, time is of the essence in playing this game, and with each passing second that the prisoner remains free, his chances for success increase, while the search party's chances decrease.

Remember those 400 men surrounding the bull's eye? Well you can start fanning them out now in groups of 5's and remember that all groups must search in the areas that their colors specify: the red north, the yellow south, the blue east, and the green west.

The prison sits in the middle of an open field about a mile from the surrounding woods and as these men trudge through the rain and thick grass, mud caking up around their boots, the party atmosphere slowly evaporates and for the first time since they joined this search party they begin to realize that this is a real man that they're hunting, a real blood and bones man, a man who was tried and convicted of commiting a crime or crimes unknown and who said "Fuck the Government; I'm not going to pay," a man whose hands can hold a gun and squeeze a trigger just like theirs, a man who could be sitting in the woods watching them right now and waiting for them to get just one step closer before he squeezes off that round. And they are afraid. The closer the men get to the woods, the further away they get from each other, and when the lightning strikes you can see all of these five man squads stop at once and when the thunder roars in you can feel their hearts stutter, and at this point little things begin to take on great significance: the rain that is falling so thick and heavy that you can hear it tap dancing on ever-widening puddles of water that lie camouflaged beneath the foot high grass; the sky that's been painted a blackish gray by a melancholy artist who felt no need to separate day from night; and the muffled squawking of the prison's siren that reverberates inside the men's heads like the echo from a nightmare that suddenly startles you awake and then dares you to fall back to sleep; and in the distance the trees and shadows are one and you know that if you enter those woods you'll never come out again. So you look around hoping someone, anyone, will call this whole thing off and tell you that it was just a game, but then they don't and you knew that they wouldn't because you know that this is not a game; it's an act of desperation by two desperate forces and you're convinced that he's more desperate than you are. And you're afraid. But once you enter the woods you're more afraid to turn around and go back than you are to keep on going, so you keep on walking clumsily along staring bug-eyed like everybody else, praying that this demonic killer is not in your area but someone else's, and you know that if you can just make it through the night you won't be back tomorrow. . . .

Elder sets the narrative scene first and suggests with his tone how the game will move from an abstract, exciting fantasy to a dreary, fear-filled reality, involving many people. He summarizes the situation in the first paragraph, then steps forward with his gameboard analogy in the second paragraph, as if stopping the story and stepping up to the blackboard to draw the circles and explain their meaning and discuss the analogy with us. How does the gameboard analogy strengthen our understanding of how the search is conducted? How does this approach differ from that of Jacobs, who deploys her analogy in the first paragraph and then begins the concrete telling of how the street works, adding to and modifying the concept as the essay progresses?

Notice the tense change from the first paragraph to the second paragraph, from the narrative past tense to the present tense of an expository demonstration. The "you" changes persona and character a few times. Locate and follow those changes. The narrative also gives a model-telling of the first part of the search, in the present tense. How does the author's attitude become evident? What is the tone he gives the piece?

What other comparisons does the author use within his broad gameboard analogy?

Writing Your Model Comparison
(Analogy, Simile, Metaphor, Figure)

Write extended comparisons that are part of your how-it-happens subject or come from outside of it—*anything that takes your attention, that you see in your mind*. In your how-it-happens subject, there are almost certainly mechanisms or activities, or patterns of activity, with which you are familiar but most of your readers are not. The right comparisons could make them clear to your readers. The comparison will come as a discovery to you and then to your readers.

When comparisons occur to you, either in talking to others or while musing to yourself, write them in your journal. When you notice yourself using gestures to communicate concepts, see those gestures in your mind and see what imagery or comparisons will communicate the gestural concept in writing to your reader. Wherever you feel your audience may not understand or be familiar with the experience of your how-it-happens subject, see in your mind possible comparisons to familiar elements of the reader's experience.

Write short comparisons, analogies, metaphors, similes, figures.

Write an extended comparison, analogy, metaphor, or figure.

Model-Character-Telling

In the model-character-telling, you concentrate on developing the imagery and narrative scene that reveal the characteristic patterns of behavior of a person or a fictional character. Think of someone you've known for long enough that you recognize patterns of their behavior. You can see the way they come into a room the same way again and again, or the way they meet a person, or their characteristic mannerisms and gestures. When you think about them, you see their ways of dealing with people, situations, authorities, work, play, anything. What catches your attention about the person? Make notes. As you begin to write about him or her, you'll begin to notice other patterns that you've barely verbalized to yourself. You'll begin to see the person more clearly, and the person will stand up and move in your imagination.

The model-character-telling gives the more or less full character of the person in short compass, say from a paragraph or two to two or three pages.

The model-character-telling does not confine us to a moment-by-moment telling of what a person does. For instance, in "Clare," we find out more about Clare in a couple of pages, see her more fully, than if we were only given a couple of pages of an incident in which Clare played a part. The model-character-telling makes us quickly, knowledgeably, familiarly acquainted with the person.

"Clare" is an excerpt from a much longer work, a novel, about Louie's family. Obviously, the necessities of the longer work play a part in producing this particular model-character-telling. Similarly, our excerpt from "Cool Willie" is the introduction to a longer tale in which Willie finally becomes the victim of his own myth, reduced to weakness, ineffectiveness, and desolation as soon as he gets into a situation in which people simply pay no attention to his COOOOL. "Route Manager" is a model-character-telling that was developed within the author's general exploration of many basic forms in his how-it-happens subject of the paper route and a boy's sexual awakening.

"Clare"
From ***The Man Who Loved Children***
Christina Stead

Model-character-telling

If Miss Rosalind Alden was the heavenly love, Clare was the alter ego. Everyone knew about her: the older ones thought her a crazy kid, while the younger ones wondered who was that dirty, ragged girl full of shouts and horseplay. When she came in through the school gate, without a hat (her hat had at last fallen to pieces), she would rip off the ragged overcoat and, showing its ripped lining and hanging seams, she would begin to sell it, ducking and grinning solicitously, smoothing down its burst seams and expatiating on its beauty, and she would offer it at auction for a dollar, fifty cents, ten cents. One day a youngster offered her ten cents for it, and she sold it, took the ten cents, and refused to take the coat back; no, it had gone under the hammer and been parted with fair and square, said this tragic muse. She trudged home to her home in a yard in Compromise Street, in Annapolis, without a coat, although it was a gray November day, with a sneaking, damp breeze and snow threatening, and the next day came in a man's coat that a neighbor, an old man, had lent her. She herself had gone in and borrowed the coat till he should ask for it. She turned out the pockets before half the school, finding string, tickets and a mucus-streaked handkerchief which she flung away from her with a magnificent gesture of loathing, and all the time, unself-conscious, amused at herself.

Narrative example and illustration

"Look at this now—a bit of string to hang myself with: but my neck's too thick—he didn't think of that! And the pocket's—where's the pocket? Ouch! I can feel my knee—my knee's in the pocket. But who said anything about pockets? Look, just air—it's lined with air: but that's a swell style, the latest thing: there are more wearing pockets of air and linings of air at this minute than linings of silk. Who cares for the naval dears with their plackets and braid? The best part of mankind wears overcoats entirely of air. First a suit of skin, then a decoration of hair, then an overcoat of air!"

Then deciding that she was dissatisfied with her overcoat, air or no air, she would shuffle off a few steps, and Louie, who would have been standing, grinning but dissatisfied, sometimes rather stern, at the edge of the crowd, would take her arm and say, "Clare, Clare!"

"What, Louie?"

"Clare—" Louie knew that Clare only behaved like this when her poverty rankled worst; Clare's poverty was no secret to anyone—she came of a brilliant family that after the death of father and mother had come into the hands of a poor, stiffnecked maiden aunt. One eldest sister was even now at work, helping to keep the two younger sisters and small brother. As soon as Clare graduated, she would take up the burden. Half the weeks in the year it was a question whether Clare would have a roof over her head at all. What was there to say? Clare would smile at her ruefully and grip her hand.

Model-character-telling

"Ah, Louie, what do I care? When I get through I'll earn; but where will I be still? There's my sister and brother and two mortgages—the only thing that worries me is the boys: the brutes won't look at a poverty like me! What does it matter what I am?"

Louie was silent. Then stupidly she would say,

"Well, you're only fourteen, Clare—" Clare would open her arms wide, spreading the loose garments that fell about her, with a gesture that somehow recalled the surf beating on a coast, the surf of time or of sorrows.

"Look at me? Will I ever be any different?" Clare resolutely refused to visit Louie at her home and would never even cross the bridge to Eastport for fear of meeting Louie with her family; she would always refuse, hanging her head and smiling to herself, though at what, Louie could never make out.

"You don't want me, Louie: I'll see you at school."

One day, just before Christmas, she came, without galoshes, but dragging, on a stockinged foot, a completely ruined shoe. Her toes peeped through holes in the stockings. Some of the girls who were hanging about exclaimed, pointed, and others running up commenced to make a great hullabaloo. Clare stopped in her tracks and, laughing at the great fun, picked up the shoe out of the muddy snow and began swinging it round and round her head: suddenly it flew loose and seemed to fly into the sky, but it landed on the roof instead and while they all stood laughing hysterically, holding their bellies and going into shrieks of laughter, Clare rushed into the janitor's room, took a ladder, scrambled up to the roof, and began mounting it towards the shoe, making a fall of snow,

Narrative example and illustration

but still going up carefully on hands and knees. Her patched and tired underwear could be seen all over the grounds. An old teacher (Clare was her protégée) came running and, in a stern high voice, cried out to Clare to come down quickly, while the janitor with a long pole began to poke after the shoe. Clare, looking round, and greeting her audience with a flustered laugh, began to back down again—the shoe slid towards her, she tweaked it off the roof and sent it flying down to the ground. She happened to be looking at her friend, the old teacher, and so the shoe struck the woman in the face. She started back but said nothing, only blushed and rubbed her face; and then she stooped and picked up the miserable object, and stood with it dangling in her hand until Clare had reached the ground again. The children, much struck, had fallen silent, and as Clare sheepishly came up to the woman and said, "I'm sorry, I'm sorry," and they looked from one to the other, they saw that Miss Harney (the mistress) was crying. She took Clare under the arm, upstairs and into her own room. Louie trailed after her, and because Miss Harney also liked her, she was allowed to remain there.

Narrative
example and
illustration
cont.

"Have you no other shoes?"

"No, ma'am," said Clare brightly.

"Why not?"

"No money, ma'am!"

"Don't call me 'ma'am,' Clare."

"No, ma'am—Miss—ma'am—Miss . . ."

Miss Harney shrugged, "I am going to send to get you a pair of shoes."

"No need, ma'am: no need at all, thankee kindly."

"Stop acting the fool, Clare."

"No'm, yes'm thankee'm."

Miss Harney, very tall, spare, spectacled, with iron-gray hair, struggled with a smile, "Clare, you don't have to go through this, surely? I'll write to your aunt. You have friends here: we'll gladly help you."

"Don't want any help: no'm," Clare said.

Soon the school was talking about it and saying the teachers had got together and bought Clare a blouse, skirt, and so forth, and that the very next day, out of pride, no doubt, Clare had come back in the former sordid outfit—but this protest did not last. She wore the better clothes, and during the winter Miss Harney looked after her constantly, for Clare had developed a bad cough. She parodied the cough too, of course: it was a great source of inspiration to her. Just before they broke for Christmas, Clare tied the draw cord of the Venetian blind round her neck and accidently fell out of the window.

When examination results were posted, Clare appeared in most lists at the top or as a runner-up. Most often she would be "sick" the day before a test, or her aunt would be sick the week before a term examination. On the morning of the examination, Clare would turn up, ragged, but with a clean blouse and cheerful as ever. She would throw balls of paper about the room, write hard, begin early, and end late. . . .

Summary-telling

The single incident of the shoe on the roof means much more to us because we've received the model-telling of how Clare acts with flamboyant defensiveness with her ragged clothes and the model-telling of how she takes exams. If the telling began with the shoe incident, it would not have as much impact for us. Because of the model-tellings before and after it, the shoe incident resonates more strongly and movingly for us. Similarly, the model-telling of how Clare takes exams gains strength from everything that precedes it and gives closure and reverberation of strength to the whole passage.

Christina Stead's exaggeration, focusing on Clare, brings forth the charming flamboyance that Clare cultivates to handle her desperation. Exaggeration focused on Louie brings forth Louie's shy, awkward, romantic qualities, and her clumsy strong ambition. Exaggeration brings forth strong telling verbs, adverbs, and adjectives: "When she came in through the school gate, without a hat (her hat had at last *fallen* to pieces), she would *rip* off the *ragged* overcoat and, showing its *ripped* lining and *hanging* seams, she would begin to *sell* it, *ducking* and *grinning solicitously, smoothing* down its *burst* seams and *expatiating* on its *beauty,* and she would *offer it at auction* for a dollar, fifty cents, ten cents." Exaggeration heightens the alternating patterns of these passages. What do you notice about tenses and conditional mood (would) in relation to model-tellings and narrative examples?

What gives you the sense and feeling of the author telling these passages with her own voice and perception? Compare the diction of Stead's dialogue with the diction of her prose.

*   *   *

Watch and listen how the talltale language and hyperbole in "Cool Willie" gives a mythological dimension to the effect of Willie's characteristic entrance into a pool hall.

Cool Willie
Ronald Booze

Cool Willie was from Philly. He was from Philly and he was COOOOL. Not cool, but COOOOL. Ice-cool, supercool, pimpin'-down-the-street-with-a-layer-of-frost-on-his-blood-red-Pierre Cardin-three-piece-suit-and-three-icicles-hangin'-off-the-super-wide-brim-of-his-blood-red-Dobbs-gangster-skypiece cool. Cool Willie was from Philly, he was COOOOL, and he shot some *meeeean* pool. Tha's right. Cool Willie's game was Poison Eightball, and he kicked ass, all over town. Whenever Cool Willie pimped through the door of a pool hall in Philly, the joint went dead quiet. Tha's right, stone cold silent as the morgue at midnight, a flat, fearful quiet that froze the spectators to the walls and straightened upright every hack and hustler bent over the green felt. Yeah, they stood up, sticks in hands, palms gettin' clammy on the cheap pockmarked ash, and they smelled their own sweat, and smiled weak, cheap smiles as the screen door slam, slam, slammed closed behind the stridin' red suit. Tha's all they saw, too, a headless red crushed velvet suit, movin' through the neck-high light, pullin' wisps of the thick cloud of cigarette and cigar smoke that filled the pool hall behind him. Everybody's eyes rode those wisps, too, watchin' that suit move straight smack-dab up the middle of the hall like it was gonna walk right through the first table. But it never did. It always turned right and went around that first table, makin' its way to the middle of the hall, to the middle table. And that's when the left sleeve of that red suit would move up past the neck and out of the light, and come back into the light with that blood-red Dobb's, gently held in the long brown fingers of the sleeve's left hand, and somebody would take it and set it down on one of the other tables (after clearing the balls, of course). It would be safe there, 'cause nobody was going to shoot any pool anywhere else anyway, not while the red suit was there.

Then, quick-smooth and sudden, the right sleeve of the red suit would flash up onto the end of the table, resting a maroon alligator-skin case there (where the hell did he find a red alligator?) and then both sleeves would come up, resting the long brown fingers on top of the shiny smooth case. The fingers would rest there for a second or so, just long enough for the light to flash and flicker off the ruby pinkie ring on the left hand the diamond-in-white-gold on the middle finger of the right. Then those fingers would sliiiiiiide, slow and easy as y'please, out to the latches on the front of the case, and with one quick "click!" that filled the pool hall and made everybody jump, the latches would pop open, and the fingers would gently lift the top of the case.

Well, if any of the rookies up in the hall hadn't dropped jaw at the sight of the red suit, or the sight of the alligator case, or at the sight of the diamond-ringed, ruby-ringed brown fingers, they sure loosed them jowls when the case was opened up. There, sittin' in two grooves of the softest, plushest red velvet any earth born creature had ever laid eye or fingertip on, were two halves of deep, jet-black polished-to-a-shine-to-make-a-man-go-blind ebonite pool cue. The neck-high tablelights shot flickering sparks and streaks of yellow off the two gleaming halves, and the shadow-hidden eyes of every man in the pool-hall would run from tip to crew of the narrow tapering top half, and from butt to gold-ringed top of the lower half of what was the baddest piece of pool shootin' equipment any of them would ever lay eyes on.

Then, the red suit's right sleeve moved to the front of the jacket, where the fingers unbuttoned it, and the sleeves would both drop down and behind the suit, and somebody would slowly sliiiiide that blood-red jacket off, and *hold* it, "don't hang it, got t'keep it in sight," Cool Willie would say, and whoever was holdin' that jacket, folded neat down the middle of the back and draped on his arm, made *sure* that he was somewhere in Cool Willie's line of sight *all* night.

Then, Cool Willie would reach into the right vest pocket, and pull out a pair of red split-leather gloves ("where the hell did he find a red cow?") and pull each glove on slooooooowly, carefully, lovingly, so delicate that somebody would sigh the sigh of a satisfied lover (yeah, pool players are lovers, too) at the sight of those long brown fingers sliding in. He'd flex those fingers, three times, each hand, then slowly, carefully, lovingly lift the fat bottom half of the stick from the case, hefting and admiring it in his left hand, his pencil-thin mustache just barely curling its ends upward in a smile that nobody could see in the shadows, and the pool hall was so quiet you could hear a flea fart. Then he'd take that slim, tapering top half from *its* red velvet groove, and heft it, and lift it to the light. Then he'd join the halves, and the scrsssh, scrsssh, scrsssh of the threaded peg screwing into the hold of the bottom half would fill the pool hall, and when both halves were firm together, with that thin line of gold at the joint, Cool Willie would lower the stick till it stood upright at his right, resting its rubber butt on the floor, and smile, lettin' his glossy whites shine just a line under that lip and up-edged pencil-thin, and say, softly,

"Anybody f'r a game a poison eight?"

Exaggeration of language and imagery brings forth the character of Willie and patterns of people's reactions to him. Note the author's special techniques to get across Willie's characteristic appearance and effect. Special visible arrangements of the printed word, such as "COOOOL," "*meeeean*," "Sliiiiide," and "scrssh, scrssh, scrssh," indicate how words should be sounded, exaggerated, and what weight and value should be given to them. Hyphenated modifiers also give special effects, such as "quick-smooth," and "two halves of deep, jet-black, polished-to-a-shine-to-make-a-man-go-blind ebonite pool cue."

Note the exaggerated imagery with which Booze emphasizes the mythical aura about Cool Willie: "Tha's all they saw, too, a headless red crushed velvet suit, movin' through the neck-high light, pullin' behind him wisps of the thick cloud of cigarette and cigar smoke that filled the pool hall."

Find the special effects that heighten the mythical COOOOL aura of Willie, including the special language effects. Note the "mixed diction," the mixture of colloquial speech and Standard English. Compare the voice and diction of "Clare" and "Cool Willie."

* * *

Now watch carefully from whose point of view "Route Manager" is seen and felt.

Route Manager
James Hall

Other paper boys had brought their erotic excitements along with them, young as they were. Here was Henderson, and Joe, and Hank from next door. They showed up sleepy-eyed at the shopping center to pick up their newspaper bundles, but each with a girl in his front seat with him. The girls stayed lazily in the front seats, sometimes examining their faces in the rear-view mirrors, the light from inside the cars spilling out upon the curb, while their boyfriends plunked, plunked their heavy newspaper bundles into the trunks of their stud cars. Everyone assumed an intimacy between these boys and their girlfriends. That's what having a girl in the front seat next to your thigh meant.

Richard always reported to the bundle drop alone.

Ed Davies, the route manager, standing there in the shopping center before the laundromat windows, checking in each of his hired hands as they reported for work, had it in for the studs or the sissies alike if you were late. Three thirty sharp, no excuses. Ed Davies chewed on his dead cigar, a real ranch-foreman, a long-time bachelor with burly forearms, his girlfriends the subject of speculation among the boys, although none ever showed up sitting next to him, thigh to thigh. Or such a woman as would have slept with him night after night the boys would have termed a "loser," for Ed Davies was a beast, the boys all knew.

There he would stand, in front of the laundromat windows in the deserted shopping center at three-thirty sharp, barking out each boy's last name, all of them having left their cars to gather round, all raggedly dressed, some with old shoes on, or none, Richard in ragged shorts, Hank in his tuxedo pants dragged out from a party, too scared of Ed Davies to be drunk, barechested, all of the boys trying to remain as cool, as much asleep as possible through Ed Davies' barks, so that when you hit the bed again in a coupla hours you could lapse right back into sleep before Mom called, and the school day began, or more truly to *affect* a sleepy look on their faces so that they would not betray how frightened and contemptuous of Ed Davies they were. If you appeared bright-eyed or ambitious, everyone would be contemptuous of you, especially Ed Davies, because then he would not be allowed to play out with you his only role of boss, and his fierce act would butt out just like his dead cigar, and he would be reduced to the cheap nobody the boys all knew him to be anyway with his little rent house (a landlady!). All the newspaper boys had come from posh suburban homes and that's why Ed Davies hated them so. The boys *had* it (or their fathers' did) and Ed Davies didn't. They had their paper routes, if you want to know the truth, in order to maintain their fancy stud cars (which were quickly ruined anyway) so they could sit thigh to thigh with their girlfriends. Their fathers would send them to college when they graduated from high school, but for now they maintained their cars. Ed Davies had his job as route manager because it would be the best job he would ever have.

Then he'd retire (the boys all knew) to his little rent house and sit with his burly forearms on his ruined football knees spread wide by his paunch, and curse all his monied, late-sleeping boys in his dreams, his girlfriends (had he ever had one?) having long dumped him for being such a beast. He'd eat bar-b-que alone at night from the take-out stand.

Anyway, after the boys had picked up their bundles, then slowly, one by one, the cars would pull off, without headlights, cruising through the deserted shopping center, here a trunk open on a bursting pile of bundles, there a tailpipe dragging the pavement sending bursts of red sparks into the dark, Joe's door ajar as he kissed his girl deeply and steered with one hand, Hank's foot dragging from his car, making the corner as if on his motorcycle—all wrecked stud vehicles loaded to the brim with tons of newsprint, and boys, and boys' girlfriends, a cocky hand on her knee by now (would they park beyond the first turn-off to continue their kissing and risk Ed Davies' wrath for finishing late, or would they wait until mid-route when the bundles were out of the back seat so they could have more room?).

And Ed Davies would stand in solitude in front of the laundromat window once again at his bundle drop surveying it all. His boys, and he a strict ranch-foreman, all *his* boys chugging off into the night. And pity the poor bastard who'd overslept—he'd incur Ed Davies' burly early morning wrath, yelling savagely through his dead cigar butt, the sucker fully awake. "That'll wake you up, you bastard!" Ed Davies would yell, the boy standing there in gym shorts with one tennis shoe, his pajama tops a shirt.

"Three lates and you're through!" Ed Davies would yell, and his voice would rubber around in the vacant air of the deserted shopping center. And Ed Davies would punish you to boot, which was worse than being fired because for Ed Davies to treat his boys decently (but never as a friend) meant that you were a man, not a sissy, and that was worth all the sleepiness and boredom and fright, an esteem to be valued and earned. Then having chewed up and spit out the tardy boy, Ed Davies would get in his own late-model car (how he kept it so clean of the newspaper ink the boys never knew, and how he managed to make enough money to trade in his car as soon as it began to look like a paper-route car the boys had not the imagination to entertain), he would get in his late model car and deliver his own five hundred or so papers (the best paper route in the district—all in one high-rise—do it in fifteen minutes), go home to his bachelor rent-house on the ragged edge of the boys' lush suburb, and over coffee, await six-thirty, when his "kicks" (a customer complaint, second sin only to arriving late at the bundle drop) would begin to light up his telephone like a fire alarm.

Anyone could get a "kick," the studs, the sissies, even Ed Davies himself, although the boys would never learn about that. Staying sleepy insured you'd miss one house every now and then. The best safeguards—NoDoz, a girlfriend's company or chatter, staying up all night, counting out your papers before you began each block, or the fear of Ed Davies' wrath—would crumble at least once a month, cutting you out forever from the Newsboy-of-the-Month Award.

If you'd earned a "kick," Ed Davies would call you up at your home. Mom had been instructed to let you get the early morning rings, and Ed Davies would announce in a gruff voice, and without saying hello, "You have a kick at . . ." and then he'd give you the address in his flat voice, no "goodbye," no "kiss my ass," just the address of the kick. Lord help you if you had two "kicks" or god-a-mighty, *three*. "What was wrong with you this morning—you gotta be half-dead to miss three houses!" Ed Davies' voice getting flatter and meaner over the phone.

And then the next morning, yes you would have to confront Ed Davies every morning of your life, for the rest of your life, he would look at you with the meanest eyes God gave a pig and you would imagine that those burly forearms could mash you up against those laundromat's windows and crush your head like a grape.

If you felt gutsy, you'd have your Mom answer the phone and say sweetly, "No, Richard has already left for school," what a lie, pretending she doesn't know who the hell she's got on the other end of that line, and what teenager anyway leaves for school at six a.m.? "May I take a message for him?" sweetly into the phone, and there'd be a click and Ed Davies would have hung up without a pip, and you would have stolen your desperate half-hour of sleep, and Ed Davies would have delivered the "kick" himself, and Mom would have said through her pinched eyes at you over breakfast, "Don't you *ever* put me in that position again," and Ed Davies next morning (which always came too soon) would let you know in his flat voice and by not meeting you in the eyes that he had known you were there in your bed when your mother answered but he could never prove it, and his voice would further let you know you were a child, a sissy, and anyway why weren't you well on your way toward collecting football knees like he had so you could be a route manager and sit on a front rented porch and have a landlady, and why didn't you have a girlfriend, and you could eat bar-b-que alone from the take-out stand later when you were sixty.

So that morning, gathering his resentment and levelling his voice at Richard as he loaded up the last of his bundles into his trunk, Ed Davies crossed his burly forearms in front of his chest and said, "Richard, you move like a damn girl." Why *that* had come at him Richard hadn't the courage to ask. But Richard wasn't a girl, was in fact one of the best paper boys Ed Davies had, was accurate more than most, paid his bill each month on time, was loyal, faithful, and true. Was slender. Was scared.

Richard hadn't said anything, but had loaded up his few remaining bundles and had driven off into the summer dark.

Workers on a job often wonder and speculate about the behind-the-scenes life of their bosses, and also what life will be like for the boss in the future. In "Route Manager," Hall has inventively taken the point of view of the boys' speculations about their boss's behind-the-scenes life and future. From their social position, the boys know rather clearly what Ed Davies' future will probably be like, so their imaginings become the actuality of his future in this telling. Examine the tenses, the use of exaggeration, and anything else that particularly takes your attention in "Route Manager."

How and where does "Route Manager" take Ed Davies's imagined point of view too?

Writing Your Model-Character-Telling

In your how-it-happens subject, find persons who attract your attention, interest you, stand out in your mind, persons you like, dislike, or feel ambivalent about. You can write model-character-tellings about people you know or about imagined characters, or about characters drawn partly from real people and partly imagined. You'll find yourself writing about how these characters relate to other people and how other people relate to them. Write about them first in your journal.

Start writing without doing much thinking about the character. Simply pick out a person and begin telling and writing the images that give you the patterns of that person's characteristic actions, attitudes, appearances, ways of doing things. Include single incident examples and illustrations. Find out what you know about the person as you write. Your telling may begin to make a point about that person, about people in general, about living, which may cause you to go back and start over again with that point in mind.

Some writers want to make notes about things that take their attention about a particular subject and then let their notes tell them directions and possibilities for the writing. They then rewrite their notes. Some work first in pencil, then on the typewrit-

er. A few work on the typewriter alone. You should experiment to find what works best
for you.

Model-Type-Telling

The model-type-telling may use either the model-telling or summary or a mixture
of summary and model-telling to present the characteristic patterns of a group of persons that make up a type. In the model-type-telling, we compare instances of figures to
find the pattern of the type, selecting a significant basis for our comparison, such as
grouping people as financial barons, union leaders, funeral directors, high school princi-
pals, running backs, "warlords" of street gangs, or whatever. In "The Silent Rich," Josephson compares examples to show the characteristic patterns of the personalities of
the financial barons of the late nineteenth and early twentieth centuries.

Contrast his model-type-telling with Patricia Sexton's "Union Leader," in which
summarizing statements are made about income, social, and personality patterns of average union leaders.

"The Silent Rich"
From **The Robber Barons**
Matthew Josephson

But against the instance of Whitney or the diverting H. H. Rogers, who was the
friend of Mark Twain, the masters of money and industry such as Morgan, Vanderbilt,
Harriman, Stillman, William Rockefeller, were all of them typically "great silent men"
with little enough to say in polite conversation, save on the score of their business oper-
ations. James Stillman, the narrow-eyed "sphinx" of the banking world, rigid in manner,
and wearing always the "cold smile of a Japanese statesman," confessed in his last
years, when he had gone into retirement, that he knew not how to enjoy himself. *"I
have never in all my life done anything I wanted,"* he said, *"and cannot now."* Stillman
relates that his friend William Rockefeller, who was almost as rich as John, would sit in
perfect silence at home with him, for fifteen minues on end, and assured the banker that
he loved him because he did not have to speak to him at all. Harriman too wore a mask
of silence perpetually. One night he asked Stillman to leave the opera with him between
the acts and return to his "den." Stillman thought that Harriman was going to unfold
some great affair to him. But the railroad nabob merely sat smoking silently for long
minutes. Fatigued, evidently craving company or consolation of some sort, he nevertheless had nothing to say, and his colleague parted from him with scarcely a word. But the
most laconic of all these men was J. P. Morgan who carried his manner to a systematic
rudeness.

There were subjects of course upon which they could talk freely either in private
or in general society. Carnegie playing golf with the publisher of books, Frank Doubleday, asked him: "How much did you make last month, Frank?" It was impossible to tell
but once a year, the publisher replied. "I'd get out of it!" said Carnegie firmly. The immortal donor of free libraries who was the most articulate of the industrialists had no

further thoughts upon the making of books than the cash profit to be derived from them.

These men were scarcely fit to bring up their own children. They, who expended all their energy in the exploiting of a railroad system, of machinery, of a power plant for the new continent, had "had no time for thought," as Henry Adams said. William Lloyd recalls having heard one of the greatest business geniuses of the country say to his son: "I will be perfectly satisfied with you if you will only always go to bed at night worth more than when you got up this morning." Yet unlike Roman fathers they reared their sons in most cases as indolent princelings. Jay Gould, for instance, brought up his eldest son George "in the lap of luxury," as befitted the heir of a railroad and telegraph monarch; in a manner which caused even the denizens of Wall Street to raise their eyebrows. . . .

The lives of the colossally rich were generally "no more worth living than those of their cooks," said Henry Adams, who respected both money and social position. His friend Cabot Lodge, the scion of New England "Brahmins," professed himself shocked by the emptiness and the vulgarity of the talk he heard everywhere in society. It was no longer taboo to speak of one's own money or one's neighbors', of the cost of Mrs. Belmont's "rope of pearls" or Mrs. Drexel's "sunburst" or Mr. Morgan's notorious Raphael—was it genuine?—or Mr. So-and-So's disease. Even the beauty of land and sea, as at a Florida beach, or the thought of unprospected Heaven itself, as Frederick Townsend Martin tells us in his "Passing of the Idle Rich," brought up suggestions of railway projects still to be carried out!

"Union Leader"
From *Blue Collars and Hard Hats*
Patricia Sexton

The truth about union leaders is that as a class, they are rather quiet men who, away from their jobs, simply fade into the general lower-middle-class landscape. Very likely less than 5 percent of full-time union officials make as much as $20,000 a year. Nor are huge incomes hidden behind fat expense accounts. The highly publicized International Presidents and Secretary-Treasurers who receive $50,000 a year are the rare specimens. There are not more than twenty of them. Compared with leaders of other large institutions, even these are not grossly overpaid. Our most informed guess is that the average salary of full-time union officials is probably around $15,000 a year. [1973]

Take an average American worker, imbue him with some sense of class injustice, make him somewhat more militant than average, bless him with the capacity to articulate his grievances and with some everyday political skills, and you will have an approximation of the average union leader.

You could draw upon library research or personal experience or both to write a model-type-telling that emphasizes a different aspect of the present-day rich or the union leader or any other character type.

Writing Your Model-Type-Telling

Look for the typical figures of a grouping of people who have a significant basis in common in your how-it-happens subject. Or research a character type that interests you, whether or not it is part of your how-it-happens subject. Note the characteristics of these people. Give examples of their characteristic behavior, statements of their patterns, and develop a model-type-telling.

Model-Place (and Model-Instrument)-Telling

The model-place-telling is a specialization of the model-telling that deals with the surroundings, use, and happenings of a place. Many places, humanly constructed, are also instruments, tools, such as the Eskimo winter house. So we can also speak of a model-instrument-telling, which, because it deals with the environment and results of the instrument's use, differs from the simpler description of a mechanism. In this section, we have model-tellings both of places that are humanly built and of larger geographic places. I have juxtaposed selections of more or less unemotional technical telling and appreciative emotional technical telling and used the method of comparison and contrast to throw into relief their differences and similarities. For instance, we compare an appreciative, sometimes humorous, technical description of the Eskimo winter house to a more or less unemotional technical description of the Eskimo snowhouse and the process of constructing it. Next, we compare a fictional description of the Galapagos Islands with a scientific description of the same islands.

"The Eskimo Winter House"
From **Book of the Eskimos**
Peter Freuchen

The familiar igloo is used by the Polar Eskimos only as a temporary shelter during travels. Most of the winter they live in permanent winter houses made of stones and peat. Permanent, that is, for the winter, for each spring they are left by the inhabitants and automatically become public property the next fall.

You enter the winter house through an entrance tunnel, usually about fifteen feet long so as to provide both ventilation and protection against the outside cold. Since the house usually faces the sea, it is on a hill which the horizontal tunnel cuts into. The floor of the tunnel is laid with flat stones, the walls are piled-up stones, and the ceiling is made of flat stones covered with peat or turf. It is low, so that you have to crawl in on your hands and knees.

In the tunnel, you will find a strange little instrument, a little saber of wood or bone, called a *tilugtut*. When snow is falling or drifting outside, thousands of snow crystals will be lodged in the long hair of your skin clothes. If you enter the warm house like that, they will melt and make your clothes wet and heavy. Moreover, if you soon have to go out again, they will freeze. The tilugtut is used to beat the clothes free of snow while still in the entrance tunnel. During this procedure, it is a good idea to call out a few remarks, like: "Somebody comes visiting, as it happens!" so that the people inside are prepared to see you. It is true that an Eskimo home is open to visitors at almost any time of day or night, but there are strained relationships everywhere in the world, and it is neither wise—nor polite—to show up in the house without a word of warning!

The entrance tunnel ends up just inside the front wall of the house itself, and you find yourself a couple of feet below the level of the floor, which you then step onto. Now you are in a room, rarely more than fifteen feet in diameter and roughly circular, inasmuch as the wide front wall, the converging side walls, and the narrower back wall of the house are curved evenly into each other. It is about nine feet high from floor to ceiling, but the roof slants toward the back wall. Besides, the whole back half of the room is filled from wall to wall by a big platform about three feet high. Since the house is sunk a little into the earth to give it extra protection against the gales, the platform usually represents the level of the ground outside. It is laid with flat stones which are extended along the front edge so as to create an overhang, under which there is storage space. On the sides, they extend into two side platforms that rest on stone supports, but also have storage space under them. What is left of the floor, which is also laid with flat stones, is then only a space about seven feet square in the front center part of the house. It serves well when game or frozen meat has to be brought in for the family meals.

The walls of the house are double, two layers, of stones with peat or earth filled in between them. The roof is made of flat stones, deftly built up and overlapping each other, at last reaching so far toward the center that a main stone slab can rest on them, their outer ends being weighed down with boulders for stability. The size of a house largely depends upon how many large flat stone slabs can be found for their purpose. Only when an extra large house is wanted will the Eskimos solve the problem by building pillars up from the platform to support the ceiling.

Lumber in sizes sufficient to support a roof was rare before the white man came to Thule. Sometimes the Eskimos could barter a few little pieces of wood from the whalers, precious objects that they guarded with their lives. Also, they would find a little driftwood on their shores, and some of them believed that it came from forests that covered the bottom of the ocean like those in the white man's country. Actually, the driftwood was supplied by the rivers of Siberia and had drifted across the Polar Basin. After several years in salt water, it had chipped and was hard and difficult to work with. But its presence caused the Eskimos never completely to forget the use of wood.

The platform in the house is the family's sleeping bunk. Here they sleep in a neat row with their feet toward the back wall. Against the back wall are usually piled extra clothes and skins so that it isn't too cold. The bunk is covered with a thick layer of dried grass, upon which skins of musk ox and caribou are spread. The family and its eventual guests sleep under blankets made of fox, hare, caribou, and elder duck skins. The natural colors of these animals' feathers and fur are used to make beautiful patterns.

Only when it is overcrowded are the side bunks used for sleeping, but they are less desirable because they are colder. Otherwise, the blubber lamps are placed on the side bunks. One of them may be used to place a piece of meat or game on for everybody to nibble on. Then there is a bucket or sealskin basin for ice to thaw in for drinking water. Whenever possible, the lady of the house gets this ice from one of the icebergs floating in the fjord by the beach. That water tastes fresh and sweet. A dipper is placed in the basin or bucket for everybody to use when drinking, and this dipper is usually passsd around after each meal.

On the other side bunk, there would then be knives, trays, and other household gear. The storage space under the bunks is used for skins and other property. On the walls may be pegs of caribou ribs or antler for hanging things on. Under the ceiling is suspended a framework of wood or bones. As it is for drying clothes on, it is directly above one of the blubber lamps. It is very important especially for the kamiks and stockings. Every evening, when the master of the house comes home from the day's hunting, his wife takes his kamiks and stockings and hangs them up to dry overnight. In the morning she chews them carefully till they are pliable and soft enough for his feet, and she puts new dried grass in between the soles.

For this purpose, the women go every fall up to the rocks to cut grass off, dry it in the sun, and carry it home. The best harvest is naturally around the bird cliffs, and they have to get a whole year's supply for their families before winter.

Both men and women are usually undressed around the house. The wife is only in her scant foxskin panties, and she sits placidly on the main bunk most of the time. Her cooking pots are suspended from the ceiling over the blubber lamp; every thing is within her easy reach, and no bustling around is necessary. Since she has to cut and sew the skin gaments of the entire family, that is what busies her most. Like a Turkish tailor, she sits with her legs stretched out at right angles to the body, her favorite position, with her work between her toes. Her most important tool is the *ulo,* a curved knife with a handle in the middle of the blade. From intuition, she cuts her skins in the proper pieces and sews them together, rarely measuring anything. The furs of the blue and the white fox are woven together in intricate patterns, and her work puts the finest Paris furrier to shame. With small, hardly visible stiches she weaves her narwhal sinew thread in and out until the skin pieces look as if they had grown together.

No wonder the needle is one of the most important Eskimo tools. It can be fatal, during a trip, if a torn garment cannot be repaired to protect against the cold, or new garments cannot be sewn. It is perfectly truthful to say that the lack of needles has caused the death of many travelers in the Arctic. For this reason, the woman's ability to sew well is one of her chief attractions.

The husband also undresses in the house. He may keep his bearskin trousers on, or he may be in the nude. When his clothes have dried, he ties them together in a bundle with a thong and hangs them up under the ceiling by a hook. That is in order to get as few lice in them as possible.

The house has one window, which is in the front wall above the entrance. The windowpane is made out of the intestines of the big bearded seal, which are split and dried and sewn together, then framed with sealskin, and the whole thing is put in the wall opening and fastened to the sides. One cannot see through such a window, but it lets quite a good light through. At one side there is a little peephole to look out of. More important, the ventilation of the house is provided through another and larger opening in the upper corner of the windowpane. Fresh air comes in through the entrance tunnel and is often regulated by a skin covering the entrance hole. This skin, when weighted down with a couple of stones, will also keep the dogs out of the house when the family is asleep. The dogs are rarely allowed in the house, anyway, but in very rough weather they may be resting in the entrance funnel.

The flow of air out through the hole in the windowpane is regulated by a whisk of hay stuck in it. It is easy to see when the air is getting close because the flame in the blubber lamp starts to burn low. And although no draft is ever felt, the house is always well ventilated.

Although the blood and blubber from the killed game smeared over floor and side bunks often give the new observer the impression of an animal cave, he will soon realize that the stone house is ingeniously suited to the arctic conditions. And it is well heated and lighted by the blubber lamps.

"The Eskimo Snowhouse"
From *Eskimos and Explorers*
Wendell H. Oswalt

When the English arrived at the village, Lyon was charmed by what he saw. "Our astonishment was unbounded, when, after creeping through some long low passages of snow, to enter the different dwellings, we found ourselves in a cluster of dome-shaped edifices, entirely constructed of snow, which, from their recent erection, had not been sullied by the smoke of the numerous lamps that were burning, but admitted the light in most delicate hues of verdigris green and blue, according to the thickness of the slab through which it passed. The natives were evidently in their best apparel, and made a very neat appearance; the darkness of their deer-skin dresses affording a strong contrast to the brilliancy of their habitations. To attempt giving a description of all we saw in one visit would be ridiculous; suffice it to say, we were much pleased." Lyon soon learned that the five-house cluster, with from one to three domes per house, sheltered 64 persons from 13 families.

Snowhouses typically are identified with the Central Eskimos, and because of their uniqueness these structures deserve further attention. A man preparing to build a snowhouse used a thin wooden rod to probe snowdrifts as he looked for snow of a uniform consistency that was neither hard, soft, nor layered. Soft snow crumbled, hard snow was difficult to work, and layered snow tended to break apart. The blocks were cut with an ivory snowknife, and the better the quality of snow the larger the blocks that could be removed. Blocks cut from superior snow were about 30 inches long, 18 inches high, and 7 inches thick. For a house 10 feet in diameter about 35 blocks were used, and one man could build it in an hour and a half. Under favorable conditions two men could build a similar snowhouse in about 45 minutes. After about 10 blocks had been cut, construction was begun. The foundation blocks were arranged in a circle and were shaped to fit together as well as to lean slightly toward the interior. All of the remaining blocks often could be cut from within the circle. They were set in place and shaped with a snowknife to fit on an ever-increasing incline until the topmost block was shaped and dropped into place. After the dome was completed, the openings between blocks were chinked with snow, and if a dwelling was to be used for very long, snow was shoveled over the structure with a special shovel. Finishing touches included a window of fresh-water ice, a vent hole in the roof, and an entrance passage. Household furnishings were meager: stone lamps, lamp stands, stone cooking pots, a rack to dry clothing, and various containers. The people in a dwelling such as this attempted to keep the temperature slightly below freezing to prevent the roof from melting and dripping on the inside. A temporary remedy for a drip was to cover it with a piece of snow to absorb the moisture.

When a number of families were establishing a relatively permanent camp, they built numerous separate and interlocking snow domes for living areas, storage, and dog shelters. One large snowhouse complex visited by Lyon was entered through a long tunnel wide enough for two persons to pass but so low that it was necessary to stoop when walking along. A dome-shaped anteroom was entered by stepping up through a hole in its floor. Off this room were three dome-shaped dwellings, each about 15 feet in diameter and as much as 7 feet high. If two families lived under one dome, they each had a bench on one side of the entrance. Benches were covered with baleen strips or pieces of sealskin and with skin blankets.

From the outside a snowhouse was a glistening dome, but on the inside the snow soon lost its whiteness. Smoke from lamps blackened the interior, and since seals were butchered inside, the floor was covered with blood and oil. During warm spells the dome might thaw, dripping water on everything. If this happened, a new dome might be built over the old one during the next cold spell and the former snowhouse removed from the inside. As the top of a snowhouse began melting in the spring, skins replaced the upper part of the dome as roofing. This was a very uncomfortable period because the house floor was always wet from the thaw.

Notice the use of the "you" and the present tense in "The Eskimo Winter House." Notice the past tense and third person ("a man") in "The Eskimo Snowhouse," and the difference between Lyon's quoted personal reaction and the historian's process telling of snowhouse construction.

With the "you," Freuchen moves you into the winter house and makes you a participant in the telling. But once you've stepped into the room in the fourth paragraph, the features of the house become the "characters" in the telling. Notice, that Freuchen uses many "is" and "are" linking verbs. Try to convert many of them to active verbs. What problems do you encounter? How do you feel about your results?

What does the telling of the Eskimo winter house highlight about human beings as creatures who have spread to all parts of the earth? In a very real sense, *Book of the Eskimos* was a how-it-happens subject for Peter Freuchen, in which he wrote about his years of experience with Eskimos.

What do you learn about the Eskimo snowhouse from Lyon's personal reaction that you do not get from the historian's unemotional description of snowhouse construction? This description most closely approximates a how-it's-done process telling. Why? What do you notice about tenses and pronouns? Do you feel that, with some experimentation, you might be able to use this description to guide you in the building of a snowhouse? At what points does the description suggest that considerable experience and "feel" for the skill were needed to build a snowhouse successfully?

Go to the library, look up Eskimos in the catalog, find a number of accounts of Eskimo life by anthropologists, explorers, and other writers, and compare various descriptions of Eskimo winter and summer houses. Research an essay that would compare the ways in which different peoples, particularly so-called primitive peoples, have solved the need for shelter in different parts of the world.

* * *

Now read two descriptions of the Galapagos Islands.

From

The Encantadas or Enchanted Isles
Herman Melville

Take five-and-twenty heaps of cinders dumped here and there in an outside city lot; imagine some of them magnified into mountains, and the vacant lot the sea; and you will have a fit idea of the general aspect of the Encantadas, or Enchanted Isles. A group rather of extinct volcanoes than of isles; looking much as the world at large might, after a penal conflagration.

It is to be doubted whether any spot of earth can, in desolateness, furnish a parallel to this group. Abandoned cemeteries of long ago, old cities by piecemeal tumbling to their ruin, these are melancholy enough; but, like all else which has but once been associated with humanity, they still awaken in us some thoughts of sympathy, however sad. Hence, even the Dead Sea, along with whatever other emotions it may at times inspire, does not fail to touch in the pilgrim some of his less unpleasurable feelings.

And as for solitariness; the great forests of the north, the expanses of unnavigated waters, the Greenland ice-fields, are the profoundest of solitudes to a human observer; still the magic of their changeable tides and seasons mitigates their terror; because, though unvisited by men, those forests are visited by the May; the remotest seas reflect familiar stars even as Lake Erie does; and in the clear air of a fine Polar day, the irradiated, azure ice shows beautifully as malachite.

But the special curse, as one may call it, of the Encantadas, that which exalts them in desolation above Idumea and the Pole, is, that to them change never comes; neither the change of seasons nor of sorrows. Cut by the Equator, they know not autumn, and they know not spring; while already reduced to the lees of fire, ruin itself can work little more upon them. The showers refresh the deserts; but in these isles, rain never falls. Like split Syrian gourds left withering in the sun, they are cracked by an everlasting drought beneath a torrid sky. "Have mercy on me," the wailing spirit of the Encantadas seems to cry, "and send Lazarus that he may dip the tip of his finger in water and cool my tongue, for I am tormented in this flame."

Another feature in these isles is their emphatic uninhabitableness. It is deemed a fit type of all-forsaken overthrow, that the jackal should den in the wastes of weedy Babylon; but the Encantadas refuse to harbor even the outcasts of the beasts. Man and wolf alike disown them. Little but reptile life is here found: tortoises, lizards, immense spiders, snakes, and that strangest anomaly of outlandish nature, the *iguana*. No voice, no low, no howl is heard; the chief sound of life here is a hiss.

On most of the isles where vegetation is found at all, it is more ungrateful than the blankness of Atacama. Tangled thickets of wiry bushes, without fruit and without a name, springing up among deep fissures of calcined rock, and treacherously masking them; or a parched growth of distorted cactus trees.

In many places the coast is rock-bound, or, more properly, clinker-bound; tumbled masses of blackish or greenish stuff like the dross of an iron-furnace, forming dark clefts and caves here and there, into which a ceaseless sea pours a fury of foam; overhanging them with a swirl of gray, haggard mist, amidst which sail screaming flights of unearthly birds heightening the dismal din. However calm the sea without, there is no rest for these swells and those rocks; they lash and are lashed, even when the outer ocean is most at peace with itself. On the oppressive, clouded days, such as are peculiar to this part of the water Equator, the dark, vitrified masses, many of which raise themselves among white whirlpools and breakers in detached and perilous places off the shore, present a most Plutonian sight. In no world but a fallen one could such lands exist.

Those parts of the strand free from the marks of fire, stretch away in wide level beaches of multitudinous dead shells, with here and there decayed bits of sugar-cane, bamboos, and cocoanuts, washed upon this other and darker world from the charming palm isles to the westward and southward; all the way from Paradise to Tartarus; while mixed with the relics of distant beauty you will sometimes see fragments of charred wood and mouldering ribs of wrecks. Neither will any one be surprised at meeting these last, after observing the conflicting currents which eddy throughout nearly all the wide channels of the entire group. The capriciousness of the tides of air sympathizes with those of the sea. Nowhere is the wind so light, baffling, and every way unreliable, and so given to perplexing calms, as at the Encantadas. Nigh a month has been spent by a ship going from one isle to another, though but ninety miles between; for owing to the force of the current, the boats employed to tow barely suffice to keep the craft from sweeping upon the cliffs, but do nothing towards accelerating her voyage. Sometimes it is impossible for a vessel from afar to fetch up with the group itself, unless large allowances for prospective lee-way have been made ere its coming in sight. And yet, at other times, there is a mysterious indraft, which irresistibly draws a passing vessel among the isles, though not bound to them.

"Galapagos Archipelago"
From **The Voyage of the Beagle**
Charles Darwin

Culpepper I.

Watman I.

Abingdon I.

Tower I.

Bindloes I.

James I.

Narborough I.

Indefatigable I.

Chatham I.

Barrington I.

Albemarle I.

Charles I.

Hood's I.

September 15th.—This archipelago consists of ten principal islands, of which five exceed the others in size. They are situated under the Equator, and between five and six hundred miles westward of the coast of America. They are all formed of volcanic rocks; a few fragments of granite curiously glazed and altered by the heat, can hardly be considered as an exception. Some of the craters, surmounting the larger islands, are of immense size, and they rise to a height of between three and four thousand feet. Their flanks are studded by innumerable smaller orifices. I scarcely hesitate to affirm, that there must be in the whole archipelago at least two thousand craters. These consist either of lava and scoriae, or of finely-stratified, sandstone-like tuff. Most of the latter are beautifully symmetrical; they owe their origin to eruptions of volcanic mud without any lava: it is a remarkable circumstance that every one of the twenty-eight tuff-craters which were examined, had their southern sides either much lower than the other sides, or quite broken down and removed. As all these craters have apparently been formed when standing in the sea, and as the waves from the trade-wind and the swell from the open Pacific here unite their forces on the southern coasts of all the islands, this singular uniformity in the broken state of the craters, composed of the soft and yielding tuff, is easily explained.

Considering that these islands are placed directly under the equator, the climate is far from being excessively hot; this seems chiefly caused by the singularly low temperature of the surrounding water, brought here by the great southern Polar current. Excepting during one short season, very little rain falls, and even then it is irregular; but the clouds generally hang low. Hence, whilst the lower parts of the island are very sterile, the upper parts, at a height of a thousand feet and upwards, possess a damp climate and a tolerably luxuriant vegetation. This is especially the case on the windward sides of the islands, which first receive and condense the moisture from the atmosphere.

In the morning (11th) we landed on Chatham Island, which, like the others, rises with a tame and rounded outline, broken here and there by scattered hillocks, the remains of former craters. Nothing could be less inviting than the first appearance. A broken field of black basaltic lava, thrown into the most rugged waves, and crossed by great fissures, is every where covered by stunted, sunburnt brushwood, which shows little signs of life. The dry and parched surface, being heated by the noonday sun, gave to the air a close and sultry feeling, like that from a stove: we fancied even that the bushes smelt unpleasantly. Although I diligently tried to collect as many plants as possible, I succeeded in getting very few; and such wretched-looking little weeds would have better become an arctic than an equatorial Flora. The brushwood appears, from a short distance, as leafless as our trees during winter; and it was some time before I discovered that not only almost every plant was not in full leaf, but that the greater number were in flower. The commonest bush is one of the Euphorbiaceae: an acacia and a great odd-looking cactus are the only trees which afford any shade. After the season of heavy rains, the islands are said to appear for a short time partially green.

In your notebook make lists of the differences and similarities between Melville's and Darwin's descriptions of the Galapagos Islands. Their visits to the islands were only a few years apart. Make a list of those things on which they agree, such as sights, atmosphere, and other information. In another list, compare those things on which they seem to disagree. Then compare the emotional or mood elements in "The Encantadas" with whatever emotional or mood elements you find in "Galapagos Archipelago."

Find descriptions in Darwin's account that correspond to such Melville metaphors as "Take five-and-twenty heaps of cinders dumped here and there in an outside city lot," "the chief sound of life here is the hiss," "Plutonian sight," and so forth. How does figurative language help technical description? Locate as many expressions as you can in which Melville gives the feeling that mysterious powers of enchantment are at work in this place.

Read Melville's full story, "The Encantadas," and the chapter, "Galapagos Archipelago," in Darwin's *The Voyage of the Beagle*, and write a comparison and contrast paper of the two authors' accounts.

* * *

Here's a model-place-telling of a completely different nature. "Blackhawk" is an excerpt from a story-length model-telling of a family's life shortly after they moved from Georgia to Chicago—of how they get up in the morning, of the atmosphere of the basement apartment, of the young narrator's desperate loneliness and nostalgia for the home they've left, of the mother's and father's going off to work each morning, of the boys' going to school. What do you notice about "you" and other pronouns? About tenses, present and future?

Notice how Bailey's model-telling seems to be a single scene that is played every winter morning, in what the narrator later calls "this five-room smelly ice cube that someone cut from a hole in the earth and stuck together with a bunch of dead-looking bricks."

From

Blackhawk
George Bailey

You go to bed thinking tomorrow won't be so mean—maybe someone will stick out a huge warm hand and take you up and pet you until he knows that you are not afraid any more, or maybe someone will come and put in a real window pane and take away the plywood and rags so you can see the rats running about the back yard from garbage can to garbage can cultivating their taste upon trash strewn around the side of the house; the oil heater might even come and you won't have to stand out in the morning's cold, waiting for the coal truck to come singing down the black suppressed streets with four big black hulks of coal dust turned human riding in the truck's bed, stamping their feet and slapping their shoulders to keep warm.

It's 6 A.M.; the reason I know it's 6 A.M. is because there's a man on the radio talking in a clean white voice about getting rid of all credit problems with just one friendly visit to friendly Bob Adams on Milwaukee Avenue. After the music plays a little more, Mama will get up and go to the bathroom and hawk and spit out all of the night; she'll rinse out her mouth and wash her face. The sound of cold water running down the drain pipe will try to put me back to sleep again, but the sleep urge will be broken by Daddy screaming through the rank basement chill of morning, telling me or Saul to get up and make a fire in the heater. We will turn and face each other in bed, trying to see who can stand whose stiff morning breath the longest.

"It's your turn," I say. "I've made the fire two mornings straight."

Once again a voice that gives clear images of belts and extension cords cracks the air, restating most firmly his wishes to have a fire in the heater.

"I don't care which one of you do it, but it better be done by the time your mama starts cooking."

The day has begun. I get out of bed on a cold linoleum floor, cold and razor sharp on its torn edges. Mama already has the flour bowl on the table and is kneading dough by the time I get through splitting kindling and wadding the grate with paper. The coldness never seems to bother her—maybe she doesn't think about it as much as I do, or maybe she has a lot of blood. She moves around the kitchen that looks like an enclosed stable without straw like it was the kitchen she had at home, but this whole house is so far from home and Daddy says that this is home now, so I guess that's why she moves around so nice in it. The fire is growing. I put bigger pieces of wood and small chunks of coal into its belly and shut the door just as the grease in the frying pan starts to pop.

Daddy is up now, going through the same ritual of putting the night he had in his mouth into the toilet. He walks out of the bathroom tucking his thick shirt into a pair of faded brown overalls that are frayed at the cuffs. His work shoes with rawhide laces clump as he walks upon small chunks and slivers of coal strewn around the heater on his way to the kitchen.

"Why is it so hard to git y'all up in the morning?" he says, fastening the shoulder straps of his overalls. "I've never seen such grown-ass chillun with no git-up about 'em in my whole life."

This kind of talk frightens me in the evenings and on Saturdays and Sundays, but in the morning it just don't matter. I know that he will soon have his breakfast and rush off to work, so I never listen to his faraway wisdoms of teaching me how to grow up in the morning. We both just don't have the time for it.

I open the door of the heater again to put in larger chunks of coal. It's a good fire. A thin ribbon of red has begun to work its way around the lower part of the belly, and rainbows swirl around in the blue-black stove pipes. Saul peers around the couch cover that is nailed to the door of our bedroom.

"Is the floor out there warm yet?"

"Come out and see for yourself," I say, closing the door to the heater.

Find examples of "mixed diction" in "The Eskimo Winter House," "The Eskimo Snowhouse," "The Encantadas," "Galapagos Archipelago," and "Blackhawk." Compare them.

Writing Your Model-Place-Telling

In your how-it-happens subject area, you'll find many different places, man-made and geographic. Of course, these two kinds of places can overlap. For instance, geography crucially influences the construction of the Eskimo winter house and snowhouse. Nevertheless, we can make rough distinctions between large geographic places (such as the Galapagos) and places of human construction and use (such as the Eskimo winter house) and between smaller and larger places. The model-place-telling can show whatever catches our attention about the place and its use. You could give, for instance, a model-place-telling of the complex of buildings that make up a Main Post Office in a large city (as affected by the geography of the surroundings), a model-place-telling of the use of a relatively small room devoted to the sorting of mail, and a model-instrument-telling of the function and effect of a conveyor belt (the way people use it and the way they act because of it). Such a model-instrument-telling should include an active description of the mechanism, its effects upon its surroundings, and patterns of people's behavior associated with it.

Write in your journal about the place or instrument. Make notes about it. You may wish to try the model-place or instrument-telling as a letter.

IV
Point-of-View

Point-of-View

One of the first misconceptions that troubles the writing of new writers, and often of any writer, is that somehow the writing should be done without anyone's being responsible for it. No one else can do it for you. You cannot, by sleight of hand, try to show that it somehow got told without your acting as teller. When authors try this vanishing act, what disappears is the essay or story, as well as the writer and the writer's voice. So first of all *permit* yourself to be the teller of the story or essay. Take the responsibility for telling what you have to say. Take *the overall point of view of the teller*.

Another mistake that diminishes the writing of many new writers is the lazy, weary attempt to tell it all from the outside: through a recital of external facts without commitment of your voice and perception and without exploring the point of view of the reader, who should be allowed to share in the teller's point of view. Much of what you have to say will be discovered through the exploration of the teller taking the *vantage point* or *internal point of view* of certain characters, and the "you" and "we" of the reader implicitly or explicitly.

The obsessive pursuit of a sort of internal monologue to the exclusion of the teller's overall dramatic point-of-view also distorts writing. When you lock yourself into the internal monologue, you often lock out most of what you have to say in your writing.

Another misconception that diminishes writing is that the storyteller or essayist should have no *attitude*. There's probably no such thing as impersonal or wholly objective knowledge. The attempt to exclude your attitude will exclude much important perception, voice, knowledge. When we try to make such an impossible and undesirable goal actual, we censor and suppress most of what we have to say. The *attitude* of your point of view opens up many possibilities for creatively organizing and presenting what you have to say.

There's a right, unique variation of point-of-view for every piece of writing. You can see in some stories that, if you change the point-of-view, the story will not work so well. For instance, in one class we made an attempt to tell Kafka's "Metamorphosis" in the first person. The students saw that it would not be funny. Another story of bizarre, fantastical events and transformations might work well in the first person. Other stories may be dull in the first person and then come alive in the third person. Dostoevsky wrote a first person rough draft of *Crime and Punishment* that, after several hundred pages, he realized simply wasn't working, so he went back and retold it in the third person, which made a big change in the dramatic immediacy of the events for the reader.

Reread a novel or other story that made a strong impression on you. Change the point-of-view as you read, from third person to first, or first to third. What happens to the effect of the story? Of course, more is involved in point-of-view than simply changing from one pronoun to another. However, if you change pronouns as you reread a story you'll begin to hear clues that will tell you why the original choice works so well.

In this section, we examine the basic structure of point-of-view rather than the variety of point-of-view innovations. For instance, we cannot here deal with such first-person variations as monologues, soliloquies, stories-within-a-story (see section by that name), epistolary first person (see Letters section), "stream of consciousness," internal monologues, memoirs, and so forth. Nor can we deal with all the variations of the third person, of the collective "we," and so on. Here we deal with the basic structure of point-of-view for narrative and expository writing.

In the following written accounts of oral tellings, we see the fundamental point-of-view structure of any kind of telling, story or expository. That is, we see the tale-teller taking *the overall point-of-view and responsibility for the tale* while simultaneously enacting characters, seeing things from their *vantage points,* taking *internal points-of-view* of perception, feeling, and thought, giving the reactions of characters, taking the listener's (or reader's) point-of-view, and employing an *attitude* toward the subject and the tale. From this basic dramatic point-of-view structure of oral tale-telling comes the tremendous expansion of point-of-view dimensions, useful in essay as well as in expository narrative and fictional writing. In the course of any single writing, the tale-teller and essayist touch the original ground of oral telling in the compositional theater of the mind again and again, drawing from the wellspring of the basic structure of point-of-view.

From
"Problems of Collecting Oral Literature"
MacEdward Leach

The Anansi stories of the Negroes of the Caribbean, for example, as found in such collections as those of Jekyll and Beckwith, are poor things when read. There is little characterization; there is sameness of style; the action is hard to follow, and so on. It is, however, an unforgettable experience to hear an Anansi tale told by a good native teller of tales to an appreciative audience. Typical is the tale of "Anansi and the Tiger" which I heard in the Blue Mountains of Jamaica a few years ago. Men, women, and children were crowded into the small room and overflowed onto the narrow porch. Some squatted on the floor; some stood around the walls; children, black eyes wide, sat at their parents' feet; the bed in the corner was loaded with women and babies. All were silent, intent on the story-teller, Arthur Wyles. Mr. Wyles was sixty-one, hair white and kinky like sheep's wool. His eyes were unforgettable—very large, very black, and remote, expressionless. He stood throughout the story, constantly moving about. First, he would be at one side of the room taking the part of Anansi; then he would jump quickly to the other and face back he took the role of Tiger. His voice was whining and ingratiating as Anansi; his face took on a smirk; his words were given a wheedling twist. But when he became Tiger, he drew himself up stern and dignified and majestic; his voice was deep and powerful and his walk stately. This story ends with a fight between Tiger and Death. Mr. Wyles, voice full of excitement, arms flailing, staged the fight, blow by blow, taking the parts alternately of Tiger and Death. When the climax was reached and Tiger delivered the knock-out blow conquering Death, the narrator over-reached himself and his clenched fist hit the door jamb a cruel blow that bloodied his knuckles. He seemed to feel nothing but went into the very realistic death throes of Brother Death. Though the audience had heard this story many times, they sat enthralled, eyes shining, audibly satisfied with the ending. Here, then, in the *telling* is the characterization and the drama, absent in the story when merely read, now abundantly supplied.

* * *

In the telling of an Anansi tale, Mr. Wyles acts as the overall storyteller (no one else can do it for him). He is aware of the listeners' point-of-view, enacts each charac- ter, sees things from the vantage point of either Brother Death or Tiger, probably sticks fairly consistently to Tiger's *point-of-view,* but gives reactions of different charac- ters, suggests their internal feelings, and may occasionally give internal thoughts such as "Brother Death, he think to get over on Tiger, but . . ." You've seen this happen when your friends are giving accounts of events, anecdotes, stories. It could be an on- the-job telling, a football player's story, an account of what happened with a boy and girl, etc. Cassius Clay (now Muhammad Ali) gives the same kind of telling of an encounter with Sonny Liston in a Las Vegas casino, as told in writing by Tom Wolfe. The encoun- ter came before the Clay-Liston fight, and the telling comes after Clay's victory.

From
The Kandy-Kolored Tangerine-Flake Streamline Baby
Tom Wolfe

One minute Cassius would be out in the middle of the floor reenacting his "High Noon" encounter with Sonny Liston in a Las Vegas casino. He has a whole act about it, beginning with a pantomime of him shoving open the swinging doors and standing there bowlegged, like a beer delivery man. Then he plays the part of the crowd falling back and whispering, "It's Cassius Clay, Cassius Clay, Cassius Clay, Cassius Clay." Then he plays the part of an effete Las Vegas hipster at the bar with his back turned, suddenly freezing in mid-drink, as the hush falls over the joint, and sliding his eyes around to see the duel. Then he plays the part of Cassius Clay stalking across the floor with his finger pointed at Sonny Liston and saying, "You big ugly bear," "You big ugly bear," about eighteen times, "I ain't gonna fight you on no September thirtieth, I'm gonna fight you right now. Right here. You too ugly to run loose, you big ugly bear. You so ugly, when you cry, the tears run down the back of your head. You so ugly, you have to sneak up on the mirror so it won't run off the wall," and so on, up to the point where Liston says, "Come over here and sit on my knee, little boy, and I'll give you your orange juice," and where Cassius pulls back his right and three guys hold him back and keep him from throwing it at Liston, "And I'm hollering, 'Lemme go,' and I'm telling them out the side of my mouth, 'You better *not* lemme go.' " All this time Frankie Tucker, the singer, is contorted across one of the Americana's neo-Louis XIV chairs, breaking up and exclaim- ing, "That's my man!"

* * *

In the following selection, we see the point-of-view structures of oral telling trans- ferred to writing, then modified, developed, and expanded.

"Sam Spies Through the Window"
From **The Man Who Loved Children**
Christina Stead

He loved this Thirty-fourth Street climb, by the quiet houses and under the trees. He had first come this way, exploring the neighborhood, a young father and widower, holding his year-old Louisa in his arms, with her fat bare legs wagging, and, by his side, elegant, glossy-eyed Miss Henrietta Collyer, a few months before their marriage; and that was ten years ago. Then afterwards, with each and all of the children, up and down and round about, taking them to the Observatory, the parks, the river, the woodland by the Chesapeake and Ohio Canal, or walking them out to Cabin John, teaching them birds, flowers, and all denizens of the woodland.

Now Old David Collyer's Tohoga House, Sam's Tohoga House, that he called his island in the sky, swam above him. A Constellation hanging over that dark space midmost of the hill, which was Tohoga's two acres, was slowly swamped by cloud.

He came up slowly, not winded, but snuffing in the night of the hot streets, looking up at the great house, tree-clouded. Now he crossed P Street and faced the hummock. On one side the long galvanized-iron back fence of his property ran towards Thirty-fifth Street and its strip of brick terrace slums. Over this fence leaned the pruned boughs of giant maples and oaks. The old reservoir was away to the right. A faint radiance showed Sam that the light in the long dining room was on. He ran up the side steps and stole across the grass behind the house, brushing aside familiar plants, touching with his left hand the little Colorado blue spruce which he had planted for the children's "Wishing-Tree" and which was now five feet high.

He was just on six feet and therefore could peer into the long room. It ran through the house and had a window looking out at the front to R Street. A leaved oak table stood in the center and at the table, facing him, sitting in his carving chair, was his eldest child, Louisa, soon twelve years old, the only child of his dead first wife, Rachel. Louie was hunched over a book and sat so still that she seemed alone in the house. She did nothing while he looked at her but turn a page and twist one strand of her long yellow hair round and round her finger, a trick of her father's. Then without Sam having heard anything, she lifted her head and sat stock-still with her gray eyes open wide. She now rose stiffly and looked furtively at the window behind her. Sam heard nothing but the crepitations of arboreal night. Then he noticed that the window was sliding gently down. Louisa advanced jerkily to this magically moving window and watched it as it fitted itself into the sill. Then she shook her head and turning to the room as if it were a person she laughed soundlessly. It was nothing but the worn cords loosening. She opened the window and then shut it again softly, but leaned against the pane looking up into the drifting sky, seeking something in the street. She had been there, and Sam, whistling softly *Bringing Home the Sheaves,* was about to go inside, when a thin, dark scarecrow in an off white wrapper Henrietta, his wife—stood in the doorway. Through the loose window frame he heard her threadbare words,

"You're up poring over a book with lights flaring all over the house at this hour at the night. You look like a boiled owl! Isn't your father home yet?"

"No, Mother."

"Why is your knee bleeding? Have you been picking the scab again?"

Louie hung her head and looked at her knee, crossed with old scars and new abrasions and bruises: she flushed and the untidy hair fell over her face.

"Answer, answer, you sullen beast!"

"I bumped it."

"You lie all the time."

The child straightened with wide frowning eyes, pulled back her arms insolently. Henny rushed at her with hands outstretched and thrust her firm bony fingers round the girl's neck, squeezing and saying, "Ugh," twice. Louisa looked up into her stepmother's face, squirming, but not trying to get away, questioning her silently, needing to understand, in an affinity of misfortune. Henrietta dropped her arms quickly and gripped her own neck with an expression of disgust, then pushed the girl away with both hands; and as she flounced out of the room, cried,

"I ought to put us all out of our misery!"

Louisa moved back to her chair and stood beside it, looking down at the book. Then she sank into the chair and, putting her face on both hands, began to read again.

Sam turned his back to the house and looked south, over the dark, susurrous orchard, towards the faint lights of Rosslyn. A zephyr stole up the slope as quietly as a nocturnal animal and with it all the domestic scents, wrapping Sam's body in peace. Within, a torment raged, day and night, week, month, year, always the same, an endless conflict, with its truces and breathing spaces; out here were a dark peace and love.

"Mother Earth," whispered Sam, "I love you, I love men and women. I love little children and all innocent things, I love, I feel I am love itself—how could I pick out a woman who would hate me so much!"

Surefooted he moved way down to the animal cages, heard them stir uneasily, and spoke to the raccoon,

"Procyon! Procyon! Here's little Sam!" But the raccoon refused to come to the wire. He went up the slope again, thinking, *Fate puts brambles, hurdles in my path, she even gives me an Old Woman of the Sea, to try me, because I am destined for great things.*

When Sam came into the hall there was no light anywhere on the ground floor. The saffron dark through his sitting room at the head of the first flight of stairs showed that Louie was in her bedroom. She had heard his whistle and had rushed upstairs with her book.

"Why, why?" thought Sam. "She could have waited to hear what her daddy has been doing all day. She is so dogged—and she has her little burdens."

Try telling this passage out loud and let yourself use gestures wherever gestural impulses come to you. You can watch this happen in class during oral recall after an oral reading of this passage. Or imagine yourself orally telling the passage to a friend.

First, the oral tale-teller would place Sam on the "Thirty-fourth Street climb" and give us access to Sam's history, then gesture to place Tohoga House, "his island in the sky," that "swam above him." The oral tale-teller would enact, visibly express, Sam's "snuffing in the night" and "his looking up at the great house." That is, the tale-teller would see Sam and tell it so we could see Sam, and sometimes see things from Sam's *vantage point* and feel them occasionally from Sam's *internal point-of-view.*

When the tale-teller sees from Sam's *vantage point*, it's as if she stands beside Sam or looks directly over his shoulder and sees things as he sees them, but not necessarily with access to his feelings. When she gives the internal point-of-view, we *feel* it as Sam *feels* it; we have access to his thoughts, feelings, perceptions, history, etc., but still with the distance of the *storyteller's overall point-of-view.* In this context, we perceive Sam's point-of-view with possible ironies and reverberations of wider knowledge. From Sam's vantage point, the oral tale-teller would gesture toward parts of the scene, for instance, toward the "faint radiance" that showed Sam "that the light in the dining room was on." The oral tale-teller would probably gesture with hands or body to show how Sam "ran up the side steps" and give another gesture or bodily expression for how he "stole across the grass" and touched "with his left hand" the spruce.

In the next paragraph, the oral tale-teller would place Sam in front of the window, gesturing with hands and enacting with her body how Sam, because of his height, can see over the window sill into the long dining room; then she would see everything from his vantage point as if standing beside him or just behind him looking over his shoulder, giving suggestions of his internal point-of-view. If she were telling it *orally*, as did Mr. Wyles and Cassius Clay, she would move to Louie's side of the spatial relationship and enact her reading, turning a page while twisting "one strand of her long yellow hair," sitting stock still when the window on its worn cords moves "magically" downward behind her, then advancing jerkily to the window and laughing to the room as if the room were "a person." At the same time, the oral tale-teller would let us know that we are seeing the enactment of Louie from Sam's vantage point. The author suggests Sam's internal point-of-view in phrases such as "without Sam having heard" and "he noticed." Oral tellers would also give gestures for the striking entrance of Henrietta and the exchange of dialogue and action between Louie and Henrietta.

Following the above structure, we can explain a seeming anomaly to many readers who feel that Sam is not sufficiently sensitive to read Louie's expression as she "looked up into her stepmother's face, squirming, but not trying to get away, questioning her silently, needing to understand, in an affinity of misfortune"; it is the tale-teller's interpretation from Sam's vantage point, over his head, so to speak.

With this structure, the rest of the written telling can be followed clearly, and we see how it would have been orally told and how it was told in the theater of composition in the author's mind. Sam speaks briefly in the soliloquizing manner of the theater, which fits the way he dramatically (or melodramatically) represents his own feelings to himself. This is the way in which theater originally gave internal point-of-view beyond the storytelling point of view of chorus or narrator. At the end of the passage, Sam's internal point-of-view comes through with the special hurt and poignancy that he feels.

What should be evident is that though much writing could all be told orally by oral storytellers, it would take much more time than it takes to read it (though not necessarily more than it takes to write and rewrite it).

The transfer of oral telling techniques to the different dimensions of written telling is the challenge of writing. The writer must find written correspondences for Mr. Wyles's gestures, enactments, tones of voice, to accomplish a powerful connection of oral telling and writing. If not, the tale goes flat as Leach suggests in his account of the Anansi tale. By now we can see that writers who have tried to give written accounts of orally told tales have often missed, in writing, the correspondences for gestures and expressions used in the oral versions that would make the story come alive. Look, for instance, at Zora Neale Hurston's successful rendering of the originally orally told "Why Women Always Take Advantage of Men" (See p 297), in which she finds the correspondences for gestures and expressions, indeed, finds everything that makes the orally told tale work on paper. Writing opens up dimensions of "sustained speech" or "sustained oral telling" that are still being discovered: What should also be evident is that these natural techniques develop in *the compositional theater of the mind*. When you're writing successfully, you more or less see, sense, feel, imagine yourself doing all the things that would be done by the oral teller and you find the ways to get them into writing.

Compare the third-person telling of "Sam Spies Through the Window" to the first-person telling of *The Adventures of Huckleberry Finn* by Mark Twain or *Black Boy* by Richard Wright, or of a number of short stories your teacher can suggest and any of the letters in the Letter Section.

*   *   *

Finding the right variation of point-of-view is always a discovery. The pictorial analogy that led Einstein to the General Theory of Relativity also became the central demonstration of the theory. Here we see point-of-view principles used for scientific discovery.

"The Man Falling in the Box"
From **Einstein: The Life and Times**
Ronald W. Clark

This was a repetition of the situation which had led to the photoelectric paper and to the theory of Special Relativity. In the first, Einstein had started by drawing attention to the contradictions between the corpuscular and the field theories which science had been content to leave rubbing up against one another with little more than an occasional comment. And the famous relativity paper had begun by drawing attention to the discrepancy between the observational and the theoretical aspects of Faraday's law of induction. Now here, once more, was a curious state of affairs which science had either not noticed or had thought it better to leave alone.

Einstein's reaction was typical. He visualized the situation in concrete terms, in the "man in a box" problem which appears in different guises in most discussions of General Relativity. Einstein's illustration was basically simple—although it appears more so now, when men have been shot out of the earth's gravitational field, than it did some half-century ago when space travel was only a theoretical fancy.

In the first place Einstein envisaged a box falling freely down a suitably long shaft. Inside it, an occupant who took his money and keys from his pocket would find that they did not fall to the floor. Man, box, and objects were all falling freely in a gravitational field; but, and this was the important point, their temporary physical situation was identical to what it would have been in space, far beyond any gravitational field. With this in mind, Einstein then mentally transported both box and occupant to such a point in space beyond the pull of gravity. Here, all would have been so before. But he then envisaged the box being accelerated. The means were immaterial, since it was the result that mattered. Money and keys now fell to the bottom of the box. But the same thing would have happened had the box been at rest in a gravitational field. So the effect of gravity on the box at rest was identical with the effect of acceleration beyond the pull of gravity. What is more, it was clearly apparent that if a centrifugal force replaced acceleration the results would be the same. As it was later described by Professor Lindemann, a friend of Einstein for more than forty years, it would be as impossible for the man in the box "to tell whether he was in a gravitational field or subject to uniform acceleration, as it is for an airplane pilot in a cloud to tell whether he is flying straight or executing a properly banked turn."

Thus logical reasoning showed that the effects of gravitation were equivalent of those of inertia, and that there was no way of distinguishing acceleration of centrifugal force from gravity. At least, this appeared to be so with money and keys and other material objects. But what would happen if one thought, instead, in terms of light? Here it was necessary to change the "thought-experiment." Once again there was the closed box. But this time, instead of dropped keys and money it was necessary to envisage a ray of light crossing the box from one side to the other while the box was being accelerated. The far side of the box would have moved upwards before the ray of light reached it; the wall would be hit by the light ray nearer the floor than the point at which it set out. In other words, to the man in the box there would have apparently been a bend in a horizontal ray of light.

But it was the very substance of Einstein's conception that the two situations—one produced by nonuniform motion and the other produced by gravity—were indistinguishable whether one used merely mechanical tricks or those of electrodynamics. Thus the ray of light, seen as bent by the man in the box when the box was subject to acceleration, would surely be seen in the same way if gravity were involved when the box was at rest. From one point of view this was not as outrageous as it sounded. In 1905 Einstein had given fresh support to the idea that light consisted not of waves but of a stream of minute machine gun bullets, the light quanta which were later christened photons. Why, after all, should not these light quanta be affected by gravity in the same way as everything else?

But even as the idea was contemplated its implications began to grow like the genie from the lamp. For a straight line is the path of a ray of light, while the basis of time measurement is the interval taken by light to pass from one point to another. Thus if light were affected by gravity, time and space would have two different configurations—one when viewed from within the gravitational field and one when viewed from without. In the absence of gravitation the shortest distance between A and B—the path along which a light ray would travel from A to B—is a straight line. But when gravitation is present the line traveled by light is not the straight line of ordinary geometry. Nevertheless, there is no way of getting from A to B faster than light gets along this path. The "light line" then *is* the straight line. This might not matter very much in the mundane affairs of the terrestrial world, where the earth's gravity was for all practical purposes a constant that was a part of life. But for those looking out from the earth to the solar system and the worlds beyond, the principle of equivalence suggested that they might have been looking out through distorting spectacles. Einstein's new idea appeared to have slipped a disk in the backbone of the universe.

As the overall tale-teller, Einstein-as-scientist-viewer-listener-reader not only sees from the *outside* what is happening with the man in the falling (or accelerating) box but simultaneously sees it from the *vantage point* of the man *inside* the box, with access to his *internal* point-of-view. In other words, without this basic point-of-view structure of our minds Einstein would have been unable to come up with the General Theory of Relativity. To the outside teller, the beam of light does not bend because we see it and the box in movement over time, but we see simultaneously from the vantage point of the man in the box that the light beam does bend, because he is *unaware* of the falling or accelerating movement that alters the appearance of the beam of light in time. If he holds up keys, the keys do not drop. We can easily imagine Einstein's playful imaginative sense, seeing the expression on the man's face when keys and money do not fall. From the teller's point-of-view, we know that the box and the keys and the money and the man are being pulled by gravity at the same rate. Such ironies, between what the teller and the reader know in contrast to what a character knows, occur also in oral and written literature.

* * *

In science and literature, point-of-view is discovery by means of seeing something from different points, simultaneously, as we do in our imaginations, as the following piece reveals.

Wordsworth's Visioning and Re-Visioning
Randall Albers

In the notes to his "Intimations Ode," Wordsworth tells how, as a young boy walking to school, he would suddenly begin to feel as if the objects around him were as airy and insubstantial as the images of his inner life. It was as if his inner dream world were reaching outward and encompassing the external world. At such times, he says, he was "unable to think of external things as having an external existence," and he would often need to reach out and grasp at a wall or a tree in order to recall himself from this "abyss of idealism" back to the real world. While, at the time, the abyss filled him with fear, in later life, he came to see that this idealistic rendering of the world was less an "abyss" than a refuge, a place that the individual could—must—seek out in order to re-fuel and sustain his hope, his desire, and his imagination:

> In later periods of life, I have deplored, as we all have reason to, a subjugation of an opposite character, and have rejoiced over the remembrances, as is expressed in the lines, 'Obstinate questionings,' &c. To that dreamlike vividness and splendour which invest all objects of sight in childhood, every one, I believe, if he would look back, could bear testimony. . . .[1]

If, as Goethe says, all healthy movement is from internal to external, Wordsworth's adult is constantly threatened by the reverse—that is, by the external impinging upon the internal. In other words, if the young Wordsworth must reach out to a tree to ground (literally and figuratively) his airy, expanding dream, the older Wordsworth worries that the mundane and soul-less world of the ordinary and the rational will reach out and stifle the ability to dream, stifle even the memory of what it meant to dream as a child.

Wordsworth's poetry, particularly *The Prelude,* in one way or another always addresses this central problem: How can the adult re-discover—even re-vision—the "vividness and splendour" of the childhood dream? How can he avoid succumbing either to the siren-call of the ideal or to the suffocation of the mundane? Or, perhaps more correctly, how can the dream and dreamlike states of mind be used to discover the universal and the infinite within the mundane? . . .

Near the beginning of *The Excursion,* as he does so often in *The Prelude* and in so many other places, Wordsworth relates an instance of a young boy coming under the influence of nature. Much like the young Wordsworth on his way to school, this boy, satchel in hand, returns from school night after night alone, and each night he sees the hills grow larger in the distance and the stars coming out overhead. As in *The Prelude,* where he steals a boat and rows to the middle of the lake, only to have the mountains rise up and pursue him back to shore, or, where, after a bit of frenzied ice skating, he suddenly leans back on his heels, stops, and feels the cliffs wheel by him with a life of their own, this young boy on his way home from school feels the objects of nature lying upon his mind "like substances," and for the remainder of his young years, compares all other memories, thoughts, objects, and the like with these earlier experiences until

> . . . being unsatisfied with aught
> Of dimmer character, he thence attained
> An active power to fasten images
> Upon his brain; and on their pictured lines
> Intensely brooded, even until they acquired
> The liveliness of dreams. (I. 143–48)

For the young child, Nature itself evokes the child's dream and actually becomes part of that dream. As the child grows into adulthood, he loses the ability to immerse himself in dream. As Wordsworth indicates elsewhere, this movement constitutes a kind of "fortunate fall" because the ability to reflect upon the images seen may deepen the experience of the images in a way that the dream does not allow. Nevertheless, without the experience of the images themselves initially, reflection is impossible. It is for this reason that Wordsworth lets himself be led to the memory, the object, or whatever is worthy of reflection by its analogy to "the liveliness of dreams."

How and where do you find the storyteller-essayist's overall point-of-view established in the first paragraph? How and where does the first paragraph tell from Wordsworth's vantage point? Where does the author assume Wordsworth's internal point-of-view?

Analyze each paragraph for the presence of one or more of the fundamental components of point-of-view structure. Analyze the paragraph in which "the mountains rise up and pursue him back to shore" and "he suddenly leans back on his heels, stops, and feels the cliffs wheel by him with a life of their own. . . ." The author's *attitude* is inquiring as well as authoritative, as he lays out what he feels is sufficient evidence to support his thesis. What would happen to "Wordsworth's Visioning and Re-Visioning" if the author did not tell some of the material from Wordsworth's point-of-view? What would happen if he tried to tell *all* of it from Wordsworth's point-of-view?

The author's *attitude* is an important dimension of point-of-view. It helps generate and organize the material as well as influence the presentation of it. What is the attitude of Mr. Wyles toward his story? How is MacEdward Leach's attitude toward Mr. Wyles affirmative, admiring, persuasive, and "objective" at the same time? What is Cassius Clay's attitude toward what he's telling? What is Ronald Clark's attitude toward Einstein's accounts of his discovery? What do you sense was Einstein's own attitude in his point-of-view experiment? What do you sense about Albers's attitude toward Wordsworth, Wordsworth's dreams, and dreams, poetry, and criticism of poetry in general?

Examine "Let's Spoil the Wilderness," "The Sermon," "When Will You Be a No-Till Farmer," "Everything but the Squeal—the Use of Spoiled Meats," and any other selection for the *attitude* of its author.

Your attitude about your subject, along with and influenced by your sense of audience, gives you a place to stand, a tone, and a perspective from which to organize and set forth the argument.

In any reading selection in this book, watch how the presentation and juxtaposition of facts indicate the author's attitude toward the material.

Using Point-of-View Structure in Your Writing

Look over your how-it-happens subject. Give a telling, factual or imagined, of how a character in your subject tells a story to one or more listeners, complete with gestures, facial expressions, and other actions similar to Mr. Wyles's or Cassius Clay's telling. You can mix factual and imagined materials. Tell it in writing with all the gestures and actions, enactment of characters, taking of point-of-view, awareness of listeners, that the teller would use.

How do you hit on the right point-of-view? The first strong imagery that comes to you may be a good indicator. You can also try switching points-of-view. If you're writing in the first person, switch to the third person (try "he" or "she" for a while on separate sheets of paper or in another part of your journal) and see how the seeing, the telling of the material comes across to you. Rather than simply retell the passage, go ahead with the movement by telling it from a different person's point-of-view.

Start a *point-of-view* shifts exercise by emphasizing the storyteller-essayist's overall point-of-view, then switch to a character's vantage point or internal point-of-view (the character who most immediately attracts your attention), then switch from first person to third person or third to first, then switch to a person whose point-of-view you would be unlikely to take (someone you would not feel sympathetic with), then to a form *and* point-of-view shift such as a monologue, a script, or other form that attracts your attention. Keep the narrative moving through all of these shifts.

Frequently, you may find that the telling comes alive with a point-of-view or form switch. Sometimes the clue resides in how you first saw and felt the imagery in your mind, from whose point-of-view, in what person. The first impulses sometimes possess the right point-of-view for exploration. In this point-of-view switch experiment, find which change is strongest and try telling the whole story that way. Move about and give the gestures of your characters to get yourself into their points-of-view.

Opposites

Many of the great characters of literature have been opposites of the author, e.g., the powerful monomaniacal whaling captain Ahab (Herman Melville), the family-life woman Mrs. Ramsay (Virginia Woolf), the young murderer Raskolnikov (Dostoevsky), the flamboyant moralistic father Sam Pollit (Christina Stead), the runaway Huckleberry Finn (Mark Twain), the rebellious murderer Bigger Thomas (Richard Wright), and many others. Your opposite may be a moral, style-of-life, behavioral, or social background opposite. Yet something about the opposite attracts—and keeps attracting—your attention. We deal with opposites on our jobs, in our schools, families, neighborhoods, just about anywhere. Sometimes we even have to persuade our opposites to help us in some way.

As you read the following selections, think of opposites of yours that you've known: jock vs. bookish student, terrorizer vs. victim, sexually alive person vs. prudish person, promiscuous person vs. abstinent person, violent person vs. peaceful person, person of colorful language vs. person of unmemorable language, strong personality vs. mild personality. These obviously contrasting (and rather stereotyped) paired opposites may lead you to see, remember, and imagine other opposites you know. We want to emphasize the character who is *your* opposite.

Morgan
John Schultz

Sfc Lewis Morgan, who had a rep as the best mess sergeant in the KComZ, always played a game in the streets of Pusan to see just how close he could nip the foot-traffic with the fender of his jeep. He managed at last to kill a gook, a baby boy slung on the small of its mother's back. "Shit, boysan," one of Morgan's buddies said, late the next day, after all hell broke loose around the headquarters compound of the 68th Engineers, "she'd a froze to death long before this if the American Army wasn't here. Why, you better mother-fuckin' believe it, sarge." Morgan himself never said so much. His glasses flashed as he looked up at his buddy and his smile was meant to please and threaten. His smile was straight as the side of his hand. He went back to planning menus, sitting alone at a table in the middle of the empty messhall, while his buddy shuffled uncomfortably away. Morgan had a black belt in judo, and it put a stamp of license on anything he did. GIs went out of their way to visit friends in the 68th so they could eat in Morgan's messhall, where the food was good and everything was clean.

In the streets, people tumbled to get out of his way, and heavy bundles rolled and spilled apart. Morgan particularly enjoyed two things, the steep, narrow streets where he could make a man jump for his life, spread out flat and quivering against a wall as the jeep whipped by. And the other was the spider-men. These were men with no legs, amputees at the hip, who walked by swinging their torsos between their arms. They used thick gloves on their hands and their torsos were padded at the bottom. They were always black with filth, and you could not tell their skin from their clothing. With incredible agility they darted in front of vehicles, among people's legs, everywhere. Morgan swerved his jeep and tried to tick the spider-men so they would lose their remarkable control and fall over in the street. More than once, in his rearview mirror, he saw people helping one of the spider-men get his arms and torso into position again, though usually they were quite able to do it themselves. "Jee-e-e-e-sus, *Christ,*" buddies riding with Morgan would hiss and holler, scared and glad he'd done it. "Whooo-eeeee, look at old mama-san go." If it were a couple of whores in Western dress he would send them scurrying off the road, stop the jeep abruptly, back up, smile at them, and the jo-sans might tell him off in the finest pidgin cussing and even then end up climbing into his jeep. . . .

I can testify that Morgan is indeed an opposite of mine, in part based upon an actual person and actual events. The first draft of the events that went into the making of this story was a first-person "I" account and, though it was clear enough, it simply didn't work, didn't have movement or story meaning. After rereading it and finding that it didn't work, I laid it aside. A few months later, while walking down a street, I began to imagine and see and feel vividly, from Morgan's point of view, the beginning movement that is presented here. The point of view shifted to the storyteller, the third person, and to Morgan. That is, I saw the event as the overall storyteller and also from Morgan's vantage point, over his shoulder, so to speak, and felt his internal point-of-view. A strong, undeniable sense of story movement and meaning took hold. Events that had been flat in my earlier first-person account became vividly present in the new version. As the overall storyteller, I became aware of the space around and between characters, in the context of events. My taking Morgan's point-of-view led to my taking other characters' points-of-view, and the story gained strength with each point-of-view. The story ceased to be autobiographical. As a character, I dropped out of it. I became the storyteller. Another character, also an opposite, was created in my place. The "facts" of many events and characters remained the same, though imaginatively changed by point-of-view, voice, tone.

The opening movement of "Morgan" gives aspects of him that made him feared, admired, respected, and hated by many people. In the second paragraph, the storyteller sees things as Morgan sees them. Where do you find instances and facts that show how Morgan was feared, admired, respected, and hated? Follow the variations of the storyteller's point of view and of the storyteller taking Morgan's point-of-view.

From
The Informed Heart
Bruno Bettelheim

. . . In the winter of 1938 a Polish Jew murdered the German attaché in Paris, von Rath. The Gestapo used the event to step up anti-Semitic actions, and in the camp new hardships were inflicted on Jewish prisoners. One of these was an order barring them from the medical clinic unless the need for treatment had originated in a work accident.

Nearly all prisoners suffered from frostbite which often led to gangrene and then amputation. Whether or not a Jewish prisoner was admitted to the clinic to prevent such a fate depended on the whim of an SS private. On reaching the clinic entrance, the prisoner explained the nature of his ailment to the SS man, who then decided if he should get treatment or not.

I too suffered from frostbite. At first I was discouraged from trying to get medical care by the fate of Jewish prisoners whose attempts had ended up in no treatment, only abuse. Finally things got worse and I was afraid that waiting longer would mean amputation. So I decided to make the effort.

When I got to the clinic, there were many prisoners lined up as usual, a score of them Jews suffering from severe frostbite. The main topic of discussion was one's chances of being admitted to the clinic. Most Jews had planned their procedure in detail. Some thought it best to stress their service in the German army during World War I: wounds received or decorations won. Others planned to stress the severity of their frostbite. A few decided it was best to tell some "tall story," such as that an SS officer had ordered them to report at the clinic.

Most of them seemed convinced that the SS man on duty would not see through their schemes. Eventually they asked me about my plans. Having no definite ones, I said I would go by the way the SS man dealt with other Jewish prisoners who had frostbite like me, and proceed accordingly. I doubted how wise it was to follow a preconceived plan, because it was hard to anticipate the reactions of a person you didn't know.

The prisoners reacted as they had at other times when I had voiced similar ideas on how to deal with the SS. They insisted that one SS man was like another, all equally vicious and stupid. As usual, any frustration was immediately discharged against the person who caused it, or was nearest at hand. So in abusive terms they accused me of not wanting to share my plan with them, or of intending to use one of theirs; it angered them that I was ready to meet the enemy unprepared.

No Jewish prisoner ahead of me in line was admitted to the clinic. The more a prisoner pleaded, the more annoyed and violent the SS became. Expressions of pain amused him; stories of previous services rendered to Germany outraged him. He proudly remarked that *he* could not be taken in by Jews, that fortunately the time had passed when Jews could reach their goal by lamentations.

When my turn came he asked me in a screeching voice if I knew that work accidents were the only reason for admitting Jews to the clinic, and if I came because of such an accident. I replied that I knew the rules, but that I couldn't work unless my hands were freed of the dead flesh. Since prisoners were not allowed to have knives, I asked to have the dead flesh cut away. I tried to be matter-of-fact, avoiding pleading, deference, or arrogance. He replied: "If that's all you want, I'll tear the flesh off myself." And he started to pull at the festering skin. Because it did not come off as easily as he may have expected, or for some other reason, he waved me into the clinic.

Inside, he gave me a malevolent look and pushed me into the treatment room. There he told the prisoner orderly to attend to the wound. While this was being done, the guard watched me closely for signs of pain but I was able to suppress them. As soon as the cutting was over, I started to leave. He showed surprise and asked why I didn't wait for further treatment. I said I had gotten the service I asked for, at which he told the orderly to make an exception and treat my hand. After I had left the room, he called me back and gave me a card entitling me to further treatment, and admittance to the clinic without inspection at the entrance.

Here Bettelheim argues the potential benefits of being able to identify with your opposite, of accepting the opposite as a human being, rather than fixing him as a rigid defensive construct of your own mind. Meeting the opposite (or any person) without preconceived notions, so Bettelheim argues, may be the best way to allow an actual relationship to develop and work for you. Just so, in writing about an opposite you need to let yourself identify with the opposite, come what may.

If we want to persuade an opposite to do something to help us, we need to be able to identify with and cultivate our relationship with that person. Bettelheim succeeded in relating to his opposite, the SS guard, as, in the LETTER ON BEHALF OF YOURSELF section, we'll see how Hart Crane succeeded in relating to an opposite of his, the editor of *Poetry*. Bettelheim's telling is also a how-to-do-it-better (see HOW-TO-DO-IT-BETTER section), showing the standard way that prisoners proposed to approach the guard, the ineffectual results of the standard way, his proposal for a better way, and the better results of his way.

"How Bigger Was Born"
From **The Introduction to Native Son**
Richard Wright

So, at the outset, I say frankly that there are phases of *Native Son* which I shall make no attempt to account for. There are meanings in my book of which I was not aware until they literally spilled out upon the paper. I shall sketch the outline of how I *consciously* came into possession of the materials that went into *Native Son*, but there will be many things I shall omit, not because I want to, but simply because I don't know them.

The birth of Bigger Thomas goes back to my childhood, and there was not just one Bigger, but many of them, more than I could count and more than you suspect. But let me start with the first Bigger, whom I shall call Bigger No. 1.

When I was a bareheaded, barefoot kid in Jackson, Mississippi, there was a boy who terrorized me and all of the boys I played with. If we were playing games, he would saunter up and snatch from us our balls, bats, spinning tops, and marbles. We would stand around pouting, sniffling, trying to keep back our tears, begging for our playthings. But Bigger would refuse. We never demanded that he give them back; we were afraid, and Bigger was bad. We had seen him clout boys when he was angry and we did not want to run that risk. We never recovered our toys unless we flattered him and made him feel that he was superior to us. Then, perhaps, if he felt like it, he condescended, threw them at us and then gave each of us a swift kick in the bargain, just to make us feel his utter contempt.

That was the way Bigger No. 1 lived. His life was a continuous challenge to others. At all times he *took* his way, right or wrong, and those who contradicted him had him to fight. And never was he happier than when he had someone cornered and at his mercy; it seemed that the deepest meaning of his squalid life was in him at such times.

I don't know what fate of Bigger No. 1 was. His swaggering personality is swallowed up somewhere in the amnesia of my childhood. But I suspect that his end was violent. Anyway, he left a marked impression upon me; maybe it was because I longed secretly to be like him and was afraid. I don't know.

If I had known only one Bigger I would not have written *Native Son*. Let me call the next one Bigger No. 2; he was about seventeen and tougher than the first Bigger. Since I, too, had grown older, I was a little less afraid of him. And the hardness of this

Bigger No. 2 was not directed toward me or the other Negroes, but toward the whites who ruled the South. He bought clothes and food on credit and would not pay for them. He lived in the dingy shacks of the white landlords and refused to pay rent. Of course, he had no money, but neither did we. We did without the necessities of life and starved ourselves, but he never would. When we asked him why he acted as he did, he would tell us (as though we were little children in a kindergarten) that the white folks had everything and he had nothing. Further, he would tell us that we were fools not to get what we wanted while we were alive in this world. We would listen and silently agree. We longed to believe and act as he did, but we were afraid. We were Southern Negroes and we were hungry and we wanted to live, but we were more willing to tighten our belts than risk conflict. Bigger No. 2 wanted to live and he did; he was in prison the last time I heard from him.

There was Bigger No. 3, whom the white folks called a "bad nigger." He carried his life in his hands in a literal fashion. I once worked as a ticket-taker in a Negro movie house (all movie houses in Dixie are Jim Crow; there are movies for whites and movies for blacks), and many times Bigger No. 3 came to the door and gave my arm a hard pinch and walked into the theater. Resentfully and silently, I'd nurse my bruised arm. Presently, the proprietor would come over and ask how things were going. I'd point into the darkened theater and say: "Bigger's in there." "Did he pay?" the proprietor would ask. "No, sir," I'd answer. The proprietor would pull down the corners of his lips and speak through his teeth: "We'll kill that goddamn nigger one of these days." And the episode would end right there. But later on Bigger No. 3 was killed during the days of Prohibition: while delivering liquor to a customer he was shot through the back by a white cop.

And then there was Bigger No. 4, whose only law was death. The Jim Crow laws of the South were not for him. But as he laughed and cursed and broke them, he knew that some day he'd have to pay for his freedom. His rebellious spirit made him violate all the taboos and consequently he always oscillated between moods of intense elation and depression. He was never happier than when he had outwitted some foolish custom, and he was never more melancholy than when brooding over the impossibility of his ever being free. He had no job, for he regarded digging ditches for fifty cents a day as slavery. "I can't live on that," he would say. Ofttimes I'd find him reading a book; he would stop and in a joking, wistful, and cynical manner ape the antics of the white folks. Generally, he'd end his mimicry in a depressed state and say: "The white folks won't let us do nothing." Bigger No. 4 was sent to the asylum for the insane.

Then there was Bigger No. 5, who always rode the Jim Crow streetcars without paying and sat wherever he pleased. I remember one morning his getting into a streetcar (all streetcars in Dixie are divided into two sections: one section is for whites and is labeled—FOR WHITES; the other section is for Negroes and is labeled—FOR COLORED) and sitting in the white section. The conductor went to him and said: "Come on, nigger. Move over where you belong. Can't you read?" Bigger answered: "Naw, I can't read." The conductor flared up: "Get out of that seat!" Bigger took out his knife, opened it, held it nonchalantly in his hand, and replied: "Make me." The conductor turned red, blinked, clenched his fists, and walked away, stammering: "The goddamn scum of the earth!" A small angry conference of white men took place in the front of the car and the Negroes sitting in the Jim Crow section overheard: "That's that Bigger Thomas nigger and you'd better leave 'im alone." The Negroes experienced an intense flash of pride and the streetcar moved on its journey without incident. I don't know what happened to Bigger No. 5. But I can guess.

The Bigger Thomases were the only Negroes I know of who consistently violated the Jim Crow laws of the South and got away with it, at least for a sweet brief spell. Eventually, the whites who restricted their lives made them pay a terrible price. They were shot, hanged, maimed, lynched, and generally hounded until they were either dead or their spirits broken.

There were many variations to this behavioristic pattern. Later on I encountered other Bigger Thomases who did not react to the locked-in Black Belts with this same extremity and violence. But before I use Bigger Thomas as a springboard for the examination of milder types, I'd better indicate more precisely the nature of the environment that produced these men, or the reader will be left with the impression that they were essentially and organically bad.

In Dixie there are two worlds, the white world and the black world, and they are physically separated. There are white schools and black schools, white churches and black churches, white businesses and black businesses, white graveyards and black graveyards, and, for all I know, a white God and a black God. . . .

This separation was accomplished after the Civil War by the terror of the Ku Klux Klan, which swept the newly freed Negro through arson, pillage, and death out of the United States Senate, the House of Representatives, the many state legislatures, and out of the public, social and economic life of the South. The motive for this assault was simple and urgent. The imperialistic tug of history had torn the Negro from his African home and had placed him ironically upon the most fertile plantation areas of the South; and, when the Negro was freed, he outnumbered the whites in many of these fertile areas. Hence, a fierce and bitter struggle took place to keep the ballot from the Negro, for had he had a chance to vote, he would have automatically controlled the richest lands of the South and with them the social, political, and economic destiny of a third of the Republic. Though the South is politically a part of America, the problem that faced her was peculiar and the struggle between the whites and the blacks after the Civil War was in essence a struggle for power, ranging over thirteen states and involving the lives of tens of millions of people.

But keeping the ballot from the Negro was not enough to hold him in check; disfranchisement had to be supplemented by a whole panoply of rules, taboos, and penalties designed not only to insure peace (complete submission), but to guarantee that no real threat would ever arise. Had the Negro lived upon a common territory, separate from the bulk of the white population, this program of oppression might not have assumed such a brutal and violent form. But this war took place between people who were neighbors, whose homes adjoined, whose farms had common boundaries. Guns and disfranchisement, therefore, were not enough to make the black neighbor keep his distance. The white neighbor decided to limit the amount of education his black neighbor could receive; decided to keep him off the police force and out of the local national guards; to segregate him residentially; to Jim Crow him in public places; to restrict his participation in the professions and jobs; and to build up a vast, dense ideology of racial superiority that would justify any act of violence taken against him to defend white dominance; and further, to condition him to hope for little and to receive that little without rebelling.

But, because the blacks were so *close* to the very civilization which sought to keep them out, because they could not *help* but react in some way to its incentives and prizes, and because the very tissue of their consciousness received its tone and timbre from the strivings of that dominant civilization, oppression spawned among them a myriad variety of reactions, reaching from outright blind rebellion to a sweet, other-worldly submissiveness.

In the main, this delicately balanced state of affairs has not greatly altered since the Civil War, save in those parts of the South which have been industrialized or urbanized. So volatile and tense are these relations that if a Negro rebels against rule and taboo, he is lynched and the reason for the lynching is usually called "rape," that catchword which has garnered such vile connotations that it can raise a mob anywhere in the South pretty quickly, even today.

Now for the variations in the Bigger Thomas pattern. Some of the Negroes living under these conditions got religion, felt that Jesus would redeem the void of living, felt that the more bitter life was in the present the happier it would be in the hereafter. Others, clinging still to that brief glimpse of post-Civil War freedom, employed a thousand ruses and stratagems of struggle to win their rights. Still others projected their hurts and longings into more naïve and mundane forms—blues, jazz, swing—and, without intellectual guidance, tried to build up a compensatory nourishment for themselves. Many labored under hot suns and then killed the restless ache with alcohol. Then there were those who strove for an education, and when they got it, enjoyed the financial fruits of it in the style of their bourgeois oppressors. Usually they went hand in hand with the powerful whites and helped to keep their groaning brothers in line, for that was the safest course of action. Those who did this called themselves "leaders." To give you an idea of how completely these "leaders" worked with those who oppressed, I can tell you that I lived the first seventeen years of my life in the South without so much as hearing of or seeing one act of rebellion from *any* Negro, save the Bigger Thomases.

But why did Bigger revolt? No explanation based upon a hard and fast rule of conduct can be given. But there were always two factors psychologically dominant in his personality. First, through some quirk of circumstance, he had become estranged from the religion and the folk culture of his race. Second, he was trying to react to and answer the call of the dominant civilization whose glitter came to him through the newspapers, magazines, radios, movies, and the mere imposing sight and sound of daily American life. In many respects his emergence as a distinct type was inevitable.

In "How Bigger Was Born," Richard Wright tells about the five "Bigger Thomases" that he knew who combined in his imagination to become the separate figure and character of Bigger Thomas in the novel *Native Son*. He makes clear that he disliked the Biggers, feared them, and yet secretly admired them. Many of us secretly admire the opposites whom we fear or hate. In this essay, Wright also gives his theory of the novel as being about "character destiny."

After his tellings of the five Biggers, Wright discusses the social and historical background that peculiarly influenced each variation of the pattern. Examine the images and examples that demonstrate what Wright has to say about the five Biggers. Where do you find short model-tellings embedded in the accounts?

In Wright's account of how his thinking and feeling about Bigger Thomas came together in his writing, you find important clues about writing itself as well as clues to the way he identified with his opposite at the same time that he maintained the storyteller's point of view. For instance, later in the essay, in passages not included here, he tells how he tried twenty or thirty times to write a beginning scene, then went to a scene that felt alive and compelling to him and started writing there. He speaks of discovery of meanings he was not aware of until they "spilled out onto the paper." In rewriting, he says that he was "both reader and writer, both the conceiver of the action and the appreciator of it."

Marge
Sharon Weber

The scrawled, jittery handwriting is unrecognizable to the man. He turns it over in his hands; finding no return address, he opens it.

Dear Jim,

Why didn't you come and visit me in the hospital? I waited and waited. You never came. I wasn't contagious, you know. Were you so ashamed?

Well, you haven't asked, but the hospital was awful. I thought those were the worst 21 days of my life. How wrong I was. It's the 21 days after the hospital that have been the worst. In the hospital, you know you can't get a drink. You know it's not in your grasp. Out here, it's all around you. Signs jump out: "JB $4.98 a fifth," "Grab for all the gusto you can." Billboards show tall, cool sweating glasses of Bloody Marys or gin and tonics, glasses that look so real you want to reach out and grab it. You want to feel it drip down your face as you pour the liquid down your parched throat.

There's no way to get around it. I can't tell anyone about this. Anyone but you, Jim, although you *did* desert me. But, dear brother, you're elected to hear me out. Ed is so busy; he has to work double shifts to pay all the bills. Kevin and Jill are so busy with their own friends. And I know I've hurt them enough. I know they probably hate me. I don't even like me, Jim. Do you? Probably not.

I hope you're not telling the rest of the family about me. I'm not proud of myself. I'm not a proud drunk. I was not a social drinker gone too far. I was a sneak drinker, Jim. Not like Grandma, running to the pantry to take a sip of cold beer on a hot day. No, I used to hide bottles in my drawers. Used to take them out after Ed and Kevin and Jill left in the morning. First it was just a sip to get the blood flowing. Pretty soon the sip lasted until after lunchtime. Then I'd stop and spend a normal evening—Ed would watch TV, Kevin and Jill would dash out to various friends. Pretty soon I'd start finding odd jobs to do in the bedroom, like cleaning out the drawers. But the only thing I'd clean out would be the bottle I'd stashed.

It wasn't long before I couldn't stop, before I couldn't hide it. They began to notice. Sometimes I just couldn't stand up. And what do you do with something that doesn't work anymore? You take it to be fixed, of course. So I was taken to the drunk-garage. And they fixed me up. Oh, they fixed me up fine. But the trouble is, I don't feel fixed. Ed thinks I'm OK, I guess. As long as I lay off the bottle, I'm good old Marge. To hell with the fact that my kids run from the house as fast as they can. Forget about how hard it is for me to wake up in the morning knowing there are no more little bottles to float me through the day. Forget that I'm pouring out my troubles to my brother, who didn't come to visit me in the hospital and who probably would like to be an only child right now.

I suppose I've taken enough time out of your busy day. Just do me a couple of favors, Jim. Have a drink on me and really enjoy it. And kiss Elaine very passionately today. Hold her and tell her you love her and make her feel good. Then take those kids out for ice cream before they get too old and don't need you anymore.

Love always,
Marge

Books and papers were strewn about the kitchen table, and while Karen's blonde head was bent over in concentration, Jill's brunette head was up, her eyes staring straight ahead at the white refrigerator. There were little magnets shaped like fruit—a banana, an apple, a cluster of grapes—tacked in no special order on the stark white refrigerator door.

"Jill, why do we have to study all this nonsense just for one test?" Karen looked up and saw that Jill was staring straight ahead. "Hey, you're not even studying! What's wrong?"

"I know for sure." Jill pulled her eyes away from the refrigerator and looked at Karen with no expression on her face. "I know for sure that my mother is drinking again. I went home after school and before I came here. She was—I don't know, asleep or passed out, I guess—on the couch. I called to her, but she didn't wake up. At first I thought, maybe she's sick. She's been complaining about having headaches a lot lately, so I figured I'd let her sleep. When I walked into the kitchen, it was a mess. Well, like I said, I thought she had been sick, so I cleaned up. I went into the front room to collect all the glasses so I could clean up all the dishes." Jill looked down at a bare spot on the table. "There was an empty glass next to the couch. And an empty bottle. It was Smirnoff vodka." She took a deep breath. "I didn't know what to do. I wanted to run out of there. I wished that I'd never gone home, but I picked up the glass and the empty bottle and I took them back into the kitchen. I scrubbed the glass good. I threw the bottle in the garbage can. Then I took the garbage out to the alley." She looked up at Karen. "I don't know who I was trying to cover up for—for her, for having gotten drunk again or for me, finding her like that. Anyway, I wrote her a note. Told her that I had cleaned up the kitchen and was coming here. I didn't mention the bottle."

*   *   *

Marge was still sitting on her bedroom floor, clutching the bottle like it was a life preserver. Her mind still told her that everything was OK.

She looked down at the miraculous bottle she held in her hands. She felt safe. Nobody knew. Nobody knew that she had a drink every now and then in the afternoons. Because she brought her own bottles of J.B., nobody found any liquor missing.

An alarm went off in her head. J.B.? She searched back in her mind. She didn't drink J.B. anymore. She was positive that she had had vodka that afternoon. Smirnoff vodka. The clear liquid in the clear bottle flashed in her mind. Yes, It *was* vodka! Marge's hands began to tremble. She hadn't drunk J.B. for months. Not since before the hospital. Then she had craved J.B., but since then, her tastes had changed. She stared blankly at the bottle shaking in her hands. This had to be an old, forgotten bottle from ages ago. Then where was that empty, clear bottle of Smirnoff's?

Weber, a young woman, imagines her opposite as an alcoholic woman who is a mother of teenage children. She writes the letter that she imagines the opposite would write. Do you feel Marge has a special intention in writing to her brother Jim? What feeling about herself does she show in the letter? What do we learn about Marge in the point-of-view shift to her teenage daughter? What do we learn, in the next instance, from Marge's own internal point-of-view?

*   *   *

Opposites often liberate strong imaginative movements and enforce clear seeing of their independence of being. They generate events. Understanding of opposites is often a key to persuasion. When you can identify with the opposite, your sense of address to the opposite is more sure, more accurate, more persuasive. Such empathic identification helps you understand the person to whom you addressed a letter in which you try to persuade that person to do something for you. Yet, despite your identification with the opposite or even your secret admiration of the opposite, the opposite *is* an opposite, not simply a projection or embodiment of deep feelings of yours.

Writing Your Opposites

The first unfortunate tendency of many writers is to make fun of the opposite from the outside rather than identify with the person and see everything from his or her point-of-view. It's a cheap and often self-defeating way of maintaining your self-esteem. Obviously, however, there can be creative, perceptive satire or parody of opposites. If the writing is going to be funny, it will often emerge naturally in the writing. Write seriously in the opposite's language. That may be the best way to let the opposite make fun of himself or herself.

In your how-it-happens subject, you can find several opposites. Take the ones that attract you most strongly—also repel you, perhaps—and write about them: someone you've known on a job, in school, in the neighborhood, in your family, wherever. Sometimes the more powerful opposites are those you fear, hate, admire, despise, or feel to be dangerous. Or someone who is inept, awkward, never reads human signals correctly. Or someone who is magnetically compelling. A gang leader. An administrator. A union leader. A business executive. A linguistic opposite, whose speech and background is different from yours, one to whom you may have listened a good deal. A person who is everybody's scapegoat. A person who is somebody's scapegoat. A person whom everyone makes fun of, or persecutes. Everybody may have been a scapegoat at one time or another. Get into the opposite's point of view. See and feel things as the opposite sees and feels them. Listen to the opposite's voice in your voice. Write a letter as written by the opposite in the opposite's language. Let the opposite be the teller of a story or of an account to a fictional audience. Explore the opposite's personality in his or her language. Look for characteristic gestures, objects, actions, places; patterns of behavior, actions, voice, attitude; patterns of reactions from other people. Tell something, in class or to yourself, about your opposite, what he or she is, what he or she does, why he or she is an opposite. Give brief sights, images. Make notes about patterns of behavior as you write your way into the opposite's point of view.

Do a four-stage writing in one sitting about the opposite: first, write about the opposite as you see him or her from the teller's point of view; second, see and write from the opposite's point of view (as "he" or "she"); third, write in the first person in the opposite's own language; fourth, write a letter that you imagine the opposite writing, perhaps a letter that the opposite writes on his or her own behalf. You could do other point-of-view *and* form shifts that attract your attention as you write. Write about five to seven minutes in each stage.

Do the four-stage point-of-view writing as completely as you can in longhand, unless you must work on a typewriter. As you shift points-of-view *and* forms, let the events keep moving; let each stage be about a new part of the story or essay, rather than telling the same event four different ways. Conceivably, you could get interesting results in telling the same passage four different ways, but your greatest benefit will come to you from letting the story move through the four stages. Read the four stages aloud to the class or a friend. Then, when you've found the strongest form and point-of-view retell the whole piece accordingly. Do it as soon as possible. The same day, if possible.

To get a sense for the spatial relationship in your mind between your opposite and you as storyteller, hold one hand out in front of you to indicate the point of view of the opposite and the other by your head to indicate the position of the storyteller. See and be aware of anything heard, seen, smelled, felt against the skin, thought, remembered, by the opposite. Make notes for the writing that will come. See the opposite from toe to head, see the space around him or her, see the gestures and stances and actions of the other people to whom the opposite relates. Listen to the opposite's voice and speech mannerisms.

Do gestures to get the sense of your opposite's stance and characteristic physical movements, and at the same time let yourself see the opposite and everything around him or her from back aways in your mind, too. For instance, when you recall "Morgan," let yourself hold onto the steering wheel as Morgan does at the moment he tries to make a "spider-man" lose his balance; see him looking (and look yourself) into the mirror at the Koreans helping the "spider-men" get to their feet. See the space around Morgan in the jeep and in the messhall. See and feel the storyteller's point-of-view further back from Morgan. Where does the storyteller's view almost merge with Morgan's?

Students, seeing and telling and writing about their opposites, have often commented that their seeing of the opposite gives them a sense of distance, of space between them and around the opposite. "The opposite is more separate from you than other characters." "You can see the opposite clearly." "The opposite sharpens your sight of character." "You realize that you could see characters more clearly if you saw them as opposites." "Looking for the characteristics of opposites makes you see the heightened characteristics of a person."

If it's not possible for you to read your four-stage writing to your class, then read it to a friend or try to hear it yourself. By hearing it yourself in relation to an audience, you can often feel the stronger point-of-view take hold in your voice. Retell the events covered by all four stages in the form and point-of-view that you've chosen (or that has chosen you). Actually, the stronger point-of-view may be the best beginning. Go on with the writing. All of us occasionally have an unfortunate tendency to try to make our pet ideas or intentions override the evidence of our eyes, ears, and feeling. *Go with the evidence of what comes through most strongly in your voice, to your audience, to yourself as audience, to your imagination.*

Continue with the opposites writing, let it move into areas not yet covered by the first four stages.

Story-Within-a-Story

The story-within-a-story is a story or account told by one character to another character or larger audience. From Homer to present day authors, from Odysseus's story of the Cyclops to Portnoy's long complaint to his psychiatrist, the story-within-a-story has been magically persuasive and stimulating to use. Frequently, the character tells the story to the fictional audience with a particular purpose, desired effect, or argumentative intention in mind. Story-within-a-story provides writers with a special opportunity for charming, vivid, downright seductive argumentation. Your opposite often crops up with this form, as the teller of the story or as the main figure in it.

Writers and critics have commented on the peculiarly compelling nature of the story-within-a-story, when, in fact, we have no reason to believe that the teller is any more truthful than other human beings. Writers of all kinds have experienced, in the engagement of the story-within-a-story, the powerful independence of story. The mask, persona, and voice of the character telling the tale unlocks the author's imaginative powers of telling.

In fact, the story-within-a-story has probably been so effective for tale-singers and writers for thousands of years because it objectifies, puts into the song where you can hear it or onto the page where you can see and hear it, the mind's actual internal structure of telling the story, the account, the essay—an imagined structure of speaker, subject, audience and occasion.

New writers often have their first strong writing experience when they see a character in a situation telling a story, see the audience, and see the story being told and the fictional audience's reactions to it.

* * *

Frequently, authors retell in a story-within-a-story form traditional stories, such as Biblical tales, giving them special twists to illustrate the authors' argumentative intentions. The two reading selections here retell Biblical stories.

"The Sermon"
From **Moby Dick**
Herman Melville

Father Mapple rose, and in a mild voice of unassuming authority ordered the scattered people to condense. "Starboard gangway, there! side away to larboard—larboard gangway to starboard! Midships! midships!"

There was a low rumbling of heavy sea-boots among the benches, and a still slighter shuffling of women's shoes, and all was quiet again, and every eye on the preacher.

He paused a little; then kneeling in the pulpit's bows folded his large brown hands across his chest, uplifted his closed eyes, and offered a prayer so deeply devout that he seemed kneeling and praying at the bottom of the sea.

This ended, in prolonged solemn tones, like the continual tolling of a bell in a ship that is foundering at sea in a fog—in such tones he commenced reading the following hymn; but changing his manner toward the concluding stanzas, burst forth with a pealing exultation and joy—

"The ribs and terrors in the whale,
    Arched over me a dismal gloom,
While all God's sun-lit waves rolled by,
    And left me deepening down to doom.

"I saw the open maw of hell,
    With endless pains and sorrows there;
Which none but they that feel can tell—
    Oh, I was plunging to despair.

"In black distress, I called my God,
        When I could scarce believe him mine,
He bowed his ear to my complaints—
        No more the whale did me confine.

"With speed he flew to my relief,
    As on a radiant dolphin borne;
Awful, yet bright, as lightning shone
    The face of my Deliverer God.

"My song for ever shall record
    That terrible, that joyful hour;
I give the glory to my God,
    His all the mercy and the power."

Nearly all joined in singing this hymn, which swelled high above the howling of the storm. A brief pause ensued; the preacher slowly turned over the leaves of the Bible, and at last, folding his hand down upon the proper page, said: "Beloved shipmates, clinch the last verse of the first chapter of Jonah—'And God had prepared a great fish to swallow up Jonah.'

"Shipmates, this book, containing only four chapters—four yarns—is one of the smallest strands in the mighty cable of the Scriptures. Yet what depths of the soul does Jonah's deep sealine sound! what a pregnant lesson to us is this prophet! What a noble thing is that canticle in the fish's belly! How billow-like and boisterously grand! We feel the floods surging over us; we sound with him to the kelpy bottom of the waters; sea-weed and all the slime of the sea is about us! But *what* is this lesson that the book of Jonah teaches? Shipmates, it is a two-stranded lesson; a lesson to us all as sinful men, and a lesson to me as a pilot of the living God. As sinful men, it is a lesson to us all, because it is a story of the sin, hard-heartedness, suddenly awakened fears, the swift punishment, repentance, prayers, and finally the deliverance and joy of Jonah. As with all sinners among men, the sin of this son of Amittai was in his wilful disobedience of the command of God—never mind now what that command was, or how conveyed—which he found a hard command. But all the things that God would have us do are hard for us to do—remember that—and hence, he oftener commands us than endeavors to per-suade. And if we obey God, we must disobey ourselves; and it is in this disobeying ourselves, wherein the hardness of obeying God consists.

"With this sin of disobedience in him, Jonah still further flouts at God, by seeking to flee from Him. He thinks that a ship made by men, will carry him into countries where God does not reign, but only the Captains of this earth. He skulks about the wharves of Joppa, and seeks a ship that's bound for Tarshish. There lurks, perhaps, a hitherto un-heeded meaning here. By all accounts Tarshish could have been no other city than the modern Cadiz. That's the opinion of learned men. And where is Cadiz, shipmates? Cadiz is in Spain; as far by water, from Joppa, as Jonah could possibly have sailed in those ancient days, when the Atlantic was an almost unknown sea. Because Joppa, the mod-ern Jaffa, shipmates, is on the most easterly coast of the Mediterranean, the Syrian; and Tarshish or Cadiz more than two thousand miles to the westward from that, just outside the Straits of Gibraltar. See ye not then, shipmates, that Jonah sought to flee world-wide from God? Miserable man! Oh! most contemptible and worthy of all scorn; with slouched hat and guilty eye, skulking from his God; prowling among the shipping like a vile burglar hastening to cross the seas. So disordered, self-condemning is his look, that had there been policemen in those days, Jonah, on the mere suspicion of something wrong, had been arrested ere he touched a deck. How plainly he's a fugitive! no bag-gage, not a hat-box, valise, or carpet-bag,—no friends accompany him to the wharf with their adieux. At last, after much dodging search, he finds the Tarshish ship receiving the last items of her cargo; and as he steps on board to see its Captain in the cabin, all the sailors for the moment desist from hoisting in the goods, to mark the stranger's evil eye. Jonah sees this; but in vain he tries to look all ease and confidence; in vain essays his wretched smile. Strong intuitions of the man assure the mariners he can be no innocent. In their gamesome but still serious way, one whispers to the other—'Jack, he's robbed a widow;' or, 'Joe, do you mark him; he's a bigamist;' or, 'Harry lad, I guess he's the adulterer that broke jail in old Gomorrah, or belike, one of the missing murderers from Sodom.' Another runs to read the bill that's stuck against the spile upon the wharf to which the ship is moored, offering five hundred gold coins for the apprehension of a parricide, and containing a description of his person. He reads, and looks from Jonah to the bill; while all his sympathetic shipmates now crowd round Jonah, prepared to lay their hands upon him. Frighted Jonah trembles, and summoning all his boldness to his face, only looks so much the more a coward. He will not confess himself suspected; but that itself is strong suspicion. So he makes the best of it; and when the sailors find him not to be the man that is advertised, they let him pass, and he descends into the cabin.

"'Who's there?' cries the Captain at his busy desk, hurriedly making out his papers for the Customs—'Who's there?' Oh! how that harmless question mangles Jonah! For the instant he almost turns to flee again. But he rallies. 'I seek a passage in this ship to Tarshish; how soon sail ye, sir?' Thus far the busy Captain had not looked up to Jonah, though the man now stands before him; but no sooner does he hear that hollow voice, than he darts a scrutinizing glance. 'We sail with the next coming tide,' at last he slowly answered, still intently eyeing him. 'No sooner, sir?'—'Soon enough for any honest man that goes a passenger.' Ha! Jonah, that's another stab. But he swiftly calls away the Captain from that scent. 'I'll sail with ye,'—he says,—'the passage money, how much is that?—I'll pay now.' For it is particularly written, shipmates, as if it were a thing not to be overlooked in this history, 'that he paid the fare thereof' ere the craft did sail. And taken with the context, this is full of meaning.

"Now Jonah's Captain, shipmates, was one whose discernment detects crime in any, but whose cupidity exposes it only in the penniless. In this world, shipmates, sin that pays its way can travel freely, and without a passport, whereas Virtue, if a pauper, is stopped at all frontiers. So Jonah's Captain prepares to test the length of Jonah's purse, ere he judge him openly. He charges him thrice the usual sum; and it's assented to. Then the Captain knows that Jonah is a fugitive; but at the same time resolves to help a flight that paves its rear with gold. Yet when Jonah fairly takes out his purse, prudent suspicions still molest the Captain. He rings every coin to find a counterfeit. Not a forger, anyway, he mutters; and Jonah is put down for his passage. 'Point out my state-room, Sir,' says Jonah now, 'I'm travel-weary; I need sleep.' 'Thou look'st like it,' says the Captain, 'there's thy room.' Jonah enters, and would lock the door, but the lock contains no key. Hearing him foolishly fumbling there, the Captain laughs lowly to himself, and mutters something about the doors of convicts' cells being never allowed to be locked within. All dressed and dusty as he is, Jonah throws himself into his berth, and finds the little state-room ceiling almost resting on his forehead. The air is close, and Jonah gasps. Then, in that contracted hole, sunk, too, beneath the ship's water-line, Jonah feels the heralding presentiment of that stifling hour, when the whale shall hold him in the smallest of his bowel's wards.

"Screwed at its axis against the side, a swinging lamp slightly oscillates in Jonah's room; and the ship, heeling over towards the wharf with the weight of the last bales received, the lamp, flame and all, though in slight motion, still maintains a permanent obliquity with reference to the room; though, in truth, infallibly straight itself, it but made obvious the false, lying levels among which it hung. The lamp alarms and frightens Jonah; as lying in his berth his tormented eyes roll round the place, and this thus far successful fugitive finds no refuge for his restless glance. But that contradiction in the lamp more and more appals him. The floor, the ceiling, and the side, are all awry. 'Oh! so my conscience hangs in me!' he groans, 'straight upward, so it burns; but the chambers of my soul are all in crookedness!'

"Like one who after a night of drunken revelry hies to his bed, still reeling, but with conscience yet pricking him, as the plungings of the Roman race-horse but so much the more strike his steel tags into him; as one who in that miserable plight still turns and turns in giddy anguish, praying God for annihilation until the fit be passed; and at last amid the whirl of woe he feels, a deep stupor steals over him, as over the man who bleeds to death, for conscience is the wound, and there's naught to staunch it; so, after sore wrestlings in his berth, Jonah's prodigy of ponderous misery drags him drowning down to sleep.

"And now the time of tide has come; the ship casts off her cables; and from the deserted wharf the uncheered ship for Tarshish, all careening, glides to sea. That ship, my friends, was the first of recorded smugglers! the contraband was Jonah. But the sea rebels; he will not bear the wicked burden. A dreadful storm comes on, the ship is like to break. But now when the boatswain calls all hands to lighten her; when boxes, bales, and jars are clattering overboard; when the wind is shrieking, and the men are yelling, and every plank thunders with trampling feet right over Jonah's head; in all this raging tumult, Jonah sleeps his hideous sleep. He sees no black sky and raging sea, feels not the reeling timbers, and little hears he or heeds he the far rush of the mighty whale, which even now with open mouth is cleaving the seas after him. Aye, shipmates, Jonah was gone down into the sides off the ship—a berth in the cabin as I have taken it, and was fast asleep. But the frightened master comes to him, and shrieks in his dead ear, 'What meanest thou, O sleeper! arise!' Startled from his lethargy by that direful cry, Jonah staggers to his feet, and stumbling to the deck, grasps a shroud, to look out upon the sea. But at that moment he is sprung upon by a panther billow leaping over the bulwarks. Wave after wave thus leaps into the ship, and finding no speedy vent runs roaring fore and aft, till the mariners come nigh to drowning while yet afloat. And ever, as the white moon shows her affrighted face from the steep gullies in the blackness overhead, aghast Jonah sees the rearing bowsprit pointing high upward, but soon beat downward again towards the tormented deep.

"Terrors upon terrors run shouting through his soul. In all his cringing attitudes, the God-fugitive is now too plainly known. The sailors mark him; more and more certain grow their suspicions of him, and at last, fully to test the truth, by referring the whole matter to high Heaven, they fall to casting lots, to see for whose cause this great tempest was upon them. The lot is Jonah's; that discovered, then how furiously they mob him with their questions. 'What is thine occupation? Whence comest thou? Thy country? What people?' But mark now, my shipmates, the behavior of poor Jonah. The eager mariners but ask him who he is, and where from; whereas, they not only receive an answer to those questions, but likewise another answer to a question not put by them, but the unsolicited answer is forced from Jonah by the hard hand of God that is upon him.

" 'I am a Hebrew,' he cries—and then—'I fear the Lord the God of Heaven who hath made the sea and the dry land!' Fear him, O Jonah? Aye, well mightest thou fear the Lord God *then!* Straightway, he now goes on to make a full confession; whereupon the mariners become more and more appalled, but still are pitiful. For when Jonah, not yet supplicating God for mercy, since he but too well knew the darkness of his deserts,—when wretched Jonah cries out to them to take him and cast him forth into the sea, for he knew that for *his* sake this great tempest was upon them; they mercifully turn from him, and seek by other means to save the ship. But all in vain; the indignant gale howls louder; then, with one hand raised invokingly to God, with the other they not unreluctantly lay hold of Jonah.

"And now behold Jonah taken up as an anchor and dropped into the sea; when instantly an oil calmness floats out from the east, and the sea is still, as Jonah carries down the gale with him, leaving smooth water behind. He goes down in the whirling heart of such a masterless commotion that he scarce heeds the moment when he drops seething into the yawning jaws awaiting him; and the whale shoots to all his ivory teeth, like so many white bolts, upon his prison. Then Jonah prayed unto the Lord out of the fish's belly. . . .

Father Mapple gives sea-commands to the seafaring folk in the congregation (men on one side, women on the other) and uses sea-language to tell his story and argue his points. Not only did Melville alter a known hymn in a kind of parody to suit his story, he based the character of Father Mapple upon a well-known New Bedford preacher. With his own and the audience's seafaring language, the preacher tells the story to illustrate and argue his points about people's duty to the commands and will of God. His tale acts as a foreshadowing for what happens when people deny the will of God.

Read the foregoing excerpt from "The Sermon" out loud (in class, if possible) seeing objects, imagery, actions, characters, anything that catches your mental sight, and listen to Father Mapple's voice in your voice. Exaggerate all the perceptions, images, verbs, metaphors, all the special language effects, as you read it aloud. You will feel times when your eyes are naturally pulled up to look at the congregation. Let yourself look up at the congregation (your classmates) as Father Mapple looks at them and sweeps them with his eyes, meeting the eyes of individuals here and there. You'll find the story coming alive with this audience sense and being suppressed if you try to keep the story and its voice to yourself.

Notice and exaggerate verbs such as "He *skulks* about the wharves of Joppa . . . ," "There *lurks* . . . ," imagery such as "slouched hat and guilty eye," "a swinging lamp slightly oscillates in Jonah's room . . . ," and metaphors such as "panther billow leaping over the bulwarks," "terrors that run shouting through his soul," and "whirling heart of such a masterless commotion."

The excerpt ends with Jonah's imprisonment in the whale. After reading the following excerpt from the King James Bible, which covers as much of the story of the Book of Jonah as is covered by the excerpt from "The Sermon," read the full story of "The Sermon" in *Moby Dick*.

From

Jonah

Now the word of the Lord came unto Jonah the son of Amittai, saying, "Arise, go to Nineveh, that great city, and cry against it; for their wickedness is come up before me."

But Jonah rose up to flee unto Tarshish from the presence of the Lord, and went down to Joppa; and he found a ship going to Tarshish; so he paid the fare thereof, and went down into it, to go with them unto Tarshish from the presence of the Lord.

But the Lord sent out a great wind into the sea, and there was a mighty tempest in the sea, so that the ship was like to be broken. Then the mariners were afraid, and cried every man unto his god, and cast forth the wares that were in the ship into the sea, to lighten it of them. But Jonah was gone down into the sides of the ship; and he lay, and was fast asleep.

So the shipmaster came to him, and said unto him, "What meanest thou, O sleeper? arise, call upon thy God, if so be that God will think upon us, that we perish not."

And they said every one to his fellow, "Come, and let us cast lots, that we may know for whose cause this evil is upon us." So they cast lots, and the lot fell upon Jonah.

Then said they unto him, "Tell us, we pray thee, for whose cause this evil is upon us; what is thine occupation? and whence comest thou? what is thy country? and of what people art thou?"

And he said unto them, "I am a Hebrew; and I fear the Lord, the God of heaven, which hath made the sea and the dry land."

Then were the men exceedingly afraid, and said unto him, "Why hast thou done this?" For the men knew that he fled from the presence of the Lord, because he had told them. Then said they unto him, "What shall we do unto thee, that the sea may be calm unto us?" for the sea wrought, and was tempestuous.

And he said unto them, "Take me up, and cast me forth unto the sea; so shall the sea be calm unto you: for I know that for my sake this great tempest is upon you."

Nevertheless the men rowed hard to bring it to the land; but they could not: for the sea wrought, and was tempestuous against them. Wherefore they cried unto the Lord, and said, "We beseech thee, O Lord, we beseech thee, let us not perish for this man's life, and lay not upon us innocent blood: for thou, O Lord, hast done as it pleased thee."

So they took up Jonah, and cast him forth into the sea: and the sea ceased from her raging. Then the men feared the Lord exceedingly, and offered a sacrifice unto the Lord, and made vows.

Now the Lord had prepared a great fish to swallow up Jonah. And Jonah was in the belly of the fish three days and three nights. Then Jonah prayed unto the Lord his God out of the fish's belly. . . .

*　　*　　*

The following story was written in response to a story-within-a-story assignment subsequent to a reading of "The Sermon."

Adam and Eva Mae
Reginald Carlvin

I was about halfway through my weekly haircut, bored as I don't know what, from listening to almost the entire Third Pentecostal Unitarian Church of the Resurrection deacon and usher board discuss the Bible (in between watching the ball game, and gossiping about everybody's business almost as bad as their wives, whom they were hiding out from in this barbershop) when Sweet Daddy Seeky came in. I knew things were going to pick up now.

Now Sweet Daddy Seeky is the coolest dude—correction, make that coolest dude I know, period. No party ain't hip unless he's there, no club or jook joint is really jooking unless he makes the scene. The cleanest, baddest ride, the baddest finest women, plenty of money—that's Sweet Daddy. Maybe that's why all those other dudes his age (somewhere on the other side of fifty) didn't like him. Sweet Daddy never married, saying that there were too few of him to allow one woman to have a monopoly.

Okay. So anyway, Sweet Daddy strutted in, wearing his tailor made, all red outfit, twirling his ever-present gen-u-ine solid mahogany cane, and tossed his floppy gangster-hat over on the hat rack.

"Good afternoon, gentlemen one and all," he smiled, and the six or seven deacons and ushers mumbled something in unison.

"I just came in to get my 'fro fixed up," Sweet Daddy said, gently patting his six-inch silver natural. "Don't let me interrupt your conversation."

"We were discussing the Bible," one of the deacons said like that was supposed to scare Sweet Daddy.

"One of my favorite subjects," Sweet Daddy said, heading for an empty chair. "Matter of fact, I used to teach Bible class over at Third Pentecostal until all the hypocrites joined the church. That was about the same time you came in, right Brother Dixon?"

Now Brother Dixon didn't quite know how to take that, 'cause he didn't quite know how it was intended, but I did, and it was all I could do to keep an untimely laugh from exploding from deep in my gut.

"What subject were you discussing?" Sweet Daddy asked.

"Sin," somebody offered.

"One of my favorite subjects," Sweet Daddy offered casually.

"I bet it is," an usher made the observation, and they all started snickering among themselves. Sweet Daddy ignored this.

"Everybody talks about sin," he began slowly, "but they don't really know what they talking about. As long as you follow the Golden Rule, you can't commit no sin, for example . . ."

"You mean to say that the original sin was not a sin," a deacon objected.

"No, no," Sweet Daddy said, "the original sin was indeed a sin," he agreed, and I was disappointed. Usually, Sweet Daddy would go off on one of his wild tangents, making up some funny ass story just to irritate them. Even if he did agree with them he would disagree just for argument's sake. I thought he had let me down until he said, "But it isn't a sin for the reason everybody thinks it is. Now I could explain what I mean, but I don't want to bore you gentlemen . . ." he trailed off, waiting for them to "coax" him into telling his story, which is what he had in mind all the time.

"Awright, you talked me into it," Sweet Daddy said. There was total silence in the room. Sweet Daddy had the spotlight, the floor and every ear and eye.

"As it says in Genny-sees, first chapter, first verse, in de beginning, God created the heaven and the earth, and the moon, and sun and the stars, and the plants and trees and rocks and birds, and water and fish and on the seventh day he rested. Then about Wednesday or Thursday of the next week, God made the first Afro-American."

"You mean God created Adam," someone amended.

"That's what I said," Sweet Daddy answered. "God made the first Afro-American."

"How do you know Adam was a Negro?" someone asked.

"Adam was not no 'nee-gro.' You can say Adam was a black man, an Afro-American, or that Adam was a nigger, but he wasn't no 'nee-grow'." Sweet Daddy further punctuated his statement with a wave of his cane.

"Awright then," the speaker amended himself, "How do you know Adam was black?"

"Because," Sweet Daddy said slowly, "it says, right there in Genesis, second chapter, seventh verse, 'And the Lord formed man from the dust of the ground.'" Now the dust of the ground is dirt, 'cause that's what the ground is made of, right? Now there's black dirt, and brown dirt, and red dirt, and even gray dirt, but did you ever see any white dirt?"

"At the beach," somebody offered, but Sweet Daddy said, "That's sand, not dirt," to no contest.

"Anyway, the Garden of Eden was in Ethiopia, and nothing but niggers live in Ethiopia.

"So anyway," Sweet Daddy continued, "God made Adam, and then he made the Garden of Eden somewhere in Ethiopia, so Adam would have a place to stay. Now Adam was a cool brother, looked kinda like my man over there," he pointed to me, and I felt honored to be included as part of Sweet Daddy's stories, "but he was kinda slow sometimes. Now since he didn't have anything else to do, God let Adam name all the animals, which is why so many of them got messed up names today. But anyway, pretty soon, Adam had named all the animals and there he was, with nothing to do all over again, nothing to do to pass the time.

"Now God sends one of His angels to look after Adam, you know, to kinda check up on him every now and then. This particular angel's official name was 'The Archangel and Guardian Spirit of the Cold Northern Wind,' but everybody called him 'Cool Breeze' for short.

"So, Cool Breeze comes hopping through the Garden, halo cocked to one side, leaning hard on his wings, dressed in his white on white tailor-made double knit robe, while Adam was having his dinner: Barbecue and Kool-Aid."

"It don't say in the Bible that Adam ate barbecue and kool-aid," some purist objected.

"I know that," Sweet Daddy smoothly said; "they only had two chapters to tell the story in, so they had to leave out a lot of the details. Now as I was saying, Cool Breeze said to Adam, 'What it is, soul-brother?' to which Adam replied, 'Ain't nothing hap'nin,' (which it wasn't). So the Angel said, 'You sho'do like yourself some bobby-q, don't cha Adam?' to which Adam replied, 'Mumrmph,' 'cause his mouth was full.

"Now, you know how people get lazy and go to sleep as soon they eat and Adam was no exception, so while he was asleep, Cool Breeze got an idea, which he took back to the Head Man, which was, why not make Adam a helper so he could have somebody to talk to and what all, and the Head Man said, 'Whyeth not'eth?'

"Now here's where a lot of confusion comes in," Sweet Daddy digressed in his narrative. "Most people think that they literally mean Eve was made from one of Adam's ribs, which is illogical. You have 26 ribs in your body, 13 on each side. If one of them had been used to make the first woman, you might have thirteen on one side and twelve on the other, or thirteen on one side and fourteen on the other, but not thirteen on both sides. And even if man did originally have 27 ribs, where did that spare one go on the cage? Now that is the answer to the question." Sweet Daddy had us confused.

"Like I said before, Adam was fond of barbecue, so Cool Breeze gathered up the bones from Adam's barbecued ribs—spare ribs, get it?—and from that the first woman was made. And even today, a good woman is like a good slab of spareribs: pretty and brown on the outside, hot, juicy, tender, spicy, sweet, lots of meat on the bones, but not too much fat and gristle, well done, but not tough, and good in your mouth." Sweet Daddy was just getting warmed up now and he knew he had us going.

"So, when Adam woke up the next morning, there was Eva Mae. In the Bible, they just call here Eve, 'cause they couldn't translate the 'Mae' part into Hebrew.

"Now Eva Mae was built kinda healthy in the chest," Sweet Daddy said, indicating a good 42 inches, "and she wasn't too bad everywhere else, either. Adam liked this even though he didn't know exactly why. I told you he was kinda slow.

"So, Adam and Eva Mae lived happily in the Garden, counting animals all day and eating barbecue and drinking kool-aid (any flavor) all night, but after two weeks of this, they got bored again; after all, just how much barbecue and kool-aid can you stand?

"Now one day, Eva Mae was walking through the garden when she came up on the Snake. Now, in addition to having legs in those days, they were horny bastards too, 'cause after all, what is a snake other than a long skinny psychedelic penis with teeth and tongue?" Nobody offered any comment on Sweet Daddy's observation, so he continued.

"So, the Snake would try to screw anything; in fact, the day before, he had screwed a turtle, two porcupines, and a nearsighted giraffe, and today, he was gonna try to get down on Eva Mae. His plan of attack was a good one; he knew Adam had told Eva Mae it was forbidden to eat the fruit of the Tree of Knowledge, which happened to be an apple tree. Now let me explain to you about that," Sweet Daddy digressed again.

"Like I said, Adam was a nice enough dude, but he was kinda slow sometimes. Whenever Cool Breeze came down to visit with him, Adam would take up all of his time asking dumb questions just to make conversation, since he wanted some company and didn't have nothing else to do. On the other hand, Cool Breeze did and he wasn't up for all those idle conversations. One day, while Adam was asking Cool Breeze, 'Can I eat out of this here tree?' and 'Can I eat out of that there tree?' Cool Breeze was thinking about how much he'd like to be up in heaven, playing his electric harp and drinking MAD DOG WINE and watching comets blow up lady angels' gowns, and the more he thought about it, the more bored he got listening to Adam, so he decided to put an end to all of that crap, so when Adam asked him if he could eat of the fruit of the apple tree, Cool Breeze told him 'HELL NO!'

"Why not,' Adam asked him, and Cool Breeze said that that was the Tree of Knowledge and he was forbidden to eat of its fruit, and that if he did, he'd have to leave the garden, and Adam didn't want to do that since there was nowhere else to go.

"Now Cool Breeze took off for heaven, leaving Adam to think about that for a while, figuring that Adam would catch on to the joke and have a good laugh, but Adam didn't, since he didn't have the knowledge to know that he didn't have nothing to gain knowledge of. They didn't have no cars, no TV's, no atom bombs, no electricity, no modern conveniences, no money, so there wasn't anything to know about that he didn't already know about. But like I said, Adam was kinda slow, so he didn't know that he knew." Sweet Daddy smiled at us and said, "Do you all understand that?" and before we could answer, he continued.

"So anyway, Adam took this seriously, and he told Eva Mae, and Mr. Snake knew this, so he was gonna have Eva Mae eat his apple, then threaten to tell Adam unless she got up off a piece. But when Eva Mae bit into the apple, it was such a change from everything else she'd been used to eating, she ran off to tell Adam before Mr. Snake could run his game down on her. Not to be outdone, Mr. Snake just shrugged and slipped off to proposition a hippopotamus.

"When Eva Mae showed the apple to Adam, the brother almost had a fit. 'Mr. Snake said it was okay.' Eva Mae told him, but Adam didn't trust the Snake ever since the Snake tried to proposition him. See, in addition to being horny, the Snake was AC/DC, too.

"But Eva Mae, not to be outdone, said to Adam, 'How can *you* trust the Snake when you always got one hanging around you?' Adam said, 'Where?' and Eva Mae pointed between his legs and said, 'Right there.'

" 'That ain't no Snake,' Adam told her, and she said, 'Alright then, what is it?' to which Adam replied, 'I don't know,' which he didn't. Would you know even today what your di—uh, I mean penis was if nobody had told you?" Sweet Daddy asked the embarrassed deacons and ushers who were looking at one another for support.

"Well," Sweet Daddy continued, "even if Adam didn't know what it was, Eva Mae thought she did, so she said, 'It is too a snake, and looks like you gonna have two more soon, 'cause this one's got eggs.'

" 'For the last time,' Adam said exasperated, 'this ain't no Snake and these ain't no Snake eggs. If you don't believe it, come and see for yourself. And Eva Mae did.

"Now, Eva Mae had been examining Adam's Snake and snake eggs for about two or three minutes when something strange started happening. Right before their very eyes, Adam's 'Snake' started to grow—to about ten inches. Since Adam had never felt a particular part of his body get solid before he didn't know quite what to do. Did you know what to do the first time you became solid?" Sweet Daddy challenged the deacons and ushers.

"Now Adam knew that he would have to explain this to Cool Breeze, who was due to come by in a few minutes, but since he didn't know what was happening, he didn't know how to explain it, so he decided to try and hide it.

"He could have taken a cold shower, except that they didn't have any showers, so he did the next best thing, which was sticking it in a stream, but the fish thought it was just a big worm, so that didn't work.

"Next he tried to beat it down with a stick, but his 'eggs' weren't much up for that. He tried to bury it in the sand, but the only available sand was on an ant hill, so that didn't work. Finally in desperation, he got an idea.

"Now as I've said before, Adam was basically slow, but he did have his movements. He wondered how Eva Mae kept her 'snake' under control, when he suddenly realized that she didn't have a 'snake'. Instead, she had a little cave or hole of some kind. Now Adam knew that gophers lived in holes, and that rabbits lived in holes, and if Eva Mae had a hole between her legs where he had his 'snake', then that must be a 'Snake hole'. So, with a tackle Mean Joe Green would be proud of, Adam put his 'Snake' in Eva Mae's hole'.

"Well, needless to say, Eva Mae didn't know what was jumping off, or rather, why Adam was jumping on, so she tried to push his 'snake' out of her 'hole,' and Adam, afraid Cool Breeze would see it, tried to push it back in. This kept up for about three or four minutes, him trying to push it in and her trying to push it out; then, it seemed like he was trying to pull it out and she was trying to pull it in; and after that, they didn't really care who was pushing and who was pulling, just so long as they kept it up.

"Now about the time that Adam and Eva Mae had come to a cli-uh I mean halt, Cool Breeze came up and said, 'What do you think you're doing?' To which Adam and Eva Mae both replied, 'We don't know,' but Cool Breeze sure did, so he ran back and told the Head Man, who realized that it was too late now, since the original sin had been committed, which was a sin, but not for the reasons people think it is. He told Adam he would have to work hard all his life and Eva Mae that she would have to go through hard labor, which she would have anyway, but He just wanted to make her feel guilty, just because they had committed the original sin."

"You still haven't told us what that was," an anxious but exasperated usher quickly said.

"I'm coming to that now, no pun intended," Sweet Daddy said, slightly annoyed at being interrupted.

"After they left the garden, Adam knew Eva Mae, which is a fancy way of saying that he fu—uh, made love to her," Sweet Daddy corrected himself, "and pretty soon, they had Cain and Abel. After Cain offed Abel, Cain went out and found himself a wife and she had Ireal, who found a wife and she had Methujael, who found a wife who had Methusael, who found a wife and had Lamech, who went out and found two wives and they had Jabal and Tubalcain . . . Don't you see what I'm getting at?" The assembly silently and collectively shook their heads no.

"Don't you see? Eva Mae was the only woman the Bible mentions being created, yet Cain, Enoch, Ireal, Methusael, and Lamech all went out and found wives. They don't tell you where they came from, but they were there. Don't you get it? As soon as brothers and sisters found out about sex, they started fuc-uh, practicing so much, they let things get out of hand. Folks was practicing so much, 'til pretty soon brothers and sisters were being born so fast 'til they was coming out of nowhere." That was so beautiful, I wanted to applaud.

"So, Lamech and Jabal and Tubalcain, and in the meantime, Adam and Eva Mae were still at it, so they had Seth, and Seth 'begat' Enos, and Enos begat Cainan, and he begat Mahalaleel, and he begat Jared, and Jared begat Enoch, and he begat Methuselah, and he begat so many sons and daughters 'til they only mentioned Noah, since he was the only one to do something important other than beget Ham, Shem, and Josepheth.

"Pretty soon, there were black people, white people, brown people, red people, and yellow people all over the place, drinking and gambling and throwing beer cans in the Euphrates and the world was one big ghetto. Maybe that's why they say 'The World is a Ghetto,' " Sweet Daddy said reflectively.

"Anyway, the world was in such a messed-up state 'til God got mad and decided to evict all of the present tenants the hard way, and that led to the Great Flood, which a lot of people have a misunderstanding about," Sweet Daddy said, and stopped. There was an awed silence in the room as everyone waited for Sweet Daddy's next sentence.

"Well," a senior usher said timidly, "what happened next?"

"I would like to oblige you gentlemen," Sweet Daddy said apologetically, "but I must go elsewhere to discuss the wages of sin." And with that, he recovered his sky and cane and joined the baddest looking hammer I'd seen in a long time who was waiting for him outside on the sidewalk, wearing an outfit that left very little to the imagination but a whole lot to the temptation. He topped his hat to us, linked arms with her, and together they walked off down the street, with, I am sure, much the same expression that Adam and Eva Mae had the second time they practiced.

Notice how Carlvin in the first sentence sets the scene of the barber shop, introduces the teller of the tale, and prepares the way for Sweet Daddy Seeky to tell his version of a Biblical tale and make his point about it. The ending sentence of the first paragraph ("I knew things were going to pick up now") gives a boost of anticipation.

How does the two-part audience, composed of "the board of ushers and deacons" and our narrator in the barber chair, help the story? How would the story be different if we had only a friendly or an unfriendly audience? How does it work for the argument of the story when Sweet Daddy Seeky agrees that "the original sin was indeed a sin" and disappoints his admirer (our narrator) in the barber chair? What persuasive and argumentative techniques does Sweet Daddy use to answer the questions and objections of the deacons and ushers? How would you sum up Sweet Daddy's final interpretation of Original Sin?

Examine the mixed diction of the total story, the mixture of standard English and colloquial speech. The language of the story-frame is the language of our narrator in the barber chair. How does Sweet Daddy Seeky's language suit the story he tells? Could the story be told with a different setting and different characters? Why or why not? How would the story change with each kind of speech or dialect? How would the cultural references change, such as those of "kool-aid," "barbecue," "spare-ribs," and so on?

Reread the story of Adam and Eve in The Book of Genesis in the King James Bible and compare it to "Adam and Eva Mae."

Writing Your Story-Within-a-Story

Story-within-a-story writing often makes clear to nearly everyone that no writing is told without an audience, even and especially when the audience is imagined in your own mind. The sense of audience helps give the all important sense of space between the teller and the story. Students often comment on the wonderful economy of the story-within-a-story, how you plunge into the telling without preliminaries, how you strongly experience the independent movement and presence of story in this form.

Look over your how-it-happens subject and find and imagine someone telling a story or an account to someone else, to a single listener or to an audience. You can use it to retell a Biblical or other traditional or well-known tale, or you can use it to tell just about any kind of story or account that you can think of. The story-within-a-story works well with author and character opposites: Imagine your opposite as listener *or* storyteller.

In the story-within-a-story, you see and identify your internal listening with a fictional audience, your internal telling sense with the teller. See the teller from some distance back in your mind, toe to head, see characteristic gestures, objects, actions, facial expressions, the way the teller sits, stands, walks; hear his or her voice, tone, mannerisms of speech. Does he or she lean toward or back from the listener, or sit at an even, middle distance? See the space around the teller. Seeing the space often helps you perceive essential relationships that make up the strongest imagery about the scene. This sight of the space around the main character and around other characters and listeners may produce a metaphor or textural sense. Coach yourself to carry out these reminders in your writing. As you draw back, see something that catches your attention about the place in which the teller tells the story, such as characteristic objects, actions, or appearances. Exaggerate to bring out the space of the scene around the character, imagery, voice, gesture, and so forth. Exaggeration also heightens underplaying or understatement. When you get the sense of space between you and the story and around the characters and scenes in the story, you will usually experience an enhancement of your writing.

The teller of your story-within-a-story may be telling a dream or an account of something that happened, or retelling an old tale. Students often ask: Can "such and such" count as a story? *Try it and find out!* Notice the gestures that the teller uses to keep the audience's attention, to bind the audience to him or her. Keep your own storyteller's eye on the reactions of the audience. Listen to the *mixtures* of language in the teller's voice. When it seems to matter in your story, get the teller's eye contact with the audience onto the paper in some way too. How does the teller carry out intentions with everything that he or she tells? Many of you may hear and feel speech and voice permissions and actually employ them for the first time in the story-within-a-story.

Write the first draft as fully as you can, as swiftly as you can. Then type a draft, letting yourself re-live, re-experience, re-see, re-hear, re-explore and further explore everything in it, telling it as fully as you can while keeping the sense of ongoing movement.

When you do oral tellings, readbacks of inclass writings, reading aloud of your own and other students' writings, listen to the mixture of standard and colloquial language.

Suggested Assignments

- Retell a Biblical or other traditional story as a story-within-a-story, using it to argue a point, give advice, distract or influence an audience: Cain and Abel, Abraham and Isaac, Sarah and Hagar, Joseph and his brothers, Moses (several

Moses stories), Joshua, Daniel and the Lion, David and Goliath, David and Bathsheba, and so on.

- An opposite tells a story-within-a-story. Or an opposite is a listener to a story-within-a-story.
- A language opposite of yours tells a story.
- A story told as a sermon or other public speech.
- Other forms of telling a story-within-a-story: reports, memos, letters, etc.
- Develop a particular course of reasoning in any of the above suggestions.

Dialogue Form

The Ancient Greeks perfected alphabetic writing, beginning in the ninth century B.C. Because alphabetic symbols have meaning *only* as secondary forms of elements of speech, the Greeks without hesitation connected alphabetic writing to the oral forms of storytelling, tale-singing, drama, poetry, and dialogue. They developed the remarkable literature that we study today, a literature still alive to us. The dialogue was a form that particularly intrigued them.

For three thousand years the dialogue form has provided a way for a character or characters to argue a thesis, incorporating doubts, objections to the argument, and opposing arguments, into character responses. The original oral form can be found in the oral exchanges we see and hear everyday: He said this and she said that, as two people discuss or try to prove or get across a point.

With speech and interaction of two or more characters, the dialogue form develops a course of reasoning. One character usually (but not always) shows eventual mastery in convincing the other characters (and the reader) of the thesis of the argument. In telling, writing, and reading dialogues, we expect that many doubts and objections to the thesis will be asserted by a character or characters. We expect to be charmed and persuaded by the master character's force of wit and reasoning as he or she handles the objections. However, we can also conceive dialogues in which two or more characters contribute with equal strength to the success of the course of reasoning.

The dialogue may or may not contain elements of the physical scene in which it takes place. It may or may not have physical description of the characters. Sometimes the author's awareness of the physical scene, and of the appearance and gesture of the characters, comes out in the speech of the dialogue and works in some way with the dramatic development of the course of reasoning.

Imagined dialogues concerning philosophical, moral, political, or other issues commonly discussed in our speech and interaction with others can be warmly entertaining and persuasive in writing.

The Allegory of the Cave
Plato

Imagine a number of men living in an underground cavernous chamber, with an entrance open to the light, extending along the entire length of the cavern, in which they have been confined, from their childhood, with their legs and necks so shackled, that they are obliged to sit still and look straight forwards, because their chains render it impossible for them to turn their heads round: and imagine a bright fire burning some way off, above and behind them, and an elevated roadway passing between the fire and the prisoners, with a low wall built along it, like the screens which conjurors put up in front of their audience, and above which they exhibit their wonders.

I have it, he replied.

Also figure to yourself a number of persons walking behind this wall, and carrying with them statues of men, and images of other animals, wrought in wood and stone and all kinds of materials, together with various other articles, which overtop the wall; and, as you might expect, let some of the passers-by be talking, and others silent.

You are describing a strange scene, and strange prisoners.

They resemble us, I replied. For let me ask you, in the first place, whether persons so confined could have seen anything of themselves or of each other, beyond the shadows thrown by the fire upon the part of the cavern facing them?

Certainly not, if you suppose them to have been compelled all their lifetime to keep their heads unmoved.

And is not their knowledge of the things carried past them equally limited?

Unquestionably it is.

And if they were able to converse with one another, do you not think that they would be in the habit of giving names to the objects which they saw before them?

Doubtless they would.

Again: if their prison-house returned an echo from the part facing them, whenever one of the passers-by opened his lips, to what, let me ask you, could they refer the voice, if not to the shadow which was passing?

Unquestionably they would refer it to that.

Then surely such persons would hold the shadows of those manufactured articles to be the only realities.

Without a doubt they would.

Now consider what would happen if the course of nature brought them a release from their fetters, and a remedy for their foolishness, in the following manner. Let us suppose that one of them has been released, and compelled suddenly to stand up, and turn his neck round and walk with open eyes towards the light; and let us suppose that he goes through all these actions with pain, and that the dazzling splendour renders him incapable of discerning those objects of which he used formerly to see the shadows. What answer should you expect him to make, if some one were to tell him that in those days he was watching foolish phantoms, but that now he is somewhat nearer to reality, and is turned towards things more real, and sees more correctly; above all, if he were to point out to him the several objects that are passing by, and question him, and compel him to answer what they are? Should you not expect him to be puzzled, and to regard his old visions as truer than the objects now forced upon his notice?

Yes, much truer.

And if he were further compelled to gaze at the light itself, would not his eyes, think you, be distressed, and would he not shrink and turn away to the things which he could see distinctly, and consider them to be really clearer than the things pointed out to him?

Just so.

And if some one were to drag him violently up the rough and steep ascent from the cavern, and refuse to let him go till he had drawn him out into the light of the sun, would he not, think you, be vexed and indignant at such treatment, and on reaching the light, would he not find his eyes so dazzled by the glare as to be incapable of making out so much as one of the objects that are now called true?

Yes, he would find it so at first.

Hence, I suppose, habit will be necessary to enable him to perceive objects in that upper world. At first he will be most successful in distinguishing shadows; then he will discern the reflections of men and other things in water, and afterwards the realities; and after this he will raise his eyes to encounter the light of the moon and stars, finding it less difficult to study the heavenly bodies and the heaven itself by night, than the sun and the sun's light by day.

Doubtless.

Last of all, I imagine, he will be able to observe and contemplate the nature of the sun, not as it *appears* in water or on alien ground, but as it *is* in itself in its own territory.

Of course.

His next step will be to draw the conclusion, that the sun is the author of the seasons and the years, and the guardian of all things in the visible world, and in a manner the cause of all those things which he and his companions used to see.

Obviously, this will be his next step.

What then? When he recalls to mind his first habitation, and the wisdom of the place, and his old fellow-prisoners, do you not think he will congratulate himself on the change, and pity them?

Assuredly he will.

And if it was their practice in those days to receive honour and commendations onc from another, and to give prizes to him who had the keenest eye for a passing object, and who remembered best all that used to precede and follow and accompany it, and from these data divined most ably what was going to come next, do you fancy that he will covet these prizes, and envy those who receive honour and exercise authority among them? Do you not rather imagine that he will feel what Homer describes, and wish extremely

To drudge on the lands of a master,
Under a portionless wight,

and be ready to go through anything, rather than entertain those opinions, and live in that fashion?

For my own part, he replied, I am quite of that opinion. I believe he would consent to go through anything rather than live in that way.

And now consider what would happen if such a man were to descend again and seat himself on his old seat? Coming so suddenly out of the sun, would he not find his eyes blinded with the gloom of the place?

Certainly, he would.

And if he were forced to deliver his opinion again, touching the shadows aforesaid, and to enter the lists against those who had always been prisoners, while his sight continued dim, and his eyes unsteady,—and if this process of initiation lasted a considerable time,—would he not be made a laughingstock, and would it not be said of him, that he had gone up only to come back again with his eyesight destroyed, and that it was not worth while even to attempt the ascent? And if any one endeavoured to set them free and carry them to the light, would they not go so far as to put him to death, if they could only manage to get him into their power?

Yes, that they would.

Now this imaginary case, my dear Glaucon, you must apply in all its parts to our former statements, by comparing the region which the eye reveals, to the prisonhouse, and the light of the fire therein to the power of the sun: and if, by the upward ascent and the contemplation of the upper world, you understand the mounting of the soul into the intellectual region, you will hit the tendency of my own surmises, since you desire to be told what they are; though, indeed, God only knows whether they are correct. But, be that as it may, the view which I take of the subject is to the following effect. In the world of knowledge, the essential Form of Good is the limit of our inquiries, and can barely be perceived; but, when perceived, we cannot help concluding that it is in every case the source of all that is bright and beautiful,—in the visible world giving birth to light and its master, and in the intellectual world dispensing, immediately and with full authority, truth and reason;—and that whosoever would act wisely, either in private or in public, must set this Form of Good before his eyes.

To the best of my power, said he, I quite agree with you.

That being the case, I continued, pray agree with me on another point, and do not be surprised, that those who have climbed so high are unwilling to take a part in the affairs of men, because their souls are ever loath to desert that upper region. For how could it be otherwise, if the preceding simile is indeed a correct representation of their case?

True, it could scarcely be otherwise.

Well: do you think it a marvellous thing, that a person, who has just quitted the contemplation of divine objects for the study of human infirmities, should betray awkwardness, and appear very ridiculous, when with his sight still dazed, and before he has become sufficiently habituated to the darkness that reigns around, he finds himself compelled to contend in courts of law, or elsewhere, about the shadows of justice, or images which throw the shadows, and to enter the lists in questions involving the arbitrary suppositions entertained by those who have never yet had a glimpse of the essential features of justice?

No, it is anything but marvellous.

Right: for a sensible man will recollect that the eyes may be confused in two distinct ways and from two distinct causes,—that is to say, by sudden transitions either from light to darkness, or from darkness to light. And, believing the same idea to be applicable to the soul, whenever such a person sees a case in which the mind is perplexed and unable to distinguish objects, he will not laugh irrationally, but he will examine whether it has just quitted a brighter life, and has been blinded by the novelty of darkness, or whether it has come from the depths of ignorance into a more brilliant life, and has been dazzled by the unusual splendour; and not till then will he congratulate the one upon its life and condition, and compassionate the other; and if he chooses to laugh at it, such laughter will be less ridiculous than that which is raised at the expense of the soul that has descended from the light of a higher region.

You speak with great judgment.

Hence, if this be true, we cannot avoid adopting the belief, that the real nature of education is at variance with the account given of it by certain of its professors, who pretend, I believe, to infuse into the mind a knowledge of which it was destitute, just as sight might be instilled into blinded eyes.

True; such are their pretensions.

Whereas, our present argument shews us that there is a faculty residing in the soul of each person, and an instrument enabling each of us to learn; and that, just as we might suppose it to be impossible to turn the eye round from darkness to light without turning the whole body, so must this faculty, or this instrument, be wheeled round, in company with the entire soul, from the perishing world, until it be enabled to endure the contemplation of the real world and the brightest part thereof, which, according to us, is the Form of Good.

The psychologist Jean Piaget distinguishes between changes that can be simply *assimilated* and changes that must be *accommodated,* the latter requiring significant alteration in our thinking and usually causing the discomfort of moving from dimness to light. Children go through such changes in their view of the world as they grow up. Changes that require *accommodation* are the sorts of changes that Socrates discusses in *The Allegory of the Cave.*

The Allegory of the Cave gives a pictorial and narrative analogy of what happens when a person moves from one way of perceiving to a 'truer' or more comprehensive way. Socrates's analogy holds as accurately today as it did in his time. In the nineteenth century, biologists and other people resisted Darwin's theories of evolution. In the early part of the twentieth century, Newtonian physicists resisted quantum and relativity theory. We have seen resistance to change in just about every field. I had a biology teacher in high school who resolved the conflict between Darwin's theory of evolution and the story of Genesis by declaring that the theory of evolution was correct, but that God made it happen in the time span of the Genesis story. This resolution enabled her to continue doing work in her field. Physics has been convulsed with controversy over Heisenberg's Theory of Uncertainty and in a smaller way over the theory of semi-conductors. If Dick Lehnert, editor of *Michigan Farmer* is right (see "When Will You Be a No-Till Farmer?" p. 325), American farmers resist the evidence of a new and much more beneficial way of farming many crops. Any one of these subjects could be worthy of a written dialogue.

In this, one of the most famous of all the Platonic dialogues, Socrates's listener is ready to go along with him most of the way, as a good friend listens when you want to test some thinking of yours. If you read it aloud, you hear the irony and tongue-in-cheek humor of the listener's agreement, his slight making fun of Socrates's vivid, well-organized argument, the way we smile to ourselves as we listen to someone making an argument that we feel has been rehearsed for our benefit.

In other Platonic dialogues, Socrates does not have it so easy and often his listeners make seemingly sound, apparently reasonable, sometimes strongly emotional statements against what he has to say. In *The Apology,* which is Plato's dialogue account of Socrates's conviction and condemnation to death for "corrupting the minds of the young," Socrates may convince the reader of the rightness of his argument but certainly not the jury members who condemned him to death. Sometimes "rightness" of argument is not welcomed simply because it requires the listener to accommodate, to change his mind, which is, of course, the thesis of *The Allegory of the Cave.*

So we see and hear that the listener in *The Allegory of the Cave* reveals his sense of irony and is not simply a machine-like character agreeing with Socrates. This is the friendly listener. Writers of a dialogue may experience more excitement and find the writing easier with a friendly listener than with a contentious one. However, the dialogue form offers a unique opportunity to have fun with an unfriendly listener. Also, you can have friendly and unfriendly responders in the same dialogue. In *The Allegory of the Cave,* who is the figure Socrates refers to who laughs at the initiate's awkward confusion in moving from darkness to light and is called "someone" at other points?

* * *

The selection that follows is a realistic dialogue that could occur in the eating and drinking places of most campuses in this country. The dialogue occurs between two close friends, friendly opposites attracted to each other's different sensibilities; nevertheless, Elaine speaks sarcastically in her barbed way, and Louisa sarcastically in her more demure, diplomatic way. Such tones we often take with good friends. They discuss—and argue—an age-old theme, one that could have been discussed by Socrates and his friends more than 2500 years ago. Is it more satisfying to anticipate and go through the process of getting something, or to finally get it? The overall teller sees Elaine from the outside, but also has access to her point-of-view. The dialogue is interrupted by the accidentally triggered firebell, though by this time both Elaine and Louisa have made their points.

Which Is Better—Anticipating Something or Getting It?
Ann Hemenway

The ash to Louisa's cigarette was table-bent, curling like a Fu-Manchu fingernail towards the thick-varnished cafeteria table. Having dolefully checked the bill of fare at the steam tables and reckoned them, at the least, inedible, and having resorted to the only dish which was palatable—fudge ripple ice cream—Elaine slammed up to Louisa's table and the ash rolled off the cigarette and hit its mark some five inches from the tin ashtray.

Elaine glanced at Louisa's plate as she scraped into her chair. Louisa was idly picking at crusty macaroni and cheese. The macaroni and cheese, as Elaine knew, only came on the vegetarian ticket. Knowing this, she also knew that Louisa did not possess a vegetarian ticket, but a regular meal ticket; therefore she also knew that Louisa had somehow scrounged a vegetarian meal ticket from some unsuspecting soul, as only Louisa could.

"Was it worth all the trouble?" Elaine asked.

"Was what worth all what trouble?" replied Louisa innocently.

"Begging a veggie ticket from somebody."

"Ellie, it's always worth the trouble. Didn't you know that?'

Elaine looked again at the macaroni and cheese; the macaroni noodles were jelly, the cheese, cement.

"No," she said.

"Ellie, the meal ticket ain't what's important—it's the gettin' of it that's important."

Elaine dipped into her ice cream. "I don't get it."

"It's like anything else. What's more fun, the courtship or the marriage?"

"I've never been married."

Louisa sighed. "Oh, Ellie, you're bein' difficult. A true doubting Thomas. Okay then, what was moh fun—gettin' ready for the prom, or bein' at it?"

"You cheated, Louisa. I already told you. I had more fun getting ready for it."

"How come?" asked Louisa with a too innocent look.

Elaine set her spoon down and wiped her lips with her napkin. "Because I went with Norman Clancy, who had thick, black, dandruffy glasses, and walked like he perpetually had to go to the bathroom."

"Then why did you even like gettin' ready for it?" Louisa asked, stabbing a noodle.

Elaine licked a dab of ice cream off her spoon. "You asked which I liked better: going to it, or getting ready for it. Well, I didn't like getting ready for it, but I liked that a hell of a lot better than being at it."

"What a shame," sighed Louisa. "Ah had such a good time at mine. Ah think you're a very pretty girl, Ellie, Ah don't see why you had to go with a creep."

"I was a nerd in high school, Louisa. I was a weirdo. Anyway, I survived," she answered, diffident, again licking her spoon. "Besides, I don't see how this correlates to mooching a veggie ticket."

Louisa widened her eyes. "It correlates, all right. All Ah'm sayin' is, anticipation is twice as good as bein' there."

Elaine merely looked at Louisa and scraped a bit of ice cream from the side of the dish.

"Okay, Ellie, Ah'll have to explain it to ya further. Have you ever met someone and you like 'em, and then you don't know when your goin' to see 'em again, and then you do see 'em again, and it's fun, shuwah, but the excitement of wonderin' if you're goin' to see 'em again is even mowah excitin'?"

"No."

Louisa's face collapsed. "Nevah?"

Elaine shrugged. "Not that I can think of. I try not to get too excited about things like that."

Louisa lowered her eyelids demurely, looking at her plate. "Why not?" she murmured.

"Because it never turns out to be as good as you—." Elaine looked at Louisa's grinning face, "Okay Louisa, you win. But are you trying to say that the anticipation of a veggie ticket is better than getting the ticket?"

"No, Ah'm sayin' that the process of gettin' the ticket is mowah fun than gettin' the food."

"You mean it doesn't matter if the ends justify the means, the means is all."

Louisa jabbed at her cold macaroni and cheese and nodded, "It's tryin' to see if you can do it—"

Elaine interrupted, "You mean manipulate people into giving you a ticket."

Louisa smiled her wide, wide smile, "If you want to call it that."

"Do you time yourself?"

"Oh, no, Ellie, no, it's nothin' that calculated. Doo, Jesus, you're a cynical thing. When Ah get to the cafeteria and Ah see the filth they're tryin' to pass off as food—"

Elaine nodded, "Like slimey grey beef and pasty gravy . . ."

"Presahsely," said Louisa, wrinkling her nose, "That shiyut tastes like cardboard, and when Ah see that, Ah start lookin' around for someone Ah know who has a vegetarian ticket."

"Then what do you do?"

"Ah ask them if Ah can use it!"

Elaine looked at Louisa doubtfully. "It's that simple. You mean the people at this school are that generous about their veggie tickets when they're not generous about anything else? How long have you been here—"

The rest of Elaine's words were lost as the bell to the fire door went screaming into every conversation. Heads whipped around to look, forks were thrown on plates in aggravation and annoyance, and some people settled themselves flatly in their chairs and rolled their eyes. Nearly every day, some jackass would go barging through the fire doors at the back of the cafeteria and set off the alarm. Someone once proposed a fire-door firing squad: whoever barged through the door should be taken out and shot, and their body hung upside down in front of the door as a warning.

The bell screeched on.

Whoever opened the door had disappeared into the bowels of the campus unscathed. A dog that had been hiding under a back table (in the hopes of some scraps, no doubt) streaked across the carpet and fled downstairs. Elaine cringed and Louisa clapped her hands over her ears. A young man in baggy bluejeans and a long, thin ponytail yanked at the door.

The bell blared on.

A few people got up and left, others decided to scream along with it. An acquaintance of Elaine's, a round-cheeked blonde girl, caught Elaine's eye and mouthed, "I can't stand it!" Finally the balding assistant manager of Food Service, Inc. sauntered out with his lump of keys and a self-important, but ever so nonchalant demeanor (in front of these rich little college kids, thought Elaine) and with one expert turn of a particular key, switched off the alarm, and swaggered back to the kitchen.

A thick relieved silence jelled in the room like pudding, then quickly the tattoo of forks and chatter resumed.

"Jesus Mary Joseph," breathed Elaine, returning to her ice cream.

Compare "Which Is Better—?" to *The Allegory of the Cave*, the way each is told. Make lists of the differences and similarities and what these may suggest for your own writing of a dialogue.

Writing Your Dialogue

If you look around your how-it-happens subject area (or any other subject area that compels your attention), you'll find people discussing almost any issue you can think of. They may be arguing the best or better way of doing something on a job, or the morality of an issue concerned with the job. They may also be discussing where to go (and why) to school, vacation, or what kind of a job to take, or what to do about whatever concerns them.

Look at the possible characters of your dialogue. Are they contentious opposites or are they friendly opposites? Probably you should choose a friendly listener, or a friendly opposition, for most arguments, that is, give yourself a break as Plato did in *The Allegory of the Cave*. Even when we know that our writing may be read by an unfriendly audience, it helps us to imagine, as we are writing, a friendly audience that helpfully raises opposing arguments. We need to feel that our audience can be convinced, and then to find ways to do it, taking into account the audience's disposition.

Draw back in your mind and see the space around each character, see the characters from head to toe, see characteristic gestures, characteristic attitudes, tones of voice, ways of sitting or standing, body stances during a discussion. Write down statements for and against the thesis. See, play with, and rehearse your notes in your mind.

When you feel the writing going well, the characters responding, the argument developing in a lively, convincing way, you'll probably feel a spatial sense between you and the dialogue and among and around the characters of the dialogue, as with any writing that begins to "work" for you. Write your way into this imaginative spatial sense.

Write a rough draft from approximate beginning to approximate end, so you have a whole movement for retelling and rewriting, for exploration and development.

Letter on Behalf of Yourself

Frequently in life you have to make an oral or written argument to get something done for yourself. Commonly, you have to write letters on your own behalf. Experience in developing a course of reasoning in writing letters on your own behalf can also help you with oral arguments on your own behalf.

Jack London wrote the following letter to handle a nearly universally recognizable situation, the dunning of a creditor. He wrote it shortly after Wolf House, on which he and his wife Charmian had spent much time, energy, imagination, and money, burned the night before they were to move into it. Watch and listen how London defends himself and how he lays out the alternatives to his creditor and finds *a defensible line of argument*. Remember that London was famous at the time he wrote the letter.

December 29, 1913

Jack London
Glen Ellen
Sonoma Co., Cal
U.S.A.

Messrs. N. Clark & Sons,

Gentlemen:

In reply to yours of December 26, 1913, addressed to Mrs. Shepard, which Mrs. Shepard has kindly forwarded to me. I am glad to know that she forwarded to you the letter I sent her the other day.

Before we get into the business end of it, let me tackle the mental end of it, namely, your inability to understand my remark that if you had collected the $1000 when it was due, I would not be pinched for it now. The funniest thing is, that it is just that $1000 I am pinched for now. Put yourself in my place: Mrs. Shepard had charge of the house building and the bill paying. I earned the money. Mrs. Shepard always let me know roughly what bills and expenses were paid each month. Anything that was left over I spent. Naturally, since the $1000 was not collected at the time that it was due, it was left over, and I spent it. You know what "dead horse" is—this $1000 is now dead horse to me. I cannot unspend the spending of it in other directions. Please know that I am very busy, that I travel around a great deal, and that I do not keep up from moment to moment in the details of work performed for me by others. Not until the house burned down did I learn that a first payment due you had not been requested by you.

Now to the business end of it. Here is the situation in a nutshell: I have had what I call a real hard year. No drunken sailor ever spent money more lavishly than I have been compelled to spend it in the past several months on law and lawyers, in a battle line that encircled the globe. Every copyright I possessed was attacked, and I was being robbed by pirate motion picture companies, not only of rights, translation rights, second-serial rights, reprint rights, and all other rights whatsoever. I have just now won that fight. Please believe me when I tell you that I am still nursing my financial wounds. By the opening months of 1914, money will be pouring in on me. But I haven't any $1000 in cash right now that I can rationally afford in using to pay dead horse. On the other hand, if I should be sued, I would see my way to paying the money, plus the legal court expenses and costs, and shrug my shoulders & get along all right.

But you have so far been eminently kind & satisfactory (too eminently kind, for that matter), that I feel impelled to make a suggestion builded upon your own suggestion, namely, of a note. If you will take a note from me for the total sum of money at stake, payable in six months, I will have that note lifted before the six months are up.

I can only tell you that we are going ahead as fast as possible for the rebuilding

of the house. Men are chopping down the trees at the present time, which will go
into the new house.

Sincerely yours,
Jack London

* * *

The next selections, poem and letter, tell of a situation which many writers would
relish: an offer by an editor to defend his or her story, poem, or essay and, if the defense is convincing, publication of the piece of writing in question. The letter is addressed to Harriet Monroe, the editor of *Poetry Magazine,* who published many of the
best poems in the English language in the first few decades of this century. Read the
poem first and then the letter. In the course of studying the letter, refer back to the
poem. Watch, first of all, how Crane addresses—and deals with—Monroe, how carefully and respectfully he sets up his differences with the issue she has raised. Watch how
he finally chooses and states a *defensible line of argument,* and then supports it.

At Melville's Tomb
Hart Crane

Often beneath the wave, wide from this ledge
The dice of drowned men's bones he saw bequeath
An embassy. Their numbers as he watched,
Beat on the dusty shore and were obscured.

And wrecks passed without sound of bells,
The calyx of death's bounty giving back
A scattered chapter, livid hieroglyph,
The portent wound in corridors of shells.

Then in the circuit calm of one vast coil,
Its lashings charmed and malice reconciled,
Frosted eyes there were that lifted altars;
And silent answers crept across the stars.

Compass, quadrant and sextant contrive
No farther tides . . . High in the azure steeps
Monody shall not wake the mariner.
This fabulous shadow only the sea keeps.

A Letter to Harriet Monroe
Hart Crane

Your good nature and manifest interest in writing me about the obscurities apparent in my Melville poem certainly prompt a wish to clarify my intentions in that poem as
much as possible. But I realize that my explanations will not be very convincing. For a
paraphrase is generally a poor substitute for any organized conception that one has fancied he has put into the more essentialized form of the poem itself.

At any rate, and though I imagine us to have considerable differences of opinion
regarding the relationship of poetic metaphor to ordinary logic (I judge this from the

angle of approach you use toward portions of the poem), I hope my answers will not be taken as a defense of merely certain faulty lines. I am really much more interested in certain theories of metaphor and technique involved generally in poetics, than I am concerned in vindicating any particular perpetrations of my own.

My poem may well be elliptical and actually obscure in the ordering of its content, but in your criticism of this very possible deficiency you have stated your objections in terms that allow me, at least for the moment, the privilege of claiming your ideas and ideals as theoretically, at least, quite outside the issues of my own aspirations. To put it more plainly, as a poet I may very possibly be more interested in the so-called illogical impingements of the connotations of words on the consciousness (and their combinations and interplay in metaphor on this basis) than I am interested in the preservation of their logically rigid significations at the cost of limiting my subject matter and perceptions involved in the poem.

This may sound as though I merely fancied juggling words and images until I found something novel, or esoteric; but the process is much more predetermined and objectified than that. The nuances of feeling and observation in a poem may well call for certain liberties which you claim the poet has no right to take. I am simply making the claim that the poet does have that authority, and that to deny it is to limit the scope of the medium so considerably as to outlaw some of the richest genius of the past.

This argument over the dynamics of metaphor promises as active a future as has been evinced in the past. Partaking so extensively as it does of the issues involved in the propriety or non-propriety of certain attitudes toward subject matter, etc., it enters the critical distinctions usually made between "romantic" [and] "classic" as an organic factor. It is a problem that would require many pages to state adequately—merely from my own limited standpoint on the issues. Even this limited statement may prove onerous reading, and I hope you will pardon me if my own interest in the matter carries me to the point of presumption.

Its paradox, of course, is that its apparent illogic operates so logically in conjunction with its context in the poem as to establish its claim to another logic, quite independent of the original definition of the word or phrase or image thus employed. It implies (this *inflection* of language) a previous or prepared receptivity to its stimulus on the part of the reader. The reader's sensibility simply responds by identifying this inflection of experience with some event in his own history or perceptions—or rejects it altogether. The logic of metaphor is so organically entrenched in pure sensibility that it can't be thoroughly traced or explained outside of historical sciences, like philology and anthropology. This "pseudo-statement," as I. A. Richards calls it in an admirable essay touching our contentions in last July's *Criterion*, demands completely other faculties of recognition than the pure rationalistic associations permit. Much fine poetry may be completely rationalistic in its use of symbols, but there is much great poetry of another order which will yield the reader very little when inspected under the limitation of such arbitrary concerns as are manifested in your judgment of the Melville poem, especially when you constitute such requirements of ordinary logical relationship between word and word as irreducible.

I don't wish to enter here defense of the particular symbols employed in my own poem, because, as I said, I may well have failed to supply the necessary emotional connectives to the content featured. But I would like to counter a question or so of yours with a similar question. Here the poem is less dubious in quality than my own, and as far as the abstract pertinacity of question and its immediate consequences are concerned the point I'm arguing about can be better demonstrated. Both quotations are familiar to you, I'm sure.

You ask me how a *portent* can possibly be wound in a *shell*. Without attempting to answer this for the moment, I ask you how Blake could possibly say that "a *sigh* is a *sword* of an Angel King." You ask me how *compass, quadrant and sextant "contrive"* tides. I ask you how Eliot can possibly believe that "Every street *lamp* that I pass *beats* like a fatalistic *drum!*" Both of my metaphors may fall down completely. I'm not defending their actual value in themselves; but your criticism of them in each case was leveled at an illogicality of relationship between symbols, which similar fault you must have either overlooked in case you have ever admired the Blake and Eliot lines, or have there condoned them on account of some more ultimate convictions pressed on you by the impact of the poems in their entirety.

It all comes to the recognition that emotional dynamics are not to be confused with any absolute order of rationalized definitions; ergo, in poetry the *rationale* of metaphor belongs to another order of experience than science, and is not to be limited by a scientific and arbitrary code of relationships either in verbal inflections or concepts.

There are plenty of people who have never accumulated a sufficient series of reflections (and these of a rather special nature) to perceive the relation between a *drum* and a *street lamp*—*via* the *unmentioned* throbbing of the heart and nerves in a distraught man which *tacitly* creates the reason and "logic" of the Eliot metaphor. They will always have a perfect justification for ignoring those lines and to claim them obscure, excessive, etc., until by some experience of their own the words accumulate the necessary connotations to complete their connection. It is the same with the "patient etherized upon a table," isn't it? Surely that line must lack all eloquence to many people who, for instance, would delight in agreeing that the sky was like a dome of many-colored glass.

If one can't count on some such bases in the reader now and then, I don't see how the poet has any chance to ever get beyond the simplest conceptions of emotion and thought, of sensation and lyrical sequence. If the poet is to be held completely to the already evolved and exploited sequences of imagery and logic—what field of added consciousness and increased perceptions (the actual province of poetry, if not lullabies) can be expected when one has to relatively return to the alphabet every breath or so? In the minds of people who have sensitively read, seen, and experienced a great deal, isn't there a terminology something like short-hand as compared to usual description and dialectics, which the artist ought to be right in trusting as a reasonable connective agent toward fresh concepts, more inclusive evaluations? The question is more important to me than it perhaps ought to be; but as long as poetry is written, an audience, however small, is implied, and there remains the question of an active or an inactive imagination as its characteristic.

It is of course understood that a street-lamp simply can't beat with a sound like a drum; but it often happens that images, themselves totally dissociated, when joined in the circuit of a particular emotion located with specific relation to both of them, conduce to great vividness and accuracy of statement in defining that emotion.

Not to rant on forever, I'll beg your indulgence and come at once to the explanations you requested on the Melville poem:

"The dice of drowned men's bones he saw bequeath/An embassy."

Dice bequeath an embassy, in the first place, by being ground (in this connection only, of course) in little cubes from the bones of drowned men by the action of the sea, and are finally thrown up on the sand, having "numbers" but no identification. These being the bones of dead men who never completed their voyage, it seems legitimate to refer to them as the only surviving evidence of certain messages undelivered, mute evidence of certain things, experiences that the dead mariners might have had to deliver. Dice as a symbol of chance and circumstances is also implied.

"The calyx of death's bounty giving back," etc.

This calyx refers in a double ironic sense both to a cornucopia and the vortex made by a sinking vessel. As soon as the water has closed over a ship, this whirlpool sends up broken spars, wreckage, etc., which can be alluded to as livid *hieroglyphs*, making a *scattered chapter* so far as any complete record of the recent ship and her crew is concerned. In fact, about as much definite knowledge might come from all this as anyone might gain from the roar of his own veins, which is easily heard (haven't you ever done it?) by holding a shell close to one's ear.

"Frosted eyes lift altars."

Refers simply to a conviction that a man, not knowing perhaps a definite god yet being endowed with a reverence for deity—such a man naturally postulates a deity somehow, and the altar of that deity by the very *action* of the eyes *lifted* in searching.

"Compass, quadrant and sextant contrive no farther tides."

Hasn't it often occurred that instruments originally invented for record and computation have inadvertently so extended the concepts of the entity they were invented to measure (concepts of space, etc.) in the mind and imagination that employed them that they may metaphorically be said to have extended the original boundaries of the entity measured? This little bit of "relativity" ought not to be discredited in poetry now that scientists are proceeding to measure the universe on principles of pure *ratio*, quite as metaphorical, so far as previous standards of scientific methods extended, as some of the axioms in Job.

I may have completely failed to provide any clear interpretation of these symbols in their context. And you will no doubt feel that I have rather heatedly explained them for anyone who professes no claims for their particular value. I hope, at any rate, that I have clarified them enough to suppress any suspicion that their obscurity derives from a lack of definite intentions in the subject-matter of the poem. The execution is another matter, and you must be accorded a superior judgment to mine in that regard.

* * *

The next letter is a vigorous petition for a job, exaggerated as a parody of a letter on behalf of yourself but also written in earnest: The writer needed a job. What is his *defensible line of argument?*

To: Ward Heeler, 51st Ward Democratic Organization
Andrew F. Hyzy

Dear Sir,

There comes a time in everyone's life when they realize that they haven't lived up to their own expectations. One will wake up some morning and realize that life is but an empty shell, a skeleton of what it could be. There are many reasons for this: dissatisfaction with one's work, love life, social standing, financial position, whatever. The reason really doesn't matter. What matters is that there is a feeling in the pit of one's stomach that loudly proclaims Failure. I implore you, please continue reading and let me explain my position.

I want to be a garbage man.

First of all, and most importantly, I am a true-blue, loyal Democrat. You will recall, sir, that I was a senior in high school and not yet eligible to vote when I first volunteered to work for the Democrats. At that time I did not have a city job and could have quite easily told you to ring your own doorbells, put up your own posters, do your own campaigning. But I didn't; quite faithfully I stuffed envelopes with campaign literature and sealed them until my tongue resembled a spoon dripping with congealed gravy. I rang doorbells for days on end, relentlessly urging people to support you at the polls. I went into houses that resembled Hiroshima after the bomb; I was attacked by mangy vicious dogs; I was insulted by vindictive Republicans who would boldly slam their front doors in my face, making me feel humiliated and ashamed. I brazenly wore your campaign buttons as I stood in the hot sun, passing out literature on street corners, the victim of verbal abuse from all angles. I didn't even stop when I was mistaken for an immigration agent and shot at by a group of illegal Mexican aliens who quickly scurried under beds and behind curtains when they saw me at the door of their hacienda. Time and time again I listened patiently as people crabbed about dead trees, potholes, broken curbs, rats, busing, the Arab-Israeli conflict, snow removal, mortgage rates, and garbage cans. In the dead of night I went through the neighborhood, ripping down your opponent's campaign posters and replacing them with yours. I even hung them where it said "POST NO BILLS UNDER PENALTY OF LAW" on the walls. In short, sir, I busted my behind to help you get elected. On election day I stayed at the polls from 6:00 A. M. until 6:00 P. M., being careful to stay 100 feet from the entrance so there would be no trouble and your name wouldn't be blackened. I patiently helped old people crippled with arthritis out of their house, into my car, out of my car, into the polling place, and back again. I said nothing when they complained about the cleanliness of my car and then proceeded to ash their cigarettes on my car floor. When the election was over, and the results were in, there was nobody happier than me when you won. This was several years ago, sir, and I have been doing it ever since. Every time there has been an election I have frantically worked like a peasant for the Regular Democratic Organization. I have bought tickets to your annual golf outing, four of them each year at $30.00 each, and I don't even golf. I, sir, am a Democrat's Democrat. I stood in line for four hours in below-zero weather to view the body of the late Richard J. Daley. Don't I deserve to be a garbage man?

Sir, I was born to be a garbage man. I am eminently qualified for this position. As a child, my favorite pastime was going through alleys, excitedly poking through muddy coffee grounds, saturated Tampax and moldy blue vegetables, seeking some sort of treasure. My parents' and grandparents' homes still bear evidence of these worthy scavenger hunts. On my grandmother's coffee table rests a large green pottery ashtray in the shape of a leaf that I distinctly remember taking from a garbage can at 88th and Kenwood in my youth. I am not afraid of dirt, sir, especially when it's useful dirt. I live for garbage, sir, and to be quite frank with you, I can no longer tolerate the job I have now. For four years I have been working steady midnights at Police Headquarters. My social life is suffering, the pay I receive is barely enough to live on, and worst of all, I have a desk job in an office with five women and four men. I have done good work where I'm at, exceptionally good work, and I don't steal paper clips, ashtrays, rubber bands, and toilet paper like some of my co-workers, yet have been passed over every time a promotion has come through. I'm trying to finish school and can take only one course per semester. I don't want to leave the city, sir, but I'm afraid that if I don't get something better in the employ of the city, I will have to look elsewhere, possibly in private industry.

In closing, I would like to thank you for reading this, and express my appreciation for anything that you can do to help. As one of your better campaign workers, I feel that I can be rest assured that I will be hearing from you soon.

* * *

With the following resume, a fresh college graduate seeks her first major fulltime job. What is the *defensible line of approach* that everything in the resume contributes to and heightens?

RESUME

Jeanette Haynes
8525 Dorchester Avenue
Chicago, Illinois 60619
(312) 221-8659

EDUCATION:

October 1977 to Present   Columbia College, Chicago, Illinois
–graduated in 1980 with B.A. in
Writing/English

Septemper 1976 to May 1977   Bradley University, Peoria, Illinois
–majored in Journalism

WORK EXPERIENCE:

October 1979 to Present   *Tutor at Columbia College, 600 South Michigan Avenue, Chicago, Illinois.*
–tutored students in reading and writing
–analyzed students' problems and developed lesson plans accordingly

April 1979 to June 1979   *Internship with Cooperative Education Program at Columbia College.*
–researched, organized, and wrote cooperative education brochure

January 1979 to April 1979   *Editor at Counsel of Mojave Inc., 1140 West Argyle Street, Chicago, Illinois.*
–edited community newsletter
–recruited and organized neighborhood children to work as reporters
–planned production schedule
–typed stencils

November 1977 to October 1979   Part-time salesclerk at Marshall Field & Company, State Street, Chicago, Illinois.

COLLEGE ACTIVITIES

–*Columbia Chronicle* reporter
–*Bradley Scout* reporter
–Fund raiser for the Romeo B. Garrett Research Committee

REFERENCES

Available upon request

* * *

One test of a letter on behalf of one's self is whether or not it succeeds. London's creditors accepted his note; Harriet Monroe not only published the poem but published the letter too; the young resume writer got a job; the "garbage-man letter" writer decided that he perhaps had a more interesting career awaiting him in writing. However, whether or not an immediate success may have been generated by a letter on one's behalf is not the only test of its value to the letter writer. The argument that does not succeed with one person may well succeed with another, or feedback from the first attempt may show you what you should do to make the argument better, stronger, more effective. It also shows your prospective employer that you can write. Many firms think that writing is the most important skill you can have, along with the main skill of the job itself. Some interesting research supports the idea that writing is your most important adjunctive skill in almost any profession. Firms are even asking to see a writing sample from prospective employees.

Each of the reading selections is very different from the others, yet they have a few essentials in common. First, they all select *a defensible line of argument.* London tells his creditor how the situation came about and explains his own position and then handles the one alternative, that of a lawsuit, which the creditor might undertake, by implying that he London could pay the money now if forced by law to do it but that the creditor would find it much more comfortable and less time-consuming to accept London's offer of a note. He draws, by clear implication, upon the credibility of his reputation to back up what he says. Describe his tone and attitude. Use examples from his letter to support your description. How do his tone and attitude help his argument?

Hart Crane postpones his temptation to argue immediately for the value he feels for his poetic devices and effects. After seven paragraphs of discussion of the issues, he settles upon a line of argument that he can defend, the issue of the apparent illogicality of many metaphors in poetry. In the first seven paragraphs, he flatters Harriet Monroe's position, defers to her ultimate power of decision, and gets her agreement with him on certain basic matters. Then he defends his perception of the issue by referring to the work of other poets, such as Blake and Eliot, whose poetry has been either traditionally or recently admired. Only when he has established this justification, to which Monroe must agree, does he proceed to defend the questioned lines and metaphors in his own poem.

Hyzy, author of the "garbage-man letter," in his petition for a change in political patronage jobs, argues that, because of his earnest and successful efforts in doing grubby but essential campaign work for the Committeeman, he should be given a better job. After swamping the Committeeman with accounts of campaign efforts on his behalf, Hyzy suggests strongly that if he does not get a better job, the Committeeman will have to look elsewhere to find someone to do such harsh, repugnant work. How do his tone and attitude help support his case?

Haynes's resume puts forward the defensible line of her educational and work experience to date. She makes clear her interest and probable abilities for doing work in which writing plays an important part. She also clearly suggests her ability to work with people. The clarity, simplicity, and forthrightness of the presentation make a winning combination. What other qualities of hers are suggested by items in the resume?

Each of the letters on behalf of yourself is characterized by a special tone. They differ sharply in the kind of tone, but are similar in taking a definite tone. Hart Crane establishes a nearly ethereal, abstract tone in his first seven paragraphs, a level to which he invites Harriet Monroe for his argument. When we read the Hart Crane letter aloud, we sense his containing and handling of strong emotion. With his tone he puts himself, the issue, and Monroe onto a plane above any personal consideration. How does this tone aid his argument?

How does Crane show a clear sense for Monroe as his opposite and for how she will act and react? Why does he establish the points of agreement between him and her before he begins to move toward answering her questions? What are the two alternatives he sets up for her? Why does he save the discussion of the imagery of his own poem to last? Why would the explication of his poem not have been so effective if he had put it first in the letter?

What is the tone of Jack London's letter to his creditor? How can you justify London's reference to spending money in a way "no drunken sailor ever spent money"? Or the tone of "You know what dead horse is—this $1000 is now dead horse to me." How do you justify the berating, self-pitying, almost threatening tone of Hyzy's "garbage-man letter"? Do you think the letter was intended solely as a parody?

How does each letter-writer show clear, definite awareness of the receiver of the letter? Find anything in the letters that reveals this awareness of the audience. How does it influence the tone, organization, choice of words, and even the choice of imagery to be included in the letter? For instance, in the Haynes resume, what words and phrases suggest—without its ever being said outright—that this person likes to work with people and works well with them?

Writing Your Letters on Behalf of Yourself

Imagine something you want to get for yourself and to whom you have to write to get it. Find a line of defensible argument. In a job resume or letter of appeal for a job, there are ways to develop a line of defensible argument for even a flimsy background, with the connotations of words, phrases, imagery, and the choice of items to mention and highlight. Conversely, the presentation of a strong background can be ruined with wrong words, phrases, and tone.

You could try a parody of a letter on behalf of yourself. Remember that in a good parody, you incorporate and fulfill the structures of the form, the need for awareness of the direct receiver of the letter, tone, choice of words and imagery, organization of the argument, etc. Make notes on things that you want to be sure to speak about.

Imagine yourself writing a letter on your own behalf addressed to someone in your how-it-happens subject area. See an opposite of yours and write the letter that the opposite writes on his or her behalf. Or imagine a problem that someone has, or something that the person needs to get done, and write the letter that this person might write. Though such a letter could be the subject of a fully developed parody, you may find the parody by trying to exaggerate the letter that the person would write. See the situation and space around the letter writer, and around the letter receiver. See characteristic objects, actions, gestures, body stances, habits, mannerisms, and tones of voice. Make note of them even if you don't actually use them in the letter.

The style of the defensible argument changes according to your subject, your background for it, the nature of the audience, your strategy. You can test the defensibility in part by taking the opposite side and poking at your line of argument. Where does it seem weak, unsupported, inappropriate?

Sound the letter to yourself, being both letter-writer and letter-receiver, as you write it in pencil or on the typewriter. See the character of the receiver of the letter and write to influence him or her.

If possible, read an early draft of the letter aloud to someone.

"Let's Spoil" Approaches to Argument and Persuasion

There's no sense in pretending that most of the writing done in argument for or against an issue is altogether fair. Unfair arguments are constantly made against one issue or another. Editorials and reportage every day treat one issue or another relatively unfairly. If our side makes a successful unfair argument, we feel good about our cleverness; if we catch the other side in an unfair argument, we are quick to criticize them; if we have actual substance in our argument about issues dear to us, we want it to be heard, we want to get it across effectively to our audience—we resent unfair argument against it. In an unfair argument, the writer usually seeks an involuntary audience response, such as laughter, hate, love, to distract readers from the substance of opposing arguments and set up a negative attitude toward the arguments and the people who espouse them. The human need to be among those doing the laughing, rather than among those being laughed at, is powerful. We have all experienced it. We've found ourselves, in a group, smiling wryly at wit directed against things we hold dear, or even laughing outright. We don't want to be among the hated, the disparaged, or to be pushed beyond the pale of the loved. Such wit can also play upon our ambivalences about most issues.

The following argument would be considered unfair by any conservationist or wilderness lover and eminently fair by any proponent of unrestricted exploitation of resources.

Let's Spoil the Wilderness
Robert Wernick

A rancher in the hills north of San Francisco saw two bald eagles, one day last spring, killing his lambs. He did what King Agamemnon, or King David, or any other sheepman mentioned favorably in our history books would have done. He killed the eagles. But this is 20th-century America, and there is a law against harming any feather on a bald eagle. The rancher was arrested, and for days he was subjected to vile abuse in the press. Right-thinking people rained down such vituperation that you would have thought he had been caught molesting little girls or sending parcels to the Viet Cong. For right-thinking people he was guilty of a gruesome crime. What crime? He was spoiling the wilderness.

The trumpeting voice of the wilderness lover is heard at great distances these days. He is apt to be a perfectly decent person, if hysterical. And the causes which excite him so are generally worthy. Who can really find a harsh word for him as he strives to save Lake Erie from the sewers of Cleveland, save the redwoods from the California highway engineers, save the giant rhinoceros from the Somali tribesmen who kill those noble beasts to powder their horns into what they fondly imagine is a wonder-working aphrodisiac?

Worthy causes, indeed, but why do those who espouse them have to be so shrill and intolerant and sanctimonious? What right do they have to insinuate that anyone who does not share their passion for the whooping crane is a Philistine and a slob? From the gibberish they talk, you would think the only way to save the bald eagle is to dethrone human reason.

I would like to ask what seems to me an eminently reasonable question: *Why shouldn't we spoil the wilderness?*

Have these people ever stopped to think what the wilderness is? It is precisely what man has been fighting against since he began his painful, awkward climb to civilization. It is the dark, the formless, the terrible, the old chaos which our fathers pushed back, which surrounds us yet, which will engulf us all in the end. It is held at bay by constant vigilance, and when the vigilance slackens it swoops down for a melodramatic revenge, as when the jungle took over Chichen Itza in Yucatán or lizards took over Jamshid's courtyard in Persia. It lurks in our own hearts, where it breeds wars and oppressions and crimes. Spoil it! Don't you wish we could?

Of course, when the propagandists talk about unspoiled wilderness, they don't mean anything of that sort. What they mean by wilderness is a kind of grandiose picnic ground, in the Temperate Zone, where the going is rough enough to be challenging but not literally murderous, where hearty folk like Supreme Court Justice Douglas and Interior Secretary Udall can hike and hobble through spectacular scenery, with a helicopter hovering in the dirty old civilized background in case a real emergency comes up.

Well, the judge and the Secretary and their compeers are all estimable people, and there is no reason why they should not be able to satisfy their urge for primitive living. We ought to recognize, however, that other people have equally strong and often equally legitimate urges to build roads, dig mines, plow up virgin land, erect cities. Such people used to be called pioneers; now they are apt to be called louts. At all events, we are faced with sets of conflicting drives, and it is up to us to make a rational choice among them.

The trouble is, it is difficult to make a rational choice when one of the parties insists on wrapping all its discourse in a vile metaphysical fog.

One cannot talk of eagles, for instance, without being told by the wilderness folk that man, vile man, has no right to destroy one of God's beautiful creatures; that the bald eagle, besides being the symbol of the United States of America, represents all the will to be free and wide-ranging quest which made life worth living for our forefathers; and finally, that killing eagles upsets the balance of nature.

These aren't arguments; they are 100 percent nonsense. The most savage nature lover thinks nothing of vindictively squashing one of God's beautiful creatures when the creature happens to be an anopheles mosquito. And yet the mosquito in every respect but size is just as awe-inspiring, just as beautiful, just as free as any eagle. The individual eagle you see stretching his great wings as he searches for a fish or a lamb to eat is quite unaware that he is a symbol of anything. And quite rightly too: The eagle on our Great Seal is a perfectly mythical creature, and could go on being a symbol even if all eagles in the land were exterminated. The British, after all, have got on quite well without Acts of Parliament to protect lions and unicorns.

As for the balance of nature, this is simply an arty phrase to denote the status quo, whatever exists in a certain place at a certain time. In truth, the status quo is always changing. On our Great Plains, for example, the balance of nature consisted for centuries of immense herds of bison browsing thunderously on buffalo grass. In the late 18th century the balance consisted of Indians, who had acquired Spanish horses, slaughtering bison. Nowadays it consists of strip-farming, beauty shops, filling stations, beer cans, etc.

Naturally some balances are more desirable for interested parties than others. From the point of view of the bison, the balance of 1750 was infinitely preferable to any balance afterward; the Indians might have preferred the balance of 1800. From the point of view of Mother Nature, it doesn't seem to make the slightest difference. In her bloody, blundering way, she has been lurching along for millions of years, wiping out whole species, drowning whole continents, burning, ravaging, destroying. Our rifles and DDT are puny compared to the forces that annihilated dinosaurs and the multicolored world of the trilobites.

The most we can do, it seems to me, is to look after our own interests as best we can, and no more consider the feelings of the eagle and the rhinoceros than they consider ours.

Of course, we make mistakes, and hurt our own interests, as when ranchers kill off coyotes and are then visited with plagues of jackrabbits. But conservationists can make mistakes too. When they saved the beaver in Montana not long ago, the busy little creatures chewed down so many trees that they caused disastrous floods.

There is actually one legitimate reason for saving the wilderness, and that is that some people enjoy it and feel thrilled and ennobled by it. They have a taste for desolate landscapes and lonely nights under the stars. There is nothing wrong with such a taste. Everyone, everywhere, in whatever culture or society, needs something to help transcend the daily round of work and grief and boredom. Some find such transcendence by driving at illegal speeds on freeways, some by chomping on sacred mushrooms. An exultant thrashing through the wilderness may be a rich human experience—not quite so rich perhaps as reading the book of Isaiah or visiting the Parthenon, but certainly more varied, and more deeply satisfying than sniffing glue.

However, let us not lose sight of the fact that the wilderness taste is definitely a minority taste. Tamed and sanitized as modern wilderness areas are apt to be, with their almost total lack of large predatory animals and hostile Indians, they are still much too sharp of fang and claw for the vast majority of people—people who have worked hard for their comforts and don't see why they should give them up for a mosquito-clouded view and an icy dip in a mountain stream.

Wilderness lovers are a phenomenon of modern time; they are not tolerated in primitive cultures; the Bible doesn't have a good word to say for Ishmael. They breed in highly developed civilizations, where men have become bored with excessive cultivation and refinement. They affect old rumpled clothes, unshaved jaws, salty language; they spit and sweat and boast of their friendship with aborigines. But this is all veneer: Underneath, they are decadents, aristocrats, snobs.

I find something quite appealing about this particular form of snobbery. Compared to folk-song snobs, foreign-movie snobs and plain old social snobs, wilderness snobs present a fine manly appearance, and I wish them all joy as they follow the spoor of the wolverine and unroll their sleeping bags under the giant ponderosa.

But I urge them to avoid the great vice of their kind, which is megalomania. A man who has been infected with the wilderness lust is not satisfied with one stretch of forest, or one uncluttered mountainside. He wants hundreds of square miles of thicket and coulee and beaver dam and white water; and he wants them all for himself.

In the full euphoria which attends this fever, all ordinary human connections are apt to be broken. You struggle, slipping angrily through chalky rock and prickly pear, to the top of a ridge, and before you are miles of sagebrush flats, with white streaks of alkali, dry lakes, purple rocks, an immensity of desolation. Your heart fills with delight and then you catch sight of a rickety service station at a forsaken crossroads, and all the beauty drains out of the scene. A single beer can will spoil a square mile of woods; and as for the lovers' initials and fraternity Greek letters painted on rocks, it takes but one such pitiful imprint of humanity to spoil a mountain.

This is very wrongheaded, though it must be admitted that there is something grandiose about the wilderness lover in full flight. No one who reads it can forget the passage in which John Muir, the great American naturalist, describes how, at the height of a tempest in the high Sierras, he lashed himself to the trunk of a giant pine and for hours heaved and swung with the great tree, while the wind howled and whole forested mountainsides quivered to its blasts. The scene has a splendid absurdity about it.

I am reliably informed that it is impossible to duplicate Muir's experience in present-day California. There is not a high tree left in the state from which you can't see the lights of cars stabbing through the night on some freeway or other. And of course that spoils everything. For the particular sensation, the *frisson,* that John Muir was after, was not simply a physical one—you could get the same by lashing yourself to the mast on the Empire State Building. It was the exultant triumphant feeling of riding the blasts, of soaring over a vast stretch of pure convulsed nature, and doing it alone, without another human soul in reach of sight or sound.

I am sure that in losing opportunities for this sensation, Californians have suffered a great loss. It is, however, a loss which I am afraid we will have to put up with. The population of California, as of the world, is growing; this population is becoming more affluent and more mobile, and as it expands and covers the land with its detritus of motels and soda bottles, there are just not enough square miles left to satisfy the wilderness lovers.

I suggest to these worthy people that they bow gracefully to the inevitable and model their conduct on that of the kings of England. William the Conqueror and his descendants were great wilderness lovers, and they turned half of England into royal forests where, through the brambles and under giant oaks, they could ride for giddy days chasing the red stag and the wild boar; and any Saxon hind who came sneaking in looking for firewood or a rabbit had his ears, or worse, chopped off.

Grudgingly over the centuries the kings gave up this demi-paradise to the uncouth people of England, who insisted on parceling it out into grubby farms and grimy factories. The loss was irreparable, but the royal huntsmen prudently swallowed their grief, and sought a replica of their old pleasures on safaris in East Africa.

Just so our modern wilderness lovers may soon have to abandon the whole North American continent to the suburbanite hordes. Barring a nuclear war, which would bring back the wilderness with a vengeance, they will have to spread their wings a little, and indulge their special tastes in Spitzbergen and the mountains of New Guinea. And if the tides of civilization lap eventually over these too, there will soon be available excursion rockets to Mars and Alpha Centauri. And there should be enough unspoiled wilderness out there for anybody's taste.

In reading this essay, particularly out loud, we almost involuntarily recognize through our laughter Wernick's caricature of the earnest attitudes of some environmentalists. Some students want to believe that the author is being parodic, that he doesn't actually intend what he's saying: they can hardly believe that they've come to laugh against policies they hold dear.

How effective would "Let's Spoil the Wilderness" be without its first paragraph? Try reading (and imagining) it starting with the fourth paragraph in which the author states the main thesis. Try beginning it with the second paragraph. What does the author do in the first paragraph that sets going the logic of his wit and argument? The first sentence of the first paragraph tells us that a rancher saw two bald eagles killing lambs. How does the second sentence shift the ground of the reader's point-of-view and provide a different attitude toward what the rancher did, the blunt statement of which the author postpones until the third sentence? What words and phrasings in the rest of the paragraph tend to make you take sides against the "right-thinking" people who malign the rancher?

To keep the record straight, bald eagles hunt mainly fish. Where, later in the essay, does the author appear to show that he is aware of this fact? How does he handle it so that it reflects back to support rather than undermine the first paragraph?

How and where does the author exaggerate to get his effects? What about the first sentence of the second paragraph, which begins, "The trumpeting voice of the wilderness lover . . ."? What about the second paragraph, in which the author appears to acknowledge a number of worthy causes of wilderness lovers, yet makes them also appear silly? And the third paragraph, in which he acknowledges the conservationist's causes to be worthy, but characterizes their attitudes as "shrill and intolerant and sanctimonious"? In the fourth paragraph, he binds together his caricature of the conservationists' attitude and his thesis, *Why shouldn't we spoil the wilderness?*

In fact, we have to agree that, from the time human beings started using tools, they have been altering the wilderness. Many techniques of conservation involve alteration of the land. In fact, Wernick concentrates his attack on a caricature of the environmentalists' most vulnerable point, the "earnest idealism" that can embarrass any political movement. He focuses on the beer cans littering the landscape, never mentioning whole rivers and canyons buried beneath sterile man-made reservoirs, ocean estuaries and lakes and rivers poisonously polluted, the pollution of the atmosphere itself, the alteration of whole watersheds, the ruinous loss of soil from our croplands, millions of acres turned into desert, massive poisoning by pesticides and herbicides. Is the power of DDT and other pesticides and herbicides really "puny" compared to the powers of nature? If we examine the evidence that went into the banning of DDT (read Rachel Carson's *Silent Spring*), we would not find that such power is "puny." The view from an airplane window as we cross the continental United States shows how we have not only altered the face of the continent but practically sculpted it to suit our needs, and sometimes in ignorance of our needs. Is that "puny"? How much wilderness land is actually involved? Who else, besides the "wilderness lover," wants control over these lands? For what purposes?

Follow the rest of the argument paragraph by paragraph, section by section. Examine sentences, sequences of sentences, timing, exaggeration, choice of words, phrases, examples. The structure of his sentences contributes to the effectiveness of his approach. "He [the wilderness-lover] is apt to be a perfectly decent person, if hysterical." Here the initial idea of the sentence gives credit to the opposition, then abruptly undercuts the reader's opinion of it with the last phrase. "Worthy causes, indeed, but why do those who espouse them have to be so shrill and intolerant and sanctimonious?" The opposition's "worthy" ideas are acknowledged, but the rest of the sentence caricatures their tone and casts suspicion on their motives. "In her bloody, blundering way, she has been lurching along for millions of years, wiping out whole species, drowning whole continents, burning, ravaging, destroying." The alliteration of the "b's" spills into the savage sequence of participles, "lurching along," "wiping out," "drowning," etc., to give a mindless, heedless, clumsy characterization of Nature.

How does he use comparisons, examples? How does the telling of John Muir's lashing himself to a tree during a High Sierra storm support Wernick's general characterization of "wilderness lovers"? If we read Muir's writings, and do some reading and research on conservation and wilderness issues and on the historical allusions in "Let's Spoil the Wilderness," we might not agree with the author's characterization. Were the lands of the English kings actually given up "to the uncouth people of England"? Find research that shows that beaver dams act as a kind of natural flood control. What political and economic approaches does "Let's Spoil the Wilderness" actually support? What reasons can you find for preserving the wilderness? How does soil conservation fit into this argument? Would dealing with the substance of these issues diminish the effect of the author's disparagement of "wilderness lovers"?

"Let's Spoil the Wilderness" is a witty, artful, well-developed, brilliant argument. The "Let's Spoil" approach is a form in itself, as well as a set of techniques. Often used in political, economic, moral, religious, etc. debates, it occurs wherever we want to move opinions and allegiances swiftly, through powerful group emotions, to one side or the other.

*   *   *

In the following selection, intended as a parody, the author carries out the essentials of the "Let's Spoil" approach from the point of view of the imagined voice telling the proposal.

Let's Give Babies Drugs
Paula G. Trent

See Junior over there, aisle three? Yeah, he's the two year old in the blue and red Winnie the Pooh coordinate suit staring down that pyramid of canned peas. He's wondering if he can snatch out the center can without the others falling. He's thinking about the time he saw Uncle Jake snatch the tablecloth from under the dinner setting while the setting remained on the table. Oh hell, here it comes.

Here comes the stockboy. The scene flashes a message to his brain; his brain translates the message to his heart; his heart is pumping blood profusely to his legs. He's running up the aisle full speed with his white apron flapping behind him, the heels of his shoes thudding into the hard wax of the supermarket floor. He's trying to prevent the scene about to occur: he knows he'll have to clean it up.

He's only two feet away. There's a chance he can stop the disaster ahead. Where's Mother?

She's in the next aisle, battling that gray-haired lady for the last package of crisp, green broccoli. It's a classic battle. The ol' bitch doesn't even like broccoli. Her only reason for the battle is that her hand touched the pack first while reaching for the lettuce. It's how she gets her jollies, and there's Mom battling for the benefit of her hard working bread-winner and the little bastard in the next aisle. She wants them to have a properly balanced and appetizing meal. She can only concentrate on one action at a time. She hears the stockboy's exclamation, "Oooooh, shit!"

The center can is sliding out. Look at the little jerk standing there, watching that avalanche of cans rushing down, as that spinning can on the left comes so close to giving him just what he deserves: It's too bad it missed. Damn, those cans sure are loud. That got his mother's attention. "Biiilly," she screams, as her head jerks in the direction of aisle three. She rushes over, snatches him by the hand, makes the necessary apologies, and picks up a few cans until the stockboy, weakened by defeat, says, "That's okay, ma'am. I'll do it."

The smirk on the kid's face would make the Marquis de Sade uncomfortable. The drool of elation is streaming down the left corner of his mouth; it passes his chin and dangles from the Pooh logo. Poor Mom.

The scene just described wouldn't have happened if Johnnie had been sedated before leaving the house. Just one of Mommie's five-gram Valiums would have done the trick. This is just one of the many reasons kiddies should be given drugs.

I hear all you double-standard, baby-babbling hypocrites. I hear you shrieking collectively, "I'm appalled! My God, she's sick!" I know who you are. You're the ones that "kitchie, kitchie coo" into some poor infant's face until he begins to give you his point of view, then you hand him to his owner or keeper.

Hell no, I'm not sick. I'm speaking up for my pint-sized buddies. You've stood between them and pleasure long enough. You have used the pleasure principle the same way drugs are used, to alter and to retain and maintain control of the little tykes.

Mothers, how many times have you stuffed a bottle into Johnnie's mouth to pacify him when you couldn't determine why he was yelling his guts out? You wanted to hear Nina, of "All My Children," confess never-ending love to Cliff Warner after their turbulent separation. It was the quickest, most effective way to shut him up until you'd heard the smacking of lips coming from the screen.

This standard practice of shoving food into the kid satisfies his unknown desire but leads the kid down the road to a cholesterol-laden heart. That's right. In these early stages of development, you have ruined the child's natural shut-off mechanism, and food becomes the answer to most of his discomforts. That's how fat kids are made, but fat babies are cute, aren't they? When puberty strikes, they catch hell, and it's all your fault.

How many times have you held his chocolate pudding ransom in lieu of his eating those icky vegetables you wouldn't be eating if someone hadn't done the same thing to you? Of all the many varieties of veggies in the world, he has to eat the ones he doesn't like. This is nothing more than Mother's own little power trip in action.

How many times have you pacified baby by adding a drop of whiskey or brandy to the nipple of his bottle? He pulled himself into a cuddly, adorable ball and nodded off to sandland, as you stood there gazing down on his peaceful face. That wasn't peace, the kid was bombed out of his mind, but you were using a society approved drug and that made it okay.

How many times have you inflicted tiny spurts of pain to alter his behavior? To hell with "Spare the rod and spoil the child," manipulation is manipulation however it takes place. Psychologically, physically, or chemically, it's all manipulation. I say, let's use drugs. At least they're an open, honest and effective method of manipulation.

Mothers, there are many advantages to giving Johnnie drugs. Let's take the diaper/Pamper problem. You know how it seems the little tyke shits in his diapers when you're most hurried, when you're arguing with the repairman, pulling his siblings apart, or cleaning up Johnnie's latest mess. The siren goes off in its loudest pitch. It's continuous and aggravates the problem. You love Johnnie, but at that moment you just wish he'd shut up, at least until the task is done.

Well, with one lude (Qualude to you novices or squares), Johnnie will merely sit there and trip off of the ooziness of the squishy pack in his diaper as it moves around his ass and privates. This will occupy him for about two hours. You can have Daddy's meal on the table when the key turns the lock of the front door, or finish that juicy item over the phone about the new slut on the block.

Downers are not the only drugs that hold advantages for parents. Oh no, there's more. If the kid is a finicky eater, blow a couple clouds of grass (marijuana for squares) up the tyke's nostrils. He'll go through Gerber's complete line, even the stuff he spits back at you.

If Johnnie is overweight, and you can't get him to stop sucking up everything in sight, give him a couple of reds. You'll see a slim, new kid in no time, but be careful. As soon as you notice a sufficient weight loss, start the kid on withdrawal. You don't want him speeding away to nothing.

For the times the little bastard gets bored with everything you put before him (toys, T.V., etc.), drop some purple microdot into his Similac. Microdots provide inward entertainment for days. It's economic, too. Because of the flashbacks, you'll only have to give it to him every two months. Remember to pad the crib. Some of the little brats tend to fulfill their masochistic desires while on the stuff.

These are just some of the ways drugs and babies can be combined. Pick a drug. Be creative. If you are one of those people who lack imagination and creativity is not your style, send away for my booklet, *The Creative Matching of Babies and Drugs.* Just send your name, address, and one pound of Hawaiian or Columbian marijuana to: Paula G. Trent, P.O. Box 101657.

Let's stop being hypocrites who cover our real motives with fake and phony pseudo-protectiveness. Let's alter and control behavior openly and directly. With drugs, the kid doesn't become caught in the psychological web of having to differentiate a thousand motives and emotions that cause, or are caused by, one single act. Give the kids a break. Let's be honest with them. Let 'em have drrrrrruuuuuggs!

How does Trent use the structure and techniques of the "Let's Spoil" approach? Why does she postpone the statement of the thesis until the seventh paragraph? How does she directly satirize the publicized programs and experiments in which drugs are used to control children's behavior? How does she make her own parodic attitude clear? Do you recognize a parody of the old TV show "You Are There"?

Examine each paragraph and the sequences of sentences in Trent's parodic argument. How does she make drug-giving seem honest and open compared to other common parental methods of "control"? What advantages of drug-use does she set forth? Reread and find each one of them. What are the cautions? How do her tellings of the advantages and cautions satirize the use of drugs to control children?

Most parents would admit to such frustration with children at times that they would "almost" condone the use of drugs. Indeed, the age-old remedy of the drop of whiskey on a pacifier makes a great many parents a kind of user of drugs to pacify children.

What opposing facts and possibilities does the author leave out of the argument?

Writing Your "Let's Spoil" Argument

Choice of the issue and of the stance toward the issue is your most important first step in making an effective "Let's Spoil" argument, whether or not the argument is parodic or you actually support it. Choose an issue or policy on which there are strongly contrasting views. Choose a stance toward the issue with which at least a part of you can identify, though you certainly don't have to admit it to anyone.

Find a rational thread on which you can string the logic of your argument, e.g., human beings have been altering the wilderness since they had hands and brains with which to do it, or that all parents make use of ingested substances (food, candy, drop of whiskey on pacifier, etc.) to control children. The "Let's Spoil" bears many resemblances to the structure and techniques of Jonathan Swift's "A Modest Proposal" (see How-to-Do-It-Better—Parodic and Satirical Proposals. Indeed, both of our "Let's Spoil" selections are "modest proposals" for how to do something better.

Find a vivid example (or make it up) that you can use to shift the reader's point of view to the logic of your argument, such as the rancher's killing of the two bald eagles or the childs toppling a tower of cans in the supermarket. Keep one eye always on the reader's point of view. Begin choosing the facts, timing your sentences, choosing your words, phrases, imagery, examples, as you draw the reader into your argument. Of course, you either leave out, undercut, or make fun of the opposing attitudes and arguments.

If you're writing a parody, let yourself identify with the voice and point-of-view of an *opposite* of yours and exploit the voice and attitude from three points-of-view: the one with which you've identified, your own as the overall author, and that of your reader. In the contrasts of these three points-of-view, you find your wit, your satire, your way of expressing things. You exaggerate the argument the way your opposite would argue it. You leave out the facts that your opposite would leave out. The wit of the "Let's Spoil" argument makes a particular demand upon your ingenuity and creativity.

In your how-it-happens subject area, you'll find possible "Let's Spoil" arguments. If you're writing about a job, you could take the boss's or an opposing worker's point-of-view about an issue, find the rational thread on which to string the argument, and then parody it by arguing it as your opposite would argue it. In a school situation, you could argue for the use of drugs to control children in grade school, or you could argue for one kind of classroom education over another. If I chose "Let's Spoil Pedestrians" as my parody, I would give an example of a powerful, healthy man in a powerful, beautiful car running down a weak old person and the conventional social reactions to it. I would string my argument on the line of the idea that nature has always maintained excellence in its species through *predation* of the strong on the weak. I would support it with certain modern anthropological ideas that the human gene pool is being weakened by people who could not stay alive without the help of modern medicine or modern laws protecting pedestrians, etc. And so on. My essay would justify legalized mayhem and murder in the streets. These parodic "Let's Spoil" arguments can be unsettling in that they force us to see uncomfortable points-of-view. My point would be that our highways, streets, and courts that deal with automobile "accidents" are close to such mayhem right now.

Have fun with your "Let's Spoil" assignment. Use every twist and turn and push of exaggeration that you can come up with. Write a full first draft in one sitting, if possible.

V

Group Address

Of course, any form in this book could be addressed to a group, from the how-to to the general essay and the how-to-do-it-better, as well as to a single person "you," or to any variation of mixed audiences. However, group address is intrinsic to certain forms, such as public issue debates, eulogies, and folktales, which we will examine and use for writing in this section.

Course of Reasoning in Support of a Public Issue

Everyday you can hear assertions of "truth" (statistics, facts, etc.) in arguments for why such and such a position concerning a public issue should be preferred to another position. Sometimes it can seem to a listener or reader that adequate, seemingly reasonable "facts" and arguments can be marshalled convincingly to support absolutely contrary positions. In many, or even in most, cases these issues are argued by special interest groups. Even the person who receives no economic gain from the success of his advocacy may anticipate ego or other emotional benefits that make his or her interest a self-interest. You can safely doubt that there is any such thing as a wholly disinterested, selfless, impersonal argument.

How are you going to make written or oral arguments on behalf of your position on various public issues? Where do you locate facts? How do you find out as much as you can about all sides (or various positions) on a particular issue? How do you present facts? If you're out to support your self-interest group, what facts do you put forward? How do you handle facts contrary to your interest? How do you handle opposing arguments? And to what self-interests in your audience do you appeal to gain their support?

The public-issue debates selected here are likely to be discussed in this country urgently in the coming years: solar energy vs. nuclear energy; handgun control vs. unrestricted gun ownership; euthanasia vs. unlimited extraordinary life support; and others mentioned later in this section. You could research and write about them yourself.

Assignment 1—Solar Energy vs. Nuclear Energy

How can you research the issue of solar energy vs. nuclear energy? You can read *The Politics of Energy* by Barry Commoner (Knopf) and peruse the Notes section at the end of his book where you will find an extensive bibliography of further materials to read. You can write or phone the major power companies in your area and ask for their legislative or public relations packets on this issue. In a matter of days, you'll receive materials in support of the use of nuclear power for generating electricity. In a few areas of the country, the power companies may also send you materials on wind, solar, and water power. Go to back issues of *Scientific American, Science,* and other periodicals (use the yearly index of each periodical to find articles in your area of interest) to develop further sources. Peruse articles in the encyclopedias and the bibliographies at the end of those articles for more leads to research materials. Within a short while, you'll find yourself sorting through fascinating "facts" and arguments from absolutely opposed positions on an issue. You will also begin to find facts and arguments that are persuasive.

Make lists about differences between opposing arguments. What contrary assertions are made by opposing writers? What do you notice about the use of examples and imagery in their arguments? Where do you find arguments to be closely reasoned and well-supported with facts and examples? How do you define a "fact"? What is a lawyer's definition of "fact"? What are the political, economic and other self-interests supported by writers with opposing views?

What ways, if any, besides nuclear power, could the power companies use to develop "bulk" electricity? Do you think it's the government's responsibility for adequate, safe disposal of radioactive waste? Why do some writers in support of nuclear power make this assertion? What argument supports it? Why did the government accept the responsibility for the Research, Design and Development of commercial nuclear power? Should the government also accept the responsibility for R, D and D of photovoltaic cells and other solar systems?

Assignment 2—Handgun Control vs. Unrestricted Gun Ownership

The issue of Handgun Control vs. Unrestricted Gun Ownership is one that you and/or your class could undertake to research for oral and written presentations. You can write or phone the National Coalition to Ban Handguns and the Institute for Legislative Action of the National Rifle Association to receive their legislative or public relations packets. They will respond promptly. You'll find that the two groups present not only opposing arguments but opposing statistics, a close examination of which can give you insight into how people use statistics on behalf of their issues. You will also see, after an initial impulse to throw your hands in the air, some statistical presentations that are more convincing, more solidly worked out, than others.

Make lists comparing the differences between the arguments of the National Coalition to Ban Handguns and the National Rifle Association. What absolutely contrary statistics and other facts are put forward by the debaters on this issue? What appeals to emotion and passional beliefs do you locate? What appeals to self-interest? What "facts" are left out or ignored? By which side? Where do you find a particularly damaging fact to one side or the other simply not mentioned by the side it hurts? How does each side handle the opposing side's arguments?

How do you read the Second Amendment? Do you think it is unclear, ambiguous? You could research the intentions of the founding fathers who wrote the Constitution. Do you believe that the banning of handguns is the first step to the registration or confiscation of all guns? How would you argue your belief either way?

Where did you find a "good" argument contradicted by an even better argument from the other side? How do you account for the apparent differences in statistical presentations on similar issues? Are some statistical presentations and discussions more convincing than others?

* * *

Here's a position paper on the third public issue mentioned earlier. The author's experience as a medical technician was a how-it-happens subject for her.

Euthanasia
Marilyn Mannisto

Advances that have been made in the practice of medicine now make it possible to save lives and to sustain bodily functions in cases where previously death was inevitable. Improved diagnostic tools, more effective drugs, and life support equipment such as respirators and dialysis machines have saved thousands of lives. However, these same advances have raised serious questions as to whether, in certain cases, it is ethical to either remove or decline to extend extraordinary measures to prolong life. In other words, does euthanasia have a place in today's system of health care?

When I was a respiratory therapy student at the University of Virginia Hospital, and serving my first rotation in the intensive care unit, a 12-year-old boy was admitted in a comatose state.

Because his mother was an invalid, the family had installed a dumbwaiter so that meals and other supplies could be easily transported to her room. A few hours earlier, John had been cleaning out the shaft of the dumbwater in the basement, stretching up and forward on his toes to reach the furthest greasy corners when someone unwittingly sent it back down to the basement. John was unable to completely back out of the shaft to safety before the dumbwaiter struck him on the head and neck. He was pinned beneath it and his trachea was forced against the edge of the shaft entrance, completely obstructing his ability to breathe.

He was deprived of oxygen for at least 20 minutes from the time of the accident until the paramedics who arrived successfully revived his heart.

Now we watched as an anesthesiologist connected him to a respirator. When he finished, we stood silently by his side. The tranquility and sense of repose that comatose persons emit is of such a supernatural quality that it can have a hypnotic effect. The surrounding activity of the medical staff, conversations, glaring lights, dropped equipment—none of it seems to penetrate the dim recesses of this subterranean level of sleep.

John's father would come to the hospital each day and sit silently by his bedside, waiting for a miracle—waiting for his son to open his eyes, to speak his name, to grasp his hand. Each evening, John's father would leave the hospital without having had any of these hopes fulfilled. As the months passed, the strain of waiting for either his son to recover or to die began to show. He became shrunken in stature, lines of worry etched his face, and mounting hospital bills contributed to the premature greying of his hair. Soon his son's body also began to degenerate: his hair thinned, ulcerous bed sores began to burrow into his flaccid flesh, and his limbs began to draw up into a fetal position as his muscles atrophied and his ligaments shortened.

For two and a half years John's heart beat, his lungs expanded, and his blood flowed, but he never awoke. He even reached the point where he could be weaned from the respirator and exist with only supplemental oxygen, but his brain was dead. Finally pneumonia extinguished his life.

Because the paramedics had revived John's heart, the hospital did not feel justified in withholding life-support systems even though he had no discernible brain activity. The accepted medical definition of death is the complete cessation of function of vital organs—that is, no heart beat, no pulse, no respiration. The hospital's fear of legal prosecution prompted them to use extraordinary means to prolong John's life even though they were sure that he would never recover from his coma.

In the highly publicized case of Karen Ann Quinlan, her parents wanted Karen's respirator withdrawn after she had been in a comatose state for several months and they had given up hope for her recovery. When the hospital refused to comply, they appealed their decision in court. In 1976, the Supreme Court of New Jersey decided that the guardian, family, and physicians of Karen could disconnect her respirator and let her die if there was "no reasonable possibility" of her ever returning to a "cognitive, sapient state." This decision was based on her right to privacy from bodily invasion.

The rights of incompetent patients such as John and Karen, who cannot express their wishes as to whether or not they want their life to be prolonged under such circumstances, need to be protected. However, medical technologies and treatments need to be used in a meaningful way and not simply for the useless prolongation of life. In 1977, the Massachusetts Supreme Court reached a decision in the case of Saikewicz that, if it was comprehensively implemented, would ensure that both of these goals are achieved.

Saikewicz was a mentally retarded ward of the state who was suffering from an incurable form of leukemia. Because he only had the mentality of a three-year-old, his physician felt that chemotherapy in his case would cause unjustifiable suffering because of Saikewicz' inability to understand the treatment. Therefore, the hospital brought the case to court to receive permission to abstain from traditional modes of treatment. The court's decision was based on the concept of substituted judgment—that is, the court and a guardian that they appointed for Saikewicz tried to determine his wants and needs and to act on his behalf. The court decided that, based on his age (67), and the opinion of physicians that although chemotherapy would prolong his life, his total life expectancy still was not expected to exceed that of one to two years, that treatment could be withheld. Within a year, Saikewicz died from complications of his leukemia.

The use of substituted judgment can resolve the conflict that arises between the need to protect the rights of the patient and the need to permit physicians to exercise their sound medical judgment. In addition, such a practice would share the burden of responsibility among the family, guardians, and physicians so that fear of legal prosecution would not override the need to act in the patient's best interests.

A few years ago in a Chicago hospital, an adult accident victim was admitted to the neurology ward. Ed had suffered severe head and neck injuries and he was paralyzed from the neck down. He was placed on a respirator and soon afterward electroencephalograms showed that he had no brain activity.

When I came on duty a few hours later and checked the settings of his respirator, I found that the volume had been turned down to zero. Standing by Ed, you could hear him faintly gasping for breath above the sounds of the machine. I quickly readjusted the settings and reported what I had found to the resident on duty. He informed me that when they found out that Ed had no brain activity and apparently no family to consult, they had decided to "speed up" the inevitable—namely, his death.

As he told me this, he kept his eyes averted as he read a medical chart and his back half turned to me. "I will need written orders to that effect," I said as he began to walk away. Hesitantly I followed him until he paused by another patient's bed. "Listen," I said, "I'm responsible for making sure that all of the respirators on this floor are functioning properly. You will have to write orders to have the volume decreased or else to completely remove the respirator." I have to admit that my legal responsibility was the reason why I had the audacity to force the issue. The class distinctions in a hospital are as clearly defined as the caste system in India. For a lowly therapist to question the actions of a resident was equivalent to a pariah speaking disrespectfully to an Indian Brahman priest. However, my boldness was surprising enough to capture his attention and force him to acknowledge me. "Ok, Ok," he muttered, and rapidly strode down the hall.

An hour later when I came back to the ward, Ed was gasping for breath, the respirator was making all the correct noises but not delivering any air, and orders had not been written in the chart. This time the resident said, "I'm just following the head neurologist's orders—this guy's brain is dead and we need the bed for patients that we can help." We stood glaring at each other at a complete stand-off—he had brutally but effectively disclaimed responsibility for his action.

I called in my supervisor, explained the situation, and he set off to find the head neurologist. Finally, he was located and persuaded to authorize the removal of the respirator, but only after the resident and I had spent four hours playing tug-of-war over the respirator controls.

The next day, a new patient was in Ed's bed, Ed's file was marked "deceased," and nothing was noted in Ed's chart except for his cause of death—"respiratory arrest."

There was no "reasonable hope" for Ed's recovery, but there also was no one who cared if Ed died with dignity or not. Because of their fear of legal prosecution, the physicians charged with his care decided to act in their own interests rather than those of their patient. They tried to commit a covert act of euthanasia and they succeeded because Ed's chart never documented the hours that he lay gasping for breath because his respirator was tampered with or the fact that the cause of his death was a direct result of the removal of his respirator. To the uninformed, it would appear as though Ed died despite the use of extraordinary means to try and sustain his life. If brain death was an accepted substitution for the current definition of death, this entire situation could have been averted, and Ed's suffering would not have been exacerbated and prolonged.

The cases of euthanasia that have been discussed so far have all involved incompetent patients who could not voice their own wishes, but what of the patients who can voice their wishes and who do not desire further medical treatment but prefer to die a natural death? To date, courts have found that "the state's interest in preserving life weakens, and the individual's right to privacy grows, as the degree of bodily invasion increases and the prognosis dims." However, if the patient's prognosis improves or if they do not have a life-threatening disease, their right to refuse treatment can be overruled by the hospital and the state legislature.

A 73-year-old terminally ill man in Florida repeatedly tried to disconnect himself from his respirator, but his attempts were thwarted by the hospital staff. He was forced to petition the court to grant his wishes to refuse extraordinary means of medical treatment. Based on his right to privacy and his terminally ill condition, his wishes were granted, the respirator was removed, and he died a short time later.

Obviously our courts are too over-burdened to handle all of the cases in which patients want to exert their right to refuse treatment. This makes it that much more important that patients do know what their rights are and that these rights are clearly defined and publicized.

I became aware of the consequences of not knowing your rights to refuse medical treatment when I became acquainted with the case of a woman who had incurable breast cancer. Edith was in her late 60's and her cancer had spread until both her liver and her spine were riddled with tumors. Her doctors decided to treat her with chemotherapy after both surgery and radiation treatments had failed to halt the progression of her disease. The devastating side effects of the drugs that she received included the loss of most of her hair, the development of painful ulcerations in her mouth and throat, and the impeded ability of her bone marrow to produce red blood cells. As a result, she began to wear a wig, eating became a painful experience, and she frequently had to receive blood transfusions. She would come to the hospital each week to receive the drugs intravenously, and the nausea and vomiting that they evoked would last for days afterward.

Her husband of 25-years had to care for her as if she were his child: rocking her in his arms when the morphine failed to ease the pain, helping her bathe, supplying her with clean bed pans, and coaxing her to eat when the sight of food made her nauseous. Within a year she had dropped from 150 to 80 pounds as the cancer ravaged her body and her appetite abated. She could no longer cook, clean, shop, visit friends, take trips, or even exist without her husband's continual presence and support.

After six months of chemotherapy treatments, Edith did not want to continue receiving the drugs. She accepted the fact that they would only prolong her life and not cure her disease. Her physician persuaded her to continue the treatments, telling her that he had a legal responsibility to see that everything humanly possible was done to curb her cancer. Reluctantly she agreed and received the drugs for an additional six months without substantial or lasting benefits. Her physician finally gave up hope and further treatments were suspended. Edith received only morphine for relief of her pain.

As higher and higher doses of morphia were required to be effective, she began to live a drugged existence that was pierced only by the pain that wracked her body between injections.

One day her clouded mind temporarily cleared and she begged her husband to end her suffering and to give her an overdose of morphia. She wrote a brief declaration of suicide that was meant to protect him from legal prosecution, and he prepared the overdose and helped her to administer it. Her husband was charged with voluntary manslaughter but he received a suspended sentence.

Essentially, this was a case of "active" euthanasia, which is illegal and considered to be equivalent to murder because an action was taken with the express purpose of ending life. However, it is not unreasonable to assume that if Edith had known that she had the right to refuse further treatment and pressed her case in court her suffering would not have been as severe or as prolonged and perhaps she would not have felt desperate enough to ask her husband to help her end her life.

The findings of the courts that have examined the issue of euthanasia need to be uniformly applied on both a federal and state level. The application of the concept of "substituted judgment" used in the Saikewicz case could successfully protect the rights of incompetent patients such as John and Ed as well as prevent the shady manuevers that Ed was subjected to. The equal sharing of responsibility among a coalition of decision-makers that included physicians, family members, and court-appointed guardians would not only serve the best interests of the patient, but remove the fear of litigation that frequently prohibits the exercising of sound medical judgment. Furthermore, the substitution of brain death for the current common law definition of death would prevent the useless extension of life-support measures and allow persons who are in a vegetative state to die a natural death. Finally, the right of terminally-ill persons to choose whether they want to continue to receive medical treatment or not needs to be considered as a basic constitutional right.

Even with the implementation of the above measures, however, euthanasia will continue to be a hard issue to confront. The full burden for such decision-making cannot be delegated entirely to either physicians or the courts. We must all share the responsibility of seeing that today's medical technologies and medical treatments are properly applied. To this end, we all have an obligation to support legislation that both establishes euthanasia as an acceptable practice and which clearly defines the ethical limitations of its practice. If we do not, cases like those of John, Ed, and Ethel will continue to exist and one day we may experience first-hand the same anguish and despair that their loved ones did or the same humiliation and suffering that they did.

Mannisto summarizes in her first paragraph how, in the historical development of medical technology, we have come to a point where the human heart and respiratory system can be sustained in ways that were not previously possible, even when the patient's brain waves are "flat." In short, the new technology has generated new ethical issues. Using illustrative examples from her own experience as a respiratory therapist, and examples from research through reading, she argues for a new legal definition of death, "brain death."

In order to explain her audacity in challenging the intentions of a resident, she gives a comparison to the caste system of India. She uses positive exaggeration to give the sense of a comatose person: "The tranquility and sense of repose that comatose persons emit is of such a supernatural quality that it can have a hypnotic effect." Such exaggeration brings forth positively what people actually feel as they look down at a person in a coma. Metaphorically, it emphasizes the removal of the comatose person to another sphere, a sphere where perhaps other rules should be made to apply.

Writing Your Side of a Debate

First, find a public issue that interests you.

Here are a few examples of current public issues: Should fossil fuel producers (oil companies) be made into public monopolies as the telephone company and utilities have been? Why or why not? Should the responsibility of postal mail delivery be turned over to competitively commercial carriers? Should biology teachers be forced to give "equal time" to competing "beliefs" about human and life origins? Should auto companies be turned into public monopolies and required to meet very high safety standards? What causes fatalities in automobile crashes? What is a fair profit? Should social benefits be considered a part of fair profit and be required and rewarded accordingly? Should we reduce military spending? Should we nationalize transportation? Should railroads and housing be supported in the same way that the national highway system is government supported? Should we have national health insurance? How should we treat issues raised by genetic engineering? Should certain educational techniques be supported in mass education? Who should be responsible for the strict management of chemical waste? How should radioactive waste be managed?

Any one of these issues can be researched. You can argue one side of an issue, or you can compare and contrast and sum up all sides. For instance, if you've chosen the issue of the management of chemical waste, you can write or phone chemical companies to get material that sets forth their side of the issue. Write or phone the Environmental Protection Agency of the Federal government. Write or phone the Environmental Defense Fund for its "legislative packet." Most lobbying agencies concerned with public issues will readily send their legislative or public relations packets, which contain a small avalanche of articles, essays, and other presentations of facts and arguments on behalf of their position. What is the self-interest of EDF? What is the self-interest of EPA? What is the self-interest of the chemical companies? What is the nation's interest? What is your interest?

In your how-it-happens subject area you will find issues already being debated. Are open classrooms more educationally effective than rigidly disciplined question-and-answer classrooms? How do you define open classrooms compared to permissive classrooms? Should workers have more voice in the control of production and services of their place of work? Does efficiency actually rise in factories where workers participate in decision-making? Should the nutritional effects of fast foods be published where they're sold? Should nutritional contents be clearly stated on any packaged foodstuffs?

You can argue for or against any one of these issues and find research and opinion to back up your argument.

    Once you've done some research on an issue, and taken notes on your research, you might find it helpful to lay out your notes and write a letter to a friend, to a member of the class, to an imagined person, organizing the material as you try to tell that person what you've found out and come to believe. You could make use of opposites principles and take the "devil's advocate" position and argue or parody the opposing position on a particular issue, that is, exaggerate how the other side would argue it.

Eulogy of a Normally Uncelebrated Object

What do you say to praise a whale's tail? A matchbook? A hambone? A tunafish sandwich? An anchor? A broom? A toilet brush? How would you find *anything* to say in praise of these objects? To eulogize such an object makes you *look* at the object and find the relationship between your perceptions and your control of metaphor, imagery, allusions, and any other language possibilities. For instance, if you hold up a book of matches by its edge and look into its inner contents, what do the rows of the heads of matches remind you of? "Turning the book on its edge, you can see the inner contents; is it a mummified choir? a petrified garden of extra-terrestrial flowers? a visible catacomb of the dead? Look closely; as from one stem, four overlapping rows of stalks tipped by ovular heads rise from the blade-edge of the cover to nestle in the broad back-edge, like seeds in a seed pod." What are you reminded of when you *feel* the book of matches? "Let us pause and see what we can find written in the book itself. Feel its outer skin— smooth, like plastic, as though oiled. What other book has so many colors and such varied artifice upon its cover?"

The Book of Matches
Chris Sweet

Consider the most marvelous book of all, the book of matches. Matches: the name alone summons to consciousness a dream of perfection—for what *is* a match? A match, in the broadest sense, is unity within plurality, the formal cause of all philosophy, the answer to all faithful men's prayers, the impalpable palpable, and the undulating, imperturbable body of what we can know and what we cannot know, yin and yang, the marriage of light and darkness. At the mere mention of match, the mind flies to a last vision of Adam and Eve, there upon the plain under the eastern gate of Eden, fended forever from their recent seat of bliss by the fiery sworded angel, our first parents, who

> ". . . hand in hand, with wandering steps and slow
> Through Eden take their solitary way."

Was there a more perfect match? Woe to the serpent! Our wandering parents walk hand in hand, yet solitary, united, yet not as once they were, but forever two singular beings.

    I sing of the metaphorical match, the match of redemption through suffering. Was ever a match consummated that was not first struck, and roughly so? All matches first must be torn out and scraped along the raw, sand-textured striking strips of this life, if they ever are to confound oblivion and *live*! One thinks of the poet who sings of his old age and failing powers as he gazes into the fading furnace of his hearth, reduced now to glowing charcoal:

"In me thou see'st the glowing of such fire
That on the ashes of its youth doth lie
As the deathbed whereon it must expire,
Consumed with that which it was nourished by."

Just so, the rough scrapes and raging fires that nourish youth do finally consume the body that delighted in them. Yet, without the first striking consummation, can one ever say, "I live"?

I sing also of the allegorical match, the match of our divine origins. For who cannot conceive a match, the ideal match, perfect in all matchness? And are not all matches manufactured in some likeness of this ideal match? Yet look deeply into the book of matches; is not each plagued by an imperfection, a falling away from the ideal? Here the cardboard was cut unevenly; there one accumulated less sulfur upon its head than the others; another stretches taller; another bears a longer, more tapered neck. Some swell to red-tipped heads, some green-tipped, some hoary white-tipped. Yet all bear the image and stamp of the one, true match. Who has not observed at first striking how the sparks leap up, the flame shoots skyward, seeking from the moment it takes life to give itself back to the splendid face of divinity? Thus are men born shining babes, trailing wreaths of cloud, as it were, that point to our diviner origin. The first sparks and burst of flame—the idealism of inspired youth—last but a second; failing to touch the sky, the match forgets what it once knew and burns steadily towards its end. At last, in old age, it shrinks, it fails, it swells, it dies; poof! Thus all transient things return to their elements.

But let us descend from these heights of Promethean Caucasus to view the match in the dimmer light of everyday, a tiny fire stick, useful in a myriad of small, human endeavors. With a match you can pick up a girl in a bar, while her ". . . Soule transpires/ at every pore with instant fires." With a match you can find a lost contact on a dark stairwell, unfreeze a frozen car door lock, revive the doused pilot light. Yet in this mundane fact lies a great truth concealed: just as every fiery romance is also an ordinary affair between ordinary people, so the match is at once philosophic and extraordinarily ordinary.

Let us pause and see what we can find written in the book itself. Feel its outer skin—smooth, like plastic, as though oiled. What other book has so many colors and such varied artifice upon its cover? Its variations outnumber all the species of fish in the fresh and salt pools of the globe. Yet each book of matches is the shadow of its ideal, the one book from which all others take form. At first, it appears as two flat, rectangular surfaces back to back, yet not flat against one another, but somewhat farther apart at the top edge than at the bottom, shaped like a wedge or the head of an axe, to enclose a space that is roomier in the head than at the feet. This skin of the book is called the cover, for it covers the book's contents. On the cover you see the celebrated colorations and designs which mark the species—collectors value the cover above all else, for often the sight of a rare, long-missed cover shakes free the memories of past pleasures—a trip, a dinner, or a seduction. Upon the seamless plane of the cover is laminated a band of rough, fine grit—the striking board or striking strip, a surface designed for friction, and contrasting with the oily, glossy skin of the cover itself. Its sole purpose is to create enough heat through friction with the match head to ignite the match, called *striking the match*, or *giving a light*. But let us delve deeper inside to unlock further secrets of the book.

Turning the book on its edge, you can see the inner contents; is it a mummified choir? a petrified garden of extra-terrestrial flowers? a visible catacomb of the dead? Look closely; as from one stem, four overlapping rows of stalks tipped by ovular heads rise from the blade-edge of the cover to nestle in the broad back-edge, like seeds in a seed pod. Peering into the book from the side like this, you experience the same revelation as when cutting into the guava fruit for the first time, to reveal a hive of black, umbilically tied seeds; just so the head of the matches—for that is what they are—appear umbilically tied to the center of the book, from which they radiate like the seeds of the guava-womb.

Open the book by sliding the moveable portion of the cover upward with your thumb and peeling it back. The first thing you notice is that the cover consists not of two pieces at all, but a single strip wrapped around the matches and, when closed, tucked in upon itself, so that the unresistant match heads are completely ensconsed. Not only that; the striking strip on the outside stretches along the blade-edge of the book while the heads nuzzle a safe distance away under the folds of the broad-edge; moreover, the striking strip traverses the back of the book (though, to speak rightly, the book has neither true front nor true back, for it can be read from either direction, but since it must be entered from the tucked-in side, and since our concept of "frontness" implies the gates of access, and when we show our backs it is as if to say, "Keep away, don't come near, I wish to be alone, I wish to deny you access to me," I will call the tucked in face of the book—though truly whether it has a face or not one may dispute—call this face of the book, its front) so that there is no way a striking match could pass over its unexposed brothers to ignite them, and striker, in a painful and injurious conflagration.

But let us return to our investigation of the interior structure of the book. The inner surface of the cover is to the outer, as is mere paper to plastic. The surface feels less smooth, and not at all oily. The inner skin soils easily, and it cannot be cleaned, except by wearing away, through friction, as one does when erasing pencil marks from paper with a rubber eraser. Having both texture and form of paper, the inner cover of the book often serves for jotting down names and phone numbers, significant dates, poems, and messages of all sorts, for which (because of its smallness) it is often found more convenient than a journal. In this respect it contrasts with the outer cover, which will not take the inky impressions of a ball point, as though you tried to write over a grease spot or a peeled stick of margarine; press harder, you'll only crease the surface with invisible lines.

Now look at the exposed match heads from the top down and you will see four parallel rows of staggered oval heads; those four rows spring from two strips of cardboard stapled at the base, and the staggering effect results from the heads being broader, due to their accumulation of sulfur, than the stalks upon which they stand. Looking at the stalks from this vantage point, one cannot escape being reminded of broccoli, whose tiny seed heads are similarly attached by filaments to the great, muscular central stalk of the plant; the seed heads of broccoli being larger than their stems, they, too, flower out and spread themselves broadly, like these matches, although there be only twenty matches to a book but countless thousands of seed heads to a single stalk of the vegetable.

Proceed now to the great lynch-pin, the fragment of extruded steel which clawlike grips the cover and sandwiches the match stems between its circling arms, the prime principle of unity in the book: the small staple. Its arms hold everything together; take it out and the book falls apart in your hands, and no glue can replace it, no reinsertion can bring back the firm unity that was before. The process of extracting the staple may not be reversed. Taken apart, the book reveals itself as no more than a twisted particle of wire and three unmatched pieces of cardboard. Once the mathboards are out of their protective casing, they rapidly decay from moisture, friction, and bending; moreover, they become a safety hazard. Lose the cover, and you lose the best of striking surfaces, rendering your matches unusable. Better to leave the complex structure as it is, clasped in the circle of wire, tight as a loving woman's arms hold the object they love and keep it from flying apart like a universe bereft of gravity and all natural laws. In shape the staple nearly makes a full circle, but its ends stay perpetually an eighth of an inch apart, like two hands nearly touching, though they are one and the same staple. Numberless are the works of art bound by the feminine encompassing principle: to name but two, there is Lena in Faulkner's *Light in August,* and there is Molly Bloom in *Ulysses,* who begins her day with a sleep-muffled "No," and ends with "yes I said yes I will Yes." Just so, the looping staple and the book itself contain all yes and no, all birth and death, all opposites. All this you may read in the book of matches.

With the word "match" itself, the author conjures up meanings—allusions and other associations—that discover for him the parodic theme of unity in diversity. Then, throughout the main body of the eulogy, he develops the comparisons that come to him from setting the direct perceptions of the matchbook side by side in his mind with the thematic allusions from the word "match." He makes the struck match the metaphor for life itself. "Was ever a match consummated that was not first struck, and roughly so?" The book of matches also becomes a metaphor for our relationship to our divine origins, in which direct perceptions of matches feed into the metaphor of our relation to the ideal. "And are not all matches manufactured in some likeness of this ideal match? Yet look deeply into the book of matches: is not each plagued by an imperfection, a falling away from the ideal? Here the cardboard was cut unevenly. . . ." The sequence of perceptions, as well as the themes, influence the sentence structure. "Open the book by sliding the movable portion of the cover upward with your thumb and peeling it back. The first thing you notice is that the cover consists not of two pieces at all. . . ." Sweet ends by making a final binding metaphor with the staple of the matchbook. "Its arms hold everything together. . . . In shape the staple nearly makes a full circle, but its ends stay perpetually an eighth of an inch apart, like two hands nearly touching, though they are one and the same staple." His themes are always worked off his direct perceptions, giving direction to the style.

Writing Your Eulogy of a Normally Uncelebrated Object

How do you select the normally uncelebrated object? Choose an object that somehow particularly attracts your attention. You may find out which object really does so when you start writing about it. If the object and your associations with your perceptions of it tickle your sense of humor, that's a good sign. Something about the object, your awareness of the reader's probable perception of it, may take your attention as a first issue to deal with: for Sweet it was the allusions generated by associations with the name "match." Dwell upon your direct perceptions of the object as you look at it in your mind, or as you actually handle it. In the interplay of your perceptions and associations, you'll discover your theme. When you discover it, you'll experience an even stronger interplay between the theme and perceptions and associations.

Exaggerate. Exaggerate. Exaggerate to find hyperbole, imagery, alliteration, any trick of language or perception that comes to you. Let any metaphor or other phrasing suggest other devices of language for the eulogy, a kind of chain-reaction.

When you rehearse the eulogy in your mind, when you play with perceptions and associations and theme, and when you begin to write, get the sense of yourself holding forth to an immediate audience—to your class, or to one person in it, or to an audience you imagine. Let perceptions, associations, and theme influence your sentence structure.

The eulogy of a normally uncelebrated object particularly challenges your sense of the relationship of your perception to your style.

Folktale

Originally, folktales were told to a small group of people who sat within easy voice range and eye contact of a teller. The sense of the audience is usually broader than in a how-to in which the "you" is assumed to be the learner and doer. You can see an example of the original situation of a folktale telling in the point-of-view selection, "The Telling of an Anansi Tale." The structure of folktales—their repetitions, their imagery, their overall *style*—varies from culture to culture; but each culture's folktales use devices that not only aid memory-storage but also give form to carry the meaning. Many of the Grimms' tales have a three-stage climactic structure. Other peoples used vivid imagery in narrative sequences without climax, as in Eskimo tales. Frequently, particular characters show up again and again in folktales, such as Jabbo, Big John, Mike Fink, Dick Whittington, Coyote, and the tricksters indigenous to almost every culture. The fact that stories change from one teller to another verifies that oral culture treats its literature dynamically as well as seeks stability for it with the memory-aid structures.

Storytelling is natural to human beings. All peoples tell stories or narratives of one kind or another. Folktales told by oral storytellers are one of the main means by which a preliterate people understood itself to be a people, with identity, morality, history, legacy of beliefs and myths. Such storytelling is restorative, entertaining, instructive, and revivifying of individual and communal imagination and feeling. In the broadest sense, story is the rescue of what would otherwise be lost. Whether we get our stories from an oral teller or from a book, magazine, movie, radio, television or oral reading, we see everywhere examples of the human need for story.

When a small group, such as a class, recalls a folktale that it read aloud or heard told, say, a week before, it is remarkable how, when one person remembers *some*thing from any part of the story, and another person carries it further in proper sequence, yet another person remembers something *else,* so that the repeated patterns, imagery, sequences, and special reversals of pattern come back and can be put together in proper order. Imagery, associated with overall structure, is one of the principal memory aids. Sometimes repeated phrases with a special new twist with each repetition are associated with the different parts of the structure, as in the "Tar-Baby" story.

* * *

The strongly defined structural elements of orally told folktales make us aware of the source in ourselves for the structure of written essays and stories. You can see such memory-aid structure in the three-task or three-part form of many of the Grimms' tales, such as "The Master Thief."

The Master Thief
The Brothers Grimm

One day an old man and his wife were sitting in front of a miserable house resting awhile from their work. Suddenly a splendid carriage with four black horses came driving up, and a richly dressed man descended from it. The peasant stood up, went to the great man, and asked what he wanted, and in what way he could be useful to him? The stranger stretched out his hand to the old man, and said, "I want nothing but to enjoy for once a country dish; cook me some potatoes, in the way you always have them, and then I will sit down at your table and eat them with pleasure." The peasant smiled and said, "You are a count or a prince, or perhaps even a duke; noble gentlemen often have such fancies, but you shall have your wish." The wife went into the kitchen, and began to wash and rub the potatoes, and to make them into balls, as they are eaten by the country folk. While she was busy with this work, the peasant said to the stranger, "Come into my garden with me for a while, I have still something to do there." He had dug some holes in the garden, and now wanted to plant some trees in them. "Have you no children," asked the stranger, "who could help you with your work?" "No," answered the peasant, "I had a son, it is true, but it is long since he went out into the world. He was a ne'er-do-well; sharp, and knowing, but he would learn nothing and was full of bad tricks; at last he ran away from me, and since then I have heard nothing of him."

The old man took a young tree, put it in a hole, drove in a post beside it, and when he had shoveled in some earth and had trampled it firmly down, he tied the stem of the tree above, below, and in the middle, fast to the post by a rope of straw. "But tell me," said the stranger, "why you don't tie that crooked knotted tree, which is lying in the corner there, bent down almost to the ground, to a post also that it may grow straight, as well as these?" The old man smiled and said, "Sir, you speak according to your knowledge, it is easy to see that you are not familiar with gardening. That tree there is old, and misshapen, no one can make it straight now. Trees must be trained while they are young." "That is how it was with your son," said the stranger, "if you had trained him while he was still young, he would not have run away; now he too must have grown hard and misshapen." "Truly it is a long time since he went away," replied the old man, "he must have changed." "Would you know him again if he were to come to you?" asked the stranger. "Hardly by his face," replied the peasant, "but he has a mark about him, a birthmark on his shoulder, that looks like a bean." When he had said that the stranger pulled off his coat, bared his shoulder, and showed the peasant the bean.

"Good God!" cried the old man, "you are really my son!" and love for his child stirred in his heart. "But," he added, "how can you be my son, you have become a great lord and live in wealth and luxury? How have you contrived to do that?" "Ah, father," answered the son, "the young tree was bound to no post and has grown crooked, now it is too old, it will never be straight again. How have I got all that? I have become a thief, but do not be alarmed, I am a master thief. For me there are neither locks nor bolts, whatever I desire is mine. Do not imagine that I steal like a common thief, I only take some of the superfluity of the rich. Poor people are safe, I would rather give to them than take anything from them. It is the same with anything which I can have without trouble, cunning and dexterity—I never touch it." "Alas, my son," said the father, "it still does not please me, a thief is still a thief, I tell you it will end badly." He took him to his mother, and when she heard that was her son, she wept for joy, but when he told her that he had become a master thief, two streams flowed down over her face. At length she said, "Even if he has become a thief, he is still my son, and my eyes have beheld him once more." They sat down to table, and once again he ate with his parents the wretched food which he had not eaten for so long. The father said, "If our Lord, the count up there in the castle, learns who you are, and what trade you follow, he will not take you in his arms and cradle you in them as he did when he held you at the font, but will cause you to swing from a halter." "Be easy, father, he will do me no harm, for I understand my trade. I will go to him myself this very day." When evening drew near, the master thief seated himself in his carriage, and drove to the castle. The count received him civilly, for he took him for a distinguished man. When, however, the stranger made himself known, the count turned pale and was quite silent for some time. At length he said, "You are my godson, and on that account mercy shall take the place of justice, and I will deal leniently with you. Since you pride yourself on being a master thief, I will put your art to the proof, but if you do not stand the test, you must marry the rope-maker's daughter, and the croaking of the raven must be your music on the occasion." "Lord count," answered the master thief, "think of three things, as difficult as you like, and if I do not perform your tasks, do with me what you will." The count reflected for some minutes, and then said, "Well, then, in the first place, you shall steal the horse I keep for my own riding, out of the stable; in the next, you shall steal the sheet from beneath the bodies of my wife and myself when we are asleep, without our observing it, and the wedding ring of my wife as well; thirdly and lastly, you shall steal away out of the church, the parson and clerk. Mark what I am saying, for your life depends on it."

The master thief went to the nearest town; there he bought the clothes of an old peasant woman, and put them on. Then he stained his face brown, and painted wrinkles on it as well, so that no one could have recognized him. Then he filled a small cask with old Hungary wine in which was mixed a powerful sleeping drink. He put the cask in a basket, which he took on his back, and walked with slow and tottering steps to the count's castle. It was already dark when he arrived. He sat down on a stone in the court-yard and began to cough, like an asthmatic old woman, and to rub his hands as if he were cold. In front of the door of the stable some soldiers were lying round a fire; one of them observed the woman, and called out to her, "Come nearer, old mother, and warm yourself beside us. After all, you have no bed for the night, and must take one where you can find it." The old woman tottered up to them, begged them to lift the basket from her back, and sat down beside them at the fire. "What have you got in your little cask, old lady?" asked one. "A good mouthful of wine," she answered. "I live by trade, for money and fair words I am quite ready to let you have a glass." "Let us have it here, then," said the soldier, and when he had tasted one glass he said, "When wine is good, I like anoth-er glass," and had another poured out for himself, and the rest followed his example. "Hallo, comrades," cried one of them to those who were in the stable, "here is an old woman who has wine that is as old as herself; take a draught, it will warm your stomachs far better than our fire." The old woman carried her cask into the stable. One of the soldiers had seated himself on the saddled riding horse, another held its bridle in his hand, a third had laid hold of its tail. She poured out as much as they wanted until the spring ran dry. It was not long before the bridle fell from the hand of the one, and he fell down and began to snore, the other left hold of the tail, lay down and snored still louder. The one who was sitting in the saddle, did remain sitting, but bent his head almost down to the horse's neck, and slept and blew with his mouth like the bellows of a forge. The soldiers outside had already been asleep for a long time, and were lying on the ground motionless, as if dead. When the master thief saw that he had succeeded, he gave the first a rope in his hand instead of the bridle, and the other who had been holding the tail, a wisp of straw, but what was he to do with the one who was sitting on the horse's back?

He did not want to throw him down, for he might have awakened and have uttered a cry. He had a good idea, he unbuckled the girths of the saddle, tied a couple of ropes which were hanging to a ring on the wall fast to the saddle, and drew the sleeping rider up into the air on it, then he twisted the rope round the posts, and made it fast. He soon unloosed the horse from the chain, but if he had ridden over the stony pavement of the yard they would have heard the noise in the castle. So he wrapped the horse's hoofs in old rags, led him carefully out, leapt upon him, and galloped off.

When day broke, the master galloped to the castle on the stolen horse. The count had just got up, and was looking out of the window. "Good morning, Sir Count," he cried to him, "here is the horse, which I have got safely out of the stable! Just look, how beautifully your soldiers are lying there sleeping; and if you will but go into the stable, you will see how comfortable your watchers have made it for themselves." The count could not help laughing, then he said, "For once you have succeeded, but things won't go so well the second time, and I warn you that if you come before me as a thief, I will handle you as I would a thief." When the countess went to bed that night, she closed her hand with the wedding ring tightly together, and the count said, "All the doors are locked and bolted, I will keep awake and wait for the thief, but if he gets in by the window, I will shoot him." The master thief, however, went in the dark to the gallows, cut a poor sinner who was hanging there down from the halter, and carried him on his back to the castle. Then he set a ladder up to the bedroom, put the dead body on his shoulders, and began to climb up. When he had got so high that the head of the dead man showed at the window, the count, who was watching in his bed, fired a pistol at him, and immediately the master let the poor sinner fall down, and hid himself in one corner. The night was sufficiently lighted by the moon, for the master to see distinctly how the count got out of the window on to the ladder, came down, carried the dead body into the garden, and began to dig a hole in which to lay it. "Now," thought the thief, "the favorable moment has come," stole nimbly out of his corner, and climbed up the ladder straight into the countess's bedroom. "Dear wife," he began in the count's voice, "the thief is dead, but after all, he is my godson, and has been more of a scapegrace than a villain. I will not put him to open shame; besides, I am sorry for the parents. I will bury him myself before daybreak, in the garden that the thing may not be known, so give me the sheet, I will wrap up the body in it, and bury him as a dog buries things by scratching." The countess gave him the sheet. "I tell you what," continued the thief, "I have a fit of magnanimity on me, give me the ring too—the unhappy man risked his life for it, so he may take it with him into his grave." She would not gainsay the count, and although she did it unwillingly she drew the ring from her finger, and gave it to him. The thief made off with both these things, and reached home safely before the count in the garden had finished his work of burying.

What a long face the count did pull when the master came next morning, and brought him the sheet and the ring. "Are you a wizard?" said he. "Who has fetched you out of the grave in which I myself laid you, and brought you to life again?" "You did not bury me," said the thief, "but the poor sinner on the gallows," and he told him exactly how everything had happened, and the count was forced to own to him that he was a clever, crafty thief. "But you have not reached the end yet," he added, "you have still to perform the third task, and if you do not succeed in that, all is of no use." The master smiled and returned no answer. When night had fallen he went with a long sack on his back, a bundle under his arms, and a lantern in his hand to the village church. In the sack he had some crabs, and in the bundle short wax candles. He sat down in the churchyard, took out a crab, and stuck a wax candle on his back. Then he lighted the little light, put the crab on the ground, and let it creep about. He took a second out of the sack, and treated it in the same way, and so on until the last was out of the sack. Hereupon he put on a long black garment that looked like a monk's cowl, and stuck a gray beard on his chin. When at last he was quite unrecognizable, he took the sack in which the crabs had been, went into the church, and ascended the pulpit. The clock in the tower was just striking twelve; when the last stroke had sounded, he cried with a loud and piercing voice, "Hearken, sinful men, the end of all things has come! The last day is at hand! Hearken! Hearken! Whoever wishes to go to heaven with me must creep into the sack. I am Peter, who opens and shuts the gate of heaven. Behold how the dead outside there in the churchyard are wandering about collecting their bones. Come, come, and creep into the sack; the world is about to be destroyed!" The cry echoed through the whole village. The parson and clerk who lived nearest to the church, heard it first, and when they saw the lights which were moving about the churchyard, they observed that something unusual was going on, and went into the church. They listened to the sermon for a while, and then the clerk nudged the parson and said, "It would not be amiss if we were to use the opportunity together, and before the dawning of the last day, find an easy way of getting to heaven." "To tell the truth," answered the parson, "that is what I myself have been thinking, so if you are inclined, we will set out on our way." "Yes," answered the clerk, "but you, the pastor, have the precedence. I will follow." So the parson went first, and ascended the pulpit where the master opened his sack. The parson crept in first, and then the clerk. The master immediately tied up the sack tightly, seized it by the middle, and dragged it down the pulpit steps and whenever the heads of the two fools bumped against the steps, he cried, "We are going over the mountains." Then he drew them through the village in the same way, and when they were passing through puddles, he cried, "Now we are going through wet clouds," and when at last he was dragging them up the steps of the castle, he cried, "Now we are on the steps of heaven, and will soon be in the outer court." When he had got to the top, he pushed the sack into the pigeon house, and when the pigeons fluttered about, he said, "Hark how glad the angels are, and how they are flapping their wings!" Then he bolted the door upon them, and went away.

Next morning he went to the count, and told him that he had performed the third task also, and had carried the parson and clerk out of the church. "Where have you left them?" asked the lord. "They are lying upstairs in a sack in the pigeon house, and imagine that they are in heaven." The count went up himself, and convinced himself that the master had told the truth. When he had delivered the parson and clerk from their captivity, he said, "You are an arch-thief, and have won your wager. For once you escape with a whole skin, but see that you leave my land, for if ever you set foot on it again, you may count on your elevation to the gallows." The arch-thief took leave of his parents, once more went forth into the wide world, and no one has ever heard of him since.

First we notice that the imagery is strong and vivid, but places and people are not described in the sort of detail that we expect from many written narratives. An oral teller of "The Master Thief" would use spontaneous, exaggerated gestures to place people and give their actions, see the story from the vantage points and points-of-view of certain characters, and show how the three tasks are carried out, in much the same way that Mr. Wyles gives the vantage points, points-of-view, enactments, and reactions in "The Telling of an Anansi Tale." The details are told when they are memorable, forceful, and essential to the story. For instance, in the first few sentences we have the strong contrast of the "miserable house" and the "splendid carriage." Two elements of imagery heighten the overall scene, "the four black horses" and "The stranger stretched out his hand to the old man. . . " The characters do not, in this story, have personal names; they are identified by their positions in society, that is, the peasant, the master thief, the count, his wife, the soldiers, parson, sexton, and so on. Examine the universal place and character elements in the following imagery: "The parson crept in first, and then the clerk. The master immediately tied up the sack tightly, seized it by the middle and dragged it down the pulpit steps, and whenever the heads of the two fools bumped against the steps, he cried, "We are going over the mountains . . . ."

The character of the master trickster, the imagery of the story, all the techniques, come together in the three tasks that the thief performs. These three tasks are told as single-event how-it-was-done process sequences. What other basic forms elements do you find directly or indirectly in the telling of the story?

In some passages of "The Master Thief" the translators and editors have joined related sentences with a comma in what is often called the "comma splice." If you read the story aloud, how do you hear such punctuation working? Ordinarily, a writer will use a period or semicolon to separate such sentences.

*   *   *

Find the differences and similarities between "The Master Thief" and the following story, "Why Women Always Take Advantage of Men."

"Why Women Always Take Advantage of Men"
From *Mules and Men*
Zora Neale Hurston

"Oh, yes, womens is got sense too," Mathilda Moseley jumped in. "But they got too much sense to go 'round braggin' about it like y'all do. De lady people always got de advantage of mens because God fixed it dat way."

"Whut ole black advantage is y'all got?" B. Moseley asked indignantly. "We got all de strength and all de law and all de money and you can't git a thing but whut we jes' take pity on you and give you."

"And dat's jus' de point," said Mathilda triumphantly. "You *do* give it to us, but how come you do it?" And without waiting for an answer Mathilda began to tell why women always take advantage of men.

You see in de very first days, God made a man and a woman and put 'em in a house together to live. 'Way back in them days de woman was just as strong as de man and both of 'em did de same things. They useter get to fussin' 'bout who gointer do this and that and sometime they'd fight, but they was even balanced and neither one could whip de other one.

One day de man said to hisself, "B'lieve Ah'm gointer go see God and ast Him for a li'l mo' strength so Ah kin whip dis 'oman and make her mind. Ah'm tired of de way things is." So he went on up to God.

"Good mawnin', Ole Father."

"Howdy man. Whut you doin' 'round my throne so soon dis mawnin'?"

"Ah'm troubled in mind, and nobody can't ease mah spirit 'ceptin' you."

God said: "Put yo' plea in de right form and Ah'll hear and answer."

"Ole Maker, wid de mawnin' stars glitterin' in yo' shinin' crown, wid de dust from yo' footsteps makin' worlds upon worlds, wid de blazin' bird we call de sun flyin' out of yo' right hand in de mawnin' and consumin' all day de flesh and blood of stump-black darkness, and comes flyin' home every evenin' to rest on yo' left hand, and never once in all yo' eternal years, mistood de left hand for de right, Ah ast you *please* to give me mo' strength than dat woman you give me, so Ah kin make her mind. Ah know you don't want to be always comin' down way past de moon and stars to be straightenin' her out and its got to be done. So give me a li'l mo' strength, Ole Maker and Ah'll do it."

"All right, Man, you got mo' strength than woman."

So de man run all de way down de stairs from Heben till he got home. He was so anxious to try his strength on de woman dat he couldn't take his time. Soon's he got in de house he hollered "Woman! Here's yo' boss. God done tole me to handle you in which ever way Ah please. Ah'm yo' boss."

De woman flew to fightin' 'im right off. She fought 'im frightenin' but he beat her. She got her wind and tried 'im again but he whipped her agin. She got herself together and made de third try on him vigorous but he beat her every time. He was so proud he could whip 'er at last, dat he just crowed over her and made her do a lot of things she didn't like. He told her, "Long as you obey me, Ah'll be good to yuh, but every time yuh rear up Ah'm gointer put plenty wood on yo' back and plenty water in yo' eyes."

De woman was so mad she went straight up to Heben and stood befo' de Lawd. She didn't waste no words. She said, "Lawd, Ah come befo' you mighty mad t'day. Ah want back my strength and power Ah useter have."

"Woman, you got de same power you had since de beginnin'."

"Why is it then, dat de man kin beat me now and he useter couldn't do it?"

"He got mo' strength than he useter have. He come and ast me for it and Ah give it to 'im. Ah gives to them that ast, and you ain't never ast me for no mo' power."

"Please suh, God, Ah'm astin' you for it now. Jus' gimme de same as you give him."

God shook his head. "It's too late now, woman. Whut Ah give, Ah never take back. Ah give him mo' strength than you and no matter how much Ah give you, he'll have mo'."

De woman was so mad she wheeled around and went on off. She went straight to de devil and tole him what had happened.

He said, "Don't be dis-incouraged, woman. You listen to me and you'll come out mo' than conqueror. Take dem frowns out yo' face and turn round and go right on back to Heben and ast God to give you dat bunch of keys hangin' by de mantel-piece. Then you bring 'em to me and Ah'll show you what to do wid 'em."

So de woman climbed back up to Heben again. She was mighty tired but she was more out-done than she was tired so she climbed all night long and got back up to Heben agin. When she got befo' de throne, butter wouldn't melt in her mouf.

"O Lawd and Master of de rainbow, Ah know yo' power. You never make two mountains without you put a valley in between. Ah know you kin hit a straight lick wid a crooked stick."

"Ast for whut you want, woman."

"God, gimme dat bunch of keys hangin' by yo' mantel-piece."

"Take 'em."

So de woman took de keys and hurried on back to de devil wid 'em. There was three keys on de bunch. Devil say, "See dese three keys? They got mo' power in 'em than all de strength de man kin ever git if you handle 'em right. Now dis first big key is to de do' of de kitchen, and you know a man always favors his stomach. Dis second one is de key to de bedroom and he don't like to be shut out from dat neither and dis last key is de key to de cradle and he don't want to be cut off from his generations at all. So now you take dese keys and go lock up everything and wait till he come to you. Then don't you unlock nothin' until he use his strength for yo' benefit and yo' desires."

De woman thanked 'im and tole 'im, "If it wasn't for you, Lawd knows whut us po' women folks would do."

She started off but de devil halted her. "Jus' one mo' thing: don't go home braggin' 'bout yo' keys. Jus' lock up everything and say nothin' until you git asked. And then don't talk too much."

De woman went on home and did like de devil tole her. When de man come home from work she was settin' on de porch singin' some song 'bout "Peck on de wood make de bed go good."

When de man found de three doors fastened what useter stand wide open he swelled up like pine lumber after a rain. First thing he tried to break in cause he figgered his strength would overcome all obstacles. When he saw he couldn't do it, he ast de woman, "Who locked dis do'?"

She tole 'im, "Me."

"Where did you git de key from?"

"God give it to me."

He run up to God and said, "God, woman got me locked 'way from my vittles, my bed and my generations, and she say you give her the keys."

God said, "I did, Man, Ah give her de keys, but de devil showed her how to use 'em!"

"Well, Ole Maker, please gimme some keys jus' lak 'em so she can't git de full control."

"No, Man, what Ah give Ah give. Woman got de key."

"How kin Ah know 'bout my generations?"

"Ast de woman."

So de man come on back and submitted hisself to de woman and she opened de doors.

He wasn't satisfied but he had to give in. 'Way after while he said to de woman, "Le's us divide up. Ah'll give you half of my strength if you lemme hold de keys in my hands."

De woman thought dat over so de devil popped and tol her, "Tell 'im, naw. Let 'im keep his strength and you keep yo' keys."

So de woman wouldn't trade wid 'im and de man had to mortgage his strength to her to live. And dat's why de man makes and de woman takes. You men is still braggin' 'bout yo' strength and de women is sittin' on de keys and lettin' you blow off till she git ready to put de bridle on you.

B. Moseley looked over at Mathilda and said, "You just like a hen in de barnyard. You cackle so much you give de rooster de blues."

Mathilda looked over at him archly and quoted:

Stepped on a pin, de pin bent
And dat's de way de story went.

———

Notice that we see the story in the simulated context of an original telling, such a wonderful retelling *in writing* that the credit for it must be given to Zora Neale Hurston. Hurston carefully mixes dialect with elements and conventions of standard written English in ways that unobtrusively enhance the sense of the story's being told in dialect speech. Examine any sentence word by word for the mixture of dialect and standard written English. See Sandra Crockett's "Cat and Chick Hooked Up" for an example of modern Black urban dialect mixed with elements and conventions of standard written English. When telling a dialect story, you usually do such mixing of language intuitively.

How is "Why Women Always Take Advantage of Men" similar to "The Master Thief" in its economical use of detail, its suggestion of universal scenes, its making you see imagery without tying you down to specific place or person? How is it dissimilar in its use of language? How does the dialect rendering become as much a part of the story as the imagery and narrative line? What do the man and woman "climb" to get to God? How is the power of God suggested and characterized by the man and by the woman? How are the images given of the house and the events without describing fully developed realistic scenes? How does the dialect speech help give the action of the relationships of man-woman, man-God, woman-God, woman-Devil, woman-man, and so forth?

Notice the narrative principle that once God has given something it can't be taken away. How does that principle give narrative force to the story?

Examine imagery and sequence of events in the story for how Hurston does in writing, with writing's different methods, everything that Mr. Wyles and Mathilda do in oral-gestural telling.

How To Melt, Blacken, and Break
Betty Shiflett

There was once a woman who feared to cherish any good fortune that came to her, lest it be lost, and she the sadder for rejoicing in it. To safeguard herself from loss of joy, she invented a thousand excuses, any one of which miraculously snatched her from all temptation to find pleasure in her possessions, her family, or the weather. Always she said, "It will tarnish," or "He will grow sickly," or, when everything else failed, "It will surely rain."

Such was her fever to avoid all pleasures, and therefore all pain, that she fell to ceaseless cleaning and scrubbing to avoid the fear of the fear of pleasure, which more and more stole into her heart when her hands were empty. While sweeping the floor one day for the fifth but by no means last time (it was only noon), she was delighted to recall that she'd been neglecting her duties under the bed. She almost gave way and called this a good piece of luck, when she remembered that the dust there would surely be in short supply and likely not fill more than a few extra minutes of her day. She proceeded in the only way she knew, and began to stir up the dust under her bed. No sooner had she lifted the counterpane and raked the floor once with her broom, than she struck a hard something that chimed. When she withdrew her broom, the straw smoked and burst into a shower of flame so brilliant the room blushed orange from stoop to rafters. Kneeling, she felt among the dust puffs for whatever it might be, so wondrous hid behind her thin counterpane. Her fingers turned about a candlestick of leaded cut crystal flashing with rainbow prisms, the like of which she'd never seen. When she pulled it out, the alabaster candle at its center sneezed delicately, and the slenderest of flames wound itself around the wick.

As she tiptoed to lay it upon the mantle above the hearth, she sighed, "Oh, it's beautiful all right, but it won't last. It will go the way of all candles. The alabaster is surely only common tallow and will melt. The lovely flame will wane and leave only a black thread of a wick. As for the dazzle of cut crystal, there is no glass that will not shatter and lose its colors."

Days came and weeks passed. Rain fell from radiant skies, silver tarnished in the chest amid camphor, and well children took cough medicine, but the alabaster candle continued to burn in its crystal socket, undiminished and sparkling as the day the woman first heard its chime. Each time she passed by it she muttered imprecations: "It will melt; it will blacken; it will break!" Her disappointment knew no bounds, but she kept herself in check lest she begin to rejoice in her bountiful disappointment.

She attacked the floors with broom and mop more furiously than ever, and carefully tucked up the counterpane, thinking to discourage any new disaster that might breed in the darkness under her bed. For good measure she strapped her husband and two little boys in mustard plasters, as they were notorious cold-catchers, and though it was the midsummer drought season, she never went to town without a beetling black umbrella. Her husband and children actually did take to their beds, so heavy were their chests with mustard plaster, leaving their chores to fall upon the poor woman's shoulders.

Her husband displayed a sinful fondness for gazing at the candlestick as he lay under his blankets, and would watch it wink its rainbow prisms from mantle to ceiling for a span of hours. What else could he do? His wife remonstrated with him, and warned him that soon he would corrupt their sons, but in candle gazing, if in nothing else, he was unswerving. No amount of window washing or rug beating on her part could divert him. Worse yet, he became so immune to her tongue-lashings that she began to suspect he lay in bed under a mustard plaster not to ward off his inevitable fall cold, but simply as a pretext to keep the rainbow candlestick with its alabaster candle and clear flame in his eye forever. And in all this time, it did not melt, blacken, or break.

While the woman's troubles multiplied, her patience thinned. She began to push fate along the way. Whenever she dusted the mantle, which was often, she threatened the abomination with angry jabs of her feather duster, and when she hoped it wasn't looking, she would give it a sly whack with her steely elbow, but not once did the candlestick oblige her by toppling, or even trembling.

Once her husband broke silence to remark that the room and all its furnishings had taken on a startling luster, and it was true. The clear flame light had accomplished what all her polishings and waxings could not. It had washed a softly vibrant sheen over each dish and stick she owned. Moreover, the faces of her two little boys had firmed from sickly pallor to freckles, as though they had been under the sun all day. This last terrified the poor woman, for she knew better than anything she knew that bursting good health only masked impending death. She doubled their dosage of cough medicine, treated them to warm bricks at their feet in July, and prayed the candle should melt, the wick blacken, and the crystal break into a million pieces and be scattered on the wind like dust. Without ceasing she prayed, but all to no purpose.

Then one night she lay beyond sleep, turning events in her mind. Her eyes itched to hide from the terrible candle's light, but they could not blink it away.

"This is intolerable," she whispered. "I fear for the lives of my husband and children. They are bewitched, doomed by this candle, and if I don't take matters into my own hands, I will surely have the pleasure of burying them come spring."

So saying she whipped off her counterpane and held it wadded behind her back as she crept to the mantle, humming, "Melt, blacken, break." With one billowing thrust she snared the alabaster candle and its crystal socket in a balloon of white counterpane, upon which she pounced, wringing and knotting it with her hands until dark filled the room. When she'd finished, she stepped to the door and whirled the counterpane with its treasure three times around her head, meaning to toss it far onto the road where feet and wheels could powder it. But it flew from her hand and was sucked up in the black night.

"Fine!" she said. "I couldn't have done better myself. Wherever it lands, it is sure to break." Then she returned to her bed in sweet darkness and slept. Toward dawn she was awakened by the silver shattering of glass on her roof, and when the neighbors passed by on their way to church next morning, they found the house fallen to ashes. All that was left of it lay in a circle of blackened grass tufts, and in the charred beds they were amazed to find four molten pools of common tallow.

———

This is a wholly original, modern folktale. The woman's earnestly pessimistic attitude that everything will fail, tarnish or grow sickly, indeed, *must* fail, tarnish, or grow sickly, is opposed to the indestructible light of the candle that comes into her and her family's life. Finally, her inability to tolerate the strain of the good feeling and pleasure brought to her life by the candle causes her to attempt to destroy it. Though her attempt seems to be initially successful, it backfires and destroys her and her family. What do you think the candle could be a symbol of? Often tales were told or sung, in the court of a ruler, in which the meaning of the symbols were known to a few of the listeners but concealed from the ruler and others in power. What could be the meaning of the candle here?

How does Shiflett, using folktale techniques, repeat characteristic behaviors of the woman, so that the repetition emphasizes the character of the woman, enhances the imagery, moves the story, and acts also as a memory-aid? What other repetitions occur? How are the images of the candle both repeated and changed? How does the woman relate to the candle? How does her relationship to it change? Why does the room "blush" orange? What is the meaning of the "clear flame light" accomplishing what "all her polishings and waxings could not"? How is the candle's magical power further emphasized in the end? Notice the three-stage reversal at the end: break, blacken, melt. Locate the author's use of vivid verbs and richly evocative modifiers, in nearly every sentence.

How is "How to Melt, Blacken, and Break" similar to, and different from, "The Master Thief" and "Why Women Always Take Advantage of Men"? How could the fact that this story was first written make it different from a story that was first orally told?

* * *

Here's another of the Grimms' tales that demonstrate, in retellings and parodies, the ways that stories are continually transformed.

The Cat and Mouse in Partnership
The Brothers Grimm

A cat, having made acquaintance with a mouse, professed such great love and friendship for her that the mouse at last agreed that they should live and keep house together.

"We must make provision for the winter," said the cat, "or we shall suffer hunger. And you, little mouse, must not stir out, or you will be caught in a trap."

So they took counsel together and bought a little pot of fat. Then they could not tell where to put it for safety, but after long consideration the cat said there could not be a better place than the church, for nobody would steal there. And they decided to put it under the altar and not touch it until they were really in want. So the little pot was placed in safety. But before long the cat was seized with a great desire to taste it.

"Listen to me, little mouse," said he. "I have been asked by my cousin to stand godfather to a little son she has brought into the world. He is white with brown spots, and they want to have the christening today. So let me go to it, and you stay at home and keep house."

"Oh yes, certainly," answered the mouse. "Pray go, by all means. And when you are feasting on all the good things, think of me. I should so like a drop of the sweet red wine."

But there was not a word of truth in all this. The cat had no cousin and had not been asked to stand godfather. He went to the church, straight up to the little pot, and licked the fat off the top. Then he took a walk over the roofs of the town, saw his acquaintances, stretched himself in the sun, and licked his whiskers as often as he thought of the little pot of fat. And then when it was evening he went home.

"Here you are at last," said the mouse. "I expect you have had a merry time."

"Oh, pretty well," answered the cat.

"And what name did you give the child?" asked the mouse.

"Top-off," answered the cat dryly.

"Top-off!" cried the mouse. "That is a singular and wonderful name. Is it common in your family?"

"What does it matter?" said the cat. "It's not any worse than Crumb-picker, like your godchild."

A little time after this the cat was again seized with a longing for the pot of fat.

"Again I must ask you," said he to the mouse, "to do me a favor and keep house alone for a day. I have been asked a second time to stand godfather, and as the little one has a white ring round its neck, I cannot well refuse."

So the kind little mouse consented, and the cat crept along by the town wall until he reached the church, where he went straight to the little pot of fat and ate half of it.

"Nothing tastes so well as what one keeps to oneself," said he, feeling quite content with his day's work. When he reached home, the mouse asked what name had been given to the child.

"Half-gone," answered the cat.

"Half-gone!" cried the mouse. "I never heard such a name in my life. I'll bet it's not to be found in the calendar."

Soon after that the cat's mouth began to water again for the fat.

"Good things always come in threes," said he to the mouse. "Again I have been asked to stand godfather. The little one is quite black with white feet, and not any white hair on its body. Such a thing does not happen every day, so you will let me go, won't you?"

"Top-off, Half-gone," murmured the mouse. "They are such curious names, I cannot but wonder at them."

"That's because you are always sitting at home," said the cat, "in your little gray frock and hairy tail, never seeing the world, and fancying all sorts of things."

So the little mouse cleaned up the house and set it all in order. Meanwhile the greedy cat went and made an end of the little pot of fat.

"Now all is finished one's mind will be easy," said he, and came home in the evening quite sleek and comfortable. The mouse asked at once what name had been given to the third child.

"It won't please you any better than the others," answered the cat. "It is called All-gone."

"All-gone!" cried the mouse. "What an unheard-of name! I never met with anything like it. All-gone! Whatever can it mean?" And shaking her head, she curled herself round and went to sleep. After that the cat was not again asked to stand godfather.

When the winter had come and there was nothing more to be had out of doors, the mouse began to think of their store.

"Come, cat," said she, "we will fetch our pot of fat. How good it will taste, to be sure?"

"Of course it will," said the cat. "Just as good as if you stuck your tongue out of the window."

So they set out, and when they reached the place they found the pot, but it was standing empty.

"Oh, now I know what it all meant," cried the mouse. "Now I see what sort of partner you have been! Instead of standing godfather you have eaten it all up. First Top-off! Then Half-gone! Then—"

"Hold your tongue!" screamed the cat. "Another word, and I eat you too!"

And the poor little mouse, having "All-gone" on her tongue, out it came, and the cat leaped upon her and made an end of her. And that is the way of the world.

In "The Cat and Mouse in Partnership" we see a three-stage structure and the essential techniques of folktale telling carried out swiftly and economically, with the three-stages repeated in the reversal at the end.

* * *

You can follow the same three-stage structure in "A Cat and a Chick Hooked Up" with essential folktale elements and techniques parodied in a modern situation.

A Cat and a Chick Hooked Up
Sandra L. Crockett

This cat, after getting next to this chick, was rapping for days over his love jones for her. The chick finally got her head bumped and agreed that they would shack together.

"We got to stock up on some grub before the hawk gets to cutting," the cat said, " 'cause I might get laid off from the gig again. All of the hustlers and the pimps going be recruitin' real tough 'bout now 'cause I know they need the extra dough. Little Mama, I want you to stick pretty close to the crib, or else they sho nuff will try to catch you in their trap."

So they started shacking and then they bought a whole lot of red beans and rice just in case the cat got laid off. They didn't have any room to put all of it because they only had a one room walk up. So after talking it over they decided to keep it over his partner's house who had much more room and who also happen to live over a storefront church. They also decided to wait until the shit really hit the fan before they touched it. Pretty soon, the fat cat decided to get greedy. What was once a love jones became a red beans and rice jones.

"Check this out, Mama," he said, "I got this cousin who is so old timey that she wants me to become her little baby's god-daddy. They going to have the baptism today and it's goin to be at the same little storefront church. Let me deal with this and you stay put and watch the crib."

"You got it," the chick said, "Go do yo' thang. And when you are smackin' yo' jaws over all that good grub I know they going to have, think of me. At least try to sneak me a bottle of Ripple back."

But the cat was lying his fat ass off. No cousin had asked him to do nothing. He went upstairs over the church to his partner's place and cooked up a pot of red beans and rice. Then he walked the streets, cruising. He passed a bunch of buddies who were standing on the street corner shooting crap. Every time he thought of red beans and rice, his mouth watered. Deciding that it was nothing on the streets worth picking up, he eased on to the crib.

"It's about god damn time," the chick said. "I know you been doing some partyin.' "

"Just a touch," the fat cat said.

"What's the name of the kid?" the chick asked.

"Sly," the cat answered with a crooked smile.

"Sly," the chick shrieked. "Well at least it ain't the same old Tom, Dick, or Harry type of name that's common yo' family.

"What's the difference?" the cat said. "It ain't no worse than Pot-Gut, yo' god-baby."

A couple of weeks went by and the cat started craving for the red beans and rice again.

"I got to bring it to you again, Mama," he told the chick. "Stay here and keep yo' eyes on things 'cause another cousin asked me to be god-daddy fo' her kid. You know how jealous them bitches are of each other so you know I got to do it."

So the naive, dumb chick agreed, and the slick cat slunk along the streets until he came to the church. He went straight upstairs, cooked a pot of food and ate. Feeling like a pig he cooked some more and ate that up. Pretty soon, he found he had wiped out damn near half of it.

"What she won't know won't hurt, and there going to be more for me." He felt like he had got away with something this time. Back home, the chick asked what name this kid had been given.

"Slick," the cat said.

"Slick!" the chick yelled. "Brother, you got to be jivin'."

Now, only three days passed before the cat began to want a taste of the stash.

"I know you ain't gone believe this," started the cat, "but my favorite cousin who also just dropped a load, wants me be god daddy. And you heard that she was my favorite so it ain't no way under the sun that I can say no."

"Sly, Slick," thought the chick aloud. "With some weird names like that, you damn right I ain't gone believe this."

"Hey, lady," said the cat, "You ain't up on nothing in this world. All you do is sit here watching the boob tube day in and day out. How you 'spect you going know anything?"

So the chick picked up around the house, bored stiff. She was beginning to wonder if she had made the right decision after all. She was not a bad looking chick, she reminded herself. If this turkey didn't start acting like he had some sense, she would space.

"Well, you ain't got to worry 'bout no more brats being brought up." he said after coming home to the house. "I ain't even got no mo' cousins."

The first thing the chick wanted to know was the name.

"You ain't going to like it no better than the others," the cat said, "His name is Wicked."

"Wicked!" yelled the chick. "Get out of here, fool! I ain't never heard of such. "Wicked, huh? I got a feeling that I am missing something." Scratching her head, she got undressed, cut the tube on and fell sound asleep. And the cat was right. He never was asked to be godfather any more.

When the hawk began to tear down the streets like an icy razor blade, the cat also got laid off from the gig.

"Come on, sugar," said the chick, "Go on over and get the stash. In fact I think that I'll just mosey on over there with you."

"You got it," the cat said.

So they put their stuff on and walked over to the little storefront church. They headed straight upstairs for the food.

"What the hell!" said the chick. "We been robbed! Or have we? Wait one cotton pickin' minute here. We ain't been robbed and you ain't been nobody's godfather. The Sly, Slick and the Wicked ain't nobody but you, you dirty, rotten son of a. . . ."

"Now wait a goddamn minute here yo'self," screamed the cat. "You better shut yo' trap or I am going to give you one 'cross yo' head."

And the naive little chick, had the word "bitch" on her tongue, and it came right on out. At that point, the cat jumped on the chick, knocked her dead in her skull and brought down the final curtain. That's the way it is.

In both the original Grimms' tale and this modern parody of it, the story ends with a "that's the way of the world" conclusion: Strength and violence win out over devotion and loyalty.

Compare the two stories line by line, stage by stage, character by character. Watch how Crockett stays inventively with the structure of "Cat and Mouse in Partnership," but varies it slightly, using Black urban dialect as she moves the basic story into a parodic telling of a modern situation.

What story would *you* tell in parody of "Cat and Mouse in Partnership"?

* * *

Folktales have often been told in order to make moral or practical points, or to illustrate principles. An example of such follows.

"Prologue" to Basic Research Methods in Social Science
Julian Simon

Cast your mind back 450 years. The Governor of Rodera—a small Asian principality—decided to find out why the country's tax collections were not higher. Here is a classic problem for research, and much of mathematics and many of our social-science techniques were originally invented to improve taxation procedures.

The Governor first consulted an adviser who had studied in Europe and had learned something of Aristotelian logic. The adviser reasoned that good citizens willingly pay as much tax as they are able to, that the folk of Rodera were very good citizens, and that, therefore, the tax collections *could* not be higher.

The Governor immediately dismissed this syllogistic thinking as pure nonsense because he had no faith in the premises. Even without special training he was smart enough to understand the weakness of bad logic.

Next, the Governor called in the regional tax collectors and put the problem to them because they were experts in the tax-collection field. After consultation the consensus among the tax collectors was that the people of the country simply could not afford to pay any more taxes. To support this statement the tax men stated that they had already used every possible technique to extract higher taxes—raising valuations of property, checking on hidden assets, and the like—and even their best efforts could not raise more money.

The Governor recognized that the tax men's analysis of the situation might well be a self-seeking attempt to make themselves seem competent and hard-working, and he therefore disregarded this "expert opinion."

The Governor then concluded reluctantly that he would have to find out the answers for himself. He instructed an aide to bring him a handful of typical citizens. The people brought in were those who were closest at hand. They included a few beggars who had been loitering nearby plus the aide's brother and two young guards. It was obvious that these people were not representative of the population, and therefore it was useless to question them. To put it in modern terms, the Governor recognized that he had a badly biased sample.

The aide was therefore instructed to bring in some "typical" peasants and townspeople, which he did. The Governor then asked them, "Why don't you pay more taxes?" The first few answers showed the folly of the question for what he heard were excuses, complaints, entreaties—everything except what seemed to be sensible answers.

The Governor then confined his questions to factual matters. He asked about each person's property, his crops, family size, and the amount he paid in taxes. Assuming that the answers were true and that he could have them checked, the Governor thought he was getting somewhere.

The information obtained from such a small handful of people was not enough, however, because the group did not include any rich men, any people from the far provinces, any foreign residents, or any representatives of other important classes of people. Nor could the Governor tell from this sample how many people of each class there were. Therefore, the Governor ordered a nation-wide house-to-house census.

Now the data for a complete nation-wide United States census can be collected in months. But transportation and communications were poorer then, and few literate people could be found to collect information. The census therefore required twelve years.

By the fifth year, the Governor grew impatient and decided to experiment with the effect of new pressures to increase tax collections. He ordered that anyone who did not pay half again as much tax as in the previous year would have his cattle confiscated. In fact the total taxes paid did not increase. All the crops were bad that year, and the Governor could not determine whether or not the taxes would have been as high or higher than otherwise if the crops had been normal. The trouble was that his experiment was uncontrolled, because he had not kept the old tax system in effect in some areas for comparison—that is, his experimental design was incomplete. And worst of all, many people slaughtered their cattle to avoid confiscation, which ruined the country's meat supply for several years.

By the time the data were all in hand at the end of the twelfth year the national situation had changed, and the data collected in early years no longer meant much. (Nowadays we know how to take samples to reduce error and avoid long time periods during which the picture may change.) Furthermore, after twelve years the tax-census data filled a whole warehouse, and another ten years would have been required to interpret them. The Governor gave up the task in disgust and retired to his harem.

The point of this story is that knowledge is often not easy to come by because there are many obstacles in one's path. And common sense alone is not enough. But by now social science has accumulated a body of tested experience on how best to overcome the obstacles and acquire empirical knowledge efficiently and safely. This book presents some of this accumulated experience.

———————

With a variation of folktale structure, Julian Simon makes a point about how and why modern social science has accumulated a body of techniques for acquiring reliable empirical data. Successively, in the guise of the governor's insights into the weaknesses of various proposed approaches to improve his tax collections, Simon deals with specific naive approaches to empirical data-gathering and why they are not reliable. In this way, he identifies the basic problems in gathering fairly dependable empirical research data. Rephrase each of the approaches and its weakness in your own words.

Writing Your Folktale

Retell an old folktale in a modern setting.

Parody a folktale in a modern situation.

Write an original folktale.

Write a folktale to illustrate a principle, moral or otherwise.

Write a folktale framed by the context of one person telling the story to other persons, in the story-within-a-story form.

Use the language of a particular dialect or form of speech in telling a folktale. Examine, sentence by sentence, how Sandra Crockett connects the power of speech to writing and renders the Black city dialect with standard written English conventions.

In your how-it-happens subject area, you may find a character and situation suitable for either a folktale or a talltale. You may also find moral or practical principles that can be illustrated by a folktale. You could use folktales to argue for or against solar energy, nuclear energy, handgun control, unrestricted gun ownership, abortion, government regulations, profit making, government spying, arms races, military spending, student aid, health insurance, food and shelter aid, and so forth.

You could go to the Grimms' tales to find stories that offer good possibilities for parody or retelling. Suggestions: "Cinderella," "Snow White," "The Master Thief," "Cat and Mouse in Partnership," "The Juniper Tree," "The Young Man Who Could Not Shiver and Shake," "The Robber Bridegroom," "Goose Girl," and any other Grimms' tale that engages your imagination. American talltales and folktales also offer good, tempting characters and patterns for parody, such as "John Henry," "Big John," "Davy Crockett," "Jabbo," and "Mike Fink."

Undergraduates have done parodies or retellings of folktales as diverse as "The Juniper Tree," "John Henry," and "Cat and Mouse in Partnership." They have developed new stories for Jabbo. John Henry has been transformed into a punk electric guitar player, a stud who will not die "with his hammer in his hand," and a President of the United States who "bugs" everyone's conversations and asks to be buried with "his tapes in his hand." Original folktales done by students in writing classes, sometimes drawing on remembered folk elements, have dramatically illustrated why shadows do not walk alone, why evergreens got that way, why we have two names, the thing that went bump in the night, and so on.

Imagine yourself telling the story to a small group within easy voice range and eye contact. Imagine the gestures and enactments you would use. If you do not directly imagine the telling of the story to a small group, get the sense of it as much as possible. Remember that the folktale does not usually describe the particular place or develop the scene with a great deal of realistic detail, but uses objects, relationships, characters, and actions with the same economy that you would use in an oral telling to a small audience about an event you saw happen somewhere.

VI

How-It-Happens—Instance-Collections and General Essays

How-It-Happens Instance-Collections

The instance-collection can be a form in itself, one very accessible and productive for new writers. One of the following instance-collections deals with a job and one with a long experience with neighborhood gangs on Chicago's south side. Though the authors could have begun at any point in the how-it-happens subject area, their instance-collections show a chronological order. An overall movement connects the different instances.

The authors undertook the same sort of assignment that you're being asked to do, to choose and explore a job or any other prolonged experience or observation of repeated behaviors. In fact, the author of "D to the Knee! Stone to the Bone!" began by writing about another subject area. By going to whatever was taking his attention most strongly in the in-class oral tellings and writings, he discovered and remembered an area of experience that was more compelling for him. In his case, and in other such cases, the authors needed the positive reactions of the audience, of teachers and classmates, to tell them that the material of that "awful old job" or that "time I'd just as soon forget" was powerful, vivid, meaningful to the listening audience and, so the authors found, meaningful to themselves. This should alert you that your prolonged "awful" or "miserable" or "oppressive" experience may be redeemed in writing in an especially beneficial way.

An instance can be any length from a one-line phrase to a whole basic forms essay or short story. We call them instances, passages, journal entries, sections, or whatever. Indeed, a pattern of short one-line instances, or a comparison of short instances, could constitute one entry of a full instance collection. Each of the entries usually deals with a central incident, seen and told fully in the form that has attracted the author's attention for that material or that "instance." A part of the assignment is to explore instances with different forms, points-of-view, techniques. Imaginative approaches and fictional treatments of the personally observed material are welcome, encouraged. If the teacher has assigned a particular form—say, a model-character or model-comparison telling—look over your how-it-happens subject and see what incidents or material are attracted to this form, and then try the form in writing.

How People Relate to Cancer
Marilyn Mannisto

It was her second day working as a physician's assistant for a group of Head and Neck Cancer surgeons. The first day had been a blur of names, instructions, strange instruments, phones ringing, and a charged atmosphere of energy and importance that thoroughly captivated her.

Mr. Ricco, whom she had seated just ten minutes earlier had removed his eye patch and was reclining in a chair facing her. A cavity was visible through an opening the size of a golfball, where his right eye formerly was. After the initial opening, it widened out to the bridge of his nose on one side and his ear on the other. It reached upwards to the middle of his forehead, downward to the lowest part of his cheekbone and backwards in depth until parallel with his ear. Unconsciously, she leaned against the door frame and placed one hand over the raging internal tide of gastric juices that she could feel pelting the lining of her stomach. She had known she would be working with severe cases of cancer, but "severe" did not adequately describe the rampaging disease that she was now face to face with.

Dr. Singer had not noticed her appearance and he and his intern continued firing questions at Mr. Ricco as they poked and pried within the cavity. "Bled lately? Still using an antiseptic solution on your packing inside this cavity? Lost any weight since last month? Is the pain better?" He was answering all the questions, but meantime she noticed that he had been observing her. When she first realized that she was being watched, and looked into his one good eye, she fancied she saw something like pity flick across it. Dr. Singer called her forward to explain what was needed.

He was using an instrument called a cauterizer which burns the skin closed to stop sites that are bleeding. It is the common instrument used in operating rooms to stop bleeding veins because it is so much quicker than suturing them closed. However, the smell is undiluted and unmistakeably that of burning flesh.

She was to take a suction hose, which is similar to a tiny vacuum, and suck away the smoke caused by cauterizing the tissue inside the cavity so that Dr. Singer's view would be unobstructed and so that the smoke would not irritate Mr. Ricco's good eye.

As she leaned forward receiving her instructions she noticed that the cavity was square-shaped and filled with patches of pink subcutaneous tissue, as well as patches of grey, brown and green skin which represented healing areas. In several places bright red waterfalls of blood were oozing down and forming small lakes on the floor of the cavern.

As he began to cauterize, smoke billowed out of the cavity. It was extremely tedious work to try and capture even the majority of it. She was thankful, for this absorbed her attention and she had no time to think of her surroundings, the gaping hole in Mr. Ricco's head, or the pain that he must regularly suffer.

Suddenly a low tenor voice broke into song; "Don't let the smoke get in your eyes, don't let the moon break your heart." Mr. Ricco was singing a parody of some old broadway show song. Startled, she leaned backward to look into his face. His one blue iris flashed in the surgical light. He winked, began studying the hair on his knuckles, and continued to hum the tune and smile whenever he caught her eye.

*　　*　　*

Uncomfortable, she was pushing herself against the back of her chair as her dark-haired friend drooped forward in his. He had one foot raised upwards onto the bar connecting the two front legs of his chair. His head was stooped towards the hand holding his cigarette positioned on his right knee. "What's the most common type of cancer? Or, no wait a minute . . . what are the three most common types?" he asked. She wasn't used to statistical questions, and that is all that Pizz had been asking all evening. None of the usual things about varieties of emotion, the stages of acceptance of the disease, or different methods of treatment. It took her a while to recall exactly what the answer to his question was. "Lung, Breast, and Colon," she murmured, "but I'm not sure about the order anymore, it's probably changed since I was in school." "Lung, really?" he queried, as he put out his cigarette. She chuckled and commented on his transparency. His girlfriend Sue broke from her intense concentration on the woven rug at her feet for the first time in many minutes and smiled. Just as she was beginning to feel a bit of the lightheartedness that had characterized their greetings, Pizz said, "Well, isn't it easy to detect cancer, and don't you get symptoms early enough to be cured in most cases?"

Sue dropped her eyes to the rug again, and their friend covered a sigh and began, "Well the severity of the symptoms varies from individual to individual. Some have a huge weight loss, coughing, night sweats, pain, etc. On the other hand another person may have a more advanced stage of disease that was only discovered on a routine chest X-ray or he may have experienced a little indigestion for enough days to make him be concerned enough to see his physician."

At the end of each couplet of question and answer, Pizz slumped a little further into his chair and the look on his face became a little more bewildered, a trifle more serious and stern. He opened his mouth to ask another question.

"No, Mike," his friend said. "I refuse to talk about this anymore. This always happens to me. Someone asks me what I do, someone else asks me a few questions, and in record time I can change a roomful of laughing, joking, happy people into depressed uncomfortable hypochondriacs who are starting to experience all the symptoms we talked about, and who can see no way to prevent getting the "Dreaded Disease" themselves. From now on, I'm a secretary, or a sales clerk . . . anything but working in cancer research."

* * *

Mr. Brunswick was waiting for her to open up the office this morning. You could give him a 6:00 a.m. appointment and he would arrive at 5:00 a.m. He is that anxious to get his clean bill of health and continue with his life.

He had just returned from a trip to Mexico and came in with ashtrays made out of centavos for Arlene and her. A truck driver friend of his came along. He is still battling with his employers, trying to get his position back, but it seems like he has made little progress, if any. His boss believes that cancer is contagious and despite the numerous letters that Dr. Bittel has written to him, he refuses to change his unscientific position, whether because of pride or superstition. She has no idea.

Mr. Brunswick was found to have a carcinoma of his lower lip two years ago. They had to do extensive surgery around his mouth and jaw, for it was a large tumor, but now he only comes in for check-ups to make sure there is no recurrence of disease and to see the plastic surgeon who is gradually rebuilding the chin and lip into their former contours.

One day Mr. Brunswick asked her if she had ever seen how he brushed his teeth, and proceeded to pull back his bottom lip, revealing a layer of grey whiskers along its inside surface. "Isn't that something?" he asked. "They took this skin off my cheek and it doesn't know yet that it is growing inside my mouth now. But the doc said that eventually all those whiskers will drop out and it will be like my old lip was before." She asked one of the doctors about it and he verified that. She guessed the same thing happens when they take grafts from a man's chest and use the skin to repair defects in the neck, mouth, or throat.

Mr. Brunswick is never shy with any of the girls in the office or the doctors. Whenever other patients begin to arrive before she has a chance to seat him inside, he will stand up in the furthest corner of the waiting room, with hat in hand, and stare down at the floor in front of him. The only time his disfigurement causes him concern is when it may make other people uncomfortable. Yet he is not offended by their inability to accept him. He knows that they cannot understand what he has gone through, or realize how happy he is to be breathing and alive, no matter what he looks like. It is sad, though, and she tries to put him into an empty room as soon as possible. He is such a large man, with a huge six-foot frame and long swinging arms, that it is impossible for him to be obscure in a small room. Once he is among people who are familiar with him, however, he relaxes completely. He has found within himself complete acceptance of his disease and his limited chances for a long life. He makes each moment count.

*   *   *

Although a conference was in progress, she slipped into the small auditorium and surreptitiously began to sweep the floor. She had her orders and this room had to be cleaned before the medical school dean arrived for his talk at 3:00 p.m.

She paused as the speaker caught her attention and stared at the illuminated screen which held an X-ray picture of someone's lungs. She squinted up her eyes and peered hard and fast at the right lung he was pointing to, but she couldn't see anything that resembled a tumor. Yet everyone else in the room acted like it was huge and plain as day. So she took their word for it. With each second this doctor was getting more and more excited and he was trying harder and harder to appear calm. It made her suspicious that he was trying to fool all of them, that there really wasn't a mass; or at least, if there wasn't, he had something up his sleeve. He kept shifting his weight from one foot to the other, waving the pointer wildly in the air, and his face was swelling with his own anticipation.

He told how they brought this man into the hospital and cut him in half to get inside the bad lung (which is what he said is called a thoractomy). But once they got inside, all they could see was fine, healthy tissue. There wasn't anything that looked a trifle suspicious. Puzzled, they closed him up again and sent him back to his room. After he recovered a little, they sent him back down to get another X-ray. He said that this one looked exactly like the first. In fact the mass was even a little larger, which made it even more likely that this man had cancer of the lung.

He paused and looked around at the puzzled, pondering faces of his audience. A couple of people came up and took a closer look at the picture but walked away, remaining convinced that there was definitely a tumor in the right lung.

She was getting more puzzled by the minute, so she set her broom down and leaned against the back wall to see if this doctor could explain why he didn't find a tumor when he kept swearing that there was one on the X-ray.

He let the suspense hang in the air a little while longer before he told how he went down to the X-ray department and talked with the technician who developed the film. Seems that the technician was puzzled; both times he had had to turn the X-ray around because it kept coming out of the machine backwards. The doctor scanned the crowd to see if anyone suspected the climax he was coming to. Then he said that this man had a congenital defect that had never been diagnosed before. His heart was on the right side of his chest. Which is why the technician had to turn around the film in order to label the right and left sides respectively and which is why, when they looked at the right lung, it was normal and healthy.

It ended up that they had to bring that poor man back to the operating room and open him up on the other side and cut that tumor out. It turned out that basically the poor guy was cut in half.

You can't blame the doctor, and not really the technician either, for who would suspect such a thing? But she swept out of that room with a grave heart. Who knows, someday she may prove to be an exception to the general rule; and those doctors in there, why they're only human and just as puzzled as she was. She thinks maybe it's not too smart to think of doctors the way she used to, that is, as knowing all the answers and being above mistakes, but you know, it sure is a much more comfortable feeling.

* * *

Mr. Pelham lay reclining in the larger surgical chair. The small opening near his eye that led into his maxillary sinus was uncovered and oozing a clear, runny liquid. His face held a sickly yellow hue and his head lay enfolded in his shoulder, completely oblivious of his surroundings or his own lack of comfort.

She hadn't seen him in the office for at least three months. He had been in the hospital most of that time due to another recurrence of his cancer, more severe than before. But once she heard that he was discharged, she imagined that he was back up to par again and working at the gas station that his son had taken over. Now that she saw him, all of these illusions fled and she escaped into the back supply room to allow herself time to think about how she could support him, now that the end was evidently so near for him.

Dr. Becker called her to help him repack the sinus with clean gauze and solution. They worked quietly, without looking at each other or chatting as usual. Mr. Pelham looked quietly from one to the other as they worked. She couldn't bring herself to ask him the usual questions about his prize-winning roses or "Pappy," the Irish wolfhound he had brought in one day when no patients were scheduled so she could meet him. She narrowed her eyes as she watched the opening being filled with packing and squinted until her eyes were partly screwed shut and the tears had less chance of forming and falling and giving her emotion away.

Finally he was through packing. She quickly put a cover bandage on and ran into the supply room. She bent over the sink and laid her forehead against the soap dispenser mounted on the wall. If this is what it will be like getting to know and love these people and then helplessly sitting by and watching them die, she won't be able to take it. She can't help but get involved with them, and she can't stand to feel so helpless that she ignores them later on, at the times when they need her support the most.

Soft steps were heard in the hallway. Dr. Becker peered in at her over the swinging doors. This was his first year of practice and he realized part of what must be going through her mind. He walked in.

"What's the matter?" Without looking up, she said, "He is dying, that's obvious, what else could be the matter?"

He sighed and replied, "Yes, after that last recurrence, he has failed in every area, under every different treatment we have tried. But we have tried, Jane. There is nothing left for us to do but make him comfortable and of course support him and be cheerful and yet sensitive to his needs when he can't voice them. All we are doing in here now is depressing each other, while Mr. Pelham sits in the next room and he's depressed too."

Suddenly she realized what a valuable asset some defenses were. Otherwise you didn't solve anything, you simply created more bad feelings and dismay when you could have been playing up the positive aspects of what has gone on before and what has been learned from people like Mr. Pelham. Quickly she dabbed at her eyes and plunged the instruments into the sink. Then she went into Mr. Pelham's room. "So, I bet Pappy has an easy time with you lately, I bet you've even been letting him sleep with you!" Mr. Pelham looked up and smiled with one corner of his mouth. Well, she thought, that's a start.

* * *

Three wigs of different lengths and colors were perched on top of the faceless styrofoam heads in the medicine room. Two patients lay connected to dripping bottles of toxic drugs with small plastic basins lying next to their heads in case their nausea should become too powerful. An oncology nurse came in to check the flow rate of the drugs and pulled up a stool next to a middle-aged woman who was taking chemotherapy for the first time. "Now," she started, "you had to sign a consent form that told you what kind of side effects you might experience with the particular drugs you are taking. Right?"

"Yes," the woman whispered.

"Have you experienced any of these after your first course of drugs last week?" the nurse asked, while checking her arms and face for changes in pigment or severe symptoms of weight loss.

"Well, yes, I had a lot of nausea for the first three days, and then my hair started coming out in large clumps whenever I brush it. So, I have stopped brushing it except when it gets so tangled that I have no choice."

"Well, you will probably lose almost all of your hair while you are on this medication, but you will also probably regain most of it once your treatment is over with. In the meantime, we can supply you with the wig that most closely resembles your hair style and color. I'll leave you with these to try on over the next few minutes, and when you have chosen one, I'll make out an order for it and we'll have it for you to pick up by next week."

* * *

She witnessed an operation for the first time last week. With a class, she goes from one case to another every morning for two hours with the head anesthesiologist as part of clinical training. The first day, they saw an entire section or lobe of a man's left lung removed because of cancer.

At first she felt queasy as the surgical knife split open around an inch of yellow, bilious fatty tissue which lay on top of the ribs. An incision was made from the top of the shoulder, all the way down the man's side and inward to his backbone, so that he was for all practical purposes cut in half. Underneath, the pulsing sponge of blue and pink tissue began to expand outward, since the skin and tissue no longer held it captive inside. Toward the bottom of the lung, the tissue changed to a dark black color and little fungating portions of tissue could be seen growing in mounds and disrupting the shape of the lung.

The surgeon worked slowly, cutting a portion away from the healthy lung; stopping to tie and clip severed veins with hemostats (which are curved scissors without sharp edges that lock into the position in which you close them), using sponges of gauze to sweep up the blood that obstructed their view. All of these sponges are tossed into a special basket on the floor and it is from them that the blood loss during an operation is estimated. If it is completely soaked with blood, that equals 100 cc's of lost blood, if only partially covered, then it is 50 cc's, etc.

No one is present without rubber gloves with a fine white powder inside to keep his hands from sweating too profusely; a green elastic shower cap on his head, a green surgical cotton gown on, the common mask extending over the mouth and nose, and even paper booties which completely cover his shoes like galoshes.

The floors are rubber to prevent electrical fires, since rubber is not conductive. The lights and tile walls make the rooms seem even colder than the 60 degrees that they are kept at (to inhibit bacteria).

The surgeons, at least many of them, do joke around while they work. For someone who cuts into lungs and stomachs every day, five and six times a day, it becomes as routine as filing or correcting test papers. But you can also be sure that if an unexpected problem arises, they are giving their entire concentration to solving it before serious repercussions are felt.

* * *

The steel voice of the microphone bounced up to the ceiling, vibrated among the chandeliers, and dropped with a whisper to the floor. At the same moment the double doors at the back of the hall were opened and a small, thin man rushed forward. The hallway's breath swept up to the podium and disarranged the speaker's hair. The small man reached the stage and began to adjust his microphone, which uttered a high, shrill protest.

The woman moderator at the right hand side of the stage glanced at the middle-aged model who was frozen in her previous position during this interruption. One hand rested on her left hip while she hugged the back of her neck with the other.

Each moderator stood behind paper-flower and sash-bedecked podiums of brilliant springtime colors. These decorations lent a stale, gaudy accent to the proceedings. They were in gross contrast with the white linen table cloths, elegant wallpaper and crystal chandeliers of the banquet room.

The small woman lifted her chin to the microphone and, while on tip-toe, resumed the fashion show. "This smart three-piece suit is perfect for that special weekend get-away. Though you may spend hours on the road, you'll arrive fresh and wrinkle-free due to its permanent-press finish. Available at the Casual Corner of Sears."

The model twirled to show the front, back, and sides of her outfit. However, her spins were quite rapid and by the time the moderator finished her recital, she stood wavering with a slight attack of vertigo.

Dr. Paul, the other speaker, boomed into the speaker: "This patient had both breasts removed in 1974. Afterwards she received a year of chemotherapy utilizing a combination of three different investigational drugs. Now she is receiving no treatment whatsoever, and merely coming in for periodic checkups."

A group of the women sponsoring the show from the Ladies Club began to clap. The embarrassed model made a slight curtsey and exited quickly off stage.

Barb and she looked at each other with rolling eyes. Who was this Dr. Paul? He represented the typical medical authority who looked upon people as being extraneous to the disease. Just the type who would never remember your name, but would read it to you off of your chart each time you came into the office.

The banquet room was crowded with tables of four, each marked with a small lamp and festooned with a floral arrangement composed of paper flowers identical to those onstage.

At an adjacent table, the administrator of the Cancer Center (which was to receive the money made from this affair) was loudly expressing her delight with the show. "Weren't the fashions lovely? The women chosen to model were terrific. I'm well acquainted with Dr. Paul; doesn't he have a striking figure?" On and on she blabbed, stifling all other conversation in a radius of five feet. Her assistant sat egging her on with monosyllabic replies and a set smile: "Oh yes, they certainly are; So true; Really?" while all the time she was looking for the appropriate moment to mention her upcoming merit review and give herself a plug for a higher raise than usual. "Heaven knows I deserve it," she thought as Irene's voice droned on.

As the finale of the show approached, a man who had been hired to entertain the guests while they were served could be heard tuning up his Stradivarius violin. All eight models came out in bathing suits, surprisingly enough, and looked quite good considering that their average age was 45. At this point Dr. Paul smiled widely and, with some feigned emotion, proclaimed these "patients" as indications of the great strides being made in the detection, treatment, and eventual cure of cancer.

First, notice that, though the author is writing from her personal experience as an assistant to Head and Neck Cancer surgeons, she tells the instances in the third person. The instances are, nevertheless, personally observed. The third person gives her a distance that enables her to see the events and the young woman (who was herself) more clearly; the third person liberates her story sense. This distance is both psychological and perceived spatially in the mind, that is, the third person separates the events and the characters from the author as storyteller.

She tells about patterns of personality reaction to serious, prolonged disease, about the signs and behavior that show how people relate to their cancers, and about doctors' and technicians' reactions. In one incident, she switches from the young technician's point-of-view to the point-of-view of a cleaning woman, to give a summary of a story-within-a-story about a mistaken X-ray reading that resulted in a patient having the wrong side of his body opened up by the surgeon. What forms, modes, and other essay and narrative techniques does she use to give the patterns of observed behavior toward cancer?

From

D to the Knee! Stone to the Bone!
Dino Malcolm

It was cold and a light snow was falling. Jughead and I were sipping white port and Kool-aid while we stared out the front window of the enclosed porch that was connected to Jughead's living room. About half a block away we could see four members of the Rangers approaching us. There was Hawk, a tall skinny guy with scars across his nose. Saint, a short stocky dude who walked like he had a grudge on his shoulders. Mack was the oldest and tallest and the ugliest. Also with them was Rosco-boy; he was the one who carried the pistol because he was the youngest. If any of the others carried the gun and got busted they could get time in the joint. But Rosco-boy was only twelve. Jughead and I would usually represent our club when we would see the Stones. We were both members of the East side Bostonian Pimp Disciples. Jughead was war counselor because he was known for doing crazy things. This was a perfect time to represent our club as the Blackstone Rangers came nearer to our window. We were located on the second floor, so we had a good view of the area. Across the street was the Kimbark Plaza and the Stones were trying to run it. They would be over there every night extorting money from businesses and customers. We finished the wine as the Rocks came nearer to the building. I cracked a window open about an inch and a half, just enough so that snow wouldn't come inside the apartment, but it was enough so that we could represent our club. The Stones were directly in front of our window and I was the first to shout out, "D's run it!" The four stopped in their tracks and then ducked behind a parked car that was covered with snow. Jughead and I ducked down under the window as one of the members looked in our direction. The Stones were confused. They didn't know whether a passing car full of D's said it or whether some of us were hiding in gangways waiting to shoot them on sight. They stayed behind the parked car as the four canvassed the area carefully. Jughead was anxious to represent us so he stood up in the window and opened it wider. This made the snow come into the house and all over me. I tried to tell him to get away from the window but it was too late. "D's thang! D to the knee! Stones ain't shit!" Jughead said in a commanding voice as he beat his fist against his chest twice. This was our code. The Stones had one also, they would use one hand against their chest. All four Stones saw him and heard him. About the same time Head's mother entered the front room from the rear of the apartment. "What's all that noise, Darryl?" Darryl was Head's real name. She was a big woman who didn't take shit from anyone. She ordered us out of the living room but first commanded Jughead to close the window. I was still sitting on the floor trying to watch the Stones and Head's mother at the same time. Jug closed the window. By this time, Rosco-boy had given the gun to Hawk who was aiming it up at the window, at Head. I grabbed at Head and yelled for him to get down. Head fell to the floor at the sound of broken glass. The shot sounded like a car backfiring. Jughead's mother also fell to the floor and the room shook a little. The bullet had broken the window and left a hole the size of a silver dollar a few feet from where Head's mother was standing. Little pieces of glass mixed with snow were everywhere, all in my hair and clothes. A piece of glass was sticking out of Jughead's hand. Jughead and I crawled on the floor over to where his mother was. She was all right except for a little shock. I crawled back to the window and inched my head up to the ledge and peeked out to see if the Rangers were still there. There was no one in sight. All I could see was four sets of tracks in the freshly fallen snow. Here I was, sixteen; and getting shot at was nothing new, but I was scared. I was scared because an innocent person could have gotten shot. Me and Head knew what to expect, we have been D's for three years and before it was over we would be shot at a lot more. Maybe killed. But this was the first time we had jeopardized his mother's life; she wasn't with anybody.

Jughead moved the following week and I became a little more careful, watching my back wherever I went. Hawk and Saint got busted for a stolen car and were sent to Cook County Jail. Mack was trying to start a new club in the neighborhood. Rosco-boy got his in the back one night in front of the YMCA; he was thirteen.

* * *

The five of us were in a basement under Darryl's apartment making zipguns. We heard that the Stones were coming down on us that night so we wanted to be prepared. We had been members of the D's now for three months and we were experts. At least we thought we were. Every time I tried to make a zip gun it would never work. Either I had too many rubber bands or the bullet was too long or short. Darryl's zip gun was made from an old Mattel derringer cap gun. Sometimes it worked and sometimes it didn't. I remember one time we put a .22 long bullet in the gun and it exploded in Darryl's hand. He had to get five stitches in the hospital. Still, he was convinced that this time it would work. Russell was looking out the basement window watching for the police. The last time we were in a basement the landlord called the cops. We barely got away that time. The basement was as long as the apartment complex. You could enter it from one door and exit from three others or vice-versa. The concrete floor was scarred up and dirty from the coal that lined the walls by the furnace. Darryl loaded his zip gun with a .22 short bullet about the same time a police car pulled up to the window. "The Man," said Russell as he ran past us and out the door. Darryl dropped the gun on the floor and it went off making a loud echo throughout the basement. Everybody split up. Darryl and I decided not to go out any doors and instead we climbed out of a window that was facing the alley. Once outside we peeked around the corner of the building and could see the cops taking Russell, who was in handcuffs, to jail. We ran around the side of the building and quickly entered a hallway that was only five feet from us. I started ringing bells until someone buzzed us in. We dashed up to the third floor and sat down on the steps. All you could hear was our heavy breathing. It was only a few minutes, but seemed like hours, when we heard someone enter the building. We don't know how he got in because no one buzzed him in. He started climbing the stairs very carefully, pausing after every few steps. Darryl and I became very quiet, we didn't move a muscle. The footsteps kept getting louder and louder until they finally stopped at the bottom of the stairway where we were sitting. The noise had belonged to the policeman who was staring at both of us. He first asked us if we lived here and when we said yes, he knocked on an apartment door near us. The woman who answered told him we didn't. He handcuffed both of us together, then took us downstairs and outside to the waiting cars. By this time three squad cars were parked in a row. Russell was inside of the first one. The other two guys that were with us sat quietly in the second car. Darryl and I were put in the last car. A policeman came out of the basement carrying Darryl's zip gun.

At the police station the arresting officers tried to blame us for the shooting of a lady a week before on Dorchester Avenue. Officer Glazier, a six-foot-four, two-hundred-fifty-pound Gang Intelligence Unit cop persuaded his fellow officers that we weren't the ones that had gone over to that area because that was the Stones' hood. Only Stones would shoot innocent people and only D's would shoot Stones. Glazier made us sign a huge wooden stick that was as big as a bat with our nicknames. He then hit each of us with it across our rumps. The stick had many names on it. Some of the names belonged to the D's and Stones and other club members. After being hit with the stick I personally couldn't sit down for two or three days. He told us he didn't want to see us again. That was the first time I saw Glazier but it wasn't the last. . . .

* * *

T-Shirt Red was the only person from our club who got killed by the Rangers. He was ambushed on a rainy Sunday night while he and Lil' Ron stood in a courtway on the corner of 51st. They were waiting for the Cottage Grove bus. Ron told us that when he stepped into the restaurant that was next to the courtway, a blue Buick pulled up to the bus stop sign and fired two shots. Ron ran back out to find T-shirt lying halfway in the courtway and halfway on the street. The blood was mixed with the rain as it moved down Red's body and into the gutter. T-Shirt Red caught both barrels in the chest. By the time the ambulance came he was dead. He was seventeen and had been one of the original Pimp-D's.

The next day the Gang Intelligence Unit came down on us as we were standing on the corner mourning our comrade's death. They were so friendly—as a matter of fact, too friendly. The Gang Intelligence Unit was part of the Chicago Police Department. They were supposed to stop the fighting between us. One of the officers was known as the Green Hornet because he drove a green unmarked police car. He offered to give Jughead, Ron, Bull and myself a lift to the outpost. The outpost was the headquarters of the east side Disciples. We dropped the Devil a few years back. Every member of the D's from the west side and east side of the city held meetings at the outpost. After meetings we would get high and party. On our way to the outpost the Green Hornet and his pal were telling us that we should do something to the Stones for killing our friend. One cop told Ron he would let him use his gun if he could because he also hated the Stones. I couldn't believe this madness. Here we are, four D's sitting in the back of a police car being driven by two Gang Intelligence Members who are supposed to be out trying to stop gang killings, and they're telling us to go get even. They dropped us off in front of the outpost and we stood outside and watched as they pulled away from the curb.

* * *

I don't know whether it was a series of gang-related incidents or one major event that changed my ideas about gangs. I probably just got tired of looking behind my back and ducking behind doors and cars every time I walked down the streets. All of this eventually added up to my leaving the D's alone. I had just turned 19 and my love for money was growing more and more. I was dressing clean every day with my tailor-made clothes and panama hats. I was getting chosen every day by the young ladies. I was even looking for a job, even though the nickle bags of reefer I was selling were keeping money in my pocket. I was buying liquor in the stores for myself and for the younger guys in the hood who couldn't cop. My political views on life were also changing. I had stopped going to the weekly meetings our club used to have and I wasn't the only one who had left the gangbanging to the youngsters. A lot of my friends had stopped going to the meetings also. I remember one time there was a bad rumor going around the neighborhood that the D's were going to come down on the people who had stopped going to meetings and that we had turned into P Stones, but it never happened. The D's weren't like the Stones. There were a lot of grown men in the Stones who took that shit seriously. I mean 29, 30 years old, still beating their chests. I remember one incident that changed my whole outlook on life. I would say, now that I think about it, it was "the icing on the cake."

It was a very hot summer day in the middle of July, and I had just come from the hospital visiting Jughead. He had gotten shot in a crossfire at the Starlite Lounge about a week before. The shooting was over whose woman was whose. We had already missed the last three meetings and we were debating on staying in the D's. The Pimps had broken up and Shylow, Mike, and Prince had joined the Woodlawn D's. They wanted Head and myself to do the same. Head was telling me he was going to pimp whores when he got out of the hospital and I was trying to boost my reefer sales. Even though we weren't representing the club, we would still hang out with people who were still known Disciples because they were still our friends.

It was so hot that day that people were walking around with their shirts off. When I saw Rat and his two henchmen walking towards me I wanted to explain to them that I was no longer a D, but it was too late. Rat was a tall skinny guy with a big Afro. He only had about three teeth in his mouth. When he was by himself he would always use "Brother" in his conversations. "How you doing, Brother?" "We've got to get together, Brother," or "Peace, Bro." When he was with his boys he was Stone to the Bone. I started to speak but Rat and his two Stones had surrounded me. "How you doing, you D?" Rat said with a smile on his face. I said, half smiling, "I ain't that shit anymore, I'm selling reefer now. Want to cop?" One of the other guys spoke. "You a D? We don't like D's. Stones run this from State to the lake." The other guy started pointing. "We ought to fuck this D up." We were standing near a row of apartment buildings and a gangway. I saw that these assholes were in the mood to fuck somebody up and I just happened to be in the wrong place at the wrong time. I sure could use a cop about now but they are never around when you need them.

I decided to make a run for it but before I could do anything they pushed me into the gangway. Rat kept his hand under his shirt as we entered the dark area. The gangway was dark as the three men shoved me against the brick wall. My knees became weak from the load they were carrying. Rat kept telling me he hated D's and I kept trying to tell him with my hands and mouth that I wasn't a D anymore. The other two men were standing at the entrance of the gangway, watching and acting very nervous. "Come on, Rat, hurry up and get this shit over with," one of them said. Rat pulled a small blue steel gun from under his shirt and jammed it into my stomach. I stopped talking. "Stones run it!" Rat said as he pulled the trigger. I tried to brace myself against the wall to catch the impact of the bullet. A lot of things flashed across my mind at that moment: how I was going to fix the flat on my mother's car; my lady would be mad at me because I wasn't going to pick her up from work; how am I going to get rid of the reefer in my pocket?

Click. Rat and his friends looked confused as Rat pulled the trigger again. Click, Click, Click. Either he forgot to load the revolver or it was jammed. I wasn't staying around to find out. I had to get the fuck out of there and right now. I made my break for the other end of the gangway. The three tried to follow me but I was too fast for them. I ran faster than I've ever run before. I leaped over a ten foot wooden fence with ease. I twisted my body through some more narrow gangways. I didn't stop until I had reached the hood where I would see somebody I knew. As I separated myself from the Stones, all I could think of was revenge. I thought about getting my pistol and calling Shylow. I was going to go up on the try (63rd Street) and get some more D's, and then we were going to fuck up any Stone we saw.

I was supposed to be getting away from this shit. I wasn't a D anymore. I sat down on some steps to decide what my next move was going to be. I figured that even though I was scared and almost got killed, I came out of it without a scratch. I had had a lot of close calls before. So I decided to play it off as if nothing happened. I went to the liquor store and bought myself a pint of rum and a Coke. I sat in the park that was behind the shopping center and thought about what just happened and how Somebody was looking out for me. . . .

———

This instance-collection begins with an incident that shows the power of group loyalty in conflict with another group, revealing the all-absorbing, demanding, dangerous game played between these two gangs and the game that each participant plays with himself. What forms are used to tell each of the incidents or entries? What points or particular meanings are illustrated or developed by each incident?

Compare "How People Relate to Cancer" and "D to the Knee! Stone to the Bone!" for language (mixed diction), forms, points-of-view, attitudes of the authors, techniques, and anything else that takes your attention.

Writing Your How-it-Happens Collection of Instances

The selection of content is important, content that is important to you, whether it's neighborhood gangs or an expensive private college. The way the content is perceived and told is also important. Either can exercise the main force in making story or essay meaningful to the audience. So you may, while writing in your journal or telling and writing in your class about possible how-it-happens subject material, become aware of a more compelling job or other experience that you've set aside or avoided up to now. Wide-ranging journal writings, oral tellings, and in-class writings may uncover strong material.

The authors of the instance-collections take the time to tell what they see in their mind's eye, what they have to say, in the forms they've chosen, rather than simply sketch or rush the passages. They take the time to tell it fully and make the effort to get it across to themselves as the first audience and to the readers and listeners. They probe to find what the experience is telling them, the patterns of the experience, what they discover about it. They explore different forms, points-of-view, and techniques to tell the various incidents. Remember, they also wrote many more incidents and passages than are published here.

In your how-it-happens collection of incidents, instances, passages, journal entries, etc., you can explore and develop any form that we've discussed in this book. Indeed, a strong how-it-happens subject area will be particularly responsive to your forms attempts. Try each form in your journal, even if you do not finally carry them so far as rewriting and typing. You may read some of them from your journal in the class.

You can fictionalize events, as much as necessary, in order to fulfill each form, point-of-view switch, the narrative needs of your essay or "story." Use your imagination for events, characters, interaction of characters, and forms. You may well come to understand the "real" personally-observed events better that way. You can also stick strictly to what you have personally observed, as in the case of Schaller's telling about gorilla behavior or Holt's telling about children in school-learning situations or my own telling about parents and children, depending upon what you perceive to be the main purpose of your how-it-happens writing.

General Essays—Combining Personal Observation, Research Through Reading, and other Research Methods

Speeches

The speech (setting forth a subject and arguing a view of it) is the antecedent oral form of the expository essay. The "General Essays" section begins with speeches, a lecture, and a speech-like essay-editorial that demonstrate the explicit, out-front audience sense of good expository and argumentative writing, with use of the personal pronouns ("you," "we," "I") characterizing most of the essays.

In these essays, as in other essays in this book, the authors combine forms and modes to tell what they have observed, researched, have to say, and what they want us to come to believe and do. The rhetorical modes—Comparison and Contrast, Cause and Effect Analysis, Definition, Division and Classification, and so forth—are ways of thinking and ways of talking about what we think, expressed in a basic form or combination of basic forms. The basic forms are at once ways of thinking and flexible forms of expression. The rhetorical modes are revealed within the overall basic forms combination of the essays.

Though each author of the following essays draws material from more than one kind of research, each relies in large part upon personal observation. Overall, these essays present a rich mixture of personal observation and research through reading, interviewing, and examination of other records, as a demonstration of the necessary interweaving of forms and ways of thinking. Each of the essays shows a pronounced "story sense," an intuitive sense of telling a "story" to an audience, which helps the authors discover, organize, and express what they have to say. Each of the essays begins with a vivid image or statement that seizes the reader's attention, suggests what the essay is about, and gives an organizing impulse.

* * *

We begin with the written transcriptions and translations of two speeches.

Oration by Chief Seattle
From *Northwest Gateway*
Archie Binns

Every part of this soil is sacred in the estimation of my people. Every hillside, every valley, every plain and grove, has been hallowed by some sad or happy event in days long vanished. The very dust upon which you now stand responds more lovingly to their footsteps than to yours, because it is rich with blood of our ancestors and our bare feet are conscious of the sympathetic touch. Even the little children who live here and rejoice here for a brief season love these somber solitudes and at eventide they greet shadowy returning spirits. And when the last redmen shall have perished and the memory of my tribe shall have become a myth among the white man, these shores will swarm with the invisible dead of my tribe and when your children's children think themselves alone in the field, the store, the shop, upon the highway or in the silence of the pathless woods, they will not be alone.

On the Murder of His Family
James Logan (Tah-gah-jute)

I appeal to any white man to say if ever he entered Logan's cabin hungry, and he gave him not meat; if ever he came cold and naked, and he clothed him not. During the course of the last long and bloody war, Logan remained idle in his camp, an advocate of peace. Such was my love for the whites that my countrymen pointed as I passed and said: "Logan is the friend of the white man." I had even thought to have lived with you, but for the injuries of one man. Colonel Cresap, the last spring, in cold blood, and unprovoked, murdered all the relations of Logan, not even sparing my women and children. There runs not a drop of my blood in the veins of any living creature. This called on me for revenge. I have sought it. I have killed many. I have fully glutted my vengeance. For my country, I rejoice at the beams of peace; but do not harbor a thought that mine is the job of fear. Logan never felt fear. He will not turn on his heel to save his life. Who is there to mourn for Logan? Not one.

These two short courses of reasoning, which were public speeches, show the remarkable economy accomplished by oral arguments when done by preliterate people who were conditioned to expect themselves to be good at it, and who knew they had to get their messages firmly and clearly into the audience's memories. Examine how each sentence makes concentrated use of imagery, concrete references, metaphorical references, and a statement of argument. When Chief Seattle addresses "you" in "The very dust upon which you now stand . . . ," he *places* his audience right before him, in the context of history, and in touch with what he has to say.

Examine Logan's argument, sentence by sentence, how he uses concrete references such as "cabin" and "meat" to symbolize large meanings, how the structure of the brief, vivid story of his life becomes the structure of his argument, how he presents with a climactic turn Colonel Cresap's massacre of his family, then states his need for vengeance, and uses imagery as a metaphor for his final attitude, "He [Logan] will not turn on his heel to save his life." What do you make of his referring to himself in the end in the third person?

* * *

You are probably familiar with deductive proof and inductive conclusions in mathematics, in which the inductive generalization is formed from what appears to be true of many examples. Such inductive generalization may be shown to be inadequate when counter-examples show up. However, in scientific investigation, inductive methods offer the main means for discovery; and inductive generalization is used in a deductive way until a better generalization is formed. The following "lecture" by Sigmund Freud uses inductive approaches.

"Parapraxes" from Lecture II
From *Introductory Lectures on Psychoanalysis*
Sigmund Freud
translated by James Strachey

LADIES AND GENTLEMEN,—We will not start with postulates but with an investigation. Let us choose as its subject certain phenomena which are very common and very familiar but which have been very little examined, and which, since they can be observed in any healthy person, have nothing to do with illnesses. They are what are known as 'parapraxes',[1] to which everyone is liable. It may happen, for instance, that a person who intends to say something may use another word instead (a *slip of the tongue* [*Versprechen*], or he may do the same thing in writing, and may or may not notice what he has done. Or a person may read something, whether in print or manuscript, different from what is actually before his eyes (a *misreading* [*Verlesen*]), or he may hear wrongly something that has been said to him (a *mishearing* [*Verhören*])—on the assumption, of course, that there is no organic disturbance of his powers of hearing. Another group of these phenomena has as its basis *forgetting* [*Vergessen*]—not, however, a permanent forgetting but only a temporary one. Thus a person may be unable to get hold of a *name* which he nevertheless knows and which he recognizes at once, or he may forget to carry out an *intention*, though he remembers it later and has thus only forgotten it at that particular moment. In a third group the temporary character is absent—for instance in the case of *mislaying* [*Verlegen*], when a person has put something somewhere and cannot find it again, or in the precisely analogous case of *losing* [*Verlieren*]. Here we have a forgetting which we treat differently from other kinds of forgetting, one at which we are surprised or annoyed instead of finding it understandable. In addition to all this there are particular sorts of *errors* [*Irrtümer*], in which the temporary character is present once more; for in their instance we believe for a time that something is the case which both before and afterwards we know is not so. And there are a number of other similar phenomena known by various names.

All these are occurrences whose internal affinity with one another is expressed in the fact that [in German] they begin with the syllable '*ver*'.[1] They are almost all of an unimportant kind, most of them are very transitory, and they are without much significance in human life. Only rarely does one of them, such as losing an object, attain some degree of practical importance. For that reason, too, they attract little attention, give rise to no more than feeble emotions, and so on.

It is to these phenomena, then, that I now propose to draw your attention. But you will protest with some annoyance: 'There are so many vast problems in the wide universe, as well as within the narrower confines of our minds, so many marvels in the field of mental disorders, which require and deserve to have light thrown upon them, that it does really seem gratuitous to waste labour and interest on such trivialities. If you could make us understand why a person with sound eyes and ears can see and hear in broad daylight things that are not there, why another person suddenly thinks he is being persecuted by the people of whom he has hitherto been most fond, or puts forward the cleverest arguments in support of delusional beliefs which any child could see were nonsensical, then we should have some opinion of psycho-analysis. But if it can do no more than ask us to consider why a speaker at a banquet uses one word instead of another or why a housewife has mislaid her keys, and similar futilities, then we shall know how to put our time and interest to better uses.'

I should reply: Patience, Ladies and Gentlemen! I think your criticism has gone astray. It is true that psycho-analysis cannot boast that it has never concerned itself with trivialities. On the contrary, the material for its observations is usually provided by the inconsiderable events which have been put aside by the other sciences as being too unimportant—the dregs, one might say, of the world of phenomena. But are you not making a confusion in your criticism between the vastness of the problems and the conspicuousness of what points to them? Are there not very important things which can only reveal themselves, under certain conditions and at certain times, by quite feeble indications? I should find no difficulty in giving you several examples of such situations. If you are a young man, for instance, will it not be from small pointers that you conclude that you have won a girl's favour? Would you wait for an express declaration of love or a passionate embrace? Or would not a glance, scarcely noticed by other people, be enough? a slight movement, the lengthening by a second of the pressure of a hand? And if you were a detective engaged in tracing a murder, would you expect to find that the murderer had left his photograph behind at the place of the crime, with his address attached? or would you not necessarily have to be satisfied with comparatively slight and obscure traces of the person you were in search of? So do not let us under-estimate small indications; by their help we may succeed in getting on the track of something bigger. Furthermore, I think like you that the great problems of the universe and of science have the first claim on our interest. But it is as a rule of very little use to form an express intention of devoting oneself to research into this or that great problem. One is then often at a loss to know the first step to take. It is more promising in scientific work to attack whatever is immediately before one and offers an opportunity for research. If one does so really thoroughly and without prejudice or preconception, and if one has luck, then, since everything is related to everything, including small things to great, one may gain access even from such unpretentious work to a study of the great problems. That is what I should say in order to retain your interest, when we deal with such apparent trivialities as the parapraxes of healthy people.

———————

In an inductive argument, the author, rather than stating a thesis and then giving the proving argument for the thesis, involves the audience directly in the investigation of the observed instances to see what may be discovered, what "thesis" may be worked out. The inductive argument parallels and simulates the actual process of discovery. If Freud were employing a deductive argument in this essay, how would he deductively state and prove the thesis differently from the way he works here?

Freud wrote and delivered this essay on the psychology of errors as a lecture, as he wrote the other chapters of *Introductory Lectures on Psychoanalysis*. So, when he wrote alone in his study, he imagined himself speaking to the mostly friendly but also skeptical audience of young doctors and other persons interested in psychoanalysis. He imagined the audience's reactions as he wrote: their questions, doubts, and how they could come to see and believe new ways of thinking. Employing all of the pronouns of address ("we," "I," "you," "he," "she," "they") he incorporates the concrete situation of the lecture dramatically into the writing. Who is the "we" in his lecture?

He emphasizes the scientific principle of examining the anomaly of the patterns (the occurrence that does not fit the pattern), in order to find another important pattern. Thus, if we compare and contrast like instances and throw out the ones that do not "fit," as we are often advised to do by some teachers of rhetoric, we may well have thrown out the anomalous instance that could help us find other similar instances that could lead to a revealing discovery of another series that will make a pattern. How do you know when to exclude and when not to exclude instances? You have to rely on your sense for connections, of which Freud speaks, which can eventually. connect the small with the "great." You see one instance connecting with another similar instance. Your sense of connections, the sense of *what takes your attention,* needs your stimulation and encouragement.

* * *

The following essay-editorial is organized and expressed with an audience of farmers specifically in mind. How closely does it resemble and sound like a public speech? Point out words, phrases, ways of speaking, and passages that support what you say. What is the author's tone, attitude? Where do you find it aggressive? Where humorous? Where factual? Find the three main parts of the structure of the argument.

When Will You Be a No-Till Farmer?
Dick Lehnert

After growing up on a farm and then spending 15 years dealing with farmers as a staffer here at Michigan Farmer, I take pride in being able to understand the kinds of questions farmers are asking and being able to help find answers.

But when it comes to the concept of no-till farming, you've really got me puzzled.

I wrote my first article on no-till in 1969, accompanied with pictures, charts about fuel and soil savings and a success story about a farmer who used it. Then I sat back to wait for the tide to swell.

It didn't. And over the 11 years since, we've had at least one or two articles per year on no-till. According to figures from the Soil Conservation Service, no-till acreage in Michigan has "swelled" to roughly 50,000.

Good grief! I've mulched that much area with newsprint on the subject.

So this issue, we're trying another approach. You see, I'm convinced beyond the shadow of a doubt that no-till will work for you and save you money, time and soil. Obviously, you're not.

I used to think that maybe you'd go to no-till when your old corn planter wore out and you had to buy a new one. That's a logical time to change. But you've been through several planters since 1969, and you didn't change.

I thought maybe as tractors got bigger and more costly you'd sooner or later decide to level off horsepower and change tillage systems, but you haven't. The equipment companies tell me they're just following your demand—and that I shouldn't fault them because you can hardly find no-till equipment if you look. They say you're not looking.

I thought those of you on the sandy ground would get sick and tired of watching your corn roll up each summer and you'd go to no-till to mulch the soil and save moisture. But instead you piled your dough into irrigation equipment.

I thought fuel costs would get to you and you'd gradually cut back tillage, but you're gradually tilling more, primarily because you're incorporating more herbicides.

I thought you'd get tired fighting compaction and soil crusting, but you just buy bigger tractors and more rotary hoes and buck your way on through.

Despite my being so "out of step," I stick with my guns. You'll be a no-till farmer by 1990 or sooner.

Persistent Trends

There are a number of trends that will ultimately force you that direction. The price of fuel is going to continue to rise. The price of machinery continues to rise and so does the interest rate on the money you borrow to buy it. If you can use older, smaller machines to no-till, ultimately that should have an impact upon you.

But the most noticeable trend, from where I sit, is the persistence of the environmentalists. Farmers have gotten off easy to date. They were able to exempt themselves from environmental legislation, but many of those "exemptions" were merely delays.

It now appears that the 1973 Michigan Environmental Erosion and Sedimentation Control Act will be implemented on farms and that the federal government is dead serious about its goal of clean water by 1983.

I realize that conservation seems to make dull copy and small headlines, but if you're not attuned to what's been happening on that front in the last three years, you should be. The federal government has finished an appraisal of the nation's land and water resources and is seriously talking about a 50-year, $200 billion program to improve them. It's under review right now.

There's an interesting bit of logic involved that goes like this:

Farmers get price supports based in part upon the cost of production of various commodities. Therefore, the public, which pays these costs, has reason to involve itself in determining how commodities are produced.

You don't farm in a vacuum. If you're losing pesticides and fertilizers from your land by using farming methods that produce erosion of more than five tons per acre per year, why should the public bear the costs in higher food prices and higher support prices? Why should they swim in poorer quality water just because farmers want to keep methods that cause erosion?

It makes a pretty fair point. There's a very serious movement afoot to insure that you use what are called "best management practices" on your land. And while you may think you already do, many people—even many farmers—do not agree.

As we published in our last issue, you've got until March 28 to make your points about what you think the government should do to achieve conservation objectives. But remember this: Those conservation objectives have already been set. And one clear aspect is, soil losses in excees of five tons to the acre each year will not be acceptable.

Almost no farmer can meet that acceptable level using a combination of fall plowing and spring tillage.

But that's enough about threats. You are being threatened, but before you get out your pen to write, you really ought to look at the other side. You ought to evaluate your farming methods and ask yourself some really basic questions, like "Why do I plow?" "How much erosion do I cause?"

In this issue, we hope we've outlined the kind of information that will allow you to undertake an "affirmative action" program that will assure you can meet the changing times without undue stress—like having your farm surrounded by government agents who chain your plow to a tree.

The first step is to put some pressure on Michigan State University. Insist that the Crops and Soils Department get on the stick to do a careful evaluation of no-till in Michigan. It's senseless that our no-tillers look to Ohio for leadership.

Secondly, take a look at the list we've published of the "farm consultants" hired by Chevron Chemical Company and try to make contact with one of them. Remember they are busy farmers, and they get a very modest fee for their no-till aid. But you might want to take a look at what they're doing and how they do it. Watch them at planting time.

Next, contact your local Soil Conservation District. In almost every district they're pushing no-till. Some districts, in fact, have bought no-till planting equipment you can rent.

If you can find a machine (there are only about 450 of them in Michigan at last count), try it out on your farm. Just try a plot and see how it works. Then you can give serious thought to what kind of planter you buy next time. A no-till planter costs 10% to 20% more than a conventional planter, but it plants both conventionally and no-till. Once you have the planter, you can continue your experiments and gradually increase no-till acreage.

Give it a fair test. A lot of people who've tried no-till saw it as a great method to plant some old swamp they could never plow. Obviously, they got less than perfect results.

The experts stress that it takes a good manager to no-till. But I might add, it takes a good manager to farm these days.

There's a great difference of opinion today about what kind of land can be no-tilled. MSU experts narrowly define land suitable for no-till as the hilly, sandy stuff. The Soil Conservation Service, asked what kind of Michigan land can be no-tilled, answered, "All of it."

Even if we take MSU's cautious advice and start on the sands and the hills, at least we'd start. Once started, we can stop wherever common sense tells us.

In the first part, the author not only makes fun of himself and the farmers in his audience and of his efforts on behalf of the better approach, but also gives once again the arguments for why farmers *should* undertake this better, more economical form of crop production. In the second part, he develops strongly the trends that he feels will "force" the "you" (the farmer) into the better way. How does his tone change here? Then, beginning with "But that's enough about threats," he lays out a positive program that will enable the farmer without great risk to acquaint himself with the methods and results of no-till. He concludes with a conservative, small-risk appeal. How do the progressive changes of tone, associated with particular parts of the argument, aid the persuasion?

Compare Lehnert's tone and sense of audience to Freud's, Logan's and Chief Seattle's.

From
The Gospel of St. Mark

Chapter 4

And he began again to teach by the sea side: and there was gathered unto him a great multitude, so that he entered into a ship, and sat in the sea; and the whole multitude was by the sea on the land.

And he taught them many things by parables, and said unto them in his doctrine, Hearken; Behold, there went out a sower to sow: And it came to pass, as he sowed, some fell by the way side, and the fowls of the air came and devoured it up. And some fell on stony ground, where it had not much earth; and immediately it sprang up, because it had no depth of earth: But when the sun was up, it was scorched; and because it had no root, it withered away. And some fell among thorns and the thorns grew up, and choked it, and it yielded no fruit. And other fell on good ground, and did yield fruit that sprang up and increased; and brought forth, some thirty, and some sixty, and some an hundred.

And he said unto them, He that hath ears to hear, let him hear.

And when he was alone, they that were about him with the twelve asked of him the parable. And he said unto them, Unto you it is given to know the mystery of the kingdom of God; but unto them that are without, all these things are done in parables: That seeing they may see, and not perceive; and hearing they may hear, and not understand; lest at any time they should be converted, and their sins should be forgiven them. And he said unto them, Know ye not this parable? and how then will ye know all parables?

The sower soweth the word. And these are they by the way side, where the word is sown; but when they have heard, Satan cometh immediately, and taketh away the word that was sown in their hearts. And these are they likewise which are sown on stony ground; who, when they have heard the word, immediately receive it with gladness; And have no root in themselves, and so endure but for a time: afterward, when affliction or persecution ariseth for the word's sake, immediately they are offended. And these are they which are sown among thorns; such as hear the word, And the cares of this world, and the deceitfulness of riches, and the lusts of other things entering in, choke the word, and it becometh unfruitful. And these are they which are sown on good ground; such as hear the word, and receive it, and bring forth fruit, some thirtyfold, some sixty, and some an hundred.

These parables were originally told orally. The "story" incorporates the scene of Jesus's telling of the parables to an audience, a series of brief stories-within-a-story, followed by his more informal speech to his disciples explaining their meaning. The metaphorical examples and illustrations get the principles across to our minds, with radiating implications. How are the techniques similar to those of Chief Seattle's and Logan's speeches? How does the method of comparison and contrast work in Jesus's organization of the parable into three parts? What gestures can you see the teller using with the image? Find modern examples for each of the parables and each interpretation. You could use the experience of your how-it-happens subject area, or any other experience that you know or have read or heard about.

Definitions

Two Definitions of "Weed"

> **weed** (wēd) n. 1. a. A plant considered undesirable, unattractive, or troublesome; especially, one growing where it is not wanted in cultivated ground.
> *The American Heritage Dictionary*

What is a *weed?* I have heard it said that there are sixty definitions. For me, a weed is a plant out of place. Or, less tolerantly, call it a foreign aggressor, which is a thing not so mild as a mere escape from cultivation, a visitor that sows itself innocently in a garden bed where you would not choose to plant it. Most weeds have natal countries, whence they have sortied. So Japanese honeysuckle, English plantain, Russian thistle came from lands we recognize, but others, like gypsies, have lost all record of their geographic origin. Some of them turn up in all countries, and are listed in no flora as natives. Some knock about the seaports of the world, springing up wherever ballast used to be dumped from the old sailing ships. Others prefer cities; they have lost contact with sweet soil, and lead a guttersnipe existence. A little group occurs only where wool waste is dumped, others are dooryard and pavement weeds, seeming to thrive the more as they are trod by the feet of man's generations. Some prized in an age of simpler tastes have become garden *déclassés* and street urchins; thus it comes about that the pleasant but plebeian scent of Bouncing Bet, that somewhat blowsy pink of old English gardens, is now one of the characteristic odors of American sidewalk ends, where the pavement peters out and shacks and junked cars begin.—DONALD CULROSS PEATTIE; *Flowering Earth.*

Three Definitions of "Work"

> **work** (wûrk) n. 1. Physical or mental effort or activity direct-
> ed toward the production or accomplishment of something;
> toil; labor.
>
> *The American Heritage Dictionary*

An Engineer's Definition

One of the fundamental units which applies to electricity as well as other things is the unit of *work*. In engineering, work is defined as the product of the force times distance. It is measured in foot pounds. If you lift a weight of 55 pounds up ten feet, you have ten times 55, or 550 pounds of foot-pound work. Likewise, if you push a box across the floor with a steady force of 55 pounds against friction, when you have moved it ten feet you have again exerted 550 pounds of work.

A Sociologist's Definition

Work may be viewed as that which a person does in order to survive. Narrowly conceived, work is simply the way in which a person earns a living. From a broad perspective, a person works in order to maintain or enhance any of the statuses that are his by virtue of his membership in a multiplicity of groups. A person may be happy in his survival tasks or he may be woefully miserable. He may work merely in order to receive his weekly paycheck, or he may perform some activities for no reason other than sheer joy in the task. However, as long as the person defines, or has defined for him, the activities in which he is engaged as in some manner related to his survival, either physical or social, then we can say that person is working. (Lee Braude, *Work and Workers*)

*   *   *

First, we have short definitions of "weed" and "work" taken directly from The American Heritage Dictionary, then longer definitions of the two subjects. What important qualification of the definition is made by Peattie when he says, "For me, a weed is . . ."? What is similar in his definition to the dictionary definition of "weed"? What more have you learned about weeds from Peattie's definition? How does he compare and contrast instances and kinds of weeds? Where does he sum up patterns of weed behavior? How does he use illustrative examples and imagery?

How is the engineering definition of work similar to and different from the dictionary's definition? How is the sociologist's definition similar to and different from the engineering and dictionary definitions?

How is the following definition of the crystal laser similar to and different from the "word" and "work" definitions?

There are many types of lasers already in existence and research gives promise of even more to come. However, the type that is probably most familiar is the ruby laser, which is a form of a larger classification known as crystal lasers. The crystal in the ruby laser is a synthetic ruby made from aluminum oxide with an impurity added in the form of a minute quantity of chromium atoms. It is the chromium which gives the ruby laser its characteristic pink or red color. The crystal is about the diameter of a pencil and has a fully mirrored surface on one end and a semi-mirrored surface on the other.

Surrounding the ruby is a flashtube—a pulsed light source similar to that used in electronic flash units for cameras. As the flash tube fires, the light energy it gives off stimulates the atoms in the crystal. Ordinarily the atoms of aluminum oxide are very stable but in the ruby crystal, the addition of the chromium creates an instability in the crystal atoms. Light energy from the flash tube is absorbed by the unstable atoms, causing their energy level to be increased. Eventually the energy level becomes so high that some of the energy must be released by the atoms. The released energy is in the form of light waves which bounce up and down the crystal, reflected at each end by the mirrored surfaces. As the light moves, it strikes more unstable atoms causing even more light energy to be released. When a sufficiently high level is reached, the light escapes from the semi-mirrored end of the crystal and the laser has "lased." This method of stimulation is called optical pumping.

Laser light is very different from ordinary light. The light from a flashlight, for example, is incoherent, that is, it travels in all directions. Laser light is coherent, which is to say that the outer edges of the beam are almost perfectly parallel to each other. A laser beam one-half inch in diameter will diverge to become only three inches in diameter after traveling more than one mile; or, to look at it another way, that half inch beam if fired from the earth to the moon would illuminate an area on the lunar surface only slightly greater than one mile in diameter. By focusing the laser beam through a lens system, even smaller areas of coverage can be achieved.

Laser light, in addition to being coherent, is also monochromatic. Ordinary light is polychromatic, which means it consists of all light frequencies ranging from infrared to ultraviolet. Laser light normally consists of only one frequency or at most a few frequencies.

One of the drawbacks to the ruby laser and many of the other early lasers was their inability to operate continuously. Light was emitted in pulsed bursts and the crystal developed excessive heat. A newer crystal consisting of neodymium yttrium aluminum garnet uses less power than the ruby and lends itself to water cooling, thereby making continuous operation possible.

To get some idea of the potential power of the laser, consider this: The electrical power used in the home is measured in kilowatt-hours, that is, an expenditure of one thousand watts of energy over a one-hour duration. A laser can take that energy, concentrate it and release it in one burst of one one-billionth of a second duration. It is difficult to conceive the amount of energy contained in that single burst, but for that short interval the laser beam would be releasing energy in the order of a gigawatt (one billion watts). That is more energy than is generated in a comparable length of time by the combined output of all the power generating stations in the United States.

Sounds good, doesn't it? Sounds like we may be well on our way to beating the energy crisis. Things are not so rosy, however, as the surface indicates. The laser is not that efficient; it always requires considerably more power input than it is able to output. Therefore high power lasers require power sources which are far larger physically than the laser itself. Technology is working to overcome this shortcoming and perhaps soon there will be lasers or power sources of increased efficiency. (Harry Partin, "The Laser: Humanitarian Hope or Doomsday Device?")

You could write your own definition of "weed," "work," or "laser." You could do straightforward, parodic, or metaphorical definitions of key terms within your how-it-happens subject area.

Go to dictionaries, encyclopedias, and other books in your school library (look under the subject names in the card catalog) and compare definitions—and extended definitions—of "love," "anger," "automobile," "dedication," "chair," "play," etc.—any word you choose.

Cause and Effect

Do most cause and effect essays reason from cause to effect, or from effect to cause? How does the reasoning happen in the following article, "Hard Starting—Causes and Cures"? Think of other subjects of everyday troubleshooting and diagnosis for writing assignments.

Hard Starting—Causes and Cures

Starting problems come in two basic forms: starting system failure, which means that the engine will not crank or cranks too slowly; and failure of the engine to fire or to continue running under its own power.

The battery, starter, starter solenoid, starter drive and the starter control (including the ignition switch, automatic transmission neutral safety switch and wiring) comprise the starting system. Of these, the battery and its cables are undoubtedly responsible for the majority of starting system failures.

Go or No Go

Suppose you hop into your car to go to work. When you turn the key to "start," nothing, not even a click, is heard. This should tell you two things immediately. Either battery current is not reaching the starter solenoid or the starting system isn't getting the message from the ignition switch.

Switch on the headlights. If they do not light, the battery is dead or the battery cables are not in good electrical contact with the battery posts. If the headlights are bright but go out as soon as you turn the ignition to "start," you have cable terminal trouble and not a discharged battery.

Battery-testing hydrometers are inexpensive, but they're common enough that every garage and service station has one. You may even be able to borrow one to use on the premises, but if the attendant does the testing for you, the fee will be small. Don't forget that batteries contain volatile gases that may be present outside the battery case, *so under no circumstances should you smoke around a battery or do anything to create a spark.*

Battery cases are often thin and flexible. If you remove the battery, use a lifting strap; otherwise, acid could be forced out of the vent holes if you squeeze the case. This would result in holes in your clothing and serious injury to your skin or eyes, depending on where acid splashes.

Jam the tip of the screwdriver into the joint between the battery post and the terminal and have someone in the car try the starter. If it's still no go, try the same trick on the other battery post. This should produce action. If you have the necessary tools aboard, you can clean the battery terminals. But if not, you'll at least be able to reach a service station where the job can be done. When cable trouble is indicated but improving contact with the battery posts doesn't do the job, check the connections at the other end of the cables.

A push-start might still get you going even if the battery is weak, but it won't tell you why the battery is flatter than a three-day-old beer. If your car has an ammeter, try to recall whether it's been reading in the "charge" range for the past several weeks. If so, it's an indication that the battery was headed for failure, due either to old age or very low electrolyte level, and could no longer accept a full charge. When a battery is fully charged, the ammeter will read "zero" while driving. If the ammeter has been showing a discharge or if the generator warning light has been coming on or staying on, then it's likely that the charging system needs attention.

Plan "B"

If the battery and terminals prove to be all right, check the control circuit. If the car has an automatic transmission, try starting it in both "park" and "neutral." Sometimes the neutral safety switch will fail to operate in one position but will still work in the other. If all remains silent, place the transmission in neutral, turn the ignition on, then short between the large terminal on the starter solenoid (which receives the cable from the battery) and the small terminal (which receives the control circuit wire coming from the ignition switch). Pliers handles are good for this. If the ignition switch, neutral safety switch or control circuit wiring is faulty, you should be able to start the engine in this way. Unfortunately, the starter and solenoid on some cars with V-8 engines are almost impossible to reach.

If the headlights are bright but grow dim when the ignition switch is turned to "start," the solenoid or starter drive may be jammed. There may be a slight clicking sound. Try the ignition switch repeatedly. If the solenoid has jammed (usually due to dirt on its plunger), it may eventually free itself and engage the starter. Jammed starter drives can often be freed by placing cars equipped with a manual transmission in 2nd gear and then rocking the car backward by hand. If a clicking sound is heard when the key is turned to "start," but the headlights nearly go out, your problem is a discharged battery. . . .

Foolin' with Fuel

Most starting problems originate in the ignition system. Very often, however, the malfunction is something that a thorough tune-up would have prevented. Wide plug gaps, worn out spark plugs, or distributor points which have closed their gap excessively due to rubbing block wear are often the cause. Carburetion problems (such as a sticking or faulty automatic choke) or an air filter that's restricted by dirt can also cause hard starting and would have been corrected by a tune-up.

If the engine is being flooded with too much gasoline, there will be a definite odor of raw gas during your starting attempts. If removing the air cleaner shows the choke to be opening properly, the odor of unburned fuel may be caused by an ignition fault which is failing to ignite the mixture. If the engine has become flooded merely due to carburetor "percolation" or errors in starting procedure, depress the accelerator pedal fully and *leave it there* for a minute or two before trying the starter again. Do not release the pedal for any reason. If the engine doesn't start, wait another minute and try again. Don't lift your foot until the engine begins running on its own power.

Holding the accelerator down on a flooded engine will not "give it gas," as many uninformed people assume. Instead it gives the engine *air* by holding both the throttle and choke valves open. This allows excess fuel to evaporate quicker and provides more air for easier combustion of the too-rich mixture when you try to start up. If all drivers understood this condition there'd be fewer cars stalled in traffic on hot days.

Comparison and Contrast—Division and Classification

If you take a box-full of wooden blocks and spill them onto the floor, you can look them over, compare them, and then begin to divide them into other piles, classifying them according to shape, color, kind of wood, etc. If you have a pile of books on the floor, you can divide and classify them into subject areas and then alphabetize them within subject headings. You compare and contrast the notes of your observed instances by seeing them side by side with each other, either in your mind or in print, and then you divide and classify according to your sense for significant connections. Of course, we carry out this process everyday with what we see in our minds without ever resorting to writing. Writing, because the medium is permanent, enables us to do complicated work in comparison and contrast and in division and classification of instances of behavior. I divided and classified the instances of laughter according to who laughed, when, at what, and further according to how those groups acted in other situations such as their voting in the jury room deliberations. Later, my interviews with two of the jurors revealed that four jurors (as predicted by the patterns of their laughter) actually voted twice to find the defendants innocent, which would have hung the jury. When a judge receives a message from a deliberating jury, he is supposed to convene the prosecution and the defense to reveal and discuss the content of the message. Judge Hoffman did not do this. When the jury story was published, he was ordered by the Appellate Court to hold a hearing examining marshals and jurors concerning the "hung jury" messages and to send the transcript of the hearing to the upper court. The information in this transcript contributed to the upper court's overturning the verdict of Judge Hoffman's court.

In the following excerpt, I compare and contrast instances of jurors' laughter and then divide and classify them, correlating patterns of jurors' laughter with patterns of jurors' other attitudes and actions, in order to make an argument (and tell a story) about the function of laughter in human affairs. The essay uses novelistic characterization to develop the arguments. What do you notice about the pronouns "you" and "I"?

"The Struggle for the Laugh in the Courtroom"
From Motion Will Be Denied
John Schultz

The different levels in the courtroom were so unobtrusive and yet so definite in their relationships, that they appeared to suggest certain attitudes appropriate both to promoting and mitigating the appearance of absolute authority. Only a lawyer examining a witness, or a lawyer objecting to something said or done, or a marshal guarding aisles or entrances, felt the clear right to stand erect. Most people tended to hunch or stoop a little when they got up to leave in the middle of proceedings. The defendants scurried around their table to confer with one another as if the air above their heads were filled with flying bullets. The court reporter sat in front of the witness box to the right of the judge. You did not realize until Miss Reporter's voice broke sweetly upon a quick, strong exchange between attorneys or witnesses and attorneys—"Mr. Kunstler, I'm sorry, you're going too fast"—that the speed of her fingers on the steno machine set the limits for the possible pace of the recorded verbal action.

When the marshal assigned to the court called, "Everyone rise," Judge Hoffman often rose as if he were, by sympathetic magic, pulling the audience to its feet. The arbitrary power of this man to control people's lives was deadening.

Nevertheless, the people in this courtroom—jurors, press, spectators, lawyers, marshals, everyone—found themselves being divided by their own laughter and terror, the kind that you feel cold or good in the gut, into two audiences. You could sit and listen to the two inside your head, as if the courtroom were a soul on display. The two audiences, perhaps two cultures, or two sides of one culture, were physically different, and they laughed at different things said by different people. Yet they came out, one against the other, one in relation to the other, one with the other, in and of the same society. The two sides had different feelings about children, about fucking, about learning, about noise, about bathrooms, about courtesy, about honor, about intelligence, imagination, duty, authority, entertainment, barbecue, money, hair, skin, blood, and laughter. It has something to do with the feeling and concept of your body, and of the bodies of others, and the way you act with that feeling and concept on issues that affect the life and future of your society.

I sat and watched how the jury came out, how it began to laugh, and who laughed and smiled at whose wit and witticism, and who gave only slight indication of a turn of the lips. The map of the "hung" jury, that stayed "hung" for four days and nights until a verdict was "negotiated," was there to be seen.

Richard Schultz, a solid young prosecutor who was always being sprung up and out by his own tensions, gibed one morning at the defense, "We have no objection to another objection." There was wit enough of the moment in it that members of both audiences smiled. But the upholder of the convict-on-all-counts end of the jury smiled big at the Assistant U.S. Attorney's remark. Edward Kratzke, an elderly man who would be the jury's elected foreman during its deliberations, never laughed at wit of the defense, and sometimes that wit pained him to the point of forcing upon him a deeply red face. Mrs. Jean Fritz, on the "acquittal" end, hardly smiled, sometimes looked down, at the wit of the prosecution. But she greatly enjoyed the wit of the defense, often holding her hand to her mouth and bending with laughter. Laughter regularly affirmed allegiances that were perhaps heretofore only hinted in a person's life. With one notable exception, the jurors voted in the deliberations as their earlier smiles and laughs would indicate.

The defendants and their attorneys were proud of the comparison of the "unholy clutter" of their table with the untroubled expanse of the prosecution's table. They also considered themselves to be a clutter of life-styles around their table beside the close-clipped, but never crew cut, hair, and the suits the colors of metal and camouflage, of the prosecutors. The defendants tried to answer letters and keep up with the speeches and talks that they were giving all over the country with grinding regularity to nurture their cause and the number of their supporters and to raise funds. Tom Foran doodled horses' heads and other items when Richard Schultz was handling an examination. Kunstler claimed after the trial that the defense had some marijuana on the table under a copy of the Berkeley *Tribe*, for one day, in a silent dare to the court and the marshals to do something about it. . . .

Witnesses on the stand for the government could take advantage of wit, too, not necessarily because their relation to their testimony was so pure. Deputy Superintendent of Police James M. Rochford was a large man, with a large sloping forehead and thinning reddish hair that he combed straight back, and his ears appeared to point back. Kunstler asked Rochford, who was in general command of police around the Conrad Hilton and in Grant Park during Convention Week, to explain why a request for a permit to march to the Amphitheatre was denied on Wednesday afternoon, August 28. Rochford had said that he himself could let a march happen if he judged it to be safe. That took the mayor off the hook for having denied crucial permits. Rochford said that one of the reasons the march was denied was that its route would go through areas of "lower socio-economic groups." Laughter came at such insight into the mind of the government. "We had information . . ." and Kunstler cut him short, "I know you had lots of information." Rochford, taking just a moment to be incensed, said snappily, "A great deal," and turned the put-down back at Kunstler. The jury's future foreman, Edward Kratzke, smiled at Rochford's comeback.

Kunstler continued cross-examining Rochford about the time when police stopped Dellinger's "nonviolent" march inside Grant Park along Columbus Drive. The jurors looked apathetic and weary, except for Mrs. Fritz and Kay Richards. Kunstler said to the Deputy Superintendent, "You saw the crowd?"

"Yes. They were dribbling about."

"Were you aware of gas from the National Guard?"

"Yes."

Kunstler now began to stake out his ambush. "Did you order any arrests made?"

"No."

"Did you see any arrests made?"

"No."

"You didn't see any reason for arrests, is that right?"

Rochford grinned. "I sure did." He explained about the "massive movements of people," implying that the police did not make legitimate arrests in order to avoid provoking the demonstrators. Rochford grinned at the jury. Once again the future foreman of the jury smiled at Rochford's comeback. Kunstler did not look good. He often overreached in his questioning and undercut his own point.

Rochford continued to testify in a low voice that he had not used so gently in front of the Conrad Hilton in August, 1968. Defendant Lee Weiner, who was usually reading a work in social science, looked up and spoke quietly to Kunstler: "Bill, the executioner is mumbling. Could you have the judge tell him to speak up?" Kunstler delivered the request. Judge Hoffman, apparently unaware of Weiner's quiet remark, asked Rochford to raise his voice. Then Foran, scorekeeper of contempt possibilities, rose, stooping, and asked that Weiner's remark be put into the record. This would be Specification 5, for which Lee Weiner would be sentenced one month in his contempt citations.

With his great head of springy black hair and black beard, he stood up and willingly repeated his remark in a raised voice for the judge. "I said, 'Bill, the executioner is mumbling. Could you have the judge tell him to speak up?'" In the jury box, Mrs. Jean Fritz, who had not heard the remark the first time, ducked her head and laughed behind her hand. Beside her, Kay Richards also laughed. Kay Richards talked and whispered only with Mrs. Fritz in the jury box, in an especially friendly way.

Now Foran protested what he called the defendants' constant flippant interruptions and heckling and harassment. Kunstler, on the other hand, protested what he called Foran's "constant schoolhouse episodes" and called Foran a "schoolmarm"—echoing frontier-western movies—for the offense he took at "mirth" in the courtroom, especially if the "mirth" was at the government's expense. At the "schoolmarm" remark of Kunstler's, Jean Fritz and Kay Richards ducked their heads and laughed. Two other jurors, who would be among the "holdouts" for acquittal, also smiled. The other jurors and the jury's future foreman looked glumly upon the scene. . . .

Rochford would also not admit in his testimony that the use of tear gas changed the character of the crowd in Grant Park. Weinglass then read from the report that Rochford wrote on the day of the event. "Frontal attack and release of gas caused complete collapse of order." Rochford now testified that he did not see either the police attack or the gas, and he did not appear to be embarrassed by the apparent contradiction.

Reluctantly, after prodding from Weinglass and becoming aware that the government would not object to the question, Rochford said, "Yes," that the demonstration parade marshals were keeping very good order in the march in Grant Park up to the point when the march was stopped by police. Then it began to disintegrate.

Kunstler, in questioning Rochford about the "intelligence" information that caused him to consider the defendants dangerous and to deny marches, said, "Did you also hear about ten thousand naked people walking on the waters of Lake Michigan?" Great laughter came from the audience for the defense, even from some jurors who ordinarily laughed on the side of the prosecution. Kay Richards and Mrs. Fritz enjoyed themselves. But the deep end of the convict-on-all-counts jurors looked pained, and the word and image of "naked" possibly pained them as much as the laughter itself. Miriam Hill, a large blond woman, always folded her arms and looked about the courtroom huffily at such images and such laughter. . . .

The prosecution, toward the end of its case, put another city official, Albert Baugher, onto the stand to testify about permit negotiations. Baugher was there to corroborate the earlier testimony of David Stahl, and to firm up the foundation for all the rest of the prosecution's case. Baugher was a man with a large mustache and an evident sense of humor. Kunstler was questioning Baugher once again about the fabled ploy of Abbie Hoffman: "Give us a hundred thousand dollars and we'll leave town." The prosecutors must have felt that many of the jurors, no matter what they believed about the question, would at least be hostile to its flippancy.

Kunstler said, "Did Abbie Hoffman say give us the money and we'll go away? Did you take that seriously?"

"I took it seriously," Baugher said.

"Did he tell you that Spiro Agnew offered him two hundred thousand dollars to come to Chicago?"

Oh, there was laughter in the courtroom, and Kay Richards and Jean Fritz were laughing, and Shirley Seaholm and Frieda Robbins were smiling. Miriam Hill folded her arms and looked huffily about. But, oh, the prosecution's witness, Albert Baugher, with the large mustache, he too was laughing. Prosecutor Foran must have felt a cold fear upon his heart and he had to do something about it. He had to give his witness an obvious signal.

Foran rose and objected, and said that Baugher was laughing at Kunstler and not at the remark. Kunstler immediately asked Baugher, and Baugher said, nodding, laughing, that he was laughing at the remark. Foran went smooth and chagrined before the acknowledgment of his own witness, and sat down without a word. Baugher once told some defendants during Convention Week, "Shove it"; no reason why he wouldn't say the same thing to the United States attorney, even though they were both comrades in Mayor Daley's Cook County Democratic party machine. But Foran should not have been so unhappy. The witness for the government looked good. Foran's objection showed his fear that the persuasive power of laughter might be greater than the substance and appearance of testimony.

Laughter enabled people to discover to which audience they most belonged, and then sharpened the aggressive division and regularly affirmed each audience's consciousness, of itself and of its representatives and its opposition.

———————

Imagery gives the revealing contrast of a particular personality's different behaviors. "Mrs. Jean Fritz, on the 'acquittal' end, hardly smiled, sometimes looked down, at wit of the prosecution. But she greatly enjoyed the wit of the defense, often holding her hand to her mouth and bending with laughter." The image "The defendants scurried around their table to confer with one another as if the air above their heads were filled with flying bullets" lets you see the situation and also suggests (from the correlation with other observed instances of stooping in the courtroom) that a kind of involuntary submissive behavior is taking place.

"Everything But the Squeal—Use of Spoiled Meats"
From The Jungle
Upton Sinclair

With one member trimming beef in a cannery, and another working in a sausage factory, the family had a first-hand knowledge of the great majority of Packingtown swindles. For it was the custom, as they found, whenever meat was so spoiled that it could not be used for anything else, either to can it or else to chop it up into sausage. With what had been told them by Jonas, who had worked in the pickle rooms, they could now study the whole of the spoiled-meat industry on the inside, and read a new and grim meaning into that old Packingtown jest—that they use everything of the pig except the squeal.

Jonas had told them how the meat that was taken out of pickle would often be found sour, and how they would rub it up with soda to take away the smell, and sell it to be eaten on free-lunch counters; also of all the miracles of chemistry which they performed, giving to any sort of meat, fresh or salted, whole or chopped, any color and any flavor and any odor they chose. In the pickling of hams they had an ingenious apparatus, by which they saved time and increased the capacity of the plant—a machine consisting of a hollow needle attached to a pump; by plunging this needle into the meat and working with his foot, a man could fill a ham with pickle in a few seconds. And yet, in spite of this, there would be hams found spoiled, some of them with an odor so bad that a man could hardly bear to be in the same room with them. To pump into these the packers had a second and much stronger pickle which destroyed the odor—a process known to the workers as "giving them thirty per cent." Also, after the hams had been smoked, there would be found some that had gone to the bad. Formerly these had been sold as "Number Three Grade," but later on some ingenious person had hit upon a new device, and now they would extract the bone, about which the bad part generally lay, and insert in the hole a white-hot iron. After this invention there was no longer Number One, Two, and Three Grade—there was only Number One Grade. The packers were always originating such schemes—they had what they called "boneless hams," which were all the odds and ends of pork stuffed into casings; and "California hams," which were the shoulders, with big knuckle joints, and nearly all the meat cut out; and fancy "skinned hams," which were made of the oldest hogs, whose skins were so heavy and coarse that no one would buy them—that is, until they had been cooked and chopped fine and labeled "head cheese"!

It was only when the whole ham was spoiled that it came into the department of Elzbieta. Cut up by the two-thousand-revolutions-a-minute flyers, and mixed with half a ton of other meat, no odor that ever was in a ham could make any difference. There was never the least attention paid to what was cut up for sausage; there would come all the way back from Europe old sausage that had been rejected, and that was moldy and white—it would be dosed with borax and glycerine, and dumped into the hoppers, and made over again for home consumption. There would be meat that had tumbled out on the floor, in the dirt and sawdust, where the workers had tramped and spit uncounted billions of consumption germs. There would be meat stored in great piles in rooms; and the water from leaky roofs would drip over it, and thousands of rats would race about on it. (It was too dark in these storage places to see well, but a man could run his hand over these piles of meat and sweep off handfuls of the dried dung of rats.) These rats were nuisances, and the packers would put poisoned bread out for them; they would die, and then rats, bread, and meat would go into the hoppers together. This is no fairy story and no joke; the meat would be shoveled into carts, and the man who did the shoveling would not trouble to lift out a rat even when he saw one—there were things that went into the sausage in comparison with which a poisoned rat was a tidbit. There was no place for the men to wash their hands before they ate their dinner, and so they made a practice of washing them in the water that was to be ladled into the sausage. There were the butt-ends of smoked meat, and the scraps of corned beef, and all the odds and ends of the waste of the plants, that would be dumped into old barrels in the cellar and left there. Under the system of rigid economy which the packers enforced, there were some jobs that it only paid to do once in a long time, and among these was the cleaning out of the waste barrels. Every spring they did it; and in the barrels would be dirt and rust and old nails and stale water—and cartload after cartload of it would be taken up and dumped into the hoppers with fresh meat, and sent out to the public's breakfast. Some of it they would make into "smoked" sausage—but as the smoking took time, and was therefore expensive, they would call upon their chemistry department, and preserve it with borax and color it with gelatine to make it brown. All of their sausage came out of the same bowl, but when they came to wrap it they would stamp some of it "special," and for this they would charge two cents more a pound.

What does the frequent use of the conditional ("would") tell you about the form of this piece? What device does the author use, coming out of the story material itself, for gathering the observed instances of the uses of spoiled meats? In what way are the instances a series of little stories-within-a-story summed up by the overall author? What rhetorical modes are employed?

You may find that several people in your how-it-happens subject could piece together the story of how a process is carried out throughout an industry, an institution, or a large social group.

Cairo, U.S.A. 1971
Betty Shiflett

"Daughter," said a man one night when the bullets were flying, "go up and turn down my bed." In a few minutes she went up. Then she came back down with a warm bullet in her hand. It had gone through two walls before she found it on the bed. . . .

That incident tells the quality of sleep for black people in Cairo, Illinois (pronounced Kay-ro like the syrup), the town that has seen enough gunfire due to racial conflict, 150 nights in the past twenty-three months, to qualify as an insurgency in the minds of the heads of state government.

"Business was never better!" white businessmen tell reporters. But seven businesses have closed during a boycott now in its twenty-third month, and the black community shows no sign of weakening. White businessmen like Bob Cunningham, whose lumberyard has burned twice (the second fire occurring the same night the serviceman Wiley Anderson was fatally shot in Pyramid Courts, the black housing project), complain loudly about their arson losses, while fifty-one major fires in twenty months have led to a confusion of charges and countercharges from blacks and whites. Cunningham's lumberyard, burned to its charred foundations, sits directly across a narrow side street from the Cairo Fire Department. Cunningham says he collected $35,000 on a $50,000 loss for the first fire, and $100,000 on a $200,000 loss for the second. He is gracious to reporters now. He shrugs and lets his boyish face and light, transparent eyes show a smile as he confesses that he "can't hold out forever." It was he who saw Al Farmer—the black candidate for mayor and a social worker with an M.A.—in a downtown picket line with his five-year-old son Rodney, and could not resist addressing him with a loaded "Hi, *boy!*": Farmer stood his ground toe to toe, tall and black and radiating hard-earned middle-class respectability while Cunningham shoved the insult up another notch—"Hello, *nigger!*" Farmer remembers, if he had stepped out of that picket line, Cunningham "would have been dead." Then he took Rodney and drove home to tell his wife Charlotte, "I'm not going downtown [to march] again, because I'm not a non-violent person." On the picket line many a black man has gone the route of Al Farmer, galvanized by the public slur in a Bob Cunningham's voice. "These things just recruit a movement for you," says Preston Ewing of the NAACP about the January 21 episode when sheriff and state police came to Pyramid Courts beating down doors and beating up people in search of arms, ammunition, and dynamite. (When nighttime firing down into the black community begins from three sides—from the overlooking Ohio River levee, from atop towering piles of scrap metal in the city dump, and from the cupola of the Cairo Police Station—black families from the more flimsy housing of the surrounding area flee into Pyramid Courts where the walls are slightly thicker.)

Chuck Koen, young minister and leader of the United Front, the black umbrella organization, calls events in Cairo "a slave uprising." Ironically, black slaves built the levees now used by whites to fire down at blacks in Pyramid Courts.

Six hundred homes have been "burned, bombed, or torn down" in the past ten years and only ten new homes have been built. Outside Pyramid Courts, dwellings for black people are apt to be shacks trembling on wooden piers, some with second-story outhouses, which means outdoor toilets on the second-floor back porches. Many frame houses are so rotten they are patched with bits of wood, tin, and iron, or so charred by fires that they are only fine black cinders shifting in the wind around the rusty old strips of metal strewn here and there. But bankrupt or burned-out, Cairo maintains one avenue of paint-fresh, grounds-trimmed mansions of antebellum curlicues and frills, all made locally famous by the one called Old Magnolia Mansion. A sprinkling of terrifically glossy three-story magnolia trees defends the reputation of this neighborhood.

Cairo, city of fires, city of guns.

Bob Lansden and his older brother Dave, who maintain the one-hundred-and-twenty-year-old law office of Lansden and Lansden, have had so many occasions to use their courage in Cairo that they seem to deserve a better designation than "white liberals." In 1954 Dave Lansden was arrested and thrown in jail for escorting black children to school—they were being run up on the curbs at intersections by white drivers—during Cairo's first school integration attempt. In 1945 the Lansdens collaborated with Thurgood Marshall to prosecute the civil rights case which won equal pay for black teachers. Corneal Davis, the black state legislator who filed the case in spite of threats to his life, was responsible for bringing Thurgood Marshall to Cairo. Hattie Kendrick, then president of the NAACP, was fired before her retirement age for securing a petition signed by all Cairo's black teachers requesting the suit—"Cairo's first United Front"—and Dave Lansden's neighbor was so vexed at having hometown white lawyers assisting the case that he put up a neon sign in his yard with a flashing arrow pointing to "the house where the niggerlovers live."

"The basic weakness of the white leadership in Cairo," says Bob Lansden, "is if you disagree with them, they want to kill you."

In 1969 Larry Potts, the good-looking minister of the Cairo Baptist Church, led virtually all the white families out of the public schools after integration in 1967, and into a specially formed all-white "freedom school" named, appropriately, Camelot. Potts insists the United Front made sure school integration wouldn't work in Cairo. "We tried it," he says. "It's chaos." In 1968, one year before he rose to the leadership of Camelot, Larry Potts clubbed a seventy-two-year-old black man to death with a baseball bat in the parsonage; he said he had caught him trying to "attack" his wife. Later, with the earnestness he really believes, he told a Springfield legislative investigative unit inquiring into Cairo's racial affairs that, on second thought, he wondered if the old man wasn't sent to his home by "the militants," whom he does not hesitate to call "revolutionary communist anarchists." Rev. Potts was never brought to trial, and Mrs. Potts, now divorced from her husband and the alleged victim of the alleged rape, has never testified under oath in any judicial proceedings as to the crime of the old black man, a small man and a gassed World War I veteran who used to speak to everyone on the streets of Cairo, white or black.

"It doesn't matter what we say, you always make us sound like racists," white people in Cairo complain to reporters.

I could not be seen arriving for interviews with white people in cabs driven by black people. There would be no interview. A regular white cab took me to Bob's Restaurant on Washington, where a huge young man at a back table kept a revolver stuck under his belt, half-hidden by a fat belly. From Bob's I could walk around the corner to the black United Front. Often at night two cabs were necessary with a neutral switch point in between. The black cab would be crowded with many people and silent because of my unexplained presence. With one notable exception, the white drivers called me "Baby" in an intimate, gritty way. The necessity behind the cloak-and-dagger performance rapidly took on the weight of a stone.

But to the visitor coming into this dreary town during a cease-fire period nothing is so vibrant as the charges and countercharges that flash up from both sides. I tried to search out the small incident from which each was shaped, but like Aaron's golden calf made from melted rings, in nearly every case, the white charges seemed to have come wholly from the fires of the tellers' imagination. All are vivid, well told. Among white people it is OK to lie about black people, and an unsweated, nerveless calm comes over the master tellers as the story lives vividly for them, too. For instance, the "black guerilla attack in three waves" on the police station the night of October 23 never happened, but was picked up by the wire services and later printed around the nation. Only later was it disproved after careful investigation by Jan and Henry De Zutter in the December issue of the *Chicago Journalism Review,* a publication of limited circulation. It seemed, after much sifting, that only the black charges had substance, perhaps again suggesting that the oppressed know more about the oppressor than the oppressor knows about the oppressed. Another time, the avuncular Mayor Thomas twinkled at me, explaining that his "kill statement" made on TV meant "kill [only] the revolutionaries" and did not refer to all the black community; he freely admits his orders to Cairo Police to return any firing, even muffled flashes they might see in the night, may risk innocent lives. State's Attorney Peyton Berbling snapped that Front leaders are profiting hugely and personally from funds contributed by "bleeding hearts" church councils and foundations—that is the cornerstone of white belief: therefore, the white corollary is that the United Front cannot afford to seek peace. But Front staff say they haven't had salaries since September, which isn't so hard to believe if you study their eating habits, provided you can catch them eating often enough to do so. On March 31, 1969, the White Hats, an earlier white vigilante group, now headed up by lumberyard owner Bob Cunningham and reincarnated under UCCA, United Citizens for Community Action, made their first move. As a Saturday rally was leaving St. Columba's church, White Hats fired into the wrong car thinking it was United Front leader Koen's, police attacked and beat heads, and the people fell back to Pyramid Courts, where a ring of armed white men surrounded the buildings and a bullhorn commanded, "All women and children come out!" A little black lady came out on her porch with a cane in one hand and a rusty shotgun in the other and said, "If we can't get along, then let's get it on!" and twenty-two months of firing began.

Later, talking to Chuck Koen around his lawyers in the packed booth in J. and L. Soul Food, we began to understand each other at the same point—when he told me that the government would never be able to prove a "black attack" in Cairo because "black folks gonna come out with their hands up," and he raised his hands in the booth as we grinned over the dirty dishes and cigarette smoke. The young Rev. Charles Koen, reared in Cairo and ordained in the National Missionary Baptist Church, used his hands again to speak with solemn humor about the Old Testament's Nehemiah building the wall with "one hand on the building and other on his gun."

The official United Front poster shows a pistol resting on a Bible. The United Front wants to be the catalytic agent to take Cairo's regional roots of Bible, Church, guns, prohibition, labor wars and family feuds and use them in a way that will lift Cairo out of its parochialism and into the Front's understanding that the political economic system is screwing everybody.

Bob Cunningham with the light curly hair and twice-burned lumberyard thinks pretty highly of guns, too—"Yes, I, everyone has guns"—and hopes whites still have the guts to defend themselves. He leaves the question to swell, and the light, transparent eyes flash briefly behind their glasses. When we talked at a little red table in his temporary headquarters at Cook's Lawn Mower Repair Shop, I did not mention the proximity of his lumberyard to the fire station, and he treated me with the style of southern kindness that says, "We might make something out of you yet, if you pay attention." He held his cigar so neatly I forgot it was there, and his shrugs were aimed to achieve an air of disarming frankness, a goal almost impossible for a southerner. I decided that the red lights and buzzers of the formidable telephone installation on the desk behind him must have more to do with his presidency of UCCA than with his defunct lumberyard. He explained how disappointed UCCA members were when no black people came to their open-air organizational meetings, held only sixty days after the White Hats were forced to disband. Bob Cunningham is baffled by any kind of risk that isn't a calculated money risk. The kinds of risks black people are beginning to take defy his notion of *sense,* his business yardstick. Yet he, businessman and bargainer, professes not to understand the black militant language of negotiation, arguing in one and the same breath that he never sold anything in his life he didn't have to negotiate, then contradicting himself by demanding, "How do you negotiate a *non*negotiable demand?" Cunningham seemed to interpret the blacks' demand that the whites negotiate with them as a "nonnegotiable" demand. Yet the mayor's earlier "Peace and Progress Offer" appeared to be a "*non*negotiable demand" and had been turned down by black leadership as "tokenism."

Don't forget Peyton Berbling, along with Mayor Thomas, named as part of the Koen assassination conspiracy and an ex-White Hat—no deterrent to becoming state's attorney. Under a shock of white hair Berbling's jaw hangs a little loose, a little sore-looking, and a lavender flush covers his face; but he is still active and powerful, even when such lawyers as the black, urbane Eugene Pincham and Life-Saver-chewing Sam

Adams (known for the acquittal of the Chicago Blackstone Rangers in the killing of policeman Alfano) tore apart Berbling's too loose but hopeful indictment against Chuck
Koen. Its wording failed to specify the behavior Koen allegedly engaged in to "put the
complainant, Cairo Fire Marshal Seawright, *in fear of battery*" when he and his men answered a false alarm in Pyramid Courts last August and got chased out by residents.

Adams and Pincham enjoyed an open, energetic exchange with Judge Dennis, a
peppery Southerner far more inclined to deny a government objection than Julius Hoffman [of the Chicago Conspiracy Trial]. "Pettifogging, pettifogging!" Berbling bellowed
at the defense. When court adjourned, he launched yet another public scorification, this
time at "the reporter"—me—whom he saw earlier driving up to the courthouse with
United Front staff. I had splurged and taken the quickest ride, then compounded my sin
by sitting in court on the same bench with them. Berbling denounced me loudly in the
courthouse hall for talking to people on both sides.

I left the Alexander County Courthouse sore with the knowledge that it is impossible not to betray the Peyton Berblings of this world. When I came back to civil rights
leader and retired school teacher Hattie Kendrick's living room to pick up a little sanity,
she said, "What's the matter? Is the white folks gettin' you down?"

Saturday afternoon the United Front rally swelled until it filled the pews at St.
Columba's church, around two hundred people, and up front a red-robed choir of young
people including children was pealing out "I Got One More River to Cross." By ownership, St. Columba's is a Catholic church, but the rolling music was pure black Protestant. Political banners were everywhere and all kinds of decoration from a red day-glo
Soul Santa to the mammoth burlap strip inscribed "Before I'll Be a Slave, I'll Be Buried
in My Grave," with bright felt flowers sprinkled around the word *grave*.

The crowd was all ages and kinds, from mothers with babies to women with hair
curlers, young folks with naturals and flowing African styles, dry old men hunched in
their work jackets, and gray-headed preachers and grandmothers. I quit wondering if
the Front contained a cross section of the black community and began to wonder how
they did it. Their formula is eminently right in all its aspects for Cairo, a town where
church is still big and vibrant for black people. The rally, which some would have called a
service, made better listening than most political rallies *or* straight church services because the slogans and shibboleths were mercifully absent and something sounder and
more vital had swarmed in, perhaps during Koen's hoarse-shouted prayer—"Let all the
bad spirits go out the window; let the Spirit come down and fill us!"

The rally had barely gotten underway before a man made public churchstyle confession before the crowd that Jim Aveary, black tavern owner, Golden Gloves champion
and former Cairo policeman, the black choice of the white power structure in the upcoming mayoral race, had been using him. The MC asked the crowd for "forgiveness for
others' hangups." Leon Page of the United Front talked about the system's failing everybody and about "false pride" that won't let poor whites admit they're poor. Then he
got around to the big point about how "dumb" the mayor is in not applying to get the first
$40,000 of $5,000,000 in federal money that Cairo *can* get for housing, when "a lot of
poor white people could use that money too." The dancing voice of Chuck Koen, no longer hoarse and shouting, promised that God "was going to *take* people" who tried to
repress the movement "before they want to go!" He was strong, he had an expert's
touch, he was treated like a Biblical David and often referred to as one by the older
preachers who took the mike.

Getting young folks off the street, "away from guns" in the street sense, and back
into the church was a central theme that accomplished several ends; the Front does not
intend to quarrel with Cairo parents, they know what will please them, and it was obvi-

ous from a glance around the pews that they had no shortage of young people in the movement. It is understood that not having the temptations of the middle road is a blessing, if a harsh one, with "no place to go but up!"

It was a memorial service for King, and names of the martyrs were swept through the hall—Jesus, Malcolm X, Martin Luther King—before Sister Lois sang King's "Precious Lord, Take My Hand" to a swelling, throbbing fare-thee-well, while the crowd clapped its hands in bursts with the pianist and pointed heavenward. The NAACP's ordinarily cool field staff educational director, Preston Ewing, came on fiery in church, celebrating his TV debate with Jim Aveary, the great white hope, and closing with King's "If you have not found something worth dying for, you are not fit to live"; strong words where gunfire is a nightly occurrence and the way of life. The offering came by in a basket and I couldn't understand the words of the humming congregation until a man's voice broke over the mike announcing a workshop in first aid, and suddenly I got the hymn words clear. They were, "I'll Go." A white strip sign pasted on the double doors said, "Since we're called niggers, I'm a United Nigger."

Preston Ewing predicted, with hands folded over his chest until excitement caught him up in what he was saying, that the bridge which will cross the Mississippi at Cairo and bypass the town on the way to Missouri when Interstate 57 is completed will also close every motel and most every filling station and restaurant in town. But according to Dick Couper and Francis Ward of the *Los Angeles Times,* a check of county real estate records for '68, '69, and '70 shows that several prominent businessmen have bought up land along River Street and Ohio Street near the Ohio levee where the bridge will go up, and even more along the right of way for Interstate 57 itself, though so far not in big enough blocks to prove anything. However you put it together, a significant number of leading white businessmen, many of whom are also members of UCCA, are demonstrating commendable faith in the future of "dying Cairo." Taking advantage of racial conflict to drive land values down so property can gradually be bought up cheaply makes sense where little else does in Cairo. It's a businessman's risk, one his yardstick measures well. Storefront lots in the business district go now for as low as $1,000 and $2,000, and homes sell at one-fifth the price they commanded five years ago. The governor of Illinois could use the arm-twisting of state funding as hard in five minutes to force negotiations as he has already used "force" in the form of state police and the armored car used for a nocturnal attack on St. Columba's and its rectory where Front staff are housed. [Cairo's streets were patrolled by *two* armored cars, one owned by the city.]

There were many things I expected would frighten me in Cairo, but nothing prepared me for the deadly chill that clapped about me in Larry Pott's church on Sunday morning. The theology of fascism is very gentle in its expression and exceedingly violent in its outcome, as everything indicated from the pretty Jesus hip-deep in water at the back of the baptistry while John the Baptist's hand is raised over his head, to the children with coloring books learning to be demure like their mothers at their sides in the pews, and the soft yellow walls and seating arranged for intimacy. This is the church where the preacher has clubbed an old black man to death with a baseball bat.

For prayer the wavy-haired minister closes his eyes and leans across the pulpit in an infinitely tender way to whisper affectionately, sometimes audibly, into his goose-necked mike while the organ plays "O Love That Will Not Let Me Go" and the collection plates slip decorously from hand to hand through the congregation, piled with small envelopes containing checks.

The rhetoric of Protestant piety began inevitably to repeat itself in God's own Camelot English. The appeal to hard work was the same for black revolutionaries as for white Anglo-Saxon Protestants, and the priestly warning that only God's reward counts and not the rewards of people turned up in both sermons. Naturally both crowds were exhorted to righteousness.

"You've got a lot of living to do," he had said for his Call to Worship, but the air in that room smelled of perfumed people, dead. By the time we sang "Rock of Ages" I was the only one keeping up with the music, but I knew them all, the doxologies and the hymns, and I sang them better than the congregation, and Potts knew it.

For the Children's Hour, the principal and chaplain of the Camelot Schools showed the little children gathered around his pulpit a shiny hypodermic needle and warned them to run and tell their parents if they saw anyone "but the doctor or his pretty nurse" using it. He called drugs "the number one sin in the nation" and said young folks today "are asking for grass when what they want is a chocolate soda with two straws." A lovely young woman sitting quite alone in the second row with her fur coat thrown open luxuriously around her on the pew caught each word on her upturned face as if it were dew.

At sermon time Potts changed the printed topic from "The Gathering Storm" to "Questions on Immortality" because the first—and I felt he'd changed it for me—was "too depressing about current events." But he waved a hand over the national scene anyway with a few statistics. Every nineteen minutes there's a murder—I think of the old man he's killed. Every forty minutes a forcible rape—I think of the attack he said he'd saved his wife from. My mind was doing somersaults with all the images and contradictions of what he was saying and what he has done and what white people are doing in Cairo. He hurried to shove in the rest of his credo, about the Supreme Court handcuffing the wrong people, and "the biggest lie in the country" told by the U.S. Commission on Pornography. I'm scared for my life. To Larry Potts, *Evergreen Review* might be considered risque, to say the least. He says the lie about pornography is a bigger lie than the one about getting along with the communists in Red China. I remember the hundreds of times I've heard that word *lie* from black lips and white lips since I came to this place.

I had barely recovered when the new sermon put the old question about "Where will we go when we die?" Will we recognize a "fellow Christian," know a grandmother, a father, an aunt? He hits them all but husband and wife, as if that's what he's rubbing out, not the old black man he's killed, and at the end of that long list of relatives he asks, "What about that little baby?" and there's a beat in his sermon, too, and a peak I climb on top of, and I freak out completely, seeing the rage that must have freed this preacher to kill that old black man, and I wonder if he wonders where that black man is now?

Cold fear shivers around me. In the church nothing is moving, yet I feel I'm in a mob. I am stunned by this minister who understands not his words or himself, this man all rage inside held together by a careful, precious manner. And I am stunned guiltily at myself. Not only have I betrayed Larry Potts as I was obliged to betray Peyton Berbling, I have tricked him *gladly* by showing up at his worship service, and by having succeeded (against his better judgment) in interviewing him at Camelot two days before—he'd told me that he never gave interviews anymore. In this pretty little church where teenagers are giggling across the aisle, I tremble for my life.

The sermon over, I start looking for a side door and find one, but I don't use it. I talk myself out of it, and sing Pott's song, the last hymn, and prepare my line for him as the music waltzes to an end.

At the door he took my gloved hand as if it would reach out and strike him. Chilly air blew in around our ankles and I told him, "I felt I should be here" in unimpeachable church parlance. He hoped I'd "gained something from worshiping" with them, but there was pain moving behind his flat brown eyes.

With fear whistling about me I walked the main streets and cold burned-out lots of Cairo, Illinois, and the words of Larry Potts's last hymn—"He hideth my soul in the cleft of a rock that shadows a dry thirsty land"—made me laugh and weep for America.

"Story-sense" organizes what we have to say for our audience. Sometimes story-sense emerges from the overall content and instances, as if it were coming up from underwater, an amorphous but possible shape that finally pops out clearly. Freud could say, "I have a story to tell you about apparently trivial human errors . . ." Story is the organizing sense with which Shiflett discovers the movement of perceptions that she has to tell to her audience.

Because of her "story-sense" for the personally observed and researched through records content, she chooses a beginning image that could have been chosen by an accomplished oral teller as well as by a writer. With the first image, the "warm bullet" in the palm of the hand, she puts us right into the midst of the conflict. In the next paragraph, she summarizes the overall conflict, so that we receive a view of its prolonged occurrence.

Having compared and contrasted instances, divided and classified them, she finds significant groupings clustering about the white side of the conflict and the black side of it. In the third paragraph, she tells about the white side, giving glimpses of the black responses, as she contrasts white liberals, white leadership, and white preachers, then summarizes in more detail the effects of the prolonged conflict upon the community.

Shiflett's first person voice emerges in a model-telling of how, for an interview with a white person, she must avoid being seen arriving in a cab driven by a black person. This model-telling structurally provides a bridge, in the essay, between the white side and the black side, at the same time giving us an acute sense for the concentrated, violent, intractable nature of the conflict. At the end of her discussion of the clustering of instances about the black side, she tells an incident in which she was actually publicly denounced in an adjourned courtroom for seeking information from *both* sides!

She contrasts the imagery, events, and what she's researched about the black church with her final narration of a service in the white church, whose minister has clubbed an old black man to death. In the final scene, in which she becomes a full participant in the white church service and in the story, she finds a special awful perception about the conflict and the white side of it. With "fear whistling about" her as she "walked the main streets and cold burned-out lots of Cairo, Illinois," feeling the irony of the words of the church service's last hymn, she laughs and weeps "for America."

What basic forms does Shiflett use in telling her story? What rhetorical modes do you find at work in it? What is the effect of the use of names of persons and places in this story of racial conflict?

Einstein and Frankenstein
Michael Finger

For a period of two years I observed the habits and lifestyle of the African clawed frog (Xenopus laevis). I owned two of the species, and they inhabited a ten gallon aquarium. The frogs were given names that seemed to match their personalities. One frog who was perpetually busy, and quite aggressive, was named Frankenstein. The other frog was passive by comparison, and quite a brooder. I called him Einstein.

A little should be mentioned about the general habits of this species of frog. Unlike all other frogs, the clawed frog has no tongue. In order to obtain food this frog must skim the bottom of his habitat with mouth open wide, pushing and stuffing any loose matter into the opening. The frog will eat almost anything, living or dead; the good is quickly swallowed and the bad is spit back out. This species of frog lives entirely under water, coming up only for air which it must breathe through its lungs. The frog can grow up to five inches in length, but most are only three inches or less. Frankenstein was the larger of the two and was approximately three inches long. Einstein was about half an inch shorter. Because it lives underwater, the clawed frog is an extremely good swimmer and can outmaneuver most fish, a staple in their diet.

I acquired the frogs through a pet shop and they were somewhat domesticated. They had been born and raised in an aquarium and were accustomed to being fed regularly. The only food known to them appeared daily in the form of frozen brine shrimp. At first I maintained this diet. Then, after a period of three months, I introduced them to live food.

Brine shrimp comes in flat, frozen rectangular packages. If it is not kept in the freezer it will soon rot and not even a ten pound box of Arm & Hammer will absorb the smell. The frozen shrimp is cut into ¼" squares and these squares are dropped into the aquarium. They float for about thirty seconds, then they begin to break apart and settle to the bottom of the tank. It only takes the frogs about ten seconds to know it's feeding time. They smell the shrimp and immediately begin fanning water into their mouths. Their short arms work furiously, trying to find the food to pump into their mouths. The frog's eyes are situated on top of his head, which is wide and elongated. Therefore they can only see what is above and around them, not what lies under them or their mouths. Often the frog will pass over a lump of shrimp lying directly under his body because he cannot see it. Frankenstein was quick to learn feeding times and often waited for me to appear with the shrimp. Floating on the water's surface with only his eyes and nose in the air, he would watch the shrimp hit the water and immediately attack it, stuffing large quantities into his mouth. Frogs have no manners or dining etiquette, the only rule being to get as much as one could eat before any other frog comes along. After a few months of steady feeding Frankenstein would take the shrimp out of my fingers, leaping out of the water to snap it with his toothless jaws. If I kept my finger in the tank long enough he would try to swallow that as well, his fore limbs and mouth gently tugging until I removed the finger. I was surprised that the coldness of the shrimp never seemed to bother the frogs. If they waited at least a minute the shrimp would completely dissolve and raise to the temperature of the water. But they just couldn't wait to eat. Whereas Frankenstein would come to the surface of the aquarium to greet me, Einstein would quickly dive to the bottom left corner of the tank every time I appeared. He never seemed to get used to my presence, even with a regularly scheduled feeding time. He would wait until the shrimp settled upon the gravel and then would move out of his corner and scavenge the bottom. Although Einstein never ate as much as Frankenstein, I don't think this had anything to do with his smaller size. Einstein didn't move that much about in the tank. He preferred to remain motionless in his corner, resting upon one of the plastic plants anchored to the aquarium floor or sitting patiently in the hole bored in the middle of a thick branch. Frankenstein never sat still and was always playing or digging in the gravel. He had the habit of racing around the tank's bottom when a light was suddenly turned on, pushing anything and everything, including Einstein, out of his way. He moved three times faster than a cockroach when you're trying to step on it. When I first got the aquarium I stocked it with real plants and anchored them securely under the gravel. Little did I know how much the clawed frog likes to dig. It didn't take more than three days for them to uproot all the plants, and I came home to find them floating atop the water and Frankenstein underneath them, a smug look upon his little face. After that it was strictly plastic plants for them, and Frankenstein tried his best to dig these up as well.

I noticed after awhile that the frogs, Frankenstein in particular, were getting overly plump on their diet of brine shrimp. I concluded that they were in need of exercise. But how does one exercise a frog? You cannot take them for a walk, for if they were removed from water for only a short period of time their skins would dry up and shrivel and they would die. A hamster is fortunate to have a wheel to run around in and spin with glee, but no such device exists for frogs. You can dangle yarn before a kitten but try that in an aquarium and the yarn starts to unravel and the bored frog turns red from the running dye. A parakeet even owns plastic dumbbells to lift, but what has a frog? There is nothing man has manufactured to bring exercise to his friend the frog. So I had to devise a method of trimming the bellies of my bulging pets. The only way was to logically utilize the natural instincts of the animal and its characteristic nature as an aggressive predator. If I put small fish in with the frogs they would chase the fish to eat them; the chase would be exciting, with a number of attempts before success, and the frog, by means of the chase, would get exercise. It seemed like it would work, but I had to verify my hypothesis. I contacted the expert who sold me the frogs and he agreed it would be a good idea. It seems that the small fish known as the guppy (Lebistes reticulatus) is frequently served to domesticated frogs. I smiled and purchased a half dozen.

But would my frogs actually go after and swallow the fish? After all, they had never seen other animals, and the only food they were familiar with came dead and frozen. Would their primordial instinct to kill be suddenly recalled from the dark and untested regions of their little brains? There was only one way to find out, and that was to put the guppies into the aquarium.

I brought the guppies home in a plastic bag and set them on the kitchen table while I removed my jacket. I got my aquarium net and took the bag of fish over to the kitchen sink. I undid the knot in the bag and slowly poured the water out of the bag and into the net. This is done because it is unhealthy to mix the waters of different aquariums. The guppies were now in my net, six jumping and squirming little fish. They were very thin, almost transparent, and their mouths opened and closed rapidly as they wondered where their air had gone and what the hell was happening to them. I walked with them over to the aquarium and opened its lid. Einstein dove to his corner and Frankenstein was resting on the gravel. Neither had been fed that day and it was four hours past their accustomed feeding time. I slowly lowered the bag of the net into the water, but kept the rim of the net above the surface so they could not escape. This was it; the hour of instinct had arrived. I looked at Frankenstein and he looked up at me, and in my best Jack Nicholson voice cooed, as I released the guppies, "Medication time."

The guppies, happy again to be in water but puzzled at their experiences, remained grouped together for fifteen seconds, and then began to explore, in clusters of two and three, their new aquatic home. Their instincts were to go to the darker areas of the tank, the log and the plants. They hovered around the air stone and the fizzing bubbles it released. Frankenstein was the first to move. He cautiously eyed the visitors and swam slowly, moving only a few inches. When he moved, the fish watched him carefully, but without apparent alarm. They kind of hovered in the water, wiggling their little bodies back and forth like exotic dancers. Frankenstein surfaced for air and floated for about thirty seconds, then he quickly dove to the bottom of the tank. For awhile nothing happened. I was getting impatient. I wanted to see a frog swallow a fish and that's all there was to it. I was seriously considering changing Frankenstein's name to something less harsh, when he made his move. It was quick. A smaller guppy, dying of curiosity, swam right up to Frankenstein's nose and opened his "O" shaped mouth repeatedly, as if greeting the frog with his own silent language. Frankenstein's reply was brief. It consisted of a lightning swift lunge forward, an even quicker opening and closing of his own mouth, and a single swallow. The fish was gone. The magical frog had made the simple guppy disappear. For the first time in his life Frankenstein felt the strange movement of live food in his stomach. It must have struggled to escape for awhile, but I didn't observe any outward disturbances on Frankenstein's underside. He didn't seem to have any bad reactions to his quick meal. He moved to the bottom of the tank and sat watching the remaining five guppies. Einstein, on the other end of the tank, did nothing, and didn't seem to notice anything different in his tank-mate's behavior. But there was. The taste of food, new food with a different taste, must have been a welcome relief to Frankenstein. In twenty seconds he was up for air, and ready to capture yet another guppy. Three of the fish seemed to know what was going on right away, and whenever Frankenstein moved they swam, or tried to swim, out of his way. The other two guppies were either stupid or suicidal, because they also swam right up to Frankenstein's nose, offering themselves to sacrifice. Never one to refuse an offer, Frankenstein greedily accepted one of the guppies as swiftly as the first one. In a flash it was gone.

Now two guppies is really quite a meal for one frog, especially when that frog is no more than three inches in length and the guppies are about one and half inches long. After his two dinners Frankenstein settled on the bottom of the tank and began the task of digesting his feast. The remaining four fish, cursing me I'm sure, learned their lesson and tried to avoid either frog. Einstein did not eat that day. He watched the fish with wonder, not hunger, and contented himself with scavenging the bottom of the tank for leftover shrimp. It was about a week later when I saw him finally lunge at a guppy. He wasn't as swift as Frankenstein and he missed. He tried once more but failed again. In all my observations of live feeding I never saw Einstein swallow any guppies. He was happy enough to swim alongside them and share their food when it was sprinkled atop the surface of the tank. It was Frankenstein alone who tried his best to keep the rapidly breeding guppy population to a minimum.

Using the method of comparison and contrast, Michael Finger tells a story of observation that shows us that even lowly creatures have a degree of individuality in their "characters," a revelation that also suggests that the power of natural selection depends upon such individual variations. The first paragraph sets up the basic situation of the experiment. Then point by point, throughout the essay, the author compares the individual "characters" of the two frogs as revealed in their actions. What other points does he make in observing the progress of the experiment? How does exaggeration through personification help the scientific observer?

Writing Your Essays—Content, Clustering of Instances, and Organization

---

If you've looked at your how-it-happens subject area and felt, "This is too much!" or "I have nothing to say!" you've responded exactly as virtually every writer responds to the vastness of his or her subject. Your dwelling upon the material, your mulling it over in your own mind, your awareness of things and events and behaviors that stick out, will begin to cause clusterings of instances. You can begin to write about these clusterings.

In Chief Seattle's and Logan's speeches, the speakers use the methods of preliterate peoples to concentrate perceptions of patterns into metaphorical imagery e.g.: "The very dust upon which you now stand responds more lovingly to their footsteps than to yours, because it is rich with blood of our ancestors and our bare feet are conscious of the sympathetic touch." And: "I appeal to any white man to say if ever he entered Logan's cabin hungry, and he gave him not meat; if ever he came cold and naked, and he clothed him not." Whole histories of clusters of instances are summed up in these images.

In "The Parable of the Sowing of the Seed," the instances cluster around each of the poles of like meaning for each illustration in the parable, which achieve their full meaning in comparison and contrast of one to another. These clusterings, long perceived and dwelt upon by Jesus, suggest the metaphorical illustrations. The great economy and heightening of the parables show the tremendous power of preliterate methods to distill and concentrate the meaning of the clusters of like and opposed instances into metaphorical forms that can be effectively delivered and easily recalled with the meaning intact.

In "Parapraxes," writing and speaking in an actual and imagined lecture situation, Freud shows a carefully aggressive perception of the relationships between his groupings of instances concerning error, what he has to say about his perceptions of error, and the sensitive persuasive needs of his audience. He divides and classifies instances of errors into patterns that show *kinds* of error, slips of the tongue, slips of the pen, misreadings, mishearings, temporarily forgetting something, etc.

In "When Will You Be a No Till Farmer?" Dick Lehnert perceives instances clustering in an overall pattern of Michigan farmers' lack of response to no-till's promise of benefits. Within the overall pattern, he perceives patterns of dependence upon herbicides, of using no-till to "plant some old swamp they could never plow," of fuel costs, and so forth. These clusterings of instances, his perceptions of their meaning and their relationships to each other, his comparison of them, provide the substance of what he has to say, and suggest organization, tone, and patterns for positive persuasion.

How does the perception of content, clustering of instances, sense of the audience, affect the organization of a piece of writing? Certainly my essay, "The Struggle for the Laugh in the Courtroom," had to combine my perceptions of chronology of events, patterns of laughter, "sense" and meaning of the trial into a nonlinear kind of storytelling. During my mulling over and thinking about my many notebooks on the trial, plus 22,000 pages of transcript and an avalanche of other reportage and research (I was wondering how on earth I could cope with it), a sudden thought caused me to type up the laughter incidents and cut them into strips and paste them into groupings of similar instances and opposing patterns. A definite interplay occurred between the material and my thoughts about it. The groupings themselves began to suggest further combinations and organizational structure. Hence my excitement, as the meanings of the numbers of instances condensed into the images and narrative examples of the patterns. When I rewrote the first drafts, the material became too cumbersome. I then used the core meanings of the instance clusters to help reduce and cut the manuscript to heighten the movement from beginning to end.

Donald Culross Peattie, in his definition of "weed," picks and chooses from his knowledge of weeds and gives thoughts and perceptions about them, as many as the purpose of his definition and the space available will allow. The technical writer's engineering definition of work shows the interplay between the kind of content and the purpose of the definition. In this case, the *measurements* of work effort are as much a part of the content as the effort itself.

In our perception of content, instances appear to group almost magnetically around poles of like and opposed meanings. The magnetism comes from the sense in our own minds of unverbalized meaning which in turn causes us to perceive the instances in patterns. Sense of the audience, character of the message, temperament of the writer come together in a sort of emotional chemical reaction that produces the author's attitude and tone. Thus, we understand the importance of the principle: *Be alert for what takes your attention for whatever reason;* for it may be telling you something important, such as perceiving the central organizing inductive "thesis" of a pattern.

You can apply these suggested techniques of clustering instances to the essay that you write out of your how-it-happens subject. Or you can choose a subject outside your how-it-happens area for the essay.

For a futher discussion of essay writing approaches, refer to "Getting Started, Build-Up, Continuing, and Rewriting" (pages 57–64).

General Essays—How-It-Happens—Research Through Reading

The following researched-through-reading essays use all of the techniques that we've seen at work in the personally-observed general essays and in the other essays under the various basic forms heading: techniques of imagery, clustering of instances, positive exaggeration, example and illustration, and all of the basic forms and modes of thinking that we've worked with.

How do you go about researching a subject through reading? How would you research tropical insects and their effect on people? Where would you look in the library's card catalog, where in the encyclopedia? How would you research the notion that kings evolved from magicians? How, in modern times, would you research the effects of the length of the working day? How would you research the historical causes and effects of slavery and racism in the United States? The use of visualization in invention and design? The history of number? The characters in a particular novelist's books? The gathering of material, note-taking, journal-writing and mental mulling over of research through reading often constitutes a large portion of a writer's skills.

How do the following essays resemble speeches to groups of people? How do they resemble letters? How and where do they use personal pronouns? How would you characterize the authors' sense of their audiences? Friendly? Cautious? Skeptical? Curious? Unfriendly? Tell anything that takes your attention about the audience sense of each essay.

When you read these essays, think about how you would research their subjects and how you would research through reading some aspect of your own how-it-happens subject, or any other subject that you may choose.

"Tropical Insects"
From **The Art of Survival**
Cord Christian Troebst

The real danger of the tropics are the insects. Many species carry parasites and spread epidemics, and are thus a greater menace than a whole zoo of wild animals turned loose. In 1939, for instance, only two hundred people in the whole of India were killed by tigers, while four million died of typhoid. The number of human victims devoured by wild animals during the past few hundred years is probably smaller than the number of malaria deaths in a year.

So the survivor in the tropics is more likely to succumb to an infectious disease or blood-poisoning than to hunger, thirst, or attack by wild animals. He must therefore take great care of his health and do everything to protect himself from insects. By all accounts the worst of the diseases they spread is malaria, which is carried by mosquitoes. The Stead trainees are given a long list of instructions on how best to avoid mosquitoes: for instance, never pitch your camp near swamps, the breeding places of mosquitoes; use your mosquito nets; use the ointments in your first-aid kit; take off as few clothes as possible.

Earlier it was mentioned how Bertram and Klausmann were plagued by mosquitoes. Ito and Minagawa were so badly stung that their faces and arms were constantly swollen. They could squash twenty mosquitoes every time they slapped their foreheads, but the spot would immediately be covered by a new lot. "Each morning our hands were bloody on both sides. This was another reason why we fled from the coast and deeper into the jungle. We were simply afraid of losing too much blood."

Then there was the American pilot who had to make a crash landing in New Guinea during World War II in a swamp only twenty miles from the airfield. He was sure he could get back on foot to his unit, so he set off eastward, leaving his emergency equipment in the wrecked plane. Soon he got into a bog, which quickly became very deep. After only three miles he was stuck and sank in it up to his shoulders. When a search party finally found him thirty-six hours later, he was covered with mosquitoes from the waterline to the top of his skull. They had bitten him so severely that his ears had swollen to shapeless lobes and he could hardly open his eyes. When he spoke, his nostrils and lips hurt. He was so much weakened that he could not walk unaided.

He had neglected to cover his face and the top of his body with mud, the simplest protection against mosquitoes (as the instructors of survival schools are always stressing). This, often mixed with burned cow dung or the dung of water buffalo, is used with great success by natives of the tropics. It also helps to rub in certain oils, from coconuts or lemon grass. Coconut oil is used, too, by the natives of tropical islands to protect them against head lice, and so is tobacco juice; while the savages of New Guinea and New Caledonia rub lime juice into their hair. This makes the hair turn red, but castaways from the West who had tried it out say it is as effective as modern synthetic preparations.

To keep off flies and bugs, the natives in the Philippines take breadfruits to bed with them. The inhabitants of New Guinea rid themselves of ants by storing lemons in damp places till the fruit is covered with mold. Then they quarter the rotten fruit and put the pieces on top of anthills. The ants clear off at once and don't go back there.

Some pilots after crash landing pitched their camp near an anthill or spent the night on an ant path: this was bad luck for they were naturally attacked by the ants and badly bitten. The South American fire ant, which has also penetrated into the southern states of North America, is so vicious that it makes calves and cows charge off lowing wildly to save themselves from its bites; farmhands there refuse to work in fields where there is a mound of fire ants. Many tropical ants live in the branches of certain trees, so one should sleep neither in a tree nor on the bare ground. In fact survival trainees are told how to construct a bed several feet above the ground; they are also warned to keep their shoes on at night and always be careful where they put their hands.

A man whose parachute got entangled in a tree in the Burmese jungle tried hastily to get to the ground, but lost his balance; one of his feet got caught in the noose, so that his head dangled a few inches above an anthill. Later, a rescue party found that with a little will power, and a realization that his situation was not hopeless, he could probably have freed himself from the noose. But the bites of the disturbed ants threw him into complete panic, and when a native party reached the place an hour later, he was already hanging dead from the tree—having put a bullet through his head.

Then there are the tropical parasites which bore into a man's skin to feed on his blood. "The ticks were terrible," said a pilot rescued in the tropics, "especially when I sat down on a place covered with grass. Sometimes I discovered dozens of these disgusting creatures on my body within a few minutes. Every day I had to strip completely to check my body for them from tip to toe. I had no iodine with me to put a drop on where the tick was biting, in order to get its head out of my skin. The only thing to do was to use a cigarette, holding its burning end to the insects hindquarters. They let go at once, and I could snip them off. Once, though, a tick's head came off in my skin, and the place became inflamed at once. When I was found by a search plane, it had already turned into an ugly wound."

Marston Bates, in *Where Winter Never Comes*, writes of another unpleasant creature: "I have had a great deal of experience with one tropical worm, the human bot-fly, or Dermatobia. This is the larva of a fly that develops in a boil-like sore on the skin of men or of various other animals (especially cattle)." It is carried by mosquitoes, and when the mosquito comes onto a man or warm-blooded animal to bite, "the larva drops off and burrows into the nearest sweat-sore, where it starts to eat and grow.

"The victim first notices a small bump like that resulting from some insect bite. But the bump persists and gets larger, and after a week or so there will be an occasional sharp pain at the infected spot. The little larva that is growing there is big at one end and tapering at the other; and the big end is armed with a series of sharp black spines, that make the whole thing look like an Indian war club. I suspect that the sharp pains result when the worm turns over, grating some nerve ends with these spines. If the spot is examined with a hand lens, it will be found to center in a tiny hole, where the worm periodically comes up for air.

"We got quite expert at getting the worms out, which is something of a trick, because they hang on inside with those spines. If the worm is broken and part of it left inside, infection is likely to result. We had many methods of extraction, but the neatest was to hold a lighted cigarette close to the skin, making the worm uncomfortably warm so that he relaxed his hold and, with an appropriately timed squeeze, could be popped out. This required considerable skill, and a more routine method was to cover the worm hole tightly with adhesive tape. The worm would then be smothered in about twenty-four hours and, dead, it could easily be squeezed out."

A person "attacked" by such worms may actually feel as though he is being eaten alive sometimes. At least this is what Juliane Koepcke felt, a seventeen-year-old German girl who on Christmas Day of 1971 was the sole survivor of a plane that crashed into the dense jungle of Peru. The plane, with ninety-two passengers on board, had been on a flight from Lima to Pucallpa when, apparently, it was hit by lightning. When

Juliane came to, she found herself still strapped in her seat, but thrown clear of the wreckage. Her mother was dead, no other passengers were to be seen (although some did survive apparently for a few days), and so Juliane started to walk out of the jungle alone.

From her father, who for many years had directed a jungle research station, Juliane had learned: "If you get lost in the jungle, look for the watercourse. It will lead you to larger ones, and they in turn will lead you to rivers. Rivers are the highways of the jungle—and will lead you to safety." And Juliane had also learned that "in the jungle, danger does not come from big animals—like jaguars, or tapirs, but from small ones—like spiders, ants, mosquitoes, flies, and other insects."

Within hours Juliane was stung by dozens of flies. "After a few days I had worms everywhere in my skin, and they hurt with every movement. Every now and then I operated on myself with a wooden splint, once extracting thirty-five worms in one hour. Where I had hurt myself (during the crash) the worms were particularly nasty: they had eaten so much out of the cut that I could put a finger in it."

On the tenth day after the crash, struggling along a river, Juliane was found by two men. Her body was swollen from mosquito bites, and thirty more worms were pulled out of her skin, this time with the aid of a few drops of gasoline.

Other survivors have reported that a favorite spot for fleas to settle and lay their eggs was under the toenails; they could only be scraped out with a sterilized knife, after which the wound had to be treated at once with iodine to stop an inflammation. One survivor of the Burma campaign recalled that "Mites also settled in our skin round our hips. They caused a terrible itching, but we knew we mustn't scratch. We covered the places with iodine, and the itch gradually stopped."

Of course there are a great many other tropical insects and parasites, which cannot all be listed here. But these few examples will show that survivors have often been able to protect themselves by simple methods (like tobacco juice and lighted cigarettes), and have also taken care to avoid inflammations. For in tropical heat even the smallest scratch can very quickly turn into an ugly wound. Cases of blood poisoning are quite common—although the natives are seldom affected by this.

Frequently, I've coached students through a reading of "Tropical Insects" and then asked, "How did the author get his information?" Most students stop, shocked, for at least a moment in considering the matter. A few of them will say that the author got the information from personal experience, simply because the writing comes across with such vivid imagery. How, they ask, could he make it so vivid if he hadn't experienced it himself? Yet there is no indication that Troebst ever got nearer the tropics than the stacks of a good library. How do any of the writers of the general essays in this section make you experience their subjects, "put you there," as if they had been there themselves?

"Tropical Insects" is a virtually complete essay, though it is excerpted from and certainly influenced strongly by the overall material, theses, purposes, organization and movement of the complete chapter "Survival in the Tropics" in the yet longer movement of the complete book *The Art of Survival*. Similarly, the involvement of your how-it-happens subject area can generate the material for the various forms of writing we've discussed so far.

Where do you find positive exaggeration used to make the examples and statements clear? What basic forms does Troebst use? Where do you see the rhetorical modes of definition, how-it's-done, comparison and contrast, cause and effect, division and classification, example and illustration, and argument?

At some point in the process of research, the observed patterns suggest directions and generalizations to the investigator. The first level of that research process is called inductive, such as Troebst's original researching of material about survival in the tropics, a gathering and figuring out of meaningful patterns of the instances and then stating generalizations drawn from those patterns. In writing about the patterns, the author becomes complexly involved with them and they become powerfully suggestive and emerge more clearly. The pattern may finally be stated as a thesis statement, and some of the researched instances are then used to provide examples and supports for the argument, strongly suggesting "proof" of the inductive thesis. Such a statement and support of thesis is never as elegantly airtight as deductive proof in logic and mathematics. Indeed, most thinking is not deductive or syllogistic. Most thinking, scientific and otherwise, is inductive.

Here is a suggestion for research: How would you research the effects of the length of the working day in modern times? Or the effects of different time-periods on working performance? Where would you go in the library? Which organizations would you approach for their research? What have you personally observed on jobs you've had?

Why Nothing Seems to Work
Rasa Gustaitis

San Francisco commuters are still complaining that their space-age, multi-million dollar BART (Bay Area Rapid Transit) is a malfunctioning boondoggle, if not downright dangerous.

And pedestrians in downtown Boston still look apprehensively skyward when passing the towering John Hancock Building, for fear those popping windows will one day hit a target.

Why is it that so many of our most sophisticated technological achievements continue to be plagued by near disasters? Why doesn't anything work anymore?

Eugene S. Ferguson, curator of the Hagley Museum in Greenville, Del., believes he has the answer. The problem, he says, is that the engineers who design today's technological behemoths no longer conceive them visually. The computer has been substituted for human vision.

Ferguson predicts that the problem will only get worse. "The more complex the machinery, the more often it will be out of order," he says.

"Something that the man in the street knows but most of our technicians don't is that much of machinery is out of order much of the time. The assumption of the engineer is that it will work."

In engineering schools visual design courses that cultivate perception are being squeezed out by scientific analysis and computer mathematics, Ferguson has observed. Consequently, engineers can calculate but often can't use their designs in relation to their context.

This failure to see whole pictures leads to fiascos such as those that have afflicted the highly automated BART system, which has malfunctioned in alarming ways. Doors have opened while trains were moving. Trains have zoomed past stations, without stopping, carrying anxious commuters to the end of the line. Electronic monitors have failed to detect a train on a track, threatening rear-end collisions.

The management finally resorted to a very old-fashioned safety measure: phoning ahead, station to station, to warn of on-coming trains.

BART "is a classic result of systems engineering uninformed by minds that can visualize the mundane things that can go wrong," Ferguson wrote in a recent issue of

Science magazine. "Absurd random failures that have plagued automatic control systems are not merely trivial aberrations; they are reflections of the chaos that results when design is assumed to be primarily a problem in mathematics."

Much creative thought in design is visual. Its language is in pictures that cannot be translated into words or equations.

"Pyramids, cathedrals and rockets exist not because of geometry, theory of structure of thermodynamics, but because they were first a picture—literally a vision—in the minds of those who built them," Ferguson argues.

Many of the great technological designers in history have also been artists. Leonardo da Vinci may be the best known among them, but in his time he was not alone. In Renaissance engineering, art—not science—was the guiding discipline, according to Ferguson.

Even into the 19th century, some of the great technological designers were also artists. Benjamin Henry Latrobe, a prominent consulting engineer and architect, was an accomplished watercolorist. Robert Fulton, known for his steamboat, and Samuel Morse, inventor of the electric telegraph, turned from careers in art to technology.

Using their intuitive sense of rightness and fitness, designers created the suspension bridge, the clock, the motorcycle. The notion that scientific information alone shaped them is "a bit of modern folklore," says Ferguson.

Yet in recent decades, as the scientific component of technology has expanded, the trend has been away from nonverbal thinking and toward verbal and mathematical analysis. Nonverbal thought is now generally viewed as less rigorous and useful than cognitive reasoning.

"There may still be engineering graphics courses in some schools," says Ferguson, "but they are going out as the new breed comes in and the old dies out."

Engineering students used to be assigned exercises that required them to think in ways that could not be reduced to mathematics: design a container for an egg that will let it drop three stories without breaking; design a wheelchair that will go up stairs. They used to work a lot with three-dimensional models.

Now, says Ferguson, engineers learn the computer approach to drafting and designing. This requires them to convert mathematical descriptions to pictures in their minds. In the process, they can easily lose sight of the whole amid the scattered parts.

Ferguson began to understand the problem, he says, one snowy day when he boarded the modern high-speed Metroliner in New York only to find that all trains that day were being pulled by slow 40-year-old engines. The new engines were out of service because the designers of the sophisticated control gear had failed to consider that, during a snowstorm, the fan that sucks in air would also suck in snow.

He realized that failure to consider such simple possibilities also lay behind many of the failures of BART. It also helped him understand why the John Hancock Building in Boston kept popping out windows until an expensive stabilizer was devised on top.

The current "systematic but intellectually impoverished engineering approach" to design is leading to a technology that is devoid of a "sense of fitness," says Ferguson. For instance, it is not fitting during this time of high unemployment, he argues, that automatic fare cards be used in transit systems instead of human ticket salespeople.

It also is not reasonable, he says, "that a man who earns $6 an hour on an assembly line should be forced to have someone come in to replace a part on his washing machine. That machine could be designed simply so he could fix it himself by changing a washer, but to do so would be bad corporate policy."

———

In large part, this article is summarized from a much longer article, "The Mind's Eye: Nonverbal Thought in Technology," by Eugene S. Ferguson, in *Science* (August 1977, vol. 197). It appears that Gastaitis may have interviewed Ferguson, too—perhaps by telephone. How do the examples support the perception of a lack of adequate visualization in modern engineering? What argument does the article make? How does it resemble a report to a small group?

"Imagination in Scientific Discovery"
From **The Art of Scientific Investigation**
W. I. B. Beveridge

"With accurate experiment and observation to work upon, imagination becomes the architect of physical theory."

—JOHN TYNDALL

Productive Thinking

This chapter and the next contain a brief discussion on how ideas originate in the mind and what conditions are favourable for creative mental effort.

Dewey analyses conscious thinking into the following phases. First comes awareness of some difficulty or problem which provides the stimulus. This is followed by a suggested solution springing into the conscious mind. Only then does reason come into play to examine and reject or accept the idea. If the idea is rejected, our mind reverts to the previous stage and the process is repeated. The important thing to realise is that the conjuring up of the idea is not a deliberate, voluntary act. It is something that happens to us rather than something we do.

In ordinary thinking ideas continually "occur" to us in this fashion to bridge over the steps in reasoning, and we are so accustomed to the process that we are hardly aware of it. Usually the new ideas and combinations result from the immediately preceding thought calling up associations that have been developed in the mind by past experience and education. Occasionally, however, there flashes into the mind some strikingly original idea, not based on past associations or at any rate not on associations that are at first apparent. We may suddenly perceive for the first time the connection between several things or ideas, or may take a great leap forward instead of the usual short step where the connections between each pair or set of ideas are well established and "obvious." These sudden, large progressions occur not only when one is consciously puzzling the problem but also not uncommonly when one is not thinking of anything in particular, or even when one is mildly occupied with something different, and in these circumstances they are often startling. Although there is probably no fundamental difference between these ideas and the less exciting ones that come to us almost continually, and it is not possible to draw any sharp distinction, it will be convenient to consider them separately in the next chapter under the title "intuitions." In this section we will draw attention to some general features of productive or creative thinking.

Dewey advocates what he calls "reflective thinking," that is, turning a subject over in the mind and giving it ordered and consecutive consideration, as distinct from the free coursing of ideas through the head. Perhaps the best term for the latter is daydreaming; it also has its uses, as we shall see presently. But thinking may be reflective and yet be inefficient. The thinker may not be sufficiently critical of ideas as they arise and may be too ready to jump to a conclusion, either through impatience or laziness. Dewey says many people will not tolerate a state of doubt, either because they will not endure the mental discomfort of it or because they regard it as evidence of inferiority.

"To be genuinely thoughtful, we must be willing to sustain and protract that state of doubt which is the stimulus to thorough enquiry, so as not to accept an idea or make a positive assertion of a belief, until justifying reasons have been found."

Probably the main characteristic of the trained thinker is that he does not jump to conclusions on insufficient evidence as the untrained man is inclined to do.

It is not possible deliberately to create ideas or to control their creation. When a difficulty stimulates the mind, suggested solutions just automatically spring into the consciousness. The variety and quality of the suggestions are functions of how well prepared our mind is by past experience and education pertinent to the particular problem. What we can do deliberately is to prepare our minds in this way, voluntarily direct our thoughts to a certain problem, hold attention on that problem and appraise the various suggestions thrown up by the subconscious mind. The intellectual element in thinking is, Dewey says, what we do with the suggestions after they arise.

Other things being equal, the greater our store of knowledge, the more likely it is that significant combinations will be thrown up. Furthermore, original combinations are more likely to come into being if there is available a breadth of knowledge extending into related or even distant branches of knowledge. As Dr. E. L. Taylor says:

"New associations and fresh ideas are more likely to come out of a varied store of memories and experience than out of a collection that is all of one kind."

Scientists who have made important original contributions have often had wide interests or have taken up the study of a subject different from the one in which they were originally trained. Originality often consists in finding connections or analogies between two or more objects or ideas not previously shown to have any bearing on each other.

In seeking original ideas, it is sometimes useful to abandon the directed, controlled thinking advocated by Dewey and allow one's imagination to wander freely—to day-dream. Harding says all creative thinkers are dreamers. She defines dreaming in these words:

"Dreaming over a subject is simply . . . allowing the will to focus the mind passively on the subject so that it follows the trains of thought as they arise, stopping them only when unprofitable but in general allowing them to form and branch naturally until some useful and interesting results occur."

Max Planck said:

"Again and again the imaginary plan on which one attempts to build up order breaks down and then we must try another. This imaginative vision and faith in the ultimate success are indispensable. The pure rationalist has no place here."

In meditating thus, many people find that visualising the thoughts, forming mental images, stimulates the imagination. It is said that Clerk Maxwell developed the habit of making a mental picture of every problem. Paul Ehrlich was another great advocate of making pictorial representations of ideas, as one can see from his illustrations of his side-chain theory. Pictorial analogy can play an important part in scientific thinking. This is how the German chemist Kekule hit on the conception of the benzene ring, an idea that revolutionised organic chemistry. He related how he was sitting writing his chemical text-book:

"But it did not go well; my spirit was with other things. I turned the chair to the fireplace and sank into a half sleep. The atoms flitted before my eyes. Long rows, variously, more closely, united; all in movement wriggling and turning like snakes. And see, what was that? One of the snakes seized its own tail and the image whirled scornfully before my eyes. As though from a flash of lightning I awoke; I occupied the rest of the night in working out the consequences of the hypothesis. . . . Let us learn to dream, gentlemen."

However, physics has reached a stage where it is no longer possible to visualise mechanical analogies representing certain phenomena which can only be expressed in mathematical terms.

In the study of infectious diseases, it is sometimes helpful to take the biological view, as Burnet has done, and look upon the causal organism as a species struggling for continued survival, or even, as Zinsser has felt inclined to do with typhus, which he spent a lifetime studying, personifying the disease in the imagination.

An important inducement to seeking generalisations, especially in physics and mathematics, is the love of order and logical connection between facts. Einstein said:

"There is no logical way to the discovery of these elemental laws. There is only the way of intuition, which is helped by a feeling for the order lying behind the appearance."

W. H. George remarks that a feeling of tension is produced when an observer sees the objects lying in his field of vision as forming a pattern with a gap in it, and a feeling of relaxation or satisfaction is experienced when the gap is closed, and all parts of the pattern fit into their expected places. Generalisations may be regarded as patterns in ideas. Another phenomenon which may be explained by this concept is the satisfaction experienced on the completion of any task. This may be quite unassociated with any consideration of reward, for it applies equally to unimportant, self-appointed tasks such as doing a crossword puzzle, climbing a hill or reading a book. The instinctive sense of irritation we feel when someone disagrees with us or when some fact arises which is contrary to our beliefs may be due to the break in the pattern we have formed.

The tendency of the human mind to seek order in things did not escape the penetrating intelligence of Francis Bacon. He warned against the danger that this trait may mislead us into believing we see a greater degree of order and equality than there really is.

When one has succeeded in hitting upon a new idea, it has to be judged. Reason based on knowledge is usually sufficient in everyday affairs and in straightforward matters in science, but in research there is often insufficient information available for effective reasoning. Here one has to fall back on "feelings" or "taste." Harding says:

"If the scientist has during the whole of his life observed carefully, trained himself to be on the look out for analogy, and possessed himself of relevant knowledge, then the 'instrument of feeling' . . . will become a powerful diving rod . . . in creative science feeling plays a leading part."

Writing of the importance of imagination in science Tyndall said:

"Newton's passage from a falling apple to a falling moon was an act of the prepared imagination. Out of the facts of chemistry the constructive imagination of Dalton formed the atomic theory. Davy was richly endowed with the imaginative faculty, while with Faraday its exercise was incessant, preceding, accompanying and guiding all his experiments. His strength and fertility as a discoverer are to be referred in great part to the stimulus of the imagination."

Imagination is of great importance not only in leading us to new facts, but also in stimulating us to new efforts, for it enables us to see visions of their possible consequences. Facts and ideas are dead in themselves and it is the imagination that gives life to them. But dreams and speculations are idle fantasies unless reason turns them to useful purpose. Vague ideas captured on flights of fancy have to be reduced to specific propositions and hypotheses.

How does Beveridge use the examples of the work of scientific investigators (and direct quotes from them) to draw the reader into a consideration of the essential use of imagination in scientific discovery? Who is the "we" of his audience address?

"Faulkner's People"
From **The Introduction to The Portable Faulkner**
Malcolm Cowley

Popeye himself is one of several characters in Faulkner's novels who represent the mechanical civilization that has invaded and conquered the South. He is always described in mechanical terms: his eyes "looked like rubber knobs"; his face "just went awry, like the face of a wax doll set too near a hot fire and forgotten"; his tight suit and stiff hat were "all angles, like a modernistic lampshade"; and in general he had "that vicious depthless quality of stamped tin." Popeye was the son of a professional strike-breaker, from whom he had inherited syphilis; he was the grandson of a pyromaniac, and he had spent most of his childhood in an institution. He was the man "who made money and had nothing he could do with it, spend it for, since he knew that alcohol would kill him like poison, who had no friends and had never known a woman"—in other words, he was a compendium of all the hateful qualities that Faulkner assigns to finance capitalism.

Sanctuary is not a connected allegory, as George Marion O'Donnell condemned it for being—he was the first critic to approach it seriously—but neither is it a mere accumulation of pointless horrors. It is an example of the Freudian method turned backward, being full of sexual nightmares that are in reality social symbols. It is somehow connected in the author's mind with what he regards as the rape and corruption of the South.

In his novels dealing with the present—I am speaking of those written before 1945—Faulkner makes it clear that the descendants of the old ruling caste have the wish but not the courage or the strength to prevent his new disaster. They are defeated by Popeye (like Horace Benbow), or they run away from him (like Gowan Stevens, who had been to college at Virginia and learned how to drink like a gentleman, but not to fight for his principles), or they are robbed and replaced in their positions of influence by the Snopeses (like old Bayard Sartoris, the president of the bank), or they drug themselves with eloquence and alcohol (like Quentin Compson's father), or they retire into the illusion of being inviolable Southern ladies (like Mrs. Compson, who says, "It can't be simply to flout and hurt me. Whoever God is, He would not permit that. I'm a lady."), or they dwell so much on the past that they are incapable of facing the present (like Reverend Hightower of *Life in August*), or they run from danger to danger (like young Bayard Sartoris) frantically seeking their own destruction. Faulkner's novels are full of well-meaning and even admirable persons, not only the grandsons of the cotton aristocracy, but also pine-hill farmers and storekeepers and sewing-machine agents and Negro cooks and sharecroppers; but they are almost all of them defeated by circumstances and they carry with them a sense of their own doom.

They also carry, whether heroes or villains, a curious sense of submission to their fate. "There is not one of Faulkner's characters," says André Gide in his dialogue on "The New American Novelists," "who properly speaking, has a soul"; and I think he means that not one of them exercises the faculty of conscious choice between good and evil. They are haunted, obsessed, driven forward by some inner necessity. Like Miss Rosa Coldfield, in *Absalom, Absalom!* they exist in "that dream state in which you run without moving from a terror in which you cannot believe, toward a safety in which you have no faith." Or, like the slaves freed by General Sherman's army, in *The Unvanquished,* they blindly follow the roads toward any river, believing that it will be their Jordan:

> They were singing, walking along the road singing, not even looking to either side. The dust didn't even settle for two days, because all that night they still passed; we sat up listening to them, and the next morning every few yards along the road would be the old ones who couldn't keep up any more, sitting or lying down and even crawling along, calling to the others to help them; and the others— the young ones—not stopping, not even looking at them. "Going to Jordan," they told me. "Going to cross Jordan."

All Faulkner's characters, black and white, are a little like that. They dig for gold frenziedly after they have lost their hope of finding it (like Henry Armstid in *The Hamlet* and Lucas Beauchamp in *Go Down, Moses*); or they battle against and survive a Mississippi flood for the one privilege of returning to the state prison farm (like the tall convict in "Old Man"); or, a whole family together, they carry a body through flood and fire and corruption to bury it in the cemetery at Jefferson (like the Bundrens in *As I Lay Dying*); or they tramp the roads week after week in search of men who had promised but never intended to marry them (like Lena Grove, the pregnant woman of *Light in August*); or, pursued by a mob, they turn at the end to meet and accept death (like Joe Christmas in the same novel). Even when they seem to be guided by a conscious purpose, like Colonel Sutpen, it is not something they have chosen by an act of will, but something that has taken possession of them: Sutpen's great design was "not what he wanted to do but what he just had to do, had to do it whether he wanted to or not, because if he did not do it he knew that he could never live with himself for the rest of his life." In the same way, Faulkner himself writes, not what he wants to, but what he just has to write whether he wants to or not.

And Faulkner loves these people created in the image of the land. After a second reading of his novels, you continue to be impressed by his villains, Popeye and Jason and Joe Christmas and Flem Snopes; but this time you find more place in your memory for other figures standing a little in the background yet presented by the author with quiet affection: old ladies like Miss Jenny Du Pre, with their sharp-tongued benevolence; shrewd but kindly bargainers like Ratliff, the sewing-machine agent, and Will Varner, with his cotton gin and general store; long-suffering farm wives like Mrs. Henry Armstid (whether her name is Lula or Martha); and backwoods patriarchs like Pappy Mac-Cullum, with his six middle-aged but unmarried sons named after the generals of Lee's army. You remember the big plantation houses that collapse in flames as if a whole civilization were dying, but you also remember men in patched and faded but quite clean overalls sitting on the gallery—here in the North we should call it the porch—of a crossroads store that is covered with posters advertising soft drinks and patent medicines; and you remember the stories they tell while chewing tobacco until the suption is out of it (everything in their world is reduced to anecdote, and every anecdote is based on character). You remember Quentin Compson, not in his despairing moments, but riding with his father behind the dogs as they quarter a sedge-grown hillside after quail; and not listening to his father's story, but still knowing every word of it, because, as he thought to himself, "You had learned, absorbed it already without the medium of speech somehow from having been born and living beside it, with it, as children will and do: so that what your father was saying did not tell you anything so much as it struck, word by word, the resonant strings of remembering."

Faulkner's novels have the quality of being lived, absorbed, remembered rather than merely observed. And they have what is rare in the novels of our time, a warmth of family affection, brother for brother and sister, the father for his children—a love so warm and proud that it tries to shut out the rest of the world. Compared with that affection, married love is presented as something calculating, and illicit love as a consuming fire. And because the blood relationship is central in his novels, Faulkner finds it hard to create sympathetic characters between the ages of twenty and forty. He is better with children, Negro and white, and incomparably good with older people who preserve the standards that have come down to them "out of the old time, the old days."

From his reading of Faulkner's novels and short stories, Malcolm Cowley clusters instances that illustrate patterns of how Faulkner's characters come to be defeated, how they submit to their fate, how they are driven to pursue impossible goals, how some are characterized with quiet affection, how some use family feeling and warmth to try "to shut out the rest of the world." In thinking about, clustering, and writing about the instances concerning Faulkner's characters, Cowley discovered the patterns. How does he state the patterns in writing and support them with instances?

Workerology
Reginald Carlvin

Author's Note:
    Countless books and articles have been written on the science of Management, and they are, without exception, on management of subordinates by superiors. The existing professional literature, startling as this may be, contains no studies whatsoever on problems of management of superiors by subordinates, specifically on the problem of the performance of the former from the point of view of the latter. This represents a glaring and intolerable void, and is also the cause of a totally unjustified neglect of the great potential of subordinate jobs.
    A number of readers might think at first that "Workerology" will be a divisive influence and will lead to great conflicts and more strife between superiors and subordinates, to the detriment of the corporate organization. Quite to the contrary, one of its main objectives is to bring the subordinate into the management process and make him a responsible partner in organizational decision-making. Inevitably, this will give the subordinate a better understanding and appreciation of the superior's role and function, and make possible more efficient and harmonious teamwork between the two. True, the superior may initially fail to see things this way, but this is only to be expected, because adjustment to something different usually takes time.

Selecting the Right Subordinate Position

O, let us love our occupations,
Bless the shoeshine man and his relations,
Live upon our daily Kennel-Rations,
And always know our proper stations.
    Jabbo: A Street Corner Philosopher

Jobs, as all elements and some wives, make good servants and bad masters. And now that we have neatly disposed of the subjects of weather and matrimony, we can confine our attention in the remainder of this section to the selection of subordinate jobs alone.

Expertise, Not Ability

Some subordinate jobs are better than others in that they make it easier to secure and maintain independence. Consequently, they also provide better leverage in the application of Workerology. It is important, however, to know that whatever occupation the subordinate chooses, it is not ability he should demonstate, but expertise. Ability makes one promotion-prone, and is therefore treacherous, while expertise is a very stabilizing influence that helps anchor a man to the job he happens to be in. Direct advertising of one's expertise is one of the recommended methods of building a professional reputation.

Expertise is best established in some esoteric or narrowly specialized technical field such as the development of numbering systems for spare parts, the composition of account numbers, registry, archives and library codification work, updating of equipment maintenance manuals, laboratory quality-testing in a single-product large chemical plant, etc. These fields are gingerly approached by Superiors and subordinates alike. A normal executive will not only delegate but gladly altogether relinquish his authority to a numbering systems expert if only to keep the subject matter of the expert's specialty at arm's length. And the prospect of being compelled to fill a vacancy of the kind just described can induce a state of deep depression in many an ill-informed executive. Jobs with these and like descriptions are bastions of autonomy for the incumbent.

The Superiority of Unpopular Jobs

The less inviting or more repugnant a job appears to be to the uninitiated, the more irreplaceable the subordinate doing it will be considered, and the more independence and job satisfaction he can win for himself. In a job that is nobody's glass of Kool-Aid, the incumbent has an unusual opportunity for making it what he really wants it to be, with a virtual guarantee of immunity from outside interference, and with adequate breaks for various extracurricular activities which are a legitimate part of the "job-enrichment" concept (e.g., keeping tab on the racetrack to add variety to the job content, or dabbling in real estate to compensate for chronic inequities in subordinate salary scales). To these activities the subordinate has an inalienable, if sometimes still disputed right, and he should exercise his right freely and regularly for, as the Turkish proverb says, "Baklava is not for the man who likes it, but for the one who is accustomed to it." Outmoded and reactionary personnel management concepts notwithstanding, a healthy part of the workday devoted to hobbies greatly contributes to high employee morale. And a satisfied work force, as everybody knows, is the foundation on which a successful organization stands. The subordinate who by any means available to him seeks fulfillment at work can rejoice in the knowledge that he is at the same time also helping his employer.

The leverage of a judiciously selected job and the validity of Workerology are well demonstrated in the application of the "I am quitting" threat gambit, so dear to our hearts, and so often resorted to without proper credentials. A well-placed subordinate can use it with impunity, to finagle some advantage for himself and even, occasionally, to indulge in a pique. Any executive hates to lose an expert who is most difficult to replace and who, in addition, represents no threat to him. He may think the threat is a bluff, but he seldom will dare call it. One should also add that, for the threat to be effective, indispensability need not be proved, but only implied. The proper subordinate job, by virtue of the job title alone, assures this. In contrast, the Superior must daily give proof or semblance of performance, and endlessly exert himself just to show that he need not be fired and replaced.

Enough Good Jobs to Go Around?

We now have some kind of idea of the kind of job the subordinate should be looking for, but the problem of finding such jobs still remains. Are there enough of them to satisfy any demand? On this score we can confidently put the reader's worries to rest. Such categories of work abound, as even a superficial survey will disclose. With technology on the march, and its administration more than keeping step, there is no danger of the bountiful supply of seemingly repulsive jobs drying out in the foreseeable future. (Remember the computer, heralded as the bane of drudgery and the greatest laborsaving device of all time, which ended up creating many more unpopular jobs than it ever eliminated?) A subordinate with only modest powers of observation should have no trouble in finding for himself a highly rewarding occupation. The fact that there is neither demand nor competition for such work only shows how little common sense people have, or how uninformed they are.

A Case in Point

The criteria described in this chapter for selecting subordinate jobs, which boil down to a recommendation to look for seemingly uninviting jobs and acquire an expertise (real or presumed) in them, may appear unusual and novel. They have, nevertheless, been valid for at least as long as recorded history. There is no better proof of this than the saga of ancient Babylon's sanitation workers. By far the best and most renowned in Mesopotamia (and at a time when sanitation was not taken for granted as it is today), they contributed in no small measure to the comparative attractions of daily life of their sophisticated city. But while keeping Babylon clean, salubrious, and with nothing to offend the refined nostrils of its urbane citizens, they also fed the envy of Babylon's neighbors, Assyrians in particular, whose capital, Nineveh, had no sanitation to speak of. A fetid stench hung without reprieve over Nineveh, and literally drove Assyrian kings and their armies out of city walls, with nothing much to do but engage in military conquest.

Unable to contain their long-simmering envy any more, the Assyrians, in 689 B. C., unleashed a savage attack on Babylon, sacked the city, and put its population to the sword. But Babylon's sanitation men were all spared, on strict orders from Sennacherib, the Assyrian king. He offered them better pay, subsidized housing and, among other fringe benefits, separate and guaranteed seating in temples and at games, if only they would come and work in Nineveh. This, of course, was an offer they could not refuse, and so to Nineveh they went and arrived there amid great popular rejoicing. Nor did they disappoint their newly adopted city, for in a very short time they cleaned it up thoroughly and made of it a place fit to breathe in. And now the king and his army found life in Nineveh so much to their liking that they rarely, if ever, ventured out of it. With

Assyrians comfortably ensconced in their capital, the fear in the hearts of their vassals and enemies gave way to security; security gave way to confidence, confidence to courage, and courage to brazenness, and soon the Assyrians found themselves with a full-scale rebellion on their hands. In 612 B. C., an allied force of Medes and Babylonians (who by now had somewhat recovered politically and militarily, but not sanitation-wise) laid seige to Nineveh, stormed it and slaughtered its citizens or sold them into slavery. But no one laid a finger on our sanitation workers. Both Medes and Babylonians bid for their services, offering them terms even better than those Assyrians had given them. The Medes outbid the Babylonians, and Nineveh's sanitation workers went to their capital, Ectabana. And there, when in 539 B. C. Ectabana fell to Cyrus, the Persian king, their story repeated itself again.

The story just told took place more than twenty-five centuries ago, but the situation hasn't changed much since: Sanitation work is still not popular, but the sanitation workers' welfare is still given due consideration, and their demands carry as much weight as ever (and anybody who has lived through a sanitation strike will readily agree with that). Workerology is as valid now as it was then.

The Use of Rules and Regulations

Any fool can make a rule
and every fool will mind it.
Thoreau: *Journal*

Once the subordinate has selected the proper job, he should learn how to use the many weapons inherent in his position. One of the most effective of these weapons at his disposal is the use of rules and regulations, the story of which should be a priority item on his agenda.

No one questions the wisdom of a rule or regulation that has long been in existence. With time, a rule of regulation dissociates itself from the fallibility of its human creator and mysteriously becomes endowed with a dogmalike quality of its own, whether it makes sense or not. In fact, the less sense it makes, the less likely it is to be questioned. Traces of logic in a rule or regulation are telltale signs of its human origin, and thus only tend to undermine its authority and credibility.

But, then, it is not the function of rules and regulations to make sense or, as so-called management experts would have us to believe, to make it possible for an organization to perform some alleged service for society at large. The only genuine reason for establishing rules and regulations in an organization is to provide a stable system of interpersonal relationships in which life is predictable and simple, and where there are no dilemmas and dangers as long as the rules and regulations are observed.

Every bureaucracy has, collectively, a vested interest in such havens of security and stability, and any violator caught breaking rules and regulations and disturbing the peace and order of organizational life is prosecuted with all the zeal and fury with which the Inquisition prosecuted a heretic. No Superior is unaware of this, and his respect for rules and regulations is deep and genuine, and often bordering on awe and worship. The case is known, for instance, of a high Ministry of Finance Official, of a government we shall leave unnamed, who would not accept bribes until he assured himself that regulations allowed remuneration for services rendered, from sources other than his employer, of up to 30 percent of his annual Civil Service pay. And then he made sure never to go over his 30 percent limit.

The only executive who will break rules and regulations irresponsibly and set precedents is the "raider" type of executive, who typically has not come through the ranks, and who knows of his authority but not of his duties to the organization. He is, fortunately, a comparatively rare and short-lived phenomenon, and the antidote needed for this irritant is a little patience and Christian forbearance, to give him time and rope enough to hang himself (which he efficiently and invariably does, even without anybody's help). The typical Superior, however, obeys the rules, and plays it safe, like the husband who follows the time-tested advice of the Arab proverb which says "Beat your wife every morning: If you don't know why, she does." But while the executive seeks the protection of rules and regulations he at the same time, by obeying them, surrenders much of his freedom of action and no subordinate who is aware of this should have trouble running circles around a Superior witlessly hobbled of his own will. A case history, briefly told, will illustrate what we have in mind:

In the Incoming Mail Unit of a large East Coast utility, the Unit's new supervisor, a certain Mr. Turnipp, was loathed by the mail clerks, and for good reason: He was a fanatic for following proper procedure, a stickler for detail, and he liked nothing better than to look over his subordinates' shoulders and breathe down their necks. For this he had plenty of time as there was nothing for him to do, except personally to examine, according to the established rule, mail marked "confidential," and decide on its disposition. This he did willingly and without fail because it made him feel important, but there just wasn't enough of it until the day the mail clerks got their heads together and bought themselves a dozen or so "confidential" rubber stamps (all of a different type, so as not to arouse suspicion), and, when Turnipp was not around, started gradually marking more and more pieces of correspondence with their newly acquired tools.

Within a few months Turnipp, sitting at his desk behind a large pile of "confidential" mail that never seemed to get smaller, had hardly enough time to go to the men's room and barely take notice of his staff. He was cursing under his breath and often wondering aloud why on earth should some pieces of mail have ever been marked "confidential." But he went on with his toil, for rules are rules and must be obeyed, and he did all of it by himself because he was certainly not going to share his special "privileged" responsibilities with any of his staff. And so, while the boss was minding the rules, the subordinates were taking it easy and reaping the rewards of a proper use of rules and regulations.

And now, after these general introductory remarks, we should go back to the specifics, to give the reader a few pointers of practical value. To better achieve this, it might prove useful to divide our subject matter into some logical subcategories, as follows:

Written Rules and Regulations

A careful perusal of rules and regulations in a large organization will disclose that for every conceivable rule and regulation there is a counterrule and counterregulation, as if always to provide an escape clause for human imperfection and also to reward the diligent student of the science of Management of Superiors. Almost any decision of a Superior that encroaches on the prerogatives of subordinates can be demonstrated to be in flagrant conflict with some explicit organization rule or regulation. Without delay, the Superior should be alerted to this; and if he is of genuine executive caliber (and not a rules and regulations expert himself) he can be counted upon to turn around and beat a full retreat.

It would be a grave mistake to underestimate the practical value of the proposition just formulated. This proposition is, in fact, the explanation for the continued existence of much of what the management likes to describe as "feather bedding." Many a management plan supposedly intended to increase efficiency and cut costs (at the expense of subordinates, of course) has come to nought because it ran afoul of some existing rule or regulation that the rank and file could invoke in defense of their interests, and this is why we have available today such wonderful subordinate jobs as those of firemen on diesel and electric trains, elevator operators in automatic elevators, and in some places, town criers in this age of TV, radio, and telephone.

But occasionally, even in the largest and oldest organizations, there will be no rule or regulation exactly answering the need of the subordinate. This, however, should not bother him unduly, for as every serious student of Workerolgy knows, proper interpretation of rules and regulations greatly extends their scope and usefulness. To give an example that easily comes to mind (and that the reader, having probably had personal experience with this sort of thing, will readily recognize), mention can be made of the flexible interpretation of what constitutes sickness, which assures an employee the full benefit of his company's sick-leave provisions. Similarly, an imaginative interpretation of the rules governing the filing of expense claims assures that sufficient mileage is gotten out of expense accounts. There is no need for the subordinate to practice deception (and risk killing the goose that lays the golden egg) if he knows how to interpret the truth.

As already explained, the purpose of rules and regulations is to assure stability, which also means to preserve the status quo. As such, they are practically suitable for blocking action, although occasionally give excellent results in securing positive action as well. To explain this in more dynamic terms, the use of rules and regulations in the application of Workerology is more defensive than offensive, more in the nature of judo than karate. The subordinate who, for example, strictly observes the 9–5 office hours, and files his nails in the interval, is less exposed to the executive frame-up than the poor devil who slaves at his desk but is occasionally late in the morning. As long as the subordinate's activities can be represented as sanctioned by rules and regulations he is safe, and he walks through the treacherous organizational corridors dressed in impenetrable armor plate.

Unwritten Rules

The validity of observations made at the beginning of this section is not restricted to written rules and regulations, but applies to unwritten rules and established practices as well. Not rarely is it just because it is so sacrosanct that an established practice can be written up. If the typical executive has true respect for written rules and regulations, he is often no less terrified by the unwritten ones. Can anyone think, for instance, of a Superior with a key to the top management rest room patronizing the rank and file toilet? A thorough knowledge of unwritten practices is an absolute must for a qualified subordinate. It can tell him, to give just one of so many examples, how to bring on, when it suits his purpose, a wholesale top management crisis by simply jamming the lock to one single door.

Precedents

The executive's fear is also not limited to breaches of existing rules and regulations, both written and unwritten. He is equally afraid, if not more, of breaking new ground and establishing a precedent (and that is why he often likes to run in circles, on a familiar, safe, and well-trodden path). A precedent, while it may not be in conflict with any existing rules and regulations, is also outside their protection, and no executive worth his salt is going to risk his future with a decision he may later be called upon to justify. A subordinate who knows his rules and regulations will very often have no trouble in identifying a harmful decision as a precedent. The offending Superior is then alerted, preferably through a third party, that he is entering dangerous uncharted territory (the key word *precedent* must be pronounced). The decision will be rescinded in no time, and most probably written off as just a misunderstanding. I recall an incident concerning a columnist in a news agency which is a case in point:

The columnist had announced his intention of recommending a raise in pay for one of his research assistants whose only merit was that he had done his utmost to ingratiate himself with his boss. Hearing of this, the other assistants were understandably furious, but they decided to use their heads rather than give in to their feelings in fighting this sort of blatant favoritism. They made no useless verbal protests and wrote no letters of complaint of dubious value. Instead, they all signed a memorandum to the columnist, lauding his decision to recommend a raise in pay for one of them, and adding that such a pay raise would represent a justified, if belated, recognition of the importance of their responsibilities, and a welcome precedent they fully intended to use in pressing for an upward pay reclassification for all of them. Needless to say, the columnist went back on his word, never made his intended recommendation and was left pondering over some other way of rewarding his by now thoroughly disgruntled favorite.

A Recommendation

This preceding information should have left little doubt in the mind of the reader about the great potential of rules and regulations as a tool of Management of Superiors. But whether this potential will be realized will depend entirely on the subordinate's mastery of his own organization's rules and regulations. He should stint no effort in learning all there is to know about them, for there is no more rewarding field of study, quite apart from the intrinsic interest of their subject matter. And lest there be some misunderstanding, we hasten to add that the subordinate should study rules and regulations not better to obey them, but better to compel the Superior to toe the organizational line when this is beneficial to the subordinate cause. He himself should use his learning to sidestep the line whenever needed, and thus make out of executive command, only more subtly, thoroughly and efficiently, what the Italians made out of Mussolini's dictatorship-"a tyranny tempered by the complete disregard of all laws."

To conclude, we can well nigh guarantee to the subordinate who does his homework well, and is ready to apply his knowledge, that he will always find corporate rules and regulations to be one of his most effective instruments of redress in the Organization—which left to itself, without corrective measures, will typically lavish its favors and attention on Superiors and subordinates in roughly the same proportion the average housewife divides hers between her fingernails and her toenails.

Much of the research for "Workerology" came from Carlvin's personal experience in a large corporation's mailroom and his perusal of the corporation's day-to-day in-house correspondence, which cannot be footnoted in the conventional way. So, in that sense, the author uses a combination of personal observation and research through reading.

Why does Carlvin suggest that the reader should pick a subordinate job? How does the historical example of the sewage workers support this notion? How would you describe the author's tone and attitude? Why is a supervisor in one anecdotal example named Mr. Turnipp? How does Carlvin's tone and attitude affect his choice of examples, his wording, and his historical allusions?

Where does Carlvin state the thesis for "Selecting the Right Subordinate Position"? In which sentence does he state the thesis for "The Use of Rules and Regulations"? Which examples seem to come from personal experience, which from hearsay, and which from research through reading? How do the sub-categories, "Written Rules and Regulations," "Unwritten Rules," "Precedents," and "A Recommendation," organize the essay to support the thesis? How does the tone of the essay make it permissible for the author to use a hearsay example? What kind of reading do you think the author has done on the subject?

How does "Workerology" resemble a speech or report to a group of people? Point out any phrasings that suggest a speech. How would you characterize the audience? What rhetorical modes does he use?

Writing Your General Essay—How-It-Happens— Research Through Reading

Often an essay combines personal observation with research through reading and other forms of research, such as interviewing. When you undertake to research through reading your personally observed how-it-happens subject, or some aspect of it, you can go to the library, look up your subject, and find the books, articles, and other materials listed in the subject area. You can use the bibliographies at the end of the articles in *Encyclopaedia Britannica* to guide you in finding other books, articles, and materials. Cross-referencing will send you into special collections.

The use of knowledge collected in libraries, which includes books, microfilm, computer data banks, etc., is one of the main skills of writers and researchers of all kinds. The doctor who knows nothing of the research in medicine since he was in medical school finds the world of medicine growing increasingly distant, strange, and unintelligible to him. In solving a problem of design, an engineer goes to the library and researches what others have written about similar problems. The undergraduate who, in trying to research a subject, does not know how to look it up and pursue it in the library's card catalog, drifts and bumps helplessly in a current that he or she does not comprehend.

Research in the library is detective work and asks that you use detective techniques. First, ask questions. I've yet to meet the librarian, even an irritable one, who was not willing to answer almost any question about procedure, how to do it, where to go, what to look for. Most librarians regard answering questions, from the simplest to the most technical, as an essential part of their jobs. It comes with the territory, one of the ways they make their profession useful. You should have no reason to fear asking a question that you think may show your naiveté or inexperience. If a librarian hassles you, ask somebody else. (Libraries occasionally offer short tours and lecture-demonstrations in how to use the library. Ask the librarian when such a demonstration will take place.)

The card catalog organizes the library and, if maintained, keeps it organized. If you don't know how to use the card catalog and try to hide it, you'll only frustrate and defeat yourself. Make your questions specific to your immediate needs. Rather than ask, "Can you give me a course in how to use the card catalog?" (to which the answer will be "Not today, my dear"), look the librarian frankly in the eye and ask, "Can you help me find material on such and such subject?" Most librarians will answer specific questions and help you find specific books in the card catalog.

The names of authors, subjects, and titles in the card catalog are in writing so your old friend the alphabet organizes virtually all catalogs within an overall numbering system, such as the Dewey Decimal or the Library of Congress systems. You need to know the alphabet and how to spell reasonably well in order to use a card catalog. If spelling becomes a problem with any name, title, or subject (this problem occurs for just about everyone at one time or another, particularly with names) ask the librarian to help you.

You can also take advantage of other reference systems and reference works within the library, such as encyclopedias, dictionaries, directories, etc. For instance, if you had to write a paper on a subject such as how pumps work, you could first look it up in the *Encyclopaedia Britannica* under the heading Pumps. The Encyclopedia's article gives you a summary discussion, then a bibliography of titles of books, articles, and names of authors that you can look up in the card catalog where you'll find other works on the subject by the same or different authors. You can also look up your topic in the subject catalog; however, the subject catalog may not be divided and classified with fine, comprehensive precision.

You may find that you need to narrow and focus your subject, bring it down to manageable size, magnify portions and themes of it for your reader. For instance, if your subject were Archery, you would find the whole subject larger than any book you could write. If your subject were methods of shooting in archery, you could give a brief history of techniques of shooting, and then concentrate on your own experience with Instinctive Shooting and research and compare other methods. If your subject were Youth and Neighborhood Gangs, you could research in the sociology collection (ask the sociology librarian) the history, sociology, and reportage on gangs, summarize them, and then concentrate on the development of leadership in gangs, or compare leaders with followers, or show how the gang is important to a gang member. There are many flexible ways that subjects can be narrowed according to your interests, perceptions, and what you find out about the subject. Appropriate basic forms help you narrow and focus the subject.

For many essays that you'll write in college, your teachers will want footnotes and bibliographies. You need to know how to form them acceptably. The conventional style for footnote citations differs from bibliographic citations.

The footnote cites the source (book, article, etc.) from which you've drawn particular information. It should not be tagged at the bottom of a page simply to prove that you've read a book. In principle, it cites the reference and gives credit where credit is due. It's a way of telling your reader that you didn't simply make up the information, but got it from a particular source. It enables your reader to go to that source, check your reference, and read further about it.

Here's a conventional form for a footnote:

7. *Personal Knowledge,* by Michael Polanyi, New York: Harper & Row, 1958, p. 49.

The number 7 indicates that it is the seventh footnote in the chapter. The body of the footnote italicizes the title of the book referred to, then gives author, place published, name of publisher, date of publication, and page number where the information can be found. In typewritten or handwritten manuscript, underlining is used in place of italics.

If it's an article published in a periodical rather than a book that's being cited, the conventional form is:

5. Richard Bolles, "Training for Transition," *Change* (July–August 1979), p. 43.

The title of the article is placed between quotation marks; the name of the magazine or journal is italicized. Sometimes the volume and issue numbers of the journal or magazine are included.

The footnote may embody a comment of yours:

4. *Imagination,* by Harold Rugg, New York: Harper & Row, 1963, p. 36. As Jacob Bronowski was fond of pointing out, imagination in this sense forms a category that embraces on one side that "logical" maneuver, the inductive leap, and on the other, ways of remembering: "The first gift of human imagination is the ability so to recall the past that it has a visual or symbolic impact." *The Visionary Eye,* Cambridge, MA, The MIT Press, 1978, p. 82.

In the above footnote, the author not only makes a comment on the first source cited, but cites another source and gives the reference for it. You can see that the footnote's easy, aside address to the reader can make it an interesting form in itself.

Sometimes authors and publishers, rather than printing the citations at the bottom of the pages as footnotes, print a list of notes at the end of each chapter or at the end of the book. Popular magazines tend to want the citations incorporated into the body of the article itself or simply cut out, not mentioned, so as not to interrupt the flow of the reader's attention. So, though many of your teachers have demanded that footnotes be included in your essays, they have not recognized that most of the reading that you've done does not show the citations. Certainly, the proper use of footnotes is respectful of and useful to the reader, and respectful of the origin of information or ideas.

A bibliography, appearing at the end of your essay, gives the books, articles, and other main sources that you've used for your background material. The citation of a background source in a bibliography has a conventional form, somewhat different from the footnote. The bibliography lists materials alphabetically by authors' last names, that is, the author's name comes before the book, last name before the first name and middle initials. For example:

Abercrombie, M. L. J. *Anatomy of Judgment,* New York: Basic Books, 1960.
Baker, Sheridan, Barzun, Jacques, and Richards, I. A. *The Written Word.* Rowley, MA: Newbury House, 1971.

After the author's name comes the title (italicized in print, underlined in manuscript), the place of publication, the name of the publisher, and the date of publication. If more than one work by a particular writer is cited, you list the author's works alphabetically by title, with the author's name used with the first citation and dashes or a line in place of the author's name for each subsequent citation of a book or article by him or her.

Joos, Martin. *The English Verb: Form and Meanings.* Madison, WI.: University of Wisconsin Press, 1968.
——————. *The Five Clocks.* New York: Harcourt, Brace and World, 1961.

If an article is cited in the bibliography, the title of the article appears between quotation marks. The title of the journal or magazine is italicized in print or underlined in manuscript.

Schultz, John. "The Story Workshop Method: Writing from Start to Finish." *College English,* December, 1977. Urbana, IL.: National Council of Teachers of English.

Sometimes a writer may make comments on the individual books listed in the bibliography, providing a sort of guide for the reader.

Britton, James. *Language and Learning.* Harmondsworth, England: Penguin,

1970. A description of the process whereby children acquire and develop their skill with language. Synthesizes much current knowledge on language learning in a way that meets the needs of teachers.

Most of the above bibliographic examples are taken from *Errors and Expectations, A Guide for the Teacher of Basic Writing,* by Mina Shaughnessy, New York, Oxford University Press, 1977.

As you find information that begins to build the "story" and the argument of your essay, make notes either on cards or in a notebook, or on a convenient sheet of paper. Include the title of the book and page number beside the note so you can cite it or go back and reread it, that is, have the bibliographic information about the book listed right with your notes.

In your reading and notetaking, you will begin to find clusterings and patterns of instances and a sense of how the researched-through-reading material works in combination with your personal observations. When you write, address it as a letter to a friendly someone or as a speech to a friendly group with one or two friendly experts in it who are keeping an eye on your performance. Combine your personally observed experience with the research through reading you've done.

Often, your attitude, the way you choose to relate the material to the audience, helps you find the right examples, allusions, and phrasing. Your attitude comes from your personal feeling about the subject and your sense of the audience. You may find that the attitude you've discovered and want to cultivate comes and goes erratically in the course of writing the first draft. That happens to professional writers, too. Keep on writing.

Frequently, we are surprised to find in reading our writing aloud to an audience that the attitude and strengths of certain passages show so much more clearly than they did when we read the writing silently. When you find the passages that come through clearly, they will help you reorganize and rewrite the essay, to cut some passages, to rephrase or condense or expand others, according to what you've noticed. If the attitude that works is deadpan irony, you can cut, reduce, or retell those passages that are more dull than deadpan. On the other hand, in another essay, you may find that attempts at humor really do not work as well as your more straightforward prose.

The important thing is to stimulate and encourage the interplay of your research, perception, writing about the content, sense of telling it to someone, in the process of retelling and rewriting.

VII

How-To-Do-It-Better

How-to-Do-It-Better—Technical Form

"Why Nothing Seems to Work" emphasized the practical, creative effort of seeing in your mind not only how things *do* work but how they *will* work, and, by a slight extension of your imagination, how they might, should, or *can* work in a better way. Bruno Bettelheim's telling of how to get permission from an SS guard to receive medical treatment for frostbite is a how-to-do-it-better as well as an opposites telling. Possibly, you'll get your first major break on a job, or even build a career for yourself, by seeing and developing how a process or method can be done in a better way.

When you imagine how something might be done better, you're exercising a fundamental human capacity. Without the perception of how to do something better, without the ability to *express* such perception to elicit the help of others in carrying out the perception in *practice,* we otherwise ill-equipped human creatures could not have survived, could not have come to the point of actually being able to change the face of whole continents. Our ability to *see,* visualize, imagine possibilities, that is, our ability to see and alter the objective world *in our minds,* comes together with our ability to express this perception persuasively in oral-gestural language. So when you find yourself imagining something, *seeing* it in your mind, even "silly" things, you are practicing *the doing of* the most essential human work.

The how-to-do-it-better form is an aggressive, imaginative, argumentative extension of the how-it's-done process and how-to forms, occurring naturally in everyday oral telling. It makes particular use of the rhetorical modes of how-it's-done, comparison and contrast, cause and effect analysis, division and classification, and argument. It shows up frequently in technical, expository, and fictional wriitng. Look for the how-to-do-it-better's four-part structure in the reading selections included in this section.

* * *

Here are two selections from *Moby Dick,* first a brief narrative of the process of chasing and harpooning a whale from the chapter that precedes "The Dart" and then "The Dart," itself, a how-to-do-it-better essay.

From
Stubb Kills a Whale

The sudden exclamations of the crew must have alarmed the whale; and ere the boats were down, majestically turning, he swam away to the leeward, but with such a steady tranquillity, and making so few ripples as he swam, that thinking after all he might not as yet be alarmed, Ahab gave orders that not an oar should be used, and no man must speak but in whispers. So seated like Ontario Indians on the gunwales of the boats, we swiftly but silently paddled along; the calm not admitting of the noiseless sails being set. Presently, as we thus glided in chase, the monster perpendicularly flitted his tail forty feet into the air, and then sank out of sight like a tower swallowed up.

"There go flukes!" was the cry, an announcement immediately followed by Stubb's producing his match and igniting his pipe, for now a respite was granted. After the full interval of his sounding had elapsed, the whale rose again, and being now in advance of the smoker's boat, and much nearer to it than to any of the others, Stubb counted upon the honor of the capture. It was obvious, now, that the whale had at length become aware of his pursuers. All silence of cautiousness was therefore no longer of use. Paddles were dropped, and oars came loudly into play. And still puffing at his pipe, Stubb cheered on his crew to the assault.

Yes, a mighty change had come over the fish. All alive to his jeopardy, he was going "head out;" that part obliquely projecting from the mad yeast which he brewed.

"Start her, start her, my men! Don't hurry yourselves; take plenty of time—but start her; start her like thunder-claps, that's all," cried Stubb, spluttering out the smoke as he spoke. "Start her, now; give 'em the long and strong stroke, Tashtego. Start her, Tash, my boy—start her, all; but keep cool, keep cool—cucumbers is the word—easy, easy—only start her like grim death and grinning devils, and raise the buried dead perpendicular out of their graves, boys—that's all. Start her!"

"Woo-hoo! Wa-hee!" screamed the Gay-Header in reply, raising some old war-whoop to the skies; as every oarsman in the strained boat involuntarily bounced forward with the one tremendous leading stroke which the eager Indian gave.

But his wild screams were answered by others quite as wild. "Kee-hee! Kee-hee!" yelled Daggoo, straining forwards and backwards on his seat, like a pacing tiger in his cage.

"Ka-la! Koo-loo!" howled Queequeg, as if smacking his lips over a mouthful of Grenadier's steak. And thus with oars and yells the keels cut the sea. Meanwhile, Stubb retaining his place in the van, still encouraged his men to the onset, all the while puffing the smoke from his mouth. Like desperadoes they tugged and they strained, till the welcome cry was heard—"Stand up, Tashtego!—give it to him!" The harpoon was hurled. "Stern all!" The oarsmen backed water; the same moment something went hot and hissing along every one of their wrists. It was the magical line. An instant before, Stubb had swiftly caught two additional turns with it round the loggerhead, whence, by reason of its increased rapid circlings, a hempen blue smoke now jetted up and mingled with the steady fumes from his pipe. As the line passed round and round the loggerhead; so also, just before reaching that point, it blisteringly passed through and through both of Stubb's hands, from which the hand-cloths, or squares of quilted canvas sometimes worn at these times, had accidentally dropped. It was like holding an enemy's sharp two-edged sword by the blade, and that enemy all the time striving to wrest it out of your clutch.

"Wet the line! Wet the line!" cried Stubb to the tub oarsman (him seated by the tub) who, snatching off his hat, dashed the sea-water into it. More turns were taken, so that the line began holding its place. The boat now flew through the boiling water like a shark all fins. Stubb and Tashtego here changed places—stem for stern—a staggering business truly in that rocking commotion. . . .

The Dart

A word concerning an incident in the last chapter.

According to the invariable usage of the fishery, the whaleboat pushes off from the ship, with the headsman or whale-killer as temporary steersman, and the harpooneer or whale-fastener pulling the foremost oar, the one known as the harpooneer-oar. Now it needs a strong, nervous arm to strike the first iron into the fish; for often, in what is called a long dart, the heavy implement has to be flung to the distance of twenty or thirty feet. But however prolonged and exhausting the chase, the harpooneer is expected to pull his oar meanwhile to the uttermost; indeed, he is expected to set an example of superhuman activity to the rest, not only by incredible rowing, but by repeated loud and intrepid exclamations; and what it is to keep shouting at the top of one's compass, while all the other muscles are strained and half started—what that is none know but those who have tried it. For one, I cannot bawl very heartily and work very recklessly at one and the same time. In this straining, bawling state, then, with his back to the fish, all at once the exhausted harpooneer hears the exciting cry—"Stand up, and give it to him!" He now has to drop and secure his oar, turn round on his centre half way, seize his harpoon from the crotch, and with what little strength may remain, he essays to pitch it somehow into the whale. No wonder, taking the whole fleet of whalemen in a body, that out of fifty fair chances for a dart, not five are successful; no wonder that so many hapless harpooneers are madly cursed and disrated; no wonder that some of them actually burst their blood-vessels in the boat; no wonder that some sperm whalemen are absent four years with four barrels; no wonder that to many ship owners, whaling is but a losing concern; for it is the harpooneer that makes the voyage, and if you take the breath out of his body how can you expect to find it there when most wanted!

Again, if the dart be successful, then at the second critical instant, that is, when the whale starts to run, the boat-header and harpooneer likewise start to running fore and aft, to the imminent jeopardy of themselves and every one else. It is then they change places; and the headsman, the chief officer of the little craft, takes his proper station in the bows of the boat.

Now, I care not who maintains the contrary, but all this is both foolish and unnecessary. The headsman should stay in the bows from first to last; he should both dart the harpoon and the lance, and no rowing whatever should be expected of him, except under circumstances obvious to any fisherman. I know that this would sometimes involve a slight loss of speed in the chase; but long experience in various whalemen of more than one nation has convinced me that in the vast majority of failures in the fishery, it has not by any means been so much the speed of the whale as the before described exhaustion of the harpooneer that has caused them.

To insure the greatest efficiency in the dart, the harpooneers of this world must start to their feet from out of idleness, and not from out of toil.

The natural structure of the how-to-do-it-better form involves statements, imagery, and discussion of (1) the standard way of doing whatever it is, (2) the unsatisfactory results of the standard way, with explanation of its flaws or inadequacies, (3) the proposed better way, emphasizing all the how-to-points that show how-to-do-it-better, and (4) the anticipated good results of the better way, plus a pertinent final boost of persuasion. When you see the better way clearly and see how the audience needs to see it, you tend to find the imagery that will get the better way across to the audience. You use any language device or method that calls attention to important points, helps persuade the audience, helps emphasize the argument, for instance, the parallel build-up of the "no wonder" clauses in "The Dart" and the careful instruction to "you" in "How to Play Pinball Better," which follows.

How to Play Pinball Better
Kevin Kotowski

Everyone, young or old, rich or poor, male or female, thinks they know how to play pinball. They sidle up to the machine, slip a quarter into the slot as cool as you please, pull the plunger, bunch up their muscles and watch as the ball oh so gently checks out on them. They mutter, punch the flippers a few times, and quietly go on their way to repeat the same tired process over and over and over again in bars, hot dog stands, chili parlors, brothels and gas stations throughout the nation. No, make that the world. Pinball, my friends, is a planet-wide disease you'd best be on the lookout for. The cure is to know how to play the game and play it well.

Playing pinball, like driving a car, is simple. But playing well, like driving a Grand Prix racer at Monaco, is an art form that demands a high level of skill, patience, and determination.

Now, I know that all you pessimists out there believe that the introduction of electromechanical devices such as bumpers, kick-out holes, thumper-bumpers, and flippers, combined with the extraordinary sensitivity of modern-day tilt mechanisms, have taken all the old-fashioned body English out of pinball. Nothing could be further from the truth.

While it is true that these devices have changed the game significantly, there's still a lot of room left for the learning and refinement of fundamentals and the development of individual playing styles.

The first rule of pinball is know the machine. Nobody, but nobody, goes in and racks up six-figure scores on a machine they've never played before. Whether you're in front of a Captain Fantastic or a Fireball or an Old Chicago, you should play it at least a half dozen times before you even try going for the big scores.

Watch where the targets are, and the slope of the playfield, and the direction the ball tends to go, and the power of the thumpers, and the angles in which the flippers send the ball spinning.

Let your eyes get accustomed to the pulse and color of the lights and your ears to the tone and melodies.

The secret is not to ignore the aural and visual effects but to wire yourself into them, flow with them, become one with the machine, an extension of the microtransistors inside.

Play any one machine enough and you'll feel an energy surge everytime you place your palms alongside its flippers. And to dispel any Freudian thoughts nagging at your mind—yes, it is a sexual feeling. And I bet that sends you running to the nearest amusement arcade.

Once you've gotten adjusted to the ways and whims of the individual machine, you're ready to play in earnest.

Stand about 3 feet in front of the machine, your shoulders relaxed, one foot slightly in front of the other for balance. If you stand too close, you'll find that the power has to come from your arms, which wastes most of your body strength. You'll find that you get slightly more power from your middle finger on the flipper buttons, slightly more control from your index finger. You pays your money, you takes your choice.

Rest the heels of both palms on the corners of the cabinet. Your palms are your secret weapons in the pinball wars. A blow to the cabinet, called a nudge or nudgie, will reinforce the rebound of the ball of a bumper or kicker. But a nudge is useless unless the ball is touching a solid surface at the precise moment you hit the machine. The trick is to nudge the machine hard enough to impart force to the ball without setting off the tilt mechanism within. Practice, yes indeedy, makes perfect.

The true pinball artist assimilates everything that governs the direction and velocity of the ball into his style of play. And keeping a ball in play is the only way to score points.

Timing and hand and eye coordination are the all-important tools you should cultivate. The flippers begin to feel like extensions of your hands. Just remember, the money's in the bonuses and free games, not just bouncing the ball around. Take some time to really learn how to play and I guarantee St. Peter will have your wizard's cap ready when you finally roll into that big pinball parlor in the sky.

————————

Imagery makes clear the flaws of the "standard" way in each of the selections: "In this straining, bawling state, then, with his back to the fish, all at once the exhausted harpooneer hears the exciting cry . . . etc . . ."; "They sidle up to the machine, slip a quarter into the slot as cool as you please, pull the plunger, bunch up their muscles and watch as the ball oh so gently checks out on them. . . ." The imagery and the reader's seeing of the standard or usual way with its flaws and inadequacies lays the foundation for making clear the proposed better way.

Aggressive phrasing puts across the argument: " . . . for it is the harpooneer that makes the voyage, and if you take the breath out of his body how can you expect to find it there when most wanted!"; "Playing pinball, like driving a car, is simple. But playing well, like driving a Grand Prix racer at Monaco, is an art form that demands a high level of skill, patience, and determination."

Review the imagery that makes clear *how* to do it better: "The headsman should stay in the bows from first to last; he should dart both the harpoon and the lance, and no rowing whatever would be expected of him, except under circumstances obvious to any fisherman. . . ."; "The first rule of pinball is know the machine. . . . Watch where the targets are, and the slope of the playfield, and the direction the ball tends to go, and the power of the thumpers, and the angles in which the flippers send the ball spinning. . . ."

Read aloud the special language and presentational effects: " . . . when the whale starts to run, the boat-header and harpooneer likewise start to running fore and aft, to the imminent jeopardy of themselves and everyone else."; "The secret is not to ignore the aural and visual effects but to wire yourself into them, flow with them, become one with the machine, an extension of the microtransistors inside."

Exaggerated imagery and humor give a push to some of the final persuasive boosts: " . . . the harpooneers of this world must start to their feet from out of idleness, and not from out of toil."; "Take some time to really learn how to play and I guarantee St. Peter will have your wizard's cap ready when you finally roll into that big pinball parlor in the sky."

The four-part form of the how-to-do-it-better is strict, yet it permits, even demands, invention in every line.

Read the following how-to-do-it-better silently by yourself and aloud in class, if possible. What do you notice about the four-part how-to-do-it-better structure, exaggeration, precision, and audience? What is this essay about, i.e., what is its underlying concern?

How to Eat a Hostess Ho Ho Better
Sue Ferraro

If you crave that creamy, chocolatey snack and a tall glass of milk, search your pantry for that coveted box or package of Hostess Ho Ho's. If you are a fanatic about that chocolate-covered cake roll, most likely you will choose the box of twelve with each separate morsel wrapped in aluminum foil, although if this desire is a once-in-a-while feeling, the package of two should be sufficient to satisfy the hunger that gnaws inside. No matter which category you place yourself under, the Ho Ho hallucination may come at any time of the day or night. You may crave one as you wake at the crack of dawn, or as the bus breaks down half way to your destination. It may come at the least expected moment. Maybe in the middle of a midterm, or after two hours of a ten-hour plane trip. Or, most dreaded, as you sit cozily with your boyfriend and he turns to say something romantic. You reply uncontrollably, "I'm starved. I've got this sudden craving for a Ho Ho." The memorable moment begins.

The important thing is not that the desire hits, but how you plan to *fill* the desire. The normal way of eating a Ho Ho, I'm sorry to say, is boring. There's no other way to describe it. You go to the pantry in search of something, anything, to eat. There is a debate in your mind as to which food to pick. There are cookies, potato chips, candy, crackers, donuts and Ho Ho's. It just so happens that the Ho Ho's catch your eye.

You pick up the package or box and place it on the kitchen table. Milk goes best with chocolate cake, so you go to the cabinet and grab a glass. Looking into the refrigerator, you get the gallon of milk and pour yourself a tall, cold glass and set it next to the Ho Ho's. There's nothing else to do except start eating.

You sit down with all the necessary gear in front of you. If it's a new box, you must tear off the perforated strip that holds the box closed. If the box is already open you've saved yourself a step and a few seconds. Remove the foil-wrapped Ho Ho with the thumb and first two fingers of your right hand. In no particular manner you tear the aluminum foil from the tiny package. If you deal with the package of two, you first tear the seal off the top, put the thumb and first two fingers in the package, and pull out a Ho Ho. The twin pack is much simpler to deal with 'cause it comes already shed of its foil wrap.

Now comes the part you've been waiting for! Eating it. First clutch the cake around its middle gently, so as not to squeeze it out of shape or force it to melt in your hand. Then, start biting from either end until it has been entirely consumed. Boring . . .

There's no technique, it goes by so fast. It has no grace, no poetry. You can't really admit you've enjoyed it. And the chocolate melts on your fingers and the palms of your hands. Too messy.

The proper way to eat a Ho Ho demands all the grace and class of a ballet. First you must know that it's a Ho Ho that you want to eat. The feeling must be such that if you find no Ho Ho's in the pantry or cupboard, you will be willing to trudge through rain or sleet or snow or dark of night until you find the treasure at a neighborhood grocery store.

When you finally find them, you pay the cashier with the last coins in your pocket. You ask her to put it in a brown paper bag so you won't look too conspicuous. With the energy you have left you rush home, anticipating the snack to come. All the while you should be careful not to squeeze the package and bruise the delicate morsels within. When you arrive at home, you gently set the package on the table and prepare for the ritual.

First you pour yourself a tall glass of milk and bring it to the table. After sitting down, you remove the box or package from the brown bag. If you have the box to deal with, the procedure is much like the standard way. You tear the perforated strip to open the box. Then remove the individually wrapped Ho Ho from its surroundings. You do this gently so as not to crack the chocolate frosting. Then neatly remove the aluminum foil so you won't tear it. You then place the cake on a plate and proceed to deal with the foil. The best way of doing this is to smooth the foil between the first two fingers of your right hand to get out as many wrinkles as possible. Then you fold it with your thumb on one flattened end of the log and your index finger on the other end, with the bottom end (seam) closest to you. Then you sink your teeth into the chocolatey layer, no farther. Piece by piece you remove the frosting with your teeth rotating the log with every bite. Savour the taste. After all the chocolate has been removed from the surface, you must then gently hold the Ho Ho around its middle and proceed to consume the chocolate from either end. The remainder is cake and cream.

However, there remains another technique. You notice the cake can be unrolled into one flat piece smeared generously with cream. But be careful when doing so, so the cake will not crumble. After unrolling the cake you hold it unrolled with your left hand. With the index finger of your right hand you scrape the creamy, white frosting from the surface. Then you put your finger to your mouth, opening your mouth enough to allow the cream-covered finger to go in. As the final knuckle of the finger enters the mouth, close your lips around it and slip your finger out. Savor the delight in your mouth. When the taste is gone and only the memory remains, eat the cake part with your own discretion. But—enjoy, enjoy.

In this way you're not eating it, you're EATING it. You'll smile, and the process will leave you feeling good all over. You may think, "It's an awful lot to go through just to eat a Ho Ho." I guess it might be, unless you're out to enjoy even the littlest things in life. A Ho Ho is just a small part of the Land of Hostess.

Writing Your How-to-Do-It-Better Technical Form

You may be reminded immediately of a perception you had on a job, or when involved in a sport, a hobby, a school, a business, of how a process could have been done in a better way. You can begin to write it now, or you can look over your how-it-happens area for perceptions of how something might be done in a better way. Perhaps you sense that something could be done in a better way without yet being able to see it clearly or express it clearly. You may discover it in writing about it.

You may want to try a parodic technical how-to-do-it-better. ("The Dart" and "How to Play Pinball Better" have their tongue-in-cheek attitudes too.) In a parody of a technical how-to-do-it-better, you carry out the basic steps of the structure fully. If you do a parody of a how-to-do-it-better, you may be surprised at what you learn about any human activity, no matter how seemingly trivial.

Most activities, work , sport, hobby, whatever, occur in a place. See the place, make notes about what catches your attention about the activity. See several instances of the activity over a period of hours, days, weeks, months, whatever. Explore the activity with seeing, hearing, smelling, tasting, touching. See the objects of the activity, the tools, the way they're used. See the objects in relation to the boundaries and other limitations of the activity. With your imaginative seeing, probe how it can be done better. Make notes about your four-part structure.

What is the approach, tone, attitude that will be most effective with your audience? Remember that people tend to resist change, so you must make a particular effort to persuade your audience. Remember Dick Lehnert's editorial, "When Will You Be a No-Till Farmer?" It, too, argues how some farming could be done in a better way.

Use positive exaggeration, irony, sense of humor, vivid imagery, metaphor, timing, whatever will help persuade your audience and make them see how a process is ordinarily done and how to do it better. During your writing and rewriting, stress and re-stress to yourself the basic four-part structure and how to relate it to your audience.

How-to-Do-It-Better—Parodic and Satirical Proposals

The how-to-do-it-better parodic and satirical proposal follows flexibly the basic four-part structure of the technical how-to-do-it-better: (1) the usual or current way of doing something, such as the usual way of letting children starve as they follow their indigent begging mothers about the streets (in Swift's "A Modest Proposal"); (2) the harmful or undesirable effects of the usual or standard way; (3) the proposal of the better way, the reasons for employing the better way, and the justification of it when compared to other proposals; and (4) the benefits—the desirable effects of implementing the proposal. The author may also argue his or her own particular authority for making the proposal, or argue that he or she has only the general social benefit in mind.

This form makes a wide range of imaginative demands upon the writer, including the fun of creating the major irony of the essay, the simulation of the attitude of the persona.

* * *

Each of the following how-to-do-it-better proposals fulfills the requirements of the how-to-do-it-better form. Each writer pretends to be serious, or to write about the proposal in the attitude of a seriously concerned persona, such as the persona of the Chairman of the Board of Trustees of the Ford Motor Company. Examine how each maintains the attitude of the persona throughout the essay, yet puts forward statements of imagery that let you know his true feelings. Watch for moments that suggest the writer's true feelings, heightening the irony.

A Modest Proposal
Jonathan Swift

For Preventing the Children of Poor People in Ireland from Being a Burden to Their Parents or Country, and for Making Them Beneficial to the Public

It is a melancholy object to those who walk through this great town, or travel in the country, when they see the streets, the roads, and cabin-doors crowded with beggars of the female sex, followed by three, four, or six children, all in rags, and importuning every passenger for an alms. These mothers, instead of being able to work for their honest livelihood, are forced to employ all their time in strolling to beg sustenance for their helpless infants: who, as they grow up, either turn thieves for want of work, or leave their dear native country to fight for the Pretender in Spain, or sell themselves to the Barbadoes.

I think it is agreed by all parties, that this prodigious number of children in the arms, or on the backs, or at the heels of their mothers, and frequently of their fathers, is in the present deplorable state of the kingdom, a very great additional grievance; and, therefore, whoever could find out a fair, cheap, and easy method of making these children sound and useful members of the commonwealth, would deserve so well of the public, as to have his statue set up for a preserver of the nation.

But my intention is very far from being confined to provide only for the children of professed beggars; it is of a much greater extent, and shall take in the whole number of infants at a certain age, who are born of parents in effect as little able to support them as those who demand our charity in the streets.

As to my own part, having turned my thoughts for many years upon this important subject, and maturely weighed the several schemes of other projectors, I have always found them grossly mistaken in their computation. It is true, a child, just dropped from its dam, may be supported by her milk for a solar year with little other nourishment; at most, not above the value of two shillings, which the mother may certainly get, or the value in scraps, by her lawful occupation of begging; and it is exactly at one year old that I propose to provide for them in such a manner, as, instead of being a charge upon their parents or the parish, or wanting food and raiment for the rest of their lives, they shall, on the contrary, contribute to the feeding, and partly to the clothing, of many thousands.

There is likewise another great advantage in my scheme, that it will prevent those voluntary abortions, and that horrid practice of women murdering their bastard children, alas, too frequent among us, sacrificing the poor innocent babes, I doubt more to avoid the expense than the shame, which would move tears and pity in the most savage and inhuman breast.

The number of souls in this kingdom being usually reckoned one million and a half, of these I calculate there may be about two hundred thousand couple whose wives are breeders; from which number I subtract thirty thousand couple, who are able to maintain their own children (although I apprehend there cannot be so many, under the present distresses of the kingdom); but this being granted, there will remain an hundred and seventy thousand breeders. I again subtract fifty thousand for those women who miscarry, or whose children die by accident or disease within the year. There only remain a hundred and twenty thousand children of poor parents annually born. The question therefore is how this number shall be reared and provided for which, as I have already said, under the present situation of affairs, is utterly impossible by all the methods hitherto proposed. For we can neither employ them in handicraft or agriculture; we neither build houses (I mean in the country) nor cultivate land: they can very seldom pick up a livelihood by stealing until they arrive at six years old, except where they are of towardly parts; although I confess they learn the rudiments much earlier; during which time they can, however, be properly looked upon only as probationers; as I have been informed by a principal gentleman in the county of Cavan, who protested to me, that he never knew above one or two instances under the age of six, even in a part of the kingdom so renowned for the quickest proficiency in that art.

I am assured by our merchants that a boy or a girl before twelve years old is no salable commodity; and even when they come to this age they will not yield above three pounds or three pounds and half-a crown at most, on the exchange; which cannot turn to account either to the parents or kingdom, the charge of nutriment and rags having been at least four times that value.

I shall now, therefore, humbly propose my own thoughts, which I hope will not be liable to the least objection.

I have been assured by a very knowing American of my acquaintance in London, that a young healthy child, well nursed, is, at a year old, a most delicious, nourishing, and wholesome food, whether stewed, roasted, baked, or boiled; and I make no doubt that it will equally serve in a fricassee or a ragout.

I do therefore humbly offer it to public consideration, that of the hundred and twenty thousand children already computed, twenty thousand may be reserved for breed, whereof only one-fourth part to be males; which is more than we allow to sheep, black cattle, or swine; and my reason is, that these children are seldom the fruits of marriage, a circumstance not much regarded by our savages, therefore one male will be sufficient to serve four females. That the remaining hundred thousand may, at a year old, be offered in sale to the persons of quality and fortune through the kingdom; always advising the mother to let them suck plentifully in the last month, so as to render them plump and fat for a good table. A child will make two dishes at an entertainment for friends; and when the family dines alone, the fore or hind quarter will make a reasonable dish, and, seasoned with a little pepper or salt, will be very good boiled on the fourth day, especially in winter.

I have reckoned, upon a medium, that a child just born will weigh twelve pounds, and in a solar year, if tolerably nursed, increaseth to twenty-eight pounds.

I grant this food will be somewhat dear, and therefore very proper for landlords, who, as they have already devoured most of the parents, seem to have the best title to the children.

Infant's flesh will be in season throughout the year, but more plentifully in March, and a little before and after: for we are told by a grave author, an eminent French physician, that fish being a prolific diet, there are more children born in Roman Catholic countries about nine months after Lent than at any other season; therefore, reckoning a year after Lent, the markets will be more glutted than usual, because the number of popish infants is at least three to one in this kingdom; and therefore it will have one other collateral advantage, by lessening the number of papists among us.

I have already computed the charge of nursing a beggar's child (in which list I reckon all cottagers, labourers, and four-fifths of the farmers) to be about two shillings per annum, rags included; and I believe no gentleman would repine to give ten shillings for the carcass of a good fat child, which, as I have said, will make four dishes of excellent nutritive meat, when he has only some particular friend, or his own family, to dine with him. Thus the squire will learn to be a good landlord, and grow popular among his tenants; the mother will have eight shillings net profit, and be fit for work till she produces another child.

Those who are more thrifty (as I must confess the times require) may flay the carcass; the skin of which, artificially dressed, will make admirable gloves for ladies, and summer-boots for fine gentlemen.

As to our city of Dublin, shambles* may be appointed for this purpose in the most convenient parts of it, and butchers we may be assured will not be wanting; although I rather recommend buying the children alive, and dressing them hot from the knife, as we do roasting pigs.

A very worthy person, a true lover of his country, and whose virtues I highly esteem, was lately pleased, in discoursing on this matter, to offer a refinement upon my scheme. He said, that many gentlemen of this kingdom, having of late destroyed their deer, he conceived that the want of venison might be well supplied by the bodies of young lads and maidens, not exceeding fourteen years of age, nor under twelve; so great a number of both sexes in every country being now ready to starve for want of work and service; and these to be disposed of by their parents, if alive, or otherwise by their nearest relations. But, with due deference to so excellent a friend, and so deserv-

---

*butcher shops.

ing a patriot, I cannot be altogether in his sentiments; for as to the males, my American acquaintance assured me from frequent experience, that their flesh was generally tough and lean, like that of our schoolboys, by continual exercise, and their taste disagreeable; and to fatten them would not answer the charge. Then as to the females, it would, I think, with humble submission, be a loss to the public, because they soon would become breeders themselves: and besides, it is not improbable that some scrupulous people might be apt to censure such a practice (although indeed very unjustly) as a little bordering upon cruelty; which, I confess hath always been with me the strongest objection against any project, how well soever intended.

But in order to justify my friend, he confessed that this expedient was put into his head by the famous Psalmanazar, a native of the island Formosa, who came from thence to London above twenty years ago; and in conversation told my friend, that in his country, when any young person happened to be put to death, the executioner sold the carcass to persons of quality as prime dainty; and that in his time the body of a plump girl of fifteen, who was crucified for an attempt to poison the emperor, was sold to his Imperial Majesty's prime minister of state, and other great mandarins of the court, in joints from the gibbet, at four hundred crowns. Neither indeed can I deny, that if the same use were made of several plump young girls in this town, who, without one single groat to their fortunes, cannot stir abroad without a chair, and appear at playhouse and assemblies in foreign fineries which they never will pay for, the kingdom would not be the worse.

Some persons of a desponding spirit are in great concern about that vast number of poor people who are aged, diseased, or maimed; and I have been desired to employ my thoughts what course may be taken to ease the nation of so grievous an encumbrance. But I am not in the least pain upon that matter, because it is very well known, that they are every day dying, and rotting, by cold and famine, and filth and vermin, as fast as can be reasonably expected. And as to the younger labourers, they are now in almost as hopeful a condition: they cannot get work, and consequently pine away for want of nourishment, to a degree, that if at any time they are accidentally hired to common labour, they have not strength to perform it; and thus the country and themselves are happily delivered from the evils to come.

I have too long digressed, and therefore shall return to my subject. I think the advantages by the proposal which I have made are obvious and many, as well as of the highest importance.

For first, as I have already observed, it would greatly lessen the number of papists, with whom we are yearly overrun, being the principal breeders of the nation as well as our most dangerous enemies; and who stay at home on purpose with a design to deliver the kingdom to the Pretender, hoping to take their advantage by the absence of so many good Protestants, who have chosen rather to leave their country than stay at home and pay tithes against their conscience to an idolatrous Episcopal curate.

Secondly, the poorer tenants will have something valuable of their own, which by law may be made liable to distress, and help to pay their landlord's rent; their corn and cattle being already seized, and money a thing unknown.

Thirdly, whereas the maintenance of an hundred thousand children, from two years old and upwards, cannot be computed at less than ten shillings a piece per annum, the nation's stock will be thereby increased fifty thousand pounds per annum; besides the profit of a new dish introduced to the tables of all gentlemen of fortune in the kingdom who have any refinement in taste. And the money will circulate among ourselves, the goods being entirely of our own growth and manufacture.

Fourthly, the constant breeders, besides the gain of eight shillings sterling per annum by the sale of their children, will be rid of the charge of maintaining them after the first year.

Fifthly, this food would otherwise bring great custom to taverns; where the vintners will certainly be so prudent as to procure the best receipts for dressing it to perfection, and, consequently, have their houses frequented by all the fine gentlemen, who justly value themselves upon their knowledge in good eating: and a skillful cook, who understands how to oblige his guests, will contrive to make it as expensive as they please.

Sixthly, this would be a great inducement to marriage, which all wise nations have either encouraged by rewards, or enforced by laws and penalties. It would increase the care and tenderness of mothers towards their children, when they were sure of a settlement for life to the poor babes, provided in some sort by the public, to their annual profit instead of expense. We should soon see an honest emulation among the married women, which of them could bring the fattest child to the market. Men would become as fond of their wives during the time of their pregnancy, as they are now of their mares in foal, their cows in calf, or sows when they are ready to farrow; nor offer to beat or kick them (as is too frequent a practice) for fear of a miscarriage.

Many other advantages might be enumerated. For instance, the addition of some thousand carcasses in our exportation of barrelled beef; the propagation of swine's flesh, and improvement in the art of making good bacon, so much wanted among us by the great destruction of pigs, too frequent at our tables, which are no way comparable in taste or magnificence to a well-grown, fat yearling child, which, roasted whole, will make a considerable figure at a Lord Mayor's feast, or any other public entertainment. But this, and many others, I omit, being studious of brevity.

Supposing that one thousand families in this city would be constant customers for infants' flesh, besides others who might have it at merry meetings, particularly weddings and christenings, I compute that Dublin would take off annually about twenty thousand carcasses; and the rest of the kingdom (where probably they will be sold somewhat cheaper) the remaining eighty thousand.

I can think of no one objection that will possibly be raised against this proposal, unless it should be urged, that the number of people will be thereby much lessened in the kingdom. This I freely own, and it was indeed one principal design in offering it to the world. I desire the reader will observe that I calculate my remedy for this one individual kingdom of Ireland, and for no other that ever was, is, or I think ever can be, upon earth. Therefore let no man talk to me of other expedients: of taxing our absentees at five shillings a pound: of using neither clothes nor household-furniture except what is of our own growth and manufacture: of utterly rejecting the materials and instruments that promote foreign luxury: of curing the expensiveness of pride, vanity, idleness, and gaming in our women; of introducing a vein of parsimony, prudence, and temperance: of learning to love our country, wherein we differ even from Laplanders, and the inhabitants of Topinamboo: of quitting our animosities and factions, nor act any longer like the Jews, who were murdering one another at the very moment their city was taken: of being a little cautious not to sell our country and consciences for nothing: of teaching landlords to have at least one degree of mercy towards their tenants: lastly, of putting a spirit of honesty, industry, and skill into our shopkeepers; who, if a resolution could not be taken to buy only our native goods, would immediately unite to cheat and exact upon us in the price, the measure, and the goodness, nor could ever yet be brought to make one fair proposal of just dealing, though often and earnestly invited to it.

Therefore I repeat, let no man talk to me of these and the like expedients, till he hath at least some glimpse of hope that there will ever be some hearty and sincere attempt to put them in practice.

But, as to myself, having been wearied out for many years with offering vain, idle, visionary thoughts, and at length utterly despairing of success, I fortunately fell upon this proposal; which, as it is wholly new, so it hath something solid and real, of no expense and little trouble, full in our own power, and whereby we can incur no danger in disobliging England. For this kind of commodity will not bear exportation, the flesh being of too tender a consistence to admit a long continuance in salt, although perhaps I could name a country which would be glad to eat up our whole nation without it.

After all, I am not so violently bent upon my own opinion as to reject any offer proposed by wise men which shall be found equally innocent, cheap, easy, and effectual. But before something of that kind shall be advanced in contradiction to my scheme, and offering a better, I desire the author, or authors, will be pleased maturely to consider two points. First, as things now stand, how they will be able to find food and raiment for a hundred thousand useless mouths and backs? And, secondly, there being a round million of creatures in human figure throughout this kingdom, whose whole subsistence put into a common stock would leave them in debt two millions of pounds sterling, adding those who are beggars by profession, to the bulk of farmers, cottagers, and labourers, with the wives and children who are beggars in effect; I desire those politicians who dislike my overture, and may perhaps be so bold as to attempt an answer, that they will first ask the parents of these mortals, whether they would not at this day think it a great happiness to have been sold for food at a year old, in the manner I prescribe, and thereby have avoided such a perpetual scene of misfortunes as they have since gone through, by the oppression of landlords, the impossibility of paying rent without money or trade, the want of common sustenance, with neither house nor clothes to cover them from the inclemencies of weather, and the most inevitable prospect of entailing the like, or greater miseries, upon their breed for ever.

I profess, in the sincerity of my heart, that I have not the least personal interest in endeavouring to promote this necessary work, having no other motive than the public good of my country, by advancing our trade, providing for infants, relieving the poor, and giving some pleasure to the rich. I have no children by which I can propose to get a single penny; the youngest being nine years old, and my wife past child-bearing.

Dear Henry
Daniel Andries

Dear Henry,

Your design plans for building a small, personal horseless transport (what did you call it, automobile?) looked very interesting. Getting rid of the horse was, in my estimation, the real stroke of genius. Horses are a pain; always wanting grain and water, crapping all over the street, getting spooked, turning carriages over, and taking off on the spur of the moment; the driver is at the mercy of that miserable beast. Horrible. My Aunt Bertha was trampled by one of the stampeding mongrels just last week. But that's another story.

Despite all these overwhelming assets, Henry, there are a number of problems with your design which negate the advantages that are inherent in the mere pondering of the idea of a horseless, self-propelled vehicle. Let me review the plans you sent us to make sure that we are both clear as to what it is specifically that I'm objecting to.

There is a basic carriage. It has a seat in the front for the driver. It has four wheels, two on each side. Behind this driver is an engine, a gas propelled engine. Behind this first carriage is a second four wheeled wagon so to speak. This wagon has two benches, with a total seating capacity of four people. Now, through the back of the carriage and into the bottom of the wagon sticks a rod. You call this a crankshaft. Suits me fine. To start the automobile, the driver turns a key in a lock system that starts a burst of electricity. The electricity travels down some wires to the wagon in back.

In this wagon sit four men. Each man has a metal ring strapped to his neck, and clipped to the ring are the wires. Each one of these men, as you specified in your plans, have had their heads shaved and are wearing wet packs upon their bald scalps to keep them moist. (Your studies with electricity have revealed that water is an excellent conductor.) The wire travels above the wetted cranium and back down to the other side of the metal ring. The wire is then connected in a similar manner to the other three men before it travels on back to the front of the automobile.

These four men, if we are to go by what you have written in your blueprint, Henry, are sitting back in that wagon to get the crankshaft turning. The point of the electricity? You state: A) Most importantly to give each man more energy, thereby giving a bigger and faster start to the crankshaft, and B) To wake up any of the men who may have fallen asleep back in the wagon. You go into a lengthy discussion of the utter boredom of this job which I shall not reprint here. I shall instead merely refer to it. You claim the job is dull. I'd say it's rather electrifying, but that's neither here nor there. You state often, after traveling a great distance over the plains with little to do but watch the scenery, the crankshaft men, for lack of a better title, may fall asleep. Yet, they may be needed at a moment's notice to start the automobile. It would be foolish and entirely uneconomical in any sense of the word to go back and wake each one up individually. So, you suggest that by running the electricity through their bodies, you should certainly have them wide awake in little or no time at all.

Directly behind the driver, on a small wooden platform with a hole in the center of it, sits another man. The hole in the center of the platform is connected via a funnel to the engine block where the gasoline, which propels the craft, ignites, thereby getting the engine going. The man on the platform sits above the hole. He has at his disposal approximately three cans, each containing two gallons of gasoline. His job is to pour that petrochemical fuel through the hole and into the funnel to keep the engine fed with gasoline. When he has emptied the first two containers and is pouring the contents of the third into the engine, he is to yell "One gallon left." The driver, according to your plans, should then pull over into a gas station to get more gas. This part of your plan thoroughly confused me. Henry, what in God's name, may I ask you, is a gas station and where does one find one? (We were also wondering where one would keep the key to the public restroom in one of these gas stations.)

We finally get back to the front of the automobile, where the driver, who has set everything in motion, should be ready to drive the automobile. To get the thing in motion, he must first push a stick forward, which will, you say, put the automobile in gear, or, in laymen's terms, make it ready to roll. The car moves. The speed of its motion is determined by how much gasoline is being poured into the engine at any given moment by the man who's sitting behind the driver. The driver also has an apparatus strapped to his head which helps to direct the car in the direction he wishes it to go. It is a canvas strapping that goes around the back of the head. The strap is connected to a metal bar, which is finally connected, after a complicated system of hinges and rods, to the axle on which the wheels turn. All the driver has to do, one would suppose, is to turn the head in the direction one wishes to go. The car should then bear in that direction. For a turn around a corner, for instance, the driver would turn his head a full 90°.

The vehicle is now moving, heading in different directions and accelerating at the whim of the gasoline pourer. The question of how to stop this eight wheeled, six passengered automobile (let me take this moment to commend you on the title you chose for this contraption, Henry: self-propelled, as auto denotates; moving vehicle, as mobile so subtly suggests) remains unanswered. Let us then apply ourselves to your solution of that problem.

You have added two more people to the automobile. They are positioned one on each side of the driver. But these two men have no seats to sit in (the least of their worries). They have instead been placed on the outside of the vehicle on two long boards that run along the sides of the carriage. These boards are called (once again, may I commend you on your cleverness, Henry) running boards. They stand on these running boards, hanging on the sides of the carriage, and when they are so told by the driver, they either do one of two things to stop the automobile. They can: A) grab onto the bar that is sticking out of the side of the car and hang down to the ground, dragging their feet and legs along the road, thereby causing friction, which should slow the vehicle down and eventually stop it, or B) for quicker stops, climb to the front of the carriage and throw themselves down by the wheels.

You claim to have devised the method for merely slowing the car down by observing some young children at a playground. They were playing on one of those nauseating merry-go-rounds. To stop themselves and the playground device, they dragged their bodies along the sides of it, using the friction caused by their bodies interacting with the ground.

I like your application of the scientific method of observation in tackling the problem of stopping your invention. Shows a keen and open mind, Henry. But I believe it also reveals one of your biggest flaws. That is that your analytical mind never thought of the practicalities involved in your current design. You obviously never built and tested a model of your automobile. But we did.

Let us take first things first, Henry. The matter of the four baldheaded men in the back with wet scalps who get an electrical current sent through their bodies. There are a number of problems with this idea.

First off, when you run that electric current down that wire, into that metal ring, up over their heads, back down, into the next metal ring, and through the next man in a likewise fashion, you end up with more than a crankshaft turning at a rapid rate. You end up with four perfectly dead men. You kill them. They die. They fry right before your eyes. While this has unlimited potential in terms of family barbecues and night lighting, and while it's true that the crankshaft is sent spinning, you now have four dead people in the back of your automobile. And here in Michigan, killing people by running electrical charges through their bodies and driving them off into the countryside is definitely considered a crime that is punishable by law. As a matter of fact, Henry, we may all get to experience the feeling of electricity running through our bodies if we continue to run an automobile in this fashion.

We've tested this method for starting a car twice now, thinking that maybe the first time we'd made some technical error in setting up the apparatus. But the only mistake we made was believing in your plans and in your judgment as an inventive genius. We are now preparing eight funeral services and consoling eight widows and approximately 45 children who no longer have fathers. That's quite a responsibility; I really don't believe that this is any way to start out the Ford Motor Company.

From a pure practical standpoint, Henry, dead men in the back of the vehicle are of no use to anybody. They can never start the automobile again. In fact, they can't do much of anything again. It's truly a one-shot deal. As for the fact that it will certainly wake them up, I believe the facts bear witness that it just might have been a little more economical to go back there and wake each one up individually. The electricity, I assure you, will put them into a state of slumber that no driver will be able to cope with.

There is next the matter of the man who sits on the platform behind the driver and pours gasoline into the engine to keep it going and to get the automobile moving faster.

There is a very interesting effect that occurs whenever one pours gasoline over anything hot. It explodes. And if it does not explode, it ignites, sending flames shooting high into the sky. While one must admit that one cannot help but be fascinated and intrigued and attracted by the sight of a 20-foot flame rising high into the night air, that is hardly the subject at hand: I will agree that you wanted the gasoline to explode, for that was the phenomenon by which you got your automobile mobile. I do, however, believe that it was your intention for the explosion to be controlled and contained within the engine block itself. This was not at all the result. The engine exploded and caught fire, burning the poor man on the platform, setting the platform on fire, setting the automobile on fire. Pieces of metal, gaskets, rings, washers, driers, whatever, went flying in every direction. It was what one would call a genuine honest-to-God mess, Henry, yes, that's what it was. And Henry, I can see no redeeming social value in having pistons and gaskets and springs flying from here to there and back again. If you can come up with such a value, please contact me immediately. I'd be very interested in hearing what you'd have to say.

We now get to the steering device, which I described as being strapped to the head of the victim, I mean driver and otherwise intrepid pilot of this flaming hearse, which now carries a total of five dead bodies in it. The first time we tested the appartus, it pulled the driver straight down and wrapped him quickly around the axle. It only took one revolution of the axle to do it. Not a very sporting way to spend a leisurely afternoon. The second time we tested the apparatus, the driver was able to remain in his seat and was not pulled down to the bottom of the vehicle. Instead, when he attempted to turn his head, he broke his neck. This second driver was luckiest of all the people who helped to test this wonderful new invention of yours. He lived. His neck is broken, he's paralyzed for life, but he lived.

There are a number of problems with this steering apparatus that have nothing to do with broken necks and twisted bodies. If, by some freak accident of nature, this contraption for steering an automobile worked with some degree of accuracy, any slight motion of the driver's head would send the vehicle swerving off in directions the driver didn't wish to go. If he turned to look back at his gasoline pourer, say he should live too, to tell him to cut the gas, or to increase the flow, for that matter, the results would be catastrophic. The vehicle would swerve and crash. And to talk to the gasoline pourer, or even to the running board men, you have to look in their general direction and yell. The noise of the engine makes any normal communication impossible and the speed of the car in the wind also cuts down on the ability to hear while maneuvering the auto or receiving commands from the driver. Actually, I believe that the title of 'driven' would be more appropriate for him at this point in time.

We finally get to the men who stand on the running boards. The problems of scraped knees which you most likely encountered when you observed the school children at play is the least of one's worries here. By hanging from the side of the car, clinging onto a bar to stop the automobile, the men received broken hips, lacerations of the skin, slipped discs, and there was much blood and often death. When the automobile deaccelerators climbed in front of the carriage, and when they flung themselves in front of the wheels, once again, like the other parts of your automobile, it did not achieve the purpose it was designed to achieve. It merely resulted in the death of two more loyal employees, and I assure you, Henry, loyal employees will be even harder to find after this. They were crushed underneath the wheels by the sheer weight and momentum of the automobile, and they succeeded in setting the vehicle further off course and finally, on its side. It very definitely came to a halt, but in no kind of efficient or orderly manner.

So picture, if you can, Henry, your invention. A key is turned. Four bald-headed men with 45 children between them all light up and die. The engine catches on fire and the vehicle begins to accelerate at a rapid rate. The engine blows up, giving the carriage a further boost. The wagon hits a rock and goes flying off in another direction, breaking the crankshaft. The driver turns to see what has happened and the car takes a sharp left towards a small farm house. This flaming rocket on wheels is heading towards private property now. It's heading toward Bible Belt Republicans, Henry. The two men on the running board jump off the front of the carriage; it runs over them, and still on fire, mind you, turns over and rolls into the side of the house. The entire automobile blows up, and the farmer's daughter and his horse are killed. So, all totaled, first and second trial run, the death toll lies at sixteen people and one horse dead. One seriously injured.

Henry, while you claim to have been poorly educated in the humanities, and know little of literature, especially European literature, I find it hard to believe that you are not familiar with the writings of the Marquis de Sade. While you lack the erotic touch that made de Sade so fascinating, you make up for that inadequacy by the sheer force of your imagination. The only use I can see for this automobile as it now stands is that which the state would put it to. I'm sure the Michigan State Prison Authorities would see its value as a viable alternative to the electric chair. You can kill off eight at once. Due to the visual thrill involved in watching this spectacle, you could certainly bring into the State of Michigan much needed revenue by just charging 50 cents a head, 25 cents for students with IDs and senior citizens, to watch the execution. My only concern lies in the fact that the sport would die out as quickly as the condemned prisoners would.

Beyond that, I can see no practical use for this death trap of yours. The horse is beginning to sound much more attractive, and the shit on the streets is certainly preferable to dead bodies falling out of the back of the automobiles as they go rocketing off to a certain end in the corner of farmhouses, or trees, brick buildings, or even rivers, which would be preferable, for the fire would be extinguished. There is nothing safe nor sane about this invention as it now stands. In fact, I will go so far as to say that this automobile of yours is unsafe at any speed.

Let us digress for a moment, and assume, most assuredly in a state of temporary insanity, that this automobile worked in a safe and orderly fashion without threat to life and/or property. Where would one get the seven men besides the driver (who would of course be under the impression that he was driving it for pleasure) who would be needed to get the car started, control the acceleration, and stop the thing? One would have to keep a veritable army of slaves, fed, and in good health, to merely take a leisurely drive through the country side. It would be entirely uneconomical. Furthermore, the sheer weight of all those men would make it vary hard for the automobile to move at all, much less turn corners and accelerate. Assume that each man weighed 165 pounds. That would total 1320 pounds. The engine alone weighs a good 200 pounds. The car would surely be overloaded, and not only would a horse be faster, it would be entirely feasible to carry eight people in a carriage drawn by a horse. Merely add another horse. To add another engine to your automobile would require another five men at least, and hence defeat the entire purpose of using another engine.

We've carefully considered your design, as you can tell. Henry, we wish to show you that we have faith in you. I don't know why, but we do. Therefore, we've come up with a list of suggestions to improve the design of your automobile.

First off, I'd suggest destroying the concept of relying heavily on human beings to start, stop and accelerate the car by themselves. We suggest placing a hand crank on the front of the car which would be hooked up to a spring, and when turned in a clockwise manner and released would release the tension of the spring and start the crankshaft turning. Much safer. The gas could be held in a tank, and there could be a pump of some kind that the driver could control to oversee the flow of gasoline and hence the speed of the car. Furthermore, the driver could have a steering device that he could operate with his hands, leaving his head free to think, observe its surroundings, and react to the different situations it might encounter while driving. And finally, a stick on the driver's left that would be connected to stoppers, like door jams or hard rubber bricks, would, when pulled back, engage the bricks and stop the car (by means of friction, by the way). I believe that if these suggestions are taken to heart, something can be worked out in that head of yours, Henry. We eagerly await your reply and your new set of design plans. Good luck Henry, and thank you.

> Sincerely,
> Chairman of the Board of Trustees
> Ford Motor Company

P.S. If you're still interested in talking to the authorities of the possible use of your present design as a means of execution, that address is: Michigan State Prison Authority, Rock and Strown Toads Road, Barn Falls, Michigan. We'd also like you to know that despite threats of possible litigation against us, we are refusing to give out your first name and your address to the families of those killed while testing your design. We suggest you keep a low profile in the weeks to come, for your own well-being.

Each essay begins with imagery or statements that put the particular situation before you: "It is a melancholy object to those who walk through this great town, or travel in the country, when they see the streets, the roads, and cabin-doors crowded with beggars of the female sex, followed by three, four, or six children. . . ." (Swift frames one image as "cabin-doors crowded with beggars," using the image principle of relating one thing to another thing so we can see it clearly); "Your design plans for building a small, personal horseless transport (what did you call it, automobile?) looked very interesting. Getting rid of the horse was, in my estimation, the real stroke of genius. Horses are a pain. . . ." How does the ensuing imagery of the horses' objectionable behavior in the streets remind us of what happens in our streets with automobiles?

Imagery heightens the impact of the proposal and the situation being satirized: "although I rather recommend buying the children alive, and dressing them hot from the knife, as we do roasting pigs"; "First off, when you run that electric current down that wire, into that metal ring, up over their heads, back down, into the next metal ring, and through the next man in likewise fashion, you end with more than a crankshaft turning at a rapid rate. You end up with four perfectly dead men. You kill them. They die."

Each of the writers develops some part of the proposal with especially careful deadpan satirical reasoning. For Swift, it's the social and economic benefits of treating the children of the poor as a national food resource; for Andries, it's the careful, precise imagery and model-telling of how Henry Ford's horseless carriage performs.

Examine "Let's Give Babies Drugs," by Paula Trent, in the "Let's Spoil" section, as a parodic and satirical how-to-do-it-better proposal.

Examine how the authors combine forms and modes in their essays, with particular attention to each persona's desire to persuade the audience.

Writing Your Parodic and Satirical How-to-Do-It-Better Proposal

If you look over your how-it-happens subject, or any other part of your life or any part of our national life, you'll easily recognize a social, political, or economic situation that makes you angry with its obvious senselessness. If you were writing about schools in your how-it-happens subject, it might be the way courses are taught, or the way homework is regarded, or the priorities of the administrators. You tell them how they can achieve their apparent goals in a "better" way. If you were writing about a job, it might be the lack of safety precautions, overtime hours, or other impositions, dangers, deprivations, or indignities. From your own concerns and perceptions, you can come up with many issues, and you can see them and phrase them in the way that is most satirically meaningful.

For instance, we decry and regard as a mark of extreme barbarism the Aztecs' sacrifice of several thousand people every year to feed the god of the sun. Yet we do not similarly decry or regard as barbaric or ask questions about the 50,000 fatalities in automobile crashes each year, or why such a large proportion of those fatalities are males younger than 25. Given such discrepancies between our beliefs and actual behaviors, a how-to-do-it-better proposal seems in order. Is a sacrificing happening here? Which god is fed by these deaths? How could the god be satisfied in a better way or the deaths be made more useful? You could research the patterns of highway fatalities and automobile construction, and of the attitudes of drivers.

This parodic and satirical how-to-do-it-better asks that you make strong use of point-of-view, opposites, and let's spoil principles.

The key to writing a parodic and satirical proposal is the use of deadpan exaggeration throughout as you develop the attitude of the person and voice you pretend to be. In the "Dear Henry" letter, Henry's horseless carriage is proposed as a form of transportation better than the horse-powered transport, and the letter itself ends with yet another how-to-do-it-better proposal that, when carried out, will get us into our modern situation with the automobile. How does the "Dear Henry" letter achieve the tone of a "personal" rather than a "formal" letter from the Chairman of the Board of the Ford Motor Company?

See the situation as your opposite (the person "writing" the proposal) sees it, and see the benefits of the situation as the opposite sees them, and then, identifying with your opposite's point-of-view, show how the situation could be developed imaginatively to be even more beneficial, how the children of Ireland can be used to the benefit of the nation, how a horseless carriage can be constructed, so that all "thinking" people must agree.

You needn't wait for a full imaginative vision. Write your way into it. When your identification with the attitude of the persona takes hold and you feel the imaginative flow and irony of your proposal, carry it all the way through in one sitting if at all possible. Such an imaginative movement is precious and powerful and may not easily return intact. In most writing, you can work your way back into the feeling of a particular movement, but if you're feeling a strong imaginative conceptual movement, you should follow it as soon and as long as you can, to the end of the first draft of the essay if possible. Many students, when they get a strong writing start in the class, go immediately to the library, or the stairs, or a study room, or home, or back to the dorm, and take advantage of the impetus of the state of mind by continuing the writing. If you have to go to another class or other appointment, get back to the movement of the writing at your first opportunity.

About the Author

and the Story Workshop Method

John Schultz, Chairman of the Writing/English Department and head of the Master's Program in the Teaching of Writing and The Master's Program in Creative Writing at Columbia College (Chicago), originated and developed the Story Workshop method of teaching writing in 1965. Articles about it have appeared in *College English:* by Betty Shiflett (November 1973), Pat Stoll (December 1973), and John Schultz (December 1977). Schultz, with co-presenter Betty Shiflett, gave a detailed presentation at the SUNY (Buffalo)-NCTE Research on Composing Conference in November 1975, which was subsequently published in *Points of Departure: Research on Composing,* edited by Charles Cooper and Lee Odell (NCTE 1978). Schultz's books include *The Tongues of Men* (stories and novelle) Big Table 1969, *No One Was Killed* (about the 1968 Democratic Convention) Big Table 1969, *Motion Will Be Denied* (about the Chicago Conspiracy Trial) William Morrow 1972, and the short novel *Custom,* in *3 × 3* and *4 × 4*, Grove Press. He was a contributing editor of *Evergreen Review* and has given presentations at conferences of CCCC, MLA, and other major English organizations.